WITHDRAWN

MESOAMERICA'S
CLASSIC HERITAGE

Mesoamerican Worlds: From the Olmecs to the Danzantes

MESOAMERICA'S
CLASSIC HERITAGE

▼

FROM TEOTIHUACAN TO
THE AZTECS

EDITED BY

DAVÍD CARRASCO, LINDSAY JONES,
AND SCOTT SESSIONS

UNIVERSITY PRESS OF COLORADO

© 2000 by the University Press of Colorado

Published by the University Press of Colorado
5589 Arapahoe Avenue, Suite 206C
Boulder, Colorado 80303

The University Press of Colorado is a cooperative publishing enterprise supported, in part, by Adams State College, Colorado State University, Fort Lewis College, Mesa State College, Metropolitan State College of Denver, University of Colorado, University of Northern Colorado, University of Southern Colorado, and Western State College of Colorado.

The paper used in this publication meets the minimum requirements of the American National Standard for Information Sciences—Permanence of Paper for Printed Library Materials. ANSI Z39.48–1984

Library of Congress Cataloging-in-Publication Data

Mesoamerica's classic heritage : from Teotihuacan to the Aztecs /
edited by Davíd Carrasco, Lindsay Jones, and Scott Sessions.
p.   cm.
Includes bibliographical references.
ISBN 0-87081-512-1 (cloth : alk. paper) — ISBN 0-87081-637-3 (pbk. : alk. paper)
1. Teotihuacán Site (San Juan Teotihuacán, Mexico) 2. Indians of
Mexico—Antiquities. 3. Mexico—Antiquities. I. Carrasco, Davíd.
II. Jones, Lindsay, 1954–   . III. Sessions, Scott.
F1219.1.T27M46   1999
972'.01—dc21   99-11257
                                                               CIP

Front cover: José María Velasco, *Pirámide del Sol,* 1878 (courtesy of the Banco Nacional de Comercio Exterior and the Museo de Arte Moderno, Mexico City). *Back cover:* Glyphs from La Ventilla, Teotihuacan (courtesy of Rubén Cabrera Castro).

11 10 09 08 07 06 05 04 03 02   10 9 8 7 6 5 4 3 2 1

to Paul Wheatley

CONTENTS

ILLUSTRATIONS

FIGURES

TABLES

MAPS

ABBREVIATIONS

ADV:	Akademische Druck-und Verlagsanstalt
AGN:	Archivo General de la Nación
BAR:	British Archaeological Reports
CEM:	Centro de Estudios Mayas
CEMCA:	Centre d'Études Mexicaines et Centroaméricaines
CH:	Coordinación de Humanidades
CIESAS:	Centro de Investigaciones y Estudios Superiores en Antropología Social
CIS:	Centro de Investigaciones Superiores
CNCA:	Consejo Nacional para la Cultura y las Artes
ENAH:	Escuela Nacional de Antropología e Historia
FCE:	Fondo de Cultura Económica
IH:	Instituto de Historia
IIA:	Instituto de Investigaciones Antropológicas
IIE:	Instituto de Investigaciones Estéticas
IIF:	Instituto de Investigaciones Filológicas
IIH:	Instituto de Investigaciones Históricas
INAH:	Instituto Nacional de Antropología e Historia
SEP:	Secretaría de Educación Pública
SEQC:	Sociedad Estatal Quinto Centenario
SG:	Secretaría de Gobernación
SMA:	Sociedad Mexicana de Antropología
SHCP:	Secretaría de Hacienda y Crédito Público
SUNY:	State University of New York
UNAM:	Universidad Nacional Autónoma de México

MESOAMERICA'S
CLASSIC HERITAGE

Introduction

▼

Reimagining the Classic Heritage in Mesoamerica

Continuities and Fractures in Time, Space, and Scholarship

Davíd Carrasco, Lindsay Jones, and Scott Sessions

Debate concerning the unity and diversity of pre-Hispanic Middle America has been a central feature of European and American imaginings about the region since Columbus's initial arrival in the New World. Even now the dense interpretive challenges posed by the oneness and manyness of the region's indigenous peoples, and by the continuities and changes of the region's history, remain among the field's most formidable problems. Among past generations of scholars, and presently, the spectrum of explanatory responses clusters around two sorts of poles.[1]

On the one hand, numerous conceptions of this region have managed the matter of sameness and difference by accentuating the discontinuities between its various sub-regions and historical eras. Perhaps most notoriously, one early and enduring strain of Americanist studies bipartitioned the Native peoples of the Central Mexican plateau over against those of the Maya lowland zone as two fully discrete cultural entities. According to one nineteenth-century view, indigenous Mexicans and Maya were wholly separate "races" that were "distinct in origin, different in character, only similar by reason of that general similarity which of necessity arose from the two nations being subject to like surroundings, and nearly in the same stage of progress" (Daniel G. Brinton, quoted in Carmack 1981: 31). In those polarizing views, the civilizations of highland Mexico and the Maya lowlands developed as essentially isolated and independent cultural spheres with only intermittent and largely inconsequential interactions. And consequently, from that frame, it seemed entirely plausible that Mexicanist and Mayanist scholars could likewise undertake their interpretive initiatives with similar independence and noninvolvement. Mexicanist studies constituted one field, and Mayanist studies quite another.

Moreover, imagining a similar measure of discontinuity along the temporal axis, for decades scholars concentrating in both areas accentuated the (supposedly) radical disjunctions between the various historical epochs of ancient Mesoamerica, particularly between the so-designated Classic and Postclassic eras. In those still prevalent perspectives, the profound differences between the characteristic approaches to religion, art, urbanism, and authority embraced respectively by the Classic versus Postclassic Maya, or by the respective "empires" of Classic Teotihuacan and Postclassic Tenochtitlan, are far more noteworthy than the continuities. Though the adequacy of the labels was always contested, the intimation that "the Classic," whether in the Maya or Mexican area, was an age of excellence, refinement, and peaceful prosperity in contrast to the disintegration and mounting chaos of "the Postclassic" proved an irresistible heuristic scheme for imposing order on the tangled development of pre-Columbian peoples and cultural productions. In these highly serviceable, if always suspiciously disjunctive arrangements, then, the cultural geography of ancient Mesoamerica is most suitably conceptualized and examined in terms of local and largely independent processes, and the history of the region is most suitably configured in terms of a stuttering succession of fractures and ruptures, rises, collapses, and fresh starts. Here the parts, in both space and time, are more significant than the whole.

Alternatively however, an even stronger collection of academic voices has argued the contrastive case in favor of the essential unity and historical continuity of ancient Middle America. Though currently the more widespread and more respectable view, the manifold arguments for the general sameness of this portion of the pre-Columbian world have not always been made on reputable grounds. Both well before and after Paul Kirchhoff's seminal articulation of "Mesoamerica" as a unified yet distinct culture area (1943: 92–107), arguments for the essential unity of "the whole Indian family," including the Aztecs, were sometimes made, for instance, on the dubious basis of a shared participation in some relatively early, still "barbarian," evolutionary stage (Lewis H. Morgan, quoted in Keen 1971: 383). Similarly implausible, sometimes insidious arguments for the essential unity of Middle America were grounded in fanciful stories of the wide adventurings and shared ancestry of some primogenial "super race" or "mother culture," variously identified as "Toltec," Maya, or Olmec, which had in some antique epoch fanned out and asserted its influence across the entire region.[2] More recent and more reasonable arguments for unity have usually been built either on the postulate of some largely homogeneous, pan-Mesoamerican "Archaic," "Formative," or "Preclassic" cultural horizon, which formed the common substratum of subsequent cultural diversification (Jones 1995: 39), or, in other cases, on the basis of the discernment of dynamic, reciprocal, and ongoing processes of cross-regional interaction. Permutations on that theme variously foreground conquests and invasions, migrations, pilgrimages, or, most often, networks of long-distance trade and economic exchange as the principal mechanisms of integration and unification.[3]

Teotihuacan, as the seemingly most complex and impressive social and architectural assemblage in the entire region, has occupied a privileged position in some, but hardly most, of these conceptions of the unity of Mesoamerica. Particularly those depictions of a widely unified Mesoamerica that accentuate mercantile and economic exchange processes between Central Mexico and other regions, most notably the southern Maya zone, afford the extension of Teotihuacan influence a crucial role in the unification of the wider region (see Santley 1983; Ball 1983; Sharer 1983). Likewise, even those historical (re)constructions that accentuate the brash innovation and uniqueness of the Aztecs' cultural accomplishment and empire building, have tended to acknowledge an important measure of continuity between Teotihuacan and Tenochtitlan. Nonetheless, as the essays in this volume well demonstrate, the full import of Classic Teotihuacan's influence—both on contemporaneous developments in the rest of Mesoamerica and subsequently for the rest of pre-Columbian history—remains to be fully appreciated.

CENTERS, CENTROIDS, AND INTERDISCIPLINARY CONVERSATIONS, FROM THE
TEMPLO MAYOR TO TEOTIHUACAN

This collection of essays, which engage the question of the unity and diversity of pre-Hispanic Mesoamerica by focusing on the "Classic heritage" of Teotihuacan, is the fruit of the latest stage of the collaboration between the Raphael and Fletcher Lee Moses Mesoamerican Archive and Research Project and the Proyecto Templo Mayor archaeological team assembled and directed by Eduardo Matos Moctezuma. This collaboration began in 1979 when Davíd Carrasco, with the help of colleagues from Mexico and the United States, organized the first scholarly conference on the then newly emerging discoveries at the Templo Mayor, entitled "Center and Periphery: The Great Temple of the Aztec Empire," at the University of Colorado in Boulder. The success of that conference, which focused on the exemplary symbolic and economic role of the Templo Mayor in the organization and expansion of Aztec urbanism, led Carrasco and Matos to organize the Mesoamerican Archive as a research and teaching center dedicated to developing new models of interpretation on the dynamics of center and periphery in Aztec society. A succession of productive interdisciplinary conferences in Boulder and Mexico City, trained principally on the Aztecs, both sustained the collaboration and issued in several important publications (Broda, Carrasco, and Matos 1987; Carrasco, ed.,1989 and 1991; Carrasco and Matos 1992; López Luján 1994; Matos Moctezuma 1995; Jones 1995; and López Austin 1997).

Now, largely in response to the wealth of provocative new information that continues to emerge from Proyecto Teotihuacan, a major and ongoing set of archaeological investigations under the general directorship of Matos, he and Carrasco have decided to re-focus their "center and periphery model" on Teotihuacan and its rippling influence across Mesoamerica. In order to initiate and advance this new stage in the collaboration, Matos hosted a 1995 conference on "The Classic Heritage: From Teotihuacan to the Templo Mayor" on-site at Teotihuacan, which was followed by a second conference, entitled "The Classic Heritage of Mesoamerica: From Teotihuacan to the Aztecs," convened by Carrasco at Princeton University in 1996. In conceptualizing that second symposium, at which initial drafts of these essays were presented, Davíd Carrasco utilized the urban ecologist Paul Wheatley's description of urban "centroids" in *Nagara and Commandery: Origins of the Southeast Asian Urban Traditions*, where he writes:

> Most important of all, the nodes in the communications networks are situated in cities, so that the messages they transmit originate predominantly with, and in any case inevitably carry the point of view of, those who, controlling the city, reside at the hub of the network. The messages which flow outwards to the rest of society are, therefore, impregnated with urban norms. In fact, what makes the city (in early and recent times) important from this point of view is less its role as a large, dense, heterogeneous collection of non-agricultural persons (when they are non-agricultural, that is) than its control of a communications hub in that society. This is essentially what we mean when we join John Friedmann in categorizing the city as a creator of effective space, when we allegorize it as the summation of society, or when we designate it as a living repository of culture. The city, by virtue of being the site of the organizational foci of society, contrives, prescribes, modulates, and disseminates order throughout the subsystems of that society. Its most crucial export, as Scott Greer has reminded us, is control. (Wheatley 1983: 9)

Accordingly, though that international, interdisciplinary conference concentrated on the currents of continuity and change that linked the florescence of Teotihuacan and the apogee of Tenochtitlan, broader issues were also raised. That conference explored in many ways the "nodes of communication networks" located within, and transmitted beyond, the built forms of Teotihuacan as it achieved in many parts of Mesoamerica the prestige of being the site of creation of the *most effective social and symbolic space*, but also the summation of society and the great exporter of imperial authority. Participants were challenged to interrogate the proposition that Teotihuacan's heritage was a "Classic heritage" insofar as it had served as an urban "centroid" and a "canon" for the rest of Mesoamerica. Carrasco asked the discussants to consider whether Teotihuacan was, in fact, both the great classic and the great anomaly. Other questions followed from this: How did its cultural patterning interact with and get altered by its exchanges with the other influential, authoritative canons of the Toltecs, Maya, Mixtecs, Zapotecs, and so forth? Did the Teotihuacanos read and ritualize the canons of other cultures into their own worldview? How did various competing urban sites and traditions borrow, challenge, and make organizational use of Teotihuacan's power and authority? Did the Aztecs and other pre-Hispanic peoples read and reread the art, symbols, and traditions of Teotihuacan into a status of "classic"? Do we? Do we make it classical because we have such a limited understanding of what went on? A classic ignorance?

The present volume, then, which consists of revised versions of the papers delivered at that symposium, emerges from the collective effort and creative friction between archaeologists, historians of religions, ethnohistorians, art historians, archaeoastronomers, epigraphers, and, not incidentally, between Mexicanists and Mayanists, as they reflected upon these questions. Though the contributors adhere to a wide range of disciplinary perspectives and individual opinions, all are dedicated to coming to terms both with new interpretive models and with an abundance of new information. Different academic orientations notwithstanding, they are united in their willingness to entertain seriously the prospect that, despite a generalized appreciation of Teotihuacan's importance, scholars have not yet come to terms with the full force of this site's foundational and decisive influence on contemporaneous and subsequent developments throughout Mesoamerica.

Full consensus remains elusive. In the assessment of some of us, though, those conversations and these articles add force to the claim that Teotihuacan, more than any other pre-Columbian center, was a paradigmatic source that informed the art and architecture, cosmology, religious demeanor, and conceptions of urbanism and political authority for, if not all, certainly a very large portion of the ancient Mesoamerican world. The exceptionally wide influence of Teotihuacan was, so it seems, both a principal cause for and among the most seminal consequences of the essential unity of Mesoamerica. In myriad different ways that we are still just beginning to understand, Teotihuacan's "Classic heritage" both fed and fed on the dynamic interactivity of the entire area.

The intellectual advances of this collaboration, which one participant likened to a "paradigm shift" in Mesoamerican studies, have encouraged the planners to consider two future conferences, and in all likelihood two future publications: one on Teotihuacan and Oaxaca and another on Teotihuacan and the Maya.

PART I: THE PARADIGM SHIFTS IN MESOAMERICAN STUDIES

This volume is divided into four sections, the first of which is devoted solely to Alfredo López Austin and Leonardo López Luján's essay, "The Myth and Reality of Zuyuá: The Feathered Serpent and Mesoamerican Transformations from the Classic to the Postclassic." This opening piece interweaves archaeological and documentary sources to propose a daringly "global vision" of the whole of ancient Mesoamerica—a vision that is, intriguingly, maybe even ironically, more unified but also more diversified than nearly all previous depictions of the area. Though in fundamental agreement with Paul Kirchhoff concerning the essential unity of the area, these authors strongly resist any intimation that this was a monolithic and homogeneous cultural area. By contrast, they stress, on the one hand, the region's dynamically multi-ethnic, multilinguistic, multicultural, multireligious diversity, yet, on the other hand, the vigorous interactivity and "international" networks of commercial and ideological exchange that integrated the entire "super area." In their view, multi-ethnicity, which was experienced with the greatest intensity in Teotihuacan and the other urban capitals, constituted both this world's most difficult challenge and its most fortuitous potentiality. Pre-Hispanic Mesoamerica, stretching from the northern frontier to the southern Maya area, was, in their view, from the earliest eras, *many and one*.

Moreover, if ancient Mesoamerica, particularly its urban centers, was always simultaneously vexed and enriched by the tensions between religio-cultural sameness and difference, López Austin and López Luján contend that those tensions were uniquely intensified during the so-termed Epiclassic, that is, during the transitional period that connected the Classic and Postclassic eras. In formulating their new solution to the old problem of continuity and change between these two eras, they capitalize especially on ethnohistoric references to

"Zuyuá," a mythical place of origin connected to but distinct from the more famously esteemed homeland of Tollan. The "Zuyuans" (a term that corresponds to no single indigenous group, language, or region) serves as their designation for those Epiclassic innovators who were unprecendentedly successful in promulgating a style of religio-socio-political organization that was both respectful of the old and the new. The great accomplishment of the Zuyuans was the creation of a "hegemonic pattern of political control, over a broad territorial range and an ethnically heterogeneous population." This hegemonic model—which answered the double-edged challenge of, on one side, preserving and respecting the particularities of existing local religio-political systems while, on the other side, superimposing new "supra-ethnic" control—built the foundations for the eventual political and religious realities of Tenochtitlan and other Postclassic centers. Instead of working to eradicate fidelity to local patron deities, the characteristic Zuyuan strategy entailed the symbolic replication of the archetypal Tollan coupled with the superimposition of a more overarching divine authority—namely, the widely revered Feathered Serpent, manifested in one or another of his myriad localized guises—which would embrace rather than supplant the more particularistic religious, and thus political, loyalties.

Teotihuacan and the other roughly contemporaneous Central Mexican centers, according to López Austin and López Luján, provide the clearest and most thoroughly documented instances of this Epiclassic imposition of the "forced harmony" of the Zuyuan system, which facilitated the transition from the Classic to the Postclassic. Nevertheless, consistent with their ambitiously holistic vision of Mesoamerica, they argue that parallel Epiclassic processes of strategically balancing the old and the new, the local and the universalistic, the generically human and the ethnically distinct, were at work also in Oaxaca and Michoacán as well as in the Maya lowlands and highland Guatemala—that is to say, essentially across the full breadth of Mesoamerica. The Zuyuan system is, in other words, though not without importantly different regional permutations, proposed as nothing less than a pan-Mesoamerica Epiclassic phenomenon that explains, in large measure, both the profound differences and the substantial continuities between the so-called Classic and Postclassic periods.

The ambitious sweep and substance of this argument is certain to stimulate lots of debate. Though still in the tradition of Kirchhoff, this essay presents a distinctively nuanced way of conceiving of the play of Mesoamerican unity and diversity insofar as it addresses not simply continuities and discontinuities across the cultural geography of the region, but along the chronological-historical axis as well. In this essay we are afforded a signal contribution to the interminable debate over pre-Hispanic unity and diversity, and thus a new point of departure for future inquiry.[4]

The remainder of the essays in this volume, while in only a few cases directly engaging the matter of the Zuyuan system, are all significantly informed by the necessity of situating or "contextualizing" more tightly focused studies of Classic Teotihuacan and related cities within the broader frame of a very dynamically interactive pre-Hispanic Mesoamerica. This initiative to *contextualize* Teotihuacan, that is, to locate (or sometimes relocate) investigations of that specific site in relation to wider Mesoamerican realities and developments, takes at least three distinct, though overlapping, forms: the first concerns time and history; the second, space and geography; and the third, theory and method.

PART II: TEOTIHUACAN IN THE CONTEXT OF MESOAMERICAN TIME AND HISTORY

This set of essays works to resituate recent discoveries and interpretations of Classic Teotihuacan with respect to the chronological frame of Mesoamerican time and history. In these cases, it is the historical transitions from the Classic to Postclassic, largely within the confines of Central Mexico, preeminently between Teotihuacan and Tenochtitlan, that are of the greatest concern.

Archaeologist Linda Manzanilla's contribution sets the tone by reexamining and extending her earlier interpretations of the numerous "caves" of Teotihuacan in relation to the wider Mesoamerican tradition of beliefs and practices concerning the underworld, a tradition that she aptly conceives as "a long-duration process of basic core ideas and peripheral formal changing aspects." Informed by her own extensive excavations of the caverns at Teotihuacan, virtually all of which now appear to have been humanly constructed quarries and tunnels rather than natural caves, Manzanilla traces the indigenous uses and representations of subterranean spaces from Formative times, through Teotihuacan and Tenochtitlan, to the cave rituals of contemporary Central Mexican communities. More specifically, she documents the impressive (and apparently ongoing) continuity of three symbolic couplings: one that juxtaposes caves and jaguars, a second connected to amphibious toads and water deposits, and third that bears on the imagery of sacred mountains and world trees. By charting the spatial and temporal distribution of those motifs, Manzanilla reveals how Teotihuacan's famous subterranean cavities, if owing their initial formation to the largely utilitarian quarrying of building materials, a kind of construction by subtraction as it were, eventually came to serve a very wide range of ritual and domestic usages—nearly all of which nonetheless find notable counterparts in other Central Mexican contexts. Thus while it is plausible to argue that Teotihuacan constitutes a fresh departure in Mesoamerican culture history and a unique accomplishment, Manzanilla's work demonstrates the advantages, necessity in fact, of also situating the capital, and specifically its utilization of the symbolism of underground spaces, in relation to both its historical precedents and subsequent heirs.

The next two chapters explore questions concerning the Classic heritage and Postclassic endurance of Quetzalcoatl, the irrepressible Plumed Serpent. Saburo Sugiyama's article, which like Manzanilla's piece draws on sustained involvements in recent archaeological work at Teotihuacan, concentrates on the sociopolitical dimensions of feathered-serpent symbolism. Sugiyama locates the earliest known representation of Quetzalcoatl in the sculptural program of the Feathered Serpent Pyramid (or the Ciudadela), and thus argues that Teotihuacan was, in a historical as well as mythical sense, the "place of origin" for the eventually ubiquitous symbolism of Quetzalcoatl. Moreover, in addition to Quetzalcoatl's irrefutable associations at Teotihuacan with water, fertility, and celestial bodies (specifically Venus), and despite the scarcity of specifically war-related associations in the

Classic city itself, Sugiyama argues that even from its earliest conception, the Feathered Serpent was very tightly and purposefully associated with militarism, human sacrifice, and a specific concept of coercive rulership. In his view, the inheritance of feathered-serpent imagery by a whole series of Late Classic and Postclassic centers in the Mexican highlands included as well the inheritance of "a state symbolic complex," that is, a specific mode of religio-political legitimization.

In his contribution, H. B. Nicholson concurs with Sugiyama that, despite significant Preclassic prototypes for Quetzalcoatl, it was most likely in Teotihuacan's famous Ciudadela façade that fully developed representations of rattlesnakes covered with feathers made their initial appearance. Then he turns the bulk of his attention to the survey, description, and organization of the myriad and highly diversified Late Postclassic Central Mexican (particularly "Aztec" style) two- and three-dimensional representations of the Feathered Serpent. Rescuing from obscurity a whole series of little-known sculptures, reliefs, and images, Nicholson thus provides a detailed catalogue—a veritable treasure map for Quetzalcoatl aficionados, in fact—which describes the provenance, current location, and present states of disrepair for innumerable Postclassic permutations on the flying snake theme.

The next two chapters concentrate on the direct, and apparently deliberately cultivated, genealogical connections between Classic Teotihuacan and Tenochtitlan. Doris Heyden, relying especially on documentary sources, argues that, while the Aztec pursuit of a legitimating pedigree entailed the expropriation of material and ideological elements from numerous cultures, Tenochtitlan owes its greatest debt to Teotihuacan. No other site enjoyed nearly the same prestige in Aztec eyes. Her analysis urges us to appreciate, moreover, that mythology and oral traditions played a uniquely important role in holding intact and disseminating the Classic-era symbolism of colors and directions, and the elaborate veneration of such natural features as celestial bodies, caves, mountains, springs, streams, trees, and birds, all of which she sees as similarly prominent in the Teotihuacan and Aztec worlds.

Eduardo Matos Moctezuma, whose intimate acquaintance with the archaeology of Teotihuacan and Tenochtitlan stems from directing excavation projects at both sites, examines cultural linkages between the two cities in terms of their "Great Temples." He begins with a brief sketch of earlier archaeological efforts at Teotihuacan, including those of the Aztecs, that provides a context for current excavations and illustrates the various ways that the Classic center was imagined and reimagined in the centuries following its decline. Guided by insights concerning the foundation and sacralization of ancient cities drawn from the history of religions, Matos presents a comparative study of six elements that, he contends, identified the principal temple in each of the sites as respective centers of the universe. These include the landmark or sign leading to the temple's foundation, its symbolism as a sacred mountain, its astronomical orientation, its association with water and the indigenous notion of the *alteptl*, the presence of sacrificial offerings there, and the surrounding platform or wall that distinguished its heightened level of sacrality from the rest of the city. Interestingly, Matos demonstrates how recent excavations reveal that the crossing of the east-west axis and thus the symbolic center of Teotihuacan at one point was moved from the Pyramid of the Sun to the Feathered Serpent Temple, and that both of these buildings, in turn, were the focus of deliberate "desacralizing" activities before the Classic city's terminal decline. His study shows how Teotihuacan was explicitly invoked as the principal prototype for the Templo Mayor as well as the Aztec ceremonial center.

Rubén Cabrera Castro, who is the curator of the Teotihuacan Archeological Zone and has worked at the site for nearly two decades, is also concerned with cultural connections between the Classic city and Postclassic Central Mexico. Based on recent archaeological findings, he traces the appearance and development of several religious ideas related to the calendar and the cosmos, antecedents of various Postclassic iconographic motifs and glyphs, and methods of astronomical observation, many of which find their earliest known expressions in Teotihuacan and will be transmitted to subsequent cultures. In terms of astronomy, Teotihuacanos employed two types of celestial observation—a horizontal form thought to come from Uaxactún, which later spread to Tikal, Dzibilchaltún, and other sites; and a vertical method conducted in specially modified subterranean chambers thought to have been invented in Teotihuacan and exported to Monte Albán, Xochicalco, Chichén Itzá, and elsewhere. Moreover, recent excavations reveal that these astronomical caves had various ceremonial and ritual uses as well. Cabrera also identifies early representations of the Postclassic cruciform quincunx motif, related to indigenous conceptions of cosmic time and space, in such diverse examples as a group of newly unearthed pecked circles and crosses, a three-dimensional depiction embodied in the layout of Structure A in front of the Pyramid of the Moon, certain designs covering Building 1B', and the arrangement of human burials at the Feathered Serpent Temple. In the last two sections of the essay, Cabrera focuses on several painted glyphic figures and a personage identified as Xolotl recently found in La Ventilla, one of Teotihuacan's urban neighborhoods, and concludes that these represent some of the earliest known stylistic and thematic antecedents of several iconographic motifs common in Postclassic codices, as well as others that would figure prominently in Mexica iconography. Moreover, the ordered arrangement and style of these figures bear witness to a glyphic writing system in Teotihuacan that was departing from the stylistic conventions of its mural-painting tradition.

The last essay in this section comes from archaeologists Leonardo López Luján and Saburo Sugiyama, along with anthropologist and materials analyst Hector Neff, who examine the composition, context, and significance of a Classic Teotihuacan-style Thin Orange ceramic vessel recently found in an offering adjacent to the Aztec Templo Mayor. Designated as the "9-Xi Vase," due to the rare appearance of a Teotihuacan calendrical glyph on its appliquéd panels, the piece provides an excellent vehicle for exploring relationships of this Classic city with other Mesoamerican sites on several levels. Contextual data concerning its burial and the processing of its contents demonstrate this vessel's reutilization, nearly a millennium after its production, as a cinerary urn for a high-ranking Mexica official and allow the partial reconstruction of his fifteenth-century funeral ceremony in front of Tenochtitlan's Casa de las Águilas. Moreover, iconographic data from the vessel itself launch the authors into analyses of several important Teotihuacan motifs and glyphs, as well as the use of certain numerical and calendrical conventions, some thought to derive from the Zapotec area and shared (either concurrently or subsequently) with Epiclassic centers such as Cacaxtla, Xochicalco, and Teotenango. Like the glyphs at La Ventilla in the previous chapter, the *9-Xi* Vase suggests the emergence, at Teotihuacan, of a distinctive system of notational signs brought to fruition in Late Postclassic Central Mexico.

PART III: CLASSIC TEOTIHUACAN IN THE CONTEXT OF MESOAMERICAN SACRED LANDSCAPES AND PLACES

The three essays that constitute this section likewise respond to more fully integrated, dynamically interactive models of Mesoamerica by working to contextualize the influence and accomplishment of Teotihuacan's florescence in a more spatial or geographical sense, that is to say, with respect to contemporaneous developments in other regions of Classic Mesoamerica, including the Maya area.

Archaeoastronomer Anthony Aveni explores the possibility that Classic Teotihuacan, traditionally designated as the site of the mythical birth of the Fifth Sun, was, moreover, "the place where time began" insofar as it served as the point of origin for a "great ideological migration." This movement included the dissemination of distinctive methods of conceptualizing space and keeping time—a "Teotihuacan space-time canon" as it were—from the Central Mexican highlands all the way to the Petén Maya region. To make his case, Aveni refines and extends his earlier hypotheses concerning the uses and meanings of Teotihuacan's numerous pecked-cross petroglyphs, that is, those circular configurations of holes, usually centered on a pair of rectangular axes, that, though widespread throughout Mesoamerica, are uniquely prevalent in the rocks and floors around this Central Mexican site. In his view, these petroglyphs, notwithstanding other plausible usages, served principally as calendrical devices and "symbols of completion." Furthermore, in his view, the exceptionally wide distribution of similar quadripartite patterns—evidenced, for instance, in contexts and media as different as the carved petroglyphs at Uaxactún, the architectural decoration of Tikal, and the Maltese cross–like diagrams common in both Maya and Mexican codices—is the consequence of a flow of information that had its initial source in Classic Teotihuacan. Thus, according to Aveni's surmise, quite specific modes of arranging space and counting time, though derived originally from observations of the unique features of Teotihuacan's local landscape and skyscape, were eventually embraced and replicated as virtually pan-Mesoamerican conventions.

Karl Taube's article, which addresses both the Aztecs' "archaistic" evocations of Teotihuacan's symbolism of fire and war as well as generally contemporaneous celebrations of and allusions to Teotihuacan's imagery of war in Classic Maya art, features a startlingly iconoclastic interpretation of those famous goggle-eyed masks that alternate with the sculpted heads of feathered serpents on the façade of Teotihuacan's Temple of Quetzalcoatl. In the wake of recent discoveries of over two hundred sacrificial victims, most in militaristic costume, buried inside this structure, other contributors to this volume have challenged the long-standing presumption that these notoriously distinctive muzzle-snouted faces, which have served Mesoamericanists for decades as a virtual signature of Teotihuacan, represent Tlaloc, the rain god. The counterproposal holds that the reiterative element is a headdress that represents Cipactli, a primordial crocodile or caiman (López Austin, López Luján, and Sugiyama 1991; and Sugiyama, chapter 3 of this volume). Alternatively, Taube responds to the new discoveries with a different interpretive tack by identifying this zoomorphic element as the "War Serpent," a prominent component of a complex of warfare symbolism for which he finds many counterparts not only in other sculptural and iconographic media around Teotihuacan and later in Tenochtitlan, but throughout Mesoamerica, including innumerable roughly contemporary instances in the Maya area. Despite significant local variations in its highland and lowland manifestations, in Taube's view, both the Classic War Serpent and its Postclassic descendant, the Xiuhcoatl Fire Serpent, in addition to strong associations with shooting stars and meteorites, portray supernatural caterpillars, that is, pupate butterflies before their metamorphosis into splendorous winged beings. This image provides, as Taube notes, an ideal metaphor for the processes of transformation and metamorphosis that occurred when, according to the "cosmovision" of ancient Mesoamericans, slain warriors were transformed into stars and "flying butterfly spirits of the sun." If Taube is correct about the identity and significance of Teotihuacan's goggled-eyed masks, several generations of scholars have been mistaken.

The third article in this group, by Geoffrey McCafferty, focuses on the dynamically fluctuating relations between the generally contemporaneous centers of Teotihuacan and Cholula. The latter, he thinks, has too often been dismissed either as a "a secondary center" within the larger Teotihuacan empire or as "an impoverished imitation" of its larger and more famous neighbor. Instead of being simply derivative, Cholula developed, according to McCafferty, a unique mode of religiously based authority, which enabled that center not only to weather the tumultuous transition from the Classic to the Postclassic era, but actually to thrive in the transitional Epiclassic context. By contrast to those innumerable circumstances in which Mesoamerican rulers worked to legitimate and enhance their own imperial ambitions by deliberately cultivating an appearance of direct connectedness to Teotihuacan, McCafferty presents the intriguing possibility that, in some cases, the most astute strategy of statecrafting was to adopt "an ideology of distinction" or "a discourse of difference to Teotihuacan," which would deliberately distance one's religious and governmental agenda from the heritage of that great capital.

According to McCafferty's archaeology-based reinterpretation of the multistaged construction history of Cholula's Great Pyramid, late in the Classic era the Cholula architects abandoned their earlier strategy of announcing a close affiliation with Teotihuacan via abundant imitations of its architecture and monumental art. At that point, the most prudent political ploy required an aura of separation from Teotihuacan and a symbolic rejection of kinship and indebtedness to the great capital, perhaps in favor of stronger affiliations with El Tajín and the Gulf Coast region. But then in later Epiclassic remodelings of the Great Pyramid, apparently in response both to Teotihuacan's decline and to the arrival of the ethnically distinct Olmeca-Xicallanca, the architects of Cholula once again began to utilize characteristically Teotihuacanoid architectural elements, this time within "a palimpset of multi-ethnic internationalism" that may even have included considerable Maya influences. Not inconsequentially (and not unlike the exposition of the Zuyuan system delivered by López Austin and López Luján), it was in the context of this Epiclassic negotiation of unprecedented ethnic and religious diversity, as Cholula undertook to position itself as heir apparent to the fading Teotihuacan, that the feathered-serpent cult of Quetzalcoatl, which would eventually be so closely identified with this place, made its initial appearance. At any rate, this adroit tactic of intermittently jettisoning and embracing affiliations with its infamous neighbor enabled Cholula, McCafferty explains, to emerge from the Epiclassic era as the primary religious center of Central Mexico, "the Rome of Anahuac," a pilgrimage center to which nobility from across Mesoamerica looked and traveled for legitimation. With Teotihuacan in disrepair, Cholula, at that point, came to serve as an esteemed reservoir rather than a mere recipient of religio-political legitimacy.

PART IV: CLASSIC TEOTIHUACAN IN THE CONTEXT OF MESOAMERICANIST SCHOLARSHIP

The final set of essays, though also addressing very specific historical problems concerning the legacy of Teotihuacan's Classic heritage, are notable especially for contextualizing recent interpretations of Teotihuacan with respect to larger problems in the history of Mesoamericanist scholarship. Here we are alerted to Teotihuacan's pivotal role not only in the pre-Hispanic past, but in the hypothetical formulations and enduring controversies of our own academic field.

In her contribution, Elizabeth Boone, for instance, situates her own fresh discussion of Aztec understandings and perceptions of Teotihuacan with respect to the timeworn debate about the extent to which the specific site of Teotihuacan can be identified with the marvelous Tollan of Nahuatl myth and legend and with the equally marvelous Toltec priest-king, Topiltzin Quetzalcoatl. Boone first rehearses the history of ideas wherein scholars' once-prevailing identification of the legendary Tollan with Teotihuacan was, in the 1940s, largely displaced by a new orthodoxy that located the legendary Toltec capital in Tula, Hidalgo. Then she joins with those scholars who have argued in various ways that "Tollan" is best conceived, not as a single historical-geographical location, but as a concept or a metaphor for urban excellence, which was assigned to a whole series of pre-Columbian capitals, Teotihuacan being presumably foremost among them.

With that nuance, Boone then assembles sixteenth-century maps and chronicles to support her contention that the Aztecs definitely did consider Teotihuacan as *a* Tollan (one of many), and perhaps as "the greatest of all the Toltec cities." Moreover, beyond its explicitly "Toltec" affiliations, she shows that Teotihuacan enjoyed a multilayered prestige insofar as it was conceived as the place where the Fifth (and present) Sun was created by the sacrifice of the gods, where the Aztec system of government had first been constituted, and as the point of departure for many of the peoples who inhabited Central Mexico in the Late Postclassic. Furthermore, Boone supersedes earlier discussions of the "Tollan problem" by foregrounding the usually neglected fact that, although its ancient ceremonial core may have decayed well before the rise of the Aztecs, Teotihuacan actually remained a thriving city in the Late Postclassic era. Though never formally under the sway of the Triple Alliance, Teotihuacan did serve as a judicial seat for the Acolhua lords, an active and autonomous *altepetl* that was home to a widely revered oracle.

We learn from Boone, in other words, that the Aztecs' veneration for Teotihuacan was not confined simply to abstract reminiscences of a bygone era, nor even to the extensive copying and incorporation of various Teotihuacan elements into their own architectural and artistic creations. Additionally, the Aztecs maintained an active and ongoing relationship with "the home of the gods" to which they often traveled and from which they retrieved innumerable objects that were subsequently deposited in offerings at the Templo Mayor and other Tenochtitlan ceremonial precincts. Via such strategic scavenging and relocating of Teotihuacan objects, the Aztecs, in a sense, transferred "the place where the Fifth Sun was created" to their own capital, and thereby, according to Boone, "metaphorically took ownership of this Sun, for whose continuance their sacrifices and offerings were responsible."

Johanna Broda's panoramic article, which draws on the work of several of the other contributors to this volume, situates a very specific hypothesis about the calendrics and axial layout of Teotihuacan in the context of some two decades of impressive progress in the interdisciplinary field of archaeoastronomy. Broda, informed particularly by the recent interpretations of Rubén Morante López, isolates several newly emergent sets of evidence that provide a basis for fresh contributions to the long, often contentious history of debate concerning Teotihuacan's orientation: the recent discovery of three additional caves that, in her view, very likely served as "subterranean observatories"; new and more-detailed studies of the alignments of the Pyramid of the Sun; provocative suggestions that the Temple of Quetzalcoatl and the Ciudadela may have functioned as a huge "calendrical marker"; and the recent discovery just to the south of the Pyramid of the Sun of those several pecked circles that figure so prominently in the article by Anthony Aveni.

Integrating those new evidences with her previous findings, Broda agues that Teotihuacan was arranged according to "a fourfold structure" that was reflected not only in the much imitated axial layout of urban space but also in the quadripartitioning of the agricultural year with respect to four specific dates: February 12, April 30, August 13, and October 30. In her view, this four-part division of both built space and calendrical time, though an informing notion for the Classic planners of Teotihuacan, ought to be appreciated as a fundamental feature of a distinctively Mesoamerican "cosmovision" that probably has Preclassic roots and definitely operated in the Postclassic world of the Aztecs. Though she is careful to note significant discontinuities over time and the particularity of local permutations on the shared scheme, Broda adduces considerable ethnographic evidence that not only the same basic cosmological principles but even respectful acknowledgments of the same four specific dates continue to be expressed in the "highly syncretistic" seasonal rites of indigenous communities in present-day Mexico and Guatemala. In her view, then, Teotihuacan may have earned its prestige less as a place of origins in the sense of brand-new innovations and unique accomplishments than as the quintessential instantiation of a set of cosmological conceptions that was embraced both well before and long after the Classic era, throughout what Broda terms "the one great cultural tradition that was ancient Mesoamerica."

The next two entries, which signal a refreshing thaw in cold-war relations between Mayanist and Central Mexicanist scholars, explore the connections between Teotihuacan and the Classic Maya. Mapping and annotating the intellectual history of the problem, William and Barbara Fash explain that full appreciation of Teotihuacan's influence in the Maya area has been complicated, and often forestalled, by the untoward tendency to regard the Isthmus of Tehuantepec as a "great divide" not only between geographical regions but between two disturbingly independent strains of Mesoamericanist scholarship. Consequently, opinions concerning highland-lowland interactions have tended to divide between two extremes: one that granted primacy to Teotihuacan in the creation of Mesoamerican civilization, and thus relegated even the Classic Maya to "secondary state status," and the equally radical converse, far more prevalent among Mayanists (at least until recently), which insisted on the complete independence of the Classic Maya from Teotihuacan, except perhaps for the self-initiated borrowing of a few Central Mexican technological and artistic features.

Alternatively, these authors welcome the more detailed and evenhanded approaches that are at last revealing the complexity of the ongoing interactions between the two regions and, concomitantly, the tremendous prestige that Teotihuacan enjoyed in the eyes of the contemporary, and in many cases competitive, Classic Maya. In their view, the present archaeological evidence, which they regard as the most reliable source of information, continues to challenge the claim that there were ever armies of Teotihuacanos stationed in the Maya lowlands. Nonetheless, recent glyphic decipherments (including those by David Stuart in chapter 15 of this volume), coupled with the excavationary record, does, they think, demonstrate very convincingly that a number of Classic Maya rulers did claim the Teotihuacan-Toltec heritage as their own. They conclude, in other words, that several Maya kings appealed to a strategy of legitimation not unlike that pursued by their Mexica counterparts insofar as they tried very hard to prove that they had the blood of Central Mexicans coursing through their veins.

Commenting specifically on the abundance of Teotihuacan imagery on the portraits and architecture associated with the Copán lord K'inich Yax K'uk' Mo', William and Barbara Fash argue that if this Classic Maya ruler was not himself Teotihuacano—which he may well have been—he had at the very least been to the Mexican capital and "drunk deeply of its waters." Moreover, having stressed the abundance of reverential allusions to Teotihuacan in Copán and other lowland centers, they suggest, albeit tentatively, that the somewhat curious absence of similarly honorific allusions to the Maya at Teotihuacan does not undermine the likelihood that the two areas were involved in very substantial and sustained interactions, but it does shed additional light both on Teotihuacan's supremacy over the entire region and on "Mesoamerican principles of hierarchy." The Teotihuacanos were aware, in other words, that, with rare exceptions, "it does not bring prestige to oneself to mention lesser sites."

Mayanist epigrapher David Stuart likewise revisits, and then contributes to, the much debated topic of the nature and scope of the interactions between Teotihuacan and the Maya lowlands. With the continuing advancements in epigraphy, it has become increasingly clear that the extensive hieroglyphic texts at Tikal, Copán, and other Maya sites provide a singularly detailed fund of evidence with respect to the relevant historical events and even the specific individual actors; yet, as Stuart reminds us, these uniquely revealing sources have, until now, played a surprisingly small role in resolving the problem. Stuart explains how his own and others' recent glyphic decipherments not only reconfirm archaeologically derived surmises of very extensive highland-lowland interactions, but, additionally, reveal startling specific information about radical changes in the status of Teotihuacan-Maya relations over the several-century duration of the Classic period. Arguing, like others in this volume, for a fuller appreciation of Teotihuacan's pivotal role throughout an essentially unified, dynamically interactive Mesoamerican super-area, Stuart contends that the Lowland Maya were heirs to the Classic heritage of Teotihuacan, which they termed the "Place of Cattails," in two successive—though drastically different—respects.

First, contrary to the views of most Mayanists, Stuart argues, principally on the basis of his reading of inscriptions at Uaxactún and Tikal, that, in the Early Classic era, that is, during the Mexican capital's florescence, Teotihuacanos actually intruded into the Petén zone with considerable frequency, and thus played a direct, probably violent and certainly disruptive role in Maya polity and religion. Reaffirming and extending Tatiana Proskouriakoff's earlier hypotheses about "the arrival of strangers" in the Maya lowlands of the late fourth century c.e., Stuart, in fact, views this physical incursion of Teotihuacanos, which may even have eventuated in the execution of the reigning Tikal lord, as no less than "the single most important political or military episode of early Classic Maya history, when Teotihuacan established itself as a dominant force in the politics and elite culture of the central Petén."

By the Late Classic, however, following the demise of Teotihuacan as an active political force either in the central plateau or elsewhere, the Maya's very tangible connection to the once-great capital was radically transformed into a relationship of a more figurative and conceptual, though still exceptionally important, sort. Focusing, in this portion of his discussion, on the abundance of Teotihuacan-style elements in the iconography of Copán, and particularly on the representations of three prominent Copán sovereigns (including K'inich Yax K'uk' Mo') as "outsiders" with highland or western origins, Stuart explains that "Late Classic references to central Mexico are almost as numerous, though of a very different character." No longer the home base of an active player in the Mesoamerican religio-political world, Teotihuacan had by this time come to serve as an idealized element of a primordial past, a distant yet profoundly prestigious place of beginnings—as Stuart says, "a paradigm through which Maya rulers could define themselves and their historical pedigree." Thus, instead of exceptions to the wider Mesoamerican patterns of authority and legitimating self-representation, Maya rulers at this point, not unlike the rulers of innumerable "other Tollans" (and not without a very substantial historical basis), invoked Teotihuacan as their place of origin and claimed for themselves the distinction of a "Toltec" heritage.

The final entry to the collection, initially crafted as a response paper at the 1996 conference on "The Classic Heritage: From Teotihuacan to Tenochtitlan," is by historian of religions Philip Arnold. Though providing an innovative and quite specific interpretation of Mesoamericans' distinctive relationship to the land, Arnold, moreover, engages the much broader methodological problems consequent of interpreting and representing a culture so remote from our own as Classic Teotihuacan. Working to reconcile an apparent contradiction between those contributors to this volume who accentuate Teotihuacan's "earth-based cult" and those who highlight the Classic city's "warrior cult," Arnold contends that Teotihuacan, not unlike other Mesoamerican contexts, is profitably conceived as "a consumptive cosmos" in which both warfare and agriculture were "consumptive activities" animated by a "symbolism of eating" and a logic of reciprocity that required killing as an essential precondition for the continuance of human life. In his view, Classic Teotihuacan expressed a "locative" worldview wherein people found their orientation, not abstractly, but in relation to their dynamic (and "consumptive") involvements with the "materiality" of this concrete place, this living landscape.

Consequently, in Arnold's view, Teotihuacan operated as a paradigmatic city and, in his terms, a "locative canon" for the rest of the Mesoamerican world insofar as it exercised enormous influence not simply as a source of ideas that could be transferred into other contexts, but as a fixed and concrete place—"the center of the cosmos which organized, or founded, the rest of material existence." Though dubious that contemporary interpreters can suspend our own "cultural grids" fully enough to recover the "Other" mind-set of the pre-Hispanic Teotihuacanos, Arnold nonetheless regards the serious consideration of ancient Mesoamerica's "consumptive cosmology" as an eminently rewarding endeavor inasmuch as it pressures and challenges us to reconsider our own involvements in a consumerist worldview of a parallel, though very different sort.

It remains for our readers to determine whether the several claims by participants at the Princeton conference were correct when they stated that a "paradigm shift" in Mesoamerican studies was taking place within the expanded community that now makes up the Mesoamerican Archive. It does appear that the "center and periphery" model[5] forged in previous conferences has undergone a rich and perhaps radical revision in the accumulated papers herein. A new contextual understanding of Teotihuacan and the diversities and unities of Mesoamerica is emerging in these pages. We witness an exciting new sense of the interrelations of Teotihuacan with Tenochtitlan, Cholula, and the Maya ceremonial centers. This in turn reflects a new openness between Aztec scholars and Maya scholars who have been laboring hard and long in their own cultural areas. Finally, this book demonstrates the distinctive virtues of interdisciplinary collaboration (which, in the Archive setting, included an emphasis on the religiosity of Mesoamerican cultures) and may reveal by its example that in fact very few individual or collective books in Mesoamerican studies are seriously interdisciplinary or speak across disciplines. Having a series of articles by scholars from different disciplines does not make or represent interdisciplinary work. There must be moments and spaces where the differences in approach and interpretation are activated, revealed, and engaged. Such an engagement is taking place in the Archive conferences where scholars are sharing important discoveries they are making while using different sorts of resources and types of evidence. The editors are especially grateful to Eduardo Matos Moctezuma, Alfredo López Austin, Leonardo López Luján, William and Barbara Fash, Karl Taube, and David Stuart for revealing how their methods and labors help us struggle toward a more unified vision of ancient Mesoamerica. The learning process has been significantly enhanced by the Department of Religion at Princeton University and especially Lorraine Fuhrmann, Departmental Manager, and Jeffrey Stout, Departmental Chair. Also, we appreciate the generous support of Raphael and Fletcher Lee Moses, President Harold Shapiro, and Provost Jeremy Ostriker. It may be that Linda Manzanilla, emerging from the ritual caves that provided ancient and profound mysteries, said it best when she noted that the Mesoamerican tradition was "a long-duration process of basic core ideas and peripheral formal changing aspects" that had their Classic expression in Teotihuacan.

NOTES

1. Regarding the intellectual history of the problem of the unity and diversity of Mesoamerica, see, for instance, Jones 1995: 32–43.

2. For a sampling of other sources that argue for the essential unity of Mesoamerica on the basis of a common ancestry to some "mother cultures," see Jones 1995: 37–39.

3. Notable in this respect are the essays assembled in Miller 1983.

4. Maybe inadvertently, by accentuating the "multicultural" and "multi-ethnic" constitution of pre-Hispanic Mesoamerica, and thus undermining monolithic views of "the Indian," López Austin and López Luján's exposition of the Zuyuan system could have profound ramifications not only for how scholars constitute and contextualize their more tightly focused studies of Mesoamerican phenomena, but even for the ways in which Mexican national identity and ethnicity are complicated and refined, the viability of the enduring notion of the "mestizo," ostensibly constituted of a simple two-part Spanish-Indian mixture, is seriously challenged. The implication of their view is that Mesoamerica was, at least from the Epiclassic era forward—and thus remains even in the wake of the colonial encounter—in an important sense, a "multicultural society," threatened but even more enriched by the condition of ethnic and religious plurality.

5. For an overview of this model, see Broda, Carrasco, and Matos 1987; and Carrasco 1991.

REFERENCES

Ball, Joseph W.

1983. "Teotihuacan, the Maya, and Ceramic Interchange: A Contextual Perspective." In A. G. Miller, ed., *Highland-Lowland Interaction in Mesoamerica: Interdisciplinary Approaches*. Washington, DC: Dumbarton Oaks, pp. 125–145.

Broda, Johanna, Davíd Carrasco, and Eduardo Matos Moctezuma

1987. *The Great Temple of Tenochtitlan: Center and Periphery in the Aztec World.* Berkeley: University of California Press.

Carmack, Robert M.

1981. *The Quiche Mayas of Utatlán: The Evolution of a Highland Guatemala Kingdom.* Norman: University of Oklahoma Press.

Carrasco, Davíd, and Eduardo Matos Moctezuma

1992. *Moctezuma's Mexico: Visions of the Aztec World.* Niwot: University Press of Colorado.

Carrasco, Davíd, ed.

1989. *The Imagination of Matter: Religion and Ecology in Mesoamerican Traditions,* Oxford: BAR International Series no. 515.

1991. *To Change Place: Aztec Ceremonial Landscapes.* Niwot: University Press of Colorado.

Jones, Lindsay

1995. *Twin City Tales: A Hermeneutical Reassessment of Tula and Chichén Itzá.* Niwot: University Press of Colorado.

Keen, Benjamin

1971. *The Aztec Image in Western Thought.* New Brunswick, NJ: Rutgers University Press.

Kirchhoff, Paul

1943. "Mesoamerica." *Acta Americana* 1: 92–107.

López Austin, Alfredo

1997. *Tamoanchan, Tlalocan: Places of Mist.* Trans. B. Ortiz de Montellano and T. Ortiz de Montellano. Niwot: University Press of Colorado.

López Austin, Alfredo, Leonardo López Luján, and Saburo Sugiyama

1991. "The Feathered Serpent Pyramid at Teotihuacan: Its Possible Ideological Significance." *Ancient Mesoamerica* 2, no. 1: 93–106.

López Luján, Leonardo

1994. *The Offerings of the Great Temple of Tenochtitlan.* Trans. B. Ortiz de Montellano and T. Ortiz de Montellano. Niwot: University Press of Colorado.

Matos Moctezuma, Eduardo

1995. *Life and Death at the Templo Mayor.* Trans. B. Ortiz de Montellano and T. Ortiz de Montellano. Niwot: University Press of Colorado.

Miller, Arthur G., ed.

1983. *Highland-Lowland Interaction in Mesoamerica: Interdisciplinary Approaches.* Washington, DC: Dumbarton Oaks.

Santley, Robert S.

1983. "Obsidian Trade and Teotihuacan Influence in Mesoamerica." In A. G. Miller, ed., *Highland-Lowland Interaction in Mesoamerica: Interdisciplinary Approaches.* Washington, DC: Dumbarton Oaks, pp. 69–124.

Sharer, Robert J.

1983. "Interdisciplinary Approaches to the Study of Mesoamerican Highland-Lowland Interaction: A Summary View." In A. G. Miller, ed., *Highland-Lowland Interaction in Mesoamerica: Interdisciplinary Approaches.* Washington, DC: Dumbarton Oaks, pp. 241–263.

Wheatley, Paul

1983. *Nagara and Commandery: Origins of the Southeast Asian Urban Tradition.* Chicago: University of Chicago Department of Geography Research Paper nos. 207–208.

PART ONE

▼

THE PARADIGM SHIFTS
IN MESOAMERICAN STUDIES

▼

1

The Myth and Reality of Zuyuá

THE FEATHERED SERPENT AND MESOAMERICAN TRANSFORMATIONS FROM THE CLASSIC TO THE POSTCLASSIC

Alfredo López Austin and Leonardo López Luján

Translated by Scott Sessions

TO MARIANA

The Transformation from the Classic to the Postclassic

PERSPECTIVES ON THE TRANSITION

Three decades ago, there was no great discussion about distinguishing the Classic period from the Postclassic. Scholars at that time supposed a sudden transformation from peaceful societies ruled by priests to forms of secular and militaristic organization. This schematic view has given way in our day to the realization that the historical reality is far more complex. The differences between both periods, though still recognized, are less clear, especially if one takes into account the recent discoveries of the bellicose character of the cities of the Classic, the expansionist ambitions of their leaders, and the widespread practice of human sacrifice. Moreover, today we are becoming aware of the great diversity of paths that Mesoamerican societies followed in the twilight of the Classic period, in the transformation occurring between 650 and 900 C.E., and in the subsequent centuries preceding the arrival of Europeans. This leads us to inquire about the general historical processes of the Postclassic in conjunction with regional and temporal particularities within the overall setting.

Various friends and colleagues assisted us in the elaboration of this work, offering materials, criticisms, and valuable suggestions. We want to particularly thank Elizabeth H. Boone, Davíd Carrasco, Michel Graulich, Alicia Hernández, Lindsay Jones, Rex Koontz, Geoffrey McCafferty, Federico Navarrete, Xavier Noguez, Guilhem Olivier, Scott Sessions, and Karl Taube. This essay is a summarized version of our book, *Mito y realidad de Zuyuá: Serpiente Emplumada y las transformaciones mesoamericanas del Clásico al Posclásico*, Fideicomiso Historia de las Américas, Serie Ensayos (Mexico: El Colegio de México/FCE, 1999).

Already in 1959, Wigberto Jiménez Moreno had pointed out the need to define an intermediate period between the Classic and the Postclassic—the Epiclassic—which would explain the changes occurring between 600/700 and 900/1000 C.E. Although Jiménez Moreno and later Malcolm Webb (1978), in a Manichaean way, supposed the movement from theocratic to militaristic organization, they developed the models that serve as the foundation of the current debate. Obviously, not all contemporary authors agree on the defining characteristics of this period, which is reflected, among other aspects, in the multiplicity of names bestowed upon it, including the Late Classic, Terminal Classic, Proto-Postclassic, and Phase One of the Second Intermediate Period.

A NEW PERSPECTIVE

Gradually, archaeological discoveries and the decipherment of Maya glyphs have modified our appreciation of the differences between the Classic and the Postclassic. Consequently, current preoccupations are centered upon understanding a change that was not so radical or abrupt as previously supposed. Examples of this line of thinking were found in the summer seminar "Cultural Adjustments After the Decline of Teotihuacan," which took place at Dumbarton Oaks in 1984 (Diehl and Berlo 1989; see also Mendoza 1992). In spite of their different positions, the specialists insisted on four aspects that distinguished the transition: a) the emergence of new centers of power; b) population movements; c) new commercial arrangements; and d) religious and architectural innovations.

In fact, the principal signs of the time were political instability, social mobility, the emergence of new multi-ethnic centers of power, the restructuring of mercantile networks, the intensification of trade, the change of spheres of political and cultural interaction, and a distinct relationship between religion and politics. Along with many authors, we believe that the foundations of the Postclassic world reside in this period.

In the centuries following the decline of Teotihuacan, Mesoamerica became an enormous crucible where ethnic and culturally distinct peoples entered into contact and fused with one and other. The weakened power of some of the old capitals opened the way for the mobilization of broad demographic sectors. Generally, displacements of agriculturists did not involve great distances. Artisans, on the other hand, specializing in the production of prestige goods, tended to travel much farther during this period in search of elites who could patronize their activities. To these movements should be added those of merchants, warriors, priests, and rulers belonging to ethnic groups whose roles in Mesoamerican history would be decisive (Diehl 1989). In addition, we should mention the continuous migratory incursions of northern nomadic and semi-nomadic societies—bellicose groups who would forge new ways of life with the ancient inhabitants of Mesoamerica (Armillas 1964).

Everything seems to suggest that, from this time on, multi-ethnic settlements and confederations proliferated at the same time marriage alliances diversified among nobles of different dynasties. Alongside these developments, the regions of Central Mexico, the Gulf Coast, the Yucatán Peninsula, Chiapas, and Highland Guatemala became linked together in a manner still not fully understood (Webb 1978; Kowalski 1989).

One of the most impressive changes occurred in the realm of exchange. The monofocal Teotihuacan system gave way to a new mercantile structure that connected numerous production and distribution centers. This imbrication led to complex pan-Mesoamerican bonds among politically independent, cosmopolitan capitals that shared symbols of elite status and participated as equals in international exchange. Luxury goods such as fine salt, cotton, green obsidian, jewelry made of semiprecious stones, plumbate, and fine orange ceramics from many different places were traded practically everywhere in Mesoamerica (see Fahmel Beyer 1988). The system was significantly strengthened by the growing importance of maritime trade (Kepecs, Feinman, and Boucher 1994).

This richness of cultural contacts was also expressed in public art through coherent eclectic styles that spoke of real or fictitious relations (Nagao 1989; Jones 1995). In such a context the military apparatus grew in an unusual manner. This does not mean that during the Classic period constant bellicose conflicts did not exist, but during the Epiclassic, political instability assured that military concerns would permeate all aspects of social life. Thus, the new cities of this time were built on strategic sites, according to a strictly defensive plan.

Another fundamental aspect of the so-called Epiclassic—and one that lasted throughout the Postclassic—was a distinct relationship between religion and politics, a product of those times dominated by multi-ethnic political organizations. The node of this relationship was the complex formed by the primordial city of Tollan and its ruler, Feathered Serpent. Our essay focuses precisely on this politico-religious phenomenon that marked, in diverse ways and to varying degrees, the life of many Mesoamerican societies from the seventh to sixteenth centuries. Our purpose is the general characterization of this phenomenon and some of its expressions in different times and spaces. To this end, we will elaborate two explanatory models: one concerning the hegemonic groups' ideology and the other concerning the articulation of this ideology with politics.

We are aware, of course, that any model is a simplification of reality that privileges certain aspects. Our two models emphasize organizational forms and shared thinking in order to obtain a congruent description. It is evident, however, that the differences are greater than the similarities in the societies studied and that specific case studies highlighting the numerous historical particularities must follow our global evaluation of the phenomenon.

CHICHÉN ITZÁ AND TULA IN THE CENTER OF THE DEBATE

SISTER CITIES

It is well known that in Chichén Itzá, around the ninth century, Puuc style was present along with several harmoniously combined artistic elements from distant Mesoamerican regions. Accounting for the coexistence of these exogenous elements, fundamentally those from Central Mexico deemed "Toltec," has fueled one of the most passionate controversies in the history of Mesoamerican studies. More than a century ago, Désiré Charnay (1885) published his *Les anciennes villes du Nouveau Monde*, a book about his travels in Mexico and Central America between 1857 and 1882 under the patronage of the French government. Among his bizarre anecdotes and eccentric commentaries, Charnay noted an important fact that until then had eluded experts and amateurs alike: the enormous similarities between the architecture of Chichén Itzá and Tula, in spite of the hundreds of kilometers separating both sites. From this moment on, by means of archaeological excavations and quantitative analysis, researchers from the team of Alfred M. Tozzer (1957) began to uncover, one by one, the many shared characteristics, until completing an extensive inventory.

Comparisons between the two cities continue to this day. Concerning the configuration of the principal plazas of Chichén Itzá and Tula, Lindsay Jones (1993a, 1993b) has pointed out similarities in the orientation of monuments; the articulation of pyramid-raised temples over a rectangular, open courtyard in the form of an amphitheater; the correlative position of the ballcourts, *tzompantli*,[1] and platforms; the presence of large colonnaded areas (the Palacio Quemado, or Burnt Palace, in Tula and the Hall of a Thousand Columns in Chichén); and the existence of almost identical buildings (the Pyramid of Tlahuizcalpantecuhtli in the Toltec city and the Temple of the Warriors in the peninsular city).

These parallelisms, of course, are not limited to architecture; they extend to numerous cultural expressions such as myths, historical narratives, artifacts, mural painting, and especially sculpture. Similar sculptural features found at both sites include atlantes supporting lintels or altars, the so-called *chacmool* images (Figure 1.1), columns in the form of a descending feathered serpent, and standard-bearers with human or animal traits. Also abundant are the pilasters, benches, panels, and other architectural elements decorated with bas-relief motifs alluding to warfare and sacrifice, most notably, birds and felines devouring human hearts, mythical beings (part man, bird, and reptile), and processions of richly attired warriors armed with throwing-sticks and arrows.

BALANCING AN OLD DEBATE

Faced with such similarities, researchers have argued for decades, trying to explain simultaneously the kind of relations that could have existed between two cities so distant from each other *and* the nonexistence of the same type of manifestations in intermediate places between the two sites. The ongoing debate has yielded a wide range of responses that attempt to support themselves with various combinations of archaeological and written evidence.

Jones, in his monumental *Twin City Tales*, has presented a detailed historiographical study of this polemic (1995: 21–104). In the first part of his analysis, he summarizes the conceptions surrounding the relationships between the Maya and the peoples of Central Mexico. A long time ago a group of authors used to imagine the Maya and the "Mexicans" as two discrete and quite opposite units: the former more ancient, peaceful, and civilized; the latter more bellicose and less refined. More recently, ideas have changed since it is now thought that these two units derived from a more modest, common Mesoamerican descent, in constant demographic exchange of goods and ideas (32–42).

In the second part, Jones tackles three great controversies raised in turn to Tula and Chichén Itzá: the historicity of the mythical Tollan and its identification with the archaeological and historical Tula in the modern-day state of Hidalgo; the chronology of Chichén Itzá; and the connections between this urban center and Tula. Regarding the latter controversy, he brings up two groups of explanations that, in general terms, succeeded each other in time (60–75). He calls the hypotheses of the first group, those of "irreconcilable polarity." Their central idea is that a confrontation between the two different societies occurred and left one of them the loser.

In this respect, all kinds of propositions exist concerning the number of invasions, their nature, and the trajectories that followed. Charnay (1885), Daniel Brinton (1882), and Tozzer (1957) supposed the direct arrival of the Toltecs to

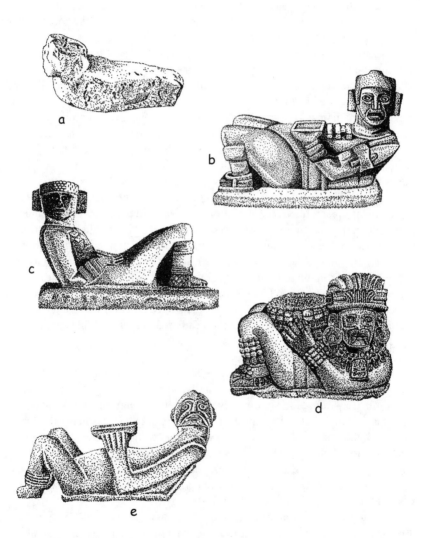

Fig. 1.1. Representations of the deity known as Chacmool: a. proto-*chacmool* from Cerro del Huistle, Jalisco (Chalchihuites culture), from Marie-Areti Hers 1989; b. Toltec; c. Maya from Chichén Itzá; d. Mexica; and e. Tarascan.

Chichén Itzá. Tozzer (1957: 53) affirmed that the Maya of Chichén were not invaded on one, but rather three successive occasions, by peoples originating from Central Mexico who had introduced—in addition to an architectural style of their own—the practices of human sacrifice, the phallic cult, and sodomy. First the Toltecs arrived, headed by Kukulcán I; then the Mexicanized Itzá from the Gulf Coast, led by Kukulcán II; and, finally, Mexican mercenaries from Tabasco. Sigvald Linné (1934), Sylvanus Morley (1947), and Tatiana Proskouriakoff (1950) proposed that peoples from Central Mexico did not arrive directly to Chichén Itzá, but rather established themselves previously in other zones of the Yucatán Peninsula, establishing relations with the local populations. Whether directly or indirectly, all these scenarios and many more perceived Tula as the indisputable motor of the process and the Maya capital as the "victim" of an invasion.

In stark contrast, George Kubler (1961) and Román Piña Chan (1980) inverted the causal equation to suggest that groups originating from the northern peninsula had founded a colony in Tula and built a modest copy of their capital there.

Jones later refers to a second group of hypotheses, those of "symbiotic polarity," which imagine more complex scenarios in which two or more societies established bonds of complementarity and collaboration, rather than coercion. In these explanations, the Itzá play a symbiotic role, and are used as "wild cards," attributing to them the most diverse ethnic affiliations, including Petén Maya, Toltecs, "Mexicanized" Maya, and Mayanized "Mexicans."

J. Eric S. Thompson (1975: 21–72) is the representative par excellence of this group. In his most refined reconstruction, he identified the Itzá with the Putún—powerful merchants and warriors of the Gulf region, who would have settled in Chichén Itzá in the tenth century, giving the city its first moment of glory. Sometime later, the Toltecs, led by Quetzalcoatl, would have fled their capital to take refuge with their Putún allies in coastal Tabasco. From there both peoples would make their way to Chichén Itzá. Thus, after this alliance was formed, the exiled Toltecs, bolstered by the power of the Putún, were able to re-create a new and more sumptuous Tula and introduce the Feathered Serpent cult in Chichén.

THE DEBATE TODAY

In recent times, the polemicists have left aside these two groups of hypotheses to explore new routes. Fundamentally, this has been possible thanks to incredible transformations in our way of conceiving Maya society. Today it is clear that Maya societies had always participated in an intense network of relations with the rest of Mesoamerica. These bonds would be strengthened in the ninth century, giving the Maya a cosmopolitan conception of the world. Along with these new scientific perspectives, many authors have supposed that the builders of Chichén Itzá were Maya who conscientiously imitated models from Central Mexico as part of a new political strategy.

Along this line of thinking, the hypothesis of Jones himself (1995: 76–78, 307–425) stands out, who in a suggestive manner thinks that the architectural and sculptural program of Chichén was eclectic and undertaken by local Maya groups, quite belligerent and knowledgeable of the outside world, given their mercantile activities. He deduces that the imitation of Toltec style could have resulted from a flow of ideas rather than that of human groups. The copy, stripped of its original significance and function, would have been integrated in this manner into a hybrid, cosmopolitan style whose purpose would be to ideologically legitimate before neighboring communities a recently attained hegemony.

Here it is interesting to compare the ideas of Jones with those of Marvin Cohodas (1989), who maintained that the "Toltec" elements of Chichén were not mere imitations of external ideas, but true esthetic innovations that created an eclectic art. The purpose that the rulers of Chichén pursued, according to Cohodas, was a political and economic relationship with Central Mexico.

OUR POSITION

Faced with this array of propositions, what is our position? Like Jones, we think that a clear intention existed in Chichén Itzá to reproduce elements of a style belonging to Central Mexico. This means that the direction of the flow—independent of those who were its historical agents—was from Central Mexico to Maya territory, because some cultural elements attributed to Tula have their antecedents five hundred years earlier in northern Mesoamerica. In fact, Marie-Areti Hers (1989) described not only a militaristic emphasis in the Classic societies of Jalisco, Zacatecas, and Durango, but also what appear to be the earliest examples of "hypostyle" halls, the *tzompantli*,[2] and, perhaps, the *chacmool*. Contrary to Kubler's proposition, she claimed that human groups from the Chalchihuites culture, together with the Nonoalca, gave origin to the Toltec tradition.

We also agree with Jones's assertion that the motives of imitation were of a political character. However, we believe that copying exogenous styles has a political meaning that goes much further than merely legitimizing a seductive cosmopolitan image. On the contrary, we think that these artistic phenomena are immersed in far more complex processes that have to do with political and ideological strategies appropriate for a new system of organization. There is another conception of power.

In this same sense, we judge that the analogies between Tula and Chichén Itzá should be analyzed in a much wider context, one that goes beyond the spatial and temporal limits of a specific case. We are referring to an historical process for which evidence seems to exist in a good portion of Mesoamerica from the Late Classic through all of the Postclassic. Written sources from many different regions continually allude to migrations, settlements, and conquests of foreign groups and contain coincidences of personages, religious symbols, and mystical journeys. Archaeology, on the other hand, reveals similarities in aspects such as settlement pattern, architectural styles, iconographic subject matter, and luxury objects. This leads us to believe that the problem is much greater than what has been posed until now.

Like all authors who have intervened in the debate, we base our proposal upon data that archaeology and history offer. However, it is appropriate to state that these data and the methodology of both disciplines have grave limitations. On the one hand, archaeologists have not developed sufficiently complex techniques for detecting the very different flows of humans and ideas that existed in Mesoamerica. The existence and nature of these flows are not necessarily revealed in the traces of demographic variations nor in the presence of exogenous cultural traits (Arnauld and Michelet 1991). On the other hand, historians are faced with very particular Mesoamerican conceptions of history that make the direct interpretation of texts and distinguishing myth, history, and political propaganda within them extremely difficult (Marcus 1992b).

A good part of the investigations that have tried to resolve this issue has proceeded from the disciplines of archaeology and history. Even in the best of cases, archaeologists have supported themselves in nonanalytical readings of texts, or historians in archaeological findings that are too specific. Lacking, in the face of these problems, has been a global, critical comparison of a considerable, diverse accumulation of historical and archaeological data.

Moreover, it seems pertinent to us that in order to breathe new life into the discussion regarding Tula–Chichén Itzá connections, the specific case must be transcended. This means studying similar phenomena that took place within the overall cultural area between 900 and 1500 C.E. The similarities, of course, are not absolute and become evident when comparing information from areas as distant as Central Mexico, Michoacán, Oaxaca, Highland Guatemala, and Yucatán. None of these regions offer all of the urban, architectural, iconographic, mythical, archaeological, and historical indicators. We are facing a *polythetic group*, whose entities share a good number of attributes, but none of them possess them *all*.[3]

To manage richer and more varied information and widen the spatial-temporal focus, we present the following two models of general explanation.

THE MODELS

AN ATTEMPT AT AN EXPLANATION OF GREATER SCOPE: THE ZUYUANS

These observations led us to formulate a proposition in an earlier book, intended to provide a global view of the indigenous past throughout the territory corresponding to modern-day Mexico (López Austin and López Luján 1996: 247–271). Particular characteristics of the work—above all, the small amount of space we had for each one of the historical periods—limited our presentation of the proposal to a mere outline. We will now develop some of its aspects.

As one might guess from the problems we posed at the beginning of this essay, research in the last few years has tended to look for:

a) A politico-ideological explanation of the problem.

b) Answers from a wider spatial-temporal range, given that the political relationships of the Postclassic present disturbing common aspects.

Various authors have preceded us in emphasizing the politico-ideological character of the problem. For example, Brinton (1890: 83–100) expressed an ideological explanation in his *Essays of an Americanist*. According to him, the process studied, which for many other specialists was produced by invasions of foreign peoples, did not necessarily occur because of population movements: what traveled were not peoples, but rather ideological paradigms and religious and aesthetic ideas. Linnea Wren and Peter Schmidt (1991), on the other hand, in studying the art of Chichén Itzá, found the simultaneity of two different styles substantiating the harmonic coexistence of ruling groups from different ethnic communities, and concluded that the so-called Modified Florescent style, rather than merely suggesting the existence of a flow, in whichever direction between Tula and Chichén Itzá, may have been the product of elites who propagated a new multi-ethnic policy of greater integration. For Jones (1995), as we have seen, there was a clear intention of reproducing architectural, sculptural, and pictographic styles of outside origin, as there was a quest for political prestige, along with a seductive propagandistic image of cosmopolitanism; copying the model of a remote capital hallowed in glory was desirable.

We can say much more about authors who have looked for a wider interpretive radius in terms of time and space. One of the first explanations that transcended the case of Chichén Itzá attributed the innovative processes emerging in northern Yucatán and Highland Guatemala to a single group of people. This was the position of Thompson (1975: 21–72), followed by many other researchers, which identified this group of people as the Putún or Chontal Maya of the coast of Tabasco and Campeche.

Marie-Charlotte Arnauld and Dominique Michelet (1991) also attributed a common cause to processes occurring in distinct regions of Mesoamerica. They demonstrated that a background of radical sociopolitical transformation exists in indigenous Tarascan and Quiché migration stories that should not necessarily be explained in terms of invasions.

We will reconsider both explicative currents. The historical event studied, in fact, has a profound political nature. In it one can observe—with particular shades of temporal, regional, and historical diversity—the confrontations between those who tried to maintain the ancient forms of sociopolitical organization and those who looked for a definitive change. As in different Mesoamerican political movements, the innovators supported their conception of dominion and control in a mythological and ritual complex derived from millenarian religious traditions, but in this case, under a new interpretation that fulfilled the political functions of the moment. This was not an exceptional phenomenon, inasmuch as Mesoamerican religion was utilized as a component of political action. And, of course, the new religious interpretation did not depend upon universal acceptance. In some written sources it is said that during the conflicts those who disagreed were denounced as heretics and sinners.

The fundamental purpose of this essay is to find a link between political action that attempted to make changes in regional relations and an ideological complex that served to support them. For many years, specialists—especially Mayanists—have recognized the ideological nucleus: the Tollan-Quetzalcoatl duality.[4] This duality constituted a paradigm of the primordial order of society, religion, and authority (Carrasco 1992: 1–2, 106). Our problem now is to determine how politics, religion, mythology, and ritual were related.

The historical scenarios and times were diverse (see Map 1.1). Among them would be found:

a) Central Mexico, with its privileged position in Tula, Cholula, and the Basin of Mexico.
b) Michoacán, with Tarascan expansion.
c) Oaxaca, with disputes among the Mixtec kingdoms.
d) Northern Yucatán, with majestic Chichén Itzá at its head.

e) Highland Guatemala, with the aggressive expansion of the Quiché, Cakchiquel, and Rabinal Maya.

Concerning the actors, these were:

a) on the one hand, original peoples with conservative tendencies
b) on the other hand, innovators who could just as well be native groups as immigrants or invaders.

The problem of naming half of the actors arises.[5] Taking into account that current investigations dismiss the idea of indispensable military flows penetrating the affected regions to impose their dominion, what name would be generically suitable to give to these innovators? Fray Diego de Landa (1982: 16) quite inappropriately called the aggressive outsiders who supported the illegitimate government of the Cocom in Mayapán, "Mexicans." Centuries later, Thompson (1964: 114–144) would perpetuate the absurd name, comparing them with the destructive honey moth that had invaded the industrious Maya beehive, and one still hears the term.[6] The terms "Toltec" and "Chontal-Putún" are inadequate because they do not extend to the realities of Michoacán and Oaxaca. In fact, any names with ethnic content are limited when facing the possibility that at least some of the political innovators were natives of the affected zones. In short, we cannot give a name to these actors that indicates an ethnicity, language, or place of origin, because other aspects besides ethnic, linguistic, and those of ideological origin are crucial for understanding the historical process.

If this process is of a profoundly political character and is based in myth, our designation of the innovators should come from their own discourse. Given that the reference that they themselves had to a place of origin exists as a common denominator, and that one of the many names of this place is *Zuyuá*, we believe it is accurate to call them *Zuyuans*.

DEFINITION OF THE ZUYUAN POLITICAL SYSTEM

We understand the Zuyuan system as a form of sociopolitical organization and suggest that its primary characteristic is control, on the part of an organic hegemonic complex of settlements of diverse ethnicities who inhabited a region, through a system that assigned an economic and political place and function to each one of the subordinate political entities. This system tended to the maintenance of (traditional ethnic) internal public order and respected the ideological foundations of power in each one of the units; but superimposed a multi-ethnic apparatus as the head of the global organization.[7]

The Zuyuan system differed from the forms of political organization of the Classic in at least three spheres:

a) The type of multi-ethnic structure.
b) The type of hegemonic influence and dominion of some political units over others.
c) The type of bellicose action.

First, we will look at the ethnic sphere. From the indigenous perspective, each human group had a patron deity, a profession received from this deity, and a language. Gentillic identity was a principle of the first order in the political life of

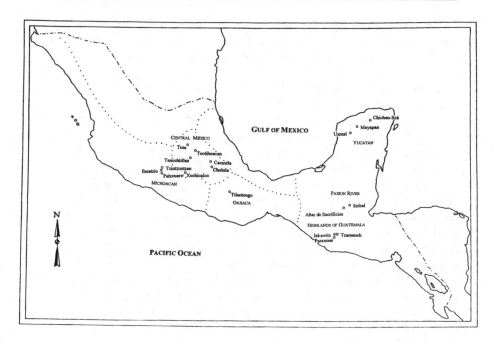

Map 1.1. Mesoamerica: Some capitals of the Classic, Epiclassic, and Postclassic.

Mesoamerican peoples. Externally, on the one hand, this identity regulated permanent political relationships among the different political units. Internally, on the other hand, it was one of the pillars of governmental authority.

Much of the iconographic and epigraphic evidence from the Classic period reveals that royal authority was based on the supposed proximity between sovereign and patron deity. The sovereign not only operated as the intermediary between the patron deity and the protected collectivity, but he also retained within himself such an affinity with the deity that he was considered superhuman, the very image of the numen over the earth. The sovereign was the "elder sibling" of his subjects, on a level of kinship that legitimated his sacred power over them.

The sacrality of the ruler through his proximity to the deity finds its prototype in the Classic Maya. The great splendor of the Maya kings was not reached in any other Mesoamerican region. This system of the sacralized "elder sibling," however, does not seem to have been sufficient in Teotihuacan. Elsewhere, we have suggested that Teotihuacan was confronted, from very early times, with the necessity of integrating diverse ethnic units under a common government (López Austin 1989; López Austin and López Luján 1996: 112–114). Ethnic composition required the fulfillment of two conditions: first, the necessity of maintaining the principle of authority of different "elder siblings," or representatives of the respective patron deities of each of the units being integrated; second, the constitution of a supra-ethnic, organic, governing collective that, without ignoring the legitimacy of the ethnic rulers and their religious foundations, was sheltered under the divine protection of a global patron deity. We have supposed that the solution was located for the most part in the character of the exalted patron: He had to be situated at the top, not strictly as a supra-ethnic deity, but as the "territorial patron deity."

If our proposition is correct, then a combination of the two systems of government would have been produced: the traditional, based on the kingship ties of the community with their patron deities (in each of the units within the political system), and the global, based on territory. By means of the first system, power would be exercised over individuals by their ethnic dependency, independent of where they were located; in the second, it would be exercised over all the settlements of a territory, independent of their ethnic group. If this combination of two systems of dominion had been initiated in Teotihuacan, similar solutions may have endured in some Mesoamerican states on until the sixteenth century. In fact, these two forms of power (gentillic and territorial), did exist simultaneously in the Mexica state and in many others on the eve of the Conquest (López Austin 1985: 232–234; López Austin and López Luján 1996: 205–208).

The Zuyuan system, as we shall immediately see, also tried to resolve the problem of ethnic integration with respect to diversity. But this was done by reducing it, ideologically, with the conception of the essential unit of humankind under a divine order that had produced several different human groups. Each group was considered a complementary element of a human complex in service to the gods. Humans, as collaborators of the gods, were agents of divine will over the earth; each different human group had a specific function it had to carry out as its particular mission.

We now move on to the second sphere: the way in which some political units influenced and dominated others. The Maya regimes of the Classic period were characterized by their dispersion. Supra-statal cohesion was attained through alliances and conquests; but a strong autonomous position within the diverse political units and relative instability when facing their neighbors prevailed. Permanent bonds between a metropolis and its dependents and allies could be cemented by extending its ruling lineages. Tikal came to dominate an area of 30,000 km², either directly, by sending nobles of the royal lineage as rulers, or through alliance, by sending royal women to become the marriage partners of neighboring sovereigns (Marcus 1992a). In Oaxaca during the Classic period, Monte Albán had successfully achieved an extensive dominion through military expansion. However, we still know little of its level of cohesion and system of domination. On the other hand, Teotihuacan had economic superiority and political influence over nearly all of Mesoamerica. Although the stages of its ascendancy varied, this seems to have been cemented for the most part in the control of production and mercantile exchange, not in a formalized political framework.

After the fall of Teotihuacan, new forms of political organization seem to have been produced. For the Epiclassic, the "celestial sign" glyph has been interpreted as indicative of a more formal pact between powerful states (Marcus 1992a). It consists of a rectangle from which two open hands emerge, and may also contain the nose and fauces of a jaguar. This glyph is found associated with others depicting weapons, giving it the possible meaning of a military alliance.

The glyph developed between 650 and 900 C.E. in Monte Albán, Zaachila, Xochicalco, and Cacaxtla.

The Postclassic regimes that we are calling Zuyuan, in contrast to those preceding them, attempted regional dominion through the imposition of a thoroughly formalized politico-economic structure. Their confederations of hegemonic capitals were not merely military alliances, but jurisdictional organs of great administrative complexity.[8]

Finally, we will mention what corresponds to the third sphere of political difference: the bellicose. Numerous researchers have contributed in the last fifteen years to refute the utopian idea of a Teotihuacan and Maya Classic period of peace and tranquillity. Nevertheless, there is little doubt that the Zuyuan system exceeded the limits of Classic-period bellicosity, above all, because it was not only a warrior regime, but also a militarist regime.

In summary, the Zuyuans constructed a system whose cohesion was based on two apparently contradictory principles. On the one hand, they followed an ideological path that was reinforced by maintaining a peace and harmony among peoples that supposedly was a reflection of universal order. On the other hand, Zuyuan states developed powerful military bodies of control and undertook aggressive campaigns of expansion against weaker ones. The Zuyuan system was an enterprise of enforced harmony.

THE NECESSITY OF FORMULATING MODELS

One reason, of an ontological character—the historical and cultural unity of Mesoamerica—and another, of an epistemological character—the limitation of the sources for knowing what they really thought—make the global study of ideology attractive and necessary. Perspectives that limit the study of a Mesoamerican tradition to an overly specific temporal and spatial scope obscure the general historical meaning of social and political events of great dimensions. Therefore, we propose a different path, divided into two methodological stages:

a) First, a global understanding of the subject, including the formulation of one or more explanatory models.
b) Second, research circumscribed to specific times, spaces, and cultures, delving deeper into the particularities of the case, but without losing its wider Mesoamerican context.

In this essay we will be concerned with covering the first methodological stage, for which we mention beforehand some specific aspects of the formulated models:

a) They derive, as one might suppose, from many earlier investigations conducted by specialists with particular foci, whose data will be integrated in such a manner that permits one to get a sense of the general historical process.
b) They are intended to be instruments of methodological orientation and not Procrustean beds; in any case, their primordial character is hypothetical.
c) Two models are offered to the reader (one corresponding to Zuyuan religious and mythological ideology and one concerning the articulation of this ideology with politics), more for facilitating exposition than for logical reasons,

since both make up an indissoluble unit.

d) First, the outlines of the model are presented; and second, the specific data that gave rise to it (in reverse order from how we proceeded) so that the reader perceives with greater clarity the historical meaning that we intend to uncover.

e) In spite of the fact that we have made use of a greater amount of space to discuss our proposition in this essay, we recognize that our presentation is susceptible to extensive additions and corrections, for which we submit it to the criticism of our colleagues.

IN SEARCH OF A MODEL OF ZUYUAN IDEOLOGY

The mythical and religious foundations of Zuyuan ideology had the characteristics of a propaganda that, in spite of the military backing of its propagators, attempted to convince rather than oppose. The act of its diffusion in those very different Mesoamerican scenarios itself tells us of its efficacy, and this, in terms of the beliefs, rituals, and imagery of the innovators, must have been presented as a sublimation of the traditional creed rather than a confrontation. In this sense, rather than thinking about this conception as a heretical deviation, we should consider it a mytho-religious adaptation to the political requirements of the innovators. They will accentuate some myths, develop others; increase or diminish the importance of specific deities; introduce or transform rituals; but always striving to maintain an equilibrium between their discourse and the beliefs and practices of the native population, faithful to their traditions and overly susceptible when faced with changes. This can be accepted in general terms; however, during the confrontations, it reached the point that each of the factions accused the other of impiety, heresy, or sin.

The ideology had to resolve a fundamental mytho-political antithesis: the unity/diversity of humans, from which derived the unity/diversity of the religious foundation of power. The mythical figure to which one could appeal to resolve the antithesis was the Tollan-Quetzalcoatl complex, one which, without negating diversity, subjugated it harmoniously.[9] We will look into the matter in greater detail.

According to Mesoamerican cosmovision, all worldly beings were composed of weighted matter and divine substance. Each living species had a particular divine substance in which resided their inherent characteristics. Human beings were more complex than the other creatures. They had, along with the divine substance that characterized them as members of the human race, that which made them belong to a particular gentillic group, defined, among other characteristics, by a language. This double ascription (to the human race and to the gentillic group) was explained through a mythology that distinguished between the common origin of humanity and the gentillic origins of human groups. Some creation myths explained how divine substance was added to give existence to the human race; others, how humanity, once created, was divided into groups that appeared in the world separately, led by their respective patron deities.

Each human group had a patron deity with whom they shared their divine substance. Mesoamericans conceived of a complex hierarchy of patron deities correlating to the social hierarchy. For example, minor patron deities were merged to form more powerful deities when the union of minor social units constituted larger groups. The fusion and fission of deities was characteristic of Mesoamerican religion, and the rank of the patrons was a reflection of social segmentation (see Table 1.1).

It is not strange, therefore, that the historical and ethnographic sources would offer us an enormous range of patron deities. The most well known are those of the Nahua *calpulli*-type or Mixtec *siqui*-type communities;[10] but minor social units such as families had patron deities, as did those of the major units, up to entire ethnic groups, such as the eponymic patron deity of all the Otomí, or Mixtecs, or Huastecs, etc. (López Austin 1994: 35–39).

The place of origin of the human groups is mysterious and shrouded in mist. The great quantity of names in the sources is surprising. This rich toponymy could be due to two nonexclusive causes: a) the place of origin had many attributes, expressed in epithets, and b) it had a complex topology that suggested specific names for each one of its compartments. The names are so numerous that it is unclear if they refer to sequences in the gestation process of the newborns, or the itineraries that the newborns followed to emerge into the world, or are merely qualifying adjectives.

Among the names given to the primogenial place are found: Where the Tree Stands Erect, The Place of the Ancestors, The Ravine, The Place of Passage, The Place of the Mountain of the Serpent, Where the Flowers Stand Up Straight,

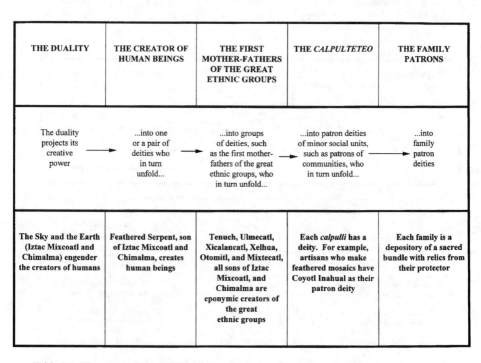

THE DUALITY	THE CREATOR OF HUMAN BEINGS	THE FIRST MOTHER-FATHERS OF THE GREAT ETHNIC GROUPS	THE *CALPULTETEO*	THE FAMILY PATRONS
The duality projects its creative power →	...into one or a pair of deities who in turn unfold... →	...into groups of deities, such as the first mother-fathers of the great ethnic groups, who in turn unfold... →	...into patron deities of minor social units, such as patrons of communities, who in turn unfold... →	...into family patron deities
The Sky and the Earth (Iztac Mixcoatl and Chimalma) engender the creators of humans	Feathered Serpent, son of Iztac Mixcoatl and Chimalma, creates human beings	Tenuch, Ulmecatl, Xicalancatl, Xelhua, Otomitl, and Mixtecatl, all sons of Iztac Mixcoatl, and Chimalma are eponymic creators of the great ethnic groups	Each *calpulli* has a deity. For example, artisans who make feathered mosaics have Coyotl Inahual as their patron deity	Each family is a depository of a sacred bundle with relics from their protector

Table 1.1. The succession of divine delegations.

Where the Curved Mountain Rises, The Place of He Who Is Adorned With Paper, Where the Blue-Green Water and the Yellow Water Flow, The Place of Reeds, The Place of the Bifurcation, In the Fauces of the Serpent, The Place of the Seven Caves, The Place of the Nine Ravines, and The Place of the Nine. Judging from the frequent confusion in the sources, it is to be supposed that the contradictions or the diversity of interpretations would already, in the past, be part of the mysterious aspect of another time-space.

The creation process in which the human groups emerge consists of three phases: the nocturnal, the auroral, and the sunrise (Table 1.2).[11]

The nocturnal phase is initiated with the formation of the species by a generic creator deity. There is a primogenial nondistinction, in that all human beings live together, speak the same language, and do not know any particular patron deities. This existence can be compared to intrauterine life, from gestation to the moment prior to birth.

In the auroral phase, the light of Venus produces the colors and with them are born order and time. Order, the colors, and time are encapsulated in the symbolism of the four cosmic trees that sink roots down into the world of the dead and support the celestial levels with their canopies. The trees are individualized by their colors, which mark their position in the cosmos.

The presence of the trees indicates the flow of the divine forces that gave rise to the world and maintain its existence. Standing out among these forces is time, also a divine substance, which extends over the earth's surface in the form of rigid calendrical order. In the primogenial place, time begins to circulate inside the trunks of the cosmic trees. The trees, therefore, record the sequence of the

```
CHICHIMECS ──────────────▶
        Wait inside Chicomoztoc
          Leave the mountain
            Learn to speak
              Learn to eat maize
                Obtain their profession-mission
                  Journey poor and naked
                    Struggle against enemies
                      Take possession of land
                        Begin ordered life
        ─────────────────────────────────▶TOLTECS

MOUNTAIN ──────────────────────────────────▶ PLAIN
```

NIGHT darkness, humidity, malleability	DAWN light, colors, order, time	SUNRISE heat, dryness, strength
Feathered Serpent creates human beings	Feathered Serpent distributes the patron deities, languages, sacred bundles, professions, and missions	The patron deities turn into stone
Feathered Serpent conciliates the extraction and cycle of maize		The first mother-fathers miraculously disappear
Nondifferentiated existence of the human groups	The first mother-fathers guide their human groups	The first mother-fathers are praised by their children in
Sin motivates the expulsion	Arrival at the promised land	leading the group

Table 1.2. Human beings, from creation to the beginning of life in the world.

deities upon their permanent entry into the world: they establish the rules of their appearance and the specific time of their influences. In other words, with calendrical time were born order, law, distribution, etc.

In the auroral phase, the various human groups started rising to the surface of the world in distinct historical moments. Often these would be multiple births of seven in seven groups.[12] The cause of birth could be imagined as a transgression committed in the primordial place that forces them to abandon the placid place of origin. This distinction occurs at the moment the light of dawn appears. Each human group acquires its coessential, patron deity, along with their language,[13] particular customs, divine image, and sacred bundle.[14] The patron presents the group with a profession—an art—that will become a sacred exercise. This phase includes their departure from The House of the Four Trees, their crossing of the waters of the sea, and their suffering great torments. According to the different myths of origin, the group is born as a multitude of humans or simply in the form of "first mother-fathers"—Edenic pairs, whose personalities come to be confused with those of the patron deities, because they are their derivations, their realization.[15] Often the story of the four "first fathers" is told and, occasionally, their consorts are mentioned. After the departure from The House of the Four Trees comes the dispersion of the human groups, who begin to journey distances on their own in search of the promised land. This stage can be compared with birth.

In the sunrise phase, the groups take possession of the land and the "first mother-fathers" disappear. This time corresponds to the beginning of life.

The first two phases of creation—the nocturnal and the auroral—are dominated by the figure of the creator deity of the human race. During the night he forms humans. After this he is the *accoucheur*, the Lord of the Dawn, the one who organizes and distributes humans in the world. Order is established under the form of a donation of goods. The creator deity is the great distributor of the riches corresponding to each group. In fact he delivers himself in the form of specific patron deities; he is projected in multiple segmentations. He gives each group the image of the patron and the sacred bundle containing the indispensable relics, cementing the direct relationship between protector and protected.[16]

The creator of humanity receives many names, among them Feathered Serpent, Our Venerable Noble, The Conqueror, Four Feet, Flower, and 1 Reed. Obviously, he is one of the most important deities in the Mesoamerican pantheon. Feathered Serpent seems, at first glance, to be a mélange of incongruous symbols: his body forms a column that supports the sky; his powers extend to the wind, light and colors, dawn, and the course of Venus; he plays an active role in human gestation; he is the inventor of the calendar and, consequently, of temporal order; he is the bandit-bestower who transfers the most precious goods (bones, fire, maize, and pulque) from the time-space of the gods to that of humans; he is the divinity of commerce, priestly knowledge, and even robbery through sorcery.

Feathered Serpent, however, could not be conceived as a divinity that accumulated attributes over the centuries. Within his range of powers exists a logic, a meaning that unifies these attributes. If we wanted to characterize Feathered Serpent in a formula, we would say that he is the divine being that causes the flow of substances between the world of the gods and the world of humans: he is the *extractor*. As the wind, he opens the way for the rains; as Venus he opens, alternately, the way to the sun and to the shadows of the night; as lord of the cosmic trees, he opens the calendrical way to the gods transformed in time; he extracts the human race, its diverse groups, and the child who is born; he extracts light, heat, and food for humankind. He transcends boundaries (see Table 1.3).

Before leaving the subject of the three phases of human creation, we want to mention the importance that geometry, colors, and numbers have in the origin of order in the universe. The cosmos was divided into three great levels: the sky, the surface of the earth, and the underworld. The three were connected by five columns or axes—usually, flowering trees—that occupied the center and each one of the four cardinal points. These five arboreal axes were distinguished from each other by a certain color and, occasionally, by other diagnostic features. In this manner, numbers and colors served as guides to the structure and mechanics of the universe.

The Flowering Tree was the central axis of the cosmos. Inside its trunk flowed two opposing, complementary forces—fire and water—into which all that existed was divided. Like the gods, the tree was projected to the four cardinal extremes in the world and, correspondingly, the two opposing forces were reproduced in pairs within each trunk. In this game of replication, the numbers one, two, four, and five stand out. With these numbers and colors, the flow of divine forces, including time, was symbolized.

ATTRIBUTES	CONDUCT		CHARACTERIZATION
GOD OF THE DAWN GOD OF VENUS GOD OF THE COLORS	*extractor*	of the light	CIVILIZER WARRIOR
WIND GOD	*extractor*	of the rains	BESTOWER REPRODUCER
COSMIC TREE COLUMN SUPPORTING THE WORLD INVENTOR OF THE CALENDAR	*extractor-organizer*	of time	ORGANIZER RULER
CREATOR DEITY OF HUMANKIND GENERAL PATRON OF HUMANITY GOD OF GESTATION	*extractor*	of human beings	REPRODUCER PROTECTOR BESTOWER
INVENTOR OF *PULQUE* EXTRACTOR OF MAIZE STEALER OF FIRE GOD OF COMMERCE	*extractor-conductor*	of the goods of humanity	BESTOWER REPRODUCER CIVILIZER MERCHANT

Table 1.3. Attributes, mythical conduct, and characterization of Feathered Serpent.

To summarize this section, the Tollan–Feathered Serpent complex constitutes the ideological essence of the Zuyuan system. Feathered Serpent, the *extractor*, creates in the night, distributes at dawn, and protects during the day. Tollan is his home, the house of the dawn, the origin of temporal, spatial, and social order. The primogenial light, arriving in Tollan at the moment when the human groups abandon it, makes the colors appear; the colors mark the points where the archetypal trees stand erect; the trees reveal the three cosmic levels that act as passageways to the gods. There in Tollan, Feathered Serpent is ruler, organizer, and distributor. And when the inhabitants of Tollan leave, Feathered Serpent, in the ultimate, auroral act, fragments and distributes himself by turning into the bestowers, the patron deities. Thus divided, he delivers a part of his own essence to humankind: he gives them different languages, he imparts to them the professions, he marks the specific ritual obligations, he situates each human group on the surface of the earth, and, when the groups are finally settled, from each unit of his divided being he makes humans and their maize plots fertile.

Finally, there is an aspect that should be emphasized: Feathered Serpent, as an astral divinity, as a being of light who defeats the powers of darkness and the night, is an aggressive, warrior deity. His figure as Lord of the Dawn is one of an armed and belligerent god.[17] Thus, another one of his names is The Conqueror.

IN SEARCH OF A MODEL OF THE ARTICULATION OF ZUYUAN POLITICS

The Zuyuans recognized and respected the internal regimes of the peoples drawn into their dominion, since this order emanated from the different patron deities. They advocated, simultaneously, the formation of a superior political example. Their innovation consisted of a center-periphery structure with a greater range, which went beyond ethnic and linguistic boundaries, without dismissing the value of their primogenial distinctions. This order was established in each region; the independent political units in constant conflict were integrated within a corporate governmental institution. This institution established the hierarchy of its components, distributed jurisdictions and functions according to a cosmic model, imposed a harmonious coexistence, and permitted the organization of a military authority for internal control, defense, and expansion.

The innovators were said to come from the source of order itself: The Place of Reeds, The Place of the Seven Caves. They were put in charge of reproducing the primordial order over the earth, of projecting Tollan in the world. This action made necessary the establishment of a network of governmental, military, and ritual functions that considerably increased administrative capacities and warrior power.

Cosmic geometry was projected in political organization. The hegemonic capitals often established their internal government upon a dualistic division. Externally, a tripartite system—which we think derived from the division of the cosmos into celestial, terrestrial, and underworld levels—commonly gave rise to an alliance among three hegemonic capitals. This allowed for multi-ethnic composition, which was one of the firmest pillars of the new power.

Inside and outside these capitals, power was distributed according to a rigid formula of functions and hierarchies. Territory customarily was segmented bureaucratically into four parts, corresponding to the divisions of the terrestrial level, and the quadrants of time and space, with their symbolic colors, organized lineages, bureaucratic bodies, functions, and power.

The earthly was a replica of the divine. For centuries rulers had been presenting themselves as spokesmen of the gods, and this arrangement had to continue. Although the traditional rulers—"natural lords," as many sources call them— were said to be privileged bearers of the essence of their respective patrons, the supreme Zuyuan ruler received the force of the generic creator of the human race: Feathered Serpent. He was the gods' replica in the world. Thus, more than a few rulers appear in history bearing some of his names: their biographies are charged with wonder and their lives follow the patterns of the Lord of the Dawn's adventures.

The ability of Feathered Serpent to be divided into various entities was also projected into the political order. As we shall see, the man-god, the earthly recipient of fire from the supreme patron (the one who presided over the man-god-patrons), was not always one individual, since the force of the generic creator could be distributed among two or more human beings to constitute a compound delegation.

The new system reproduced among the rulers the deity-creator/deities-patrons relationship, and at the same time legitimated a superior order that unified the diverse (Table 1.4). The traditional rulers, since remote times, had celebrated rituals renewing their sacred political power through the mystical path of meeting with their patron deity, the great ancestor. In the new order, the delegation of divine power formed a pyramid. Feathered Serpent, The Conqueror, Lord of the Dawn transmitted authority to terrestrial representatives, and they, in turn, authorized the charges of the "natural lords." This system obligated the supreme delegate to travel to the Place of Reeds to obtain the god's power. The written sources refer to the sovereign's legitimating journey as the miraculous crossing to another time-space, where he received as gifts the symbols of the deity's power—the sacred bundle,[18] the diagnostic adornments, the book, jewels, musical instruments, emblems, mantles, etc.—or to the sanctuary that reproduced the place of creation. In the sanctuary, a representative of Feathered Serpent, during the pilgrimage, pierced the nasal wing membrane or nasal partition to insert a jewel that identified him, in turn, as the redistributor of the sacred instruments of power and governmental legitimacy. Through ritual, both officiant and penitent achieved communion with the god, both partook of his essence.

All this appeared in a context of opposition between two cultural categories: the *chichimecayotl* and the *toltecayotl*, nomads and sedentaries, barbarism and civilization. Zuyuans extolled their nomadic Chichimec origins; but their political message was the civilized *toltecayotl*. How can this be understood? In this opposition, values from two extreme conditions experienced during the auroral phase were being expressed. When the human groups began setting auroral time in motion, when they left The Place of the Seven Caves, they were semiconscious, as if inebriated, still possessed by the forces of the night; they were described as savages, crude, ignorant of correct forms of expression. It is said that they did not even know about eating maize, one of the goods that Feathered Serpent had stolen for humans.[19] But their condition started to be transformed on their mythical

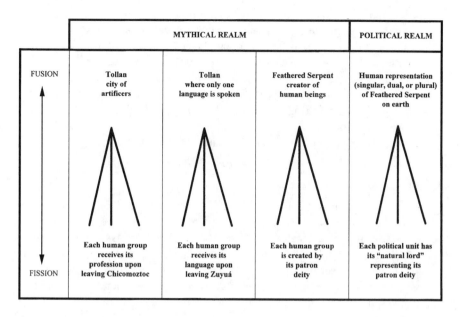

Table 1.4. Transitions between unity and diversity in the divine and worldly realms.

journey until being replaced by civilization.[20] This was reached at sunrise, that is to say, in the time of the founding of their settlements, the establishment of great order, the beginning of Zuyuan cultural and political realization.[21] We think that the ontological change between *chichimecayotl* and *toltecayotl* is not simply a confrontation of opposites, but rather a transition of the human groups in the auroral phase, the supposed transformation of the poor migrants who arrive, in the end, at the promised land to await the first rising of the sun.[22] As Fray Bernardino de Sahagún (1989, Lib. X, cap. xxix, II: 650) says, "These said Toltecs all were named Chichimecs, and had no other particular name, except for the one taken from the curiosity and excellence of the works they created, they were called Tultecas, which is the same as us saying 'refined and curious artificers,' as those now of Flanders."[23]

In the terrestrial Tollans, the primogenial order of diversity was renewed under one unique power: the power of those who personified the archetypal Toltec ruler. The name "Tula" became synonymous with "civilized metropolis."

THE ABANDONMENT OF THE ZUYUAN SYSTEM

Before testing our models with specific cases, it is necessary to mention the two ways in which the Zuyuan system or its attempted implementation came to its end.

The first way, which we may call Mixtec-Maya, was the deterioration that led to political disintegration in Oaxaca, Yucatán, and Highland Guatemala. The second, which we can call Tarascan-Mexica, was, in contrast, the surmounting of the system by more centralized and powerful regimes. Along these lines, the processes in Michoacán and in the Basin of Mexico were similar: on the political terrain, one of the hegemonic states unseated its two allies to become the superior power; ideologically, the winners declared that their own patron deity had the function of "foster father" over all the communities (López Austin 1992; López Austin and López Luján 1996: 270–271). Thus, the Tarascan and Mexica written sources, rather than referring to systems totally Zuyuan in character, illustrate a transitional process toward a more novel order that was interrupted by the Spanish Conquest: the order of Huitzilopochtli and that of Curicaueri.

MESOAMERICAN SCENARIOS

CENTRAL MEXICO

Although we have tried in this essay to relate very synthetically specific cases to the application of the models, none of the sections are as drastically condensed as this one dedicated to Central Mexico. The reasons for abbreviating are appreciable: on the one hand, the volume of data is so great that more detailed attention would offset the balance of the presentation; on the other hand, we have referred to these problems in various earlier works. We therefore will highlight only some of the important points, with the purpose of returning to the topic in the future.

Teotihuacan, Xochicalco, Cacaxtla, and Teotenango. In the Metepec Phase, when Teotihuacan lived its ultimate times of splendor and retained a population of eighty thousand inhabitants (Sanders 1989), some foretelling signs of change appeared. Cohodas (1989) has said that warfare was exalted in mural painting and funerary pottery, artistic phenomena that also occurred in Xochicalco and Cacaxtla. On the other hand, Esther Pasztory (1988) notes that, as a result of competition with Xochicalco and Cacaxtla, Teotihuacan art of the Metepec Phase turned more virtuous and complex.[24] The figurines of the period show exalted and richly attired personages, while, according to her, the mural painting emphasized individualism and nobiliary secularity.

Unfortunately, we lack written sources that speak specifically about the possible roots of Zuyuan ideology in Teotihuacan, Xochicalco, Cacaxtla, Teotenango, or Cholula. Nevertheless, some characteristics exist in these centers that could be situated within the spectrum of our study (cf. Carrasco 1992: 106).[25] The first of these is the paramount importance of Feathered Serpent. In the iconography of Cacaxtla and Xochicalco this god is represented as an ophidian with long barbs.[26] The second feature is the militaristic character of these cities: Teotenango, Cacaxtla, and Xochicalco were built at relatively inaccessible elevations and protected with walls and moats. An art style charged with symbols of war and sacrifice corroborates this bellicose exaltation (Hirth 1989; Berlo 1989b; Foncerrada 1993).[27]

Another aspect worth taking into account is the multi-ethnic condition of their populations, reflected in very diverse ways. On the one hand, calendrical notation in the Epiclassic capitals derived from the Teotihuacan system, although they did coherently combine glyphs from other distinct regions of Mesoamerica (Berlo 1989a). On the other hand, the art of Xochicalco, Teotenango, Cholula, and Cacaxtla is markedly eclectic (Marquina 1970; Nagao 1989; Foncerrada 1993).

One more element situates Xochicalco in the interpretive range of what is Zuyuan: Kenneth Hirth and Ann Cyphers (1988: 147–151) are very astute to notice that the city was founded in a valley that did not have the agricultural potential to support so large a population. Its sudden appearance and prominence could only be explained, according to these authors, by the integration of a confederation of the region's elites, attempting to consolidate regional political control after the fall of Teotihuacan.

Finally, we would like to point out that in the principal temple of Xochicalco, as is well known, the *taludes* (sloping panels) are decorated with feathered serpents and the *tableros* (vertical panels) present a succession of seated personages, individualized with glyphs that have been interpreted as onomastic of one dynasty (Nicholson 1969) or as toponyms of conquered communities (Berlo 1989a; Hirth 1989). A third possibility, however, could be considered in light of the aforementioned work of Hirth and Cyphers: the personages on the *tablero* could be local rulers integrated into a federation under the sign of Feathered Serpent. Although one could interpret this sequence as a lineage legitimated by Feathered Serpent, it could also be understood as a meeting of local lords incorporated into the Xochicalco state, members of a system of corporate government. This third reading seems more plausible if one considers it doubtful that, during the relatively short life of the city, a dynasty of thirty monarchs would have existed.

The influence of the Central Mexican Epiclassic cities on the rest of Mesoamerica should not be minimized. Gordon Willey (1977: 67) thinks it is possible that the iconography of Cholula and Xochicalco may have inspired the invaders of the Río de la Pasión region.

Tula. As we move forward in time, the archaeological and historical information from Central Mexico offers more evidence concerning Zuyuan ideology and organization. In the written sources of the sixteenth century, as Arnauld and Michelet (1991) asserted, "all roads led to Tollan or came from there." Tollan, The Place of Reeds, is the focal point of legitimacy.[28] Central Mexico possessed four great capitals whose fame, in one way or another, made them replicas of the mythical center of power: Teotihuacan and Cholula, which received the name of Tollan as an epithet; Tula, Hidalgo,[29] considered by many authors to be the prototypical Tollan; and the powerful Mexico-Tenochtitlan, the city that provides us with the most information concerning the political organization of the *excan tlatoloyan*, or Triple Alliance.[30] We will exclude the first of the four, which, at least for now, remains outside the temporal scope of our study, and will refer to the rest.

Tula—the "ugly sister" of an old polemic—astonishes us as much for the praise of its greatness made in the sources as for the contrast between these eulogies and archaeological reality. The magnificence, technical development, and treasures described by the written sources do not correspond with excavation results. But at least the archaeologists have been able to show the magnitude of the city, its relative wealth, and multi-ethnic character (Matache and Cobean 1985; Cobean and Mastache 1995),[31] crucial factors in assessing its role in history.

The explanation of the apparent contradiction between the written and archaeological sources is well known: it concerns two cities, one divine and the other worldly. Tula (Hidalgo) was one of the terrestrial replicas of the divine

Tollan (The Place of Reeds). Tollan is identified—wholly or as one of its parts—with the Tamoanchan of the newborns' formation. As we have seen, the Feathered Serpent god played a primary role in this during the nocturnal and auroral phases.

According to the written sources, in the terrestrial Tula existed one or two rulers who received the name of Quetzalcoatl, meaning Feathered Serpent, which allows us to suppose that the ones who carried the name were the representatives of the Lord of the Dawn, human vessels wherein the creator divinity deposited his force (López Austin 1973).

In addition, it is also necessary to take into account that the protagonist role of Tula exercised during the Early Postclassic period was converted into a Mesoamerican model in the realms of architecture, imagery, dress, and armaments. The confusions between Tollan and Tula derive from the Mesoamerican conception of history, but also from popular fantasy, and, above all, from political intentionality. This vagueness formed a chain in which myth, legend, and reality were reciprocally transformed (Table 1.5). As if that were not enough, the force of Tollan/Tula and Feathered Serpent/Quetzalcoatl also affected colonial historiography, in which the richest interlaces between divine adventures, legendary miracles, and terrestrial events appear.

When referring to Tula as the city of exuberance, wealth, precious birds, colors, wisdom, and the coming together of all artificers (master craftsmen), the written sources are referring to the primordial Tollan (Sahagún 1989, II: 650–655). The mythical Tollan infected the historical Tula with its fame. The archetypical place was marked not only by total abundance, but also by the joining together of the arts and human knowledge. It is well-known that the word *toltecatl* in the Nahuatl language was as equivalent to the genteel "Toltec" as it was to "artificer."[31] Under this logic, we believe that the cluster of "artificers" of Tula of which the written sources speak should be interpreted as the auroral meeting of all the human groups in the common mythical homeland: Tollan. Upon leaving there in the moment of their creation, each human group acquired a specific art as a gift from their patron deity.

Much more can be said about the ruler Quetzalcoatl: he is painted as a powerful being who repeats the heroic exploits of Feathered Serpent. Political propaganda depicts the earthly Quetzalcoatls as founders of order and sources of legitimacy. Thus, according to written sources, the royal houses of the Quetzalcoatl of Tula are four (Sahagún 1989, II: 651) and are distinguished among themselves by the colors of the cosmic trees, and in each of them are joined the cold and hot substances that constitute time (López Austin 1990: 345–347). In other words, the order imposed by the priest-ruler Quetzalcoatl is a reflection of the calendrical order established by Feathered Serpent, that is to say, the temporal sequence that rises through the cosmic columns to spread over the face of the earth.

The colonial historiography concerning the historical Tula (Hidalgo) began to be affected, moreover, by the efforts of some historians who intended to give a rational explanation to indigenous mythical passages and, at the same time, wanted to adjust the story to new myths: those of the Bible. Thus, when Fernando de Alva Ixtlilxóchitl (1975: 263–264) recounted the history of the Toltecs, he made the five cosmogonic suns merely stages in the history of humanity. He said that the peoples altered their languages, but he related the episode to the construction of a very high tower. The ancestors of the Toltecs were seven men and seven women who spoke the same language, covered great lands and seas, and arrived at Huehue Tlapallan (The Ancient Place of Painting), a site that seems to have more to do with auroral colors than with terrestrial time. In spite of its imbrication with Christian elements, this material is very useful, at least for establishing comparative links with other narratives of greater historical constancy. In this respect, the passage is interesting where the ruler Our Venerable Noble,[33] in order to establish peace with his powerful neighbors, proposes that they construct a harmonious quadripartite government and gives them a ball court. The ball court is made of precious stones: emerald, ruby, diamond, and hyacinth (Alva Ixtlilxóchitl 1975: 279). Here the reader should remember the symbolic nexus between the terrestrial level and the ball court, as well as the quadripartite division of the Zuyuan system, itself. The colors of the jewels of the ball court (green, red, white, and reddish yellow) clearly coincide with those that another source points out for houses of Quetzalcoatl (Sahagún 1989, II, 651).[34]

Cholula. As we said, Cholula also was called Tollan. It is an exhilarating case for at least three reasons. The first is the serious doubt it raises when reading

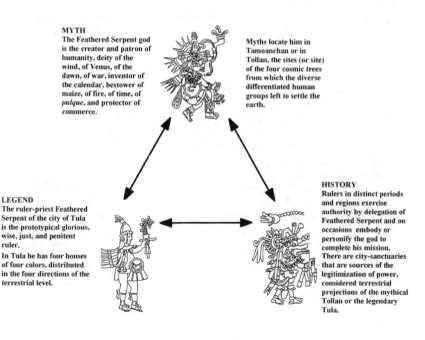

MYTH
The Feathered Serpent god is the creator and patron of humanity, deity of the wind, of Venus, of the dawn, of war, inventor of the calendar, bestower of maize, of fire, of time, of *pulque*, and protector of commerce.

Myths locate him in Tamoanchan or in Tollan, the sites (or site) of the four cosmic trees from which the diverse differentiated human groups left to settle the earth.

LEGEND
The ruler-priest Feathered Serpent of the city of Tula is the prototypical glorious, wise, just, and penitent ruler.

In Tula he has four houses of four colors, distributed in the four directions of the terrestrial level.

HISTORY
Rulers in distinct periods and regions exercise authority by delegation of Feathered Serpent and on occasions embody or personify the god to complete his mission. There are city-sanctuaries that are sources of the legitimization of power, considered terrestrial projections of the mythical Tollan or the legendary Tula.

Table 1.5. The three levels of analysis of Feathered Serpent and Tollan.

fragments in the *Historia tolteca-chichimeca* (1976) that mention the Toltec people's city of origin: To which Tula were they referring? The second has to do with the dual government of Cholula, formed by two personages who represent the Supreme Divinity and integrate the Sky/Earth pair. The third reason is the sanctuary character Cholula had along with the "nose-piercing" ceremony practiced there, the ritual legitimator of the power of other communities' rulers (Figure 1.2).[35]

We begin with the reference to Tula in the *Historia tolteca-chichimeca*. When we read the story of the Tolteca-Chichimecs and the Nonohualca-Chichimecs who left The Place of Reeds, do we not find mention of the terrestrial Tula or are we in the presence of the Tollan of myth? In spite of the very timely and careful translation of Luis Reyes García, the text is totally obscure and contains strange parts that require meticulous analysis.

We will synthesize the beginning of the narrative: Toltecs and Nonohualca were Chichimecs originating from Colhuacatepec (The Place of the Mountain of the Ancestors), where they left to occupy Tula. It is mentioned that there were four Toltecs and four Nonohualca who abandoned Colhuacatepec (*Historia tolteca-chichimeca* 1976: 132–133). It could be interpreted that there were four chiefs of the emigrants, or the four "first fathers." Everyone was settled in The Place of Reeds; but the Nonohualca-Chichimecs had to leave there during the general disbanding of the twenty groups subordinate to the Toltecs. The source says that each one of the twenty went to deserve their place of settlement.

Up to here, nothing seems too suspicious. The first problem is the time of the occupation of The Place of Reeds. The joint stay of the Tolteca-Chichimecs

a   b

Fig. 1.2. Nose-piercing ritual for insertion of the jewel of power: a. Mixtec: 8 Deer Jaguar Claw submits to the ritual on lámina 52 of the *Codex Zouche-Nuttall*; b. Cholula: Icxicoatl pierces the nose of the Chichimec chief Tecpatzin on folio 21r of the *Historia tolteca-chichimeca*.

and Nonohualca-Chichimecs in this city, which one could suppose lasted centuries based upon written and archaeological sources, is reduced to two years! In addition, the Nonohualca-Chichimecs, after the conflict, leave "The Place of Reeds" *during the night* and "take the riches of Quetzalcoatl" (*Historia tolteca-chichimeca* 1976: 132–135). These riches, perhaps, may be related to the sacred bundle (*tlaquimilolli*) that one of the chiefs carries (*Historia tolteca-chichimeca* 1976: 136–137). They leave, moreover, in seven groups, which will give rise to the foundation of seven seats of stone (*chicome teicpalli*), symbols of authority (*Historia tolteca-chichimeca* 1976: 136 and note 19).

The Tolteca-Chichimecs, now without the Nonohualca-Chichimecs, remain in The Place of Reeds until completing a total stay of fifteen years. They abandon the city according to Feathered Serpent's instructions. In fact, one of the Toltec chiefs, Cohuenan (*Historia tolteca-chichimeca* 1976: 141–144), travels to Cholula and admires its richness. Then he invokes the creator (He for Whom Is Lived, Feathered Serpent, Four Feet, The Conqueror), and asks him for a home for the Toltecs. Feathered Serpent acquiesces, and the Toltecs depart toward Cholula, where they are established in definitive form.

In summary, what is suspicious is that until this point the narrative seems to correspond to an auroral time that begins in Tollan and ends in Cholula, suggesting that these Tolteca-Chichimecs were not necessarily those of Tula (Hidalgo). Thus, there is no basis in this source for supposing invasion. Cholula would earn the name of Tula in its own right and not by the intervention of its western neighbor.[36] Many other details in the document's text and pictographs would complement this proposition, but we will leave this problem for another time and continue with the Cholula story.

In the same document, another auroral time takes place that is very well defined. Two of the four Toltec chiefs—or "first fathers"—are the most important personages in the codex: Quetzaltehueyac and Icxicoatl. They are characterized by their extraordinary longevity. Their names form, with two of their respective halves (*Quetzal-* and *-coatl*), the name of Feathered Serpent. They are depicted, moreover, with a priest's hairstyle and the long whiskers of this deity. By order of He for Whom Is Lived, both go to the place of origin, called in the codex, among many other names, The Place of the Mountain of the Ancestors, The Place of One Adorned with Paper, The Place of the Seven Caves, Where the White Reed Is, and Where the Magical Ballcourt Is Straight. Their supernatural powers allow them to do the work of *accouchers*, of initiators, for they conciliate the departure of the seven Chichimec groups waiting in the seven wombs of Chicomoztoc (The Place of the Seven Caves). The two Tolteca-Chichimec priests receive the newborns when they cannot even speak the Nahuatl language, and teach them to eat maize. The Chichimecs who went out to the world obtain the military profession, for which they were created and with which they will fulfill their obligation before the creator god, acknowledging their commitment with a sacred song. They will leave, then, their mythical mountain, to wander "through the flat land, through the divine land."[37] Quetzaltehueyac and Icxicoatl are the ones who legitimate the Chichimec chiefs through complex ritual acts, and pierce their noses to insert the jewels of power in the holes (*Historia tolteca-chichimeca* 1976: 158–171) (Figure 1.2).

One of the drawings in the *Historia tolteca-chichimeca* may provide evidence concerning the political functions of Cholula architecture. Two quadrangular buildings, found on folio 27r, are organized symmetrically with stairways in front, an arrangement that can be seen in Quiché Maya settlements. The four Chichimec chiefs are depicted in the interiors of the buildings: Quetzaltehueyac and Tezcahuitzil in one and Icxicohuatl and Tololohuitzil in the other.

We move on to the second of the interesting issues we mentioned at the beginning of this section. Before the Toltecs settled in Cholula, when it was still populated by the Olmeca-Xicallanca, the priest Cohuenan observed the lords who governed the city: the *tlalchiach* and the *aquiach*. The titles of these two lords are very interesting because we know from another source that they derive from the compound name given in Cholula to the Supreme Deity (Tlaquiach Tlachiach), as the master who came from the celestial levels and the underworld (Muñoz Camargo 1981: 72v and 197r).[38]

When using his name, both rulers should be considered the joint delegates of the Supreme Deity. But, at the same time, these rulers are identified with those instituted by Quetzalcoatl, himself:

These two Indians [Aquiach and Tlalchiach] were in a temple . . . that was called Quetzalcoatl['s], . . . founded to honor a captain who brought the people of this city, in olden times, to settle there, from very remote parts toward the west, where is not known [with] certainty. And this captain was named Quetzalcoatl, and, deceased as he was, they made him a temple, in which there were, besides these two Indians, a great quantity of priests (Rojas 1985: 129).[39]

Now then, if we take into account that the two principal personages of the *Historia tolteca-chichimeca* make up a dual authority in a city where the same type of government previously existed, and if we accept that putting together the two halves of the names Quetzaltehueyac and Icxicoatl form Quetzalcoatl, may we not suppose that the Zuyuan government in Cholula had to adapt to a local tradition of dual power?

The third of these issues relates to the sanctuary character the city had—for which it received the title of "Tula"—and to the ceremonies involving the piercing of the nose, lip, or ears, as an legitimizing act for the lords of other communities. Rojas (1985: 130), speaking of the power of the city and the attributions of the two priest-rulers who reigned there, describes that,

[l]ikewise, these two supreme priests had preeminence for confirming the status of all the rulers and kings of this New Spain, [and it was] in this manner: that those such kings and chiefs, upon inheriting their kingdom or domain, came to this city to acknowledge their obedience to the idol there, Quetzalcoatl, to whom they offered rich feathers, mantles, gold and precious stones, and other things of value. And, having made offerings, they joined together in a chapel dedicated for this purpose, where the two supreme priests honored them by piercing their ears, or their noses, or their lower lip, according to the domain they possessed, by which their authority was confirmed, and they returned to their lands . . .

Likewise, there was an order and law that, in 53 out of 53 years . . . peoples, from all the communities, who confirmed [their] authority here, came to pay tribute to the said temple . . .

> Likewise, the Indians who came from throughout the land brought these offer-
> ings because of their devotion and pilgrimage to visit the temple of Quetzalcoatl,
> because this was the metropolis and had as much veneration as Rome in Christian-
> ity, and Mecca among the Moors (Rojas 1985: 130–132).[40]

Zuyuan tradition also continued to be reflected institutionally in the Puebla-
Tlaxcala region during the Late Postclassic. We are referring particularly to the
installation ritual of the rulers called *tetecuhtin*, according to a report sent to
Spain by Viceroy Antonio de Mendoza on December 10, 1537. This report, published by Pedro Carrasco (1966), says that the future *tecuhtli* ascended to the
office in the penitential ceremony called *yacaxapotlaliztli*, or "the perforation of
the nose," an operation performed with two piercing implements, one made of
eagle bone, the other of jaguar bone. In this ceremony, the ruler was awarded two
highly significant names: the first, Motecuhzauhqui, characterized him as a penitent who attained the title of *tecuhtli*; the second identified him with the god
Quetzalcoatl himself, under his Nacxitl avocation. The text literally says, "and
four days passed, on the fifth they covered his entire body and face with soot,
and some clothes and some strips of paper and two names were given to him, one
was Motecuçauque, and the other, Naxictle, which are his designations as penitent and image of Calcoatle" (Carrasco 1966: 135).[41]

Mexico-Tenochtitlan. On the other side of the mountains, the communities
of the Basin of Mexico provide us with a vast amount of information about origin
myths, migration accounts, as well as the political organization of the hegemonic
Triple Alliance. One of the best-known myths is that of the creation of human
beings beginning with the journey of Feathered Serpent to the world of the dead,
where he takes bones and ashes—a cold substance—to mix with blood extracted
from his own penis—a hot substance (*Leyenda de los soles* 1945: 120–121).[42]
From this mixture humans would be born.

The preceding myth is complemented with another account in which it says
that, after the fourth age of the world had been destroyed, the first man and the
first woman were created, ten years before the birth of the Fifth Sun. In this
account the creator deity was named 9 Wind (Benavente 1971: 389), a name that
also corresponds to Feathered Serpent.

The myth of the origin of human beings is connected with the myth of their
sustenance. The creator of humankind begins the process of extracting maize, a
treasure that the gods had hidden away in an impenetrable mountain. This action
prompted by Feathered Serpent causes maize to begin a life-and-death cycle.
Leaving the Mountain of Our Sustenance, maize is robbed by the rain gods, the
ones who bring him to the underworld (*Leyenda de los soles* 1945: 121), and thus
will begin the cycle of the birth and rebirth of agricultural crops.

The first of the myths mentioned is fundamental for the problem that we have
taken on, because in it one can see the dividing of the creator god into the
multiplicity of the patron deities. In fact, in one variant very similar to the account
pointed out, the one who descends into the world of the dead is not Feathered
Serpent, but rather his twin, Xolotl. Instead of Feathered Serpent's blood giving
origin to human beings, it will be the blood of a group of deities; and instead of

this act occurring in Tamoanchan, the generic site of creation, it happens in Chicomoztoc, the Place of the Seven Caves (Mendieta 1945, I: 83–84).[43]

Here, the pairing from the singular to the plural is clear. On the one hand, we have Feathered Serpent creating all of humanity in Tamoanchan (the generic cradle); on the other hand, the patron deities gestate their respective human groups in Chicomoztoc (a multiple uterus of births that occur in the story).

This important leitmotif is found in other mythical accounts that refer to the birth of the children of the Supreme Pair, the Sky and the Earth (cf. López Austin 1973: 145–147). From this hierogamy is born one or various offspring.

1. According to the *Histoyre du Mechique* (1965: 112), Camaxtli (the Sky) impregnates Chimalma (the Earth) in Michatlauhco. Chimalma dies during childbirth and the son is Quetzalcoatl.
2. According to Motolinía (Benavente 1971: 10), Iztacmixcoatl (equivalent to Camaxtli)[44] has six children with Ilancueitl (equivalent to Chimalma).[45] The six are: Xelhua, Tenuch, Ulmecatl, Xicalancatl, Mixtecatl, and Otomitl. The place of origin is Chicomoztoc.

We may see in these two accounts some characteristics coinciding with the myths of the creation of human beings.

1. *Singularity/plurality*. In one of them, the protagonist is Quetzalcoatl. In the other, there is a multiplicity of personages.
2. *Multiple personages engender human groups*. In Motolinía's account, five of the six personages are clearly eponyms: Tenuch, Ulmecatl, Xicalancatl, Mixtecatl, and Otomitl, generators, respectively, of the Tenochca, Olmec, Xicallanca, Mixtec, and Otomí peoples.[46] In addition to this, Motolinía affirms that "from them great generations were produced, almost like one reads of the sons of Noah" (Benavente 1971: 10).
3. *Mythical places*. Quetzalcoatl's place of origin is Michatlauhco, while that of the eponymic deities is Chicomoztoc. It should be stated here that Michatlauhco means "In the Ravine of the Fishes," a name that we suggest is equivalent to Tamoanchan.[47]

The migration stories of the peoples of the Basin of Mexico also offer rich information. However, their proper exploitation would require a timely study of mythical births, migrations, and foundations of settlements, one that would go considerably beyond the aims of this essay.[46]

Other Mesoamerican accounts whose registers come from Central Mexico illustrate the relationship between the patron deity and his people by way of the sacred bundle. Some refer to the birth of the sun, their sovereign character in the world, and the way in which other deities were destroyed to initiate their government. "Dead" gods were converted into patron deities, each one delivering to the community a sacred bundle with their relics. These would be the link between the protector and his children. When a priest, for example, wore the clothes of the patron deity, he transformed his body into a vessel of the divinity (*Historia de los mexicanos por sus pinturas* 1965: 47). Another gift that the patron deity gave to his children—the profession—was delivered to them with the instruments of office. Thus, the Mexica received from Huitzilopochtli the necessary instruments to act as hunters of lacustrine (lake) species.

The Mexica and their contemporaries in the Basin of Mexico boasted as much about their Chichimec origin as their claim to *toltecayotl*, which might seem contradictory if one did not take into account that "Chichimec" and "Toltec" were two extremes of a people's transformation process during the auroral stage. In other words, as Carlos Martínez Marín (1963) proposed, the alleged nomadic origin of the Mexica does not correspond to a cultural reality. It is appropriate to observe here that, based on an overly literal interpretation of the sources, the originality of the Mexica as supposed Chichimecs has been exaggerated. We believe, to the contrary, that this community was thoroughly Mesoamerican at the moment of their arrival to the Basin of Mexico, and that their feigned foreignness was precisely part of the mythical paradigm common to their neighbors. Thus, the strength of Mexica art is owed more to the power they achieved in their last years of existence than to the introduction of new concepts.

The attraction that the Toltec past exerted over the Mexica remains as evident in the written sources as in the archaeological data. Their admiration was not free of political content. It is well known that the Mexica often conducted excavations in the ruins of Tula (Sahagún 1989, Lib. X, cap. xxix, II: 654; Acosta 1956–1957). They extracted numerous objects from their offerings and tombs and dismantled sculptural elements of considerable size from their buildings, all of which were transported to Tenochtitlan. In the Sacred Precinct of the city, not only did they bury Toltec treasures, but they reproduced the style of Quetzalcoatl's metropolis (Navarrete and Crespo 1971; Umberger 1987; López Luján 1989, 1993: 81–82; Fuente 1990; Solís Olguín 1990).

The mythical nexus also connected the creator deity with the Mexica nobles. They were assured that, as sons of Feathered Serpent, they were given in primogenial time the mission of governing the people.

> Here they take, they receive, our rulers, our nobles, the hair of the people, the fingernails of the people, the sons of the precious ones, of the jades, of the bracelets, the receivers of divine breath, those who come from Our Venerable Noble, Feathered Serpent. [This] was what was delivered to them, what they deserved, for which they acquired life, for which they were born: the mat, the seat;[49] [power was given to them over] the one who had to be carried, [over] the one who had to be ruled. For this they acquired life, for this they were born, for this they were created in the place where in the night it was determined, it was ordained, that they would be rulers, that they would be *tlatoque* (Sahagún 1979, Lib. VI, cap. xvi, fols. 67v–68r, 1).[50]

Concerning Mexica administrative and political organization, it is appropriate to point out three aspects: The first was the dual government that fell upon the *tlatoani* and the *cihuacoatl*. The second consisted in the division of the city into quadrants, the *nauhcampan*, each one directed by a high-ranking official. The third was the constitution of the Tenochtitlan-Texcoco-Tlacopan Triple Alliance.

Regarding this alliance, it is necessary to say, first, that the Triple Alliance was not merely a military and political league that emerged in the fifteenth century among the winners after the war against Azcapotzalco. On the contrary, it was a form of political organization with deep historical roots in the Basin of Mexico.

The written sources speak of it as a very ancient regional institution, whose origins go back to Tollan (*Anales de Cuauhtitlan* 1945: 63). Its name in Nahuatl, *excan tlatoloyan*, makes reference to its judicial character arranged around three seats. Alvarado Tezozómoc (1944: 178, 245, 267, 340) also calls it *tecuhtlatoloyan* ("the tribunal of the *tetecuhtin*"), or, in Spanish, "el tribunal de los reyes" or "las audiencias" (in English, "the tribunal of kings" or "the supreme courts"). Although this does not allow us to understand the ideological foundations of its establishment as a jurisdictional organ, accounts of its political actions reveal its role as an instrument of expansion and domination in the hands of three hegemonic states. On the other hand, it was a political body that joined the ethnic system within the territorial system. Carrasco (1996: 185) points out that "in the organization of the Triple Alliance there was no personnel dedicated exclusively to the central government," and adds that "the rulers of the three capitals assumed imperial functions, acting in unison or exercising special activities."

It is appropriate to emphasize here that the *excan tlatoloyan* not only allowed for the multi-ethnicity of its constituents, but also established a structure of an economic and political character that was a reflection of cosmic order (López Austin 1987; López Austin and López Luján 1996: 211–214). Moreover, the Triple Alliance tended to respect the internal political order of the societies integrated within its sphere of dominion, centering its attention more on tribute collection than on the administration of those subjugated. In this political context, the cultural influence of the Mexica, Texcocan, and Tlacopanecan was minimal outside the nuclear area. This is made clear by the sparse presence of Aztec III ceramics and sculpture and architecture of the so-called Imperial Aztec style in the majority of their provinces (Umberger and Klein 1993). The system tended to the conservation of internal (traditional ethnic) political order and respected the ideological foundations of power in each of the units, but it superimposed a multi-ethnic apparatus as the head of the global organization. Earlier, we stated that, at the moment of the Spanish Conquest, the Mexica were found in a transition between the Zuyuan system and a regime of more centralized power. This produced some incongruencies of a political character that would remain registered in the historical documents. Mexica historiography contains two contradictory theses concerning the source of supreme power. In the first, the Mexica recognized the authority of their patron deity, Huitzilopochtli, and that of their rulers derived from Quetzalcoatl. For example, when Tizoc was installed on the throne, it was said to him, "From today, lord, you remain on the throne, the seat that Zenacatl [One Reed] and Nacxitl Quetzalcoatl first set up . . . and in their name Huitzilopochtli came" (Alvarado Tezozómoc 1944: 247).[51] But, as a consequence of their sudden rise, the Mexica placed upon the *excan tlatoloyan* a new political conception, thus moving away from the Zuyuan model. They elevated Huitzilopochtli to the rank of "foster father," to whom the communities within reach of their military might had to be subordinated (79–80). This new conception, which quite probably would have been conducive to the development of a different type of state from the Zuyuan system, was interrupted by the Spanish Conquest. The words directed by Motecuhzoma Xocoyotzin to Fernando Cortés seem to reflect a strong ideological conflict: before the European invasion, the Mexica *tlatoani* already mistrusted his own ideas concerning the "foster father" and recognized that the time of the return of Quetzalcoatl, the god of the *excan tlatoloyan* whom the Mexican had unseated, had come.

THE MAYA LOWLANDS

The Río de la Pasión Basin. The most ancient evidence of Zuyuanism in the Maya lowlands may go back to the ninth century in the Río de la Pasión Basin of northern Yucatán. Numerous researchers have proposed that, from the ninth century on, important demographic movements related to an atmosphere of political instability took place in both regions. Concerning Río de la Pasión, the archaeological findings support the hypothesis of the arrival of foreign groups to Seibal and Altar de Sacrificios. It is not known if the intruders were Maya or not, or if they came from coastal Tabasco (which seems more probable) or from more distant regions, but it seems evident that they followed the course of the Usumacinta River from the north.

Numerous sculpted monuments from Seibal that combine typical Classic Maya elements with other exogenous ones are well known (Graham 1971, 1973; Sabloff 1973). Among these latter types of elements, the use of the square cartouche stands out, as well as the depiction of personages with non-Maya ethnic traits such as long, straight hair, mustache, and beard. In addition, they bear strange insignias and weapons: long skirts, nose ornaments, curved staffs, and throwing sticks. Some personages wear symbols of deities not worshipped before in that region; for example, one of them has a long-billed buccal mask similar to that of the Wind God, an avocation of Feathered Serpent.

A similar phenomenon is observed in the architecture and ceramics of Seibal (Sabloff 1973). Buildings with a circular plan, temples with four stairways situated in the center of plazas, and façades with barrel-shaped columns appear during the Bayal Phase (830–930). Some ritual changes are evident in the ceramics, as traditional censors and funerary vessels are replaced by spiked and ladle censers and fine paste vessels. These changes only occur in the ceramics of elites, causing Jeremy Sabloff (1973: 129) to suppose that a partial changeover in the ruling group had taken place.

At the same time, Altar de Sacrificios experienced a marked decline during the Boca (771–909) and Jimba (909–948) Phases (Adams 1973). Buildings of importance were neither constructed nor renovated, nor were stelae erected. Fine Orange and Gray ceramics, and figurines depicting foreign deities as well as armed warriors with quilted armor, rectangular shields, and feathered headdresses significantly appear.

This intrusion from the ninth century on is corroborated by linguistic data. In an interesting study, John Justeson, William Norman, Lyle Campbell, and Terrence Kaufman (1985: 49–52) have asserted that dynamic interaction took place in coastal Tabasco and surrounding areas between Nahuatl, Mixtec-Zoque, Chontal, and Yuactec Maya speakers. One of the results was that certain Nahuatl terms made their way into the Lowland Maya lexicon. Words such as *cimal* ("shield") and *tepewal* ("authority") would suggest that these contacts were not always peaceful.

Chichén Itzá. The phenomena that took place in the Río de la Pasión Basin and coastal Tabasco may have been inscribed in a much wider process that would have included the Yucatán Peninsula. The constant flows of individuals and ideas would have followed the same riverine and maritime routes as the new commercial system. Pure, crystalline, white salt, produced on the northern coast of Yucatán was one of the reasons this region was integrated into the pan-Mesoamerican network of exchange. According to Anthony Andrews (1978) and Susan Kepecs, Gary Feinman, and Sylviane Boucher (1994), Chichén Itzá reached its apogee thanks to its control of the salt marshes of the Río Lagartos estuary, the port of Isla Cerritos, and the farming settlements in the region. This permitted it not only to become master of the northern peninsula, but also converted it into an important link in a chain extending from Central Mexico to Central America. In this manner, Emal and Isla Cerritos, like Chichén, were enriched with the traffic of gold, greenstone, turquoise, cotton, fine orange ceramics, and green obsidian. With its commercial and political prominence and the religious prestige of its Sacred Cenote, Chichén Itzá acquired a cosmopolitan physiognomy.

A few decades ago no one doubted that the invaders guided by Kukulcán (Feathered Serpent) had succeeded the Chichén Maya: that is, the passing from the Pure Florescent Period to the Modified Period, from Puuc to Toltec architecture, and from Cehpech to Sotuta-style ceramics. Recent studies of the city's urbanism, architecture, iconography, and ceramics reveal no such historical succession, but rather a three-way chronological overlap between Yucatec societies and those of the so-called Terminal Classic of the Southern Lowland Maya, between Chichén Itzá and the Puuc capitals, and between the so-called Maya Chichén and Toltec Chichén (Lincoln 1986; Andrews and Sabloff 1986; Taube 1994; Jones 1995: 52–60). This suggests the cosmopolitan character of the inhabitants of Chichén Itzá.

We will not repeat here the architectural, sculptural, and pictorial characteristics that have given rise to the already more than a century-long controversy over the similitude between Chichén Itzá and Tula (see Tozzer 1957 and Jones 1995). However, there is no doubt that Chichén's inhabitants, whatever their ethnic affiliation and provenance, knew thoroughly well the dominant styles in Central Mexico. Whether direct or indirect, contact was intense. Concerning architecture, in some cases, the imitation is reduced to formal aspects, creating eclectic combinations without importing the original contextual function and logic. In contrast, other cases reveal a congruency between form and function and the imitation implicitly bears an organization of space that satisfies new functional requirements of an administrative and ritual nature. In this respect, we mention as an example the building that received the name El Mercado (The Market) (Ruppert 1943). Its plan is made up of two rectangles joined together in the form of a T. Its façade has a long, 75-meter portico with a vaulted roof, supported in front by a row of alternating columns and pillars. The portico is connected, through only one central entrance without passage to any other rooms, to a wide courtyard furnished with an *impluvium* (a large central sunken basin). Hers (1989: 157, 173–175) has noted that this type of courtyard is inappropriate for a market, since it is a partially open, poorly arranged space. Moreover, its paintings and reliefs, pertaining mostly to warfare, have nothing to do with commerce. It is an aisled cloister with its central part uncovered, similar, according to Hers, to those that appear in the architecture of Tula and the distant Chalchihuites culture. She supposed that the northern buildings—like those of Alta Vista and La Quemada (550–900 C.E.)—had a double function: congregating members of a segment of the population and distinguishing them from the rest of society.

In other words, these large spaces with their broad interiors would be appropriated to accommodate meetings of numerous, but entirely select, bodies that would be adjusted to the requirements of a political organization such as the Zuyuan system, whose governmental actions enlisted the participation of a very large number of high dignitaries.

The buildings of Chichén Itzá transmitted an equally cosmopolitan message through imagery. Here there was no categorical separation, as was previously supposed, between Maya and Toltec. On the contrary, indigenous and foreign elements are intertwined. Although the majority of the symbols are either Maya or from Central Mexico, those from the Gulf Coast and the Cotzumalhuapa region are not rare (Taube 1994). For example, the representations of Gods K and N, Chac, and the number 13 have their roots in Classic Maya, while the feathered-serpent figures (primarily repeated as a cosmic column), Tlahuizcalpantecuhtli, Tlaloc, and Tezcatlipoca belong to a clearly Central Mexican matrix. But independent of their origins, the images are interpreted in the expressive style of the city. As Karl Taube (1994) points out, there was no mere transfer of the Toltec to Yucatec lands, but rather an expression that corresponded to a new cultural and political reality.

In its time, Chichén Itzá radiated its symbols and its style. Inextricably linked to both a political exercise and a religious cult, they would begin extending themselves throughout northern Yucatán, above all in the direction of the Puuc area. Rubén Maldonado Cárdenas and Edward Kurjack (1993) proposed, on the basis of this shared iconography, a lively early interrelationship between Chichén and other large cities in the region.

In the iconography of Chichén there is a manifest intention of contrasting two military groups. The weapons and adornments distinguish these groups: the "Toltecs" wear tessera (mosaic) headdresses with standing plumes and butterfly pectorals, and carry circular shields, arrows, atlatl (throwing sticks), and tezcacuitlapilli (a large ornamental disk worn on the lower back); the "Maya" are depicted as Chac and bear rectangular shields, lances, knives, and hachas (celts). Both groups are represented, whether in stark bellicose confrontations or in peaceful scenes.

On the deteriorated images inside the Temple of the Jaguars at Chichén, "Toltecs" and "Maya" are led by personages who have been interpreted as either gods or their terrestrial representatives. These leaders often form the pair called Captain Serpent/Captain Solar Disk (Miller 1977). The first of these has a feathered serpent on his back, wears a tessera headdress and a characteristic butterfly pectoral, and carries an atlatl. The second is enclosed in a clearly Central Mexican–style solar halo; but he has a Chac mask, a long nose ornament in the form of a bar, and a jaguar throne.[52] Significantly, as Taube (1994) has noted, the motif of this pair of captains developed in Central Mexico, as they are represented in murals at Ixtapantongo and on a polychrome vessel discovered at Tula.

This duality, of course, could be explained in different ways. Arthur Miller (1977) supposed the existence of two antagonistic ethnic groups. Charles Lincoln (cited in Taube 1994) asserted that the two captains exercised complementary charges in the same government, whose roots derived from the Classic Maya. Taube, on the other hand, suggests that this duality has clearly exogenous elements: the solar captain represents the traditional Maya *ahau*, while Feathered Serpent refers to the charge of the war captain or co-ruler of Chichén. He adds that the Maya elite of this city aggressively adopted a military ideology and mode of dress from Central Mexico. For the Maya, Toltec imagery was the iconography of warrior power legitimated by a religious creed.

In the Temple of the Chac Mool, images were discovered that elucidate the governmental roles of the two mentioned groups. This council house, buried beneath the Temple of the Warriors, was decorated with mural paintings of lords adorned as different deities (Morris, Charlot, and Morris 1931). The personages depicted on the south bench are seated upon jaguar-skin cushions and present offerings or hold *hachas*, very similar to the manikin-scepters of the Southern Maya lowlands. On the north bench, in contrast, the personages rest on jaguar thrones and hold arrows and *atlatl*. While members of the first group have typical Maya hairstyles, the hairstyles in the second group are clearly Toltec. Linda Schele and David Freidel (1990: 370–371) very astutely believed that there was no preeminent person among them, but rather that they formed a gathering of nobles who governed in a corporate manner.

In our judgment, the architectural, iconographic, and ceramic data make plausible the ideas that Chichén Itzá was a center in which two or more ethnic groups (Maya or not) interacted in an ongoing manner; that these groups would have made up a corporate government; that each one of its members was represented as a god; and that the corporation in its entirety rested upon a dual cosmological principle in which Feathered Serpent played a fundamental role. Chichén had militarily conquered the neighboring peoples of northern Yucatán to incorporate them into a complex political system, legitimated by a cosmopolitan court discourse. Such plans of incorporating neighboring communities are revealed in a new style of artistic propaganda in which enemies vanquished by arms are no longer depicted naked, humiliated, and mutilated as in the old regimes of the Classic Maya; in Chichén Itzá, they are shown richly attired with their emblems of rank (Schele and Freidel 1990: 366–367), arranged, perhaps, to be assimilated into a multi-ethnic system. According to Schele and Freidel (367), the Itzá Maya preferred to absorb their enemies rather than annihilate them.

All of this profiles the government of Chichén Itzá as one more version of the system we have called Zuyuan. Although the colonial sources from Yucatán are often confusing, contradictory, and cryptic, we find data in them that strengthen our models. In fact, we took the term "Zuyuá" from colonial Maya writings. It is the name of the legitimizing capital, a city whose location is so vague that it is valid to suppose its mythical nature. It was said, for example, that from faraway Zuyuá came the riddles that the supreme rulers of Yucatán used to substantiate whether their functionaries were of a royal lineage or had received adequate education or not. At the end of each *katun*, the *halach uinic* formulated these questions to the *bataboob*. If the *batab* passed, his mandate was ratified; if not, the *halach uinic* ordered that he be bound and sacrificed (*Chilam Balam of Chumayel* 1973: 35–37; *Books of Chilam Balam* 1948: 204–219).

As in the case of Tollan, there are many names associated with Zuyuá, among them Tulán. The names also have a vague character: they confuse the identity, the vicinity, and the part for the whole. There are those that come from Nahuatl: the tradition speaks of men coming from Tulapan (The River of Reeds) or from Chiconautlan (The Place of the Nine). Resembling passages from the *Historia tolteca-chichimeca*, the *Books of Chilam Balam* (1948: 57–59, 64, 69) mention a site called Nonoual and insist that the invaders were "mountain people," as were the Chichimecs in The Place of the Seven Caves, who left their mountain to wander "the flat land, the divine land."[53]

Some names given to the creator deity in the Central Mexican sources also appear in the colonial Maya texts. In Yucatán there is memory of two great rulers, both named Kukulcán (Feathered Serpent), who governed Chichén Itzá in different periods. At least one of them was considered a god. The Maya written sources also speak of a leader named Chan Tepeu (*Books of Chilam Balam* 1948: 58), who led the Tutul-Xiu to Yucatán. His two names are very significant: Chan means "Serpent" (Barrera Vázquez and Rendón, in *Books of Chilam Balam* 1948: 58) and Tepeu comes from Tepeuhqui, that is to say, "The Conqueror," a name given to the creator deity in Cholula tradition. This causes us, again, to wonder if we are facing the figure of an historical leader or dealing with one of the mythical "first fathers." In this sense, the Maya sources state that the Itzá invaders were led by four lords who were the chiefs of the four lineages of the sky (Thompson 1975: 383).

Who were these "mountain people"? Perhaps they were military invaders, foreign merchants with old roots, or local natives dazzled by faraway traditions; most probable is that these three identities were not exclusive and that the change would have been instigated by heterogeneous groups in the dense historical complexity brought on by the deterioration of the old regimes. One of the most attractive hypotheses concerning the invading groups—though it should be taken with reservation—is one that identifies them with the Chontal or Putún Maya, the lords of coastal commerce who connected, both commercially and culturally, the Yucatán Peninsula, the Gulf Coast, and Central Mexico (Thompson 1975: 21–72).

One of the problems of political organization that has also disturbed Mayanists is that of the Yucatec "triple alliance." The written sources speak of the famous League of Mayapán. Its hegemonic cities would be Uxmal, Chichén Itzá, and Mayapán, capitals, respectively, of the Tutul-Xiu, Itzá, and Cocom Maya. A great deal of the discussion revolves around chronology, a problem that no one to date has been able to solve in any definitive manner. Whether or not the three cities were contemporaneous, necessary for the establishment of that alliance, has been discussed. In order to solve the problem, some authors propose that accounts in the sources should be interpreted as an alliance between three ethnic groups or between three dynastic lineages. Most disconcerting is that this confederation would correspond to the system we have characterized as Zuyuan. Assuming for the moment that it did exist, the league would have been dissolved around the end of the thirteenth century. Two centuries later, with Mayapán's supremacy also vanished, acute political fragmentation occurred in northern Yucatán, the situation encountered by the Spaniards upon their arrival.

HIGHLAND GUATEMALA

We know the traditions concerning the origin of Guatemalan Zuyuans principally from three extremely important texts: the Quiché *Popol vuh* and *Título de Totonicapán*, and the Cakchiquel *Memorial de Sololá*. Their descriptions of the faraway homeland and the adventures of the "first mother-fathers" aid in understanding our central problem, in spite of the fact that the texts, strongly influenced by Christianity and colonial life, present human and divine acts with many contradictions, distortions, interpolations, and reinterpretations. A study of the meaning of the migrations of these Maya peoples, based on a very timely analysis of the written sources, becomes urgent. At this time, two currents of interpretation exist. The traditional interpretation, still defended by researchers such as Robert Carmack (1981: 43–52, 125–126) and John Fox (1987: 156), maintains that the Guatemalan innovators effectively came from the Gulf Coast, identified as the legendary Tulán of Nacxit. The most recent interpretations, however, assert that sufficient elements do not exist to show the foreignness of these historical actors. Carlos Navarrete (1996), for example, points out that there are no archaeological, linguistic, or physical bases supporting immigration, and that "the testimonies in manuscripts and from oral tradition do not match the material remains." Navarrete adds that the contrary could be thought, that is, assuming a Toltec origin formed part of an ideology subsequently acquired by the Maya rulers.

We continue our brief synthesis of the relevant parts of the three books. The *Popol vuh*[54] begins the account by mentioning the creator-divinity as a duality: Tepeu and Gucumatz.

> And the Progenitors, the Creators and Shapers, who were called Tepeu and Gucumatz, said, "The time of dawn has arrived, for which the work is determined and that those who sustain and nurture us, the enlightened children, the civilized vassals, would appear; that man, humanity would appear on the face if the earth." Thus they said. (*Popol vuh* 1964: 103)[55]

We have previously encountered the first of the names—Tepeuqui (meaning The Conqueror in Nahuatl)—as the creator's name in the Cholula story and in the Yucatán story, as that of the serpent chief—The Conqueror—who led the Tutul-Xiu from Tulapan Chiconautlan to the peninsula. The second name, Gucumatz, means Feathered Serpent.

According to the *Popol vuh*, the Quiché "first mother-fathers" were created by divine prodigy. They were born looking so much like deities that the gods had to fog up their eyes by breathing on them to diminish their nature. There were four men and their wives, and together they engendered all the tribes.

The name of the place of origin was East.[56] The enormous diversity of human beings, of different races and languages, was formed there, in the dark, before there was sun or light in the world. In East they did not worship deities; they did not keep stone or wood images. There, in the mountain, they were insane,[57] and spoke only one language.

The "first mother-fathers" asked the creator to give them a lineage, a dawn, level roads over the land, peace and happiness, a good life, and a purposeful existence. They watched toward the east for the Morning Star, the female harbinger of the sun;[58] then, tired of waiting for the star to rise and lacking images of their deities and their symbols, they proceeded to a city called Tulán Zuivá, and also Vucub Pec (The Seven Caves), Vucub Zuivá (The Seven Ravines). Innumerable peoples came to Tulán, where the distribution of deities, one to each human group, began. And there the languages of the peoples were altered and they no longer could understand each other (*Popol vuh* 1964: 111).[59]

After the alteration of their languages, each group made their way on an arduous journey. In fact, during the entire time after their departure from Tulán, the Morning Star shined and the peoples did not eat. The texts describe them as being so poor that they only dressed in animal skins. This is the same image that the Central Mexican written and pictographic sources give us of the Chichimecs.

Tohil, the god who had been delivered as the patron of the first father of the Quiché "mother-fathers," presented fire to his people. The Quiché gave it to the Vucamag people, but only with the promise that they would later allow their children to be sacrificed in honor of Tohil. The Quiché peoples continued in search of the places where they would establish themselves, where the sun would rise for the first time. They took a detour to the mountain called Place of Advice[60] and agreed on an alliance, which later grew to include the Cakchiquel, Rabinal, and Tzikinahá peoples.

The Quiché groups continued on their way. Already close to the sunrise, they crossed the sea. Each group hid their deity in a safe place and settled. Then, the four "first mother-fathers" retired to a mountain to await the sunrise. Jubilant, they burned copal incense when the sun appeared. Beasts roared, birds sang, and the surface of the earth, which until then had been muddy and humid, dried out. In that moment, the patron deities turned into stone images. The sun appeared everywhere and rose for each group when they had arrived at their promised land. The source specifies that the sun rose for the Mexica when they were in Mexico-Tenochtitlan.[61]

With the Quiché already settled, the "first mother-fathers" bid their children farewell. One of them left as a memento a sacred bundle that could not be unwrapped because it did not have a seam on any side. The "first mother-fathers" descended down the mountain and disappeared miraculously to return to East.

Much later, the three sons who succeeded them set out on a journey to the sea, toward East. In East they received the investiture of the kingdom from the hands of Lord Nacxit (Four Feet),[62] "the only supreme judge of all the kingdoms." They returned with the insignias of power, including the canopy, the throne, the bone flutes, the books, the yellow beads, the claws of the wild beast, the mantles, the snail shells, and other objects of legitimacy. They brought back the government and displayed the insignias of the kingdom's greatness to the Quiché, Cakchiquel, Rabinal, and Tziquinahá peoples.

We now move to the *Título de Totonicapán* (1983: 174–196). In this book, Sewán Tulán is compared to the earthly paradise of Judeo-Christian tradition. The Great Lord created humans there, in "Wukub Pec, Wukub Siwán, which truly was in a cave, in the ravine, where [the ancestors] slept in the east." This makes one suppose that, in the *Título*, East and Sewán Tulán are the same mythical place. In the place of origin there was a violation of the law that led to the language change. Tulán is also mentioned as being on the other side of the sea and called The Yellow Mountain/The Green Mountain, which refers to the idea of the origin of the world, since the same image appears in the foundation stories from Central Mexico (see Alvarado Tezozómoc 1949: 3). The ancestors, who were "magical people," celebrated rituals in Tulán with Lord Nacxit. He personally delivered the sacred bundle, known as *pisom c'ac'al*, to them. When the four Quiché "first mother-fathers" left Tulán, they wished to cross the sea. One of them poked at it with a walking stick; the sand dried up; and thus all the groups were able to pass.

Some episodes of the painful journey toward their definitive settlement, including the origin of fire, the concealment of the patron deities before the first sunrise, and the miraculous disappearance of the "first mother-fathers," are repeated in the *Título*, more or less, as they appear in the *Popol vuh* account.

Once the Quiché groups were settled, the authors of the document give special attention to the journey that two of their leaders made in search of the sacred instruments of power that were distributed after they returned from East. One of the Quiché groups had the idea of establishing rule. They told "our messengers to go there where the sun rises, ahead of Lord Nacxit, so that the warrior factions would not conquer us, exterminate us, destroy us; so they would not diminish our power, our lineage, our name, and our presence." They sent two sons of one of the "first mother-fathers." Both were directed different ways to search for the original homeland, and one returned with the mantle, the throne, the puma and jaguar bones, the black and yellow stones, and all the rest of the instruments of power delivered by Lord Nacxit, himself. These brothers "were the first to possess authority and listen to the problems of the people." Then the instruments from the East are distributed among the different titles of the rulers. The sacred bundle is "the sign of the power which came from where the sun rises." Later on, the text speaks of the ceremony in which the nose of the most famous of the Quiché lords, Q'uikab, is pierced, and the same is done to other lords of the upper hierarchy, to insert in the orifice the precious jewel.

The Cakchiquel history told in the *Memorial de Sololá* (1950: 47–84) is very similar to the previous two Quiché documents; but, while these first two have thoroughly obscure passages, this third source excels in confusion.[63]

The story begins by telling how the two "first fathers" were to settle Tulán. But far from considering that only one Tulán existed, it speaks of four: one in the east, one in the west, one in the underworld (Xibalbay), and one supposedly in the sky, since the text situates it "where God is."

The two Cakchiquel "first fathers" were engendered in the darkness of night, in a Tulán whose gates were guarded by a bat. The text is thoroughly confusing in terms of the location of the Cakchiquel ancestors and the directions in which their journeys were made. It seems that their Tulán of origin was the one in the underworld, and their departure from there was ordained by a deity formed below the earth who was named Obsidian Stone. This god ordered the people to go to the other side of the sea to search for the lands that he offered them; he promised them valleys and mountains to make them happy. On the outskirts of Tulán, the travelers received images of their deities. The journey seems to have gone from the Tulán of Xibalbay to Zuyvá, the Tulán in the east, with a necessary crossing of the sea, but it is very difficult to distinguish in the narrative which stage of the story (the auroral or sunrise phase) these different acts occurred. Some passages simply state that the two "first mother-fathers" acted when the aurora still had not glowed; that before the sunrise no one ate, and that the peoples were distributed in the territory to await the sunrise (*Memorial de Sololá* 1950: 81–84).

As in the case of the Quiché texts, the *Memorial de Sololá* (67–68) refers to the symbols of power when it speaks of the ceremony in which two personages invested with supreme titles were legitimated by Lord Nacxit. The rite consisted of piercing these two rulers' noses and the presentation of flowers.

These three books possess a wealth of information about Zuyuan political organization in Highland Guatemala. One could say that the abundance of data concerning the structure, functions, ethnic value, and mythical origin of the different titles of dignity and power has no parallel in the rest of the written sources pertaining to Mesoamerica. Some information, however, is very difficult to process, and thanks only to the timely studies of specialists such as Carmack (1981: 156–163) and Fox (1987: 142–193) have sufficiently explanatory descriptions been obtained. The results reveal an extremely complex political body that combined ethnic and supra-ethnic functions and principles of government by distributing different dignities among the segmentary lineages that made up the assembly of authorities. It is an impressive bureaucratic edifice in which the value of cosmic numbers, spaces, colors, and times are prominent (Fox 1989). In fact, divine geometry becomes reality, converting the political world into a faithful reflection of the order of the universe. Faced with such complexity attained by lineages, Fox (1989) asserted that this type of organization shows that the dichotomy that some anthropologists make between "state" and "segmentary tribes" is mistaken.

The proper functioning of such an apparatus must have required the meeting of organs and suborgans in long but orderly sessions and ceremonies. And this, of course, lent itself to a particular arrangement, both urban and architectural, as well as, paradigmatic and functional. An idea of the complexity of this organization emerges when we take into account that the Quiché were organized in twenty-four "great houses," or heads of agnatic lineages, organized in four major lineages that, in turn, made up two halves. Those who headed each agnatic lineage hereditarily possessed a specific governmental charge with all of them together constituting the Quiché political nucleus. This nucleus, in turn, was joined with those of the allied communities (Fox 1989). According to Fox, the general organization followed a triad patron, exemplified in the confederation of the three capitals: Jakawitz of the Quiché, Tzameneb of the Rabinal, and Paraxoné of the Cakchiquel.

We see repeated in Highland Guatemala some of the ideological foundations of other Zuyuan peoples, including the existence of extraordinary sovereigns, the best example of this being the Quiché Lord Gucumatz (Feathered Serpent), famous for his power of transformation.

Some foreign influences in Highland Guatemala are clearly Nahua, including the use of certain terms to designate levels of social and political organization, such as *chinamit*. Navarrete (1976, 1996), in his meticulous inventory of architectural, pictorial, sculptural, ceramic, and lithic indicators, taking into account skeletal remains that reveal ritual practices, has concluded that Nahua influence penetrated Guatemala during the Late Classic by way of Soconusco, not via river routes leading from the Gulf of Mexico. Finally, it is appropriate to examine not only the existence of indicators common to other Zuyuan-dominated regions, but also the notable absences. Absent in Highland Guatemala are the so-called *chacmool* sculptures, columns carved in the form of Feathered Serpent, atlantes, and warriors dressed in Toltec fashion.

OAXACA

The Postclassic history of Mixtec peoples, documented primarily in the pictographic codices, is presented as a precarious balance of small independent political units in permanent effervescence. Scholars have suggested that this political atomization was due, in large part, to the nature of the mountainous terrain, fragmented into small valleys, though the decline of Monte Albán also influenced Mixtec life in the Postclassic, since the metropolis exercised considerable control over its neighbors during its time of splendor.

Keeping these Mixtec domains in a state of equilibrium depended in great measure on political alliances, based, above all, upon marriages, and a flexible tradition of heritage (Caso 1977–1979 I: 69–155; Spores 1984: 79; Byland and Pohl 1994: 108–113). Thus, for example, the emergence of too favorable a union could produce a crisis in the region due to the danger its power represented to the rest of the small kingdoms.

The codices show that, sporadically, lords of exceptional quality attempted to establish foundations for regional consolidation (Byland and Pohl 1994: 125). Some cases lead one to suppose that these rulers received foreign assistance for the realization of their designs. Assistance came from Central Mexico, as may have been the case of Lord 8 Deer, who appears dressed in Toltec style (Flannery and Marcus 1983a). However, experiments involving the centralization of power were illusory, too bloody, considerably limited territorially, and of short duration. Therefore, in Oaxaca, rather than finding a Zuyuan state, we are in the presence of a difficult succession of failed attempts at Zuyuan consolidation.

In the Mixtec codices, we begin to find evidence of ancient religious concepts that occupied a niche in Zuyuan ideology as well as anchored the Zuyuan process of political transformation. Among these beliefs, those referring to the origin of humans focused on the birth of rulers, as one might expect due to the dynastic character of the pictographic documents. Thus, in the upper right panel of lamina 14 in the *Codex Zouche-Nuttall* (1992), the royal pair 5 Flower and 3 Flint appear in a very significant scene bordered on three sides by overlapping multiple bands. The top and right sides consist of two sky bands: a) one with stars depicted in the form of eyes and b) a band of diagonally arranged colored stripes, six omega figures, and an open womb symbol in the corner. From the womb emerges a third band of footprints leading from the top right corner down the right side and to the left along the bottom. Jill Furst (1986) very astutely identified these six omegas and the womb figure as the seven caves of Chicomoztoc. The path of footprints, from the womb to the earth, completes the symbolism of the birth of these royal personages. This is a clear expression of the origin of the lineage in The Place of the Seven Caves. Another very similar example is the scene in the *Selden Roll* (1964–1967: lam. 4), which depicts the birth of 1 Jaguar, a personage who descends from the top of the mouth of the great mountain of The Place of the Seven Caves. These two pictorial representations are in accordance with the Mexica view concerning the origin of the Mixtecs, since, according to Torquemada (1975–1983, I: 49), they descended from the eponymic ancestor Mixtecatl, born in Chicomoztoc along with his brothers—Xelhua, Tenuch, Ulmecatl, Xicalancatl, and Otomitl.

A problem, facing this affirmation of the origin of the Mixtecs, emerges from an old colonial document—the account that Antonio de los Reyes (1976) provided in his Mixtec grammar. Reyes spoke of how the Mixtec people, called *tay ñuhu*, had come from the center of the earth, but also said that the primogenial ruling lineages emerged from the river of Apoala,[64] which in Mixtec is called the River of the Lineages or River Where the Rulers Emerged. On the banks of Apoala there were certain trees with particular names. As in the myth concerning the expulsion of the gods from Tamoanchan, these trees were broken. From them emerged the first heroic lords to extend themselves throughout the four regions dividing the Mixteca. They conquered, founded settlements, gave names to each place, and established law and order in the territory (Reyes 1976: i–ii).

Different accounts come from Gregorio García, a friar who incessantly inquired about human origins in the Americas. According to García (1981: 262), there were two indigenous traditions. One maintained that Quetzalcoatl, the king of Tula, after retiring to Cholula, founded the provinces of the Zapotecs and the Mixteca Alta and Baja. The other (1981: 327–328) told of the creation of the world and of the role played by the two supreme deities, 1 Deer Puma's Serpent and 1 Deer Jaguar's Serpent. This duality died near Apoala, in The Place Where the Sky Is, a great mountain with a rock-faced summit, upon which a copper ax, with the blade facing upward, held up the sky. Puma's Serpent and Jaguar's Serpent engendered two sons: 9 Wind Serpent and 9 Wind Cavern. The older of them had the remarkable ability to change into an eagle, while the younger one could become a flying serpent. Between the two they founded a garden filled with trees and flowers. There they dedicated themselves to burning copal incense in honor of their parents and pierced their ears and tongues to ask them to dry up the waters, so land could be found and clarity would exist in the world. We continue reading the account, hoping that García will tell us how time passed from the auroral phase to the sunrise, but the Dominican abruptly interrupts the story "so as not to annoy the reader with such fables and nonsense as the Indians tell" (1981: 328).

Other written sources complement the story. Francisco de Burgoa (1934, I: 274–275, 369–371), for example, referred to the trees of Apoala, speaking as

Torquemada did of the joint origin of the Mixtecs and Mexica, arriving from the west. He narrates the adventure of Mixtecatl, the eponymic leader who was led to Tilantongo with plans of conquest and when encountering the sun in the west, fired his weapons at it, hit it, and caused the fires of the sunset with the hemorrhage of the star.

The discrepancies in these origin myths have been interpreted as the confluence of two traditions. According to Bruce Byland and John Pohl (1994: 119–120), the texts reveal, on the one hand, the beliefs of a people with ancient roots in the region, who were originally created from the depths of the earth, and, on the other hand, the mythification of a wave of conquerors coming from Central Mexico who imposed themselves upon the original population, saying they emerged from the trees of Apoala.

We propose, as a hypothesis, a different explanation; but before presenting it, we must clarify the point concerning the identification of the brothers 9 Wind Serpent and 9 Wind Cavern with the creator deity of the human race. Eduard Seler (1904) made a brilliant observation concerning the calendrical name of the two divine brothers: the combination of the number 9 and the "wind" sign refers to the god, Quetzalcoatl.[65] Seler added that the divine Mixtec brothers formed a complementary pair representing light and darkness. This Mixtec creator deity's duality corresponds to the dual projection of Cholula's figures of Quetzaltehueyac and Icxicoatl. In sum, the coupled unfolding of these deities allows for the games of replication to which we previously referred, and in the case of this Mixtec myth, we encounter Feathered Serpent as a pair of complementary opposites.

We move on to our explanation concerning these different myths of origin. We propose that they are parts of the same extensive myth and that there is no need to suppose that northern invaders introduced an explanatory account of their own creation. We can accept that all the Mixtecs came from the interior of the earth, that is, that they emerged from The Place of the Seven Caves. Thus, 5 Flower and 3 Flint, even though they formed a royal pair, emerged from Chicomoztoc, as we have already seen. However, the account of the origin of human beings may be more complex. In the first stage of creation (the nocturnal phase), on the mountain, the creator duality ruled over a still-unsettled world that was dark, humid, and devoid of creatures. From the divine pair were born the creators of humanity as a pair of brothers: 9 Wind Serpent and 9 Wind Cavern. Their mission was to bring the light of the dawn, time, the colors, and order to the place of the four cosmic trees. It was necessary to introduce humans into the world before the sun rose and dried the surface of the earth. Thus, the birth could have various representations, including the departure from caves or from the four cosmic trees. It all depended on what emphasis was desired in the mythical narrative. If the second symbolic pattern was used, reference was being made to the foundation of the four lineages of Mixtec royalty.

Ronald Spores (1984: 83) has noted that the Mixtecs thought that their dead rulers were transformed into gods. At the same time, a multiplicity of founders of royal lineages, considered by some to be a reflection of noncentralized authority, stands out (Byland and Pohl 1994: 226). One could add that many Mixtec lords, in the pictographic sources, had extraordinary biographies, some of which present aspects connecting with the Zuyuan systems of their times.

The most famous in terms of miracles is Lord 9 Wind, Koo Sau (Feathered Serpent).[66] The importance of his calendrical name immediately comes to mind, since it is the same as the two divine Mixtec brothers who created humanity and, as we have said, corresponded to Feathered Serpent. His identification with Feathered Serpent has been amply studied by several authors (Dahlgren 1990: 238–239; Nicholson 1957: 204–205; 1978; Caso 1977–1979, II: 60–64; Furst 1978: 109; Anders, Jansen, and Pérez Jiménez 1992: 57–58, 90–93). This Mixtec ruler is repeatedly represented in the codices with the diagnostic features of the Wind God—the double-billed buccal mask, conical hat, rounded adornments, etc. In the *Codex Vindobonensis* (1992: lam. 48) he appears with a helicoidal-shaped body, as the Wind God is depicted in images from other parts of Mesoamerica (López Austin 1990: 488, plate 13). He is also represented carrying the sky (*Codex Vindobonensis* 1992: lam. 47), in the same manner as the Feathered Serpent–Wind God appears in pictographic documents from the Mixteca-Puebla tradition (*Codex Borgia* 1993: lam. 15; *Codex Vaticanus B* 1993: lam. 21; Nicholson 1978; Furst 1978). But, without a doubt, the most important adventure for our purposes is the journey of Lord 9 Wind to the other world (*Codex Vindobonensis* 1992: lam. 48). He goes up to the sky with the divine duality, who in this case is shown as two bearded deities.[67] Facing them, naked and orant, he receives all the objects of power, including his adornments, his buccal mask and other diagnostic features of the wind god, the sacred bundle, the quincunx staff, and the god's weapons. Now majestically dressed, loaded with presents, 9 Wind descends from the sky on a rope adorned with white plumes. He then establishes order in the world, distributing the objects of power among the Mixtec rulers, who are depicted in the codices, in their turn, carrying the conch trumpet, the fire sticks, the staff of Xipe Totec, the quincunx staff, the sacred bundle, etc.[68]

Another great Mixtec personage was the conqueror 8 Deer Jaguar Claw, who, through usurpation, marriage alliances, and warfare, dominated an extensive amount of territory in the Mixteca Alta, Baja, and the Coast during the eleventh century. 8 Deer established a complex bureaucratic state, modeled, according to some authors, after the Toltec state (Flannery and Marcus 1983b; Spores 1984: 78–79; Byland and Pohl 1994: 142). Spores (1984: 77) has pointed out that his government had four high dignitaries immediately below the sovereign, which we suggest is a Zuyuan trait.

Most notable about his government, however, was the manner in which he legitimized his power. He traveled to a sanctuary where a distinguished personage pierced his nose and implanted the jewel of power. According to Maarten Jansen (1996), 8 Deer was awarded this distinction by 4 Jaguar, a Toltec king who wore the face paint of Quetzalcoatl and had a similar pimple or tumor on his nose. The location of the sanctuary is represented in the *Codex Colombino* (1966: lam. 13) with a place-glyph in the form of a frieze of reeds and thought to be situated in either Tula, Cholula, or San Miguel Tulancingo (near Coixtlahuaca), a site of possible Toltec heritage (e.g., Byland and Pohl 1994: 147; Jansen 1996).

After the death of 8 Deer Jaguar Claw, political atomization returned to the Mixtec area.

MICHOACÁN

While the process of Zuyuanization in Oaxaca seems not to have reached its full manifestation, in Michoacán the system was rapidly overcome by another that imposed a heightened level of centralization and control, one in which a conquering patron deity provided protection to communities that submitted to his rule.

The principal actors in this historical process were the Uacúsecha, Tarascan speakers who, by their own accounts, had no remote history in the region. Their ancestors, they said, had arrived a few generations before as nomads. In other words, they were a people who took pride in their Chichimec origin. But not all contemporary authors accept this part of their story, once they consider the notion that the Uacúsecha's alleged Chichimec origin was inspired by Central Mexican traditions and that their inclusion of *chichimecayotl* heritage was aimed at projecting the image of great conquerors to their neighbors (Michelet 1989, 1995; Arnauld and Michelet 1991). This new point of view takes into account contradictions in the *Relación de Michoacán* (1977)—where, for example, these "Chichimecs" appear constructing storage bins—and recent excavations in the region of Zacapu, the origin of the Uacúsecha expansion. The archaeological work of Dominique Michelet reveals that the region was occupied around 1300 C.E. by a clearly Mesoamerican people who had little to do with the hunter-gatherers of historical tradition.[69]

The Uacúsecha initiated their process of expansion in the fourteenth century with the bellicose actions of their leader, Taríacuri, his son, and his two nephews in the Lake Pátzcuaro region. This territory, as well as the rest of the lands dominated by the Tarascans, was multi-ethnic. The Uacúsecha then organized a powerful army of different peoples in the region and launched a fervent war of conquest. According to Helen Pollard (1994), the problem of the ethnic groups' unification under one ruler was solved by means of a prophetic fiction, because they mentioned the alliance's divine resolution between the Uacúsecha god Curicaueri and the goddess Xarátanga of the Tarascans, who settled the lake islands before the arrival of the "Chichimecs." This provided the foundation for a joint enterprise. In time, the conquering army was converted into a true ethnic mosaic made up of Tarascan, Nahua, Otomí, Matlatzinca, and Chontal peoples, along with members of other ethnic groups (*Relación de Michoacán* 1977: 191).

After the death of Taríacuri, a central domain composed of three capitals—Pátzcuaro, Ihuatzio, and Tzintzuntzan, ruled respectively by his son and his two nephews—was established. Michelet (1995) has suggested that the Tarascan triple alliance lasted approximately three decades, from 1450 to 1480, as a multi-ethnic power. After this brief period of consolidation, Tzitzipandácuare, successor of the first king of Tzintzuntzan, nullified the tripartite system and concentrated power in his own capital.

The political system imposed by Pátzcuaro, Tzintzuntzan, and Ihuatzio was characterized by a complexity never before seen in the region. Speaking about the border and enclave groups, Pollard (1994) noted that many of them were not Tarascan, but often were composed of various ethnic groups. These communities had governments administered by their "natural lords," whose power derived from their own ethnic right, authorized by the Tarascan king, or *cazonci*. When a ruler died, his designation fell upon a member of his family. The new lord was ratified by the *cazonci* as the Zuyuan patron, because the representative of Curicaueri presented him the jewels that legitimated his authority.

> When a chief died in the communities of the province, his brothers and relatives came to inform the *cazonci*, and brought him the gold lip ornament, and the earspools, and the bracelets, and the turquoise necklaces, which were the lord's insignias that the *cazonci* had given him when they made him lord, and as they were bringing those jewels, they carried and placed them with the jewels of the *cazonci* ... And appearing before [the *cazonci*] were five or six relatives, brothers, sons, or nephews of the dead chief ... and [the *cazonci*] entrusted the position to the most judicious, the one who grieved the most, which is their way of telling, who is the most experienced and most obedient ... And the *cazonci* ordered he be given another new gold lip ornament and earspools and bracelets, and said to him, "Take this as the insignia of the honor that you carry with you" (*Relación de Michoacán* 1977: 203).[70]

In a few words, the system respected the order and customs of the integrated units. This occasioned—as has been pointed out for the *excan tlatoloyan*—that the cultural influence of the Tarascan nuclear area over the periphery was not significant. Acámbaro is a typical case of this. Shirley Gorenstein (1985: 27–98) has observed that the diagnostic archaeological elements of Tarascan presence are minimal in this frontier site.

As we have said before, the system's structure corresponded to the image of the cosmos. Thus, the conquered communities began to be incorporated into an arrangement in which their patron deities would be reinterpreted within the order of the four quarters (those of the four brothers of Curicaueri) and the five directions, including the center. This made Lake Pátzcuaro the navel of the universe. These four quarters and the center of the earth were associated with the colors red (east), yellow (north), white (west), black (south), and blue (center) (Pollard 1994).

Among the Tarascan archaeological remains that refer to Zuyuan ideology, the so-called *chacmool* images (Figure 1.1) and thrones in the form of carnivorous mammals stand out (see Williams 1992). Hers (1989: 74, note 20) observed that the *chacmool* figures of Ihuatzio are related to coyote thrones, as those of Chichén Itzá were linked to jaguar thrones. This led her to suppose that the Michoacán sculptures belonged to the Early Postclassic. Another Zuyuan architectural example is the *tzompantli*. In fact, written sources mention the practice of skewering the heads of sacrificed victims with wooden rods (*Relación de Michoacán* 1977: 182).

The lack of written sources for Tarascan history and culture, above all in what is referred to as their cosmovision, makes it difficult to find many more ideological foundations of Zuyuan character. These, moreover, could have remained hidden under the new ideology that made the god Curicaueri protector of all the communities. The *Relación de Michoacán* is a document that firmly reflects this ideology. According to this source, the sky deities had entrusted Curicaueri to conquer and rule the land, by which his representative, the *cazonci*, held power over the four parts of the territory (*Relación de Michoacán* 1977: 173).

CONCLUSIONS

Our two models concerning the Zuyuan system attempt to explain a thoroughly complex historical process that took place in various regions of Mesoamerica between the seventh and sixteenth centuries. This process, of course, manifested itself in very different ways through time and space. Its axis was of a political character, fundamentally consisting of a statal reorganization that attempted the creation of supra-ethnic governments that joined units of different ethnic groups, the establishment of a regional domain through confederations of hegemonic capitals, and the implantation of militarist regimes charged with maintaining and expanding the political and economic order.

We have proposed, for the study of this process, the existence of a hegemonic patron of political control, over a broad territorial range and an ethnically heterogeneous population. This patron tended to be widely accepted, from the Epiclassic on, in a good portion of Mesoamerica, with lively resistance from political units that defended their traditional and more autonomous forms of government. Among the typically Zuyuan institutions, the confederations of three capitals stand out.

We have also proposed a model that explains the ideological foundation of the Zuyuan system, crystallized as much in political institutions as in religious beliefs. The supra-ethnic centers presented themselves as those in charge of establishing order in the world. Other notable institutions were the rule of one or more sovereigns who embodied the force of the Feathered Serpent god, including Quetzalcoatl, Kukulcán, Gucumatz, and Nacxit; the consecration of royal power by means of a ceremony officiated in sanctuaries identified with the mythical place of origin; and a specific, common cult that held the different military orders together. Concerning beliefs, the Zuyuans assured that their primordial ancestors came from the same mythical place: Tollan, Zuyuá, or Tulán Sewán.

The bearers of the Zuyuan system were of a very different nature. While in some regions the system was introduced by aggressive foreigners who seized power, in others it was imposed by the local groups themselves over their neighbors. The routes of ideology may have been the same as those of commerce, an activity very important for the Zuyuan lords. Their principal interest, however, was dominating the tribute of their respective regional territories and they did this for themselves. They were not agents of remote forces established in enclaves. Thus, even in the case that some Zuyuans had originally been foreign invaders, it is logical to think that with the passage of time they became assimilated to the local cultures to the degree of losing their own language. There is no evidence suggesting the existence of a great metropolis upon which all the Zuyuan groups were dependent. We know, on the other hand, that some urban centers—such as Cholula and Mexico-Tenochtitlan—received the epithet of Tollan. In addition, it is possible that the Zuyuan system may be very old, with roots in the Epiclassic, multi-ethnic, mercantile cities of Central Mexico. Cacaxtla or Xochicalco are good candidates as cradles of this ideology.

This leads us to reiterate that Zuyuan and Toltec are not synonymous. Zuyuan does not correspond to an ethnic group, a language, or a precise region of origin. The Zuyuan system quite probably was initiated before the founding of Tula and lasted several centuries after its decline. We should not confuse, therefore, the primordial Tollan-Zuyuá with the historical Tula in the modern-day state of Hidalgo. This city, in the Late Postclassic, acquired sufficient prestige to become the terrestrial Tollan par excellence, with its fame enduring until the arrival of the Spaniards.

It is undeniable that a considerable number of characteristics of the Zuyuan system were disseminated by Tula. Today, we know that this city inherited them from very old civilizations, including those of northern and central Mesoamerica. Tula would have been able to absorb and bring together the first Zuyuans, of whom it was a member and important diffuser. This would explain the presence of its artistic models in many regions of Mesoamerica, and why certain terms of Zuyuan sociopolitical organization derived from the Nahuatl language.

In other words, Tula was not the capital of a pan-Mesoamerican empire, but rather, in its moment, the principal center of the spread of Zuyuan ideology and, perhaps, of some immigrant groups of conquerors.

We believe that with these proposed models it is feasible to deepen the studies of each one of the regions where Zuyuan systems seem to have been established. As we have seen, the form and success of the system's implantation varied considerably in time and space. This remains evident in myths, in historical accounts, in artistic styles, and in luxury objects. Not only should the similarities and differences be determined, but the specific historical processes to which they correspond will have to be explained.

One of the fundamental problems that remain, of course, is determining the historical origin of the Zuyuan system.

NOTES

1. Here we use the Nahuatl term *tzompantli*, which refers to the buildings that supported racks where the heads of sacrificial victims were hung, and we extend its meaning to buildings that depict sculpted as well as pierced skulls.

2. According to Hers, the *tzompantli* is found dating back to the sixth century in Alta Vista, La Quemada, and Cerro del Huistle.

3. "A polythetic group—is a group of entities such that each entity possesses a large number of attributes of the group, each attribute is shared by large numbers of entities, and no single attribute is both sufficient and necessary to the group membership" (Clarke 1968: 37).

4. Enrique Florescano (1993: 144–145) synthesizes this proposition of Mayanists.

5. Charles Lincoln (1986: 143) says, "While the terms *Mexican*, *Toltec*, and *Maya-Toltec* do not satisfactorily describe the distinctiveness of the art and architecture in Chichén Itzá, there is yet no other name that adequately conveys the cosmopolitan but very original character of the site."

6. Concerning the use of the term "Mexican" in the context of Maya history, see Alberto Ruz Lhuillier (1971). According to him, "the meaning of 'Mexican' implies what

in the Valley of Mexico is called archaic, Teotihuacan, Tolteca-Chichmeca, and Aztec, or in other words, the cultural manifestations that flourished in Central or Highland Mexico in the different chronological horizons." For Thompson (1964: 31), "Mexican" is a term designating non-Maya cultures, except for the Zapotecs. For Ledyard Smith (1955: 75–77), "Mexican" refers to non-Maya cultures, including those of Oaxaca.

7. See, for example, *Popol vuh* (1964: 149).

8. Pedro Carrasco (1996) says that, due to the ethnic complexity of prehispanic Mexico, internal segmentation in the political units prevailed. The Triple Alliance of the Basin of Mexico almost always respected this segmentation.

9. Concerning this issue, see the way in which Tollan was a mythical site of linguistic unity (López Austin 1990: 437–439; 1995).

10. These patrons in the Nahuatl language received the name *calpulteteo*, or deities of the *calpultin*.

11. Our conception of the paradigm of the sun's course differs from the interpretation that Michel Graulich has given in numerous works. For example, he thinks that the peoples' original migrations mythically compare to the night (Graulich 1988: 260–263). As will be seen later, we identify the migrations with the dawn.

12. There is an exception to this idea of successive births of human groups. The *Popol vuh*, as we shall see, speaks of simultaneity in the birth: it says all the human groups received the sun in the same moment.

13. The separation of languages from one original language is a pre-Hispanic mythical theme (Graulich 1988: 75; López Austin 1995).

14. Recently, Guilhem Olivier (1995) has published an extensive study of sacred bundles.

15. In demotic stories, the elements of myth, legend, and history become fused. There-fore, the ethnic (often eponymic) engenderers, on the one hand, become fused with the patron deities and, on the other hand, can be considered political founders.

16. The donation of the sacred bundle appears in the written sources in various modali-ties: a) the creator deity of humanity (Feathered Serpent or Nacxit) delivers to each group a particular bundle in the mythical Tulan of the auroral phase; b) a particular patron deity delivers to his people part of his own body, clothing, or belongings, such as legate matter of his divine substance, in the moment of his death or entry to the underworld; c) a "first mother" or a "first father" (a common ancestor of the group, a personage who is confused with the patron deity) leaves his or her people the relic in some moment during the mythical migration, often when he or she disappears before the first sunrise. In all these cases, the meaning is the same: the bundle marks the transition between myth and history, serving as a permanent connection between the divine and the worldly.

17. On the bellicose character of Feathered Serpent, see, for example, Virginia Miller (1989), John Carlson (1991), Saburo Sugiyama (1992), and Ivan Šprajc (1996: 123–168).

18. Werner Stenzel (1970) points out that sacred bundles in Mesoamerican tradition may indicate a hierarchy within the clan system and a connection to political power.

19. Many groups in the migration accounts insisted on their nomadic origins, in spite of the information from archaeological and written sources, which suggests they were agriculturists. Taking this into account, various authors have affirmed that the hunter-gatherer origin of the migrants is more a product of the mytho-historical archetype than reality. See Pedro Armillas (1964) and Brigitte Boehm de Lameiras (1986: 252–274) for the case of the Chichimecs of Xolotl; Carlos Martínez Marín (1963) for the Mexica; and Arnauld and Michelet (1991) for the Tarascans and the Quiché Maya.

20. Graulich (1988: 125) says, "We understand well: before becoming such [refined artificers] the Toltecs were Chichimecs."

21. The "first sunrise" is a very important event in the life of the human groups.

Accounts of migrations from darkness to the primogenial sunrise exist among the Chichimecs (*Anales de Cuauhtitlán* 1945: 3–4), the peoples of Michoacán (*Lienzo de Jucutácato* n.d.), the Quiché Maya (*Popol vuh* 1964: 122–123), the Tlaxcalans (Zapata y Mendoza 1995: 86–87), etc. However, in some accounts we should distinguish three types of sunrise: a) the *mythical* (the passage from another time-space to the worldly time-space, marked by the primogenial sunrise, in the moment when the human groups come to life on the surface of the earth); b) the *legendary* (a miracle that gives "definitive" possession of land to a group, according to the account that corresponds to their last migration to that of primordial time); and c) the *ritual* (a ceremony that stages or dramatizes the primogenial sunrise). Confusion among the three types of sunrise was due to ideological reasons, since their nondistinction sacralized reality.

22. Nigel Davies (1980: 72–90, 327–329) interprets the change from Chichimecas to ex-Chichimecas as passing from rags to riches.

23. "Estos dichos tultecas todos se nombraron chichimecas, y no tenían otro nombre particular, sino el que tomaron de la curiosidad y primor de las obras que hacían, que se llamaron tultecas, que es tanto como si dijésemos 'oficiales pulidos y curiosos,' como ahora los de Flandes."

24. Pasztory follows the chronology of René Millon (1981: 207), dating the Metepec Phase from 650 to 750 C.E., a period that coincides with the initial splendor of Xochicalco and Cacaxtla. Recently, however, new radiocarbon dates have been used to propose that the Metepec Phase occurred a hundred years earlier (Cowgill 1996). This proposition puts in doubt the contemporaneity of the Teotihuacan Metepec Phase with Xochicalco and Cacaxtla.

25. We are convinced that the symbol complex of Feathered Serpent has much earlier manifestations. For example, in Miccaotli-Phase Teotihuacan (150–200 C.E.), the symbols of Feathered Serpent, the creation of the world, the extraction of time, the calendar, governmental authority, and war were all joined together in one building (López Austin, López Luján, and Sugiyama 1991; Sugiyama 1992).

26. Feathered Serpent also appears on the sides of Altar 2 at Cholula (Acosta 1970).

27. In recent years, Norberto González Crespo found sculptures depicting human skulls with temporal perforations, characteristic of the *tzompantli.*

28. Davies (1974) examines the mythical and historical levels of Tula, and compares this city with the idealized image of Rome and Jerusalem of the Middle Ages.

29. For the sake of clarity, here we are calling the mythical city "Tollan," and the archaeological city located in the modern-day state of Hidalgo, "Tula."

30. These and other settlements in Central Mexico and in the rest of Mesoamerica received the name of Tollan (Davies 1977: 29–52; Carrasco 1992: 106). In the *Mapa Quinatzin*, the "tules" (reeds) glyph is associated with Teotihuacan; in the *Codex Sierra*, the same glyph refers to Tenochtitlan; Chalco was also called Tollan (Graulich 1988: 20).

31. Richard Diehl (1989) says that in the tenth century Tula was possibly the largest city in Mesoamerica.

32. Gabriel de Rojas (1985: 128) says, "[T]he Indians call [Cholula] Tullan Cholollan Tlachiuh Altepetl . . . Tullan means 'congregation of artificers of different arts' " ("llaman los indios [a Cholula] Tullan Cholollan Tlachiuh Altepetl . . . *Tullan* significa 'congregación de oficiales de diferentes of[ici]os' ").

33. "Topiltzin" was another one of the names of the feathered-serpent god.

34. The houses of Quetzalcoatl were characterized by their walls covered with minerals and seashells, or by feathers. In the first case, corresponding to the east was gold; to the west, jades and turquoise; to the south, silver and seashells; and to the north, precious red stones, jaspers, and shells. In the second case, corresponding to the east were yellow feathers; to the west, *xiuhtototl* (blue-green) and quetzal feathers; to the south, white

feathers; and to the north, red feathers. These give the values: east = yellow; west = blue-green; south = white; and north = red.

35. There is evidence that this ceremony also was practiced in Tula: see, for example, the Toltec *chacmool* bearing the *yacaxihuitl*, the distinctive turquoise nose jewel (Fuente, Trejo, and Gutiérrez 1988: 53). As we will see later, the *yacaxapotlaliztli* (nose-piercing ceremony) also was performed in Huexotzinco and Tlaxcala. Evidently, the best known descriptions of this ceremony come from Tenochtitlan (see, for instance, Durán 1984, 2: 301, 317, 399; Broda 1978: 226–231).

36. Rojas, in his "Relación de Cholula" (1985: 128–129), makes the distinction between a remote, unknown Tula, and the contemporaneous Tula, Cholula's western neighbor. Nevertheless, like many accounts from this period, he leaves unclear the context that would have favored the ideological interpretation in pre-Hispanic times: "And the Indians also say that the founders of the city [Cholula] came from a community called Tullan, *about which, being very far away and much time having [passed], nothing is known*, and that, on the way, they founded Tullan . . . and Tullantzinco." "Y también dicen los indios que los fundadores desta ciudad [de Cholula] vinieron de un pueblo que se llama Tullan, *del cual, por ser muy lejos y haber [pasado] mucho tiempo, no se tiene noticia,* y que, de camino, fundaron a Tullan . . . y a Tullantzinco." The emphasis is ours.

37. This same expression is used to speak of the Tolteca-Chichimecs who abandon Tula (*Historia tolteca-chichimeca* 1976: 144, 174).

38. The relationship of these two personages with the Sky and the Earth is corroborated in their distinguishing characteristics, since the first had the eagle, a symbol of the Sky, for his insignia while the second had the jaguar, a symbol of the Earth, as an emblem (Rojas 1985: 129).

39. "Estos dos indios [Áquiach y Tlálchiach] estaban en un templo . . . que se llamaba [de] Quetzalcóatl, . . . fundado a honor de un capitán que trajo [a] la gente desta ciudad, antiguamente, a poblar en ella, de partes muy remotas hacia el poniente, que no se sabe [con] certinidad dello. Y este capitán se llamaba Quetzalcóatl, y, muerto q[ue] fue, le hicieron un templo, en el cual había, demás de los dichos dos indios, gran cantidad de religiosos."

40. "Asimismo, tenían por preeminencia los dos sumos sacerdotes dichos de confirmar en los estados a todos los gobernadores y reyes desta Nueva España, [y era] desta manera: q[ue] los tales reyes y caciques, en heredando el reino o señorío, venían a esta ciudad a reconocer obediencia al ídolo della, Quetzalcóatl, al cual ofrecían plumas ricas, mantas, oro y piedras preciosas, y otras cosas de valor. Y, habiendo ofrecido, los metían en una capilla q[ue] para este efecto estaba dedicada, en la cual los dos sumos sacerdotes los señalaban horadándoles las orejas, o las narices o el labio inferior, según el señorío q[ue] tenían. Con lo cual quedaban confirmados en sus señoríos, y se volvían a sus tierras . . .

"Asimismo, había un orden y ley que, de 53 en 53 a[ñ]os . . . venían gentes de todos los pueblos que aquí confirmaban los señoríos a tributar al dicho templo . . .

"Asimismo, traían estas ofrendas los indios que de toda la tierra venían por su devoción y romería a visitar el templo de Quetzalcóatl, porque éste era metrópoli y tenido en tanta veneración como lo es Roma en la cristiandad, y [La] Meca en[tre] los moros."

41. ". . . i pasados los quatro dias, al quinto le entiznavan todo el cuerpo i la cara, i le hacian unas ropetas i unas ameras de papel i le ponian dos nombres, el uno era Motecuçauque, y el otro Naxictle, ques su declaracion ayunante i figura de Calcoatle."

42. It seems contradictory that, without true human beings having existed during the earlier "suns" or ages of the world, there would be two piles of bones, one of men and another of women, in the Place of the Dead. We must understand that the reading of myth is not that of a historic account: the bones are, in this case, the first cold raw material, generator of life. Mesoamericans understood that life was generated from death and led it in a cyclical process.

43. Concerning the comparison between both variants of the myth, see López Austin (1994: 35–37).

44. For the Camaxtli-Iztacmixcoatl—The Sky account, see López Austin (1973: 145–146).

45. For the Chimalma-Ilancueitl—The Earth account, see López Austin (1973: 146).

46. Xelhua, the sixth personage in Motolinía's account, was the patron of the Cholultecs (*Codex Vaticanus A* 1964: lam. 14).

47. Compare "In the Ravine of the Fishes" with another of Tamoanchan's names: Chalchimmichhuacan, The Place of Those Who Have Precious Fishes (López Austin 1994: 87–88).

48. The historian Federico Navarrete thoroughly investigates this topic.

49. The expression "the mat, the seat" signifies power.

50. "Ca njcan qujcuj, cana: in totecujoan in tepilhoan, in tetzonoan, in teiztioan, in tlaçoti in chalchiuhtin, in maqujzti in jnpilhoan: auh in jtlâpitzalhoan, in jtlaxoxalhoan in topiltzin in quetzalcoatl: a in jpan iolque, in jpan tlacatque in jmjlhvil, in jnmaceoal in petlatl, in jcpalli: in tlatconj, in tlamamalonj in çan njman iuh iolque, in njman iuh tlacatque, in çan njman iuh icoloque in canjn iooaia itoloc, iocoloc in tecutizque in tlatocatizque" (Sahagún 1950–1982, book VI, chapter 16, p. 83). (Translator's note: The English translation is based upon the authors' Spanish translation of the Nahuatl text and differs somewhat from the English translation of Dibble and Anderson: "Here the sons, the noble sons, the precious ones, the precious green stones, the precious bracelets, the sons of our lords, and the descendants of Topiltzin Quetzalcoatl—those under his spell—take it, receive it. At this time they came to life, at this time they were born; their desert, their merit is the realm, the governed. So they came to life, so they were born, so they were created where in the beginning it was determined, ordained that they would be lords, that they would be rulers.")

51. "Ya desde hoy, señor, quedáis en el trono, silla que primero pusieron Zenácatl [Ce Ácatl] y Nácxitl Quetzalcóatl . . . y en su nombre vino Huitzilopochtli."

52. Hypothetically, one could think that these two personages have a parallel in mythology. Captain Serpent would correspond to the god, Feathered Serpent, the son of the supreme pair and, as we have seen, the patron deity of humanity. Captain Solar Disk could refer to the sun, also a son of the supreme pair and ruler of all creatures in the world. Both divinities, while favored sons of the supreme pair, have notable similarities in their mythical cycles.

53. Although the traditional Maya term, translated into Spanish as "montañez" and rendered here in English as "mountain people," does not seem to have had the sense of being "barbarous" or "barbarian"; if it is found that the native population superimposed a meaning of "foreign" onto the term, it is very probable that it implied "heretic," "sinful," and "lascivious."

54. Versions of the *Popol vuh* are very different, especially due to the obscurity of the mythic language. Its interpretation not being our field of specialization, for convenience we follow the version of Adrián Recinos (*Popol vuh* 1964: 103–143), unless otherwise indicated.

55. "Y dijeron los Progenitores, los Creadores y Formadores, que se llaman Tepeu y Gucumatz: 'Ha llegado el tiempo del amanecer, de que se determine la obra y que aparezcan los que nos han de sustentar y nutrir, los hijos esclarecidos, los vasallos civilizados; que aparezca el hombre, la humanidad, sobre la superficie de la tierra.' Así dijeron." (Translator's note: Interestingly, Tedlock (*Popol vuh* 1995: 163) translates this passage: "So they spoke, the Bearer, Begetter, the Makers, Modelers named Sovereign Plumed Serpent: 'The dawn has approached, preparations have been made, and morning has come for the provider, nurturer, born in the light, begotten in the light. Morning has come for humankind, for the people of the face of the earth,' they said.")

56. In this part of the account, the place of origin seems to be divided into two different sites: East and Tulán Zuivá.

57. This state of insanity, similar to the inebriation referred to in other sources when human groups begin their journey toward life in the world, is very clear in both the Recinos (*Popol vuh* 1964: 109) and Tedlock (*Popol vuh* 1996: 150) versions.

58. Recinos (*Popol vuh* 1964: 176, n. 13) interprets her name, Icoquih, as She Who Shoulders the Sun.

59. Later on, the text will say, "Oh no! We have abandoned our language! What have we done? We are lost. Where were we deceived? We only had one language when we arrived there at Tulan" (*Popol vuh* 1964: 113). ("¡Ay! ¡Hemos abandonado nuestra lengua! ¿Qué es lo que hemos hecho? Estamos perdidos. ¿En dónde fuimos engañados? Una sola era nuestra lengua cuando llegamos allá a Tulán.")

60. Here we are following Tedlock's translation (*Popul vuh* 1996: 157).

61. The word used to designate the Mexica is *yaqui*. It derives from Nahuatl: *yaqui* (singular), *yaque* (plural) and means "those who go," "the travelers."

62. This name derives from the Nahuatl "Nacxitl" and corresponds to Quetzalcoatl.

63. Like the *Popol vuh*, the *Memorial de Sololá* was translated by Recinos (1950).

64. This comes from Nahuatl and means "in the calculation of water."

65. One could add to what Seler said, by pointing out that the name 9 Wind appears as the god Quetzalcoatl himself, in the *Codex Telleriano-Remensis* (1995: fol. 8v).

66. Ferndinand Anders, Maarten Jansen, and Aurora Pérez Jiménez (1992: 57–58, 90–93, 243) give the name Koo Sau to Lord 9 Wind.

67. Anders, Jansen, and Pérez Jiménez (1992: 92) identify them as the Grandparents from the "Place of the Sky of the Venerated Ancestors."

68. Concerning this, see Furst (1986). The Mixtec lord appears, for example, in the *Codex Zouche-Nuttall* (1992: lams. 14–17). As for the case of Cholula, the *Historia tolteca-chichimeca* (1976: lam. 26v) seems to depict a similar distribution of insignias of power in front of the principal temple.

69. This vision contradicts Paul Kirchhoff's interpretation (1956) of the conquest of an uncultured people by a refined group.

70. "Muriendo algún cacique en los pueblos de la provincia venían sus hermanos y parientes a hacerlo saber al cazonci, y traíanle su bezote de oro y orejeras y brazaletes y collares de turquesas, que eran las insinias del señor que le había dado el cazonci cuando le criaban señor, y como traían aquellas joyas, llevábanlas e poníanlas con las joyas del cazonci ... Y poníanle delante [al cazonci] cinco o seis parientes suyos, y hermanos del muerto, o de sus hijos o sobrinos ... y [el cazonci] encomendaba aquel oficio al más discreto, el que tiene más tristezas consigo, según su manera de decir, que es el más experimientado, y el que era más obidiente ... Y mandábale dar entonces el cazonci otro bezote nuevo de oro y orejeras y brazaletes, y decíale: 'Toma esto por insinia de honra que traigas contigo.'"

REFERENCES

Acosta, Jorge R.
1956–1957. "Interpretación de algunos de los datos obtenidos en Tula relativos a la época tolteca." *Revista Mexicana de Estudios Antropológicos* 14: 75–160.
1970. "El Altar 2." In I. Marquina, ed., *Proyecto Cholula*. Mexico: INAH, pp. 103–110.

Adams, Richard E. W.
1973. "Maya Collapse: Transformation and Termination in the Ceramic Sequence at Altar de Sacrificios." In T. P. Culbert, ed., *The Classic Maya Collapse*. Albuquerque: University of New Mexico Press, pp. 133–164.

Alva Ixtlilxóchitl, Fernando de
1975. "Sumaria relación de todas las cosas que han sucedido en la Nueva España, y de muchas cosas que los tultecas alcanzaron y supieron desde la creación del mundo, hasta su destrucción y venida de los terceros pobladores chichimecas, hasta la venida de los españoles, sacada de la original historia de esta Nueva España." In Edmundo O'Gorman, ed., *Obras históricas*. 2 vols. Mexico: UNAM-IIH, vol. I, pp. 261–288.

Alvarado Tezozómoc, Fernando
1944. *Crónica mexicana*. Mexico: Editorial Leyenda.
1949. *Crónica mexicáyotl*. Trans. A. León. Mexico: UNAM-IH.

Anales de Cuauhtitlán
1945. "Anales de Cuauhtitlán." In *Códice Chimalpopoca*. Trans. P. F. Velázquez. Mexico: UNAM-IH, pp. 3–118.

Anders, Ferdinand, Maarten Jansen, and Gabina Aurora Pérez Jiménez
1992. *Origen e historia de los reyes mixtecos, libro explicativo del llamado Códice Vindobonensis*. Madrid/Graz/Mexico: SEQC/ADV/FCE.

Andrews, Anthony P.
1978. "Puertos costeros del Postclásico Temprano en el norte de Yucatán." *Estudios de Cultura Maya* 11: 75–93.

Andrews V, E. Wyllys, and Jeremy A. Sabloff
1986. "Classic to Postclassic: A Summary Discussion." In J. A. Sabloff and E. W. Andrews V, eds., *Late Lowland Maya Civilization*. Albuquerque: University of New Mexico Press, pp. 433–456.

Armillas, Pedro
1964. "Condiciones ambientales y movimientos de pueblos en la frontera septetrional de Mesoamérica." In *Homenaje a Fernando Márquez-Miranda, arqueólogo e historiador de América: Ofrenda de sus amigos y admiradores*. Madrid: Talleres Gráficos Ediciones Castilla, pp. 62–132.

Arnauld, Marie-Charlotte, and Dominique Michelet
1991. "Les migrations postclassiques au Michoacán et au Guatemala: Problèmes et perspectives." In A. Breton, J.-P. Berthe, and S. Lecoin, eds., *Vingt études sur le Mexique et le Guatemala réunies à la mémoire de Nicole Percheron*. Toulouse: Presses Universitaires du Mirail, pp. 67–92.

Benavente, Fray Toribio de (Motolinía)
1971. *Memoriales o Libro de las cosas de la Nueva España y de los naturales de ella*. Ed. by E. O'Gorman. Mexico: UNAM-IIH.

Berlo, Janet Catherine
1989a. "Early Writing in Central Mexico: *In Tlilli In Tlapalli* Before A.D. 1000." In R. A. Diehl and J. C. Berlo, eds., *Mesoamerica After the Decline of Teotihuacan, A.D. 700–900*. Washington, DC: Dumbarton Oaks, pp. 19–47.
1989b. "The Concept of the Epiclassic: A Critique." In R. A. Diehl and J. C. Berlo, eds., *Mesoamerica After the Decline of Teotihuacan, A.D. 700–900*. Washington, DC: Dumbarton Oaks, pp. 209–210.

Books of Chilam Balam
1948. *El libro de los libros de Chilam Balam*. Trans. A. Barrera Vásquez and S. Rendón. Mexico: FCE.

Brinton, Daniel G.
1882. *The Maya Chronicles*. Philadelphia: D. G. Brinton Library of Aboriginal American

Literature no. 1.

1890. *Essays of an Americanist*. Philadelphia: Porter and Coates.

Broda, Johanna

1978. "Relaciones políticas ritualizadas: El ritual como expresión de una ideología." In P. Carrasco and J. Broda, eds., *Economía política e ideología en el México prehispánico*. Mexico: INAH-CIS/Editorial Nueva Imagen, pp. 221–255.

Burgoa, Fray Francisco de

1934. *Geográfica descripción*. 2 vols. Mexico: SG-AGN.

Byland, Bruce E., and John M. D. Pohl

1994. *In the Realm of 8 Deer: The Archaeology of the Mixtec Codices*. Norman: University of Oklahoma Press.

Carlson, John B.

1991. *Venus-Regulated Warfare and Ritual Sacrifice in Mesoamerica: Teotihuacan and the Cacaxtla "Star Wars" Connection*. College Park, MD: Center for Archaeoastronomy, Technical Publication no. 7.

Carmack, Robert M.

1981. *The Quiché Mayas of Utatlán: The Evolution of a Highland Guatemala Kingdom*. Norman:University of Oklahoma Press.

Carrasco, Davíd

1992. *Quetzalcoatl and the Irony of Empire: Myths and Prophecies in the Aztec Tradition*. Chicago: University of Chicago Press.

Carrasco, Pedro

1966. "Documentos sobre el rango de tecuhtli entre los nahuas tramontanos." *Tlalocan* 5, no. 2: 133–160.

1996. "La Triple Alianza: Organización política y estructura territorial." In S. Lombardo and E. Nalda, eds., *Temas mesoamericanos*. Mexico: INAH, pp. 169–211.

Caso, Alfonso

1977–1979. *Reyes y reinos de la Mixteca*. 2 vols. Mexico: FCE.

Charnay, Désiré

1885. *Les anciennes villes du Nouveau Monde: Voyages d'explorations au Mexique et dans l'Amérique Centrale, par Désiré Charnay, 1857–1882*. Paris: Hachette.

Chilam Balam of Chumayel

1973. *Libro de Chilam Balam de Chumayel*. Prologue and trans. by A. Mediz Bolio. Mexico: UNAM.

Clarke, David L.

1968. *Analytical Archaeology*. London: Methuen.

Cobean T., Robert H., and A. Guadalupe Mastache F.

1995. "Tula." In L. López Luján, R. H. Cobean T., and A. G. Mastache F. *Xochicalco y Tula*. Milan: Jaca/CNCA, pp. 143–222.

Codex Borgia

1993. Edited by F. Anders, M. Jansen, and L. Reyes García. Madrid/Graz/Mexico: SEQC/ADV/FCE.

Codex Colombino

1966. Mexico: SMA.

Codex Telleriano-Remensis

1995. Eloise Quiñones Keber, *Codex Telleriano-Remensis: Ritual, Divination, and His-*

tory. Austin: University of Texas Press, 1995.

Codex Vaticanus A
1964. "Códice Vaticano A." In Lord Kingsborough. *Antigüedades de México*. Edited by J. Corona Núñez. 4 vols. Mexico: SHCP, vol. III, pp. 7–314.

Codex Vaticanus B
1993. *Códice Vaticano B 3773*. Edited by F. Anders, M. Jansen, and L. Reyes García. Madrid/Graz/Mexico: SEQC/ADV/FCE.

Codex Vindobonensis
1992. *Códice Vindobonensis Mexicanus I*. Facsimile eds.: F. Anders, M. Jansen, and G. A. Pérez Jiménez. Madrid/Graz/Mexico: SEQC/ADV/FCE.

Codex Zouche-Nuttall
1992. Madrid/Graz/Mexico: SEQC/ADV/FCE.

Cohodas, Marvin
1989. "The Epiclassic Problem: A Review and an Alternative Model." In R. A. Diehl and J. C. Berlo, eds., *Mesoamerica After the Decline of Teotihuacan, A.D. 700–900*. Washington, DC: Dumbarton Oaks, pp. 219–240.

Cowgill, George L.
1996. "Discussion." *Ancient Mesoamerica* 7: 325–331.

Dahlgren, Barbro
1990. *La Mixteca, su cultura e historia prehispánicas*. 4th ed. Mexico: UNAM-IIA.

Davies, Nigel
1974. "Tula: Realidad, mito y símbolo." In E. Matos Moctezuma, ed., *Proyecto Tula (Primera parte)*. Mexico: INAH, pp. 109–114.
1977. *The Toltecs, Until the Fall of Tula*. Norman: University of Oklahoma Press.
1980. *The Toltec Heritage, from the Fall of Tula to the Rise of Tenochtitlan*. Norman: University of Oklahoma Press.

Diehl, Richard A.
1989. "A Shadow of Its Former Self: Teotihuacan During the Coyotlatelco Period." In R. A. Diehl and J. C. Berlo, eds., *Mesoamerica After the Decline of Teotihuacan, A.D. 700–900*. Washington, DC: Dumbarton Oaks, pp. 9–18.

Diehl, Richard A., and Janeth Catherine Berlo
1989. "Introduction." In R. A. Diehl and J. C. Berlo, eds., *Mesoamerica After the Decline of Teotihuacan A.D. 700–900*. Washington, DC: Dumbarton Oaks, pp. 1–8.

Fahmel Beyer, Bernd
1988. *Mesoamérica tolteca: Sus cerámicas de comercio principales*. Mexico: UNAM-IIA.

Flannery, Kent V., and Joyce Marcus
1983a. "Oaxaca and the Toltecs: A Postcript." In K. V. Flannery and J. Marcus, eds., *The Cloud People: Divergent Evolution of the Zapotec and Mixtec Civilizations*. New York: Academic Press, pp. 214–215.
1983b. "The Postclassic Balkanization of Oaxaca." In K. V. Flannery and J. Marcus, eds., *The Cloud People: Divergent Evolution of the Zapotec and Mixtec Civilizations*. New York: Academic Press, pp. 217–229.

Florescano, Enrique
1993. *El mito de Quetzalcóatl*. Mexico: FCE.

Foncerrada de Molina, Marta
1993. *Cacaxtla: La iconografía de los olmeca-xicalanca*. Mexico: UNAM-IIE.

Fox, John W.

1987. *Maya Postclassic State Formation: Segmentary Lineage Migration in Advancing Frontiers*. Cambridge: Cambridge University Press.

1989. "On the Rise and Fall of *Tuláns* and Maya Segmentary States." *American Anthropologist* 91: 656–681.

Freidel, David A.

1986. "Terminal Classic Lowland Maya: Successes, Failures, and Aftermaths." In J. A. Sabloff and E. W. Andrews V, eds., *Late Lowland Maya Civilization: Classic to Postclassic*. Albuquerque: University of New Mexico Press, pp. 409–432.

Fuente, Beatriz de la

1990. "Retorno al pasado tolteca." *Artes de México*, nueva época, 7: 36–53.

Fuente, Beatriz de la, Silvia Trejo, and Nelly Gutiérrez Solana

1988. *Escultura en piedra de Tula*. Mexico: UNAM-IIE.

Furst, Jill Leslie

1978. *Codex Vindobonensis Mexicanus I: A Commentary*. Albany: Institute for Mesoamerican Studies, SUNY.

1986. "The Lords of 'Place of the Ascending Serpent': Dynastic Succession on the Nuttall Obverse." In G. H. Gossen, ed., *Symbol and Meaning Beyond the Closed Community: Essays in Mesoamerican Ideas*. Albany: Institute for Mesoamerican Studies, SUNY, pp. 57–68.

García, Gregorio

1981. *Origen de los indios del Nuevo Mundo*. Intro.by F. Pease G. Y. Mexico: FCE.

Gorenstein, Shirley

1985. *Acambaro: Frontier, Settlement on the Tarascan-Aztec Border*. Nashville, TN: Vanderbilt University.

Graham, John A.

1971. "Non-Classic Inscriptions and Sculptures at Seibal." In *Papers on Olmec and Maya Archaeology*. Berkeley: University of California Press, pp. 143–153.

1973. "Aspects of Non-Classic Presences in the Inscriptions and Sculptural Art of Seibal." In T. P. Culbert, ed., *The Classic Maya Collapse*. Albuquerque: University of New Mexico Press, pp. 207–219.

Graulich, Michel

1988. *Quetzalcóatl y el espejismo de Tollan*. Antwerp: Instituut voor Amerikanistiek.

1994. *Montezuma ou l'apogée et la chute de l'empire aztèque*. Paris: Fayard.

Hers, Marie-Areti

1989. *Los toltecas en tierras chichimecas*. Mexico: UNAM-IIE.

Hirth, Kenneth G.

1989. "Militarism and Social Organization at Xochicalco, Morelos." In R. A. Diehl and J. C. Berlo, eds., *Mesoamerica After the Decline of Teotihuacan A.D. 700–900*. Washington, DC: Dumbarton Oaks, pp. 69–81.

Hirth, Kenneth G., and Ann Cyphers Guillén

1988. *Tiempo y asentamiento en Xochicalco*. Mexico: UNAM.

Historia de los mexicanos por sus pinturas

1965. "Historia de los mexicanos por sus pinturas." In Ángel María Garibay K., ed., *Teogonía e historia de los mexicanos: Tres opúsculos del siglo XVI*. Mexico: Editorial Porrúa, pp. 21–90.

Histoyre du Mechique

1965. "Historia de México." In Ángel María Garibay K., ed., *Teogonía e historia de los mexicanos:*

Tres opúsculos del siglo XVI. Mexico: Editorial Porrúa, pp. 91–120.

Historia tolteca-chichimeca
1976. Edited by Paul Kirchhoff, Linda Odena Güemes, and Luis Reyes García. Mexico: INAH-CIS.

Jansen, Maarten
1996. "Lord 8 Deer and Nacxitl Topiltzin." *Mexicon* (Berlin) 18, no. 2: 25–29.

Jiménez Moreno, Wigberto
1959. "Síntesis de la historia pretolteca de Mesoamérica." In *Esplendor del México antiguo.* Mexico: Centro de Investigaciones Antropológicas de México, vol. II, pp. 1019–1108.

Jones, Lindsay
1993a. "The Hermeneutics of Sacred Architecture: A Reassessment of the Similitude Between Tula, Hidalgo and Chichén Itzá, Yucatan, Part I." *History of Religions* 32: 207–232.
1993b. "The Hermeneutics of Sacred Architecture: A Reassessment of the Similitude Between Tula, Hidalgo and Chichén Itzá, Yucatan. Part II." *History of Religions* 32: 315–342.
1995. *Twin City Tales: A Hermeneutical Reassessment of Tula and Chichén Itzá.* Niwot: University Press of Colorado.

Justeson, John S., William M. Norman, Lyle Campbell, and Terrence Kaufman
1985. *The Foreign Impact on Lowland Mayan Language and Script.* New Orleans: Tulane University, Middle American Research Institute Publication no. 53.

Kepecs, Susan, Gary Feinman, and Sylviane Boucher
1994. "Chichen Itza and Its Hinterland: A World-Systems Perspective." *Ancient Mesoamerica* 5: 141–158.

Kirchhoff, Paul
1956. "La *Relación de Michoacán* como fuente para la historia de la sociedad y cultura tarascas." In *Relación de las ceremonias y ritos y población y gobierno de los indios de la Provincia de Michoacán.* Madrid: Aguilar, pp. xxiv–xxxii.

Kowalski, Jeff Karl
1989. "Who Am I Among the Itza?: Links Between Northern Yucatan and the Western Maya Lowlands and Highlands." In R. A. Diehl and J. C. Berlo, eds., *Mesoamerica After the Decline of Teotihuacan A.D. 700–900.* Washington, DC: Dumbarton Oaks, pp. 173–185.

Kubler, George
1961. "Chichén Itzá y Tula." *Estudios de Cultura Maya* 1: 47–79.

Lameiras, Brigitte Boehm de
1986. *Formación del estado en el México prehispánico.* Zamora, Mexico: El Colegio de Michoacán.

Landa, Fray Diego de
1982. *Relación de las cosas de Yucatan.* Mexico: Editorial Porrúa.

Leyenda de los Soles
1945. "Leyenda de los Soles." In *Códice Chimalpopoca.* Trans. P. F. Velázquez. Mexico: UNAM-IH, pp. 119–164

Lienzo de Jucutácato
n.d. Ms. in the Sociedad Mexicana de Geografía y Estadística, Mexico, D.F.

Lincoln, Charles E.
1986. "The Chronology of Chichen Itza: A Review of the Literature." In J. A. Sabloff and

E. W. Andrews V, eds., *Late Lowland Maya Civilization, Classic to Postclassic*. Albuquerque: University of New Mexico Press, pp. 141–196.

Linné, Sigvald
1934. *Archaeological Research at Teotihuacán, Mexico*. The Ethnological Museum of Sweden New Series Publication 1. Stockholm: Victor Pettersons Bokindustriaktiebolag.

López Austin, Alfredo
1973. *Hombre-dios: Religión y política en el mundo náhuatl*. Mexico: UNAM-IIH.
1985. "Organización política en el Altiplano Central de México durante el Posclásico." In J. Monjarás-Ruiz, R. Brambila, and E. Pérez-Rocha, eds., *Mesoamérica y el Centro de México: Una antología*. Mexico: INAH, pp. 197–234.
1987. "The Masked God of Fire." In E. H. Boone, ed., *The Aztec Templo Mayor*. Washington, DC: Dumbarton Oaks, pp. 257–291.
1989. "La historia de Teotihuacan." In A. López Austin, J. R. Romero, and C. Martínez Marín. *Teotihuacan*. Mexico: Citicorp/Citibank, pp. 13–35.
1990. *Los mitos del tlacuache: Caminos de la mitología mesoamericana*. Mexico: Alianza Editorial Mexicana.
1992. "La religión y la larga duración: Consideraciones para la interpretación del sistema mítico-religioso mesoamericano." *Journal of Latin American Lore* 18: 53–62.
1994. *Tamoanchan y Tlalocan*. Mexico: FCE.
1995. "Tollan: Babel." *Universidad de México*, nos. 528–529 (January-February): 3–8.

López Austin, Alfredo, and Leonardo López Luján
1996. *El pasado indígena*. Mexico: FCE/El Colegio de México.

López Austin, Alfredo, Leonardo López Luján, and Saburo Sugiyama
1991. "The Temple of Quetzalcoatl at Teotihuacan: Its Possible Ideological Significance." *Ancient Mesoamerica* 2: 93–105.

López Luján, Leonardo
1989. *La recuperación mexica del pasado teotihuacano*. Mexico: INAH/GV Editores.
1993. *Las ofrendas del Templo Mayor de Tenochtitlan*. Mexico: INAH.

Maldonado Cárdenas, Rubén, and Edward B. Kurjack
1993. "Reflexiones sobre las relaciones entre Chichén Itzá, sus vecinos peninsulares y Tula." *Arqueología*, nos. 9–10 (January-December): 97–103.

Marcus, Joyce
1992a. "Political Fluctuations in Mesoamerica." *National Geographic Research and Exploration* 8, no. 4: 392–411.
1992b. *Mesoamerican Writing Systems: Propaganda, Myth, and History in Four Ancient Civilizations*. Princeton, NJ: Princeton University Press.

Marquina, Ignacio, ed.
1970. *Proyecto Cholula*. Mexico: INAH.

Martínez Marín, Carlos
1963. "La cultura de los mexicas durante la migración: Nuevas ideas." *Cuadernos Americanos* 4: 175–183.

Mastache F., Alba Guadalupe, and Robert H. Cobean
1985. "Tula." In J. Monjarás-Ruiz, R. Brambila, and E. Pérez-Rocha, eds., *Mesoamérica y el centro de México: Una antología*. Mexico: INAH, pp. 273–307.

Memorial de Sololá
1950. *Memorial de Sololá: Anales de los cakchiqueles*. Trans. and notes by A. Recinos. Mexico: FCE.

Mendieta, Fray Gerónimo de
1945. *Historia eclesiástica indiana.* 4 vols. Mexico: Salvador Chávez Hayhoe.

Mendoza, Ruben G.
1992. "Conquest Polities of the Mesoamerican Epiclassic: Circum-Basin Regionalism, A.D. 550–850." Ph.D. dissertation, Athropology Dept., University of Arizona, Tucson.

Michelet, Dominique
1989. "Histoire, mythe et apologue: Notes de lecture sur la Seconde Partie de la *Relación [. . .] de Michoacán.*" In D. Michelet, ed., *Enquêtes sur l'Amérique moyenne, mélanges offerts à Guy Stresser-Péan.* Mexico: CEMCA/INAH/CNCA, pp. 105–113.
1995. "La zona occidental en el Posclásico." In L. Manzanilla and L. López Luján, eds., *Historia antigua de México.* Mexico: INAH/UNAM/Miguel Ángel Porrúa, vol. III, pp. 153–188.

Miller, Arthur G.
1977. "Captains of the Itzá: Unpublished Mural Evidence from Chichén Itzá." In N. Hammond, ed., *Social Process in Maya Prehistory, Studies in Honour of Sir Eric Thompson.* London: Academic Press, pp. 197–225.

Miller, Virginia E.
1989. "Star Warriors at Chichen Itza." In W. F. Hanks and D. S. Rice, eds., *Word and Image in Maya Culture: Exploration in Language, Writing, and Representation.* Salt Lake City: University of Utah Press, pp. 287–305.

Millon, René
1981. "Teotihuacan: City, State, and Civilization." In J. A. Sabloff, ed., *Archaeology: Supplement to the Handbook of Middle American Indians.* Austin: University of Texas Press, vol. 1, pp. 198–243.

Morley, Sylvanus G.
1947. *The Ancient Maya.* Stanford: Stanford University Press.

Morris, Earl H., Jean Charlot, and Ann Axtell Morris
1931. *The Temple of the Warriors at Chichen-Itza, Yucatan.* 2 vols. Washington, DC: Carnegie Institution Publication no. 406.

Muñoz Camargo, Diego
1981. *Descripción de la ciudad y provincia de Tlaxcala de las Indias y del Mar Océano para el buen gobierno y ennoblecimiento dellas.* Facsimile edition of the Glasgow Manuscript. Mexico: UNAM-IIF.

Nagao, Debra
1989. "Public Proclamation in the Art of Cacaxtla and Xochicalco." In R. A. Diehl and J. C. Berlo, eds., *Mesoamerica After the Decline of Teotihuacan A.D. 700–900.* Washington, DC: Dumbarton Oaks, pp. 83–104.

Navarrete, Carlos
1976. "Algunas influencias mexicanas en el área maya meridional durante el Postclásico tardío." *Estudios de Cultura Náhuatl* 12: 345–382.
1996. "Elementos arqueológicos de mexicanización en las tierras altas mayas." In S. Lombardo and E. Nalda, eds., *Temas mesoamericanos.* Mexico: INAH, pp. 309–356.

Navarrete, Carlos, and Ana María Crespo
1971. "Un atlante mexica y algunas consideraciones sobre los relieves del Cerro de la Malinche, Hidalgo." *Estudios de Cultura Náhuatl* 9: 11–15.

Nicholson, Henry B.
1957. "Topiltzin Quetzalcoatl of Tollan: A Problem in Mesoamerican History." Ph.D.

dissertation, Anthropology Dept., Harvard University, Cambridge, MA.
1969. "Pre-Hispanic Central Mexican Historiography." In *Memorias de la Tercera Reunión de Historiadores Mexicanos y Norteamericanos, Oaxtepec, Morelos*. Mexico: UNAM/ El Colegio de México/University of Texas at Austin, pp. 38–81.
1978. "The Deity 9 Wind 'Ehecatl-Quetzalcoatl' in the Mixteca Pictorials." *Journal of Latin American Lore* 4, no. 1: 61–93.

Olivier, Guilhem
1995. "Les paquets sacrés ou la mémoire cachée des indiens du Mexique Central (XVe– XVIe siècles)." *Journal de la Société des Américanistes* 81: 105–141.

Pasztory, Esther
1988. "A Reinterpretation of Teotihuacan and Its Mural Painting Tradition." In K. Berrin, ed., *Feathered Serpents and Flowering Trees: Reconstructing the Murals of Teotihuacan*. San Francisco: The Fine Arts Museums of San Francisco, pp. 45–77.

Piña Chan, Román
1980. *Chichén Itzá, la ciudad de los brujos del agua*. Mexico: FCE.

Pollard, Helen Perlstein
1994. "Factores de desarrollo en la formación del estado tarasco." In B. B. de Lameiras, ed., *El Michoacán antiguo: Estado y sociedad tarascos en el época prehispánica*. Zamora, Mexico: El Colegio de Michoacán/Gobierno del Estado de Michoacán, pp. 187–246.

Popol vuh
1964. *Popol vuh: Las antiguas historias del Quiché*. Trans. A. Recinos. Mexico: FCE.
1996. *Popol Vuh: The Mayan Book of the Dawn of Life*. Ed. and trans. D. Tedlock. New York: Simon and Schuster.

Proskouriakoff, Tatiana
1950. *A Study of Classic Maya Sculpture*. Washington, DC: Carnegie Institution Publication no. 593.

Relación de Michoacán
1977. *Relación de las ceremonias y ritos y población y gobierno de los indios de la provincia de Michoacán* [1541]. Facsimile edition. Transcription by J. Tudela, intro. by J. Corona Núñez. Morelia, Mexico: Balsal Editores.

Reyes, Antonio de los
1976. *Arte en lengua mixteca* [1593]. Facsimile edition. Nashville, TN: Vanderbilt University.

Rojas, Gabriel de
1985. "Relación de Cholula." In R. Acuña, ed., *Relaciones geográficas del siglo XVI: Tlaxcala*. Mexico: UNAM-IIA, vol. 2, pp. 120–145.

Ruppert, Karl
1943. *The Mercado, Chichen Itza, Yucatan*. Contributions to American Anthropology and History no. 43. Washington, DC: Carnegie Institution Publication no. 546.

Ruz Lhuillier, Alberto
1971. "Influencias mexicanas sobre los mayas." In E. Z. Vogt and A. Ruz, eds., *Desarrollo cultural de los mayas*. Mexico: UNAM-CH-CEM, pp. 203–241.

Sabloff, Jeremy A.
1973. "Continuity and Disruption During Terminal Late Classic Times at Seibal: Ceramic and Other Evidence." In T. P. Culbert, ed., *The Classic Maya Collapse*. Albuquerque: University of New Mexico Press, pp. 107–132.

Sahagún, Fray Bernardino de
1979. *Códice Florentino. Manuscrito 218-20 de la Colección Palatina de la Biblioteca Medicea Laurenziana.* Facsimile edition. 3 vols. Mexico: SG-AGN.
1989. *Historia general de las cosas de Nueva España.* Edited by A. López Austin and J. García Quintana. 2 vols. Mexico: CNCA/Alianza Editorial Mexicana.

Sanders, William T.
1989. "The Epiclassic as a Stage in Mesoamerican Prehistory: An Evaluation." In R. A. Diehl and J. C. Berlo, eds., *Mesoamerica After the Decline of Teotihuacan A.D. 700–900.* Washington, DC: Dumbarton Oaks, pp. 211–218.

Schele, Linda, and David Freidel
1990. *A Forest of Kings: The Untold Story of the Ancient Maya.* New York: William Morrow.

Selden Roll
1964–1967. "Códice Selden I." In Lord Kingsborough. *Antigüedades de México.* Edited by J. Corona Núñez. 4 vols. Mexico: SHCP, vol. I, pp. 151–338.

Seler, Eduard
1904. "Wall Paintings of Mitla: A Mexican Picture Writing in Fresco." In E. Seler et al. *Mexican and Central American Antiquities, Calendar Systems, and History.* Bulletin of the Bureau of American Ethnology no. 28. Washington, DC: Smitshsonian Institution, pp. 243–324.

Smith, Ledyard
1955. *Archaeological Reconnaissance in Central Guatemala.* Washington, DC: Carnegie Institution Publication no. 608.

Solís Olguín, Felipe
1990. "Reminiscencia y evocación de la ciudad de Quetzalcóatl entre los mexicas." In F. Sodi Miranda, ed., *Mesoamérica y norte de México: siglo IX–XII.* 2 vols. Mexico: INAH, vol. II, pp. 607–612.

Spores, Ronald
1984. *The Mixtecs in Ancient and Colonial Times.* Norman: University of Oklahoma Press.

Šprajc, Ivan
1996. *La estrella de Quetzalcóatl: El planeta Venus en Mesomérica.* Mexico: Editorial Diana.

Stenzel, Werner
1970. "The Sacred Bundles in Mesoamerican Religion." In *Verhandlungen des XXXVIII Internationalen Amerikanistenkongresses. Stuttgart-München, 12. bis 18. August 1968.* Munich: Kommissionsverlag K. Renner, vol. II, pp. 347–352.

Sugiyama, Saburo
1992. "Rulership, Warfare, and Human Sacrifice at the Ciudadela: An Iconography Study of Feathered Serpent Representations." In J. C. Berlo, ed., *Art, Ideology, and the City of Teotihuacan.* Washington, DC: Dumbarton Oaks, pp. 205–230.

Taube, Karl A.
1994. "The Iconography of Toltec Period Chichen Itza." In H. J. Prem, ed., *Hidden Among the Hills: Maya Archaeology of the Northwest Yucatan Peninsula: First Maler Symposium.* Möckmühl: Verlag von Flemming, pp. 213–246.

Tedlock, Dennis
1996. "Introduction." In *Popol Vuh: The Mayan Book of the Dawn of Life.* Ed. and trans. Dennis Tedlock. New York: Simon and Schuster, pp. 21–60.

Thompson, J. Eric S.
1964. *Grandeza y decadencia de los mayas*. Mexico: FCE.
1975. *Historia y religión de los mayas*. Mexico: Siglo Veintiuno Editores.

Título de Totonicapán
1983. *El Título de Totonicapán*. Trans. R. M. Carmack and J. L. Mondloch. Mexico: UNAM-IIF-CEM.

Torquemada, Fray Juan de
1975–1983. *Monarquía indiana*. Edited by M. León-Portilla. 7 vols. Mexico: UNAM-IIH.

Tozzer, Alfred M.
1957. *Chichen Itza and Its Sacred Well of Sacrifice: A Comparative Study of Contemporaneous Maya and Toltec*. 2 vols. Memoirs of the Peabody Museum of Archaeology and Ethnology, Harvard University, vols. 11–12. Cambridge, MA.

Umberger, Emily
1987. "Antiques, Revivals, and References to the Past in Aztec Art." *Res: Anthropology and Aesthetics* 13: 63–106.

Umberger, Emily, and Cecelia F. Klein
1993. "Aztec Art and Imperial Expansion." In D. S. Rice, ed., *Latin American Horizons*. Washington, DC: Dumbarton Oaks, pp. 295–336.

Webb, Malcolm
1978. "The Significance of the 'Epiclassic' Period in Mesoamerica Prehistory." In D. Browman, ed., *Cultural Continuity in Mesoamerica*. The Hague: Mouton, pp. 155–178.

Willey, Gordon R.
1977. "External Influences on the Lowland Maya: 1940 and 1975 Perspectives." In N. Hammond, ed., *Social Process in Maya Prehistory: Studies in Honour of Sir Eric Thompson*. London: Academic Press, pp. 57–75.

Williams, Eduardo
1992. *Las piedras sagrada: Escultura prehispánica del Occidente de México*. Zamora, Mexico: El Colegio de Michoacán.

Wren, Linnea H., and Peter Schimdt
1991. "Elite Interaction During the Terminal Classic Period: New Evidence from Chichen Itza." In T. P. Culbert, ed., *Classic Maya Political History: Hieroglyphic and Archaeological Evidence*. Cambridge: Cambridge University Press, pp. 199–225.

Zapata y Mendoza, Juan Benaventura
1995. *Historia cronológica de la noble ciudad de Tlaxcala*. Trans. L. Reyes García and A. Martínez Baracs. Tlaxcala, Mexico: Universidad Autónoma de Tlaxcala/CIESAS.

PART TWO

▼

CLASSIC TEOTIHUACAN IN
THE CONTEXT OF MESOAMERICAN
TIME AND HISTORY

2

THE CONSTRUCTION OF THE
UNDERWORLD IN CENTRAL MEXICO

TRANSFORMATIONS FROM THE CLASSIC TO THE POSTCLASSIC

LINDA MANZANILLA

The Mesoamerican tradition, a long-duration process of basic core ideas and peripheral formal changing aspects, was marked by a dicotomy: fertility and warfare. In this chapter, I will review some of the uses through time of underground spaces in Central Mexico, with particular emphasis in the inclusion of the following set: water spring or water deposit–amphibian beings–fertility inside mountains or pyramids.

I thank the following people for their participation in particular studies of my project, "The Study of Tunnels at Teotihuacan": Luis Barba and Agustín Ortiz for the geophysical and geochemical prospection, as well as for the chemical studies; Raúl Valadez for the paleofaunal analysis; Emily McClung, Rebeca Rodríguez, and Cristina Adriano for the paleobotanical data; Emilio Ibarra and Ruth Castañeda, for the pollen information; Judith Zurita and Gabriela Silva for the phytolith analysis; Cynthia Hernández and Rosanna Enríquez for the lithic analyses; Miguel Angel Jiménez and Claudia López for the ceramic distributional maps; Edith Ortiz, Rocío Arrellín, and Claudia López for the assistance in the exploration of the caves; and the Graphics Department of the Institute of Anthropological Research of the National Autonomous University of Mexico for their invaluable help. This interdisciplinary research was funded by the Institute of Anthropological Research of the National Autonomous University and by Grant no. H9106–0060 of the National Council of Science and Technology of Mexico (CONACYT), and with permission of the Archaeological Council of the National Institute of Anthropology and History (INAH). The geophysical work was also partially supported by an internal grant, IGF–02–9102. I would also like to thank doctors Zoltán de Cserna and Gerardo Sánchez Rubio of the Institute of Geology; José Lugo Hubp of the Institute of Geography; and Jaime Urrutia and Dante Morán of the Institute of Geophysics, National Autonomous University of Mexico, for their advice and suggestions at different stages of the geological research at Teotihuacan. We also thank the students of the Engineering Faculty of the university and of the National School of Anthropology and History for their participation.

CAVES, WATER FLOWS AND DEPOSITS, AMPHIBIAN BEINGS, AND
SACRED MOUNTAINS IN FORMATIVE TIMES

THE OLMEC WORLD

Three different elements that bear relevance to what will develop in Late
Formative and Classic times in Central Mexico will be traced since Middle Formative times in the Olmec world: one is related to caves and jaguars; the second
seems to be related to toads/frogs and water deposits/springs; the third is the
sacred mountain and the world tree. They will coalesce in different cults in later
times, and thus we shall speak not only of caves, but also of springs, frogs/toads,
and sacred mountains.

Caves. Contact with the deities, particularly important in the ruler's accession to the throne, occurred through cracks in mountains, the residences of the
gods (Bernal-García 1994: 114–115). Mountain peaks and caves are named the
same (*tzatAk*) in Copainalá Zoque (Harrison et al. 1981, in Bernal-García 1994:
116), and thus are seen as entrances to the underworld.

Numerous representations of caves are found in the Olmec art of La Venta
(Altars 4 and 5), San Lorenzo Tenochtitlan, Laguna de los Cerros, and Chalcatzingo
(Figures 2.1 and 2.2). Altars 4 and 5 at La Venta depict seated figures, probably
rulers, emerging from a cave, and particularly in Altar 4, the access to the underworld is a jaguar's mouth (Magni 1995a: 94). The relationship of the jaguar's face
and mouth with the subterranean world and the earth is also evident in the massive sealed serpentine offerings of La Venta (Ortiz and Rodríguez 1994:70).

At Chalcatzingo, Relief 1, the famous relief named The King depicts a male
figure in a throne inside a cave as the representation of the earth's monster (Fig.
2.2). A series of plants emerge from the four corners. Spirals that may represent

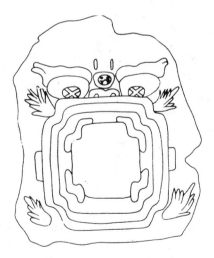

Fig. 2.1. Relief n. IX at Chalcatzingo (redrawn from de la Fuente 1996, vol. II: 25).

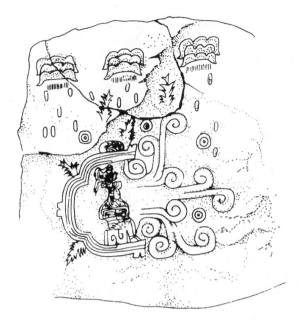

Fig. 2.2. Relieve n. I at Chalcatzingo (redrawn from de la Fuente 1996, vol. II: 25).

water or wind rise from the cave. In the upper part, three clouds full with water release rain. Thus, this representation relates the gates to the underworld with fertility cults (Ortiz and Rodríguez 1994: 75), with the main figure as the provider of rain (Taube 1995: 99), probably Tepeyollotl as the jaguar god that inhabits caves with water flows, the heart of the mountain (Angulo Villaseñor 1987b: 217). Thus, the three vertical levels of the Mesoamerican cosmos are represented in this relief (Magni 1995a: 9). Monument 9 at Chalcatzingo is related to the former, in that it represent the jaguar's mouth as a quadripartite cave entrance (see Figure 2.1).

On another line of evidence, Reilly (1994) has proposed an interesting interpretation of Complex A at La Venta, in which Tomb A, the sandstone sarcophagus (Monument 6), the sunken courtyard, and Massive offerings numbers 1 through 3, are seen as the materialization of the conception of the watery underworld, the primordial ocean, through the burial of jade celts and objects (particularly a jade frog and a jade clamshell) representing water, and fertility symbols, blue clays, organic materials, stingray spines, and shark's teeth. The entrance of Tomb A would symbolize the maw of the earth monster (Reilly 1994: 129).

Numerous caves in Guerrero offer polychrome mural paintings (Villela F. 1989). At the deepest sector of the Juxtlahuaca cave, a lordly figure stands near a smaller seating figure, probably evoking vassalage (Niederberger 1996: 96). It may suggest the connection of Olmec ancestry with caves (Grove 1970: 31).

At Oxtotitlán, one of the representations refers to a male figure dressed in a bird attire over the entrance of the cave, depicted as a feline's open mouth (Grove 1970: 8–9, frontispiece; Lombardo 1996: 6–11; Magni 1995a), a representation that

Grove (31) relates to rain, water, and fertility. The Oxtotitlán Cave would be thus seen as a shrine to water and fertility, and the nearby Quiatepec Mountain (the so-called hill of rain) would be related. Grove (14) has also suggested a relationship of the owl motif to rain, as in the Teotihuacan and Maya cultures.

Magni (1995a: 102–103, 1995b) has stated that the knuckle-duster and torch depictions in Olmec petaloid celts are related to ritual sequences inside caves, where men dressed in jaguar disguise crawl through narrow passages, imitating the jaguar's movements.

Water flows and amphibian beings. Taube has stated that the Olmecs developed "an elaborate ideology devoted to water and rain and, in addition, religious rituals of sacrifice and supplication designed to ensure agricultural abundance"(1995: 83). Thus they were the first "rainmakers," a tradition that we shall follow till the present day. Through the iconography of avian serpents, the Olmecs represented the fertilizing elements of wind, lightning, and rain, in a deity that preluded Itzamná or Ometeotl, according to Joralemon (83). Particularly in La Venta's Monument 19, the avian serpent, as a sky symbol, arches a seated male figure (87).

The Olmec Rain God is depicted with jaguarlike furrowed brows, and upper lips pulled up to the level of the nostrils (97–98). Protoclassic rain gods in the act of rainmaking may be recognized in Stela I at Izapa, as a prototype for the Maya god Chac (95).

Rain ceremonies may have involved ritual bathing, and ritual management of water and rain. Gómez Rueda (1997) cites numerous stone elements used for managing water among the Olmec: water deposits, subterranean ducts, open canals, aqueducts, control holes, fountains and troughs, gargoyles, dams, etc. At San Lorenzo Tenochtitlan, a long stone aqueduct has been excavated, moving water from a pond, and the presence of rubber balls is probably related to a cult devoted to water deities (Krotser 1973). Also at San Lorenzo, sinuous canals may be related to serpentine watery beings (Cyphers 1996: 65, fig. 3); Monument 9 is a fountain in the form of a duck. At Izapa, Chiapas, more than half of these stone monuments are related to water springs (Gómez Rueda 1997).

Particularly, El Manatí in Veracruz and Chalcatzingo in Morelos display elaborate Olmec offerings near or in springs or runoff channels at the base of the sacred mountains (Taube 1995: 99). At El Manatí, Veracruz, the mountain emerges as an island in a plain with lagoons and swamps; to the west of the mountain, springs emerge from the mountain in a bed of sandstone blocks. In the earliest phase, inside the bed of blocks, pottery vessels, stone bowls, mortars, jade axes and jade beads, and rubber balls were found. In a second phase, the Olmecs continued to place rubber balls and jade celts in clusters. By 1200 B.C.E. we see the burial of human wooden busts enveloped in mats like funerary bundles together with jade celts, hematite fragments, child bones, obsidian blades, white bowls, a staff with a shark's tooth, and another hexagonal staff with red and white paint (Ortiz and Rodríguez 1994). The relationship of child sacrifice, rubber balls, and springs evokes rain and fertility cults.

Chalcatzingo, Morelos, also has numerous elements involving water control (Angulo Villaseñor 1988): water springs with retention walls and diversion streams, water deposits in Cerro Delgado caves, enclosed water storing places, dikes and diversion structures, dams, cisterns, etc. In Cave number 4, explored by Burton, sculpted canals in the rock were found, as well as a plastered and red-painted water deposit (Angulo Villaseñor 1988: 56).

At Teopantecuanitlan, Guerrero, Martínez Donjuán (1985, 1994) has excavated a Middle Formative ceremonial site with various elements of water control: a spring area with a dam near it, a megalithic aqueduct, and a batrachian altar. This set of traits is also related to the cruciform sunken courtyard flanked by four feline sculptures that probably represents the entrance to the watery underworld, because of its form and the insertion of clays and sands of different colors.

Frogs are also represented as altars (Altars 2, 53, and 54) (Norman 1976: 242, 247, 248) at Izapa, Chiapas, related to water control devices and the spring cult.

Sacred mountains and cosmic trees. Bernal-García (1994:122) and Schele (1995: 107–108) have related the Olmec ruler to maize as the central tree, and the power of the mountain. When the ruler spoke, he did so with the voice of the baby-jaguar, the Olmec ancestor who inhabits the cave inside a mountain. Due to the fact that for the accession to power the ruler needed a mountain, and that the Gulf Coast plain does not have many, the Olmecs then built sacred mountains in their sites (La Venta) or shaped large plateaus (San Lorenzo), except where mountains were prominent, as in San Martín Pajapan, Veracruz (Joralemon 1996: 53), or Chalcatzingo, Morelos (Angulo V. 1987a: 157). The sacred mountain would be conceived of as the place where the celestial gods, the terrestrial fertility and sustenance deities, and the underworld beings met (Angulo Villaseñor 1987a: 157).

Fig. 2.3. Ritual tanks at Cuetlajuchitlán, Guerrero.

Fig. 2.4. Ritual water tanks in front of the Flower Pyramid at Xochitécatl, Tlaxcala.

The axis mundi of the Olmec cosmic model of three levels would be the world tree, the sacred mountain, or the ruler himself (Reilly 1994: 130). Horizontal space would be divided in quadrants, with a fifth point in the center, where the cosmic tree would pierce the center of the earth (Joralemon 1996: 53).

LATE FORMATIVE CENTRAL MEXICAN SITES

Cuetlajuchitlán, Guerrero, is a Late Formative planned site that continues the tradition of ritual water tanks (Figure 2.3), in groups of two, within the ceremonial precinct, related to a sweat-bath or *temazcal* and to rocks with depressions to concentrate pluvial water (Manzanilla López and Talavera González 1993; Talavera González and Rojas Chávez 1994; Manzanilla López 1996). The monolithic tanks have a seat in their western sides, and the water was channeled through a sophisticated hydraulic system (Manzanilla López 1996: photos 12, 13, 14, 15).

Similar monolithic tanks, also in groups of two, are found at Xochitécatl, Tlaxcala, in front of the Flower Pyramid (Figure 2.4); in one of them a batrachian sculpture was found (Figure 2.5), together with two anthropomorphic sculptures and a serpentine figure with an open mouth from which a human figure is emerging. Child burials of later times, associated with numerous shell beads and one greenstone bead, as well as bird bones, were found on the stairway (Serra Puche and Beutelspacher 1994: 9, 27–29, 31). This pyramid was devoted to fertility and rain cults, and probably involved the tunnels and chambers in the mound, which are cited in the historical sources of the sixteenth century.

At Totimehuacan, Puebla, Spranz (1966, 1967, 1968) excavated a 2 x 3 meter basaltic water tank, but now, for the first time, incorporated inside a pyramidal

Fig. 2.5. Frog deity found inside one of the water tanks in front of the Flower Pyramid at Xochitécatl, Tlaxcala.

construction (Tepalcayo 1) with a tunneled access (Figures 2.6 and 2.7), and with four frog representations around the basin (Figure 2.8) (Spranz 1967: 20) dated around the beginnings of the era (Spranz 1973: 63). The batrachian-water deposit complex is thus included inside the artificial sacred mountain (Spranz 1967: 21, 1968:20).

At Cholula, Puebla, the earliest structure under the great pyramid (Tlachihualtépetl) belonged to the Late Formative, and was situated on the shore of a lake fed by springs (Noguera in Dumond and Müller 1972: 1208; McCafferty 1996b: 303), although there are Middle Formative materials at the site (McCafferty 1996a: 2; 1996b: 302–303). The pyramid itself is built on top of a spring, and there is an interior chamber discovered deep inside the building (McCafferty 1996a: 3), perhaps copying Totimehuacan. The orientation of the Great Pyramid toward the setting sun on the summer solstice, and Durán's description of mountain worship to Tonacatecuhtli on top of it (McCafferty 1996a: 13–14), parallel the Pyramid of the Sun at Teotihuacan, as we shall see further on. The Tlachihualtépetl Great Pyramid of Cholula was represented in the *Historia tolteca-chichimeca* with a froglike rain deity on top of it, and a water spring at its base (see McCafferty 1996a: 3 and 4) (Figure 2.9).

Further evidence of a rain cult related to Tlaloc is also seen in the Calucan Cave in the Iztaccíhuatl volcano, with Late Formative to Aztec II ceramics; Tláloc vases were found, as well as a small water spring (Navarrete 1957: 18). On the eastern slope of the nearby Popocatépetl volcano, there are also evidences of Late Formative volcano cults, as well as some hints of a Tlaloc cult in a dispersed

village covered by a pumice eruption from the beginnings of the era. In court-
yards surrounded by three houses with *talud-tablero* architecture that preludes
Teotihuacan, small altars depicting the two volcanos are re-created, as well as the
blowing faces of its deities (Plunket and Uruñuela 1998). It is possible that due to
the large-scale volcanic eruptions around the beginning of the era, these groups
moved to the Teotihuacan Valley, where they re-created the three-mound com-

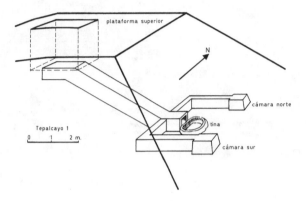

Fig. 2.6. Water basin inside a Formative pyramid at Totimehuacan, Puebla (redrawn from
Spranz 1967: 21).

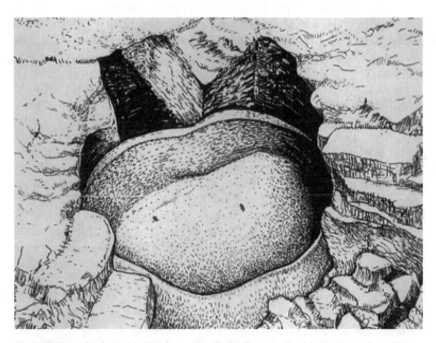

Fig. 2.7. Water basin inside Tepalcayo 2 at Totimehuacan, Puebla (redrawn from Spranz
1967: 20, Photo 15).

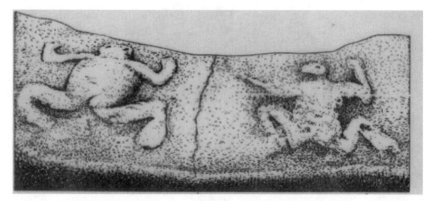

Fig. 2.8. Frog reliefs bordering the water tank at Totimehuacan, Puebla (redrawn from Spranz 1967: 20, Photo 16).

pounds in a monumental scale, and converted the volcano cult into a fertility/ sacred-mountain religion, centered in the Pyramid of the Sun, as we shall propose further on.

In volcanic environments, where natural holes (lava tubes) are rare, pre-Hispanic groups of Late Formative and Early Classic times created artificial "caves" inside man-made sacred mountains, and incorporated springs and water deposits, as well as frogs, in their wombs. In karstic environments in eastern Puebla, however, Medina Jaen (1996) has detected subterranean water flows in travertinic geology and consequent caves at different levels; some (such as the ones in the Barranca del Águila) were occupied during the Formative horizon, and were facing large Formative sites such as Xochiltenango.

In the Ticumán sector of Morelos, in a limestone environment, two caves belonging to the Late Formative period have been recently excavated (Alvarado et al. 1994; Cruz Flores and Noval Vilar 1994). In the El Gallo Cave, an outstanding abundance of preserved organic materials as offerings, including maize, squash, beans, chile, plums, *chayote*, avocado, other seeds, fibers, textiles, and a polychrome gourd, accompanied an infant's funerary bundle with a dog (Morett Alatorre and Rodríguez Campero 1996: 36; Cruz Flores and Noval Vilar 1994). Less than a kilometer farther, the Chagüera Cave also had abundant organic materials, including seeds, grasses, fibers, textiles, wood, coprolites, sandals, and corncobs, together with numerous Formative vessels and groups of human remains in mats. Some of these funerary bundles lay on top of palm mats and beds of corncobs. A total of seventeen individuals of different ages have been detected (Alvarado et al. 1994). (The relationship of child burials with dogs will be an element that we will review further on.)

THE CLASSIC HORIZON IN THE TEOTIHUACAN VALLEY

In Teotihuacan, underground cavities were places where fertility could be propitiated. Particularly in the so-called Tlalocan of Tepantitla we can observe an idol on top of a *talud-tablero* structure that is placed on top of a cave with seeds. Frogs and

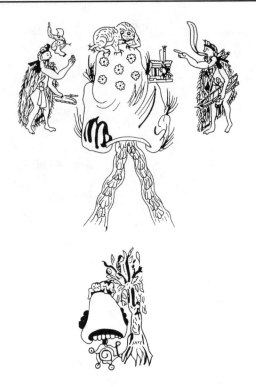

Fig. 2.9. Depictions of the Great Pyramid of Cholula (Tlachihualtépetl) from the *Historia tolteca-chichimeca* (redrawn from McCafferty 1996).

springs are also depicted in close association (see de la Fuente 1996, II: 233) (Figure 2.10).

The existence of underground holes in Teotihuacan is a well-known fact. Toponyms such as Oztoyahualco and Oztotícpac make reference to subterranean cavities.

Former archaeological research in Teotihuacan tunnels includes Linné's (1934) excavations at San Francisco Mazapa; de Terra and Bastien's (Armillas 1950) exploration of the Calaveras Pit, where thirty-five human skulls were found; Cook de Leonard (1952: 49) and Millon (1957: 12) at Oztoyahualco; Michael and Elizabeth Goodliffe's (1963) excavations in four interconnected tunnels in Purificación, with Teotihuacan, Mazapan, and Aztec II and III ceramics; Obermeyer's (1963) excavation of the Huexóctoc Cave in Oxtotícpac; Heyden's (1973, 1975; Baker et al. 1974) study of the tunnel below the Pyramid of the Sun, excavated by Acosta and used during Teotihuacan II times (first to third centuries C.E.) for ritual purposes; Basante's explorations (1982, 1986) in several tunnels and holes in the valley; and finally Soruco's exploration (1985, 1991) of a cavity probably built for solar observations, located to the southeast of the Pyramid of the Sun. In August 1992, we began the extensive excavation of four tunnels to the east of the Pyramid of the Sun (Manzanilla 1994a, 1994b; Manzanilla et al. 1996; Manzanilla et al. 1994;

Fig. 2.10. Frogs from which springs and water flows emerge are also depicted at the Tlalocan of Tepantitla (redrawn from de la Fuente 1996, II: 233).

Manzanilla et al. 1989; Barba et al. 1990; Arzate et al. 1990; Chávez et al. 1988; Chávez et al. 1994). In 1994, two other cavities were tested by INAH's *Proyecto Especial 1992–1994*, one of which is a smaller replica of Soruco's solar observatory (Moragas Segura 1994).

Soruco Sáenz's (1985, 1991) exploration of the so-called Astronomical Cave, used for solar observations and located to the southeast of the Pyramid of the Sun, revealed a basalt stela on an altar displaying a ray of light at its center during the beginnings of the summer solstice. Around it, several jars, bowls, miniatures, vases, Gulf Coast pottery, twenty prismatic blades, a Xipe Totec figurine, as well as copal resin, red and green pigments, amaranth, chile, tomato, cactus, maize, and frogs' long bones, were found. It is interesting to note the relationship of rain prediction with fertility symbols (edible plants) and with incense and frog bones, as in Formative times.

During the study of the depressions around the Pyramid of the Sun, the absence of buildings in the area between the pyramid and the depression to the east on Millon's topographic map (1973) was noted. This is unusual because all of the rest of the area surrounding this important structure is heavily occupied. If this information is considered together with the way in which depressions are formed—that is, as a result of the collapse of the roof of extraction tunnels—then it can be proposed that one of the reasons why the Teotihuacanos did not build any construction in this area was because of the risk of cave-ins. The preliminary exploration of a cave extending underground from the depression toward the pyramid, provided enough evidence to lead us to suggest the existence of similar tunnels extending throughout the zone.

Our project, "The Study of Tunnels at Teotihuacan," has provided evidence that virtually all the underground cavities of the Teotihuacan Valley were originally extraction places excavated around 80 C.E., to obtain pyroclastic construction materials; later these underground holes were used either ritually or domestically. Thus, the tunnel underneath the Pyramid of the Sun could be conceived as one of the many tunnels that run under the ancient city, in the northern part of the Valley, and not as a natural cave.

The system of tunnels and caves in the Teotihuacan Valley was originally, then, a group of quarries dated in the Patlachique or Tzacualli periods, for the extraction of porous volcanic materials, and are, thus, man-made. We therefore rectify our previous idea, derived from Heyden (1975) and Millon (1973), that they were natural, because there is no natural phenomenon in volcanic contexts that can produce large or long holes, except solid lava tubes. And this is not the case.

There are examples of C^{14} dates from our caves (Beta 69912), as well as from the lower tunnel of the Pyramid of the Sun (M–1283; Millon, Drewitt, and Bennyhoff 1965: 33) and the Temple of Quetzalcoatl (Cabrera in Rattray 1991: 12), that are placed around the year 80 C.E. This could be evidence of great construction enterprises involving the tunnels and the main pyramids. It is also possible that after the city was built, these underground spaces were conceived of as a Tlalocan, in a way similar to that of Balankanché, Yucatán (Andrews 1970).

The Pyramid of the Sun at Teotihuacan is the only structure not constructed with the porous volcanic material known as *tezontle*, and coming from the tunnels. Instead, it was built mainly with earth and small fragments of tuff (5 to 10 cm) (Rattray 1974), that generally overlie the pyroclasts.

In 1989, we interviewed old men and women regarding the caves at Teotihuacan. Different persons mentioned the myth that in olden days, in February, a man was seen coming from under the Pyramid of the Sun carrying maize, amaranth, green beans, and zucchini. Many added also that under the Pyramid of the Sun there were *chinampa*-like fields were all this foodstuff was collected.

The concept of a mountain of sustenance—the Tonacatépetl of the Nahua tradition—is frequent in Mesoamerica, and also frequent is the sacred mountain with a cave from which water emerged (Freidel, Schele, and Parker 1993: 430). Instead of housing springs, as Heyden (1975) originally proposed for the Pyramid of the Sun, which would be a very improbable phenomenon in porous volcanic materials, there were perhaps small water filtrations that were received by stone water drainages inside the tunnel; other water courses inside the tunnels could derive from vertical seepage in the northeastern sector of the valley. These courses have been mentioned in various interviews with local people. The real springs emerge in the alluvial plain in the southwestern part of the ancient city.

We propose that the Pyramid of the Sun represented the Tonacatépetl, or "mountain of sustenance"; this is reinforced by the mention made by the *Relación de Teotihuacan* in the sixteenth century (Paso y Troncoso 1979: 222) in which the idol in the summit of the pyramid was Tonacateuctli. This monumental construction is the only one built with organic soil, full with plant remains, coming from the alluvial plain, perhaps as a reaction to the violent volcanic eruptions of the Xitle and Popocatépetl volcanos, at the beginnings of the era, that changed the demographic configuration of the Basin of Mexico. Other "mountains of sustenance" were built in rain-producing mountains such as Tetzcotzingo and Mount Tlaloc, as Townsend states (1993: 38). Finally, the Templo Mayor of Tenochtitlan would be a continuation of this tradition (Broda 1987).

The Pyramid of the Sun could have synthesized three intimately related concepts: the Tonacatépetl; the main temple for the state-god Tlaloc as a fertility deity; and the sacred mountain, the center of the universe, represented as the center of the four-petal flower, as López Austin (1989) suggests.

Teotihuacan was built as a sacred copy of the cosmos. Its terrestrial plane is divided into the four courses of the universe; it has a celestial plane with the sky itself and the summits of the temples, but also an underworld represented by the system of tunnels under the northern halves of the city. Its main avenue connected the natural sacred mountain of Cerro Gordo, where Tobriner (1972) detected a cave of special significance, with the Pyramid of the Sun (the artificial "mountain of sustenance") and the spring area to the south (Townsend 1993: 41). As Townsend states, following Aveni and Broda, the east-west avenue traces the path of the Pleiades in the summer solstice.

The Late Classic site of El Zapotal in Veracruz has a mound (n. 2) within which a *mictlan* or world of the dead was re-created. Huge clay human figures represent either Mictlantecuhtli, the Lord of the Dead, or women who died during childbirth, and are deposited together with human remains (Torres Guzmán 1972). Thus, in other areas of Mesoamerica, the concept of the *mictlan* would be developing and finally would arrive in the Basin of Mexico in the Late Postclassic period.

THE EPICLASSIC AND EARLY POSTCLASSIC
PERIODS IN CENTRAL MEXICO

THE TEOTIHUACAN VALLEY

The existence of underground cavities in Teotihuacan is a well-known fact. Heyden (1981) reproduces the glyph of Teotihuacan from the *Codex Xolotl*, which represents the two large pyramids overlying a cave with a person inside. It is likely that this figure refers to the oracles that were frequently located within caves, as indicated in the *Relación de Teotihuacan* (Soruco Sáenz 1985: 107).

The general objective of our project consisted of locating and defining the tunnels and cavities that were of interest to archaeology because of their potential ritual or economic use, that is, the original extractive activities related to porous pyroclastic volcanic materials, large-scale storage, burials, offerings related to fertility rites, and domestic and manufacturing activities. Many of these functions, as well as numerous activity areas related to post-Teotihuacan occupational levels—such as hearths, hide preparation and weaving, wood cutting, bifacial obsidian production loci, etc.—were corroborated by the storage and funerary loci found in the Cueva de las Varillas and Cueva del Pirul, Epiclassic and Early Postclassic tunnel occupations behind the Pyramid of the Sun, as we shall see further on. As of this writing, we have thoroughly excavated four cavities to the east of the Pyramid of the Sun (Manzanilla 1994; Manzanilla et al. 1996).

Cueva del Pirul is the last one excavated. In different chambers of the tunnel, under Aztec structures and activity areas, we have found fourteen Coyotlatelco burials belonging to the sixth to tenth centuries C.E., including: two seated adults (one with bilobated skull, and another dated in the sixth century), two young adults in fetal positions, four sets of child burials, and six perinatal burials. A group of six burials, mainly infants, was placed around a ritually "killed" hemispherical monochrome bowl with plastic design, also named "Jiménez Sealed Brown" (Good and Obermeyer 1986: 258, plate 7; Nichols and McCullough 1986: plates 8 and 9; Cobean 1990: 194–198). This design type has been related by Cobean to the Coyotlatelco Sphere and to the Corral Complex; he suggests that these bowls were used to drink chocolate. In our excavations, we have found numerous examples of this type with different kinds of sealed motifs. Another type frequently found in contact with the disintegrated tuff is the negative-painted bowl (Good and Obermeyer 1986: plate 11).

Near two of the children and one new-born baby, three complete and articulated dog skeletons were found: two adults and a puppy, one of them with skeletal malformations. They could have been conceived of as guides to the underworld. Modest storage-bin bottoms were also found in the first chamber of this tunnel. In another sector, a newborn baby was placed inside a bowl near one of the seated adults (with a calibrated radiocarbon average date of 550 C.E.), and an eight-month-old baby in fetal position covered with another bowl (Manzanilla et al. 1996).

The third tunnel—Cueva de las Varillas, 50 m in length—has a vast entrance chamber 18 m. in diameter, with seven small niches and a tunnel that crosses three small chambers. To one side, it is connected to another chamber that had well-preserved funerary and storage contexts. In this tunnel here are some hints of a cult that involved marine and aquatic elements, such as different types of mother-of-pearl shells, a ray's cauda, and fragments of turtle shells, perhaps related to an ideal reconstruction of the Tlalocan (Tlaloc's watery underworld) that the new-born-baby burials, as well as Tlaloc sacrificial victims with amaranth masks, suggest.

Twelve Mazapa burials were found: a group of three seated-adult burials facing south were excavated underneath a pillar left in the chamber; two infant burials were placed near the adult ones at the level of their heads. All of these burials had nearly complete and ritually killed pottery vessels as offerings, as well as some projectile points. This first group appeared to be placed in the northeastern fringe of the chamber.

Higher on there were seven newborn babies, some of them in a seated position and some in fetal position; they were placed in an east-west band in the central part of the chamber, under a sanctuary. These had only triangles or rectangles of cut mica as offerings, as well as some hearths with Teotihuacan *candeleros* and projectile points.

In tunnels behind the Pyramid of the Sun, the Epiclassic–Early Postclassic people constructed a shrine for the *tlaloque* (Tlaloc's assistants), represented by the seven babies deposited in the central part of the chamber, precisely underneath a hole in the cavity's roof, a hole that may have allowed the pouring of rainwater on top of the shrine. The adult burials—probably Tlaloc's sacrificial victims—were seated with their backs to a pillar left behind to prevent the collapse of the cavity, and facing south (Figure 2.11). In some of the storage bins, amaranth was found, a plant from which masks were made for Tlaloc's sacrificial victims (Manzanilla and McClung de Tapia 1996). At San Francisco Mazapa, Linné (1934: 37) found a Mazapa house on top of a tunnel, and in this cavity, large storage jars were found. In the funerary chamber of the Varillas tunnel, we also found seven circular storage-bin bottoms distributed in different sectors and at depths corresponding to the adult burials. Fifty meters inside the tunnel, in an inner chamber, we had already found six of these storage contexts, but with no apparent association to the burials.

Thus, two of the four cavities gave us elements to confirm the three functions we expected to find for the tunnels: storage areas probably related to fertility rites in the womb of the earth; burials related to the underworld concept; and baby burials related to the rituals to Tlaloc. In all four of them we also found living-area floors, and Epiclassic and Postclassic domestic activity areas.

MORELOS DURING THE EPICLASSIC

At Xochicalco, a system of more than nineteen man-made tunnels, of which the so-called Observatory is just a part, also represent a series of quarries from which one of the two types of limestone for building the city came from. Since the eighteenth century, there are precise descriptions of the tunnels by Alzate y Ramírez (Peñafiel 1890). Togno (1903) describes nine interconnected tunnels in the north and northeastern sectors of the site. Their walls were plastered and painted in red (Krickeberg 1949: 212).

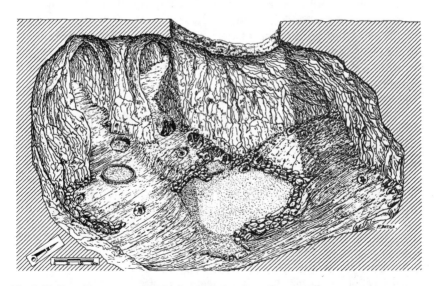

Fig. 2.11. Drawing representing the funerary chamber of the *Varillas* Tunnels to the east of the Pyramid of the Sun at Teotihuacan (drawn by Fernando Botas).

In recent geophysical work we have undertaken inside and on top of the Cueva de los Jabalíes and Cueva de los Amates (better known as the Observatory), there is evidence of interconnection between these systems, as well as a gridlike plan (Manzanilla 1993). The eastern parts of both systems continue beneath the western part of the Acropolis, suggesting continuation to the main plaza. The tunnels were excavated in different levels of the mountain, suggesting either stratification of the systems, or stairlike ascensions. The Observatory marked the zenital passage of the sun in the beginnings of the summer solstice, the rainy season, and is thus equivalent to the so-called Astronomical Cave at Teotihuacan.

THE LATE POSTCLASSIC OF CENTRAL MEXICO

The Nahuas associated three concepts with the underworld: Mictlan, Tlillan, and Tlalocan. Mictlan was located to the north, and was guarded by Mictlantecuhtli and Mictecacihuatl (Mendoza 1962). The Nahuas thought that the sun entered the Mictlan during the first month of its zenital passage, that is Toxcatl (in May), in the prelude to the rainy season (Broda 1982: 94); thus, the observatories in Building P at Monte Albán, Xochicalco, and the Astronomical Cave at Teotihuacan were used to observe these zenital passages.

In the archaeological excavations at Templo Mayor, interesting sculptures related to the Mictlan have also been found,. In 1981, a monolith of Huehueteotl, the Fire God, was found, with atypical traits such as a Tlaloc mask and aquatic symbols, and thus has been identified by López Austin (1985) as the Fire God in the world of the dead. Its other names, Ayamictlan and Xiuhtecuhtli, are mentioned in the *Florentine Codex* as related to the residence of this god: the navel of the earth, the water enclosure (López Austin 1985: 262). In recent excavations by López Luján (1996) at Templo Mayor of Tenochtitlan, two huge Mictlantecuhtli ceramic sculptures were found underneath the Eagle's Precinct, thus evidencing the re-creation of the Mictlan underneath the sacred core of the city.

For the Totonacs, the realm of the dead is an underworld where the Fire God and the Death God dwell (Ichon 1969: 138). The Popolucas conceived the underworld as a region with dangerous passages, in which two roads existed: the one to the right was narrow, difficult, debris-strewn, and ascending toward the sky; the one to the left was large, smooth, clean, and descending gently to hell (Foster 1945: 186).

With respect to the Tlillan, it is an artificial cave where the goddess Cihuacoatl dwelt. Broda (1987: 80) proposes that Cihuacoatl is an old goddess of the earth and also Tlaloc's wife. In the Mayan area, at Chichén Itzá, the so-called High-Priest Tomb also has an artificial cave excavated underneath a stepped pyramid (Thompson 1938).

According to Anderson (1988: 153–154), Tlalocan was conceptualized in many ways among the Nahuas of Central Mexico:

a) In the *Florentine Codex*, it was depicted as a place of great wealth where there was no suffering, and where maize was abundant, as were squash, amaranth, chile, and flowers. In the "Prayer to Tlaloc" of the *Florentine Codex*, translated by Sullivan (1965: 45), it is said that sustenance has not disappeared, but rather that the gods have hidden it in Tlalocan.

b) In several examples of Nahuatl poetry, it was portrayed as a place of beauty where birds with lovely feathers sang, on top of pyramids of jade.

c) It was described as a construction consisting of four rooms around a patio, with four containers filled with water. One was good and the other three were associated with frosts, sterility, and drought. Durán (1967: 82) mentions that this Tlalocan was represented on Mount Tlaloc, in the eastern fringe of the Basin of Mexico, as a walled enclosure with a patio and a figure representing Tlaloc, around which were placed other smaller figures representing the lesser mountains. Sahagún mentions that the mountain was a disguise, because it was a jar full of water.

d) Tlalocan was also thought of as an underground space filled with water that connected the mountains with the sea. It was a place where rivers originate. Furthermore, "Tlaloc" may be translated as "long cave" (Broda 1987: 101–2). Durán and Tezozómoc mention that Tlalocan and Cincalco could be the same concept: one enters them through a cave (Graulich 1987: 252). Sullivan's (1965: 55) translation of the *Florentine Codex*'s "Prayer to Tlaloc" states the following, refering to the Gods of Rain:

> And you who inhabit the four quarters of the universe,
> you the Lords of Verdure, you the Providers,
> you the Lords of the Mountain Heights, you the Lords of the Cavernous Depths

In the *Florentine Codex*, it is said that the mountains were conceived of as hollow upside-down vessels full with water, and Torquemada adds that each was inhabited by an assistant to Tlaloc (a *tlaloque*) that engendered clouds and provoked rains (de Vega Nova and Pelz Marín 1994). Thus, mountains and caves are intimately related in Late Postclassic times.

During this period, there are numerous examples of cave cults in Central Mexico. We have, for example, the Chimalacatepec Cave in Morelos (Broda and Druzo Maldonado 1994; De Vega Nova and Pelz Marín 1994), a real lava tube with various offerings: censers, vessels, polished stones, figurines, duck figures, greenstones, pendants, black-and-green idols, etc. The vessels could have been deposited to receive infiltrating water. The censers are frequently cited in water-petition ceremonies inside the caves. The idols are fertility symbols (Broda and Druzo Maldonado 1994).

On another line of evidence, the foundation of Tenochtitlan mentioned in the historical sources of the sixteenth century involved two caves with springs that were sighted when the sacred place announced by Huitzilopochtli was located; immediately afterwards, the ball court was traced, even before Huitzilopochtli's shrine was built (Tezozómoc 1975: 62 *et seq.*). Some cite the fact that the water from the springs flowed from caves or rocks (Figures 2.12 and 2.13). It was the site where the heart of Copil (the god Huitzilopochtli's nephew) had been thrown (Dahlgren et al. 1982). In recent geotechnical work under the cathedral of Mexico City, Ovando and I (Ovando-Shelley and Manzanilla 1997) have detected three springs, one of which is near the ball court.

The Tetzcutzingo Mountain near Texcoco is a rainmaking "mountain of sustenance" (Townsend 1993), where the spring-canal-water/basin-frog complex is found in open air (Figure 2.14). Thus, the Tonacatépetl, the archetypical sacred mountain, was the house of maize and of water, and the *tlaloque* were its guardians.

On the other hand, Tlaloc's half of the Templo Mayor at Tenochtitlan, the Aztec capital, was the mythical re-creation of the primordial mountain of sustenance (Broda 1989: 40). Different ceremonies that relate water and rain deities with mountains and caves have been studied by Broda (1971, 1982, 1987, 1989, 1991a, 1991b, 1994). In those related to caves, she stresses that the Tonacatépetl—the "mountain of sustenance"—was the reservoir of food and water, and water came out from Tlalocan through water springs (Broda 1971: 259).

Another fact that should be mentioned is that Xipe Totec had a temple in Tenochtitlan, called Netlatiloyan, at the base of which was a cave where the skins of the flayed were hidden (Sahagún 1969, vol. I: 237). It is interesting to note that Linné (1934; Scott 1993) found a shattered Xipe Totec sculpture associated with sixteen graves belonging to the Mazapa culture, in his excavations at Xolalpan, near the tunnels that we described in the Valley of Teotihuacan.

Fig. 2.12. Foundation of Mexico-Tenochtitlan, from the *Codex Aubin* (redrawn from Dahlgren et al. 1982: 47).

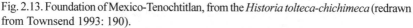

Fig. 2.13. Foundation of Mexico-Tenochtitlan, from the *Historia tolteca-chichimeca* (redrawn from Townsend 1993: 190).

MODERN TIMES AND CAVE RITUALS

At present, hail-preventing ceremonies are still held in different parts of Central Mexico: the Sierra Nevada range in the Basin of Mexico (Bonfil 1968; Glockner 1996), the Valley of Teotihuacan (Martel 1922), the Toluca Basin (Christensen 1962), and other areas. Bonfil (1968) carefully registered these rites in the Amecameca area near the Popocatépetl and Iztaccíhuatl volcanos, among the so-called *graniceros, aureros, tiemperos,* and *trabajadores temporaleños,* derived from pre-Hispanic magicians called *teciuhtlazqui* or *teciuhpeuhqui* ("those who throw or conquer hail") (Bonfil 1968: 101). Some of the most important offerings are placed in the Las Cruces cave-temple.

Sahagún described ceremonies to the water deities in the high volcanos of Central Mexico in which amaranth figures were offered during the first days of May, the Holy Cross feast (Glockner 1996: 51–52).

In San Francisco Mazapa, in the Valley of Teotihuacan, a legend was recorded in 1922 in which a cave was used to predict good or bad crops. If the stones in the mouth of the cave were humid, good weather was expected

(Christensen 1962: 247). Water-petition ceremonies are also present in the mountains of Guerrero, particularly at Ostotempa (Sepúlveda 1973), where a deep fault receives the offerings, so that four giants, representatives of the winds who live in caves, bring good rain.

In recent ethnographic work in the Sierra de Puebla, with Nahuat-speaking groups, Aramoni (1990) and Knab (1991) have shed light on a persistence of the concepts related to "Talokan," as they call it. In them, caves are entrances to this underworld, and the informants state that Tamoanchan is the deepest part of the Talokan. "Crossing the doors of the underworld and further on, in the deepness, there is a splendorous world. There the miracle of fertility resides" (Aramoni 1990: 144). In this Talokan, the future human beings, as well as all seeds and animal species, are found; from Talokan all power and wealth emerge, and are concentrated in the Heart of the Mountain, the Tepeyólot or "treasure of the mountain" (145–146). The Nahuas of Cuetzalan also speak of three roads as the final destiny of men: one with God (the sky); another under the earth (Talokan), and the last through caves, which is the devil's road, the Miktan (148).

Fig. 2.14. View of the water basins with frog sculptures at Tetzcutzingo, Estado de México.

Knab (1991) describes a myth that mentions the geography of the underworld or "Talocan," as conceived by the inhabitants of San Miguel Tzinacapan. These caves are also considered to be entrances to the underworld, as evidenced by these descriptions:

a) The mythical northern entrance, Mictalli or Miquitalan, is represented by a "cave of the winds" and accesses the world of the dead. Tobriner (1972) makes reference to a gorge on the northeastern slope of Cerro Gordo on the northern fringe of the Teotihuacan Valley, with a cave that emitted a sound of water. A map dating to 1580 represents this gorge on the southeastern portion of the hill. Tobriner also suggests that the Street of the Dead in Teotihuacan was built pointing toward Cerro Gordo because of the association of this mountain with the God of Water (113).

b) The southern entrance of the mythical cave Talocan is called Atotonican and it is a place of warmth; a hot spring that produces vapor and clouds resides in the back of the cave. On the other hand, it is well known that the area of springs is situated in the southwestern sector of the valley, another parallel with respect to the myth.

c) The mythical eastern access is called Apan, a large lake in the underworld that joins the sea. The lacustrine basin of Apan is precisely located to the east of the Teotihuacan Valley.

d) The western entrance of Talocan is a mountain called Tonalan, where the sun stops on its voyage. Mount Tonalan is actually a low mountain located on the northwestern boundary of the valley, between Cerro Gordo and Cerro Malinali.

It is possible that the myth of Nahuat-speakers in the Sierra de Puebla is derived from a version based on the sacred geography of the Teotihuacan Valley, but it is equally probable that both have their source in an archetypical Mesoamerican conception of the underworld.

Thus, the construction of sacred space is a tradition derived from Formative times, and culminated with the building of cities as models of the cosmos.

REFERENCES

Alvarado, José Luis, Jorge Luis Jiménez-Meza, Luis Morett-Alatorre, Ana María Pelz Marín, and Fernando Sánchez-Martínez
1994. "Proyecto Arqueobotánico Ticumán '94. Cueva La Chagüera. Primeros avances." In *Memoria III Congreso Interno del Centro INAH Morelos a los XX años de su fundación: en recuerdo de Guillermo Bonfil Batalla y Juan Dubernard Chauveau: celebrado en el Foro Wanda Tomassi, Casa de Maximiliano, Acapantzingo, Cuernavaca, Morelos diciembre 5 al 10 de 1994*. Cuernavaca, Mexico: INAH Centro, INAH Morelos, pp. 131–148.

Anderson, Arthur J. O.
1988. "A Look into Tlalocan." In J. K. Josserand and K. Dakin, eds., *Smoke and Mist: Mesoamerican Studies in Memory of Thelma D. Sullivan*. Oxford: BAR International Series 402(i), pp. 151–159.

Anderson, Neal S.
1981. "Solar Observatory at Xochicalco and the Maya Farmer's Almanac." *Archaeoastronomy* 4, no. 2: 23–25.

Andrews IV, E. Wyllys
1970. *Balankanche, Throne of the Tiger Priest.* New Orleans, LA: Tulane University, Middle American Research Institute Publication 32.

Angulo Villaseñor, Jorge
1987a. "10. The Chalcatzingo Reliefs: An Iconographic Analysis." In D. C. Grove, ed., *Ancient Chalcatzingo.* Austin: University of Texas Press, pp. 132–158.
1987b. "Los relieves del Grupo 'IA' en la montaña sagrada de Chalcatzingo." In B. Dahlgren, C. Navarrete, L. Ochoa, M. C. Serra Puche, and Y. Sugiura, eds., *Homenaje a Román Piña Chan.* Mexico: UNAM-IIA, Arqueología, Serie Antropológica 79, pp. 191–228.
1988. "Siete sistemas de aprovechamiento hidráulico localizados en Chalcatzingo." *Arqueología* (Mexico: Dirección de Monumentos Prehispánicos, INAH), no. 2: 37–83.

Aramoni, María Elena
1990. *Talokan tata, talokan nana: Nuestras raíces: Hierofanías y testimonios de un mundo indígena.* Mexico: CNCA/Dirección General de Publicaciones.

Armillas, Pedro
1950."Teotihuacán, Tula y los toltecas: Las culturas post-arcaicas y pre-aztecas de centro de México. Excavaciones y estudios, 1922–1950." *Runa* (Buenos Aires: Instituto de Antropología, Universidad de Buenos Aires) 3: 37–70. (Also in Teresa Rojas Rabiela, ed., *Pedro Armillas: Vida y obra.* Mexico: CIESAS-INAH, 1991, vol. 1, pp. 193–231.)

Arzate, J. A., L. Flores, R. E. Chávez, Luis Barba, and Linda Manzanilla
1990. "Magnetic Prospecting for Tunnels and Caves in Teotihuacan, México." In S. H Ward, ed., *Geotechnical and Environmental Geophysics, Volume III: Geotechnical.* Tulsa, OK: Society for Exploration Geophysicists, Investigations in Geophysics 5, pp. 155–162.

Baker III, George T., Hugh Harleston Jr., Alfonso Rangel, Matthew Wallrath, Manuel Gaitán, and Alfonso Morales.
1974. "The Subterranean System of the Sun Pyramid at Teotihuacan: A Physical Description and Hypothetical Reconstruction." Paper prepared for the XLI International Congress of Americanists, Mexico, D.F.

Barba, Luis A., Linda Manzanilla, R. Chávez, L. Flores, and A. J. Arzate
1990. "Caves and Tunnels at Teotihuacan, Mexico: A Geological Phenomenon of Archaeological Interest." In N. P. Lasca and J. Donahue, eds., *Archaeological Geology of North America.* Boulder, CO: Geological Society of America, Centennial Special, vol. 4, pp. 431–438.

Basante Gutiérrez, O. R.
1982. "Algunas cuevas en Teotihuacan." In R. Cabrera Castro, I. Rodríguez, and N. Morelos, eds., *Memoria del Proyecto Arqueológico Teotihuacan 80–82.* Mexico: INAH, Colección Científica, Arqueología 132, pp. 341–354.
1986. "Ocupación de cuevas en Teotihuacan, México." Thesis in Archaeology, ENAH, Mexico, D.F.

Bernal-García, María Elena
1994. "*Tzatza*: Olmec Mountains and the Ruler's Speech." In V. M. Fields, vol. ed., M. G. Robertson, gen. ed., *Seventh Palenque Round Table, 1989.* San Francisco: The Pre-Columbian Art Research Institute, pp. 113–124.

Bonfil Batalla, Guillermo
1968. "Los que trabajan con el tiempo: notas etnográficas sobre los graniceros de la Sierra Nevada, México." *Anales de Antropología* (Mexico: UNAM) 5: 99–128.

Brady, James E., and George Veni
1992. "Man-Made and Pseudo-Karst Caves: The Implication of Subsurface Features Within Maya Centers." *Geoarchaeology: An International Journal* 7, no. 2: 149–167.

Broda, Johanna
1971. "Las fiestas aztecas de los dioses de la lluvia." *Revista Española de Antropología Americana* (Madrid) 6: 245–327.
1982. "Astronomy, *Cosmovisión*, and Ideology in Pre-Hispanic Mesoamerica." In A. F. Aveni and G. Urton, eds. *Ethnoastronomy and Archaeoastronomy in the American Tropics*. Annals of the New York Academy of Science 385. New York: The Academy, pp. 81–110.
1987. "Templo Mayor as Ritual Space." In J. Broda, D. Carrasco, and E. Matos Moctezuma. *The Great Temple of Tenochtitlan: Center and Periphery in the Aztec World*. Berkeley: University of California Press, pp. 61–123.
1989. "Geografía, clima y observación de la naturaleza en la Mesoamérica prehispánica." In E. Vargas, ed., *Las máscaras de la cueva de Santa Ana Telóxtoc*. Mexico: UNAM-IIA, Arqueología, Serie Antropológica 105, pp. 35–51.
1991a. "The Sacred Landscape of Aztec Calendar Festivals: Myth, Nature, and Society." In D. Carrasco, ed., *To Change Place: Aztec Ceremonial Landscapes*. Niwot: University Press of Colorado, pp. 74–120.
1991b. "Cosmovisión y observación de la naturaleza: el ejemplo del culto de los cerros." In J. Broda, S. Iwaniszewski, and L. Maupomé, eds., *Arqueoastronomía y etnoastronomía en Mesoamérica*. Mexico: UNAM-IIH, Serie de Historia de la Ciencia y la Tecnología 4, pp. 461–500.

Broda, Johanna, and Druzo Maldonado
1994. "La cueva de Chimalacatepec, Morelos: Una interpretación histórica." In *Memoria III Congreso Interno del Centro INAH Morelos a los XX años de su fundación: en recuerdo de Guillermo Bonfil Batalla y Juan Dubernard Chauveau: celebrado en el Foro Wanda Tomassi, Casa de Maximiliano, Acapantzingo, Cuernavaca, Morelos diciembre 5 al 10 de 1994*. Cuernavaca, Mexico: INAH Centro INAH Morelos, pp. 101–122.

Byers, Douglas S., ed.
1967. *The Prehistory of the Tehuacan Valley*. Vol. I: *Environment and Subsistence*. Austin and London: University of Texas Press.

Chávez, René E., J. Arzate, L. Flores, Linda Manzanilla, and Luis Barba
1988. *Estudio geofísico de las cuevas y túneles de Teotihuacan*. Mexico: UNAM, Instituto de Geofísica, Serie Investigación 78.

Chávez, René E., Linda Manzanilla, Nayeli Peralta, Andrés Tejero, Gerardo Cifuentes, and Luis Barba
1994. "Estudio magnético y de resistividad en los alrededores de la pirámide del Sol, Teotihuacan, Mexico." *Geofísica Internacional* (Mexico: UNAM) 33, no. 2: 243–255.

Christensen, Bodil
1962. "Los graniceros." *Revista Mexicana de Estudios Antropológicos* 18: 87–95.

Clark, John E., ed.
1994. *Los olmecas en Mesoamérica*. Mexico: El Equilibrista/Citibank.

Cobean, Robert H.
1990. *La cerámica de Tula, Hidalgo*. Mexico: INAH, Colección Científica 215.

Cook de Leonard, Carmen
1952. "Notas del interior. Teotihuacan." *Tlatoani* (Mexico: INAH) 1, nos. 3–4 (May-August): 49.

Cruz Flores, Sandra, and Blanca Noval
1994. "Conservación del material cultural orgánico de la cueva 'El Gallo,' Morelos." In *Memoria III Congreso Interno del Centro INAH Morelos a los XX años de su fundación: en recuerdo de Guillermo Bonfil Batalla y Juan Dubernard Chauveau: celebrado en el Foro Wanda Tomassi, Casa de Maximiliano, Acapantzingo, Cuernavaca, Morelos diciembre 5 al 10 de 1994*. Cuernavaca, Mexico: INAH Centro INAH Morelos, pp. 123–130.

Cyphers, Ann
1996. "Reconstructing Olmec Life at San Lorenzo." In E. P. Benson and B. de la Fuente, eds., *Olmec Art of Ancient Mexico*. Washington, DC: National Gallery of Art, pp. 61–71.

Dahlgren, Barbro, Carlos Navarrete, Lorenzo Ochoa, Mari Carmen Serra Puche, and Yoko Sugiura, eds.
1987. *Homenaje a Román Piña Chan*. Mexico: UNAM-IIA, Arqueología, Serie Antropológica 79.

Dahlgren, Barbro, Emma Pérez-Rocha, Lourdes Suárez Diez, and Perla Valle de Revueltas
1982. *Corazón de Copil*. Mexico: INAH.

de la Fuente, Beatriz, ed.
1996. *La pintura mural prehispánica en México*. Vol. 1: *Teotihuacán*, and Vol. 2: *Estudios*. Mexico: UNAM-IIE.

de Vega Nova, Hortensia, and Ana María Pelz Marín
1994. "Informe parcial de los hallazgos arqueológicos de la cueva de Chimalacatepec, San Juan Tlacotenco, Municipio de Tepoztlán, Morelos." In *Memoria III Congreso Interno del Centro INAH Morelos a los XX años de su fundación: en recuerdo de Guillermo Bonfil Batalla y Juan Dubernard Chauveau: celebrado en el Foro Wanda Tomassi, Casa de Maximiliano, Acapantzingo, Cuernavaca, Morelos diciembre 5 al 10 de 1994*. Cuernavaca, Mexico: INAH Centro INAH Morelos, pp. 95–100.

Dumond, Don E., and Florencia Müller
1972. "Classic to Postclassic in Highland Central Mexico." *Science* 175 (March 17): 1208-1215.

Durán, Fray Diego
1967. *Historia de las Indias de Nueva España e Islas de la Tierra Firme*. Vol. 1. Mexico: Editorial Porrúa.

Evans, Susan T.
1986. "Analysis of the Surface Sample Ceramics." In W. T. Sanders, ed., *The Toltec Period Occupation of the Valley*. Part 1: *Excavations and Ceramics*. The Teotihuacan Valley Project Final Report, vol. 4. Occasional Papers in Anthropology no. 13. University Park: Department of Anthropology, Pennsylvania State University, pp. 283–365.

Ford, Richard I.
1990. "Corn Is Our Mother." Paper presented at the meeting "Corn and Culture in the Prehistoric New World," May 11–13, University of Minnesota, Minneapolis.

Foster, George M.
1945. *Sierra Popoluca Folklore and Beliefs*. University of California Publications in American Archaeology and Ethnology 42, no. 2. Berkeley and Los Angeles: University of California Press, pp. 177–250.

Freidel, David, Linda Schele, and Joy Parker
1993. *Maya Cosmos: Three Thousand Years on the Shaman's Path*. New York: William Morrow and Co., Inc.

Glockner, Julio
1996. *Los volcanes sagrados: Mitos y rituales en el Popocatépetl y la Iztaccíhuatl*. Mexico: Grijalbo.

Gómez Rueda, Hernando
1997. "Función y representación: Monumentos y sistemas hidráulicos en Izapa, Chiapas." Paper presented at the Segundo Coloquio de Antropología Simbólica, March 6, ENAH, Mexico, D.F.

Good, Kenneth, and Gerald Obermeyer
1986. "Excavations at Oxtotipac (TT82)." In W. T. Sanders, ed., *The Toltec Period Occupation of the Valley*. Part 1: *Excavations and Ceramics. The Teotihuacan Valley Project Final Report*, vol. 4. Occasional Papers in Anthropology no. 13. University Park: Department of Anthropology, Pennsylvania State University, pp. 195–265.

Goodliffe, Michael and Elizabeth
1963. Untitled ms., Departamento de Prehistoria, INAH, Mexico, D.F.

Graulich, Michel
1987. *Mythes et rituels du Mexique ancien préhispanique*. Mémoires de la Classe des Lettres, Colléction in–8o, séconde série, t. 67, fasc. 3. Brussels: Palais des Académies.

Grove, David C.
1970. *The Olmec Paintings of Oxtotitlan Cave, Guerrero, Mexico*. Studies in Pre-Columbian Art and Archaeology no. 6. Washington, DC: Dumbarton Oaks.

Hellmuth, Nicholas
1987. *The Surface of the Underworld: Iconography of the Gods of Early Classic Maya Art in Peten, Guatemala*. Culver City, CA: Foundation for Latin American Anthropological Research.

Hapka, Román, and Fabienne Rouvinez
1994. "Prospección arqueológica en las cuevas del Cerro Rabón (Sierra Mazateca, Oaxaca)." *Trace Arqueología* (Mexico: CEMCA), no. 25 (June): 47–65.

Heyden, Doris
1973. "¿Un Chicomóstoc en Teotihuacan? La cueva bajo la Pirámide del Sol." *Boletín del INAH*, segunda época, no. 6 (July-September): 3–18.
1975. "An Interpretation of the Cave Underneath the Pyramid of the Sun in Teotihuacan, Mexico." *American Antiquity* 40, no. 2 (April): 131–147.
1981. "Caves, Gods, and Myths: World Views and Planning in Teotihuacan." In E. P. Benson, ed., *Mesoamerican Sites and World Views*. Washington, DC: Dumbarton Oaks, pp. 1–39.

Ichon, Alain
1969. *La religion des Totonaques de la Sierra*. Paris: Éditions du Centre National de la Recherche Scientifique.

Joralemon, Peter David
1996. "In Search of the Olmec Cosmos: Reconstructing the World View of Mexico's First Civilization." In E. P. Benson and B. de la Fuente, eds., *Olmec Art of Ancient Mexico*. Washington, DC: National Gallery of Art, pp. 51–59.

Knab, Timothy J.
1991. "Geografía del inframundo." *Estudios de Cultura Náhuatl* 21: 31–57.

Krickeberg, Walter
1949. *Felsplastik und Felsbilder bei den Kulturvolkern Altamerikas mit besonderer Berücksichtigung Mexicos*. Berlin: Palmen-Verlag Vormals Dietrich Reijmer.

Krotser, G. Ramón
1973. "El agua ceremonial de los olmecas." *Boletín del INAH*, segunda época, no. 6: 43–48.

Lee Jr., Thomas A., and Gareth W. Lowe
1968. *Situación arqueológica de las esculturas de Izapa*. San Cristóbal de Las Casas, Mexico: Fundación Arqueológica Nuevo Mundo/Editorial Dr. Rodulfo Figueroa.

Linné, Sigvald
1934. *Archaeological Researches at Teotihuacan, Mexico*. The Ethnographical Museum of Sweden New Series Publication 1. Stockholm: Victor Pettersons Bokindustriaktiebolag.

Lombardo de Ruiz, Sonia
1996. "El estilo teotihuacano en la pintura mural." In B. de la Fuente, ed., *La pintura mural prehispánica en México*. Vol. l: *Teotihuacán*, and Vol. 2: *Estudios*. Mexico: UNAM-IIE, pp. 3–64.

López Austin, Alfredo
1985. "El dios enmascarado del fuego." *Anales de Antropología* (Mexico: UNAM) 12: 251–285.

López Austin, Alfredo
1989. "La historia de Teotihuacán." In *Teotihuacán*. Mexico: El Equilibrista/Citicorp/ Citibank, pp. 13–35.

López Luján, Leonardo
1996. "Dos esculturas de Mictlantecuhtli encontradas en el recinto sagrado de México-Tenochtitlan." *Estudios de Cultura Náhuatl* 26: 41–68.

Lowe, Gareth W., Thomas A. Lee Jr., and Eduardo Martínez Espinosa
1982. *Izapa: An Introduction to the Ruins and Monuments*. Papers of the New World Archaeological Foundation no. 31. Provo, UT.

MacNeish, Richard S.
1962. *Second Annual Report of the Tehuacan Archaeological-Botanical Project*. Andover, MA: Robert S. Peabody Foundation for Archaeology, Phillips Academy, Report no. 2.
1967. "A Summary of the Subsistence." In D. S. Byers, ed., *The Prehistory of the Tehuacan Valley*. Vol. 1., *Environment and Subsistence*. Austin and London: University of Texas Press, pp. 290–309.

MacNeish, Richard S., Antoinette Nelken-Terner, and Irmgard W. Johnson
1967. *The Prehistory of the Tehuacan Valley*. Vol. 2: *Nonceramic Artifacts*. Austin and London: University of Texas Press.

Magni, Caterina
1995a. "El simbolismo de la cueva y el simbolismo solar en la iconografía olmeca, México." *Cuicuilco* (Mexico: ENAH) 1, no. 3, (January-April): 89–126.
1995b. "Análisis del complejo iconográfico 'empuñadura-antorcha' en el arte olmeca, México." Paper presented at the XVII Congreso Internacional de lal Historia de las Religiones, August, Claustro de Sor Juana, Mexico, D.F.

Manzanilla, Linda
1993. *Macro Proyecto Xochicalco: Subproyecto estudio de los túneles y cuevas de Xochicalco*. Technical report, INAH, Mexico, D.F.
1994a. "Geografía sagrada e inframundo en Teotihuacan." *Antropológicas* (Mexico: UNAM-IIA) 11 (July): 53–65.
1994b. "Las cuevas en el mundo mesoamericano." *Ciencias* (Mexico: UNAM, Facultad de Ciencias), no. 36 (October-December): 59–66.

Manzanilla, Linda, L. Barba, R. Chávez, J. Arzate, and L. Flores

1989. "El inframundo de Teotihuacan. Geofísica y Arqueología." *Ciencia y desarrollo* (Mexico: Consejo Nacional de Ciencia y Tecnología) 15, no. 85: 21–35.

Manzanilla, Linda, L. Barba, R. Chávez, A. Tejero, G. Cifuentes, and N. Peralta
1994. "Caves and Geophysics: An Approximation to the Underworld of Teotihuacan, Mexico." *Archaeometry* 36, no. 1 (January): 141–157.

Manzanilla, Linda, Claudia López, and AnnCorinne Freter
1996. "Dating Results from Excavations in Quarry Tunnels Behind the Pyramid of the Sun at Teotihuacan." *Ancient Mesoamerica* 7 (Fall): 245–266.

Manzanilla, Linda, and Emily McClung de Tapia
1996. "Patterns of Resource Utilization in Post-Teotihuacan Tunnel Occupations." Paper presented at the 61st Annual Meeting of the Society for American Archaeology, New Orleans, LA.

Manzanilla López, Rubén
1996. "Cuetlajuchitlan: Un ejemplo de sociedad jerárquica agrícola en la región Mezcala de Guerrero." Master's thesis in Archeology, ENAH, Mexico, D.F.

Manzanilla López, Rubén, and Arturo Talavera González
1993. "El sitio arqueológico de Cuetlajuchitlan, un centro urbano del Preclásico Terminal en la región norte-este de Guerrero." In M. T. Castillo Mangas, ed., *A propósito del Formativo*. Mexico: Subdirección de Salvamento Arqueológico, INAH, pp. 105–116.

Martel, Apolinar
1922. "Los Tecihueros: Leyenda Teotihuacana." *Ethnos* 1, nos. 8–23: 246–248.

Martínez Donjuán, Guadalupe
1985. "El sitio olmeca de Teopantecuanitlan en Guerrero." *Anales de Antropología* (Mexico: UNAM) 23: 214–226.
1994. "Teopantecuanitlán: Hallazgos recientes." *Memoria III Congreso Interno del Centro INAH Morelos a los XX años de su fundación: en recuerdo de Guillermo Bonfil Batalla y Juan Dubernard Chauveau: celebrado en el Foro Wanda Tomassi, Casa de Maximiliano, Acapantzingo, Cuernavaca, Morelos diciembre 5 al 10 de 1994.* Cuernavaca, Mexico: INAH Centro INAH Morelos, pp. 77–86.

McCafferty, Geoffrey G.
1996a. "Reinterpreting the Great Pyramid of Cholula, Mexico."*Ancient Mesoamerica* 7, no. 1 (Spring): 1–17.
1966b. "The Ceramics and Chronology of Cholula, Mexico." *Ancient Mesoamerica* 7, no. 2 (Fall): 299–323.

Medina Jaen, Miguel
1966. "Informe del Registro de Cuevas en el Area de Tepeaca-Acatzingo, Puebla. Temporada: septiembre-diciembre de 1995 y enero-agosto de 1996." Proyecto Acatzingo-Tepeaca, unpublished report.

Mendoza, Vicente T.
1962. "El plano o Mundo Inferior, *Mictlan, Xibalbá, Nith* y *Hel.*" *Estudios de Cultura Náhuatl* 3: 75–99.

Millon, René
1957. "Teotihuacan." *Scientific American* 216, no. 6 (June): 38–48.
1973. *Urbanization at Teotihuacan, Mexico.* Vol. 1, *The Teotihuacan Map.* Part 1, *Text.* Austin: University of Texas Press.

Millon, René, Bruce Drewitt, and James A. Bennyhoff

1965. *The Pyramid of the Sun at Teotihuacán: 1959 Investigations*. Transactions, n.s., vol. 55, no.6. Philadelphia, PA: The American Philosophical Society.

Mooser, Federico
1968. "Geología, naturaleza y desarrollo del valle de de Teotihuacan." In J. L. Lorenzo, ed., *Materiales para la arqueología de Teotihuacan*. Mexico: INAH, Serie Investigaciones 17, pp. 29–37.

Moragas Segura, Natalia
1994. *Salvamento arqueológico en la Puerta 5: Cueva II-Cueva III-Cala II. Marzo 1993-Octubre 1993*. Technical Report, Proyecto Especial 1992–1994, INAH, Mexico.

Morett Alatorre, Luis, and Omar Rodríguez Campero
1996. "La unidad de excavación 9 de la Cueva del Gallo. Estudio arqueobotánico de sus depósitos y análisis de su significado." Paper presented at the IX Coloquio de Paleobotánica y Palinología, Resúmenes, November 25–29, Mexico, D.F.

Müller, Florencia
1948. "La Cueva Encantada." *Chimalacatlan*. Mexico: ENAH, Acta Anthropologica, vol. 3, no. 1.

Navarrete, Carlos
1957. "El material arqueológico de la Cueva de Calucan (un sitio posclásico en el Iztaccíhuatl)." *Tlatoani* (Mexico: ENAH), segunda época, 11 (October): 14–18.

Nichols, Deborah, and John McCullough
1986. "Excavations at Xometla (TT21)." In W. T. Sanders, ed., *The Toltec Period Occupation of the Valley*. Part 1, *Excavations and Ceramics. The Teotihuacan Valley Project Final Report*, vol. 4. Occasional Papers in Anthropology no. 13. University Park: Department of Anthropology, Pennsylvania State University, pp. 53–193.

Niederberger, Christine
1996. "Olmec Horizon Guerrero." In E. P. Benson and B. de la Fuente, eds. *Olmec Art of Ancient Mexico*. Washington, DC: National Gallery of Art, pp. 95–103.

Norman, V. Garth
1976. *Izapa Sculpture*. Part 2: *Text*. Papers of the New World Archaeological Foundation no. 30. Provo, UT.

Obermeyer, Gerald
1963. *A Stratigraphic Trench and Settlement Pattern Survey at Oxtotípac, Mexico*. M.A. thesis in Anthropology, Department of Sociology and Anthropology, Pennsylvania State University, University Park.

Ortiz, Ponciano, and Ma. del Carmen Rodríguez
1994. "Los espacios sagrados olmecas: El Manatí, un caso especial." In J. E. Clark, ed., *Los olmecas en Mesoamérica*. Mexico/Madrid: El Equilibrista/Turner Libros, pp. 69–91.

Ovando-Shelley, E., and Linda Manzanilla
1997. "An Archaeological Interpretation of Geotechnical Soundings Under the Metropolitan Cathedral, Mexico City." *Archaeometry* 39, no. 1: 221–235.

Paso y Troncoso, Francisco del
1979. *Papeles de Nueva España. Segunda Serie: Geografía y Estadística, Relaciones Geográficas de la Diócesis de México*. Mexico: Editorial Cosmos.

Pasztory, Esther
1993. "El mundo natural como metáfora cívica en Teotihuacan." In R. F. Townsend, ed., *La antigua América: El arte de los parajes sagrados*. Mexico: Grupo Azabache/The Art Institute of Chicago, pp. 135–145.

Peñafiel, Antonio
1890. *Monumentos del Arte Mexicano Antiguo. Ornamentación, mitología, tributos y monumentos*. Berlin: A. Asher and Co.

Pérez Elías, Antonio
1956. "Las cuevas del Valle de México (su importancia etnohistórica)." *Tlatoani* (Mexico: ENAH, segunda serie, 10 (June): 34–38.

Plunket, Patricia, and Gabriela Uruñuela
1998."Preclassic Household Patterns Preserved Under Volcanic Ash at Tetimpa, Puebla, Mexico." *Latin American Antiquity* 9, no. 4 (December): 287-309.

Rattray, Evelyn Childs
1974. "Some Clarifications on the Early Teotihuacan Ceramic Sequence." In *Actas del XLI Congreso Internacional de Americanistas, México, 2 al 7 de septiembre de 1974*. Mexico: INAH, vol. 1, pp. 364–368.
1991. "Fechamientos por radiocarbono en Teotihuacan." *Arqueología* (Mexico: INAH), segunda época, no. 6 (July-December): 3–18.
n.d.   "The Teotihuacan Ceramic Chronology: Early Tzacualli to Metepec Phases."

Reilly III, F. Kent
1994. "Enclosed Ritual Spaces and the Watery Underworld in Formative Period Architecture: New Observations on the Function of La Venta Complex A." In V. M. Fields, vol. ed., M. G. Robertson, gen. ed., *Seventh Palenque Round Table, 1989*. San Francisco: The Pre-Columbian Art Research Institute, pp. 125–135.

Sahagún, Fray Bernardino de
1968. *Historia General de las Cosas de Nueva España*. Vol. I. Mexico: Editorial Porrúa.

Schele, Linda
1995. "The Olmec Mountain and Tree of Creation in Mesoamerican Cosmology." In *The Olmec World: Ritual and Rulership*. Princeton, NJ: The Art Museum, Princeton University, pp. 105–122.

Scott, Sue
1993. *Teotihuacan Mazapan Figures and the Xipe Totec Statue: A Link Between the Basin of Mexico and the Valley of Oaxaca*. Nashville, TN: Vanderbilt University Pubications in Anthropology no. 44.

Sepúlveda, María Teresa
1973. "Petición de lluvias en Ostotempa." *Boletín del INAH* (segunda época), no. 4, (January-March): 9–20.

Serra Puche, Mari Carmen, and Ludwig Beutelspacher
1994. *Xochitécatl. Guía*. Mexico: INAH/Salvat.

Soruco Sáenz, Enrique
1985. "Una cueva ceremonial en Teotihuacan." Thesis in Archaeology, ENAH, Mexico, D.F.
1991. "Una cueva ceremonial en Teotihuacan y sus implicaciones astronómicas religiosas." In J. Broda, S. Iwaniszewski, and L. Maupomé, eds., *Arqueoastronomía y etnoastronomía en Mesoamérica*. Mexico: UNAM, pp. 291–296.

Spranz, Bodo
1966. *Las pirámides de Totimehuacan: Excavaciones 1964–1965*. Puebla, Mexico: Instituto Poblano de Antropología e Historia.
1967. "Descubrimiento en Totimehuacan, Puebla." *Boletín del INAH* 28 (June): 19–22.
1968. "Die präklassischen Pyramiden von Totimehuacan, Puebla (Mexico)." *Tribus* (Stuttgart: Linden-Museum für Völkerkunde), no. 17 (August): 17–26.

1973. "El preclásico en la arqueología del proyecto Puebla-Tlaxcala." *Comunicaciones Proyecto Puebla-Tlaxcala*, no. 7. Primer Simposio January 29–February 2, 1973. Puebla, Mexico: Fundación Alemana para la Investigación Científica, pp. 63–64.

Sullivan, Thelma D.
1965. "A Prayer to Tlaloc." *Estudios de Cultura Náhuatl* 5: 39–55.

Talavera González, Jorge Arturo, and Juan Martín Rojas Chávez
1994. "Cuetlajuchitlan." *Arqueología* (Mexico: INAH), segunda época, nos. 11–12 (January-December): 47–63.

Taube, Karl A.
1986. "The Teotihuacan Cave of Origin." *Res: Anthropology and Aesthetics* 12 (Autumn): 51–82.
1995. "The Rainmakers: The Olmec and Their Contribution to Mesoamerican Belief and Ritual." In *The Olmec World: Ritual and Rulership*. Princeton, NJ: The Art Museum, Princeton University, pp. 83–103.

Tezozómoc, Fernando Alvarado
1975. *Crónica mexicáyotl*. Mexico: UNAM-IIH.

Thompson, Edward H.
1938. *The High Priest's Grave, Chichén Itzá, Yucatan, Mexico*. Anthropological Series, vol. 27, no. 1. Chicago: Field Museum of Natural History Publication 412.

Tobriner, Stephen
1972. "The Fertile Mountain: An Investigation of Cerro Gordo's Importance to the Town Plan and Iconography of Teotihuacan." In *Teotihuacan: XI Mesa Redonda*. Mexico: SMA, pp. 103–115.

Togno, Juan B.
1903. "Xochicalco. Estudio topográfico y técnico-militar de sus ruinas." In Antonio Peñafiel, ed., *Colección de documentos para la historia mexicana. Documento de Texcoco*. Mexico: Oficina Tipográfica de la Secretaría de Fomento.

Torres Guzmán, Manuel
1972. "Hallazgos en El Zapotal, Ver." *Boletín del INAH*, segunda época, no. 2 (July-September): 3–8.

Townsend, Richard F., ed.
1993. *La antigua América: El arte de los parajes sagrados*. Mexico: Grupo Azabache/The Art Institute of Chicago.

Vargas, Ernesto, ed.
1989. *Las máscaras de la Cueva de Santa Ana Telóxtoc*. Mexico: UNAM-IIA, Arqueología, Serie Antropológica 105.

Villela F., Samuel L.
1989. "Nuevo testimonio rupestre olmeca en el oriente de Guerrero." *Arqueología* (Mexico: INAH), segunda época, no. 2 (July-December): 37–48.

Weitlaner, Roberto, and Juan Leonard
1959. "De la cueva al palacio." In J. R. Acosta, R. Noriega, C. Cook de Leonard, and J. R. Moctezuma, eds., *Esplendor del México antiguo*. Mexico: Centro de Investigaciones Antropológicas de México, pp. 933–956.

3

▼

TEOTIHUACAN AS AN ORIGIN FOR POSTCLASSIC FEATHERED SERPENT SYMBOLISM

SABURO SUGIYAMA

At the time of the Spanish Conquest, the Feathered Serpent was among the principal mythical entities in Mesoamerica. Representations characterized by specific attributes were abundant in sixteenth-century documents on Aztec religion and ritual. Numerous myths and legends associated with this entity had been diffused, especially in the Central Mexican highlands. Among the Aztecs, the Feathered Serpent was called Quetzalcoatl in Nahuatl, after the precious *quetzal*, a bird much esteemed for its long green feathers, and the *coatl*, the name for the serpent. As a god, Quetzalcoatl was associated with the wind, referred to as the sweeper of roads, as well as with dawn and the Morning Star or Venus.

The significance of Quetzalcoatl was further complicated by confusion arising from the existence of priests who were known by the same name. Aztec accounts of the mythico-historical past spoke highly of Ce Acatl Topiltzin Quetzalcoatl, a legendary Toltec priest who was described as a ruler, a god, or sometimes as Venus (e.g., Sahagún 1978; *Codex Chimalpopoca* 1992). Thus, the Postclassic Feathered Serpent seemed to constitute a symbolic complex conflating mythologies as well as political histories. In Mesoamerica, religion and politics were so tightly interwoven that it is often difficult to separate them into their distinct strands. Politics was often conceived metaphorically in terms of the interactions of sacred entities. The Feathered Serpent seems to have been an

The present paper benefited from comments and editorial corrections by Debra Nagao, to whom I am very grateful. I am also thankful to George Cowgill, who made comments on an earlier version of the paper. Misinterpretations and errors, however, remain the sole responsibility of the author. My thanks should also be addressed to Davíd Carrasco, who encouraged and invited me to join in the conference at Princeton.

example of a divine force in the universe used metaphorically to symbolize political power in society (e.g., Carrasco 1982; López Austin 1973).

This mythical-historical entity apparently has roots dating back several centuries, based on the chronology of feathered-serpent representations. However, their meanings and attributes in pre-Aztec times have not been clearly understood, due to the lack of written records from these earlier periods. For the much more remote time of Teotihuacan (100 B.C.E.–650 C.E.; Cowgill 1996), where one of the earliest identified feathered-serpent representations appears without any associated explanatory text, we are less sure how feathered-serpent imagery may have been conceived and employed by society.[1]

The present chapter explores the origins of this legendary entity and discusses the sociopolitical implications of the context of its early appearance at Teotihuacan. I attempt to delineate possible historical continuities or changes in meanings and functions of the Feathered Serpent in Teotihuacan, rather than assuming that the Mesoamerican belief system and related institutions persisted without substantial modification for more than a millennium. I first analyze a variety of feathered-serpent representations at Teotihuacan and relate them to social domains reconstructed on the basis of archaeological contexts. Although the decipherment of meanings involved in Teotihuacan images is hardly specific, certain clusters of distinctive traits associated with this mythical entity may be inferred by making structural analogies and seeking patterns of associated elements, as discussed later. Furthermore, the oldest known representation in Teotihuacan was the focus of a sculptural program covering one of the city's major monuments, the Feathered Serpent Pyramid. Recent excavations of this monument have highlighted the strong political significance of this structure.[2] Thus, feathered-serpent representations make particular sense to me when they are considered explicitly within the political context of Teotihuacan. Based on archaeological and iconographic studies of materials from the metropolis itself, the early Feathered Serpent seems to have been a symbol of political authority associated with militarism and human sacrifice carried out for the Teotihuacan state.

Theories underlying this interpretation state that symbols were essentially social products of conventional linkages relevant exclusively to members of Teotihuacan society and that public symbols, rather than being locked inside people's minds, played a particular role in determining social actions (e.g., Geertz 1973). It seems that the Teotihuacan state purposefully materialized the Feathered Serpent for the first time on a grand scale and spiritualized it through rituals conducted at the monument for political legitimization. I present a specific case of political function of symbols using the earliest example of the feathered-serpent manifestation in Teotihuacan. An analytical reading of the sculptural program on the façade at the Feathered Serpent Pyramid may be especially helpful in broadening our understanding of a state symbolic complex that had been inherited by successive rulers well beyond the collapse of Teotihuacan in Mesoamerica.

FEATHERED SERPENT REPRESENTATIONS IN TEOTIHUACAN

I start with a brief overview of feathered serpent images depicted during about four centuries of urban life (250–650 C.E.). In general, Teotihuacan representations have been described as mythological, animalistic, impersonal, anonymous, abstract, or ahistorical. The Feathered Serpent was one of the most recurrent mythical entities in Teotihuacan. In fact, there is only one representation known of a "realistic" serpent in Teotihuacan (Figure 3.1 [a]). This refers to a serpent with more or less naturalistic features, without fantastic or hybrid traits. All other figures with apparently long, serpentlike bodies include unrealistic features. For the most part, the so-called Feathered Serpent was a creature basically composed of elements combining serpent, bird, jaguar, and crocodile traits. In later periods in Teotihuacan, some representations of this creature likely became further complicated through the addition of aspects of other animals.

In addition to the realistic example and the hybrid creatures, there are also "conservative" representations of serpents with feathers on the body (Figure 3.1 [b–f]). I define the feathered serpent image as a creature with a serpent head, feathered eyes, a curling snout, a wide mouth with a series of inward-curving fangs without incisors or molars, a bifurcated tongue, eyebrows with curled-up ends, a feathered body, and a rattle tail. The Feathered Serpent with these diagnostic traits lasted until the time of the Spanish Conquest, although the style of each element seems to have changed significantly through time.

Feathered serpents defined by this criteria characteristically appear as sculptural elements with three-dimensional heads projecting from the balustrades of staircases in Teotihuacan (Figure 3.2 [a–d]). This convention eventually became a pan-Mesoamerican tradition extending well beyond Teotihuacan in both time and space, as documented in Tula, Chichén Itzá, Tenayuca, Tenochtitlan, and other ritual centers. Paintings of feathered serpents in Teotihuacan were also represented frequently on marginal parts of walls, rather than on central fields, such as on moldings or frames of *tableros* (rectangular panels) or on areas bordering *taludes* (Figures 3.1 [b, c, and e], and 3.3 [c]). This secondary position is particularly common when the entire body of a feathered serpent was depicted. These contexts imply that the Feathered Serpent played a structural role in defining sacred space invested with specific divine attributes. As pointed out by Alfredo López Austin (1990), this tendency may be better understood by Postclassic mythological accounts that Feathered Serpent brought time and structured space into this world. Therefore, they seem to have been represented at the spot defining sacred space in many Mesoamerican sites.

In Teotihuacan, feathered-serpent heads were also used as an independent iconographic element often attached to anthropomorphic figures as if to help identify the figure (Figure 3.4). It was represented in the form of a headdress (Figure 3.5) or as an element attached to headdresses (Figure 3.4 [c]). Feathered serpents were also represented frequently as the main motif on ceramic vessels, in stamps and ceramic plaques or *adornos* used as appliqué emblems on incense burners (Figure 3.6). Feathered serpents in these cases may have been used to express certain attributes of the mythical entity or may have formed part of the social identification code.

Elements associated with the Feathered Serpent contribute to defining the more specific identity of the creature. One major dimension is the militaristic aspect of the Feathered Serpent. However, this is not exclusive to the Feathered

Serpent, because several zoomorphic and anthropomorphic figures—the coyote (C. Millon 1973, 1988b), jaguar (Kubler 1972), bird (von Winning 1948), and butterfly (Berlo 1984)—had military affiliations in Teotihuacan imagery. For example, a figure carrying spears and shield, establishing his military identity, wears a feathered-serpent headdress and a feathered-serpent head at his waist, perhaps further qualifying or categorizing that basic identity (Figure 3.5 [a]). Although this creature bearing martial objects was not often represented in Teotihuacan, mythical serpents found abroad with or without feathers commonly appeared in military contexts.

In contrast to the scarcity of militaristic associations of Feathered Serpent in Teotihuacan itself, feathered serpents are often connected with bloody rituals in the metropolis. On ceramic vessels, feathered-serpent heads are often represented explicitly in association with a heart and/or droplet signs, which probably allude to heart sacrifice and blood respectively (Figure 3.7). In other cases, feathered serpents are depicted in ceremonial scenes, such as scattering rituals, without clear reference to heart sacrifice (Figure 3.3 [c]). Like the Maya, who preferred

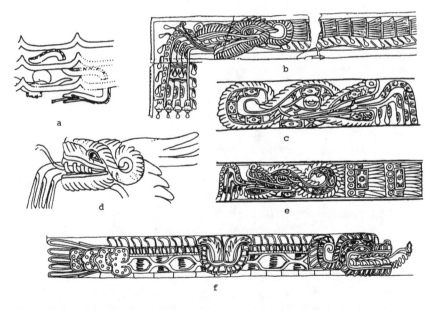

Fig. 3.1. Representation of realistic serpent and conventional, conservative Feathered Serpents; a. Representation of realistic serpent. Drawing by the author from Miller 1973: 73; b. Mural from Techinantitla, drawn by the author at the De Young Museum, San Francisco (after Berrin 1988: 138); c. Mural on altar at Atetelco (after Miller 1973: 164); d. Mural of Mythological Animals. Drawing by the author from Miller 1973: 72; e. Mural on altar at Atetelco (after Miller 1973: 164); f. Mural at Atetelco (after de la Fuente 1995: 216), the Feathered Serpent as the main motif in a *tablero* panel.

to depict victory celebrations culminating in sacrificial rituals instead of actual war scenes, the Teotihuacanos also may have stressed warfare-related rituals in visual presentation more than the wars that often preceded them. Such a perspective appears plausible within the broader Mesoamerican context, given that among the principal aims of warfare was the acquisition of sacrificial victims, rather than carnage on the battlefield.

Feathered serpents were also associated with water and fertility. In fact, water imagery surrounding them and/or flowing from their maws is a recurrent characteristic of this entity. However, in some cases the water symbols are not clearly distinguishable from blood symbols. Water symbols used with shells, suggesting water, also appear frequently in association with hearts; in these instances, the symbols most likely represent blood. Liquid symbols flowing from the mouths of feathered serpents apparently represent water, but they sometimes might have meant blood, particularly in those instances in which the stream is painted red (Figure 3.1 [b]). It is therefore probable that the Teotihuacanos metaphorically equated water and blood.

Feathered serpents in Teotihuacan were also represented as a symbol of authority. In several cases, the Feathered Serpent is shown resting on a mat (Figure 3.8), a symbol of authority and rulership well known throughout Mesoamerica (C. Millon 1988a: 119). Significantly, in Teotihuacan the mat symbol appears almost exclusively with feathered-serpent heads. Another expression of

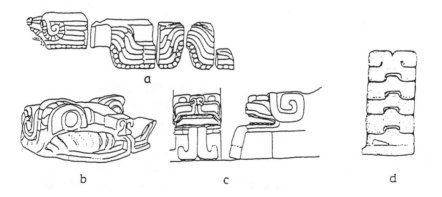

Fig. 3.2. Representation of Feathered Serpents in sculpture; a. Feathered Serpent sculptures discovered at the Quetzalpapalotl Palace. Drawing by the author from Acosta 1964: fig. 15; b. Feathered Serpent head discovered at the Quetzalpapalotl Palace. Drawing by the author from Acosta 1964: fig. 25; c. Serpent head found at the Avenue of the Dead complex. Drawing by the author; d. Carved stone representation of rattle of a serpent or feathered serpent that stood at the foot of balustrades of a staircase in Quetzalpapalotl Palace.

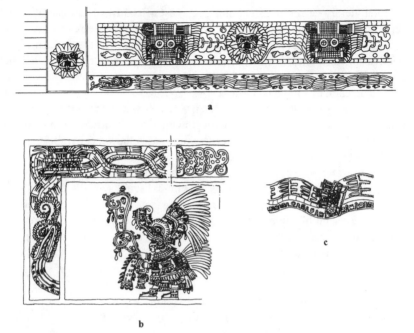

Fig. 3.3. Representations of the Feathered Serpents bearing headdresses on their bodies; a. Sculptures of Feathered Serpents and representations of headdresses at the Feathered Serpent Pyramid (Sugiyama 1989b); b. Representation of a headdress superimposed on the body of the Feathered Serpent, painted in Zacuala Palace. Drawing by the author from Miller 1973: 112–113 and Séjourné 1966a: fig. 9; c. Processional figures bordered by the Feathered Serpent with headdresses attached to its body, painted in Tepantitla. Drawing by the author from Miller 1973: 100.

authority is the association of feathered serpents with headdresses (Figures 3.3 [b–c], 3.4 [b], and 3.8 [c]). The depiction of headdresses as independent icons was so common in Teotihuacan as to suggest that headdresses had a highly specialized significance for that society (Langley 1986: 107–121). Furthermore, Clara Millon's (1973) studies have made a persuasive case for the tassel headdress as a symbol of a Teotihuacan military order or authority abroad. The Feathered Serpent Pyramid would perhaps have been the most striking and dramatic case in which the Feathered Serpent is associated with headdress signs as an expression of authority, which will be discussed in greater detail below.

Apart from these attributes, the Feathered Serpent also seems to have been related to celestial bodies, probably Venus, ever since its early appearance in Teotihuacan iconography. This is suggested by the quincunx sign that appears repeatedly on the body of feathered serpents (Figures 3.1 [c,e], and possibly 3.6 [c]).[3] It was Seler (1963, I: 188–191) who interpreted the quincunx glyph as a Venus representation (Figure 3.9). John Carlson (1991) further proposes that the quincunx symbolized the five cycles of the Venus almanac, which combined with eight cycles of the 365-day "vague year" to represent a long cycle called the Sacred Round. Another calendrical interpretation was put forth by Caso (1967), who identified the function of the quincunx as that of a year bearer (Glyph E) among the Zapotecs. Moreover, the quincunx sign, or the Maya version of the same glyph, known as the Kan-cross (Glyph 281 in Thompson 1962), has been interpreted as a symbol of terrestrial water (von Winning 1987, II: 11, 66) and of turquoise or something "precious" (Thompson 1962: 65–66; Caso 1967: 145, figure 2). Thus, although the specific meaning of the quincunx glyph is still uncertain, the association of Venus with the Feathered Serpent appears to be substantiated.

SYMBOLISM OF THE FEATHERED SERPENT PYRAMID

The review of feathered-serpent representations suggests that a series of divine attributes—warfare, heart sacrifice, water and fertility, authority, and Venus—were probably associated with the Feathered Serpent in Teotihuacan. However, it is difficult to anchor this imagery to the particular historical context in which it was created. Many motifs appear in murals or ceramics discovered in domestic contexts or without any excavation data. They appear to occur in purely mythical scenes and may not have been related to any historical social events or

Fig. 3.4. Representations of the Feathered Serpent used as independent symbols; a. Sculptures of Feathered Serpents and representations of headdresses at the Feathered Serpent Pyramid (Sugiyama 1989b); b. Drawing by the author from Séjourné 1966c: fig. 90; c. Drawing from the original (Sugiyama 1989b: 71); d. Drawing by the author from Caso 1967: fig. 34b.

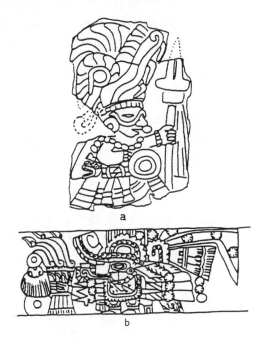

Fig. 3.5. Representations of human figures with the Feathered Serpent headdress, carrying martial objects; a. Ceramic plaques found north of the Ciudadela (Sugiyama 1992: 214); b. Traced from Séjourné 1964: fig. 8.

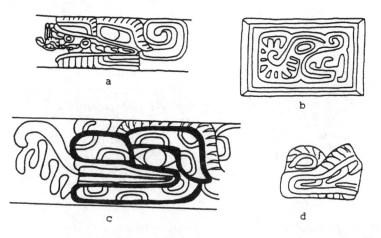

Fig. 3.6. Representations of the Feathered Serpent as the main motif on ceramics; a. Drawing by the author from Séjourné 1966b: fig. 195; b. Drawing by the author from Séjourné 1966c: fig. 140; c. After Séjourné 1959: fig. 25, and von Winning 1987; d. Drawing from original piece found north of the Ciudadela.

institutions. However, the Feathered Serpent Pyramid provides an unusual opportunity to discuss feathered-serpent representations in a specific social and historical context (Figure 3.10). A number of the features mentioned above were already linked to this mythical creature dating back to the time of the erection of the Feathered Serpent Pyramid.

Chronologically speaking, the Feathered Serpent Pyramid seems to have constituted one of the earliest representations of this creature in Mesoamerica. More importantly, the feathered-serpent representation at the pyramid is, unlike other cases, the single central focus of an exceptionally large-scale sculptural program on a major construction in the metropolis. Excavations at the Feathered Serpent Pyramid have provided extensive information on the symbolism of this early monument, in addition to data about chronology, architectural sequence, and modification and destruction processes (Cabrera, Sugiyama, and Cowgill 1991; Sugiyama 1994, 1998). We know that both architectural style and iconography at the pyramid formed the final stages of a single construction program that began with the preparation of the offerings and burial complex discovered at the

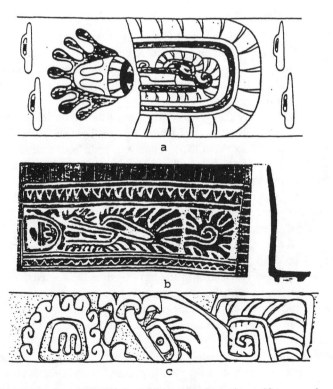

Fig. 3.7. Representations of the Feathered Serpent as the main motif on ceramics; a. After Séjourné 1959: fig. 132; b. After von Winning 1987:vol. 1, 130–131; c. Drawing by the author from Séjourné 1966b: fig. 112.

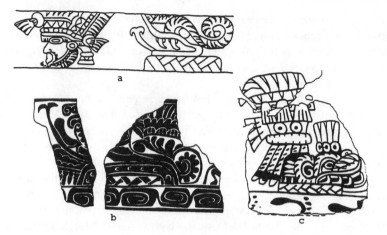

Fig. 3.8. Representation of Feathered Serpents set on mat symbols; a. Drawing by the author from Séjourné 1970: fig. 83; b. Drawing by the author from von Winning 1987:vol. 1: 130–131; c. Drawing from the original by the author (after Berrin 1988: 118).

pyramid. Therefore, it would appear to be a logical expectation to find some sort of coherent ritual meanings linking the architecture, sculptural program, and the burial and offering complexes dedicated to that structure. The following is a summary of what I believe were major ideological components that persisted through the various programs.

First of all, I believe that warfare was one of the fundamental features revealed archaeologically at the Feathered Serpent Pyramid. The Temple of Quetzalcoatl Project discovered that probably more than two hundred soldiers or soldier-priests were sacrificed and dedicated to the erection of the pyramid around 200 C.E. Many of them were found with their hands behind their back as if they were tied and buried unwillingly. We consider most of them to be soldiers, or at least soldier impersonators, based on associated materials. More than twelve hundred projectile points were discovered around not only males, but also in graves for females. Slate disks found at the waist also support their identification as soldiers, since pictorial representations of military figures in Teotihuacan and post-Teotihuacan sites carry them at their waist. Necklaces of human maxillae, real or imitated with shells (Figure 3.11), also suggest the martial aspect of individuals buried at the pyramid. These may have been a sort of war trophy for soldiers, as Mesoamerican ethnohistorical records indicate (Tozzer 1941: 120; Roys 1943: 67).

Another ideological component would be human sacrifice. Victims were not just antagonists of the state who were captured, sacrificed, and buried with their own costume. Rather, they were victims systematically prepared and buried with symbolic objects in order to manifest the significance of human sacrifice itself. Symbolic objects alluding to bloody rituals include obsidian knives

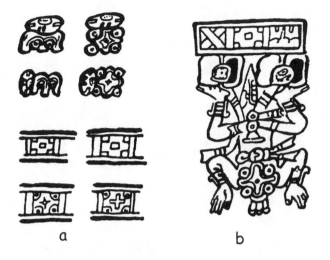

Fig. 3.9. Representation of Venus and its related signs; a. Venus signs and quincunx (after Seler 1963: vol. I: 191; b. The quincunx in the *Codex Dresden*, page 58, also formed a celestial band element (Thompson 1972: 77), from which Venus is descending (after Seler 1963: vol. I: 21).

and curved blades, possibly implements for human sacrifice, and obsidian perforators, ideal for autosacrifice. These items might have been used as tools to sacrifice the individuals with whom they were associated, but they also may have been objects buried symbolically as special paraphernalia or a type of code identifying the interred victims.

Another unique set of symbolic objects associated with the Feathered Serpent Pyramid is composed of obsidian anthropomorphic and zoomorphic figurines, and unidentified eccentrics. I believe these eccentrics blend the figure of a feathered serpent and the basal portion of an obsidian projectile point (Figure 3.12). They perhaps represent feathered serpents being transformed into projectile points, or vice versa. This implies that the Feathered Serpent itself had martial attributes, and that soldiers may have been sacrificed in honor of the Feathered Serpent.

The numbers of individuals deposited in each grave suggest that certain numbers were selected for calendrical or mythological reasons (see Figure 3.10). Recurrent symbolic numbers were 20, 18, 13, 9, and 4, which were all related to solar or ritual calendars or numbers of layers in the upperworld or underworld. This emphasis on a matrix composed of calendrical and cosmological numerals may indicate that the event was related to fundamental conceptions of time and space, such as the initiation of a new era or the recognition of a new cosmic order.

Finally, I believe that the most explicitly manifested theme at the Feathered Serpent Pyramid was rulership. A wooden staff recovered in one of the looted graves represents the Feathered Serpent and may have been used as a scepter by

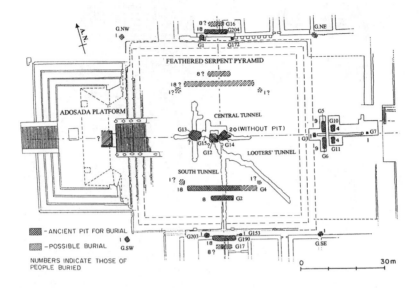

Fig. 3.10. General plan of the Feathered Serpent Pyramid, showing the distribution pattern of the burial complex. Drawing by Kumiko Sugiyama.

the ruling group (Figure 3.13). The previously mentioned tools of autosacrifice were probably also symbols of rulership; it was the duty of rulers and members of the royal family to shed blood to feed the gods in Mesoamerican societies (Stuart 1988). Individuals adorned with exceptionally rich greenstone ornaments and other objects were also discovered, although we believe many of the isolated artifacts found without clear association to a specific individual were anonymously dedicated to the monument. Luxurious objects included twenty-four greenstone nose pendants pertaining to two types, which were often represented in murals or pottery in Teotihuacan (Figure 3.14 [a–d and f]). The most richly adorned anthropomorphic figures in Teotihuacan imagery wear this type of nose pendant with other types of greenstone ornaments that are also identical to those found at the pyramid. A similar type of nose pendant is represented on the façade of the pyramid, which will be discussed in greater detail below. The same types of nose pendant were also worn by Classic Maya elites, apparently as emblems of royal status (Laporte and Fialko 1990: 53; Schele and Grube 1994: 91) (Figure 3.14 [e and g]).

Burial patterns also suggest that royal tombs, in addition to the graves of sacrificial victims, were possibly once part of this burial complex. If so, the pyramid itself would have been seen by the public as a physical resting place of rulership. One of the most probable locations for an elite burial is a pit that was found looted in front of the staircase of the pyramid. Although the deposit was exhaustively looted, several grave features suggest the distinctiveness of the burial. The same pattern of royal tomb location was apparently copied by Maya elites living at Kaminaljuyú (Kidder, Jennings, and Shook 1946). Elite graves

Fig. 3.11. Burial 5-H found with a pendant of real human maxilla on the east side of the Feathered Serpent Pyramid.

reflecting Teotihuacan influence at Kaminaljuyú seem to have been conventionally placed in association with the staircase of a pyramid, probably at the death of the principal individual in each tomb (Figure 3.15). If the practice of renovating monuments in conjunction with elite graves in this Maya city was derived from Teotihuacan, analogies would support the idea that pits found in front of the Feathered Serpent Pyramid were elite tombs rather than part of the sacrificial burial complex.[4]

Another unique grave suggesting rulership at the Feathered Serpent Pyramid was the central grave, containing twenty sacrificed males buried with the richest offerings discovered to date at Teotihuacan in quality, quantity, and variety of artifacts (Figure 3.16). I believe that this was the place where a ruler invested the treasure of the state. The bodies were placed in a highly symbolic manner with primary orientation toward the east. My analyses of spatial distributions of the offerings indicate that the majority of greenstone, obsidian, and shell objects were scattered on the mass of bodies, with certain spatial patterns (Sugiyama 1995). No similar archaeological instances of dedication burials or scattering ritual like this has been reported from Teotihuacan. However, some murals in residential compounds represent richly adorned priests scattering streams of offerings of objects from their hands that are similar to those found in the central grave (Figures 3.3 [c] and 3.14). In Aztec times, scattering precious greenstone objects was a metaphor for the dissemination of precious words "scattered" by elders, or priests, in songs, orations, rituals, and funeral ceremonies, as cited by Sahagún, Durán, and other sixteeth-century chroniclers (Sullivan 1986).

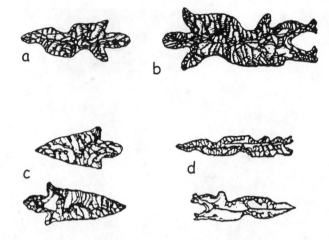

Fig. 3.12. Obsidian objects found at the Feathered Serpent Pyramid. Drawings by Verónica Moreno; a. Possible representation of a feathered serpent tail combined with a projectile point; b. Possible representation of a feathered serpent head combined with a projectile point; c. Typical forms of projectile points found at the Feathered Serpent Pyramid; d. Typical forms of the representation of the Feathered Serpent.

Furthermore, the actual scattering of precious objects may be seen in the offerings buried in the Templo Mayor, the most sacred and politically charged structure of the Aztec empire (López Luján 1994). Perhaps, the ritual that took place at the Feathered Serpent Pyramid was a prototype for Postclassic scattering rituals symbolizing authority.

In conclusion, the archaeological data at the Feathered Serpent Pyramid indicates that a monumental event took place in an early period of the city's history, with mass sacrificial burials dedicated to the Feathered Serpent, and that the burial complex and rich symbolic offerings seem to have had specific ritual meanings metaphorically entailing social implications. The glorification of warfare, human sacrifice, and rulership seem to have been major themes of this state-executed program.

FAÇADE ICONOGRAPHY

After the sacrificial graves were buried in the nucleus of the pyramid, construction work continued and concluded with a sculptural program that covered the façades on all four sides of the pyramid. These façade works were the most explicit manifestation of meaning visible to the public, who nevertheless were most likely aware of the mass interment of sacrificial victims beneath and around the structure. The following interpretation of the messages communicated through the façade imagery may shed light on additional specific·attributes of the Feathered Serpent involved in this social event.

The main figure at the Feathered Serpent Pyramid was evidently the full-bodied version of the Feathered Serpent (Figure 3.3 [a]), depicted as the principal figure on

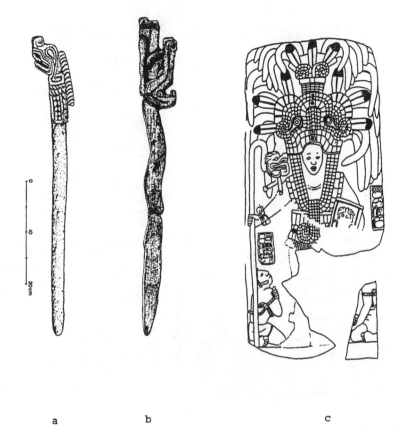

a   b   c

Fig. 3.13. Batons or staffs in the form of a Feathered Serpent; a. Carved wooden baton found complete in a looted grave at the Feathered Serpent Pyramid (Cabrera et al. 1991: fig. 7). Drawing by Maa-ling Chen and the author; b. Feathered serpent baton/scepter recovered from the Cenote of Sacrifice, Chichén Itzá, Yucatán (after Coggins 1992: 266–268); c. A Maya stela that shows a ruler grasping a feathered serpent baton/scepter, from Stela 26 at Piedras Negras (after Schele and Grube 1994: 111).

all four façades, where they filled both *tablero* and *talud* panels. Duality has been the recurrent emphasis of the work of several scholars discussing this pyramid, due to the two alternating three-dimensional "heads" repeated throughout the monument (R. Millon 1976: 237, 238; Coe 1981: 168; Drucker 1974: 16; Taube 1992a). However, when examined in greater detail, these "heads" did not occupy the same position within the context of meanings, so they cannot form a duality. In fact, rather than depicting two heads, the pair of images represent a feathered-serpent head and a zoomorphic headdress. My reading is that the Feathered Serpent is carrying on his body the headdress of the Primordial Crocodile, which

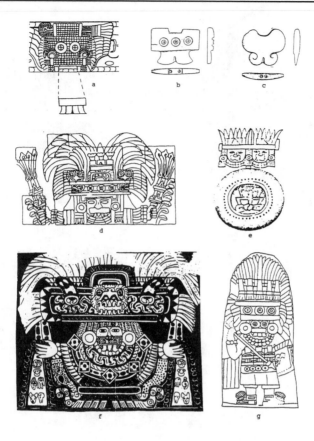

Fig. 3.14. Variety of nose pendants; a. Representation of Primordial Crocodile at the Feathered Serpent Pyramid with a nose pendant; b. Two types of greenstone nose pendants were found at the Feathered Serpent Pyramid. One type consists of a rectangular plaque with a distinctive bifurcated tonguelike projection below it. Drawing by Verónica Moreno; c. Another is the so-called butterfly type. Drawing by Verónica Moreno; d. Sculpture discovered at the Avenue of the Dead complex. Drawing by the author from Morelos 1982: 312; e. Representations of two human heads wearing nose pendants of the type shown in Figure 13c, depicted on the surface of a composite stela found in Tikal. Architecture and iconography associated with the stela indicate Teotihuacan influence (after Laporte and Fialko 1990: 53); f. Mural Painting, a so-called Jade Tlaloc, found at the Tetitla compound (after Berrin and Pasztory 1993: 49); g. Representation of a soldier who wears Teotihuacan-influenced ornaments, including a type of nose pendant shown in Figure 13b. A stela from Yaxhá (after Hellmuth 1975: 60)

had to do with the concept of the "beginning of time." (This aspect will be further discussed below.) The image of the Feathered Serpent with an independent head-dress emblem on its body is known from Teotihuacan murals (Figure 3.3), adding further credence to this interpretation. The zoomorphic headdress occupied a subordinate position to the Feathered Serpent, and provided additional attributes of this entity. I believe that this was a mythical expression of the beginning of a new era with explicit political implications.

The headdress emblems alternating with the feathered-serpent heads are somewhat enigmatic (Figure 3.17 [a]). They can be divided into two sections to facilitate analytical interpretation. The lower half of the headdress (area II of Figure 3.17 [a]) represents the head of a mythical creature lacking a lower jaw and which I called the Primordial Crocodile, an ancestral form of the Late Postclassic Mexican *cipactli*, a crocodilian earth monster with calendrical attributes as the

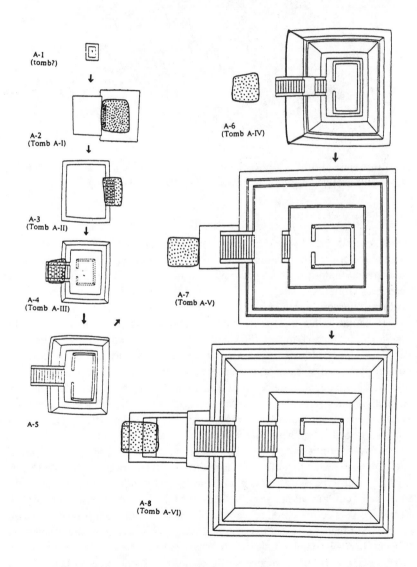

Fig. 3.15. Plan showing the process of modification at Structure A in Kaminaljuyú. Drawing by the author. Data are taken from Kidder, Jennings, and Shook 1946.

Fig. 3.16. Central section of a grave found at the center of the Feathered Serpent Pyramid, showing the distribution of offerings (after Sugiyama 1993: 119).

first date of the Aztec year. The upper half (area I of Figure 3.17 [a]) depicts the headdress worn by this mythical animal. In Mesoamerican imagery, animal heads are conventionally used for headdresses, which in turn have their own smaller headdress (Figures 3.3 [c], 3.17 [b and e]). Part of a double headdress at the Feathered Serpent Pyramid had a typical Teotihuacan form and may have had calendrical attributes, as suggested by its iconographic components, such as the bow-and-knot sign (Langley 1986: 165). When combined with two calendrical variables, the headdress head takes on a strong calendrical significance as a possibility. This may be parallel to Zapotec calendar signs in which a headdress formed a component, together with a day sign below it (Figure 3.17 [g]). This writing system was established in Monte Albán, the capital of a state friendly to Teotihuacan (Flannery and Marcus 1983: 161–162; R. Millon 1973: 42), at least by 200 C.E., when the Feathered Serpent Pyramid was constructed.

Below the representation of the Primordial Crocodile and within the mouth cavity, a nose pendant, similar to those found in the pyramid, is shown (Figure 3.14 [a]). This type of nose pendant is worn by richly-adorned anthropomorphic figures in Teotihuacan imagery, perhaps as an identification code (Figure 3.14 [d and f]). This combination of elaborated headdress and nose pendant not associated with a face was in fact a common central motif in many Teotihuacan images (Figure 3.18). This complex of symbols may have served in the identification of a person, group, or other social entity connected with authority in Teotihuacan society.

Generally speaking, the Feathered Serpent at the pyramid was represented in a watery underworld setting suggested by shell representations. Alfredo López

Austin, Leonardo López Luján, and Sugiyama (1991) proposed that the Feathered Serpent functioned as the initiator of the calendrical division and the extractor of the divine-temporal-destiny force at the Postclassic centers and probably also at Teotihuacan. The feathered-serpent image on the pyramid seems to have been emerging from the watery underworld through mirrors, which Taube (1992b) interprets as symbols of vital passageways for divine communication with the world of the living. This cosmogenic meaning seems to have been manifested for the first time around 200 c.e. at the Feathered Serpent Pyramid in an unprecedented monument.

As a whole, the façade seems to have celebrated a mythical event in which the Feathered Serpent was the culture bearer of a symbolic complex associated with the beginning of time or the calendar evoked by the emblem of the Primordial Crocodile headdress. It was the commemoration of a new era that was expressed overwhelmingly in mythological terms. Given the aforementioned archaeological information clearly indicating the involvement of the state apparatus to coordinate such a colossal ritual undertaking, the sociopolitical dimensions underlying this mythical expression require further exploration. The representation of the headdress and the special nose pendant at the Feathered Serpent Pyramid may have symbolized the sacred authority of the specific ruler who orchestrated the erection of the pyramid.[5] This political proclamation was situated in the context of the domination of the most fundamental value system: the time-reckoning complex. One particular ruler in the course of Teotihuacan's history seems to have established a form of legitimization, in which the Feathered Serpent was considered the divine entity imbued with the power to invest the living bearer (a ruler) with this headdress and nose pendant as emblems of rulership. In fact, the artistic expression of the transferal of political authority by means of a headdress granted by former authorities—whether a sacred entity, an ancestral king, or sometimes a ruler's mother—seems to have been one of the distinct pictographic strategies preferred by Mesoamerican elites (Figure 3.19). The Feathered Serpent Pyramid was probably one of the earliest example of governmental proclamation coordinated by a ruler associated with the Feathered Serpent/ Quetzalcoatl in Mesoamerica, linking his divine rulership with the ritual display of warfare and human sacrifice on an unprecedented scale.

CONCLUSION

This view of feathered-serpent symbolism at Teotihuacan focuses on the sociopolitical dimension. I believe that my reading of the façade imagery at the Feathered Serpent Pyramid is supported by the archaeological findings at the pyramid. The foundation event of this unique pyramid took place only once in an early stage of city formation in Teotihuacan, and a ruler was probably responsible for this state-sponsored ideological program. Rich individual-oriented offerings explicitly symbolizing divine authority and evidence of associated rituals strongly indicate that an individual ruler placed political hegemony under the emblem of the Feathered Serpent, although we have not yet been able to identify this ruler's body archaeologically. Thus, the association of the Feathered Serpent/Quetzalcoatl with a ruler or a group of rulers in Teotihuacan reminds us of

Postclassic legendary rulers described in the codices as the incarnation of the Feathered Serpent.

As suggested by iconographic information from the later phases at Teotihuacan, the symbolism of divine authority established at the Feathered Serpent Pyramid seems to have continued for the next four centuries at Teotihuacan, although sociopolitical circumstances may have significantly changed over the

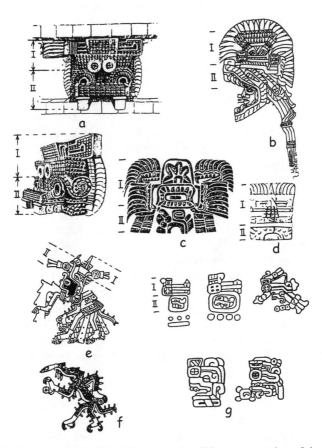

Fig. 3.17. Representations of headdresses; a. Possible representation of the Primordial Crocodile in the form of headdress at the Feathered Serpent Pyramid (Caso and Bernal 1952: fig. 184); b. Representation of Feathered Serpent in the form of headdress (drawing from von Winning 1979: fig. 24a); c. Representation of "reptile eye" and a headdress that may have been an abstract form of the Primordial Crocodile (after von Winning 1987: 70–78); d. "Manta" compound as a combination of "reptile eye" and a "headdress" including a year sign (after von Winning 1987: 78–79); e. Representation of Cipactli, which wears a headdress of year sign (after *Códice Borgia*: 1963: lám. 38); f. Representation of Cipactli, without headdress (after *Códice Borgia*: 1963: lám. 51); g. Representations of a headdress with year Bearer M, according to Urcid 1992: 139.

course of time.[6] The erection of the Feathered Serpent Pyramid also appears to have had an impact on Teotihuacan's contemporaries, such as the Maya. In contexts indicating Teotihuacan influence in Maya areas, there are substantial parallels with symbol sets found at the Feathered Serpent Pyramid. After the collapse of Teotihuacan, this cultural heritage associated with feathered-serpent symbolism seems to have persevered to a certain degree in Late Classic and Postclassic ritual centers such as Cholula, Cacaxtla, Xochicalco, Tula, and others in the Mexican highlands. By the time the Aztecs took over the region, more than eight hundred years had passed after the decline of Teotihuacan. By then, the ruined metropolis, probably an origin of the feathered-serpent symbolism, had become a

Fig. 3.18. Teotihuacan representations of headdresses with a nose pendant but with no face depicted; a. Offering scene mural at the so-called "Temple of Agriculture." Behind a cremation scene, an anthropomorphic figure wearing a headdress and a nose pendant of type B is depicted without face (after Miller 1973: 63); b. Representation on pottery of a headdress with a nose pendant of the type (Figure 14b) we found at the Feathered Serpent Pyramid (after Séjourné 1966b: fig. 95); c. Abstract stone sculpture of headdress, a nose bar and earspools without face (after Berrin and Pasztory 1993: 172); d. The central figure in the so-called Tlalocan mural at Tepantitla (after von Winning 1987, vol. 1: 138–139).

legendary place. Postclassic mythical accounts of the Feathered Serpent often hark back to the timeless past, in which the correlation of legendary accounts with historical events remains ambiguous. Consequently, we wonder to what extent Aztec myths about Quetzalcoatl can transmit chronological and spatial specifics. However, material-based archaeology indicates that these timeless legends may have had deep historical roots, dating at least back to 200 C.E. The Feathered Serpent seems to have been established, since its very inception, as a mythical entity legitimizing rulers' political authority before society. As far as is archaeologically known to date, the place of origin of this specific symbolism was Teotihuacan.

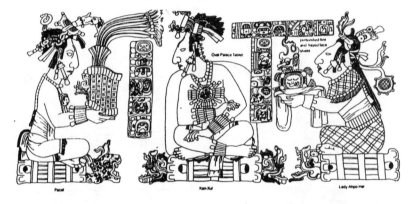

Fig. 3.19. Palace Tablet from Palenque, Chiapas, Mexico. Kan-Xul King (center) preferred to depict himself as being given the emblems of the office he is assuming. In this accession scene, his father, Pacal King (left), is giving his son the Drum-Major headdress with a large Jester God, the sign of kings (after Schele and Miller 1986: 115).

Notes

1. The cult of Feathered Serpent seems to have existed since the Middle Preclassic times (Joralemon 1971: 82–84). However, only a few pre-Teotihuacan instances that may be identified as feathered serpents are known from Olmec sites, while serpent representations are recurrent. They are significantly different from those from the Central Mexican highlands that I discuss here. In addition, the cases do not provide precise spatial, temporal, and contextual information, with which their ritual meanings and sociopolitical implications could be argued. An exceptional case (Monument 19 at La Venta) was persuasively discussed by Taube (1987), who identifies the quetzal-serpent in association with a human figure.

2. Sources mentioned herein are mainly from a joint project coordinated by the Mexican Institute of Anthropology and History and Arizona State University with funding from the National Geographic Society, the National Endowment for the Humanities, the National Science Foundation, the Arizona State University Foundation, and others. With Rubén Cabrera as director, George L. Cowgill of Arizona State University, Carlos Serrano of the Universidad Nacional Autónoma de México, and myself are preparing excavation

and analysis reports for publication (Cabrera et al. 1989; Cabrera, Sugiyama, and Cowgill 1991). The interpretations I mention here are discussed in greater detail in another publication (Sugiyama 1995). Other project members may or may not agree on all points I make, so I accept responsibility for the opinions expressed herein. In addition to these publications, a handy way to access new information on our project is available on the Internet (*http://archaeology.la.asu.edu/teo*).

3. The relationship of the Feathered Serpent with Venus is also suggested by the discovery of a mural in the Great Plaza in the Ciudadela (Cabrera 1992: figure 6). A row of double cross signs, each with a disk at its center, is painted on the *tableros* of this structure. This sign is reminiscent of representations of Venus in the *Vienna Codex* (Caso 1950). In Mixtec codices (Seler 1963, II: figure 118), a similar sign is attached as the symbol to Tlahuizcalpantecuhtli, god of Venus. Analogous symbols were also found at a Teotihuacan-style building in Tikal (Pasztory 1978: 109). In Yaxhá, a similar sign was represented on the body of an obviously Teotihuacan-type serpent, that is, overlapping with a sacrificial knife (Miller 1991: plate 4). Although the mural found in the Ciudadela has not been dated, it is logical to suppose that the mural formed an integral part of the symbolism of the Ciudadela for a certain period. These data support the idea that the Feathered Serpent Pyramid was associated with Venus, probably since the early date of this monumental construction.

4. I also believe that a grave pit might still exist under the staircase of the Feathered Serpent Pyramid. This is suggested by the fact that the upper part of the staircase and its lateral walls had once been damaged by the extraction of stone blocks, which were later repaired with small lava stones and typical Teotihuacan concrete. The evidence of destruction seems to me to indicate that a grave pit was prepared under the staircase after the completion of the pyramid, or that a grave pit covered by the pyramid was originally located under the staircase and was later looted (Sugiyama 1989a).

5. The case reminds me of the representations of Motecuhzoma II in the *Codex Mendoza* (1992, III: 38, folio 15v), to which the representations of a headdress and nose pendant were attached for his identification.

6. The Feathered Serpent Pyramid seems to have been destroyed well before the decline of the city. Architectural modification programs and the looting activities at the pyramid may reflect the changing ideological and sociopolitical transformation of Teotihuacan society (Sugiyama 1998).

REFERENCES

Acosta, Jorge R.
1964. *El Palacio del Quetzalpapalotl*. Mexico: INAH, Memorias, 10.

Berlo, Janet C.
1984. *Teotihuacan Art Abroad: A Study of Metropolitan Style and Provincial Transformation in Incensario Workshops*. 2 vols. Oxford: BAR International Series 199 (i and ii).

Berrin, Kathleen, ed.
1988. *Feathered Serpents and Flowering Trees: Reconstructing the Murals of Teotihuacan*. San Francisco: The Fine Arts Museums of San Francisco.

Berrin, Kathleen, and Esther Pasztory, eds.
1993. *Teotihuacan: Art from the City of the Gods*. New York: Thames and Hudson/The Fine Arts Museums of San Francisco.

Cabrera Castro, Rubén
1992. "A Survey of Recently Excavated Murals at Teotihuacan." In J. C. Berlo, ed., *Art, Ideology, and the City of Teotihuacan*. Washington, DC: Dumbarton Oaks, pp.113–128.

Cabrera Castro, Rubén, Saburo Sugiyama, and George L. Cowgill
1991. "The Temple of Quetzalcoatl Project at Teotihuacan: A Preliminary Report." *Ancient Mesoamerica* 2, no. 1: 77–92.

Cabrera Castro, Rubén, George L. Cowgill, Saburo Sugiyama, and Carlos Serrano
1989. "El Proyecto Templo de Quetzalcóatl." *Arqueología* (Mexico: INAH) 5: 51–79

Carlson, John B.
1991. *Venus-Regulated Warfare and Ritual Sacrifice in Mesoamerica: Teotihuacan and the Cacaxtla "Star Wars" Connection*. College Park, MD: Center for Archaeoastronomy Technical Publication no. 7.

Carrasco, Davíd
1982. *Quetzalcoatl and the Irony of Empire: Myths and Prophecies in the Aztec Tradition*. Chicago: University of Chicago Press.

Caso, Alfonso
1950. "Explicación del reverso del *Codex Vindobonensis.*" *Memoria de El Colegio Nacional* (Mexico) 5, no. 6:1–46.
1967. *Los calendarios prehispánicos*. Serie de Cultura Náhuatl, monografía 6. Mexico: UNAM.

Caso, Alfonso, and Ignacio Bernal
1952. *Urnas de Oaxaca*. Mexico: INAH, Memorias, 2.

Códice Borgia
1963. Mexico: FCE.

Codex Chimalpopoca
1992. *History and Mythology of the Aztecs: The Codex Chimalpopoca*. Translated from the Nahuatl by J. Bierhorst. Tucson: The University of Arizona Press.

Codex Mendoza
1992. Edited by F. F. Berdan and P. R. Anawalt. 4 vols. Berkeley: University of California Press.

Coe, Michael D.
1981. "Religion and the Rise of Mesoamerican States." In G. D. Jones and R. R. Kautz, eds., *The Transition to Statehood in the New World*. Cambridge: Cambridge University Press, pp. 157–171.

Coggins, Clemency, ed.
1992. *Artifacts from the Cenote of Sacrifice, Chichén Itza, Yucatan*. Cambridge, MA: Peabody Museum of Archaeology and Ethnology, Harvard University.

Cowgill, George L.
1996. "Discussion." *Ancient Mesoamerica* 7, no. 2: 325–331.

Drucker, R. David
1974. "Renovating a Reconstruction: The Ciudadela at Teotihuacan, Mexico: Construction Sequence, Layout, and Possible Uses of the Structure." Ph.D. dissertation, University of Rochester, N.Y. Ann Arbor, MI: University Microfilms.

Flannery, Kent V., and Joyce Marcus
1983. "Monte Albán and Teotihuacan: Editors Introduction." In K. Flannery and J. Marcus, eds., *The Cloud People: Divergent Evolution of the Zapotec and Mixtec Civilizations*. New York: Academic Press, pp.161–166.

de la Fuente, Beatriz
1995. *La pintura mural prehispánica en México: I Teotihuacán, Tomo I Catálogo*. Mexico: UNAM-IIE.

Geertz, Clifford
1973. "Thick Description: Toward an Interpretive Theory of Culture." In *The Interpretation of Cultures*. New York: Basic Books, pp.3–30.

Hellmuth, Nicholas M.
1975. *The Escuintla Hoards: Teotihuacan Art in Guatemala*. Guatemala: Foundation for Latin American Anthropological Research.

Joralemon, Peter D.
1971. *A Study of Olmec Iconography*. Washington, DC: Dumbarton Oaks.

Kidder, Alfred V., Jesse D. Jennings, and Edwin M. Shook
1946. *Excavations at Kaminaljuyu, Guatemala.* Washington, DC: Carnegie Institution Publication no. 501.

Kubler, George
1972. "Jaguars in the Valley of Mexico." In E. P. Benson, ed., *The Cult of the Feline*. Washington, DC: Dumbarton Oaks, pp. 19–50.

Langley, James C.
1986. *Symbolic Notation of Teotihuacan: Elements of Writing in a Mesoamerican Culture of the Classic Period*. Oxford: BAR International Series 313.

Laporte, Juan Pedro, and Vilma Fialko C.
1990. "New Perspectives on Old Problems: Dynastic References for the Early Classic at Tikal." In F. S. Clancy and P. D. Harrison, eds., *Vision and Revision in Maya Studies*. Albuquerque: University of New Mexico Press, pp. 33–66.

López Austin, Alfredo
1973. *Hombre-dios: Religión y política en el mundo náhuatl*. Mexico: UNAM.
1990. *Los mitos del tlacuache: Caminos de la mitología mesoamericana*. Mexico: Alianza Editorial.

López Austin, Alfredo, Leonardo López Luján, and Saburo Sugiyama
1991. "The Feathered Serpent Pyramid at Teotihuacan: Its Possible Ideological Significance." *Ancient Mesoamerica* 2, no. 1: 93–106.

López Luján, Leonardo
1994. *The Offerings of the Templo Mayor of Tenochtitlan*. Trans. B. R. Ortiz de Montellano and T. Ortiz de Montellano. Niwot: University Press of Colorado.

Miller, Arthur. G.
1973. *The Mural Painting of Teotihuacán*. Washington, DC: Dumbarton Oaks.

Miller, Victoria E.
1991. *The Frieze of the Palace of the Stuccoes, Acanceh, Yucatan, Mexico*. Washington, DC: Dumbarton Oaks.

Millon, Clara.
1973. "Painting, Writing, and Polity in Teotihuacan, Mexico." *American Antiquity* 38: 294–313.
1988a. "A Reexamination of the Teotihuacan Tassel Headdress Insignia." In K. Berrin, ed., *Feathered Serpents and Flowering Trees: Reconstructing the Murals of Teotihuacan*. San Francisco: The Fine Arts Museums of San Francisco, pp. 114–134.
1988b. "Coyote with Sacrificial Knife." In K. Berrin, ed., *Feathered Serpents and Flowering Trees: Reconstructing the Murals of Teotihuacan*. San Francisco: The Fine Arts Museums of San Francisco, pp. 207–217.

Millon, René
1973. *Urbanization at Teotihuacan, Mexico.* Vol. 1, *The Teotihuacan Map*. Part 1, *Text*. Austin: University of Texas Press.

1976. "Social Relations in Ancient Teotihuacán." In E. R. Wolf, ed., *The Valley of Mexico: Studies in Pre-Hispanic Ecology and Society.* Albuquerque: University of New Mexico Press, pp. 205–248.

Morelos, Noel

1982. "Exploraciones en el área central de la Calzada de los Muertos al norte del Río San Juan, dentro del llamado Complejo Calle de los Muertos." In R. Cabrera C., I. Rodríguez G., and N. Morelos G., eds., *Memoria del Proyecto Arqueológico Teotihuacan 80–82.* Mexico: INAH, vol. 1, pp. 271–320.

Pasztory, Esther

1978. "Artistic Traditions of the Middle Classic Period." In E. Pasztory, ed., *Middle Classic Mesoamerica: A.D. 400–700.* New York: Columbia University Press, pp. 108–142.

Roys, Ralph L.

1943. *The Indian Background of Colonial Yucatan.* Washington, DC: Carnegie Institution.

Sahagún, Fray Bernardino

1978. *Florentine Codex: General History of the Things of New Spain.* Book 3. Trans. A. J. O. Anderson and C. E. Dibble. Santa Fe, NM: The School of American Research/ University of Utah.

Schele, Linda, and Nikolai Grube

1994. *Notebook for the XVIIIth Maya Hieroglyphic Workshop at Texas.* Austin: University of Texas Press.

Schele, Linda, and Mary Ellen Miller

1986. *The Blood of Kings: Dynasty and Ritual in Maya Art.* New York: G. Braziller.

Séjourné, Laurette

1959. *Un palacio en la ciudad de los dioses.* Mexico: INAH.
1964. "La simbología del fuego." *Cuadernos Americanos* 135, no. 4: 149–178.
1966a. *Arquitectura y pintura en Teotihuacan.* Mexico: Siglo Veintiuno Editores.
1966b. *Arqueología de Teotihuacan: La cerámica.* Mexico: FCE.
1966c. *El lenguaje de las formas en Teotihuacan.* Mexico.
1970. *Pensamiento y religión en el México antiguo.* 2nd ed. Mexico: FCE.

Seler, Eduard

1963. *Comentarios al Códice Borgia.* 2 vols. Mexico: FCE.

Stuart, David

1988. "Blood Symbolism in Maya Iconography." In E. Benson and G. Griffin, eds., *Maya Iconography.* Princeton, NJ: Princeton University Press, pp.175–221.

Sugiyama, Saburo

1989a. "Burials Dedicated to the Old Temple of Quetzalcoatl at Teotihuacan, Mexico." *American Antiquity* 54, no.1: 85–106.
1989b. "Iconographic Interpretation of the Temple of Quetzalcoatl at Teotihuacan." *Mexicon* (Berlin) 9, no. 4: 68–74.
1992. "Rulership, Warfare, and Human Sacrifice at the Ciudadela, Teotihuacan: An Iconographic Study of Feathered Serpent Representations." In J. C. Berlo, ed., *Art, Ideology, and the City of Teotihuacan.* Washington, DC: Dumbarton Oaks, pp. 205–230.
1993. "Worldview Materialized in Teotihuacan, Mexico." *Latin American Antiquity* 4, no. 2: 103–129.
1996. "Mass Human Sacrifice and Symbolism of the Feathered Serpent Pyramid in Teotihuacan, Mexico." Ph.D. dissertation, Anthropology Department, Arizona State University.

1998. "Termination Programs and Prehispanic Looting at the Feathered Serpent Pyramid in Teotihuacan, Mexico." In S. Mock, ed., *The Sowing and the Dawning: Dedication and Termination Events in the Archaeological and Ethnographic Record of Mesoamerica.* Albuquerque: University of New Mexico Press, pp. 146-164.

Sullivan, Thelma D.
1986. "A Scattering of Jades: The Words of Aztec Elders." In G. H. Gossen, ed., *Symbol and Meaning Beyond the Closed Community: Essays in Mesoamerican Ideas.* Albany: Institute for Mesoamerican Studies, SUNY, pp. 9–17.

Taube, Karl
1987. "Early Representations of the Feathered Serpent in the Gulf Coast Region." Paper presented at the 86th Annual Meeting of the American Anthropological Association.
1992a. "The Temple of Quetzalcoatl and the Cult of Sacred War at Teotihuacan." *Res: Anthropology and Aesthetics* 21: 53–87.
1992b. "The Iconography of Mirrors at Teotihuacan." In J. C. Berlo, ed., *Art, Ideology, and the City of Teotihuacan.* Washington, DC: Dumbarton Oaks, pp.169–204.

Thompson, J. Eric S.
1962. *A Catalog of Maya Hieroglyphs.* Norman: University of Oklahoma Press.
1972. *A Commentary on the Dresden Codex.* Philadelphia: American Philosophical Society.

Tozzer, Alfred M.
1941. *Landa's Relación de las Cosas de Yucatán.* Papers of the Peabody Museum of Archaeology and Ethnology, Harvard University, vol. 18. Cambridge, MA.

Urcid Serrano, Javier
1992. *Zapotec Hieroglyphic Writing.* 2 vols. Ph.D. dissertation, Yale University, New Haven, CT.

von Winning, Hasso
1948. "The Teotihuacan Owl and Weapon Symbol and Its Association with 'Serpent Head X' at Kaminaljuyú." *American Antiquity* 14, no. 2: 129–132.
1979. "The 'Binding of the Year' and the 'New Fire' in Teotihuacan." *Indiana* 5: 15–32.
1987. *La Iconografía de Teotihuacan: Los dioses y los signos.* 2 vols. Mexico: UNAM.

4

THE ICONOGRAPHY OF THE FEATHERED
SERPENT IN LATE POSTCLASSIC CENTRAL MEXICO

H. B. NICHOLSON

One of the most striking icons ever developed in pre-Hispanic Mesoamerica, an area co-tradition noted for the richness and variety of its symbolic art, was the Feathered Serpent. This fantastic hybrid creature was, at the time of the Conquest in Central Mexico, known in Nahuatl, the dominant language of the region, as Quetzalcoatl. Quetzalcoatl literally meant "quetzal feather" (*quetzalli*)/ "snake" (*coatl*). This union of the precious green feathers of a bird, symbolizing the celestial realm, and a dangerous, slithering reptile, connoting the terrestrial sphere, this fusion of earth and sky—as in many cosmogonies—signified, above all, fertility and creativity. Certainly the deity known by this name played a major role in the cosmogonic myths, particularly in the creation of mankind and human sustenance. Creativity is the most positive manifestation of fertility, and Quetzalcoatl—particularly in his aspect as Ehecatl ("wind")—epitomized this fundamental core of the late pre-Hispanic Central Mexican religious system, both conceptually and in propitiatory ritual.

According to a rich corpus of ethnohistorical narratives, a great priest-ruler of Tollan bore, among other names and titles, including Topiltzin (Our Honored Prince), that of Quetzalcoatl, of whose cult he was reputed to have been a particular devotee. Apart from the question of some possible genuine historicity in the Topiltzin Quetzalcoatl of the Tollan tale—concerning which there has been much difference of opinion—there is considerable evidence that Motecuhzoma Xocoyotzin (Huey Tlatoani of Mexico Tenochtitlan), 1502/03–1520 C.E., was held

All figures and photographs, unless otherwise noted, are from the UCLA Aztec Archive, most of them taken by the author.

to be the direct dynastic descendant of the Toltec ruler who bore this name/title and who was believed to have been the ultimate founder and legitimist of the political order that prevailed in Central Mexico at the advent of Cortés (Nicholson 1957; 1978: 297; Carrasco 1982).

The nature of the relationship between the deity Ehecatl Quetzalcoatl and the semilegendary Toltec ruler Topiltzin Quetzalcoatl is a problem of considerable complexity (Nicholson 1979). Although for analytic purposes it is convenient to distinguish them, it is clear that at least by the time of the Conquest the two had become partially fused—which is particularly evidenced by portrayals of the Toltec ruler displaying elements of the costume and insignia of the deity Ehecatl Quetzalcoatl. This blending probably applied also to the feathered-serpent icon, which in some contexts might primarily connote the creator-fertility-wind deity and in others the Toltec dynastic founder-patron—and in still others perhaps aspects of both.

Although prototypical forms of the Feathered Serpent possibly appear in western Mesoamerica as early as the Preclassic (e.g., Taube 1995), it is at Teotihuacan, probably late in its second major phase, Miccaotli, or early in its third, Tlamimilolpa (i.e., ca. the third century C.E.), that fully developed representations of rattlesnakes with bodies covered with feathers clearly made their appearnce—most dramatically in both relief and three-dimensional stone sculpture on the seven-staged Pyramid of the Feathered Serpent in the center of the Ciudadela. Many other depictions of this avian/ophidian creature are known, primarily on ceramic vessels and wall paintings, throughout the site's history (see, especially, von Winning 1987, vol. 1: 69–70, 125–133). Whatever its precise conceptual connotations—concerning which there are diverse views—the Feathered Serpent clearly functioned as an important icon in the complex religious ideological system of the great Classic civilization of Teotihuacan.

After the demise of Teotihuacan, feathered-serpent imagery persisted, especially via Cacaxtla and Xochicalco (where another, smaller Pyramid of the Feathered Serpent displayed its image in a bold, dramatic fashion, rivaling its counterpart at Teotihuacan) into Toltec. The ubiquity of the feathered-serpent motif in the art and architecture of this Early Postclassic civilization and its congener in Yucatán is well known (see, especially, Tozzer 1957: figs. 105–115, 118–127, 129–132B). Most innovative was the feathered-serpent column, which constituted a striking feature of Toltec-style buildings at both Tula (Tollan), Hidalgo, and approximately contemporaneous Chichén Itzá in Yucatán (Kubler 1982).

In post-Toltec times, the Feathered Serpent continued to play a prominent role in the art and iconography of Late Postclassic Central Mexico—and now a wealth of ethnohistorical sources can be utilized to aid in understanding its ideological significance. What is most remarkable about the imagery of this icon in this final pre-Hispanic period is the range and variety of its manifestations, significantly greater than in any of the earlier traditions out of which it evolved. The remainder of this paper will be largely devoted to a survey and description—tapping the resources of the University of California at Los Angeles's Aztec Archive—of the diverse categories into which "Aztec"-style representations of the Feathered Serpent can be divided.

AZTEC-STYLE FEATHERED SERPENTS

The most frequent images of this icon among the surviving archaeological pieces dating to this epoch are the three-dimensional stone sculptures, often superbly carved, of coiled feathered serpents (e.g., Gutiérrez Solana Rickards 1987: láminas 22–23, 35–38, 52–58; Nicholson and Quiñones Keber 1983: figs. 57–60). Stone sculptures of coiled serpents in Central Mexico go back to Teotihuacan, but they are extremely rare until the Late Postclassic, when they proliferate. The forked tongue is standard; occasionally it is combined with the stone knife, or *tecpatl* (Figure 4.1). They sometimes display, behind the creature's head and usually in a square cartouche, the date Ce Acatl (1 Reed), the special calendric sign associated with Quetzalcoatl (Figure 4.2). One large piece, in the Museo de Santa Cecilia Acatitlan, Mexico City (Solís Olguín 1976: fig. 63), displays behind the head, now missing, the *ehecacozcatl*, or "wind jewel"—the sliced conch shell pectoral that is a standard item in the insignia of Ehecatl Quetzalcoatl. These coiled feathered snakes (e.g., that illustrated in Figures 4.1 and 4.2) also frequently display on their undersides—as do many other Aztec stone sculptures—representations of the earth monster, Tlaltecuhtli, or Earth Lord (Nicholson 1967; Nicholson and Quiñones Keber 1983: 60–61, 139–141).

On some pieces, human faces peer out of the open serpentine jaws, occasionally wearing the *epcololli*, the distinctive curved white shell ear ornaments of the deity (e.g., Nicholson and Quiñones Keber 1983: fig. 60, pp. 143–144). Another somewhat mutilated example, a large specimen found in Mexico City in the eighteenth century, uniquely features a stone knife-tongue fronting the *atl tlachinolli*, or "sacred war" symbol (Figure 4.3). In an interesting subgroup of these coiled feathered serpents, the faces wear the buccal "wind mask" of the

Fig. 4.1. Coiled feathered serpent. Museo Arqueológico Apaxco, Estado de México.

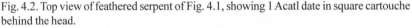

Fig. 4.2. Top view of feathered serpent of Fig. 4.1, showing 1 Acatl date in square cartouche behind the head.

wind deity Ehecatl, a major aspect of Quetzalcoatl (e.g., Baer and Bankmann 1990: 142–143; Didrichsen Art Museum 1968: 891).

The function of these coiled feathered serpents is uncertain. The larger ones possibly served as the princpal "idol" in a shrine dedicated to Quetzalcoatl. In the case of the one for which some information is available concerning its principal image, the temple of Quetzalcoatl in Cholollan, the paramount center of the cult of this deity in Mesoamerica at the time of contact, it was clearly an anthropomorphic representation of Ehecatl Quetzalcoatl (Durán 1995, II: 70–78, lám. 13). The relatively small size of most of these coiled feathered snakes might rather suggest that they served as subsidiary cult images in sacred structures, probably including temples dedicated to Quetzalcoatl—and this may also have been the case with the plain coiled serpents, of which there are also numerous surviving examples (e.g., Gutiérrez Solana Rickards 1987: láms. 20–21, 24–25, 28–34, 39–43, 47–51, 61–63; Nicholson and Quiñones Keber 1983: figs. 50–51, 54–56).

Colossal three-dimensional plumed-serpent heads used as architectural embellishments, of a type which may have originated in Teotihuacan and was particularly developed in Toltec and Toltec-related centers, continued to be important in Late Postclassic Tenochtitlan, especially as adornments of the Templo Mayor, together with other types of serpent heads, (e.g., Gutiérrez Solana Rickards 1987: láms. 73–74) (Figure 4.4). Blocky, highly stylized serpent heads with feather trimming also served as architectural adornments (e.g., Bolz 1975: tafeln CV-CVI) (Figure 4.5), but these are quite distinct in configuration from those just mentioned and probably had distinct conceptual connotations as well. Whether feathered-serpent columns of the Toltec type continued is problematic; none, at least, have so far been reported.

Two-dimensional relief carvings of feathered serpents continued to be important in this period. They closely resemble the few representations of the creature extant in the ritual/divinatory painted screenfolds and colonial manuscript copies thereof, such as that on *Codex Borbonicus* 14 (Figure 4.6). A particularly

Fig. 4.3. Coiled feathered serpent with "stone knife tongue" and *atl tlachinolli*, "sacred war" symbol. Museo Nacional de Antropología, Mexico City.

Fig. 4.4. Colossal feathered serpent head attached to the foot of the southern stairway ramp of the Stage IVb Templo Mayor of Huitzilopochtli and Tlaloc, Mexico-Tenochtitlan. Discovered by Manuel Gamio in 1913.

Fig. 4.5. Colossal stylized serpent head. Museo Nacional de Antropología, Mexico City. Discovered in Mexico City in the eighteenth century.

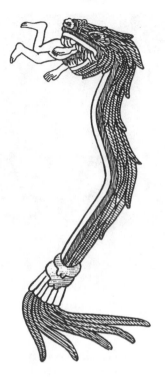

Fig. 4.6. Feathered serpent, co-regent, with Xipe Totec, of the fourteenth *trecena* of the *tonalpohualli*, commencing with 1 Itzcuintli (dog). *Codex Borbonicus* (Anders, Jansen, and Reyes García 1991), p. 14. From Seler 1904–1909, II: abb. 260.

Fig. 4.7. Drawing of lid of "Box of Hackmack." Museum für Völkerkunde, Hamburg. From Seler 1902–1923, II: 733, abb. 22.

Fig. 4.8. Side A, "Stone of Acuecuexatl." Museo Nacional de Antropología, Mexico City.

good example is carved on the so-called Box of Hackmack, in the Museum für Völkerkunde, Hamburg, accompanied by two of the calendric signs particularly associated with Quetzalcoatl: 1 Acatl and 7 Acatl (e.g., Nicholson and Quiñones Keber 1983: fig. 15, pp. 64–66) (Figure 4.7). Clear delineation of the ventral scales, prominent, voluted supraorbital plates, and feather headdresses and "taildresses" are a frequent feature of these relief depictions of the Feathered Serpent.

Three feathered serpents of a somewhat different type are carved in relief on three faces of a small parallelepiped, of unknown provenience, published by von Winning (1961, figs. 5, 7, and 11). The upper face displays the 4 Ollin (Movement) day sign, connoting the sun. The angular, undulating bodies of the feathered serpents are decorated with rectangular elements instead of feathers, but they display elaborate feather headdresses and collars. Attached to their bodies are volute motifs that von Winning, following Beyer and Krickeberg, interpreted as clouds, comparing them to similar motifs on the bodies of the undulating feathered serpents of the Pyramid of the Feathered Serpent at Xochicalco.

Four excellent examples of feathered serpents are also depicted on the large stone quadrangular monument known as the Stone of Acuecuexatl, found in 1924 when the old slaughterhouse off the Plaza San Lucas in the southern part of Mexico City was demolished (e.g., Alcocer 1930, 1935: 96–100; Wicke 1984; Quiñones Keber 1993). They accompany two representations of Ahuitzotl (Huey Tlatoani of Mexico Tenochtitlan), 1486–1502 C.E. One (Side A: Figure 4.8) is depicted to the rear of this ruler, who sits crossed-legged in profile, drawing blood from his ear with a pointed bone implement, before a leafy framework enclosing what appears to be a variant of the *zacatapayolli*, the ritual grass ball

Fig. 4.9. Side B, "Stone of Acuecuexatl." Museo Nacional de Antropología, Mexico City.

into which bloodstained perforators were thrust. The date 7 Acatl, in a square cartouche, is depicted above it. The other, slightly differently configured feathered serpent, on the other side (Side B: Figure 4.9), is fronted by another depiction of the same ruler, in the same pose and before the same leafy framework and the same date. Both human figures are identified by their well-known name signs, the semimythical aquatic creature, the *ahuitzotl*.

On the narrower top surface of the monument (Figure 4.10) is another image of the feathered serpent, facing what appears to be another version of the Ahuitzotl name sign. The serpent displays a stone knife-tongue, and its undulating body is decorated with prominent circles-within-circles, probably connoting precious greenstones, or *chalchihuitl*. Another similar feathered serpent, the fore part of whose jaws is missing, is depicted on the right side of the stone (Figure 4.11).

Nearly the whole left portion of the monument is missing, but the very small portion that remains indicates that another human figure, holding what appears to be an incense pouch, was represented on the other side of the leafy framework. The identity of this lost figure can only conjectured, but, judging from other scenes involving versions of the *zacatapayolli* that depict complementary pairs of rulers or other high-ranking personages flanking it and performing autosacrifice (e.g., Figure 4.14), it may have been another elite personage.

Alcocer, noting the presence of the date 7 Acatl, which he equated with 1499 C.E., believed that the monument commemorated completion of an aqueduct that was intended to bring additional water to Mexico Tenochtitlan from five springs, the principal one of which was called Acuecuexatl or Acuecuexco, south of the city near Coyoacan. Alcocer's hypothesis, in essence, has been accepted by many other students, including García Payón, Lizardi Ramos, Umberger, Pasztory, Wicke, and Klein. However, as I pointed out some years ago (Nicholson 1955: 14–16), he made various errors in his interpretations of the iconography of the monument, and I questioned whether the depictions on the stone really had any connection with the Acuecuexatl aqueduct. Quiñones Keber (1993), who undertook the most detailed critique of Alcocer's interpretation, definitely rejected it in favor of a possible connection of the monument with a round temple to Quetzalcoatl excavated nearby in the late 1960s, while stressing the importance of Quetzalcoatl as a dynastic patron of Tenochca royalty to possibly account for the depiction of his icon in intimate association with Ahuitzotl.

Certainly the depictions on this monument appear to indicate some special connection between Ahuitzotl and Quetzalcoatl, perhaps in the year 1499, the fourteenth of his reign—although the presence here of 7 Acatl could alternatively be explained as a date known to be particularly associated with this deity

Fig. 4.10. Top, "Stone of Acuecuexatl." Museo Nacional de Antropología, Mexico City.

Fig. 4.11. Right side, "Stone of Acuecuexatl." Museo Nacional de Antropología, Mexico City.

and not that of a particular year. The loss of nearly all of the left half of the stone greatly adds to the difficulty of correctly interpreting it. If this missing portion is ever located, hopefully a more positive interpretation can be achieved. In any case, the four depictions of feathered serpents on this monument constitute some of the most stylistically typical and at the same time intriguing Late Postclassic Central Mexican versions of this creature that have survived.

The "patron" position of the feathered serpent, undulating behind or to the rear of a human figure, that appears as early as Cacaxtla and which is particularly common in Toltec art (e.g., Covarrubias 1957: fig. 118), occurs, in addition to its presence on the Ahuitzotl monument just discussed, on a Late Postclassic cliff sculpture on what is known as the Cerro de la Malinche, near the site of Tula, Hidalgo (Figure 4.12). The profile human figure, wearing the sacred priestly jacket, the *xicolli*, and carrying an incense pouch, is drawing blood from his ear with a jeweled maguey spine and is identified by the date 1 Acatl. It has been suggested (e.g., Nicholson 1955: 17–19; Quiñones Keber 1993: 153) that the figure was intended to represent Topiltzin Quetzalcoatl, the traditional ruler of the nearby imperial Toltec center. The undulating feathered serpent behind him is close in configuration to other Aztec-style examples, while displaying a somewhat rare feature: stone knives with "demon faces" incorporated into its feathered body (cf. *Codex Vaticanus A* 1979: folio 6r).

Another striking example of the Feathered Serpent as patron is depicted on the imitation of an Early Postclassic X Fine Orange (Silho) pedestal cylindrical vessel found in Offertory Cache 14 in the platform fronting the stairway of Stage IVb of the Templo Mayor of Huitzilopochtli and Tlaloc in Mexico Tenochtitlan

Fig. 4.12. Drawing of relief carving on face of rocky cliff, Cerro de la Malinche, near site of Tula, Hidalgo. From Meyer 1939.

Fig. 4.13. Drawing of portion of banquette relief carving. Templo Mayor of Huitzilopochtli and Tlaloc, Mexico Tenochtitlan. Museo Nacional de Antropología, Mexico City. Discovered by Manuel Gamio in 1913. From Beyer 1955: fig. E.

Fig. 4.14. Drawing of central portion of Templo Mayor banquette relief carving (see caption to Figure 4.13).

(e.g., Nicholson and Quiñones Keber 1983: 96, fig. 30). In the carved panel on this vessel the creature undulates behind a profile figure that appears to be a version of the deity Tezcatlipoca (a very unusual association). Interestingly, in view of the stone knives decorating the body of the feathered serpent of the Cerro de la Malinche cliff relief, mentioned above, another patron serpent image on a similar vessel found in nearby Offertory Cache 10 is decorated with what appear to be stone knives rather than feathers (Nicholson and Quiñones Keber 1983: 95, fig. 29).

One of the earliest appearances of the icon being discussed in this paper, at Teotihuacan, was as an undulating feathered serpent framing a larger scene as a

Fig. 4.15. Carved slab discovered in or near Calle de las Escallerillas, Mexico City, 1900/01. Museo Nacional de Antropología, Mexico City.

Fig. 4.16. Left side, "Stone of the Warriors," discovered in 1897 in the southwest corner of the Zócalo, Mexico City. Museo Nacional de Antropología, Mexico City.

border image—and this position of the creature was also common on a frequent feature of Toltec architecture, projecting cornices above benches, or banquettes, that feature polychromed relief carvings of processions of warrior figures. Fragments of similar banquette reliefs were discovered in 1900–1901 in Mexico City in connection with the Calle de las Escalerillas excavations (Seler 1902–1923, II: 893, abb. 96–97), then many more by Manuel Gamio in 1913 in the southwest corner of the Templo Mayor (Beyer 1955) (Figures 4.13 and 4.14). Intact examples of the banquettes were uncovered in the Stage V rooms adjacent to and below the Precinct of the Eagle Warriors north of the Templo Mayor during the 1978–1982 Proyecto Templo Mayor (Matos Moctezuma 1988: 38–39). They closely imitated the earlier Toltec examples, complete to the undulating feathered serpents on their cornices. Very similar feathered serpents are featured on the four edges of a large rectangular slab found in 1900–1901 near the Calle de las Escalerillas (Seler 1902–1923, II: 892–893, abb. 95) (Figure 4.15)—and on a similar piece still embedded in the top of the Stage IVb platform that fronts the Templo Mayor (López Portillo, León Portilla, and Matos Moctezuma 1981: 187).

A parallel format, a procession of fourteen marching warriors converging on a *zacatapayollii*, below an upper border strip comparable to a cornice that features undulating feathered serpents, is carved on the four sides of a massive, somewhat battered parallelepiped discovered in 1897 in the foundations of a colonial building in the southwest corner of Mexico City's Zócalo during the construction of the Centro Mercantil, a large department store. On each side were depicted two types of feathered serpents, one with fully feathered body and the other with a plain body but sharing feathered crests and tails with the other type (Figure 4.16).

The significance of these bordering feathered serpents presents a considerable problem. Quiñones Keber has suggested that "although the feathered serpent is usually associated with the concepts of creativity and agricultural fertility, . . . in this context the placement of feathered serpents above the warriors . . . suggests the role of the feathered serpent as a supernatural patron of warrior activities and a possible beneficiary of the sacrificial event alluded to," citing

Fig. 4.17. Carved cylindrical monument (*cuauhxicalli?*) found in 1905 in Mexico City. Museo Nacional de Antropología, Mexico City. Photo provided by the museum.

"earlier associations of the feathered serpent with warfare and sacrifice, a recurrent Early Postclassic motif of architectural reliefs and fresco painting at such sites as Chichén Itzá and Tula, as well as the Late Classic site of Cacaxtla" (1993: 150).

Another striking monument from Mexico Tenochtitlan that bears an expertly executed relief carving of a pair of feathered serpents facing each other, bifurcated tongues touching, is a cylinder with a shallow concave depression on its top surface, perhaps a special type of *cuauhxicalli*, the vessel for sacrificed hearts and blood (Figure 4.17). It was found in 1905 in the foundations of the old convent of Santa Isabel, at the corner of Cinco de Mayo and Bolívar streets, four blocks west of the Zócalo. A very similar, somewhat smaller piece, reportedly from Tlatelolco (ex-Armour collection), is in the Chicago Natural History Museum (Figure 4.18). Both of these cylindrical monuments display plaited strips as upper and lower borders. Some years ago I photographed, in the Museo Nacional de Antropología *bodega* at Teotihuacan, a somewhat more crudely carved cylinder with a similar format of two feathered serpents meeting tongue to tongue (these photos are presently in the UCLA Aztec Archive).

Another sculpture, of green diorite, reportedly from the Basin of Mexico (ex-Armour collection), in the Chicago Natural History Museum represents a human face peering from an open serpent's mouth (Holmes 1897: plate LVI). Two human figures, one on each side, are depicted drawing blood from their ears with a bone perforator. A full-bodied feathered serpent, in typical late Aztec style, is carved on the top and rear surfaces of the piece (Figure 4.19).

Two well-carved greenstone images that appear to represent aspects of the deity bear on their backs typical late Aztec-style depictions of the Feathered Serpent. One image (British Museum, ex-Bullock collection; Baquedano 1984: 26–28, fig. 1) is an anthropomorphic figure wearing the *epcololli* curved-shell ear ornaments of Quetzalcoatl and a solar disk collar. The undulating feathered

Fig. 4.18. Roll-out of relief carving of one of the feathered serpents on a cylindrical monument, reportedly from Tlatelolco, in the Chicago Museum of Natural History. Photo courtesy of the museum (ex-Armour collection). Cf. Figure 4.17.

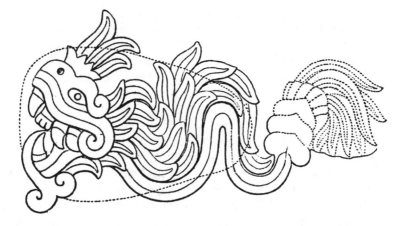

Fig. 4.19. Drawing of feathered serpent carved on the upper and back surface of a green diorite sculpture, reportedly from the Basin of Mexico, of a human head peering from a reptilian mouth. Chicago Museum of Natural History. From Holmes 1897: fig. 121.

serpent on the back is fairly standard, while the body is decorated with what are apparently cloud motifs (cf. those on the parallelepiped published by von Winning [1961], described above, and the Pyramid of the Feathered Serpent, Xochicalco).

The other image (Württembergisches Landesmuseum, Stuttgart; e.g., Seler 1902–1923, III: abb. 1–5) is a skeletal figure displaying various of the insignia of Quetzalcoatl, including the *epcololli*, and also bearing a solar disk on its back. Above the disk is a profile head of the feathered serpent, in typical style (Figure 4.20).

The UCLA Aztec Archive contains many more examples of Late Postclassic Central Mexican feathered serpents, but those just described should provide a reasonably representative sample of the most important types of this icon. Again, the considerable variety in the imagery of this fantastic creature in this area and time period is remarkable, particularly because what has survived obviously represents only a fraction of what was once extant. This variety reflects both the pantheonic importance of this ancient deity as well as the richness and diversity of Aztec iconography in general. And, as has been brought out above, a political aspect was probably also a significant factor, with the paramount rulers of the region, those of Mexico Tenochtitlan, claiming direct dynastic descent from Topiltzin Quetzalcoatl of Tollan, the traditional fountainhead of all "legitimate" royal authority in Late Postclassic Central Mexico.

One hallmark of Aztec civilization was its ability to synthesize successfully and express in diverse forms the complex iconographic and ideological traditions it had inherited from earlier civilizations. The feathered-serpent iconography was a typical example of this. Although obviously most directly derived from the most proximate of these earlier cultural traditions, the Toltec, the ultimate roots of the icon clearly went back, as part of the "Classic heritage" of Late Postclassic Central Mexico, to the first great civilization of this area, that of Teotihuacan. And, as the manner of depicting the feathered rattlesnake further evolved through the Epiclassic and Postclassic, it proliferated and diversified until, in Aztec culture, it achieved its greatest variety and range of expression.

The often beautifully carved three-dimensional coiled feathered serpents constitute the most strikingly original versions of the icon in this period—but some of the two-dimensional depictions (especially those in Figures 4.7, 4.8, 4.16, 4.17, and 4.19), although less innovative, convey equally effective expressions of the creature. The feathered serpent is Mesoamerica's best known symbol of cosmic duality. It also connotes one of its most important and complex deitiies, as well as the most mysterious and intriguing legendary ruler of ancient Mexico. Ironically, some of its most memorable images were produced not long before the arrival of Cortés/Quetzalcoatl, as he has been called, whose appearance signaled the death of Mesoamerica's outstanding artistic tradition, overall unquestionably the greatest in the history of the pre-European Western Hemisphere.

Fig. 4.20 Drawing of feathered serpent head on back of greenstone skeletal image. Württembergisches Landesmuseum, Stuttgart. From Seler 1902–1923, III: 393, abb. 4a.

REFERENCES

Alcocer, Ignacio

1930. "Piedras que hablan de nuestro pasado: Piedra de Acuecuexatl." *Revista de Revistas* (Mexico), no. 1059 (August 17): 51.

1935. *Apuntes sobre la antigua México-Tenochtitlan.* Tacubaya, Mexico: Instituto Panamericano de Geografía e Historia, vol. 14.

Anders, Ferdinand, Maarten Jansen, and Luis Reyes García

1991. *El Libro del Cihuacoatl, Homenaje para el año del Fuego Nuevo: Libro explicativo del llamado Códice Borbónico. Codex de Corps Legislatif, Bibliothèque de l'Assemblèe Nationale Française, Paris, Y 120.* Códices Mexicanos, III. Madrid/Graz/Mexico: SEC/ADV/FCE.

Baer, Gerhard, and Ulf Bankmann

1990. *Altmexikanische Skulpturen der Sammlung Lukas Vischer, Museum für Völkerkunde Basel.* [Ancient Mexican Sculptures from the Lukas Vischer Collection, Ethnographic Museum Basel.] Corpus Americanensium Antiquitatum. Union Académique Internationale. Basel: Verlag Wepf und Co.

Baquedano, Elizabeth

1984. *Aztec Sculpture.* London: Published for the Trustees of the British Museum by British Museum Publications Ltd.

Beyer, Hermann

1955. "La procesión de los señores, decoración del teocalli de piedra en México-Tenochtitlan." *El México Antiguo* 8: 1–42.

Bolz, Ingeborg

1975. *Meisterwerke altindianischer Kunst: die Sammlung Ludwig im Rautenstrauch-Joest-Museum Köln.* Recklinghausen: Verlag Aurel Bongers.

Carrasco, David

1982. *Quetzalcoatl and the Irony of Empire: Myths and Prophecies in the Aztec Tradition.* Chicago and London: University of Chicago Press.

Codex Borbonicus

1991. See Anders, Jansen, and Reyes García.

Codex Vaticanus A

1979. *Codex Vaticanus A* ("Cod. Vat. A," "Cod. Ríos"). Der Biblioteca Apostolica Vaticana. Farbreproduktion des Codex in Verkleinertem Format. Codices Selecti, Phototypice Impressi, vol. 65. Graz: ADV.

Covarrubias, Miguel

1957. *Indian Art of Mexico and Central America.* New York: Borzoi Books, Alfred A. Knopf.

Didrichsen Art Museum

1968. *Catalogue.* Helsinki: Oy Tilgmann Ab.

Durán, Fray Diego

1995. *Historia de los Indias de Nueva España e Islas de Tierra Firme.* Estudio preliminar Rosa Camelo y José Rubén Romero. 2 vols. Mexico: CNCA, Dirección General de Publicaciones.

Gutiérrez Solana Rickards, Nelly

1987. *Las serpientes en el arte Mexica.* Mexico: UNAM, Coordinación de Humanidades, Colección de Arte no. 40.

Holmes, William H.
1897. *Archeological Studies Among the Ancient Cities of Mexico*. Part II, *Monuments of Chiapas, Oaxaca and the Valley of Mexico*. Anthropological Series, vol. 1, no. 1. Chicago: Field Columbian Museum Publication 16.

Kubler, George
1982. "Serpent and Atlantean Columns: Symbols of Maya-Toltec Polity." *Journal of the Society of Architectural Historians* 41, no. 2: 93–115.

López Portilla, José, Miguel León Portilla, and Eduardo Matos Moctezuma
1981. *El Templo Mayor*. Mexico: Bancomer.

Matos Moctezuma, Eduardo
1988. *Obras maestras del Templo Mayor*. Mexico: Fomento Cultura Banamex.

Meyer, Enrique
1939. "Noticia sobre los petróglifos de Tula, Hgo." *Revista Mexicana de Estudios Antropológicos* 3, no. 2: 122–128.

Nicholson, H. B.
1955. "Aztec Style Calendric Inscriptions of Possible Historical Significance: A Survey." Duplicated paper prepared for the symposium of the Sociedad Mexicana de Antropología on Pre- Hispanic Mesoamerican Calendric Systems, December, Castillo de Chapultepec, Mexico, D.F.
1957. "Topiltzin Quetzalcoatl of Tollan: A Problem in Mesoamerican Ethnohistory." Ph.D. dissertation, Athropology Dept., Harvard University, Cambridge, MA.
1967. "A Fragment of a Relief Carving of the Earth Monster." *Journal de la Société des Américanistes* 56, no. 1: 81–94.
1978. "Western Mesoamerican Historical Traditions and the Chronology of the Postclassic." In C. W. Meighan and R. E. Taylor, eds., *Chronolgies in New World Archaeology*. New York: Academic Press, pp. 185–329.
1979. "Ehecatl Quetzalcoatl vs. Topiltzin Quetzalcoatl of Tollan: A Problem in Mesoamerican History and Religion." In *Actes du XLIIe Congrès International des Américanistes: Congrès du centenaire: Paris, 2-9 septembre 1976*. Paris: Société des Américanistes, vol. 6, pp. 35–47.

Nicholson, H. B., and Eloise Quiñones Keber
1983. *Art of Aztec Mexico: Treasures of Tenochtitlan*. Washington, DC: National Gallery of Art.

Quiñones Keber, Eloise
1993. "Quetzalcoatl as Dynastic Patron: The 'Acuecuexatl Stone' Reconsidered." In J. de Durand-Forest and M. Eisinger, eds., *The Symbolism in the Plastic and Pictorial Representations of Ancient Mexico: A Symposium of the 46th International Congress of Americanists, Amsterdam, 1988*. Bonn: Holos Verlag, pp. 149–155.

Seler, Eduard
1902–1923. *Gesammelte Abhandlungen zur Amerikanischen Sprache- und Altertumskunde*. 5 vols. Berlin: A. Asher und Co/Behrend und Co.
1904–1909. *Codex Borgia, eine altmexikanische Bilderschrift der Bibliothek der Congregatio de propaganda fide, hrsg. auf Kosten Seiner Excellenz des Herzogs von Loubat. Erläutert von Dr. Eduard Seler*. 3 vols. Berlin: Druck von Gebr. Unger.

Solís Olguín, Felipe R.
1976. *Catálogo de la escultura Mexica del Museo de Santa Cecilia Acatitlan*. Mexico: INAH.

Taube, Karl A.
1995. "The Rainmakers: The Olmec and Their Contribution to Mesoamerican Belief and Ritual." In *The Olmec World: Ritual and Rulership*. Princeton, NJ: The Art Museum, Princeton University, pp. 83–103.

Tozzer, Alfred M.
1957. *Chichen Itza and Its Cenote of Sacrifice: A Comparative Study of Contemporaneous Maya and Toltec*. Memoirs of the Peabody Museum of Archaeology and Ethnology, Harvard University, vol. 12: Reference Material and Illustrations. Cambridge, MA.

von Winning, Hasso
1861. "A Relief Decorated Aztec Stone Block." *El México Antiguo* 9: 461–472.
1987   *La iconografía de Teotihuacan: Los dioses y los signos*. 2 vols. Mexico: UNAM-IIE, Estudios y Fuentes del Arte en México no. 47.

Wicke, Charles R.
1984. "Escultura imperialista Mexica: El Monumento de Acuecuexatl de Ahuitzotl." *Estudios de Cultura Náhuatl* 17: 51–61.

▼

5

From Teotihuacan to Tenochtitlan

City Planning, Caves, and Streams of Red and Blue Waters

Doris Heyden

The Sources

The world of the people of ancient Mexico was part of nature itself, where the celestial bodies, fire and water, trees, caves, and mountains were deified; they were often considered sacred ancestors. But other sacred ancestors were real people, real places. One of these places was Teotihuacan, whose prestige as the axis mundi, the center of the world, was adopted and adapted centuries after Teotihuacan's efflorescence, by Tenochtitlan. I suggest that this continuity, with some changes, was carried out through oral tradition in the form of myth, by possible contact with material remains such as architecture and painted murals, and by relations with other ethnic groups. After their long migration from Aztlan-Chicomoztoc-Colhuacan to the Basin of Mexico, the Aztecs aligned themselves (for a time) with the Toltecs of Colhuacan, thereby acquiring instant and prestigious ancestors whose roots went back to Teotihuacan. I will deal with this heritage later. Meanwhile, in order to indicate that oral, written, painted, and sung references to ancestors and past glories claimed by the Aztecs were present in the formation of the history of these people—real or imagined—I cite some historical chronicles. Well-known sources are Fray Bernardino de Sahagún, Diego Durán, Fray Toribio de Benavente (known as Motolinía), Francisco de las Navas, Fernando de Alva Ixtlilxochitl, the *Historia de México*, and the *Historia de los mexicanos por sus pinturas*, to name a few.

We'll start with a modern historian, Jan Vansina, author of *La tradición oral* (1968), who claims that part of history has been preserved in verbal transmission, either spoken or sung; such transmissions are usually passed from generation to generation and become aids in the reconstruction of the past. Among peoples called literate, states Vansina, many historical sources, especially those rooted deeply in the past, have had their origin in oral tradition. In these groups, the memory becomes highly developed and traditions are transmitted in a disciplined manner and, following certain formulas, by specialists who are in charge of history, myths, traditions, and customs. That is, they constitute a kind of living library (Heyden 1989: 32–37). Among the Mexica, they would be called *tlamatime*, or "wise men, scholars" (Karttunen 1983: 281); one was *nemiliztlacuiloani*, "the historian" (Molina 1944: 68); a *teoyomacani*, "priest"; a *tlacuilo*, or "scribe" who conveyed knowledge through his paintings; a *toltecatl*, or "artisan, teacher" (Siméon 1988: 713). Oral and visual education was carried out not only in the schools but also in the homes. Histories were repeated over and over, both in family groups and in public. The *huehuetlatolli*, "words of the elders," existed as a norm for advice from parents to their children, and from the sovereign to his people and to the gods. These also glorified the rulers. Sahagún's informants placed an *N* (for *nombre*, or "name") where the name of the person or persons addressed were to be, thus indicating that these wise words were part of a pattern, to be filled in according to the occasion. This suggests that they must have been of long standing, probably with roots in earlier cultures.

Myths were incorporated into oral representations, whether ritual or theater, and found their way into pictorial art—mural painting, ceramic decoration, sculpture, architecture, and textile design—where they told of creation, the greatness of forebears, the hardships of migration, wars and conquests, the stars and their earthly reflections, calendrical events, gods and heroes. In short, myth and its close companions, ritual and symbol, cannot be divorced from historical fact in pre-Hispanic Mexico.

Various chronicles written in the sixteenth century mention myths and traditions inherited from earlier cultures. This heritage would have been in both oral and visual form, the latter in cult objects and sacred documents. The pictorial manuscripts, for example, "tenían memoria de sus antiguallas, así como linajes" [they remembered their ancient history and lineages through the use of pictorial codices] (Motolinía 1971: 210). Navas (n.d.: 155) tells us that the genealogy of the lords could be traced back to the beginning of the world. In order to distinguish themselves from the commoners, these men of high birth had songs composed that extolled the family tree and the feats of their ancestors. These songs were sung in public or in temples (Navas n.d.: 140, 156; *Historia de los mexicanos por sus pinturas* 1973:142).

To distinguish themselves from "people of low birth" the great lords used devices and insignia that exalted their ancestors' deeds and the "grandeur of their origins and of their genealogical tree, which were always esteemed and respected" by these noblemen (Navas n.d.: 156). Myths that spoke of ancestors, gods, and outstanding past events were inherited by one generation from a previous one. The "Myth of the Creation of the Fifth Sun," for example, originated with "the predecessors" (200).

For the reconstruction of history, nothing is clearer than a statement made by Fernando de Alva Ixtlilxochitl, descendant of Nezahualcoyotl and the royal houses of Texcoco and Teotihuacan, who wrote a history of his people and the region in the seventeenth century. Ixtlilxochitl claimed that the arduous task of reconstructing this pre-Conquest history was possible only because he had managed to rescue some ancient documents that had, in their paintings, information about "kings and illustrious persons" as well as geographical features, laws, temples, priests, deities, ceremonies, and the calendar—works of "philosophers and wise men" who had been in charge of "all the sciences known to them" (1985, 1: 524–529). An extraordinary contribution to recorded history made by Don Fernando in his work is the explanation that the information presented in pictorial form in the codices was "read" by the *tlamatime*, the "learned priests," by stimulating their memory or understanding of the images in combination with the *cantares*, the "ritual songs," whose words and rhythm clarified much of the pictorial material. As Ixtlilxochitl stated, he collected not only the codices but also the songs because they complemented each other: the visual images "gave true meaning to the songs, since these were composed with metaphors, similies, and allegories," and only by studying both codices and cantares together could he understand what they meant (1985, I: 525). I think this combination of two means of communication, common at least among the Aztecs and possibly earlier (though we have no ritual songs registered from earlier periods that I know of, they must have been passed on from one group or generation to another by oral tradition), is important and has not been sufficiently explored. Elizabeth Boone, however, in *Writing Without Words* (1994: 72) cites León Portilla, who in turn refers to a Nahuatl scholar:

> I sing the pictures of the book
> and see them spread out;
> I am an elegant bird
> for I make the codices speak
> within the house of pictures.

As another invaluable source of information, archaeology has unearthed many secrets of the past. This is vital in tracing back the Teotihuacan heritage recieved by Tenochtitlan. Other scholars with more knowledge than I discuss the archaeological remains both in Teotihuacan and in the Templo Mayor (see Matos Moctezuma and others in this volume).

THE PLANNING OF A SITE: HOW DID TEOTIHUACAN INFLUENCE TENOCHTITLAN?

The planning of a city is fequently based on a concept of the cosmos; it is the microcosmos, mirror of the macrocosmos (Wheatley 1969: 19; Eliade 1959: 26–27). The founding of a settlement can be seen as designating a sacred space, which then grows to encompass secular areas. In many cultures, geomancy—divination by means of natural geographic features and the heavenly bodies in order to locate an appropriate site for a religious-political center—has also been a determinant in the founding of cities (Heyden 1989: 43). Furthermore, an important element in the founding of an area that is sacred or profane can be traced to ancestor relations. The Mexica were not ignorant of the importance of distinguished ancestors as one means of legitimation, they may have intended, by different means, to insure their prestige as heirs of other cultures. We know that the Mexica had been of humble background, for Cristóbal del Castillo (1966: 82) states that these Aztecs (before they changed their name to Mexitin) were

Mexixikilkuani, "eaters of wild water cress"; that is, they were hungry and were forced to collect these edible plants, and they were vassals of other Aztecs, those who held the preferred lands on the shores of the rivers or lakes (Figure 5.1). This would explain their abandoning their homeland and migrating in search of greener fields, or of a watery paradise, where they would find the desired edible lake worm, the *izcahuitli*, which their tutelary god Huitzilopochtli claimed was "my flesh, my blood, my color" (Tezozomoc 1949: 33).

When they finally reached the Basin of Mexico and came in contact with other groups—with the Toltecs of Culhuacan, for example—they must have become aware of the great Teotihuacan civilization (Figure 5.2) and certainly they saw this metropolis that had been abandoned centuries earlier. Divine descent was difficult to prove (since the Mexica evidently did not possess this) but it was easy to acquire, simply by claiming it. When the Mexica had themselves become powerful, their rulers went to Teotihuacan every twenty days to offer sacrifices, and it was said that these *tlatoque* were elected here (Heyden 1975:139). But earlier, when Tenochtitlan was formally laid out, the planners and architects evidently were familiar with the myth of the Fifth Sun, wherein the world of the Mexica was created in Teotihuacan. It will be remembered that after Nanahuatzin and Tecuciztecatl threw themselves into the fire in order to create the sun and the moon, the gods faced the four directions to see where the sun would rise. The builders of Tenochtitlan, perhaps wishing to re-create the sacred space of Teotihuacan where the sun, the moon, and the world came into being, thus insuring the benevolence of the gods in their own city, based their plan on the place where divine ancestors were believed to have been present at this miraculous birth. Diego Durán describes Tenochtitlan's great square, inspired by what the Mexicas had been told about the earlier powerful metropolis, which they probably saw as the world of their forebears:

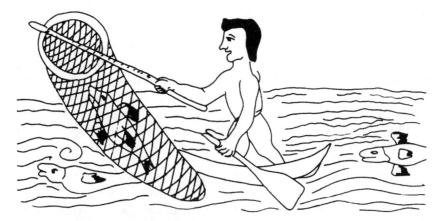

Fig. 5.1. In their original home, Aztlan, the Aztecs were fishermen. An aquatic environment was their ideal and was to influence the choice of a promised land. Redrawn from *Florentine Codex*, Sahagún 1950–1982, X: 133.

Fig. 5.2. The great metropolis, Teotihuacan, may have been seen by the Aztecs when they entered the Basin of Mexico.

[The courtyard was immense] . . . for it accomodated eight thousand six hundred men, dancing in a circle. This courtyard had four doors or entrances, one on the east, another on the west, one on the south and another on the north [see Figure 5.3]. The four main temples had entrances facing [these] . . . directions . . . [the reason for this] I shall not refrain from narrating . . . The ancients believed that before the sun rose or had been created the gods discussed lengthily among themselves, each insisting stubbornly on the direction he thought appropriate for the rising of the sun, which had to be determined before its creation . . . [Each god faced a different direction.] . . . These four doors [of the square of Tenochtitlan] existed for this reason [see Figure 5.4]. And so they spoke of the door of such and such god, each door being named for its god (1977: 78).

By planning their ceremonial and administrative precinct on the myth of the Fifth Sun and the sacred space related to this tradition, the Mexica were insuring the well-being and prestige of their capital by associating it in orientation, space, and myth with the most important and influential metropolis in the central Mexican world of the Classic period (Heyden 1989: 78).

Another legacy from Teotihuacan could have been Tenochtitlan's awareness and copying of the earlier city's "sacred direction," the skewed northeast-southwest orientation followed by the Street of the Dead, which turned up centuries later, in the Mexica period, in the *chinampas* on the southern outskirts of Tenochtitlan. After the conquest of the *chinampa* zone by the Mexica in the fifteenth century, it flourished and became the breadbasket, or rather, the tortilla basket, for the Mexica capital. According to Armillas (1971: 600, 657), at that time this entire agricultural zone was planned on a grid pattern of milpas (cultivated plots) bordered by canals. This planned grid paralleled the alignments of the larger canals, which served as the base of the grid, and whose orientation was northeast to southwest, similar to the sacred direction of the Classic city. Armillas does not mention Teotihuacan, but he does suggest that the carefully planned orientation of the *chinampas* could have been copied from an earlier plan. This replanning of the *chinampa* zone, the place of sustenance, took place during the period of consolidation of the Mexica state, when the leaders of that state—who needed the fertile agricultural area in order to feed their people—also saw the advantage of incorporating religious traditions from earlier cultures into their own (Heyden 1989: 76).

The complex of mountains, water, fields, caves, trees, and plants, is equivalent to fertility and security. This combination of natural features was usually associated with a center, whether it was a capital city or a sacred tree, rock, or cave. It was the cosmos in miniature. This was the case, too, of the founding of Tenochtitlan, where the Mexica-Aztecs believed they had found all the necessary natural elements for the center of their world (Heyden 1989: 46–47).

Fig. 5.3. The Templo Mayor had four entrance doors, oriented to the four world directions. Redrawn from the *Codex Mendoza* 1992, III: folio 2r.

Fig. 5.4. Each of the four doors to the main plaza was associated with a deity and was based on the myth of the Creation of the Suns at Teotihuacan. Redrawn from *Primeros Memoriales*, Sahagún 1993: 269 (269r).

CAVES

Everything was sacred to the people of Teotihuacan and to those who followed them, including springs, waterholes, rivers, lakes, the sea, hills, rocks, trees, and caves. Lakes and springs and the interiors of hills were the womb of the goddess of groundwater, called Chalchiuhtlicue by the Aztecs (Figure 5.5). Water that fell from the sky belonged to Tlaloc, who fertilized the earth with his moisture (Figure 5.6). He was said to be the Path Under the Earth, the Long Cave (Durán 1977: 154).

James Brady has pointed out that

it appears that most sacred locations are these that combine the fundamental elements of earth and water into a single sacred expression of the power of the earth. Because caves are geological conduits for the movement of groundwater, they tend by nature to combine these elements. As entrances into the heart of the earth, caves are places of communication with the supernatural and, therefore, are par excellence, sacred space (1994: 3).

This is true of both Teotihuacan and Tenochtitlan, although there were differences in the use of caves in these places.

A cave is the symbol of creation. Herrera mentions that both the sun and the moon were created in a cavern (1945–1947, I: 308). Mendieta (1945, I: 158) said that both gods and people were created in caves, while Pané claimed that the entire human race came out of caverns (1963: 50).

The cave beneath the Pyramid of the Sun in Teotihuacan has been the subject of much discussion. I believe I was the first person to suggest that this cave

Fig. 5.5. Chalchiuhtlicue, goddess of ground waters. Redrawn from *Codex Borgia*, Seler 1963, III: 65.

Fig. 5.6. Tlaloc, god of rain and earth's fertility. Redrawn from *Codex Borgia*, Seler 1963, III: 67.

Fig. 5.7. The Pyramids of the Sun and the Moon surround the sacred enclosure referred to as the "Oracle of Montezuma" in the *Relación geográfica de Teotihuacan, 1580*. Redrawn from Bazán 1986, in *Relaciones geográficas del siglo XVI, México*, VII: 214, map.

(discovered in 1971) may have determined the location for the building of a primitive shrine within the pyramid and consequently for the pyramid itself. In my 1975 article, I give a number of reasons for this assumption; some people now disagree with these. The remarkable work being carried out today by Linda Manzanilla and her team has shown that "my" cave actually continued to the east, that is, the exit had been blocked in Teotihuacan times, and that this and other caves at the site were actually man-made.

Returning to the religious symbolism of caves in Teotihuacan, I now cite a few lines from my 1975 article:

Since pre-Columbian myths and customs recorded in Colonial chronicles usually reflect those of earlier periods, Sahagún's sixteenth-century informants may provide us with a clue regarding the location chosen for the pyramids by their builders, that is, whether the cave as a shrine determined the site. When questioned about the origins of their people, these informants said that "Offerings were made at a place named Teotihuacan. And there leaders were elected, wherefore it is called Teotihuacan [place where lords or gods are made]. And when the rulers died, they buried them there. Then they built a pyramid over them . . . those who made them at that time were giants . . ." (Bazán 1986: 235–236) [see Figure 5.7]. Obviously the Aztecs of Mexico-Tenochtitlan of the fourteenth or fifteenth centuries were not the builders, although the *Relación Geográfica* of the Teotihuacan Valley tells us that the priests of "Montesuma, the lord of Mexico-Tenochtitlan, with the said Montesuma came to offer sacrifices [in Teotihuacan] every twenty days" (1986: 235–236) [see Figure 5.8], apparently continuing or reviving the ancient tradition of pilgrimages to the shrine.

Aztec lords were not buried under the pyramids, since it was their custom to be cremated before the image of the god Huitzilopochtli and the ashes buried next to the *cuauhxicalli*, or Sun Stone, in the Temple of the Sun at the Templo Mayor

(Durán 1994: 386). [This suggests that] rulers from earlier periods may have been buried beneath the pyramids (Heyden 1975: 139–140).

The cave may have become the focus of a shrine (Figure 5.8). A shrine attracts pilgrims, and trade routes (firmly established in Teotihuacan) are usually accompanied by pilgrimages, all of which favors a flourishing economy. Not every center of worship becomes a metropolis, but in the case of Teotihuacan the highly favorable ecological conditions were combined with the religious attraction to create the religious-economic and consequently sociopolitical situation necessary for the rise of a great center. This cavern at Teotihuacan with its natural chambers enlarged by man, although they do not number seven, may well have been a Chicomoztoc (Seven Caves). I do not say *the* Chicomoztoc, because Chicomoztoc is both a mythical and probably also a real Place of Birth and Place of Return—like Tlalocan and Tamoanchan—a paradise on earth (or, as Sahagún calls Tamoanchan, our Ultimate Home [1969, VI: 105]). Undoubtedly there were many paradises of this type, both in mythology and in fact, and more than one with the same name. Every group, every individual, has his Chicomoztoc, his place of the "good old days," the place we would like to call home (Heyden 1975: 143–144) (Figure 5.9).

Many of the suggestions for the rites performed in the cave at the Pyramid of the Sun in Teotihuacan are hypotheses. For the period of the Mexica, however, we have direct references in the colonial chronicles. Some refer to traditions, such as one mentioned by Mendieta, who spoke of the creation of the Fifth Sun in Teotihuacan thus: "[A]fter [Nanahuatzin] threw himself into the fire and was transformed into the sun, another [divine personage] went into a cave and

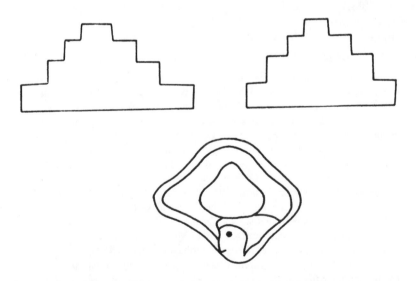

Fig. 5.8. The cave underneath the Pyramid of the Sun may have been a shrine that attracted pilgrims. The *Codex Xolotl*, sixteenth century, depicts a cave with an oracle within. Redrawn from *Códice Xolotl* 1980, map I: 3–2.

Fig. 5.9 Chicomoztoc, the place of Seven Caves, place of creation of the Aztecs. Redrawn from Diego Durán 1994, plate 3.

came out as the moon" (1945, I: 87). Creation evidently was important in association with the Teotihuacan cave, and this mythical creation continued to Mexica times, who (when they were still Aztecs) were born of caves, in Chicomoztoc, the caves "from which their ancestors had set forth," according to Durán (1994: 215). Not only did Pané state that "all humankind was created in two caves" (1974: 22, 93), but these cave-births are portrayed in pictorial codices, for example in the *Atlas de Durán* (in Durán 1994) and the *Manuscrito de Tovar* (1972).

Sahagún cites Mexica women who say that "in us is a cave, a gorge . . . whose only function is . . . to recieve . . ." (1950–1982, VI: 118), and also to give life. When a woman was about to give birth, the midwife took her to the *temazcalli*, the "steam bath," which represents an artificial cave, a place of birth (151).

Many caves, natural or artificial, were associated with sacrificial ceremonies—they were places of death, the opposite of caves seen as places of birth, of creation. A cave in the pyramid Yopico in Mexico-Tenochtitlan served as a storage space for the skins of flayed victims (Sahagún 1950–1982, II: 5). After the sacrifice, the priest wore the human skin for twenty days and then placed it in a cave at the foot of the pyramid stairway, "in an underground place . . . which had a movable stone doorway (Durán 1977: 183–184).

The statue of the goddess Iztaccihuatl was kept in a cave in the mountain of the same name, together with the figures that represented the hills that surround the White Mountain, and on the feast day of the goddess four children, two boys and two girls, were sacrificed on the mountain and their bodies placed in the cave where the goddess was kept (Durán 1977: 248–250).

When Motecuhzoma II fled from the invading Spaniards, he hid in Cincalco, a great cave that was "a place of crystalline clear water and great fertility," but was also the home of the Lord of the Underworld. For Motecuhzoma, however, this cave was not the paradise he was seeking, his refuge from menacing events. When Huemac, lord of the cave, showed him that the place was one of darkness, of "toil and sorrow," the Tlatoani had to return to the real world (485–486).

STREAMS OF RED AND BLUE WATERS, THE SACRED TREE AND BIRD

The vision of a mountain, natural or artificial, set in water (called Our Mother the Lake by Durán [1977: 168]) was the community, the city: it was the *altepetl*, "hill and water." This was the ideal place, a paradise. The Mexica Templo Mayor has been called an *altepetl*, an artificial mountain in an aquatic setting. The Tepantitla mural at Teotihuacan also depicts a hill from which water pours out in streams from a cave. The homeland of the Aztec-Mexitin—Aztlan (an island in water)-Chicomoztoc (caves)-Culhuacan (hill)—was the site where these elements were united as sacred symbols. These symbols were among those that led the people to their promised land.[1]

The insignia of the city of Mexico is an eagle devouring a snake, perched upon a nopal cactus that grows from a rock on top of a cave, and from which flow streams of blue and red water (Figure 5.10). Some of these symbols are present in the pictorial representation, while all are found in the oral tradition as reported in the historical chronicles. The founding of the capital of the Mexica, Tenochtitlan, came about, in myth, after the long migration from Aztlan-Chicomoztoc-Colhuacan. These people were led by their god, Huitzilopochtli, who informed them that they must search for the signs mentioned here. According to the myth, the nopal grew from the heart of Copil, nephew of Huitzilopochtli who slew him.

After many adventures in their travels, the Mexica-Aztecs finally reached the Basin of Mexico, where they discovered wonderful things: a white bald cypress—"and the spring came forth from the foot of the tree. Then they saw more vegetation, reeds and rushes, willows, all white, and a spring of clear water. The elders wept, claiming they had found the promised land" (Durán 1994: 40). But Huitzilopochtli appeared to Cuauhtlequetzqui, his custodian, in dreams, telling him that the people must find the eagle, the cactus, and the rock, not the white place. So the next day the people again went into the swamp to find the spring they had seen, and when they saw it the water flowed out of a cave in the rock in two streams, "one red like blood, the other so blue and thick that it filled the people with awe" (43). Having found the red and blue streams, the Mexica-Aztecs continued to search and discovered a majestic eagle pearched on a nopal, on the rock in the waters.

Fig. 5.10. The founding scene of Mexico Tenochtitlan depicts the eagle, the nopal cactus, the rock, and water. The chronicles say that streams of red and blue waters flowed from a cave beneath these natural elements. Redrawn from Diego Durán 1967, introductory plate.

In Tezozomoc's version, flaming waters flowed out from the spring in a cave that faced east and was called Tleatl-Atlatlayan (Water of Fire, Place of Burning Water). The second cave, containing a spring, faced north and was called Matlalatl-Tozpalatl (Dark Blue Water, Yellow Water, Water the Color of a Parrot) (1949: 63). These were the streams of two colors that flowed from the cave or caves beneath the rock and nopal, the sacred symbols that indicated to the Mexica the place for their home.

The symbolism of blue (or green) and red (or yellow) was important in traditional Mexican thought. For example, when a child was born, the midwife adressed Chalchiuhtlicue, advising the goddess of water that she was bathing the infant in blue water, in yellow water (Sahagún 1950–1982, VI: 175–176). Evidently these two colors (for red was synonymous with yellow, and blue with green) had deep meaning for the people.[2] As found in the mythic tradition and joined to the rock or hill, the cave and the eagle-bird form part of an important combination that represents security, sustenance, the promised land. But when the Mexica entered the Basin of Mexico at the beginning of the fourteenth century, these symbols were not new. They must have existed in oral tradition and visual representations for centuries. For example: some symbols, forms, colors, and ideas present in Aztec art and beliefs can be traced back to Teotihuacan, from whom the Mexica inherited more than they would have liked to admit. In the mural painting at Tepantitla, where a supernatural figure is represented on either side of a doorway, the great central figure has a twisted tree that appears to be growing from its head (Figure 5.11). One branch of the tree is red, one is yellow;

birds are on the branches. The central figure is a bust, placed upon a cave. Streams of two colors (red and blue) spring from the cave in round waves. Each wave is red with a blue border; water symbols, aquatic creatures, and symbols of sustenance such as seeds abound. The entire scene is bordered by interlaced red and blue waters, with heads of Tlaloc at regular intervals (Figure 5.12).

In this mural painting from ca. 650 C.E. (according to Pasztory, from a personal comunication), visual elements exist that could have been transformed by oral tradition and myth into the signs the Mexica were told by their god to seek as indicators for their sacred place. In the Teotihuacan mural, the images represent security through an abundance of water, the streams of two colors, agricultural fertility, and a benevolent and protective deity. In Tenochtitlan, they represent much the same, expressed differently. The basic elements in this picture are

Fig. 5.11. In the mural painting at Tepantitla, Teotihuacan, a sacred tree grows from the majestic central figure. Courtesy of the Museo Nacional de Antropología, INAH, Mexico.

Fig. 5.12. Streams of red and blue interlacing waters surround the Tepantitla painting. Courtesy of the Museo Nacional de Antropología, INAH, Mexico.

the cave or rock; the red and blue streams that flow from this cave; the tree that grows from the head of a supernatural figure (possibly the Mother Goddess in Teotihuacan, the heart of Copil—invisible—in Tenochtitlan); the nopal cactus, which was considered a "tree" by Sahagún; the bird on the nopal or tree; the eagle in Tenochtitlan; and the numerous birds on the branches at Tepantitla (Heyden 1989: 68–70).

An auspicious bird on a tree or plant that grows from the heart of a supernatural being is not an uncommon motif in ancient Mexican art. It can be seen on a number of plates in the *Codex Borgia* (Figure 5.13), in the *Codex Dresden*, in Palenque relief carvings, and on the back of the stone monument called the Teocalli de la Guerra Sagrada, where a cactus grows from a supernatural figure and the fruits of the nopal cactus are hearts. The eagle on the nopal holds an *atl-tlachinolli* symbol in its beak, which early croniclers may have misinterpreted as a serpent (Figure 5.14).

Tenochtitlan inherited material and ideological elements from other cultures, mainly, we believe, from Teotihuacan. As Eliade has pointed out, the sacred character of a site can be transferred to another through orientation, art, norms, oral tradition, and the magic-religious association of a people with their natural environment. How the Mexica took the elements mentioned here from the culture they considered their sacred ancestors, is not clear. They may or may not have seen some of the murals at Teotihuacan, but evidently oral traditions, which constitute an important part of history, belief, and custom, contributed much to the sacred myth and symbols of the Mexica-Aztecs. They seem to have been experts at acquiring "instant culture," and they also acquired an elite genealogy by intermarrying with the Culhua Toltecs. Then of course they molded this history, philosophy, art, and ideology into a belief system of their own (Heyden 1989: 99). It is interesting to read in Durán that when Tenochtitlan had been conquered by the Spaniards, these men began to seek the treasure that supposedly had been hidden by the Mexica and their allies:

> The Tlatelolcas, by command of their leader, had concealed it [the treasure] in a deep pool in the city that the Aztecs feared, due to a certain religious superstition. It was believed that this spring was the place discovered by their ancestors, where the red and blue waters flowed, where lived the white fish, the white frogs, the white snakes. This pool was never seen by the Spaniards nor has anyone ever discovered its exact location (1994: 558).

The Europeans did not understand that the sacred streams of red and blue water, flowing from a cave, seen in the Teotihuacan murals and constituting one of the important symbols in the Mexica foundation myth, were a metaphor for security, for riches from the aquatic environment, for stability and power in the goverment. The conquering Spaniards must have thought that this myth, still

Fig. 5.13. A bird on a tree or plant that grows from a supernatural figure is seen in a number of representations in the *Codex Borgia*. Redrawn from the *Códice Borgia*, Seler 1963, III: 51.

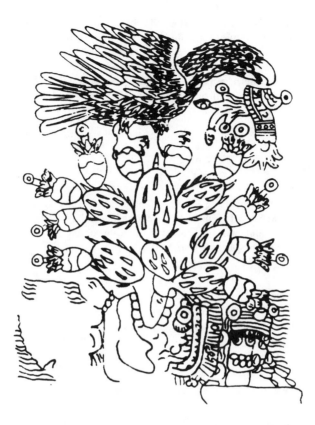

Fig. 5.14. The eagle, the cactus, and a supernatural figure are carved on the base of the Aztec Sacred War stone, Museo Nacional de Antropología. Courtesy INAH. Redrawn by A. Flores.

alive in 1521, described not a promised land but a real treasure of gold and gems. The place where the streams of two colors flowed from a rock or hill costituted an *altepetl*, an ideal place for a settlement, that the Mexica had been seeking, and this was their genuine treasure (Heyden 1989: 100).[3]

NOTES

1. The following ideas have been discussed in my books of 1988 and 1989, in my Dumbarton Oaks article of 1981, in my 1975 *American Antiquity* article (where I proposed that the cave underneath the Pyramid of the Sun was the original axis mundi of the site), in a talk presented at Colgate University in 1983, and at the Mesoamerican Archive in Teotihuacan in 1995.

2. The streams of two colors, one blue, one flaming red, could represent the *atl-tlachinolli*, "water and fire" or "flaming water," the symbol for war in Aztec-Mexica times. This, too, probably was an old motif but with a different meaning, undoubtedly related to

agriculture and the earth's benefits. Water and fire are two of the basic elements for life; plants cannot grow without water,and fire is a means of regeneration. In pictorial codices (the *Borbonicus, Borgia, Laud,* and *Fejérváry-Mayer*), the *atl-tlachinolli* is associated with deities of creation and fertility (Heyden 1989: 66–67).

3. A number of scholars have mentioned the legacy recieved by Tenochtitlan, particulary in the Templo Mayor, from Teotihuacan. See, for example, Clara Millon 1973, Leonardo López Luján 1989, and Kathleen Berrin and Esther Pasztory 1993.

REFERENCES

Armillas, Pedro
1971. "Gardens in Swamps." *Science*174, no. 4010: 653–661.

Bazán, Antonio
1986. "Descripción del pueblo de San Juan Teotihuacan, encomendado a Don Antonio Bazán, alguacil Mayor del Santo Oficio de Inquisición, hecha en dicho pueblo a primero de marzo de mil y quinientos y ochenta años." In R. Acuña, ed., *Relaciones geográficas del siglo XVI: México*. Mexico: UNAM-IIA, vol. 2, no. 7, pp. 232–240.

Berrin, Kathleen, and Esther Pasztory, eds.
1993. *Teotihuacan, Art from the City of the Gods*. New York: Thames and Hudson/The Fine Arts Museums of San Francisco.

Boone, Elizabeth Hill, and Walter D. Mignolo. eds.
1994. *Writing Without Words: Alternative Literacies in Mesoamerica and the Andes*. Durham, NC and London: Duke University Press.

Brady, James E.
1994. "The Role of Caves in Ancient Maya Cosmovision." Paper presented at the Dumbarton Oaks Pre-Columbian Roundtable: Earthly Matters II, March 12, Washington, DC.

Castillo, Cristobal del
1966. "Historia de la venida de los mexicanos e Historia de la Conquista." In *Fragmentos de la obra general sobre historia de los mexicanos escrita en lengua náuatl por Cristóbal del Castillo á fines del siglo XVI, los tradujo al castellano Francisco del Paso y Troncoso en homenaje al XVI Congreso Internacional de Americanistas que se reunirá en Viena del 9 al 14 de septiembre de 1908*. Ciudad Juárez, Mexico: Editorial Erandi. Originally published (Florence: Tipografía Salvador Landi, 1908).

Codex Borgia: see Seler

Codex Mendoza
1992. Edited by F. F. Berdan and P. R. Anawalt. 4 vols. Berkeley: University of California Press.

Códice Xolotl
1980. Edited by C. E. Dibble. Preface by M. León-Portilla. 2 vols. 2nd ed. Mexico: UNAM-IIH.

Durán, Diego
1967. *Historia de las indias de Nueva España*. Ed. Á. M. Garibay K. 2 vols. Mexico: Editorial Porrúa.
1994. *The History of the Indies of New Spain*. Translated, annotated, and introduction by D. Heyden. Norman: University of Oklahoma Press.

Eliade, Mircea
1959. *The Sacred and the Profane*. Trans. Willard R. Trask. New York: Harcourt, Brace, and World.

Herrera y Tordesillas, Antonio de
1945–1947. *Historia general de los hechos de los castellanos en las islas y tierra firme de el mar oceano. 1601*. 4 vols. Reproduction of the second edition, 1726–1730. Asunción, Paraguay: Editorial Guaranía.

Heyden, Doris
1989. *The Eagle, the Cactus, the Rock: The Roots of Mexico-Tenochtitlan's Foundation Myth and Symbol*. Oxford: BAR International Series 484.
1975. "An Interpretation of the Cave Underneath the Pyramid of the Sun in Teotihuacan, Mexico." *American Antiquity* 40, no. 2: 131–147.
1973. "Historia de México." In Á. M. Garibay K., ed., *Historia de los mexicanos por sus pinturas*. 2nd ed. Mexico: Editorial Porrúa, Sepan Cuantos, pp. 91–120.

Karttunen, Frances
1983. *An Analytical Dictionary of Nahuatl*. Austin: University of Texas Press.

López Luján, Leonardo
1989. *La recuperación mexica del pasado teotihuacano*. Mexico: INAH/GV Editores.

Manuscrito de Tovar
1972. *Origines et croyances des indiens du mexique*. Ed. Jaques Lafaye. Graz: ADV.

Mendieta, Fray Gerónimo de
1945. *Historia eclesiástica indiana*. 4 vols. Mexico: Salvador Chávez Hayhoe.

Millon, Clara
1973. "Painting, Writing, and Polity in Teotihuacan, Mexico." *American Antiquity* 38, no. 3: 294–314.

Molina, Alonso de.
1944. *Vocabulario en lengua castellana y mexicana*. Facsimile edition. Madrid: Ediciones Cultural Hispánica, 1944.

Motolinía, Fray Toribio de Benavente
1971. *Memoriales o libro de las cosas de la Nueva España y de los naturales de ella*. Ed. Edmundo O'Gorman. Mexico: UNAM-IIH.

Navas, Fray Francisco de las
n.d. "Calendario de Fr. Francisco de las Navas, de Don Antonio de Guevara y Anónimo Tlaxcalteca." Ms. in Archivo Histórico del INAH, Colección Ramírez, Opúsculos Históricos, tomo 21, no. 210, pp. 93–203. Colección Antigua, Mexico, D.F.
1984. "Calendario Indico de los indios del mar océano y de las partes de este Nuevo Mundo." In R. Acuña, ed., *Relaciones geográficas del siglo XVI: Tlaxcala*. Mexico: UNAM-IIA, vol. 4, pp. 219–285.

Pané, Fray Ramón
1963. "La relación de la antigüedad de los indios de la Española." In L. Nicolau d'Olwer, ed., *Cronistas de las culturas precolombinas*. Mexico and Buenos Aires: FCE, pp. 47–56.

Sahagún, Fray Bernardino de
1993. *Primeros Memoriales*. Facsimile. Photographed by Ferdinand Anders. Norman: University of Oklahoma Press.
1969. *Historia general de las cosas de Nueva España*. Ed. Á. M. Garibay K. 4 vols. 2nd ed. Mexico: Editorial Porrúa.
1950–1982. *Florentine Codex: General History of the Things of New Spain*. Translated from the Nahuatl by C. E. Dibble and A. J. O. Anderson. 12 books. Santa Fe, NM: The School of American Research/University of Utah.

Seler, Edward
1963. *Comentarios al Códice Borgia*. Trans. M. Frenk. 3 vols. Mexico and Buenos Aires: FCE.

Siméon, Rémi
1988. *Diccionario de la lengua náhuatl o mexicana*. 5th ed. Mexico: Siglo Veintiuno Editores.

Tezozómoc, Fernando Alvarado
1949. *Crónica mexicáyotl*. Trans. A. León. Mexico: UNAM-IH.

Vansina, Jan
1968. *La tradición oral*. Translated into Spanish by M. M. Llongueras. 2nd ed. Barcelona: Editorial Labor.

Wheatley, Paul
1969. *City as Symbol*. London: University College/Lewis Co.

6

▼

FROM TEOTIHUACAN TO TENOCHTITLAN

THEIR GREAT TEMPLES

EDUARDO MATOS MOCTEZUMA

TRANSLATED BY SCOTT SESSIONS

ANTECEDENTS

One of the cities whose characteristics have always attracted attention, even after being buried by the sands of time, is, without a doubt, Teotihuacan. We already know of the Aztecs' periodic visits in pre-Hispanic times to revere the ancient urban center, for even though it was covered with earth and vegetation, the general plan of the city, as well as the monumental complexes of the Ciudadela and the great mounds of the Pyramids of the Sun and Moon, had not disappeared. Moreover, if ceramic fragments bearing witness to the site's occupation are found here and there today, in Aztec times they must have been even more abundant and have caught the attention of new groups who saw ancestral traces without knowing with complete certainty who had created them. Thus, what was the work of humans became the work of the gods to later groups who came to know the site. From here to myth there is only one step: the old city becomes imbued with sacrality, and an extraordinary act will take place: the creation of the Fifth Sun brought about by the sacrifice of the gods.

On many occasions, we already have discussed how the quest to know more about the City of the Gods induced the Aztecs to excavate at the site. No less than forty Teotihuacan objects have been found in different offerings at the Templo Mayor of Tenochtitlan (López Luján 1989). Moreover, there is also imitation in the city's plan itself, organized as it is into four major barrios, and the presence of *talud-tablero* buildings and mural painting remind us of those at Teotihuacan. Furthermore, a sculpture of the Old God appeared near the Aztec Templo Mayor in the same position that a representation of Huehueteotl was found at Teotihuacan. To all this we suggest adding something of great importance, which is the purpose of the present study: the location, orientation, and characteristics of the principal buildings that mark or indicate the center of the city itself, the axis mundi, from which the four directions of the universe emanate. We will speak more about this later in the chapter.

After the European Conquest, indigenous buildings were destroyed. Teotihuacan, already buried after a little more than seven centuries of abandonment (except for minor occupations in a few places in the city) was not an object of this destruction, but rather attracted the attention of some sixteenth-century chroniclers who made reference to it. What is interesting about this is that these chroniclers became aware of the myth of the birth of the Fifth Sun in Teotihuacan. Thus, we read in the works of Bernardino de Sahagún (1995), Diego Múñoz Camargo (1995), the *Leyenda de los Soles* (1995), and elsewhere (see Matos, ed. 1995), about the myth that undoubtedly caused the tallest monuments in the city to be named the Pyramids of the Sun and Moon as well as assigned their dedication to these two astral bodies, even though today we are able to find associations to other important elements.

In the seventeenth century, we have an event of great importance for the history of archaeology: Carlos Sigüenza y Góngora, the learned Mexicanist, tried to excavate at the Pyramid of the Sun. Lorenzo Boturini has left us a record of Sigüenza y Góngora's attempt in his *Historia general de la América Septentrional* (1746):

> This ancient hill was perfectly square, whitewashed, and beautiful, and one used to climb to the top by way of some steps, that today cannot be seen, for having been filled in by their own ruins and earth deposited by the winds, upon which trees and thistles have sprouted. Nevertheless, I was on it and out of curiosity measured it, and, if I am not mistaken, it is two hundred *varas* tall. Thus I ordered that it be recorded on a map that I have in my archive, and walking around it I saw that the celebrated Carlos Sigüenza y Góngora had tried to bore his way into it, but had encountered resistance (Boturini 1995: 49).[1]

Along with Boturini's remarks, we must also mention those of another traveler from the end of the century, Giovanni Francesco Gemelli Careri. In his *Giro del mondo*, published in 1700 in Italy, we see how he visited the site and made several assertions that had no relation to reality, though one of them has recently attracted interest. He mentions that some of the caves found in Teotihuacan are artificial, that is, made by human hands. The traveler tells us:

> Indeed it is certain that there where they were was previously a great city, as evidenced by the extensive surrounding ruins, and by caves, artificial as well as natural, and by the quantity of mounds thought to be made in honor of the idols (Gemelli Careri 1995: 47-48).[2]

In subsequent centuries, authors such as Francisco Clavigero (1780–1781, 1995), Alexander von Humboldt (1811, 1995), Frances Calderón de la Barca (1843, 1995), José María García (1860), and Ramón Almaraz (1865, 1995) would mention Teotihuacan in their writings. Almaraz, as part of the Report of the Pachuca Scientific Commission, wrote in 1865 that he had visited the site and made the first map using precision instruments. He also referred to topics such as the orientation and construction of the pyramids and was the first to mention the "rampart" (*muralla*) that surrounds the Pyramid of the Sun. Closer to our times are the works of Désiré Charnay (1885) and Leopoldo Batres (1906, 1995) himself. Along with Batres's discoveries at the end of the nineteenth century, such as the Temple of Agriculture murals on the west side of the so-called Street of the Dead, we must add his work beginning in 1905 to shed light on the Pyramid of the Sun. The investigations initiated by Manuel Gamio in 1917, presented in his monumental *La población del Valle de Teotihuacán* (1922), and considered the first in modern Mexican anthropology, deserve separate mention. From this moment on, many researchers and institutions—foreign as well as Mexican—have carried out work in Teotihuacan, offering valuable contributions to the understanding of the urban center (see Matos, ed. 1995).

Now let us begin our study of the aforementioned topic—"From Teotihuacan to Tenochtitlan: Their Great Temples"—in which we will speak of the buildings that we think had the role of the symbolic "center" in the two cities. Although they are separated by at least six centuries, they will be joined together by a series of characteristics that we already have discussed in previous studies (see Matos 1994, 1995a).

SACRED SPACE

We know from the study of religions how the founding of ancient cities was imbued with a sacred and symbolic character. Historian of religions Mircea Eliade (1979) is clear in this respect. He explains how the place where the new city will be located is always preceded by landmarks or signs that sacralize the place. Sacred space is thus validated and clearly separated from the profane, or other surrounding space, which we prefer to call "space of less sacrality." As Eliade tells us:

> The founding of the new city repeats the creation of the world; in fact, once the place has been ritually validated, a wall is raised in the form of a circle or square interrupted by four gates that correspond to the four cardinal points. . . . The cities, like the cosmos, are divided in four; in other words, they are a copy of the universe (Eliade 1979: 374).[3]

Various archaeological and symbolic indicators allow us to determine how the pre-Hispanic peoples of Central Mexico adopted a series of elements to clearly distinguish what we have called the "center of centers" or the fundamental center of the city—inasmuch as the city itself, in its totality, was conceived of as the center of the universe, inside of which was established this space of greater sacrality which, in turn, was an image of the cosmos. These internal spaces of the city are those that we will proceed to analyze in Teotihuacan and Tenochtitlan, although it is necessary to state that in Teotihuacan we see two centers with more or less similar elements: the Pyramid of the Sun and the Ciudadela. Therefore, we have suggested that, given its greater antiquity, the Pyramid of the Sun was the center of what we call the "old city," which subsequently was moved south to the site occupied by the Ciudadela and the Temple of the Feathered Serpents or of Quetzalcoatl.

We find the following elements present in both cities:

a) A landmark or sign situating and constituting the fundamental, sacred center of the city.

b) A principal building erected on this landmark or sign, which acquires the
character of a sacred mountain where the distinct celestial, terrestrial, and
underworld levels of the cosmos meet and the four cardinal directions emanate; thus its character as the center of the universe.

c) The same orientation of this building or sacred mountain.

d) The presence of water. Inside this sacred mountain are kept the water and maize
kernels that provide sustenance for the community, which we see in its *altepetl*
or "mountain of water" character, around which the settlement is organized.

e) The presence of human sacrifice and a place of offering where the principal
myths are repeated through ritual performance.

f) A platform surrounding it or the buildings that give it its axis mundi quality.
These platforms are elements serving to distinguish the sacred from the profane or less sacred space.

Now, we will examine each of these elements.

THE LANDMARK OR SIGN FOR THE FOUNDATION OF THE CITY

In the case of Teotihuacan, archaeologists have found a cavity underneath
the Pyramid of the Sun that is thought to be what motivated the construction of
this monument. This cavity—whether natural or artificial, since Federico Mooser
(1968) considers it a geological formation while Linda Manzanilla (chapter 2 of
this volume) thinks it may be human-made—constitutes the sign indicating the
place selected by the gods. Here it does not matter if the cavity is natural, artificial, or even a combination of the two, but rather that humans "discover" and
make or adapt the place. What is important is the dual character of caves in the
pre-Hispanic world: it was the birthplace of peoples—recalling Chicomoztoc,
with which this cave shares certain characteristics (see Heyden 1975, 1995)—
and at the time it was conceived as the entrance to the underworld; thus the
duality of life and death is present there.

In the case of Tenochtitlan, the landmark or sign is the well-known image of
the eagle perched on the cactus, in addition to certain earlier Toltec symbols
that, we believe, the Aztecs appropriated to legitimate the sacred space. These
include the streams of blue and red water, which is nothing other than the *atl-
tlachinolli* or war symbol, along with the presence of the color white in fish,
frogs, serpents, reeds, and cattails, which are the same symbols that the Toltecs
saw in the sacred city of Cholula, if we accept what the *Historia tolteca-
chichimeca* (1976) tells us (aspects that we have already mentioned on another
occasion).[4]

THE CONSTRUCTION OF THE TEMPLO MAYOR

The location of the Pyramid of the Sun at Teotihuacan in relation to the
cavity doubtless means that it was intentional and motivated by the previously
stated reasons. Although we do not have written documentation for such early
times that would tell us about the character of the "sacred mountain," it has
always been suggested that the massive Pyramids of the Sun and Moon imitate
mountains in the surrounding landscape. The characteristic shape of the pyramids' four *talud* sections seek this adaptation to the natural surroundings.

Concerning the Templo Mayor of Tenochtitlan, we definitely can draw upon a greater amount of information from sixteenth-century narrative accounts and pictographs, such as plate 1 of the *Codex Mendoza* (1992), where the center of the city is the place where the eagle is perched on the nopal cactus, and we know that the Templo Mayor was erected there at that center. We also have accounts of the founding of the city and how the separation of sacred and profane space was achieved by constructing the principal temple in the middle of the sacred precinct. As for its "sacred mountain" character, in this case it is invested in a singularity consisting of two mountains: Coatepec, or the sacred mountain where the battle between Huitzilopochtli and Coyolxauhqui takes place, and Tonacatepetl, or the mountain where maize kernels are guarded by the assistants of Tlaloc, who presides over this part of the temple. In this way, the Templo Mayor resonates two principal Nahua myths, in addition to being the fundamental center of the universe in their cosmovision where the celestial levels and the underworld meet, and from which the four cardinal directions emanate.[5]

ORIENTATION OF THE PRINCIPAL BUILDINGS

The Pyramid of the Sun, the Temple of Quetzalcoatl, and the Templo Mayor of Tenochtitlan are all oriented toward the west. Evidently, the movement of the stars, especially the sun, determined the position of these temples.

THE *ALTEPETL*, OR "MOUNTAIN OF WATER"

Water, as a vital element for the subsistence of these peoples, acquired a transcendent importance that is present in myths and in the importance of the gods associated with it. It was common belief that water was kept inside mountains or hills; therefore it would not be strange that the sacred mountain would be where the liquid giving life to plants and humans would be kept. In the case of the Pyramid of the Sun, it seems, a stream of water ran inside the aforementioned cave and some stone channels have been found in its interior. The most recent archaeological excavations around the Pyramid of the Sun have resulted in the discovery of a canal, 3 meters wide, surrounding the pyramid on all sides. It has been thought that perhaps this could be a street for specific ceremonies, but the avalanche of water that would come down the sides of the pyramid during the rainy season makes us think seriously that it was a canal. The other "center" of the city of Teotihuacan, the Temple of Quetzalcoatl, has undulating serpents surrounded by snails and conch shells depicted on its façade that speak of the importance of the aquatic element. Furthermore, archaeologist Rubén Cabrera says that a looters' tunnel inside the building was discovered running into the center, where an inexplicable degree of humidity was detected, suggesting that a source of flowing water might be found just below it.

In the case of Tenochtitlan, particularly the Templo Mayor, we have already mentioned the streams of water and the maize kernels kept inside.

It would be interesting to analyze the *altepetl* character more deeply, because its relation to the community is important from the symbolic as well as social-organization, kinship, and other points of view.

THE PRESENCE OF SACRIFICE AND OFFERINGS

When Leopoldo Batres excavated the Pyramid of the Sun at the beginning of this century, he found the skeletal remains of children in each of the corners of the four sections that make up the building. This fact is particularly interesting given that we know how children were dedicated, in later times, to the cult of the water god, Tlaloc. It would not be strange that this cult would have come from Teotihuacan, since many aspects present in Tenochtitlan previously existed in the earlier city. As for the Temple of Quetzalcoatl, we have the ceremonial burials found by archaeologists Rubén Cabrera and Saburo Sugiyama in specific places and numbers. One of the characteristics of the individuals deposited there, male (nine in number) and female (in groups of four), was that their hands were tied behind their backs. This has been interpreted as human sacrifice in honor of the temple in association with the calendar and agriculture.

As for the Aztec Templo Mayor, various studies speak of the presence of multiple offerings of decapitated skulls, child burials (forty-two on the Tlaloc side in Offering 38), and ritual sacrifice by heart extraction practiced on the side dedicated to Huitzilopochtli, about which various historical sources have left us information.[6]

THE SURROUNDING PLATFORM

In Teotihuacan we see only two places inside the city with large platforms that enclosed and delineated, in our judgment, the spaces of great sacrality and buildings that were the fundamental center of the city: the Pyramid of the Sun and the Temple of Quetzalcoatl in the Ciudadela. The first of these buildings was excavated in 1993 in the Proyecto Especial Teotihuacán, although a portion of the south side, in the so-called House of the Priests, was partially excavated by Batres several years earlier. Surely it was Batres who destroyed part of the platform near the southwest corner to remove debris from the pyramid and constructed his camp on top of the south side, and its excavation has continued in recent years. Returning to the topic at hand, in the past this platform has been interpreted in several different ways. It was first mentioned in the Report of the Pachuca Scientific Commission (Almaraz 1865) on the map of the center of the city, which referred to it as a "rampart" (*muralla*). Later on, it was Batres who said that its function was to provide stability to the great mass of the Pyramid of the Sun, something that evidently did not correspond to reality. Other studies such as Gamio (1922, 1995) and Marquina (1951: 69–76; 1995) only mentioned it, without attributing to it a specific function, while Rémy Bastien (1995), who conducted a study of the Pyramid of the Sun for his 1947 thesis in the School of Anthropology, referred to three functions: 1) mechanical, seeing its absence at the Pyramid of the Moon and "its importance at the Ciudadela"; 2) aesthetic, related to the visual appearance of the complex, and 3) military, or defense. Concerning what he says about the absence of this and other elements we have mentioned from the Pyramid of the Moon, they were omitted so that the Pyramid of the Sun would be considered the "center" of the city.

As for Tenochtitlan, we have various pictographs in which we see the great platform framing the principal plaza with, according to Sahagún (1989), its seventy-eight buildings, inside. Archaeologically, sections of the platform from a later stage of the Templo Mayor have been found with walls that alternate with stairways. The same arrangement is seen at Tlatelolco, where one can examine a large section, including the inside southeast corner. In the case of Tenochtitlan, the rampart or walled-platform is clearly a delimiter of sacred space from which the great causeways running north, west, and south emanated.

In summary, we think that this platform divided two types of space: the interior, consisting of a great plaza imbued with enormous sacrality, and the exterior, profane, or less sacred space.

CONCLUSIONS

In the case of Central Mexico, all these elements had to be present to identify a building as the principal temple, as an axis mundi, with all its implications. In Teotihuacan, evidently, two fundamental centers were established: the Pyramid of the Sun and the Temple of Quetzalcoatl in the Ciudadela. There is also another important fact in relation to this second building: the excavations of Rubén Cabrera allow us to see that this second "center," in turn, was desacralized. There is evidence of a looters' tunnel penetrating the southeast corner that terminates at the center of the building. Subsequently, the building, at least its principal façade, was covered by another building stage less rich in elements than the one preceding it. Other tunnels made by Teotihuacanos themselves were found in the La Ventilla excavations carried out in the Proyecto Especial Teotihuacán. This leads us to think about the city's development, because this clearly did not occur during a time of internal peace, but rather there were many moments (at least three) in which disturbances in Teotihuacan society must have occurred. These three moments are: 1) when the "center" of the city passed from the Pyramid of the Sun to the Ciudadela, which must have been an enormous transformation with important religious and social implications; 2) when the Temple of Quetzalcoatl was covered and desacralized to such a degree that it was looted; and 3) when we see in later phases (Tlamimilopa-Xolalpan) that looters' tunnels were made in different places in the ceremonial area. All of this occured before Teotihuacan's final devastation around 700 C.E., when its preeminence ended and it passed into a form of the myth in which later peoples would transform the city into the place where the gods were born.

NOTES

1. "Era este cerro de la antiguedad perfectamente cuadrado, encalado, y hermoso, y se subía a su cumbre por unas gradas, que hoy no se descubren, por haberse llenado de sus proprias ruinas, y de la tierra que arrojan los vientos, sobre la cual han nacido árboles, y abrojos. No obstante estuve yo en él, y le hice por curiosidad medir, y, si no me engaño, es de docientos varas de alto. Ansimismo mandé sacarlo en mapa, que tengo en mi archivo, y rodeándole vi, que el célebre don Carlos de Singüenza y Góngora había intentado taladrarle, pero halló resistencia" (Boturini 1995: 49).

2. "Sí es cosa cierta que allí donde ellas están hubo anteriormente una gran ciudad, como se advierte por las extensas ruinas alrededor, y por las grutas, tanto naturales como artificiales, y por la cantidad de montecillos que se cree que fueron hechos en honor de los

ídolos" (Gemelli Careri 1995: 47-48).

3. "La fundación de la nueva ciudad repite la creación del mundo; en efecto, una vez que el lugar ha sido validado ritualmente, se eleva una cerca en forma de círculo o de cuadrado interrumpida por cuatro puertas que corresponden a los cuatro puntos cardinales. . . . Las ciudades, a semejanza del cosmos, están divididas en cuatro; dicho de otra manera, son una copia del universo" (Eliade 1979: 374).

4. The Toltec elements present in the founding of Tenochtitlan are discussed in the official guidebook of the Templo Mayor (Matos 1993).

5. For more about these characteristics of the Templo Mayor, see Matos (1986, 1995b).

6. See Juan Alberto Román Berrelleza (1990), as well as Diego Durán (1867–1880, 1994) and Bernardino de Sahagún (1989).

REFERENCES

Almaraz, Ramón
1865. *Memoria de los trabajos ejecutados por la Comisión Científica de Pachuca en el año de 1864, dirigida por el ingeniero Ramón Almaraz*. Mexico: J. M. Andrade y F. Escalante.
1995. "Apuntes sobre las pirámides de San Juan Teotihuacan [1865]." In E. Matos Moctezuma, ed., *La pirámide del Sol, Teotihuacán: Antología*. Mexico: Artes de México/ Instituto Cultural Domecq, pp. 65–75.

Bastien, Rémy
1995. "La pirámide del Sol en Teotihuacan [1947]." In E. Matos Moctezuma, ed., *La pirámide del Sol, Teotihuacán: Antología*. Mexico: Artes de México/Instituto Cultural Domecq, pp. 209–258.

Batres, Leopoldo
1906. *Teotihuacán: Memoria que presenta Leopoldo Batres . . . año de 1906*. Mexico: Imprenta de F. S. Soria.
1995. "Pirámide del Sol [1906]." In E. Matos Moctezuma, ed., *La pirámide del Sol, Teotihuacán: Antología*. Mexico: Artes de México/Instituto Cultural Domecq, pp. 100–117.

Boturini Benaducci, Lorenzo
1746. *Idea de una nueva historia general de la América Septentrional*. Madrid: Imprenta de Juan de Zúñiga.
1995. "Idea de una nueva historia general de la América Septentrional [1746]" (excerpt). In E. Matos Moctezuma, ed., *La pirámide del Sol, Teotihuacán: Antología*. Mexico: Artes de México/Instituto Cultural Domecq, pp. 49–50.

Calderón de la Barca, Frances E. I.
1843. *Life in Mexico, During a Residence of Two Years in That Country*. Boston: C. C. Little and J. Brown.
1995. "Carta XVI [1840]." In E. Matos Moctezuma, ed., *La pirámide del Sol, Teotihuacán: Antología*. Mexico: Artes de México/Instituto Cultural Domecq, pp. 59–64.

Charnay, Désiré
1885. *Les anciennes villes du Nouveau Monde. Voyages d'explorations au Mexique et dans l'Amérique Centrale, par Désiré Charnay, 1857–1882*. Paris: Hachette.

Clavigero, Francisco Javier
1780-1781. *Storia antica del Messico*. Cesena, Italy: G. Biasini.
1995. "Apoteosis del Sol y la Luna [1780]." In E. Matos Moctezuma, ed., *La pirámide del Sol, Teotihuacán: Antología*. Mexico: Artes de México/Instituto Cultural Domecq, pp. 51–53.

Codex Mendoza
1992. Edited by F. F. Berdan and P. R. Anawalt. Berkeley: University of California Press.

Durán, Fray Diego
1867–1880. *Historia de las Indias de Nueva España y islas de Tierra Firme*. Mexico: J. M. Andrade y F. Escalante.
1994. *The History of the Indies of New Spain*. Translated, annotated, and with an introduction by D. Heyden. Norman: University of Oklahoma Press.

Eliade, Mircea
1979. *Tratado de historia de las religiones*. Trans. T. Segovia. Mexico: Ediciones Era.

Gamio, Manuel
1922. *La población del Valle de Teotihuacán representativa de las que habitan las regiones rurales del Distrito Federal y de los Estados de Hidalgo, Puebla, México y Tlaxcala.* Mexico: Dirección de Talleres Gráficos.
1995. "En cuatro grupos [1922]." In E. Matos Moctezuma, ed., *La pirámide del Sol, Teotihuacán: Antología*. Mexico: Artes de México/Instituto Cultural Domecq, pp. 126–127.

García, José María
1860. "Las pirámides de San Juan Teotihuacán." *Boletín de la Sociedad Mexicana de Geografía y Estadística* 8: 198-200.

Gemelli Careri, Giovanni Francesco
1700. *Giro del mondo*. Napoli: G. Roselli.
1995. "De los cúes o pirámides de San Juan Teotihuacan [1700]." In E. Matos Moctezuma, ed., *La pirámide del Sol, Teotihuacán: Antología*. Mexico: Artes de México/Instituto Cultural Domecq, pp. 46–48.

Heyden, Doris
1975. "An Interpretation of the Cave Underneath the Pyramid of the Sun in Teotihuacan, Mexico." *American Antiquity* 40, no. 2 (April): 131–147.
1995. "Una interpretación en torno a la cueva que se encuentra bajo la pirámide del Sol en Teotihuacan [1975]." In E. Matos Moctezuma, ed., *La pirámide del Sol, Teotihuacán: Antología*. Mexico: Artes de México/Instituto Cultural Domecq, pp. 286–311.

Historia tolteca-chichimeca
1976. Edited by P. Kirchhoff, L. Odena Güemes, and L. Reyes García. Mexico: INAH-CIS/SEP.

Humboldt, Alexander von
1811. *Essai politique sur le royaume de la Nouvelle-Espagne*. Paris: F. Schoell.
1995. "Los antiguos monumentos de Teotihuacan [1807–1811]." In E. Matos Moctezuma, ed., *La pirámide del Sol, Teotihuacán: Antología*. Mexico: Artes de México/Instituto Cultural Domecq, pp. 56–58.

Leyenda de los soles
1995. "Leyenda de los soles [1558]" (excerpt). In E. Matos Moctezuma, ed., *La pirámide del Sol, Teotihuacán: Antología*. Mexico: Artes de México/Instituto Cultural Domecq, pp. 27–28.

López Luján, Leonardo
1989. *La recuperación mexica del pasado teotihuacano*. Mexico: INAH/Proyecto Templo Mayor/GV Editores/Asociación de Amigos del Templo Mayor.

Marquina, Ignacio
1951. *Arquitectura prehispánica*. Mexico: INAH.

1995. "Descripción de los edificios [1951]." In E. Matos Moctezuma, ed., *La pirámide del Sol, Teotihuacán: antología*. Mexico: Artes de México/Instituto Cultural Domecq, pp. 259–267.

Matos Moctezuma, Eduardo
1986. *Vida y muerte en el Templo Mayor*. Mexico: Ediciones Océano.
1993. *Templo Mayor: Guía oficial*. Mexico: INAH/Salvat.
1994. "Teotihuacán." *Arqueología Mexicana* 2, no. 10 (October-November): 75–79.
1995a. "La pirámide de Sol y el primer *coatepantli* conocido del centro de México." In M. H. Ruz and J. Arechiga V., eds., *Antropología e interdisciplina: Homenage a Pedro Carrasco. XXIII Mesa Redonda, Villahermosa, Tabasco, 1994*. Mexico: SMA.
1995b. *Life and Death in the Templo Mayor*. Trans. B. R. Ortiz de Montellano and T. Ortiz de Montellano. Niwot: University Press of Colorado.

Matos Moctezuma, Eduardo, ed.
1995. *La pirámide del Sol, Teotihuacán: Antología*. Mexico: Artes de México/Instituto Cultural Domecq.

Millon, René
1973. *The Teotihuacan Map*. Austin: University of Texas Press.

Mooser, Federico
1968. "Geología, naturaleza y desarrollo del Valle de Teotihuacán." In J. L. Lorenzo, ed., *Materiales para la arqueología de Teotihuacán*. Mexico: INAH, pp. 29–37.

Muñoz Camargo, Diego
1995. "Tenían ansimiso este engaño [siglo XIV]." In E. Matos Moctezuma, ed., *La pirámide del Sol, Teotihuacán: Antología*. Mexico: Artes de México/Instituto Cultural Domecq, p. 39.

Román Berrelleza, Juan Alberto.
1990. *Sacrificio de niños en el Templo Mayor*. Mexico: INAH/GV Editores/Asociación de Amigos del Templo Mayor.

Sahagún, Fray Bernardino de
1989. *Historia general de las cosas de Nueva España*. Eds. A. López Austin and J. García Quintana. 2 vols. Mexico: CNCA/Alianza Editorial Mexicana.
1995. "Historia general de las cosas de Nueva España [1565–1577]" (excerpt). In E. Matos Moctezuma, ed., *La pirámide del Sol, Teotihuacán: Antología*. Mexico: Artes de México/Instituto Cultural Domecq, pp. 29–32.

7

Teotihuacan Cultural Traditions Transmitted into the Postclassic According to Recent Excavations

Rubén Cabrera Castro

Translated by Scott Sessions

It is archaeologically confirmed that Teotihuacanos received numerous ideas and traditions in several areas of knowledge from peoples that preceded them, but many of these were also transmitted through them to later groups. Teotihuacanos initiated a strong cultural, political, economic, and religious culture that paved the way for subsequent cultures to follow in highland Central Mexico. This is confirmed every time that more data are obtained from archaeological excavations, not only from Teotihuacan but also from other sites corresponding to later periods, where materials showing similarities to Teotihuacan cultural elements are discovered. Moreover, numerous accounts referring to ceremonies, rites, and legends that allude to Teotihuacan are found in documentary sources and in the codices of Late Postclassic peoples. Many of these data find their antecedents in Teotihuacan archaeological contexts that confirm the existence of a strong Teotihuacan tradition transmitted to peoples developing in later periods. In this essay, I will refer only to some of the recent discoveries related to astronomy, the cosmos, the calendar, and glyphic writing that Teotihuacanos possessed, data that are also manifested in sites that flourished after the collapse of the great urban center.

ASTRONOMY AND THE CALENDAR

Various authors have referred to the astronomical function of some of the buildings and the development of the calendar in Teotihuacan. Mainly, they have speculated that some of the Ciudadela (Citadel) Complex buildings, due to their position and context, were closely related to astronomy and calendrics (Drucker 1974; Cabrera 1993). It has been suggested that the three temples of the East Platform of the Ciudadela Complex, due to their form and layout, may have been inspired by an architectural design derived from Group E at Uaxactún, where an artificial horizon was created by three temples located on a platform east of an observation temple with a radial plan (Building E-VII sub). Anthony Aveni (1993: 314) states that Franz Blom, in 1924, was the first to point out these buildings' astronomical function of determining solstices and equinoxes.

Other examples from archeological sites in the Maya area were derived from the Uaxactún complex. According to Rubén Morante (1996)—citing Anthony Aveni and Horst Hartung (1989: 455) and Vilma Fialko (1988)—eighteen sites with this model or pattern of horizontal astronomical observation have been located, including the complex at Dzibilchaltún and that of the Mundo Perdido (Lost World) at Tikal. With the exception of Uaxactún's Group E, the rest of these complexes, due to their architectural design relating more to the 260-day ritual calendar than the 365-day solar calendar, have been designated "astronomical commemoration complexes" (Fialko 1988).

Uaxactún's Group E complex is the oldest. The observation temple and platform situated toward the east have a chronology that runs between 600 and 500 B.C.E., but the three temples above it date to around 100–250 C.E. According to Anthony Aveni and Horst Hartung (1989), Uaxactún's Group E corresponds to the Early Classic, or perhaps a bit earlier during the Protoclassic. The rest of the examples, however, are much later. According to Fialko, some of them, including the Tikal and Dzibilchaltún complexes, are contemporaries of Teotihuacan's Ciudadela Complex. Determining the provenance and diffusion of this idea is largely a question of reexamining the dates of each of the sites. Our recent work in the Ciudadela has provided a better approximation of new dates concerning the construction of the Temple of the Feathered Serpent, which we think took place between 200 and 250 C.E. (Cabrera 1998; Cowgill 1998; Sugiyama 1998), and even though we have no exact dates for the platform that surrounds this complex, its construction seems to have occurred immediately after that of the temple. Therefore, we think this tradition of horizontal astronomical observation may have come from Uaxactún. Due to their position, various authors have suggested that the buildings forming part of this observation system are the central shrine found on the great esplanade of this architectural group and the three pyramidal foundations located on the East Platform (Figure 7.1).

CAVES WITH ASTRONOMICAL AND CEREMONIAL FUNCTIONS

Another system of astronomical observation used at Teotihuacan is the vertical method, as practiced at Building P in Monte Albán, Oaxaca, and the astronomical cave at Xochicalco in the modern-day state of Morelos. Observatories of this type were found in Teotihuacan in three caves with vertical access dug in the volcanic rock. Being older than the observatories of Xochicalco and Monte Albán, it seems that this system, utilized to perform celestial observations, was created by Teotihuacanos and the idea was transmitted to other later groups (Morante 1996: 159). The caves in Teotihuacan adapted for this purpose are shaped like giant bottles, with a narrow vertical opening in the volcanic rock that widens as it reaches the bottom, where a small altar with a stone slab or astronomical marker rising from the cave floor is illuminated by the projection of the sun's light at certain hours and periods of the year.

One of these caves, registered as Cave 1, was discovered during the Proyecto Arqueológico Teotihuacán 1980–1982 excavations and studied by archaeologist Enrique Soruco (1985 and 1991), and is located southeast of the Pyramid of the Sun in quadrant N3E1 on René Millon's map (Millon, Drewitt, and Cowgill 1973). Two others, registered as Caves 2 and 3, also found in the same place just north of Cave 1, were explored by archaeologist Natalia Moragas (1996) during the Proyecto Especial Teotihuacán 1992–1994 excavation directed by archaeologist

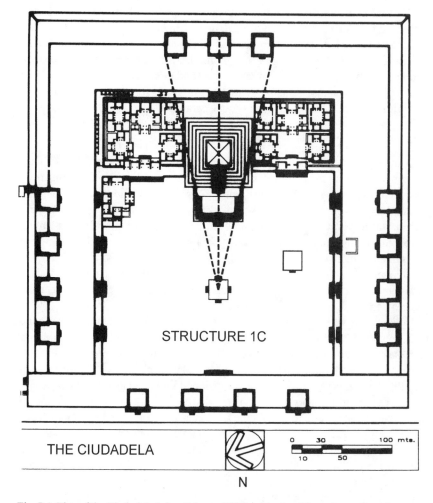

STRUCTURE 1C

THE CIUDADELA

0   30   100 mts.
10   50

N

Fig. 7.1. Plan of the Ciudadela (after Cabrera 1991), with visual lines drawn from Structure 1C illustrating the horizontal system of astronomical observation (after Morante 1996).

Eduardo Matos Moctezuma. A fourth cave, with a different type of interior, but with similar characteristics in terms of access and vertical trajectory, causing us to think it too probably had an astronomical function, was found at the summit of Cerro Malinali, on the edge of the ancient city, northeast of the Pyramid of the Sun.

Caves 1, 2, and 3 are located in a space enclosed by a thick wall, an area delimited on three of its sides, where only one entrance was found. Although its south side was not located, the site's characteristics suggest that its access was strictly controlled and the context of the caves attests that, in addition to the astronomical observations, ceremonial events were also performed there.

Caves 1 and 2 were found intact, and though the interior of Cave 1 was filled with earth containing archaeological remains from later periods, its occupation floor had not been altered. In the case of Cave 2, its entrance was found sealed, thus its interior chamber was empty of debris. Numerous offerings were found in both, along with an altar in each of them upon which a thin stone slab had been situated that functioned as an astronomical marker. In contrast, Cave 3, though its vertical access showed no signs of alteration, also had a horizontal entrance through which its interior space was enlarged and modified, and which was later used for interring human remains, primarily from post-Teotihuacan times associated with Coyotlatelco, Mazapa, and Aztec ceramics.

CAVE 1

Associated materials found in Cave 1 provide considerable evidence that, along with being an astronomical observatory, it also had a ceremonial function. As the corresponding illustration (Figure 7.2) shows, a shallow depression, surrounded by a Teotihuacan floor whose surface was constructed of mortar and stucco, was found at the bottom of the cave. In this cavity or tomb, human femurs were found painted red with their ends perforated (Figure 7.3). On the east side of this same tomb, a small rectangular altar was constructed, upon which a stone slab or stela remains in situ in a vertical position (Figure 7.4). This stone slab or astronomical marker is completely illuminated on the one day of the year when the sun crosses the sky very close to its zenith passage. According to Soruco (1991: 292), the points where the sun's light reaches the cave floor, from one year to the next, confirms that the sun returns to the same points every 365 days. In addition to these data, Soruco discovered two other positions in this cave related to solar projections corresponding to the dates of May 24 and July 20 (see Figure 7.2). On July 20, the entire altar is completely enveloped by the sun's light. This cave is considered to be the oldest of the three due to its ceramic context dating to Teotihuacan IIa, or around 200–300 c.e. This date is corroborated by numerous ceramic offerings found in its interior, with the latest materials corresponding to Early Tlamimilopa ceramic phases, found below the stuccoed floor of the cave (Soruco 1991: 294). In addition to the numerous ceramic offerings, twenty prismatic obsidian blades of excellent quality, whose number may significantly relate to the calendar, were found inside the small altar upon which the stela or astronomical marker was situated.

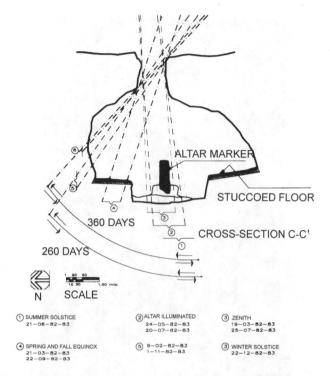

Fig. 7.2. Cross-section C-C' of astronomical Cave 1 (after Soruco 1991).

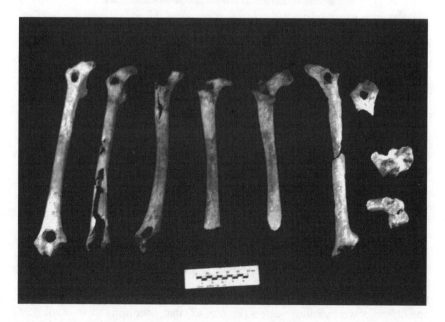

Fig. 7.3. Human femurs with perforated ends found in the interior of Cave 1 were part of a ritual performed inside the astronomical cave.

Fig. 7.4. This vertical stone slab or astronomical marker from Cave 1 is situated on a small altar and is completely illuminated on one day during the year.

CAVE 2

Its opening, found about 10 meters north of Cave 1's entrance, is also vertical and, although smaller, has similar features. Its entrance was found totally sealed, thus the greater reliability of its contents. Like the other two caves, a small circular deposit was found near the entrance that may have contained some type of liquid (Figure 7.5). Access to this cave is made through a circular hole around 80 centimeters in diameter that is quite narrow like the neck of a bottle and begins to widen at a depth of around 2.8 meters. At about 4.8 meters, a layer of packed earth is found that constitutes the occupation floor or surface. Given its characteristics and context, it is also thought to be "a ceremonial cave with astronomical connotations" (Moragas 1996: 124) with a small altar and a stone slab with similar features as those found in Cave 1 (Figure 7.6). Among the associated materials and offerings were various vessels (Figure 7.7) that, according to archaeologist Moragas, "could be ascribed to the Miccaotli to Early Tlamimilolpa Phases, nevertheless, some of them coexist with somewhat earlier forms as well as vessels with vertical supports corresponding to the Late Tlamimilolpa Phase." The chronology of this offering led her to suggest a terminal date of around 300 c.e. for the functioning of this cave.

These caves also were examined by Morante (1996: 169–170), who, based on the dates suggested by Soruco for Cave 1 and Moragas for Cave 2, thinks that Teotihuacanos invented this form of carrying out astronomical observations. Morante has been analyzing various chambers with astronomical functions from different sites in Mesoamerica, and has observed that of all the astronomical chambers reported to date, those at Teotihuacan are the oldest. Among the caves mentioned in his study are the well-known Cave of the Sun at Xochicalco, which contains a chimney through which solar rays penetrate, and Building or Mound P at Monte Albán, an area constructed around 400–600 c.e. He also refers to a well at Chichén Itzá that dates from the Late Classic, as well as an underwater cave at Xel Ha in Quintana Roo. All these sites correspond to later periods than those of the astronomical caves at Teotihuacan.

Numerous caves exist in the subsoil of the northern portion of the Teotihuacan Archaeological Zone, and thus it is very possible that in the future other similar observatories will be found, although not joined to the three aforementioned caves, since, as I previously specified, they were enclosed by a thick wall. According to the assigned chronology, these caves must have operated during Teotihuacan's earliest phases, but the causes of their closing at the end of the Late Tlamimilolpa Phase is not known. A deeper study, however, is required to better understand its functioning and the reasons why its use was terminated.

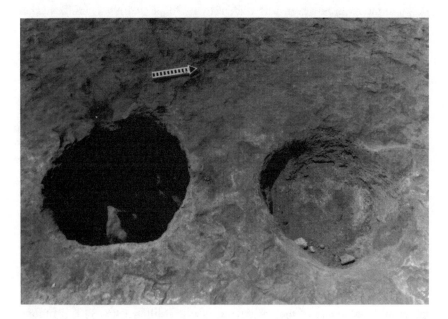

Fig. 7.5. Opening and circular deposit near the entrance to Cave 2.

Fig. 7.6. Stela or astronomical marker situated on a small altar inside Cave 2 shown behind a stone maquette or base and a Teotihuacan ceramic vessel in the foreground.

Earlier in this chapter I mentioned that another very similar cave was found on top of Cerro Malinalli, located very close to the northwest edge of the ancient city of Teotihuacan. Although no studies of it exist, this cave is really a deep vertical well dug into the rock; however, it is evident by its shape that it was utilized as an observatory to measure the passage of light projected by celestial bodies.

The So-Called Astronomical Markers

There are some other symbolic elements, though not related to astronomical measurements, that various authors have related to the calendar, the cosmos, measurements, and orientations. I am referring to the circular symbols and pecked crosses, also known as astronomical markers, that are crossed in the center by two perpendicular axes aligned toward the cardinal points and are often found in Teotihuacan and other Teotihuacan sites such as Tepeapulco in the modern-day state of Hidalgo. These figures, however, are also found in other parts of Mesoamerica, as far from Teotihuacan as Durango to the northwest and lowland Guatemala to the southeast. They usually appear on building floors, although they are also found on rocks in the nearby hills.

Due to their abundance in Teotihuacan sites, it has been suggested that this symbolic element originated in Teotihuacan (Winning 1987: 61). Because their axes, pointing toward the four cardinal directions, were found in specific points in the city, other authors have suggested that these crosses have a cosmogonic-calendrical significance, and that they may have served as instruments of orientation in the planning of the ancient metropolis (Millon 1968: 113). Anthony Aveni, Horst Hartung, and Beth Buckingham (1978; Aveni and Hartung 1982) have carried out the most extensive studies on these symbols and have pointed out their characteristics and their possible function in numerous publications. Our intention here is to emphasize what von Winning suggested—their possible Teotihuacan origin.

Although most of these figures were discovered on floors corresponding to the last level of Teotihuacan occupation, they also have been found on the floors of substructures, indicating their use in earlier phases. One piece of evidence confirming their antiquity and suggesting their possible Teotihuacan origin was recently found on a compacted *tepetate* floor belonging to a substructure in the La Ventilla architectural group (Romero 1996). The ceramics associated with this floor correspond to the Miccaotli Phase, that is to say, this figure has an known antiquity of between 150 and 200 c.e. Another figure or concentric pecked circle was found, although incomplete, on the north landing of the Temple of the Feathered Serpent, on the fresco floor from which the building rises exactly on its north-south axis, also corresponding to the Miccaotli Phase (Morante 1996: 142).

Up until a little before the completion of the Proyecto Especial Teotihuacán 1992–1994, directed by Eduardo Matos Moctezuma, around twenty-four pecked circles were known in Teotihuacan, which Aveni has identified with progressive numbers placed after the word "TEO." During the Proyecto Especial Teotihuacán excavations, however, a group of forty-four pecked figures were found in a space 20 meters long and 2 meters wide, at the foot of the south wall of the platform surrounding the Pyramid of the Sun (Matos 1995: 26–27). The figures in this

Fig. 7.7. Ceramics associated with Cave 2 situated on the occupation floor.

Fig. 7.8. Recently discovered astronomical markers situated on a Teotihuacan floor near the south wall on the south side of the platform that surrounds the Pyramid of the Sun.

unusual group vary in size and shape, including some superimposed on others that do not seem to correspond to the same chronology. Although they were executed on the same floor, some of their axes retain the same orientation, but the majority's orientations are different. Recently, Morante (1996) described some of them in a general study of these figures. Their formal analysis, however, is still pending and when completed will provide greater information for understanding their significance (Figure 7.8).

Most but not all of the axes have a 16° deviation with respect to the cardinal directions at the point where they perpendicularly cross the center of the figures, forming four quadrants or sectors. Because of this, some authors think that the cruciform motifs were utilized in the orientation of buildings and possibly contributed in the planning of the two principal axes of the city—the Street of the Dead and the East and West Avenues.

Some of these pecked figures, especially the one known as TEO 2, have shapes that seem very similar to plate 1 of the *Codex Fejérváry-Mayer* (1994), and have been related to the cruciform quincunx (Aveni, Hartung, and Buckingham 1978: 267; Aveni and Hartung 1982: 39). Symbolic figures like these are manifested repeatedly in Teotihuacan iconography in multiple variants, including the four-petaled figure and other similar symbols that may be considered antecedents of the elaborate "Maltese cross" or cruciform quincunx motifs in the iconography of Postclassic cultures, especially in some of the codices from highland Central Mexico, such as the aforementioned *Fejérváry-Mayer* image.

THE CRUCIFORM QUINCUNX FIGURE

Representations of simple or elaborate figures with the same cruciform structure pointing to the four directions and their intermediate points are found depicted in the mural painting, ceramics, and even sculpture and architecture of Teotihuacan. Many authors think that these cruciform figures or signs represent the four cosmogonic directions in indigenous thought (see Figure 7.9 [a and b]). According to this conception, the cross is the symbol of the universe in its totality. Specialists on the subject say this figure points toward the four cosmogonic regions at the same time it highlights the center. Similar figures, alluding to the

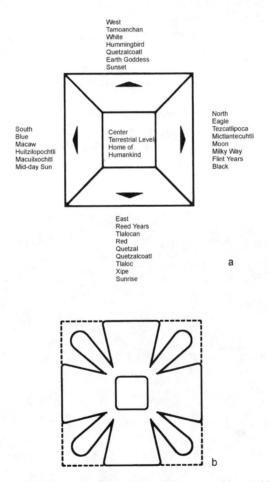

West
Tamoanchan
White
Hummingbird
Quetzalcoatl
Earth Goddess
Sunset

North
Eagle
Tezcatlipoca
Mictlantecuhtli
Moon
Milky Way
Flint Years
Black

South
Blue
Macaw
Huitzilopochtli
Macuilxochitl
Mid-day Sun

Center
Terrestrial Level
Home of
Humankind

East
Reed Years
Tlalocan
Red
Quetzal
Quetzalcoatl
Tlaloc
Xipe
Sunrise

a

b

Fig. 7.9.a. The pre-Hispanic conception of the world expressed in graphic form, with the earth as the central space surrounded by the four regions marking the cardinal points (after Gendrop 1979); b. Schematic outline of plate 1 of the *Codex Fejérváry-Mayer*, a cyclographic-astronomical figure depicting the five regions of the universe including the center according to indigenous thought.

four cosmogonic directions are found in Late Postclassic documents, primarily in the codices whose faraway antecedents of this conception of the universe may be found in Teotihuacan. In order to reinforce the hypothesis that these figures have a Teotihuacan heritage, I will present some of the many examples of iconographic motifs found in Teotihuacan that greatly resemble the cruciform quincunx figure.

THE ARCHITECTURAL STRUCTURE LOCATED IN FRONT OF THE PYRAMID OF THE MOON

The architectural form and composition of this edifice, investigated by archaeologist Ponciano Salazar from 1962 to 1964 and registered as Structure A of Zone 1, are like no other class of building found in Teotihuacan or any other Mesoamerican site (Figure 7.10). It has a square floor, around 20 meters per side, with only one entrance located on its west side. In its interior are ten small structures or altars, arranged symmetrically according to the four cardinal directions and their intermediate points (Figure 7.11 [a]). No information concerning its function exists, but it must have been very important given its unique form and its location on the Plaza of the Moon, an area of significant religious importance. Its general chronology is based on the surrounding buildings that, according to Acosta (1966: 48), are dated between 300 and 650 C.E.

The archeologist Otto Schöndube completed a general study of this building from the perspective of its possible function and significance. By way of analogy

Fig. 7.10. Architectural structure, located in front of the Pyramid of the Moon, containing a group of altars whose distribution forms a design similar to the cruciform quincunx figure.

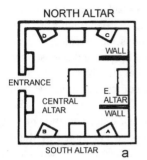

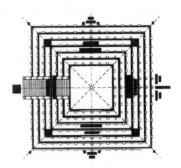

Fig. 7.11. Figures depicting symbolic elements indicating the five directions of the universe, according to archaeological data; a. Schematic drawing of the structure located in front of the Pyramid of the Moon; b. Schematic drawing of the figures represented on Building 1B' located on the esplanade of the Ciudadela; c. Schematic drawing of the Temple of the Feathered Serpent in the Ciudadela illustrating the symmetrical distribution of human burials located inside and outside of the building.

he considers that it must be related to the figure appearing in plate 1 of the *Codex Fejérváry-Mayer* (Schöndube 1975: 241). That is to say, he thinks that this architectural structure is a three-dimensional representation of the four directions of the universe and the dwelling of the gods as depicted in the codex image. The similarity can be seen when comparing the architectural structure with the general outline of the codex image (see Figures 7.9 [b] and 7.11 [a]).

THE CALENDARICAL MOTIFS OF BUILDING 1B'

Other Teotihuacan representations similar to the *Fejérváry-Mayer* image are found in the architectural substructure of the building located on the platform of the Ciudadela and registered as 1B' in the Millon project (Millon, Drewitt, and Cowgill 1973). I investigated the interior of this building from 1980 to 1982 and have already published general information concerning its characteristics (Cabrera 1982: 85, 1991: 46).

The substructure containing these pictorial motifs is called Sub–2 and corresponds to the fifth superimposition in a sequence of seven superimposed structures. The designs depicted on this building consist of two red, perpendicularly superimposed rectangles; three alternating green and black concentric circles in the center; and four narrower elements or strips superimposed on this cruciform figure, which, viewed together, point to the four directions and intermediate points, resembling the *Fejérváry-Mayer* image (see Figure 7.11 [b]). For this reason these symbolic motifs are thought to be related to the calendar and considered antecedents of other similar figures appearing in Postclassic codices of highland Central Mexico.

These figures covered the four façades of the building, and though they have not been fully examined, calculating from the space occupied by the depicted motifs, arranged one after another, there must have been at least thirty identical figures on this building organized in the following manner: three figures on each side of the stairway on the principal façade, eight on its north side, eight on its south side, and quite possibly eight on its back side.

THE SYMMETRICAL DISTRIBUTION OF BURIALS AT THE TEMPLE OF THE FEATHERED SERPENT

Another example similar to the quincunx figure is found at the Temple of the Feathered Serpent, where numerous human burials were discovered that had been sacrificed in honor of the construction of this building or to the deity venerated there. The arrangement of the burials clearly indicates their relation to the cosmos and the calendar. Inference to the 260-day ritual calendar and possibly the solar calendar is based on the number of skeletons that make up these burials. They were arranged symmetrically inside and outside the pyramid, as I have specified elsewhere (Cabrera and Cabrera 1993), in groups of four, eight, nine, eighteen, and twenty skeletons, in addition to individual burials. These numbers have been considered the most important in the Mesoamerican calendar. The symmetrical distribution of these burials and the quantity of skeletons found so far suggest that 260 people must have been buried at this building, a number corresponding to the amount of days in the ritual calendar. Its cosmogonic meaning is manifested in their arrangement, clearly related to the four directions of the universe, their intermediate points, and the center, where a burial of twenty skeletons was located, to represent the cruciform quincunx pattern (see Figure 7.11 [c]).

This important information was recently obtained from the Temple of Quetzalcoatl Project directed by Dr. George L. Cowgill and myself with the valuable assistance of Saburo Sugiyama and others. This event of large-scale human sacrifice took place when the Temple of the Feathered Serpent was erected around 150–250 C.E.

The three examples that I have presented are more than enough to consider that the idea of the cruciform pattern and the cosmogony of the pre-Hispanic peoples of Mexico summarized in the *Fejérváry-Mayer* image had antecedents in Teotihuacan. Presently, however, we are unable to assert that this figure and the cosmogonic principles it represents were a Teotihuacan invention. It is most probable that this tradition came from more ancient peoples, but it clearly had a great impact on Teotihuacan, such that it influenced the layout of the ancient city and, it seems, that of Tenochtitlan as well. In the case of Teotihuacan's layout, René Millon (1966: 73) says that the site of the Ciudadela was not only the geographic center of the city, but together with the Great Complex, it was also the cultural and political center, formed by the crossing of the East and West Avenues with the Street of the Dead. This conception, analogous to the Sacred Precinct of Tenochtitlan, is based on a religious structure that reflects cosmic order, as various persons have proposed. Referring to the Sacred Precinct of Mexico Tenochtitlan, Sonia Lombardo de Ruiz states,

> When Mexico [Tenochtitlan] took its first steps towards urban development, the presence of Huitzilopochtli was again manifested. The sources indicate that scarcely had the city grown, the god ordered the Mexicans to divide themselves into four principal *barrios*, the shrine taking the center . . . once this division was made, he ordered each section to be divided among the gods so that all of them would be worshipped (1972: 49–50).

The conception and design of the Sacred Precinct of Mexico Tenochtitlan takes as its model the figure shown on plate 1 of the *Codex Fejérváry-Mayer*, whose more ancient antecedents, as we previously mentioned, are found in Teotihuacan.

GLYPHIC FIGURES ON A TEOTIHUACAN FLOOR, THE OLDEST ANTECEDENTS OF THE CODICES OF HIGHLAND CENTRAL MEXICO

In the excavations of La Ventilla, one of the Teotihuacan barrios recently discovered during the Proyecto Especial Teotihuacán 1992–1994, a group of glyphic figures were found that surely were part of an ancient writing system. Due to their style and subject matter, I have suggested in other writings that this glyphic system represents the oldest antecedent of some of the codices from highland Central Mexico (Cabrera 1996). Before referring to this discovery, it is necessary to present some data that in a certain way are part of the general context. These glyphic figures were found on the floor of one of the architectural groups recently investigated at La Ventilla, a site covering more than 13,500 square meters, in the southwest quadrant formed by the two great axes that cross the city at the Ciudadela, more specifically located in spaces N1W1, N1W2, S1W1, and S1W2 on Millon's grid (Millon, Drewitt, and Cowgill 1973).

The area investigated in the barrio of La Ventilla shows a very important portion of Teotihuacan urbanization. Various architectural complexes of diverse categories were discovered with their own arrangements, interiors, and ambiance, different in certain ways from those already known at Teotihuacan. The newly discovered architectural groups are separated by streets that, viewed together, represent a clear example of Teotihuacan's urban complexity. As previously mentioned, it is a barrio or part of a barrio that made up the urban system of the ancient city (see Figure 7.12).

Among the discoveries, an architectural group of a civic-religious character stands out, principally consisting of pyramidal bases, patios, and shrines, enclosed by high walls and streets separating habitational complexes of various categories, including those of the residential or "palace" type of extraordinary construction and with some walls decorated with murals (see Figure 7.13). Other architectural complexes were found with smaller spaces whose exterior constructions were of a lesser quality. Some of these complexes are found associated with

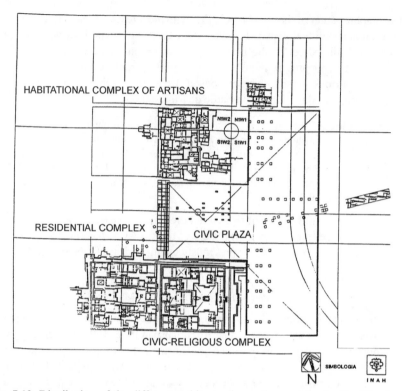

Fig. 7.12. Distribution of the different architectural complexes at the La Ventilla site, Teotihuacan.

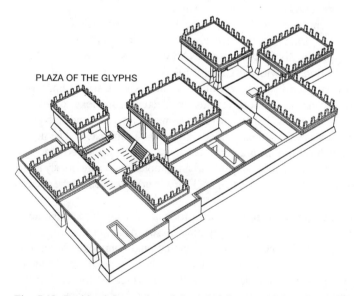

Fig. 7.13. Residential complex of the palatial type and the Plaza of the Glyphs at La Ventilla, Teotihuacan.

artisanal workshops where luxury objects made of greenstone, shell, bone, and other materials were produced. In addition to these complexes, a platform or open space without any construction on it was found in the area studied, whose function we do not know. This open space has been considered to be a possible neighborhood *tianguis* or market, a grove, possibly a lagoon, or a public plaza for social events. Determining its function of this space is not easy since the soil was subjected considerable recent cultivation. Nevertheless, soil samples obtained by the biologists who participated in this project may perhaps help determine the function that this open space might have had. Also associated with these architectural complexes was an intricate hydraulic system made up by canals, reservoirs, sewers, and drains.

As expected, the enormous area of investigation containing various architectural complexes provided valuable information and numerous objects made of ceramic, lithic, shell, bone, and other material. More than three hundred burials were recovered, including numerous sacrificed children. Many of these data are of relevant importance for understanding Teotihuacan culture, including a group of forty-two glyphic figures found in one of the habitational complexes of the residential or "palace" type. I will now present some of examples from this new information (Figure 7.14).

Of the forty-two figures, most were found painted on the floor of a small patio of one of the architectural complexes considered to be of the residential and possibly administrative habitational type. Some of these glyphic figures were painted on a small altar found in the center of this section, while others were depicted on the walls that made up this patio bordered by a pyramidal base and three colonnaded chambers. Many red spots were also found on the floors of the habitations near this patio, suggesting that this graphic system of glyphic signs consisted of a large number of figures.

This group of drawings includes representations of human figures, animals, symbolic objects, buildings, and movable objects. There are also abstract representations and other drawings that due to their poor state of preservation/conservation have been impossible to identify. With the exception of one skull depicted in profile facing west, the rest of the human and animal figures are depicted facing east, or to left of the observer standing on the north side facing south. There are other figures shown head on, such as representations of buildings and movable objects, among which there are depictions of bags, similar to those of copal, that priests and other personages are pictured carrying in Teotihuacan murals. They also include representations of the so-called *zacatapayolli*, or grass-ball receptacle for the spines or needles used for autosacrifice.

Some figures of animals are depicted with their entire bodies; among them are four small birds and two reptiles. The birds have been identified as hummingbirds due to their long beaks. Two of them appear inside receptacles as if they were sitting in their nest. Concerning the reptile figures, two serpents have been recognized wearing a deer staff on their heads, a motif that some have suggested may indicate the Nahuatl word *mazacoatl*.

Among the mammalian figures identified, four felines and one canine are depicted, only with their heads in profile, except for a dog whose body is partly

Fig. 7.14. Glyphic figures situated on a floor at La Ventilla, Teotihuacan.

shown. Nine human heads also appear; two wear no adorning elements while seven are depicted with various symbolic elements that are attributes of Tlaloc, the rain god, including large eye rings, ear ornaments consisting of a disk with hanging rectangles, mustache, and the characteristic fangs of this deity. They also wear on their heads a horizontal bow or knot, an iconographic element that has been related to the Oaxacan knot deity (Caso and Bernal 1952).

Some of the figures identified as Tlaloc are accompanied by other well-known symbolic elements in Teotihuacan iconography; for example, glyphs such as the "reptile eye," the "kindling bundle" related to the sacred fire, the so-called flaming elements, the water lily, the speech scroll, and the cruciform quincunx figure. In this group of iconographic and symbolic elements, Tlaloc is clearly the central figure as some integral part of the phrase that is possibly being expressed (Figure 7.15).

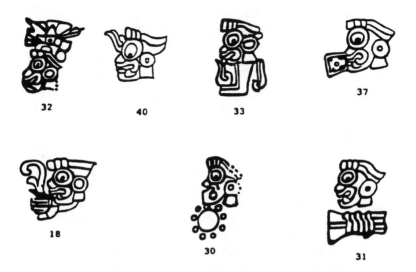

Fig. 7.15. Glyphic figures representing Tlaloc associated with various symbolic elements.

The forty-two figures may be organized in five groups:

a) Those that seem arranged from east to west, one after the other in a row or line, and separated by a succession of red lines spaced at regular intervals.

b) Those in rectangular spaces where only one figure is depicted with the same orientation facing east.

c) Those that appear in groups of three, framed within a rectangular space where the figure of Tlaloc is the principal element.

d) Those drawn on the walls of the nearby buildings, not counting the red spots found on other nearby floors outside of the Plaza of the Glyphs.

e) Those found painted on the small altar in the center of the patio.

Concerning their chronology, based on the stratigraphic context I have mentioned elsewhere (Cabrera 1996), these glyphic figures may be dated approximately to 450 C.E. A great portion of these are clearly identified as Teotihuacan glyphs. Such is the case of the glyph known as the "reptile eye" referred to in various studies, which frequently appears on many diverse archaeological materials at Teotihuacan. This group also contains, as previously mentioned, various representations of Tlaloc and other Teotihuacan iconographic elements, such as copal bags adorned with serpent rattles, the so-called flaming elements, kindling bundles, and the speech scroll. Nevertheless, the pictorial style of these figures appears to be late and their manner of expression is very different from the form of representation in Teotihuacan mural painting. Some of the figures are characteristic of the Late Postclassic, such as the depiction of skulls, very frequent in Mexica iconography. One of these skulls has a knife in its mouth and other figures representing cranial masks also have a knife thrust into the nasal passage. Because of these data, some archaeologists have doubted the antiquity of these glyphic figures, thinking that later groups perhaps may have painted them on this floor after the abandonment of Teotihuacan. Supporting our affirmation that they are from Teotihuacan times is the fact that the patio floor where they were found painted corresponds to an occupational level that was later covered by another building stage belonging to one of the last phases of Teotihuacan occupation. This latter floor was raised during our investigations because we found it very deteriorated by recent cultivation, and thanks to this act, this important information could be discovered.

I have discussed elsewhere (Cabrera 1996) that, due to these glyphic characters' linear and ordered arrangement integrated within a matrix of red lines indicating their reading order, this discovery may represent the oldest known antecedent of the pre-Hispanic codices of Postclassic highland Central Mexico. This statement is based on the presence of various clearly recognized Teotihuacan iconographic elements among this group of figures, such as the "reptile eye" glyph (identified by Caso over fifty years ago), the copal bags, the water lily, the speech scroll, and the cruciform quincunx figure, as well as the representations of Tlaloc with his characteristic eye rings, ear ornaments, and fangs. As previously mentioned, these Teotihuacan figures are associated with other late iconographic elements, often represented in Mexica iconography, such as the aforementioned skulls and the so-called *zacatapayolli* element related to autosacrifice. These and other figures are similar to those found depicted in some of the Postclassic codices, including the personage I will now discuss.

A Deity Identified as Xolotl

There is a standing personage that appears painted on the floor of a small sunken patio near the Plaza of the Glyphs, who faces east with his legs extending to the north, and thus must be viewed from the north. The figure is 70 centimeters tall and 46 centimeters wide, including its associated elements (Figure 7.16).

He has the face of an animal, with its mouth partially opened revealing its pointed fangs. Because of these features this personage has been identified as Xolotl, one of the avocations of Venus. He is shown with one of his legs slightly flexed as if he were dancing, in a field of blooming plants whose leaves look like those of maguey, but with flowers. His erect penis stands out, colored pink and ending in a more fiery tone, from which two types of liquid run in different directions. Large drops, possibly representing sacrificial blood, fall down upon the blooming plants. The other symbolic liquid leaving his masculine member shoots forward to a small opening of a drain leading to the street, referring possibly to the semen of the personage fertilizing or inseminating the plants. Because of these elements, I think that this personage may allude to fertility and fecundity.

His attire consists of a wide sash tied around the waist and dangling in back. His elaborate headdress is adorned with iconographic elements similar to personages found in Mesoamerican codices. The rest of the symbolic elements composing this scene are also characteristic in terms of their late style as well as subject matter. Among these elements, a spherical vessel stands out with a flowery speech scroll emerging upward from its opening. The vessel is adorned with concentric

Fig. 7.16. Anthropomorphic personage or deity situated on the floor of a small patio at La Ventilla, Teotihuacan.

circles along with two bows tied vertically on the sides as if they were handles. These iconographic symbols suggest that it may be related to the sacred vessels containing pulque, as represented in various Postclassic Mesoamerican codices, such as the *Borgia* (1993), *Vaticanus B* (1993), and *Borbonicus* (1991), as well as the early colonial *Codex Mendoza* (1992). It is possible that this personage and his associations may be related to this sacred liquid. A more detailed analysis of this finding by specialists, of course, will be able to define its symbolic meaning, a study whose completion is still pending. What I wish to emphasize here is that many of the iconographic elements represented in this recent discovery are already well known and appear in much later cultural contexts.

This is another example of the diverse evidence suggesting that the antecedents of a large part of the religious knowledge, ideas, and concepts of the Postclassic peoples of highland Central Mexico are found in Teotihuacan. Much of the knowledge of Classic Mesoamerica was transmitted by Teotihuacanos to cultures that succeeded them.

REFERENCES

Acosta, Jorge R.
1966. "Una clasificación tentativa de los monumentos arqueológicos de Teotihuacán." In
   Teotihuacán: Onceava Mesa Redonda, México 1966. Mexico: SMA, vol. 1, pp. 45–56.

Aveni, Anthony F.
1993. *Observadores del cielo en el México antiguo.* Mexico: FCE.

Aveni, Anthony F., and Horst Hartung
1982. "New Observations of the Pecked Cross Petroglyph." In F. Tichy, ed., *Space and
   Time in the Cosmovision of Mesoamerica.* Munich: Wilhelm Fink Verlag, pp. 25–41.
1989. "Uaxactún, Guatemala, Group E, and Similar Assemblages: An Archaeoastronomical
   Reconsideration." In A. F. Aveni, ed., *World Archaeoastronomy: Selected Papers from
   the 2nd Oxford International Conference on Archaeoastronomy, Held at Mérida, Yucatán,
   México, 13–17 January 1986.* Cambridge: Cambridge University Press, pp. 441–461.

Aveni, Anthony F., Horst Hartung, and Beth Buckingham
1978. "The Pecked Cross Symbol in Mesoamerica." *Science* 202 (October 20): 267–279.

Cabrera Castro, Rubén
1982. "La excavación de la Estructura 1B', en el interior de La Ciudadela." In R. Cabrera C.,
   I. Rodríguez G., and N. Morelos G., eds., *Memoria del Proyecto Arqueológico
   Teotihuacan 80–82.* Mexico: SEP/INAH, Colección Científica 132, pp. 75–87.
1991. "Secuencia arquitectónica y cronología de la Ciudadela." In R. Cabrera C., I. Rodríguez
   G., and N. Morelos G., eds., *Teotihuacán 1980–1982: Nuevas interpretaciones.* Mexico:
   INAH, Colección Científica 227, pp. 29–60.
1996. "Caracteres glíficos teotihuacanos en un piso de La Ventilla." In B. de la Fuente, ed.,
   La pintura mural prehispánica en México: Teotihuacán. Mexico: UNAM-IIE, vol. II,
   pp. 401–427.
1998. "La cronología de La Ciudadela en su secuencia arquitectónica." In R. Brambila and
   R. Cabrera, eds., *Los ritmos de cambio en Teotihuacán: Reflexiones y discusiones de su
   cronología.* Mexico: INAH, pp. 143-166.

Cabrera Castro, Rubén, George L. Cowgill, and Saburo Sugiyama
1990. "El Proyecto Templo de Quetzalcoatl y la práctica a gran escala del sacrificio
   humano." In A. Cardós de Méndez, ed., *La época clásica: Nuevos hallazgos, nuevas
   ideas.* Mexico: Museo Nacional de Antropología/INAH, pp. 123–146.

Cabrera Castro, Rubén, and Oralia Cabrera Cortez
1993. "El significado calendárico de los entierros del Templo de Quetzalcoatl." In M. T.
   Cabrero, ed., *II Coloquio Pedro Bosch-Gimpera.* Mexico: UNAM-IIA.

Caso, Alfonso
1937. "¿Tenían los teotihuacanos conocimiento del tonalpohualli?" *El México Antiguo* 4:
   131. Reprinted in Alfonso Caso, *Los calendarios prehispánicos* (Mexico: UNAM-
   IIH, 1967).

Caso, Alfonso, and Ignacio Bernal
1952. *Urnas de Oaxaca.* Mexico: INAH.

Codex Borbonicus
1991. *Códice Borbónico.* Facsimile editors F. Anders, M. Jansen, and L. Reyes García.
   Madrid/Graz/Mexico: SEQC/ADV/FCE.

Codex Borgia
1993. Facsimile editors F. Anders, M. Jansen, and L. Reyes García. Madrid/Graz/Mexico:

SEQC/ADV/FCE.

Codex Fejérváry-Mayer
1994. Facsimile editors F. Anders, M. Jansen, G. A. Pérez Jiménez, and L. Reyes García. Madrid/Graz/Mexico: SEQC/ADV/FCE.

Codex Mendoza
1992. Edited by F. F. Berdan and P. R. Anawalt. 4 vols. Berkeley: University of California Press.

Codex Vaticanus B
1993. Facsimile editors F. Anders, M. Jansen, and L. Reyes García. Madrid/Graz/Mexico: SEQC/ADV/FCE.

Cowgill, George L.
1998. "Nuevos datos del Proyecto Templo de Quetzalcoatl acerca de la cerámica Miccaotli-Tlamimilopa." In R. Brambila and R. Cabrera, eds., *Los ritmos de cambio en Teotihuacán: Reflexiones y discusiones de su cronología*. Mexico: INAH, pp. 185-199.

Drucker, David R.
1974. "Renovating a Reconstruction: The Ciudadela at Teotihuacan, Mexico: Construction Sequence, Layout, and Possible Uses of the Structure." Ph.D. dissertation, Anthropology Dept., University of Rochester, Rochester, N.Y.

Fialko, Vilma
1988. "Mundo Perdido, Tikal: Un ejemplo de complejos de conmemoración astronómica." *Mayab* (Madrid) 4 : 13–21.

Gendrop, Paul
1979. *Arte prehispánico en Mesoamérica*. Mexico: Editorial Trillas.

Lombardo de Ruiz, Sonia
1973. *Desarrollo urbano de México-Tenochtitlan según las fuentes históricas*. Mexico: INAH, Departamento de Investigaciones Históricas.

Manzanilla, Linda, Luis Barba, René Chávez, Jorge Arzate, and Leticia Flores.
1989. "El inframundo de Teotihuacán: Geofísica y arqueología." *Ciencia y desarrollo* 15, no. 85: 21–35.

Matos Moctezuma, Eduardo
1995. "Excavaciones recientes en la pirámide del Sol, 1993–1994." In E. Matos Moctezuma, ed., *La pirámide del Sol, Teotihuacán: Antología*. Mexico: Artes de México/Instituto Cultural Domecq, pp. 312–329.

Millon, René
1966. "extensión y población de la ciudad de Teotihuacán en sus diferentes periodos: Un cálculo provisional." In *Teotihuacán: Onceava Mesa Redonda, México 1966*. Mexico: SMA, vol. 1, pp. 57–78.
1968. "Urbanization at Teotihuacan: The Teotihuacan Mapping Project." In *Actas y memorias: XXXVII Congreso Internacional de Americanistas, Mar de la Plata, Argentina, 1966*. Buenos Aires: Buenos Aires Library, vol. 1, pp. 105–125.

Millon, René, Bruce Drewitt, and George L. Cowgill
1973. *Urbanization at Teotihuacan, Mexico*. Vol. 1: *The Teotihuacan Map*. Austin: University of Texas Press.

Moragas S., Natalia
1996. "2 003 cuevas ceremoniales en Teotihuacán: Cuevos hallazgos." *Revista Mexicana de Estudios Antropológicos* 42: 121–127.

Morante López, Rubén B.
1996. "Los observatorios astronómicos subterráneos: ¿Un invento teotihuacano?" *Revista Mexicana de Estudios Antropológicos* 42: 159–172.

Romero H., Javier
1996. "Informe de la excavación del pozo 3 en la Plaza Sur del Frente 1, La Ventilla, Teotihuacán." Ms. in the Archivo Técnico de la Dirección de Arqueología, INAH, México.

Schöndube Baumback, Otto
1975. "Interpretación de la estructura ubicada al pie de la pirámide de la Luna, Teotihuacán." In *Balance y perspectiva de la antropología de Mesoamérica y del centro de México, XIII Mesa Redonda, Xalapa, sep. 9–15 de 1973.* Mexico: SMA, vol. 2, pp. 239–246.

Soruco Sáenz, Enrique
1985. "Una cueva ceremonial en Teotihuacán." Tesis de Licenciatura, ENAH, Mexico, D.F.
1991. "Una cueva ceremonial en Teotihuacán y sus implicaciones astronómico-religiosas." In J. Broda, S. Iwaniszewski, and L. Maupomé, eds., *Arqueoastronomía y etnoastronomía en Mesoamérica.* Mexico: UNAM-IIH, pp. 291–296.

Sugiyama, Saburo
1998. "Cronología de sucesos ocurridos en el Templo de Quetzalcoatl, Teotihuacán." In R. Brambila and R. Cabrera, eds., *Los ritmos de cambio en Teotihuacán: Reflexiones y discusiones de su cronología.* Mexico: INAH, pp. 167-184.

Winning, Hasso von
1987. *La iconografía de Teotihuacán: Los dioses y los signos.* Vol. 2. Mexico: UNAM-IIE.

8

THE 9-XI VASE

A CLASSIC THIN ORANGE VESSEL FOUND AT TENOCHTITLAN

LEONARDO LÓPEZ LUJÁN, HECTOR NEFF, AND SABURO SUGIYAMA

TRANSLATED BY SCOTT SESSIONS

TO JAMES LANGLEY

Like the Babylonians, the Mexica are noted for their interest in the cultural manifestations of societies that preceded them. They felt so attracted to the past that, during the fifteenth and part of the sixteenth centuries, they made innumerable trips to the already archaeological cities of Teotihuacan and Tula (e.g., Umberger 1987a; López Luján 1989: 51–65, 1998, I: 357–364; Boone, chapter 12 of this volume). Amid the ruins, they were accustomed to make sacrifices, deposit offerings, exhume cadavers, and erect monuments. They also took advantage of their sojourns to undertake bonafide excavation campaigns in which they removed enormous amounts of debris to unearth entire buildings. These ambitious projects allowed them to copy architectural profiles, mural paintings, and sculptures in the same manner as they appropriated monolithic images and minor objects, whether supposing the works to be divine or made by legendary peoples. Returning to Tenochtitlan and Tlatelolco, the Mexica were given to the task of reproducing the old styles in markedly eclectic buildings, exhibiting some of the relics in their

The Fifth Field Season of the Proyecto Templo Mayor was carried out thanks to financial contributions from the Instituto Nacional de Antropología e Historia, the Asociación de Amigos del Templo Mayor, A.C., and the Raphael and Fletcher Lee Moses Mesoamerican Archive and Research Project (Princeton University). We would like to thank Eduardo Matos Moctezuma, Alfredo López Austin, Davíd Carrasco, and Scott Sessions for their constant support. We also want to acknowledge Laura del Olmo and José María García, who participated directly in the excavation of Offering V; Warren Barbour, Cynthia Conides, Linda Manzanilla, Debra Nagao, Evelyn Rattray, Mari Carmen Serra Puche, and Javier Urcid, who provided valuable critiques and suggestions to earlier drafts of this work; and Fernando Carrizosa Montfort and Ténoch Medina, who produced the drawings.

temples, and burying others as part of dedicatory caches and funerary offerings (Batres 1902: 61–90; Gussinyer 1969: 35, 1970: 8–10; Navarrete and Crespo 1971; Nicholson 1971; Matos 1983, n.d.; Umberger 1987a; López Luján 1989: 25–42, 1993, 137–138, 1998: 364–367; Fuente 1990; Matos and López Luján 1993; Solís Olguín 1997). As demonstrated by archaeological works carried out during the present century in the center of Mexico City, this interesting phenomenon of reutilization was not limited to Teotihuacan and Toltec antiquities; it also extended to Olmec creations (Matos 1979) and those of the Mezcala region (Angulo 1966; González and Olmedo 1990).

The fundamental purpose of this article is to make known a Teotihuacan-style vase that recently was discovered in the Casa de las Águilas (House of the Eagles), a building located within the Sacred Precinct of Tenochtitlan. We are referring to a vessel that, given its exceptional qualities, we have christened with the name, "*9-Xi.*" It is an interesting example of Thin Orange ceramic produced almost a thousand years before its reutilization as a cinerary urn for the remains of an important Mexica dignitary. This vessel is distinguished by its elevated aesthetic quality and its rich iconographic content. Its greater scientific attraction, however, stems from the appearance of two distinct calendrical dates on its sides. As is well known, this is an extremely rare phenomenon in Teotihuacan civilization. The corpus of numerals consigned by James Langley (1986: 139–143) is limited to twenty-two examples, only half of which seem beyond dispute, and Alfonso Caso (1967a: 143–163), in his celebrated and at the time controversial studies concerning the Teotihuacan calendar, proposed the identification of only a few signs in the *tonalpohualli*, or 260-day cycle, namely "Turquoise," "Eye," "Tiger," and "Wind."

THE CASA DE LAS ÁGUILAS AND OFFERING V

The *9-Xi* Vase was discovered during the Fifth Field Season of the Proyecto Templo Mayor of the Instituto Nacional de Antropología e Historia. This phase of exploration was not conceived of in the spirit of bringing to light unknown portions of the Sacred Precinct of Tenochtitlan, but rather to study integrally and in depth one of the fifteen religious buildings discovered during the 1978–1982 field season. The principal purpose of the new investigation was to analyze all tangible aspects of a specific case in Mexica sacred architecture: its original form and evolution through time, materials and techniques of construction, artistic styles and iconographic programs, special relationships with its surroundings, and associated archaeological objects. Equally important was to confront the difficult problem of functions and religious significance that builders and users had given to the architectural environment.

With these ideas in mind, the Casa de las Águilas was chosen, without a doubt, as the most promising location for gaining such information. This complex of rooms built on an L-shaped platform, is the second-largest building in the area explored by the project (Matos 1984: 19–20; López Luján 1993: 81–82). It stands out as much for its privileged location 15 meters to the north of the Templo Mayor as for its rich decoration and archaizing style (Figure 8.1). Another important reason for continuing work in the Casa de las Águilas was the presence of various large-format ceramic sculptures, codex-style mural paintings, benches with

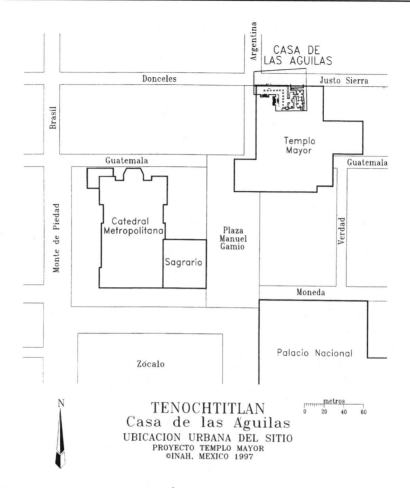

Fig. 8.1. Location of the Casa de las Águilas in the excavation zone (drawn by T. Medina, courtesy of CONACULTA-INAH-MÉX).

polychrome reliefs, and rich offerings that, in all certainty, would offer valuable clues concerning the symbol program and liturgy developed in this ritual space.

Thus, a varied range of archaeological works was carried out from 1994 to 1997 (Barba et al. 1996, 1997; López Luján 1995, 1998; López Luján and Mercado 1996; Román and López Luján 1997). A systematic plan of excavations was developed that consisted of a total of twenty operations in places scrupulously selected as much for complementing previously recovered data as for resolving new questions. In the process of these works the discovery of Offering V and, consequently, the *9-Xi* Vase were registered.

THE SPATIAL AND TEMPORAL LOCATION OF OFFERING V

The excavation of Offering V proved very advantageous for studying the functions and significance of the Casa de las Águilas (Aguirre et al. 1997; López

Luján 1998: 315–327, 500–504). As we shall later see, this rich deposit offered sufficiently abundant data for reconstructing a transcendental funeral ceremony that took place in front of the principal façade of the building (Figure 8.2). It was discovered during Operation Y, a test pit at the bottom of the stairway of the entrance to the east wing (coordinates Q'-60).

The context of this burial corresponds to Stage 3 of the Casa de las Águilas, when the fourth floor (P3/F3) of the North Plaza was in use. Through stratigraphic and stylistic correlation, it was established that the aforementioned construction phase was contemporary to Stage VI of the Templo Mayor (López Luján 1998: 54–56). This means that, if we take into account the existing chronologies (Matos 1981: 50; Umberger 1987b: 415–427), Offering V would date back to the last two decades of the fifteenth century (see Table 8.1).

We should point out, however, that the dating of a carbon sample (INAH-1517e) obtained from inside a ceramic vessel from Offering V itself resulted in a slightly earlier date: CAL AD 1432(1443)1484 with a standard deviation.

THE FUNERARY PITS OF OFFERING V

According to the register of Operation Y, the inhumation of the offering involved the removal of a floor of stone slabs with a mortar foundation (P3/F3) that was found at the bottom of the stairway. We estimated that the disturbed area measured 120 cm north to south by 150 cm east to west (see Figure 8.3). The Mexica then dug three small cylindrical pits through four mortar foundations of slab floors (F3, F4, F5, and F6), a false mortar foundation floor (F7), and five intermediate layers of clay (R3, R4, R5, R6, and R7). The pits were more or less

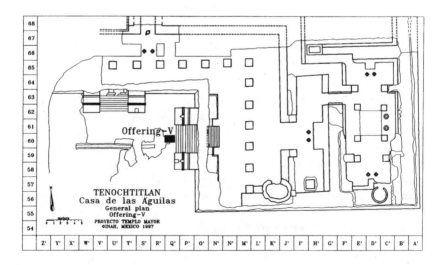

Fig. 8.2. Location of Offering V in the Casa de las Águilas (drawn by T. Medina, courtesy of CONACULTA-INAH-MÉX).

aligned in an east-west direction: the easternmost measured 60 cm north to south, 52.5 cm east to west, and 56 cm deep; the central one, 50 cm north to south, 43.5 cm east to west, and 36 cm deep; and the westernmost, 50 cm north to south, 45 cm east to west, and 39 cm deep.

Construction		Stages Chronology	
Casa de las Águilas	Templo Mayor	Matos	Umberger
1	III	Itzcoatl	Itzcoatl
1	IV	Motecuhzoma I	Motecuhzoma I
1	IVa	Motecuhzoma I	Motecuhzoma I
2	IVb	Axayacatl	Motecuhzoma I
	V	Tizoc	Axayacatl
3/4	VI	Ahuitzotl (1487–1502)	Tizoc/Ahuitzotl (1481–1502)
	VII	Motecuhzoma II	Motecuhzoma II

Table 8.1. Relative chronology of the Casa de las Águilas.

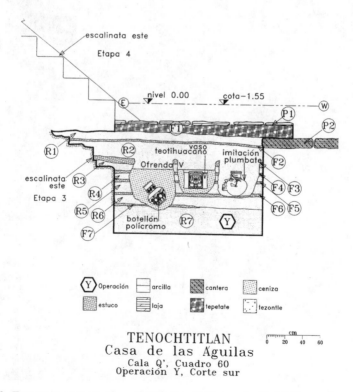

TENOCHTITLAN
Casa de las Águilas
Cala Q', Cuadro 60
Operación Y, Corte sur

Fig. 8.3. East-west cross-section of Offering V (drawn by T. Medina, courtesy of CONACULTA-INAH-MÉX).

Each of these intrusions served to accommodate a ceramic vessel, a portion of the mortal remains of a single individual, and a rich offering. After the inhumation ceremony, the three pits were covered with fragments of the previously removed stucco foundation. Finally, the stone floor at the foot of the stairway was restored, leaving no visible traces of the rite.

THE CONTENTS OF OFFERING V

With respect to the quantity and quality of the materials, Offering V rivals many of the offerings at the Templo Mayor (López Luján 1998: 560–561). This

Fig. 8.4. Offering V during the process of exploration (photo by S. Guil'liem, courtesy of CONACULTA-INAH-MÉX).

three-part deposit contained the remains of a man, a dog, a jaguar, a golden eagle, and a sparrow hawk (Figure 8.4). There were also 101 complete pieces, 32 incomplete, and 318 fragments belonging to artifacts made of ceramic, obsidian, flint, basalt, greenstone, turquoise, gold, copper, bronze, pyrite, bone, shell, copal, cotton, and palm.

Without a doubt, the most impressive objects in the assemblage were the three ceramic vessels used by the Mexica as cinerary urns. They are three fine pieces dating from different periods. The most ancient is the *9-Xi* Vase, a Classic Teotihuacan piece that we will analyze further on in this chapter. Next in terms of antiquity is an effigy jar, in the form of an old man's head, imitating Tohil Plumbate-type ceramic, and produced in the Basin of Mexico during the Early Postclassic (900–1200 C.E.). The third urn is a Mexica polychrome bottle from the Late Postclassic (1200–1521 C.E.) that has a rich decoration of hearts and flowers.

Both inside and around the urns we found a large quantity of human skeletal remains that intentionally had been broken and exposed to fire for many hours. In spite of their fragmentary state, we were able to determine that all of them belonged to one adult male who had suffered from a severe dental ailment (Román and López Luján 1997; López Luján 1998: 280–284).

The ashes and the bone fragments of this individual were accompanied by a lavish offering, a fact that led us to formulate two hypotheses at the moment of exploration. On the one hand, we thought these may have been the remains of a deity impersonator (*ixiptla*) who had been sacrificed in a large brazier and later buried in front of the Casa de las Águilas. On the other hand, he could have been a high-ranking dignitary who, after his death, was cremated and buried at our building.

The first hypothesis, however, seemed unlikely in light of Javier Urcid's (1997) recent analysis of sixteenth-century sources. According to this investigator, the historical texts clearly point out that warriors, captives, and slaves, who were hurled into fire during the festivals of Hueytecuilhuitl, Xocotlhuetzi, and Teotleco, usually did not die from this action (e.g., Sahagún 1989: 90, 92, 137, 145, 153–154). Generally, they spent only brief instances in the flames, after which they were taken to be sacrificed by means of decapitation or heart extraction. In Urcid's judgment, the nature of their exposure to fire would not have been enough to leave traces on the bone tissue. The remains recovered in Offering V, however, exhibited very serious damage, a fact that reinforced the hypothesis concerning a high-level dignitary whose cadaver was cremated.

Other evidence supports this idea. First, we cite the Mexica custom of depositing cremation remains in ceramic vessels witnessed in numerous archaeological contexts (e.g., Ruz 1968: 155, 157; López Luján 1993: 220–229) and historical sources (e.g., Sahagún 1989: 221; Durán 1984, II: 436). Second, we should emphasize the discovery of numerous cranial fragments of a dog in Offering V (Polaco 1998), an animal that the Mexica and their contemporaries often buried together with its master's cadaver for magical ends (e.g., Sahagún 1989: 221).

We must also mention the presence in Offering V of other materials that usually form a part of mortuary contexts in sites such as Tenayuca (Noguera 1935), Tlatelolco (González Rul 1979: 15, 1988: 72–73; Salvador Guil'liem Arroyo, personal communication, May 1990), and Tenochtitlan (López Luján 1993: 222, 225, 351; González Rul 1997: 52–53, 58). In Offering V these included obsidian beads in the form of duck heads, obsidian rings, flint and obsidian projectile points, ceramic spindle whorls, a greenstone bead, cords of cotton and palm, and copal.

While this assemblage of artifacts and dog bones persuaded us to infer with sufficient certainty the occurrence of a funeral in front of the Casa de las Águilas, other materials from the offering gave us some clues concerning the identity of the interred individual. Everything points to the idea that the personage in question was, in fact, a high-ranking dignitary. In this respect, we note that the cadaver was accompanied by goods used exclusively by the nobility. Among these were the fragments belonging to at least three elaborate garments with extremely fine cotton threads and decorated with exquisite brocades. Equally significant are the numerous gold-plated pendants, hemispheres, and spheres that were found together with the textiles. Possibly, these tiny pieces were sewn to some of the cotton cords, although they also could have formed part of a headdress, shield, or other adornment that did not survive the passing of the centuries (cf. Sahagún 1997: 206). It is appropriate to remember here that a good portion of the gold objects discovered in the ruins of the Templo Mayor belonged to funerary deposits of dignitaries from the highest levels of the Mexica hierarchy (López Luján 1993: 347, 351–352).

It would not be unreasonable to imagine that the marine-shell pendants, the bronze and copper bells, the copper tie clasps or brooches, and the turquoise mosaic tesseras recovered from Offering V also formed part of the rich attire of this individual. There is a certain probability that the tesseras formed part of a mosaic turquoise crown (*xiuhuitzolli*) or a nose ornament (*yacaxihuitl*). If our conjectures are correct—unfortunately we are unable to corroborate them—we would be standing before nothing less than the remains of a *tecuhtli* or of a warrior who died heroically (cf. Graulich 1992: 8; *Codex Magliabechiano* 1983: 66v–67r, 71v–72r). We should clarify, however, that he would not have been a *tlatoani* or a *cihuacoatl*, because these two supreme rulers were buried in the royal palace, the Templo Mayor, or the Cuauhxicalco, according to Fernando Alvarado Tezozómoc (1944: 174, 266, 392) and Fray Diego Durán (1984, 2: 248, 300, 369, 395).

Although with certain reservations, it is appropriate to suggest that other objects such as sacrificial knives, obsidian prismatic blades, and perforators made from the long bones of felines and birds of prey also relate to the obsequies of a dignitary. Speculating a little, we might propose that the deceased's servants and slaves were sacrificed with these knives, as mentioned in sixteenth-century sources (e.g., *Costumbres, fiestas, enterramientos* 1945: 57; Sahagún 1989: 222; Alvarado Tezozómoc 1944: 238–239, 390–391; Durán 1984, I: 55–56, II: 248, 295–297, 311, 392–394). Along these same lines, the perforators and prismatic blades were possibly the autosacrificial instruments used in the life of this personage, or by relatives during the funerals.

Unfortunately, determining the role played by other objects found in Offering V is even more difficult. For example, scepters were found with a globe on one end made of obsidian or basalt. These pieces could well be the votive representations of war clubs or of the scepters carried by Techalotl, one of the pulque gods (Nagao 1985: 74–76).

A similar thing occurs with the remains of the feline and birds of prey. During the exploration, some burned animal bones were recovered: a sparrowhawk leg; a golden eagle claw; and an axis vertebra, two secondary premolars, and two fangs of a jaguar (Polaco 1998). These various anatomical parts possibly functioned as amulets or symbols of power. This seems to have been the case with the two jaguar fangs, which were separated from the skull by means of a transversal cut between the root and the crown.

THE SEQUENCE OF THE FUNERARY CEREMONY

Through laboratory analysis we were able to determine that, before crema-tion, the cadaver of the personage and the offering that accompanied him had undergone a systematic process of intentional destruction. As a consequence, a good portion of the human and animal remains, as well as the obsidian, flint, bone, and shell artifacts, were reduced to small fragments that still preserve the impact marks. In contrast, the basalt scepters, the smaller artifacts elaborated in ceramic, obsidian, greenstone, turquoise, gold, bronze, and copper, and some of the bones from his hands and feet apparently did not necessitate such treatment or escaped fragmentation due to their lesser size.

In the case of the cadaver, the diverse fracture patterns indicate that the blows were applied directly to the bones, free of their soft tissues, yet still fresh (Román and López Luján 1997; López Luján 1998: 280–284). In the fracture zones of the long bones, vertebrae, and skull, we found clearly-defined V-shaped clefts measuring about 4 mm, most likely produced with a stone ax weighing between 350 and 500 grams. Approximately 90 percent of the fractures were made with this instrument, primarily affecting the aforementioned skeletal parts. The remaining 10 percent of the intentional fractures were made by manually twisting and flexing the humeri, ribs, ulnae, and clavicles. It is worth adding that the bone perforators also show traces of both types of fracturing.

A detailed osteological analysis revealed a lack of cut marks that would presumably result from defleshing or dismemberment. The absence of these types of marks made us ask ourselves: How were the soft tissues eliminated before the direct fragmentation of the fresh bones? On the one hand, the elimination of the soft tissue may not have been necessary, given a hypothetical state of advanced putrefaction of the cadaver. This hypothesis, however, does not seem very prob-able, because various sixteenth-century sources say that dignitaries were cre-mated within fours days of their deaths (e.g., Benavente 1971: 304). On the other hand, we could speculate that the dead body was subjected to a primary burning that eliminated the soft tissue. We propose that at the end of this cremation, the bones and the offering, partially consumed by fire, were gathered up and frac-tured with an ax and with the hands. This action would increase the efficacy of a second burning and, in time, would facilitate the introduction of the skeletal remains and other objects into the funerary urn.

Whichever the correct explanation may be, we are sure that after their inten-tional destruction, the bones and artifacts of Offering V were methodically mixed together and thrown onto an open-air pyre. In fact, when we reunited the diverse fragments of the same bone or artifact, we saw that they were not exposed to the same intensity of heat. This may be due to the fact that temperatures in this type of fire vary a great deal between interior and extremities, and in terms of the duration of combustion.

In a later stage of the ceremony, part of the residue from the pyre was brought to the bottom of the principal stairway for its interment inside the previously described pits. This residue was composed of an amorphous mixture of ashes, bones, small artifacts, and pieces of larger ones. According to the inventory of Offering V, many fragments from the person's skeleton as well as the objects making up the offering were lacking in this context. This could be due, on the one hand, to numerous fragments being reduced to ashes after their prolonged exposure to fire or, on the other hand, to the possibility that certain portions may have had different destinations than inhumation in Offering V: for example, they may have been discarded, delivered to relatives, or ritually consumed (cf. *Costumbres, fiestas, enterramientos* 1945: 57).

Concerning the rite of inhumation, we have managed to distinguish three consecutive stages. In the first, 95 percent of the largest bone fragments were separated from the mixture in an incandescent state. Immediately after this separation, part of the glowing mixture was deposited at the bottom of the easternmost pit and inside the polychrome bottle. The bottle then was placed in the cavity and was covered with more of the incandescent mixture. This produced burning on the walls of the pit as well as on the inside and outside surface of the bottle. In the second stage, the same action was repeated in the central hole and with the 9-*Xi* Vase. By this time, the mixture had cooled, for neither the pit nor this vessel were burned. The third stage consisted of depositing 95 percent of the large bone fragments, cooled ashes, and copper tie clasps or brooches inside the effigy jar, then placing this urn in the westernmost pit, oriented toward the east. It seems that this exhausted the mixture because the rest of the cavity was filled with clay. Once the ceremony concluded, the three pits were definitively covered with the fragments from the mortar foundation and the stone slabs of the previously removed floor.

THE SHAPE AND CHEMICAL COMPOSITION OF THE 9-*XI* VASE

The 9-*Xi* Vase is a large vessel measuring 20.2 cm in height and 28.2 cm in diameter at its widest point, with its sides being 0.6 cm thick (Figure 8.5). Morphologically speaking, it is a typical Teotihuacan cylindrical vase with a flat bottom, perpendicularly straight sides, and a slightly flanged rim (Figure 8.6 [a and b]). It has two small, flat rings: the upper one, 2 cm wide, is on the rim; the lower one, also 2 cm wide, is near the base. Originally, the vase had three hollow supports, although we do not know if these were in the form of rectangles or *almenas* (crenelations). Only the rectangular outlines of the supports have survived, each one measuring 10.2 cm by 3.9 cm (Figure 8.6 [c]). Two of these areas were intentionally polished, leading us to suppose that the Mexica found the vase with one of the supports broken and decided to eliminate the two remaining supports to reuse the piece as a funerary urn. However, comparing the proportions of other similar vessels, we estimate the original height of the vase to be around 24 cm.

Fig. 8.5. The *9-Xi* Vase (photo by L. López Luján, courtesy of CONACULTA-INAH-MÉX).

Typologically, the *9-Xi* Vase is a clear example of Regular or Export Thin Orange ceramic, in vogue during the Classic period and diffused by Teotihuacanos across a vast territory extending from Chanchopa in the Mexican state of Colima to Copán in Honduras (Sotomayor and Castillo 1963: 7). Numerous investigators have pursued the task of studying Thin Orange ceramic, especially from the 1940s on, when they discovered that it was not produced in the Teotihuacan Valley. At the end of the '80s, after several decades of fruitless efforts, it finally was established through archaeological, petrographic, and chemical means that the center of production was located in the Río Carnero region, about 8 kilometers south of Tepexi de Rodríguez in the state of Puebla (Rattray 1990; Rattray and Harbottle 1992). Among other things, the excavations in the residential units and potters' workshops at the site of Pedernal, Puebla, revealed that the peoples of this region—probably ethnically Popoloca—manufactured enormous amounts of this ceramic with Teotihuacan shapes and motifs during the Classic. This production was destined almost completely for exportation to Teotihuacan. Only this would explain why between 12 and 20 percent of the surface sherds found today in the City of the Gods are the remains of Thin Orange objects (Rattray 1979: 57). In addition to being the principal consumer of this type of ceramic, Teotihuacan held a monopoly on its distribution throughout Mesoamerica. With the decline of the city at the end of the Metepec Phase, however, the production of Export Thin Orange ceramic completely ceased (Sotomayor and Castillo 1963: 20; Müller 1978: 125–126; Rattray 1991: 10–11; Rattray and Harbottle 1992: 223; Cowgill 1996: 329–330). In fact, during the subsequent Coyotlatelco Phase, the inhabitants of the Río Carnero region would have only coarse incense burners in this material for local consumption (Rattray, personal communication, March 1997).

Concerning the *9-Xi* Vase, it is clear that it was produced with the same paste as the majority of Thin Orange pieces. A quick visual inspection is sufficient to tell that it is of semifine texture, porous, and of reddish-yellow color (5YR 6/6), it contains numerous nonplastic schist and quartzite inclusions (from 0.5 to 1 mm), and its surfaces have no slip (cf. Sotomayor and Castillo 1963: 10–17; Müller 1978).

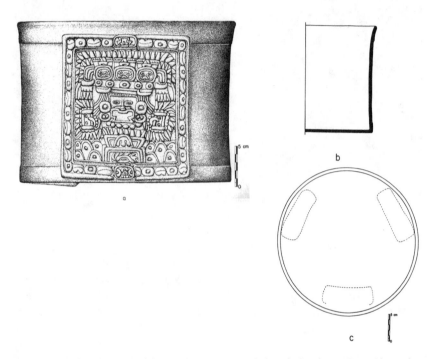

Fig. 8.6. Technical drawing of the *9-Xi* Vase: a. Frontal view; b. Section; c. Base (drawn by F. Carrizosa, courtesy of CONACULTA-INAH-MÉX).

Element	Concentration	Element	Concentration	Element	Concentration
As (ppm)	9.70	Cs (ppm)	14.10	Zn (ppm)	76.00
La (ppm)	53.00	Eu (ppm)	1.92	Zr (ppm)	226.00
Lu (ppm)	0.58	Fe (%)	3.81	Al (%)	11.10
Nd (ppm)	46.00	Hf (ppm)	6.71	Ba (ppm)	1110.00
Sm (ppm)	10.10	Rb (ppm)	193.00	Dy (ppm)	7.42
U (ppm)	3.50	Sb (ppm)	3.49	K (%)	3.80
Yb (ppm)	4.34	Sc (ppm)	18.40	Mn (ppm)	381.00
Ce (ppm)	109.80	Ta (ppm)	1.36	Na (ppm)	1830.00
Co (ppm)	11.40	Tb (ppm)	1.10	Ti (ppm)	5500.00
Cr (ppm)	100.20	Th (ppm)	17.00	V (ppm)	130.00

Table 8.2. Chemical composition of the sample (ppm = parts per million).

In order to corroborate this identification, we decided to take a minute sample from the bottom of the vase for neutron activation analysis (see Neff 1992). The sample was irradiated in the Research Reactor Center at the University of Missouri to measure its gamma spectra and determine its chemical composition.

The results were compared with numerous other Thin Orange specimens contained in the database of the Brookhaven National Laboratory. This comparison demonstrated that the composition of the *9-Xi* Vase was completely consistent for Thin Orange Ware (Figure 8.7). As Evelyn Rattray and Garman Harbottle (1992) have reported, Thin Orange has a unique chemical profile, fundamentally characterized by high concentrations of rubidium (Rb), cesium (Cs), thorium (Th), and potassium (K). In Table 8.2, observe that our vase manifests the same distinctive characteristics, thus confirming its origin in the southern part of the modern state of Puebla.

THE DECORATION OF THE 9-Xi VASE

As we pointed out, the exceptional nature of the *9-Xi* Vase is due to its particular decoration consisting of two identical appliqués in bas-relief. Made from the same mold, these two thin pieces were added onto the polished sides of the vase a short time before firing (see Müller 1978: 116, 125–126; Séjourné 1983: 165). Each appliqué is composed of a central scene measuring 13.6 cm per side and a rectangular frame, 17.9 cm per side and 2.1 cm wide (Figure 8.8).

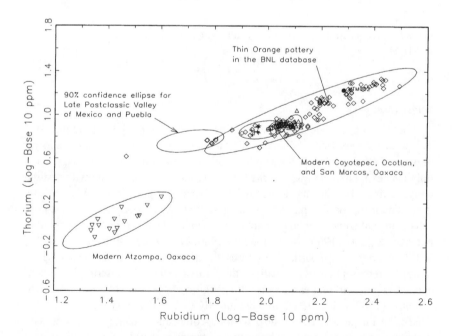

Fig. 8.7. Graphic representation of the chemical comparison between the *9-Xi* Vase sample and other Thin Orange ceramic samples (H. Neff).

Fig. 8.8. Appliqué of the *9-Xi* Vase (drawn by F. Carrizosa, courtesy of CONACULTA-INAH-MÉX).

THE CENTRAL SCENE

In the central scene is observed the frontal, symmetrical representation of a richly adorned personage. This complex image seems to emerge from the lower register of the scene, filled with an interesting series of notational signs, leaving only his head, torso, and open arms visible. He wears his hair long with straight bangs in front. His face has typically Teotihuacan, elliptical eyes and a realistic nose. The lower half of his face is covered by an enormous *yacapapalotl* nose ornament that some scholars identify with *talud-tablero* architecture or with a butterfly (Séjourné 1966: fig. 93; Langley 1986: 277; Winning 1987, I: 119, II: 59–60). The *yacapapalotl* partially obscures the facial painting on his cheeks, which in similar representations is usually in the form of a step-fret pattern. The personage wears large circular ear-spools with hanging rings. These rings, according to Winning (1987, I: 119, 124), imitate butterfly eyes that signify the individual is dead. The image in question also wears a collar and a pair of bracelets with globular beads. In his hands he holds two rectangular shields made of sticks with a plumed fringe on three of the ends.

The personage on the *9-Xi* Vase wears an ostentatious headdress in the form of a stereotyped group of notational signs (see Langley 1993: 132–136) known as the "Panel Cluster." According to Langley (1986: 139, 167–170), this group, frequently associated with the butterfly, could well be the register of a calendrical cycle. The Panel Cluster of our vase is integrated by three levels of notations and surrounded by feathers that denote sacrality or divine rank. In the lowest level are observed five *chalchihuites* superimposed on a band (Langley 1986: 282). The middle level is occupied by three *Reptile's Eye* (RE) glyphs enclosed in double oval cartouches. This glyph was employed during the Classic and Epiclassic as an iconographic element and as a calendrical day sign. Even though associations with water, earth, wind, creation, warriors, and sacrificial victims have been suggested, the exact meaning of the Reptile's Eye remains uncertain. Because of its particular shape, it has been related to the eye of a serpent, of the Cipactli monster, of a butterfly, and to flames (Winning 1961; Caso 1967a: 149, 158, 161–165; 1967b: 265–267; Langley 1986: 98–100, 280–281; Berlo 1989: 25; Miller and Taube 1993: 143). Finally, in the upper level of the Panel Cluster there are three representations of the "Manta Compound," which has strong associations with the calendar and, in particular, with the year, the New Fire, and the year of the New Fire (Langley 1986: 166; 1992: 270–273; 1998). These representations correspond to Langley's Type 3 (1986: 153–159, fig. 46): the lower section is not visible because the Reptile's Eye glyph covers it; the middle section has a trapezoidal element over a band; and the upper section is a triangle with "accessory" signs. From each side of the Panel Cluster hangs a tassel (*Tassel B*) (Langley 1986: 338) that has certain formal similarities with the motif called *Aspergillum* (Langley 1986: 230–231).

As we mentioned above, the lower register of the scene is occupied by a horizontal band of notational signs. In the center of this band, we see the *Feathered Headdress Symbol* (FHS) (Langley 1986: 107–121; 1992: 262). This symbol complex may be broken down into two halves. The lower half consists of a rectangle that encloses a *Feathered Eye*, possibly a calendrical glyph, which has been attributed to birds, serpents, felines, canines, and humans (Langley 1986: 249). This representation corresponds to Langley's Type C (1986: 250), because it only has feathers on the upper portion of the eye. In the upper half we observe a *Trapeze-Ray* ending in a row of feathers ("TR B" in Langley 1986: 293–294). This is the symbol of the year and of political authority (López Austin, López Luján, and Sugiyama 1991: 96–97). According to Langley (1986: 145–152), in Teotihuacan as well as many other Mesoamerican sites, the Trapeze-Ray usually appears as part of calendrical notations or as an attribute of government, military leadership, or sacrifice. Inside the ray of the *9-Xi* Vase there is a *Trilobe* element (cf. Winning 1987, II: 52–53, fig. 1a, 70–71, figs. 9c–d) that usually is interpreted as a set of water droplets or as streams of sacrificial blood (Langley 1986: 296–297).[1] The trapeze is flanked by two diagonal elements with divided ends, which have been interpreted as torches (Taube, chapter 10 of this volume). Finally, we point out that on each side of the Feathered Headdress Symbol there are five large *Mountain* glyphs with their characteristic circles in their interiors (Langley 1986: 274, 331; Winning 1987, II: 11–13).

In sum, the central scene depicts: a) an individual who exhibits attire and paraphernalia related by several authors to the butterfly (nose ornament, ear-rings, and headdress) and to war (shields/wings); b) who is qualified by nota-tions associated with fire, time, governmental authority, and possibly, sacrifice (Panel Cluster, Feathered Headdress Symbol, and the calendrical dates [see be-low]); and c) who emerges from a world of fertility (mountain glyphs and the rectangular frame, see below). He is a personage very similar to those who appear with many commonly shared elements everywhere in Teotihuacan iconography, in different symbol contexts, especially on Theater-type censers (e.g., Winning 1977; Berlo 1983; Manzanilla and Carreón 1991; Sugiyama 1998) (Figure 8.9), poly-chrome vases (e.g., Séjourné 1966: 38) (Figure 8.10), Thin Orange ceramic vessels (e.g., Pasztory et al. 1993: 262–263) (Figure 8.11), and stone sculptures (e.g., Pasztory et al. 1993: 126, 274) (Figure 8.12).

As is frequent in these cases, in spite of the enormous extant iconographic corpus, the identification of the personage in question is still debated. In 1922, Manuel Gamio (1979: 200) suggested that he possibly was a agricultural deity. According to Laurette Séjourné (1959: 116–128), he corresponded to a Teotihuacan version of Xochipilli, a Postclassic god related to butterflies, birds, and flowers. Years later, Caso (1967b: 259–263) called him "Quetzalpapalotl" and linked him to water and vegetation deities. Hasso von Winning (1987, I: 115–124) christened him as the "Butterfly God" and arrived at the conclusion that he was the tutelary numen of merchants and ambassadors, that is, people engaged in the external, including military, affairs of the metropolis. In addition, Winning proposed that the personages on the Theater-type censers represented the soul of the warriors and, by extension, deceased merchants and ambassadors. On the other hand, Janet C. Berlo (1983) at first held the idea of a feminine warrior divinity who prefigured Xochiquetzal or Itzpapalotl, but years later changed her opinion, assimi-lating her into the "Great Goddess" (Berlo 1992). In more recent times, however,

Fig. 8.9. Butterfly-personage from a brazier discovered by Linda Manzanilla in Oztoyahualco, Teotihuacan (Berrin and Pasztory 1993: 97, redrawn by F. Carrizosa).

Fig. 8.10. Butterfly-personage from a Teotihuacan polychrome vase (Séjourné 1966: fig. 8, redrawn by F. Carrizosa).

Fig. 8.11. Butterfly-personage. Backside of a pyrite mirror, probably from Escuintla, Guatemala. Xolalpan/Metepec Phases (Berrin and Pasztory 1993: 126, redrawn by F. Carrizosa).

Zoltán Paulinyi (1995: 82–95) has sufficiently demonstrated that the personage in question is male. According to this author, he is the "Butterfly-Bird God," an avocation of the Sun who assures the fertility of the earth and who descends into the Underworld.

To this wide spectrum of interpretations we must add other, more recent ones that link our personage to Teotihuacan military elites. Saburo Sugiyama (1998), for example, proposes that they are images of warriors, possibly specific historical individuals, or abstract representatives of a determined social group, who were symbolized with identification codes as being ritually incinerated in braziers. Langley (1998) emphasizes his symbol nexus with the martial elite, death, and temporal cycles, proposing that the Theater-type censers were used in periodic warrior rites or in martial activities related to calendrical cycles. Karl Taube (chapter 10 of this volume) specifically suggests that he was a soldier whose dead body—represented on the Theater-type censers—connotes the chrysalis or cocoon of the soul of the warrior before his transformation by way of fire into a butterfly.

In our judgment, it is imperative that an exhaustive and systematic review of these mysterious personages be undertaken, taking into account their diverse

Fig. 8.12. Butterfly-personage. Thin Orange tripod vase. Xolalpan/Metepec Phases (Berrin and Pasztory 1993: 263, redrawn by F. Carrizosa).

iconographic elements, their variants according to the medium in which they were executed (mural painting, ceramics, sculpture, etc.), and their contextual relationships. Obviously, future studies will have to explain the presence—sometimes combined, sometimes isolated—of symbolic elements related to calendrical cycles, political authority, war, fertility, the associated offerings, the passing to the other world, and the ancestors.

THE FRAME AND THE CALENDRICAL DATES

We mentioned above that a frame in the form of a rectangle delineated the personage scene. This frame is composed of two parallel lines that enclose *chalchihuites* and ovoid elements with an end split. Perhaps, the latter represent shells or seeds such as those painted in the Temple of Agriculture mural (Marquina 1979: 125, plates 27, 33; Villagra 1971: 140, fig. 8) (Figure 8.13). According to Cynthia Conides (personal communication, March 1997), the frame of the *9-Xi* Vase may represent the personage emerging from an aquatic world of fertility or else passing through a portal to the other world (cf. Figures 8.8 and 8.12).

In addition to the *chalchihuites* and ovoid elements, the frame contains the two calendrical dates that make the *9-Xi* Vase so special. The first date in the frame is found in the center of the upper border and corresponds to an oval cartouche that encloses the *Xi* glyph (Figure 8.14[a]). This serrated-shape glyph was designated with the letter *S* by Alfonso Caso (1928: 44) in the 1920s; however, Caso (1967a: 174–175) himself changed its name decades later, due to the fact that its physiognomy imitates the tail of a *xiuhcoatl*, or fire serpent. Under the *Xi* glyph on our vase we observe the number 9, represented with a horizontal bar over four dots.

Fig. 8.13. Detail from a mural at the Temple of Agriculture, Teotihuacan (Marquina 1979: lám. 27, redrawn by F. Carrizosa).

The second date in the frame is located on the opposite extreme, that is, at the center of the lower border (Figure 8.15[a]). There we see a glyph in the shape of a knot which Caso (1928: 27–28) designated with the letter *A*. An oval cartouche and eleven dots surround this glyph. According to Javier Urcid (personal communication, April 1997), this notation could be read in three different ways: a) as the date *11-A*, if we concede that the dots have numerical value; b) as the date *1-A*, if we suppose that the cartouche represents a unit and the dots are decorative elements, as is usually the case in the Ñuiñe system (see Winter and Urcid 1990: 44); and c) simply as the *A* glyph, if we assume that the cartouche and the dots have no numerical value. If the first reading were correct, that is to say, if we have the date *11-A*, our vase would combine two different numbering systems: a date from the bar-and-dot system and another one from the dots-only system. We should not consider this strange because it seems to have been a common phenomenon in Teotihuacan, at least in the few known examples, and also in other cities in Central Mexico such as Xochicalco, Teotenango, Tula, as well as Tenochtitlan (Langley 1986: 141–143; Berlo 1989: 30, 44).[2]

Today controversy still exists concerning the calendrical position of the *Xi* and *A* glyphs. With respect to the *Xi* glyph, Caso (1967a: 174–175; 1967b: 268) proposed that it could be equivalent to the 10th day (*Dog*) of the *tonalpohualli*, due to the fact that Xiuhtecuhtli had the day *1-Dog* as his calendrical name. In contrast, Edmonson (1988: fig. 15a) associate the *Xi* glyph with the 18th day (*Flint*), while Urcid (1992, I: 168–169, 197, II: 250) suggested that perhaps it corresponded to the 4th day (*Lizard*) and calls it *Xicani*, the Zapotec name of the *xiuhcoatl*. The *A* glyph is equally controversial. According to Caso (1967a: 173), greater possibilities exist that this glyph is equivalent to the 12th day (*Twisted Grass*) of the *tonalpohualli*; however, he also considered as other plausible candidates, the 4th (*Lizard*), 9th (*Water*), 10th (*Dog*), 15th (*Eagle*), and 16th (*Vulture*) days. On the other hand, Edmonson (1988: fig. 15a) identifies it with the 12th day (*Twisted Grass*), while Urcid (1992, I: 136–137, II: 250) proposes the 10th (*Dog*, for the Mexica; *Knot*, for the Zapotec).

Such discrepancies and the lack of testimonies concerning the Teotihuacan calendrical system impedes our ability to determine if the *Xi* and *A* glyphs functioned as year bearers. In this respect, we mention that Caso (1967a: 161–163) proposed that the "Turquoise," "Eye," and "Wind" signs were three of the four year bearers employed in Teotihuacan, due to the fact that at times they were associated with the Trapeze-Ray and numerical notations. On the other hand, this author (Caso 1967a: 163) and Edmonson (1988: 241–243) have suggested that the Type II (2nd, 7th, 12th, and 17th days of the *tonalpohualli*) system of year bearers prevailed in Teotihuacan. Based on these propositions, we may speculate that: a) if the Trapeze-Ray of the *9-Xi* Vase does not form part of the attributes of the personage, and b) if the *A* glyph corresponds with the 12th day, then the contiguous position of the Trapeze-Ray sign and glyph *?-A* could indicate a year in the fifty-two-year cycle. However, it is also plausible to consider that the Trapeze-Ray marks the year of the Feathered Eye glyph that is found directly below him.

The specific significance of the dates *9-Xi* and *?-A* is equally obscure. Our current state of understanding allows us only to surmise four possible types of reading: that one or both types of notation allude to: a) the calendrical name of a divinity; b) the date of a mythical event; c) the name of a historical personage, and d) the date of an historical event. If the personage of our piece turns out to be a divinity, the first two types of readings would be more viable. On the other hand, if the personage in question is, in fact, a renowned personage from Teotihuacan history, then the last two types of readings would seem more adequate.

| | Calendrical Position | | |
Glyph	Caso	Edmonson	Urcid
Xi (S or Xicani)	10th	18th	4th?
A (Knot)	12th (4th, 9th, 10th, 15th, or 16th)	12th	10th

Table 8.3. Proposed calendrical positions of the Xi and the A glyphs.

THE ANTIQUITY OF THE 9-Xi VASE

According to Rattray's (1992: 59) inventory, all the Thin Orange objects discovered in funerary and oblatory contexts at Teotihuacan until now date from the long period between the Late Tlamimilolpa and Metepec Phases. The 9-Xi Vase, however, offers certain indications that assist us in establishing its antiquity with greater precision. According to the inspection of this vase amicably conducted by Warren Barbour (personal communication, June 1997), the more rounded rather than geometric contours of the personage are appropriate for the style in vogue during the Metepec Phase. This dating is corroborated by recent investigations which affirm that Thin Orange cylindrical vases decorated with appliqué panels were one of the few innovations of the Metepec Phase (Rattray 1991: 10) and that their production did not continue into the subsequent phase (Cowgill 1996: 329–330).

In the same vein, we should point out the evolutionary study of the glyphs present on our vase. Thanks to the work of Urcid (1992, I: 168–169, II: 202–203), we know that the Xi glyph has its origins in Oaxaca during Monte Albán II (200 B.C.E.–200 C.E.), a phase in which it was represented as the tail of a fire serpent (Figure 8.14 [b]). Nevertheless, it was not until the Monte Albán IIIa–IIIb transition (450–650 C.E.) that this glyph was used in Zapotec writing (Figure 8.14 [c]). In regards to Teotihuacan, the images of the Xi glyph are extremely rare and probably quite late. One of these scarcely known cases is observed on the headdress worn by a feminine figure on a stela published by Berlo (1992: 142–143) (Figure 8.14 [d]). Unfortunately, we do not know the exact provenance of the monument. Other interesting examples include an almena in the form of the Xi found by Noel Morelos (1993: photo 1.3; cf. Peñafiel 1890, 2: 40) in the uppermost levels of the West Plaza Complex at Teotihuacan (Figure 8.14 [e]) and a petroglyph with numerical notation discovered in the Teotihuacan site of Xihuingo (Jesús Galindo, personal communication, January 1999). The most celebrated image of the Xi

a

b

c

d

e

f

g

h

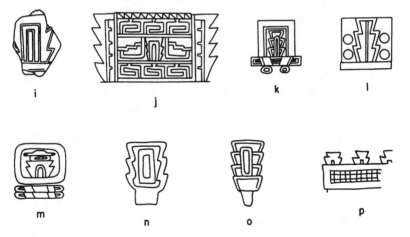

i

j

k

l

m

n

o

p

Fig. 8.14. The *Xi* glyph: a. The *9-Xi* Vase; b. As the tail of *xicani* (Urcid 1992: fig. 4.115); c. Zapotec glyph (Urcid 1992: fig. 4.114); d. Teotihuacan-style stela (Berlo 1992: fig. 17); e. Teotihuacan *almena* (Morelos 1993: photo 1.3); f. Jaguar from the Palace of Quetzalpapalotl (Acosta 1964: fig. 54); g. Face of the butterfly-personage, mural painting (Langley 1993: fig. 8); h. Face of the butterfly-personage, ceramic figurine (Caso 1967b: fig. 16.3c); i. Cacaxtla (López de Molina and Molina Feal 1986: lám. 109); j. Xochitécatl (Serra Puche, personal file); k. Río Grande (Caso 1967a: fig. 11b); l. Cerro de los Monos (Caso 1967a: 11c); m. Xochicalco (Caso 1967a: fig. 11a); n. Tula (Fuente, Trejo, and Gutiérrez 1988: fig. 150); o. Chichén Itzá (Ruppert 1935: fig. 246c); p. Tenochtitlan (González Aragón 1993: 47-48); all redrawn by F. Carrizosa.

glyph, however, comes from the Quetzalpapalotl building, in a context dated between 500 and 650 C.E. by Acosta (1964: 52–58). We are referring to the *tecalli* sculpture representing a seated jaguar. This fine object has the glyph *1-Reed* carved on its back and the *Xi* glyph on its tail (Acosta 1964: 34–35, fig. 54) (Figure 8.14 [f]). In Teotihuacan we also find suggestive formal analogies between the *Xi* glyph and the step-fret pattern facial paint characteristic of the personages we are discussing (Figure 8.14 [g and h]).

It is important to mention the existence of various examples of the *Xi* glyph in the Puebla-Tlaxcala Valley, which are contemporaneous with or slightly later than the decline of Teotihuacan. Among these, the fragment from a Teotihuacan

a

b

c

d

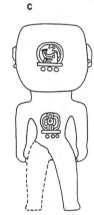

e

f   g   h   i

Fig. 8.15. The *A* glyph: a. The *9-Xi* Vase; b and c. Zapotec glyph (Urcid 1992: fig. 4.61); d. Teotihuacan (Caso 1967b: fig. 42f); e. Teotihuacan-style figurine (Urcid 1992: 4.167); f and g. Xochicalco (Caso 1967a: figs. 8a and b); h. Chalco (Caso 1967a: fig. 8d); i. Chichén Itzá (Caso 1967a: fig. 8g); all redrawn by F. Carrizosa.

"Engraved Brown" vase (variant 13, group 8) found in Cacaxtla (López de Molina and Molina Feal 1986: 51, lám. 109) (Figure 8.14 [i]), as well as a "Foso Engraved" tripod vase (Figure 8.14 [j]), and a Teotihuacan-style brazier discovered in Xochitecatl in contexts dated between 632 and 774 C.E. (Serra Puche 1998: 68–69, 83, 86, 89–90; personal communication, January 1999). Finally, we would add to this corpus of *Xi* glyph examples, the Río Grande Stela from Oaxaca; the Cerro de los Monos Stone in Guerrero; the Stone of the Four Glyphs at Xochicalco (Caso 1967a: 174–175) (Figure 8.14 [k–m]); as well as some Postclassic *almenas* (roof ornaments) from Tula (Fuente, Trejo, and Gutiérrez 1988: fig. 150), Chichén Itzá (Ruppert 1935: fig. 246c), and Tenochtitlan (Eduardo Matos Moctezuma, personal communication, December 1996; cf. *Codex Mendoza* 1992: 61r; *Codex Telleriano-Remensis* 1995: 39r; González Aragón 1993: 47–48) (Figure 8.14 [n–p]).

The *A* glyph, on the other hand, has been identified in twenty examples of Zapotec writing ranging between 200 B.C.E. and 1000 C.E. (Urcid 1992, I: 136–137; II: 147) (Figure 8.15 [b and c]). Among the rare occasions in which its presence has been registered outside of Oaxaca include the *13-A* glyph carved on a Teotihuacan piece (Caso 1967b: 275, fig. 42f) (Figure 8.15 [d]), the *8-A* glyph on a Teotihuacan-style greenstone figurine from southern Puebla (Urcid 1992, II: 258; Pasztory et al. 1993: 276) (Figure 8.15 [e]), the Palace Stone and the Pyramid of the Plumed Serpent at Xochicalco (Figure 8.15 [f and g]), and other monuments in Chalco and Chichén Itzá (Caso 1967a: 173) (Figure 8.15 [h and i]).

Although we lack many elements to fully reconstruct the development of the Central Mexican calendrical system, we may infer from this quick review that the *Xi* and *A* glyphs have Preclassic Zapotec roots, which first manifested in Central Mexican highlands at the end of Teotihuacan's dominion and reached its maximum dispersion during the apogee of the Epiclassic centers. The unusual presence of these two glyphs on the *9-Xi* Vase is explained by the late date of its production, which, we are convinced, dates back to the Metepec Phase.

CONCLUSIONS

There is a high probability that the Mexica obtained this *9-Xi* Vase in the ruins of Teotihuacan, given the archaeological richness of this metropolis, its close proximity to Tenochtitlan, and the numerous accounts concerning the activities of Postclassic peoples in the so-called City of the Gods (see Castañeda 1986: 234–236). Evidently, this does not rule out the possibility that this piece came from the ruins of another site contemporaneous with Teotihuacan, such as, for example, Azcapotzalco, Xico, or Portezuelo. Whichever the case may be, it is clear that the Mexica attributed to the *9-Xi* Vase a dual value, derived from its great aesthetic quality as well as its supposed magical quality in terms of its creation by divine or legendary beings. In addition to these two attributes, we should ask ourselves if the Mexica decided to reutilize this vase as a funerary urn for a high-level dignitary due to their relating the image of the personage with its suggested funerary, governmental, and martial symbolism.

Concerning the *9-Xi* Vase's central scene, we have noted enormous analogies with the Theater-type censers, above all on the level of the correlated presence and distribution of certain notational signs. There is little room to doubt that the appliqués of this vessel found in the Casa de las Águilas depict the mysterious personage extensively celebrated in Teotihuacan iconography, although at the end of the twentieth century he resists being fully identified.

Throughout this essay we also have stood firm in terms of the two calendrical dates on our vase. As we have said, their presence seems to be explained by the late production of this Thin Orange vessel, which we have dated to the Metepec Phase. Although it is still unclear whether the temporal boundaries of this phase are 650 and 750 c.e. (Rattray 1991: 10–11) or one hundred years earlier (Cowgill 1996: 329–330), there is common consensus that Teotihuacan experienced great transformations on the political and cultural levels at that time. The art of the city became more virtuous and complex, exalting, as never before, war, individualism, and aristocratic secularity (Pasztory 1988a; Cohodas 1989). This is precisely when the murals of Techinantitla are painted with their innovative notational signs and when the formation of the Central Mexico writing system that would lead to the Aztec system is initiated (Pasztory 1988b; Berlo 1989: 20–23; Cowgill 1992). Thus, Metepec Phase Teotihuacan—whether preceding or contemporaneous with Cacaxtla, Xochicalco, and Teotenango (cf. Molina Feal 1977: 1–5; Hirth and Cyphers 1988: 110–143; López Austin and López Luján 1996: 170)—shared many of these glyphs in common with the Epiclassic centers. This phenomenon is revealed in the *9-Xi* Vase.

NOTES

1. In this respect, the painted murals recently found at La Ventilla B are worth mentioning. Among the depicted images, a representation of the Feathered Headdress Symbol stands out, whose Trapeze-Ray encloses a blue trilobe (Néstor Paredes, personal communication, January 1999).

2. Recently, Langley (1998) has identified the row of elongated signs across the top of the V Manta Compound as fingers. He proposed that the finger would be in this context a variant of the numeral 1, as occurs in the Zapotec, Maya, and Mexica number systems.

REFERENCES

Acosta, Jorge R.
1964. *El Palacio del Quetzalpapálotl*. Mexico: INAH.

Aguirre Molina, Alejandra, Ximena Chávez, Leonardo López Luján, Juan Román Berrelleza, and Ximena Vázquez del Mercado
1997. "Consideraciones sobre la Ofrenda V." Unpublished report in the Archivo del Museo del Templo Mayor, INAH, Mexico, D.F.

Alvarado Tezozómoc, Fernando
1944. *Crónica mexicana*. Mexico: Editorial Leyenda.

Angulo Villaseñor, Jorge
1966. "Una ofrenda en el Templo Mayor de Tenochtitlan." *Boletín del INAH* 26 (December): 1–6.

Barba, Luis A., Agustín Ortiz, Karl F. Link, Leonardo López Luján, and Luz Lazos
1996. "Chemical Analysis of Residues in Floors and the Reconstruction of Ritual Activities at the Templo Mayor, Mexico." In M. V. Orna, ed., *Archaeological Chemistry: Organic, Inorganic, and Biochemical Analysis*. Washington, DC: American Chemical Society, pp. 139–156.

Barba, Luis A., Agustín Ortiz, Karl F. Link, Luz Lazos, and Leonardo López Luján
1997. "La arquitectura sagrada y sus usos: Estudio geofísico y químico de la Casa de las Águilas de Tenochtitlan." *Revista de Arqueología* 18, no. 198: 44–53.

Batres, Leopoldo
1902. *Exploraciones arqueológicas en la Calle de las Escalerillas, año de 1900.* Mexico: Tipografía y Litografía "La Europea" de J. Aguilar Vera.

Benavente, Fray Toribio de (Motolinía)
1971. *Memoriales o libro de las cosas de la Nueva España y de los naturales de ella.* Mexico: UNAM.

Berlo, Janet Catherine
1983. "The Warrior and the Butterfly: Central Mexican Ideologies of Sacred Warfare and Teotihuacan Iconography." In J. C. Berlo, ed., *Text and Image in Pre-Columbian Art.* Oxford: BAR International Series 180, pp. 79–117.
1989. "Early Writing in Central Mexico: *In Tlilli, In Tlapalli* Before A.D. 1000." In R. A. Diehl and J. C. Berlo, eds., *Mesoamerica After the Decline of Teotihuacan, A.D. 700–900.* Washington, DC: Dumbarton Oaks, pp. 19–47.
1992. "Icons and Ideologies: The Great Goddess Reconsidered." In J. C. Berlo, ed., *Art, Ideology, and the City of Teotihuacan.* Washington, DC: Dumbarton Oaks, pp. 129–168.

Berrin, Kathleen, and Esther Pasztory, eds.
1993. *Teotihuacan, Art from the City of the Gods.* New York: Thames and Hudson/The Fine Arts Museums of San Francisco

Caso, Alfonso
1928. *Las estelas zapotecas.* Mexico: SEP.
1967a. *Los calendarios prehispánicos.* Mexico: UNAM.
1967b. "Dioses y signos teotihuacanos." In *Teotihuacan. Onceava Mesa Redonda, México 1966.* Mexico: SMA, pp. 249–279.

Castañeda, Francisco de
1986. "Relación de Tequizistlán y su partido." In *Relaciones geográficas del siglo XVI.* Mexico: UNAM, vol. 7, pp. 211–251.

Codex Mendoza
1992. Edited by F. F. Berdan and P. R. Anawalt. 4 vols. Berkeley: University of California Press.

Codex Magliabechiano
1983. Edited by E. H. Boone. 2 vols. Berkeley: University of California Press.

Codex Telleriano-Remensis
1995. Eloise Quiñones Keber. *Codex Telleriano-Remensis: Ritual, Divination, and History.* Austin: University of Texas Press.

Cohodas, Marvin
1989. "The Epiclassic Problem: A Review and an Alternative Model." In R. A. Diehl and J. C. Berlo, eds., *Mesoamerica After the Decline of Teotihuacan, A.D. 700–900.* Washington, DC: Dumbarton Oaks, pp. 219–240.

Costumbres, fiestas, enterramientos
1945. "Costumbres, fiestas, enterramientos y diversas formas de proceder de los indios de Nueva España." *Tlalocan* 2, no. 1: 37–63.

Cowgill, George L.
1992. "Teotihuacan Glyphs and Imagery in the Light of Some Early Colonial Texts." In J.

C. Berlo, ed., *Art, Ideology, and the City of Teotihuacan*. Washington, DC: Dumbarton Oaks, pp. 231–246.

1996. "Discussion." *Ancient Mesoamerica* 7: 325–331.

Durán, Fray Diego
1984. *Historia de la Indias de Nueva España e Islas de la Tierra Firme*. 2 vols. Mexico: Editorial Porrúa.

Edmonson, Munro S.
1988. *The Book of the Year: Middle American Calendrical Systems*. Salt Lake City: University of Utah Press.

Fuente, Beatriz de la
1990. "Escultura en el tiempo: Retorno al pasado tolteca." *Artes de México*, nueva época, 9: 36–53.

Fuente, Beatriz de la, Silvia Trejo, and Nelly Gutiérrez Solana
1988. *Escultura en piedra de Tula*. Mexico: UNAM-IIE.

Gamio, Manuel
1979. "Esculturas esqueyomorfas." In M. Gamio, ed., *La población del Valle de Teotihuacán*. Mexico: Instituto Nacional Indigenista, vol. II, pp. 196–200.

González, Carlos Javier, and Bertina Olmedo
1990. *Esculturas Mezcala en el Templo Mayor*. Mexico: INAH/GV Editores.

González Aragón, Jorge
1993. *La urbanización indígena de la Ciudad de México: El caso del Plano en papel maguey*. Mexico: Universidad Autónoma Metropolitana.

González Rul, Francisco
1979. *La lítica de Tlatelolco*. Mexico: INAH.
1988. *La cerámica en Tlatelolco*. Mexico: INAH.
1997. *Materiales líticos y cerámicos encontrados en las cercanías del monolito Coyolxauhqui*. Mexico: INAH.

Graulich, Michel
1992. "On the So-called 'Cuauhxicalli of Motecuhzoma Ilhuicamina' the Sánchez-Nava Monolith." *Mexicon* 14, no. 1: 5–10.

Gussinyer, Jordi
1969. "Hallazgos en el Metro, conjunto de adoratorios superpuestos en Pino Suárez." *Boletín del INAH* 36 (June): 33–37.
1970. "Un adoratorio dedicado a Tláloc." *Boletín del INAH* 39 (March): 7–12.

Hirth, Kenneth G., and Ann Cyphers Guillén
1988. *Tiempo y asentamiento en Xochicalco*. Mexico: UNAM.

Langley, James C.
1986. *Symbolic Notation of Teotihuacan: Elements of Writing in a Mesoamerican Culture of the Classic Period*. Oxford: BAR International Series 313.
1992. "Teotihuacan Sign Clusters: Emblem or Articulation?" In J. C. Berlo, ed., *Art, Ideology, and the City of Teotihuacan*. Washington, DC: Dumbarton Oaks, pp. 247–280.
1993. "Symbols, Signs, and Writing Systems." In K. Berrin and E. Pasztory, eds., *Teotihuacan, Art from the City of the Gods*. New York: Thames and Hudson/The Fine Arts Museums of San Francisco, pp. 129–139.
1998. "Teotihuacan Incensarios: The "V" Manta and Its Message." *Teotihuacan Notes: Internet Journal for Teotihuacan Archaeology and Iconography*, Notes 1-3.

Archaeological Research Institute, Department of Anthropology, Arizona State University, Tempe, AZ. http://archaeology.la.asu.edu/teo/notes/JL/notes1_3.htm.

López Austin, Alfredo, Leonardo López Luján, and Saburo Sugiyama
1991. "The Temple of Quetzalcóatl at Teotihuacan: Its Possible Ideological Significance." *Ancient Mesoamerica* 2, no. 1: 93–105.

López Austin, Alfredo, and Leonardo López Luján
1996. *El pasado indígena*. Mexico: FCE/El Colegio de México.

López de Molina, Diana, and Daniel Molina Feal
1986. "Arqueología." In *Cacaxtla, el lugar donde muere la lluvia en la tierra*. Mexico: INAH/Gobierno del Estado de Tlaxcala/Instituto Tlaxcalteca de Cultura, pp. 11–208.

López Luján, Leonardo
1989. *La recuperación mexica del pasado teotihuacano*. Mexico: INAH/GV Editores.
1993. *Las ofrendas del Templo Mayor de Tenochtitlan*. Mexico: INAH.
1995. "Guerra y muerte en Tenochtitlan: Descubrimientos en el Recinto de las Águilas." *Arqueología Mexicana* 2, no. 12 (March–April): 75–77.
1998. "Anthropologie religieuse du Templo Mayor, Mexico: La Maison des Aigles." 2 vols. Doctoral thesis in Archaeology, Université de Paris X-Nanterre, Paris.

López Luján, Leonardo, and Vida Mercado
1996. "Dos esculturas de Mictlantecuhtli encontradas en el Recinto Sagrado de Mexico-Tenochtitlan." *Estudios de Cultura Náhuatl* 26: 41–68.

Manzanilla, Linda, and Emilie Carreón
1991. "A Teotihuacan Censer in Residential Context: An Interpretation." *Ancient Mesoamerica* 2, no. 2: 299–307.

Marquina, Ignacio
1979. "Primera parte. Arquitectura." In M. Gamio, ed., *La población del Valle de Teotihuacán*. Mexico: Instituto Nacional Indigenista, vol. II, pp. 99–164.

Matos Moctezuma, Eduardo
1979. "Una máscara olmeca en el Templo Mayor de Tenochtitlan." *Anales de Antropología* 16: 11–19.
1981. *Una visita al Templo Mayor*. Mexico: SEP/INAH.
1983. "Notas sobre algunas urnas funerarias del Templo Mayor." *Jahrbuch für Geschichte von Staat, Wirtschaft und Gesellschaft Lateinamerikas* 20: 17–32.
1984. "Los edificios aledaños al Templo Mayor." *Estudios de Cultura Náhuatl* 17: 15–21.
n.d. "El chac mool de la Casa del Marqués del Apartado." In press.

Matos Moctezuma, Eduardo, and Leonardo López Luján
1993. "Teotihuacan and its Mexica Legacy." In K. Berrin and E. Pasztory, eds., *Teotihuacan, Art from the City of the Gods*. New York: Thames and Hudson/The Fine Arts Museums of San Francisco, pp. 156–165.

Miller, Mary Ellen, and Karl A. Taube
1993. *The Gods and Symbols of Ancient Mexico and the Maya: An Illustrated Dictionary of Mesoamerican Religion*. London: Thames and Hudson.

Molina Feal, Daniel
1977. "Consideraciones sobre la cronología de Cacaxtla." In *XII Mesa Redonda*. 2 vols. Mexico: SMA, vol. 2, pp. 1–5.

Morelos, Noel
1993. *Proceso de producción de espacios y estructuras en Teotihuacán: Conjunto Plaza Oeste y Complejo Calle de los Muertos*. Mexico: INAH.

Müller, Florencia
1978. *La cerámica del Centro Ceremonial de Teotihuacán.* Mexico: INAH.

Nagao, Debra
1985.*Mexica Buried Offerings: A Historical and Contextual Analysis.* Oxford: BAR International Series 235.

Navarrete, Carlos, and Ana María Crespo
1971. "Un atlante mexica y algunas consideraciones sobre los relieves del Cerro de la Malinche, Hidalgo." *Estudios de Cultura Náhuatl* 9: 11–15.

Neff, Hector
1992. "Introduction." In H. Neff, ed., *Chemical Characterization of Ceramic Pastes in Archaeology.* Madison, WI: Prehistory Press, pp. 1–10.

Nicholson, H. B.
1971. "Major Sculpture in Pre-Hispanic Central Mexico." In R. A. Wauchope, gen. ed.; G. Ekholm and I. Bernal, vol. eds., *Handbook of Middle American Indians.* Vol. 10, Part 1: *Archaeology of Northern Mesoamerica.* Austin: University of Texas Press, pp. 92–134.

Noguera, Eduardo
1935. "La cerámica de Tenayuca y las excavaciones estratigráficas." In *Tenayuca.* Mexico: Departamento de Monumentos/SEP, pp. 141–201.

Paulinyi, Zoltán
1995. "El pájaro del dios mariposa de Teotihuacan: análisis iconográfico a partir de una vasija de Tiquisate, Guatemala." *Boletín del Museo Chileno de Arte Precolombino* 6: 71–110.

Pasztory, Esther
1988a. "A Reinterpretation of Teotihuacan and its Mural Painting Tradition." In K. Berrin, ed., *Feathered Serpents and Flowering Trees: Reconstructing the Murals of Teotihuacan.* San Francisco: The Fine Arts Museums of San Francisco, pp. 45–77.
1988b. "Feathered Serpents and Flowering Trees with Glyphs." In K. Berrin, ed., *Feathered Serpents and Flowering Trees: Reconstructing the Murals of Teotihuacan.* San Francisco: The Fine Arts Museums of San Francisco, pp. 137–161.

Pasztory, Esther, Clara Luz Díaz Oyarzabal, Rubén Cabrera Castro, Evelyn Rattray, Cynthia Conides, Warren Barbour, Martha Carmona Macias, and Leonardo López Luján
1993. "Catalog of Objects." In K. Berrin and E. Pasztory, eds., *Teotihuacan, Art from the City of the Gods.* New York: Thames and Hudson/The Fine Arts Museums of San Francisco, pp. 167–278.

Peñafiel, Antonio
1890. *Monumentos del arte mexicano antiguo: Ornamentación, mitología, tributos y monumentos.* 3 vols. Berlin: A. Asher & Co.

Polaco, Óscar J.
1998. "La arqueofauna de la Casa de las Águilas, Templo Mayor, México." Unpublished report in the Archivo del Museo del Templo Mayor, INAH, Mexico, D.F.

Rattray, Evelyn Childs
1979. "La cerámica de Teotihuacan: Relaciones externas y cronología." *Anales de Antropología* 16: 51–70.
1990. "New Findings on the Origins of Thin Orange Ceramics." *Ancient Mesoamerica* 1, no. 2: 181–195.
1991. "Fechamientos por radiocarbono en Teotihuacan." *Arqueología*, segunda época, 6 (June–December): 3–18.

1992. *The Teotihuacan Burials and Offerings: A Commentary and Inventory*. Nashville, TN: Vanderbilt University Publications in Anthropology, no. 42.

Rattray, Evelyn, and Garman Harbottle
1992. "Neutron Activation Analysis and Numerical Taxonomy of Thin Orange Ceramics from the Manufacturing Sites of Rio Carnero, Puebla, Mexico." In H. Neff, ed., *Chemical Characterization of Ceramic Pastes in Archaeology*. Madison, WI: Prehistory Press, pp. 221–231.

Román Berrelleza, Juan Alberto, and Leonardo López Luján
1997. "Un enterramiento en el Recinto Sagrado de Tenochtitlan: La Ofrenda V de la Casa de las Águilas." Paper presented in the IX Coloquio "Juan Comas," November 6, Museo Regional de Querétaro, Querétaro, Mexico.

Ruppert, Karl
1935. *The Caracol at Chichen Itza, Yucatan, Mexico*. Washington, DC: Carnegie Institution Publication no. 454.

Ruz Lhuillier, Alberto
1968. *Costumbres funerarias de los antiguos mayas*. Mexico: UNAM.

Sahagún, Fray Bernardino de
1989. *Historia general de las cosas de Nueva España*. 2 vols. Mexico: CNCA/Alianza Editorial Mexicana.
1997. *Primeros Memoriales*. Paleography of the Nahuatl and translation into English by T. D. Sullivan, completed and revised with additions by H. B. Nicholson, A. J. O. Anderson, C. E. Dibble, E. Quiñones Keber, and W. Ruwet. Norman: University of Oklahoma Press.

Séjourné, Laurette
1959. *Un palacio de la Ciudad de los Dioses (Teotihuacán)*. Mexico: INAH.
1966. *Arqueología de Teotihuacán: La cerámica*. Mexico: FCE.
1983. *Arqueología e historia del Valle de México: De Xochimilco a Amecameca*. Mexico: Siglo Veintiuno Editores.

Serra Puche, Mari Carmen
1998. *Xochitécatl*. Tlaxcala: Gobierno del Estado de Tlaxcala.

Solís Olguín, Felipe
1997. "Un hallazgo olvidado: Relato e interpretación de los descubrimientos arqueológicos del predio de la calle de Guatemala núm. 12, en el Centro Histórico de la Ciudad de México, en 1944." In L. Manrique and N. Castillo, eds., *Homenaje al doctor Ignacio Bernal*. Mexico: INAH, pp. 81–93.

Sotomayor, Alfredo, and Noemí Castillo Tejero
1963. *Estudio petrográfico de la cerámica "Anaranjado Delgado."* Mexico: INAH, Departamento de Prehistoria Publicaciones 12.

Sugiyama, Saburo
1998. "Archaeology and Iconography of Teotihuacan Censers: Official Military Emblems Originated from the Ciudadela?" *Teotihuacan Notes: Internet Journal for Teotihuacan Archaeology and Iconography*, Notes I-2. Archaeological Research Institute, Department of Anthropology, Arizona State University, Tempe, AZ. http://archaeology.la.asu.edu/teo/notes/SS/noteI_2SS.htm.

Título de los Señores de Totonicapán
1950. With *Memorial de Sololá, Anales de los Cakchiqueles*. Trans. D. J. Chonay and A. Recinos. Mexico: FCE, pp. 209–242.

Umberger, Emily

1987a. "Antiques, Revivals, and References to the Past in Aztec Art." *Res: Anthropology and Aesthetics* 13: 63–106.

1987b. "Events Commemorated by Date Plaques at the Templo Mayor: Further Thoughts on the Solar Metaphor." In E. H. Boone, ed., *The Aztec Templo Mayor*. Washington, DC: Dumbarton Oaks, pp. 411–450.

Urcid Serrano, Javier

1992. "Zapotec Hieroglyphic Writing." 2 vols. Ph.D. dissertation, Yale University, New Haven, CT.

1997. "Convenio con la madre tierra: La muerte ritual entre los mexicas." Unpublished report in the Archivo del Museo del Templo Mayor, INAH, Mexico, D.F.

Villagra Caleti, Agustín

1971. "Mural painting in Central Mexico." In R. A. Wauchope, gen. ed.; G. Ekholm and I. Bernal, vol. eds., *Handbook of Middle American Indians*. Vol. 10, Part 1: *Archaeology of Northern Mesoamerica*. Austin: University of Texas Press, pp. 135–156.

Winning, Hasso von

1961. "Teotihuacan Symbols: Reptile's Eye Glyph." *Ethnos* 26, no. 3: 121–166.

1977. "Los incensarios teotihuacanos y los del litoral pacífico de Guatemala: Su iconografía y función ritual." In *XV Mesa Redonda*. Mexico: SMA, pp. 327–334.

1987. *La iconografía de Teotihuacan. Los dioses y los signos*. 2 vols. Mexico: UNAM.

Winter, Marcus, and Javier Urcid

1990. "Una mandíbula humana grabada de la Sierra Mazateca, Oaxaca." *Notas Mesoamericanas* 12: 39–49.

PART THREE

▼

CLASSIC TEOTIHUACAN IN
THE CONTEXT OF MESOAMERICAN
SPACE AND SACRED GEOGRAPHY

9

▼

OUT OF TEOTIHUACAN

ORIGINS OF THE CELESTIAL CANON IN MESOAMERICA

ANTHONY F. AVENI

TEOTIHUACAN IN LAND AND SKYSCAPE

There is little question that during the Middle Classic Period (400–700 C.E.) architecture and decorative arts all over Mesoamerica were profoundly influenced by the Teotihuacan culture (Pasztory, 1978; Berlo 1992; Diehl and Berlo 1989). Lately, specific aspects of Maya iconographic imagery such as the Tlaloc-Venus war symbolism (e.g. Schele and Freidel 1990: pp 130–131; Baird 1989) and particular elements associated with burials and stelae at Uaxactún and Tikal also have been traced, with varying degrees of acceptance, to Teotihuacan (Schele and Freidel 1990: 159–164). This chapter investigates the possibility that methods of conceptualizing space and keeping time also might have followed the great ideological migration route out of the Mexican highlands.

Like Brazilia and Washington, D.C., Teotihuacan was a planned community, deliberately presented as a sort of paradise on earth with a sacred geography. It was the place, say the chroniclers, where people first emerged from the earth at the beginning of creation and the home of a powerful goddess who dwelled in natural caves. The local geography was enhanced to reflect certain aspects of the creation myth—the strict grid plan that runs against the grain of the landscape, the building of an artificial cave beneath the Pyramid of the Sun, and the careful positioning of the urban plan respecting Cerro Gordo on the north. The distinctively novel axial orientation of Teotihuacan claims for it "a new, and probably privileged, relationship to the gods" (Pasztory 1978: 49), a reflection of the sacred cosmic blueprint handed down to them.

I am indebted to my late colleague Horst Hartung, who supplied the illustrations, and to James Langley for valuable comments on earlier drafts of this paper.

First there is the mountain. No one will doubt that Cerro Gordo gives Teotihuacan's northern vista a dramatic effect, as Tobriner (1972)—and Linné (1934) and Gamio (1922) before him, and the *Relación de Tequizistlan* (1580) before them—points out. Looking north along the Street of the Dead, the Pyramid of the Moon, which mirrors Cerro Gordo both in its position and triangular shape, enhances the effect. Tobriner has stated that the placement of the city's axial grid with respect to the mountain is deliberate and that it was done to honor "the most important single factor affecting settlement in the area": water (Tobriner 1972: 107). He argues both on geological as well as iconographic grounds that Cerro Gordo was Teotihuacan's "water mountain" and that is why their city was designed to align with it.

Next there are the heavens. The axial alignment, together with the key positions of the sun and stars on the local horizon, converge in a reservoir of numerological and cosmological meaning. First of all, the sun sets along the west-east axis of Teotihuacan on April 29 and August 12. These dates were meaningful because they are separated by a period of 260 days, during which interval the sun passes to the south of that alignment, and by 105 days (= 52 + 1 + 52) when it passes to the north.

Looking along the same urban axis in the east-west direction, one would have seen the Pleiades star group set about the time Teotihuacan's grid structure was set in place. This I believe is not pure coincidence, for the Pleiades would have made their first yearly appearance in the east before dawn on the first of the two dates when the sun passed overhead (May 18). This means that for Teotihuacanos the signal that tripped the switch to mimic creation time by restarting the seasons was the reappearance of the conspicuous Pleiades star group, which, carrying on the temporal tradition, is frequently mentioned in the (later) Aztec chronicles in connection with signalling the start of a new 52-year cycle when it crosses the zenith.[1]

Finally, there is the cave, with its mouth opening in the same east-west direction beneath the Pyramid of the Sun as the Pleiades-sun alignment (see Linda Manzanilla, chapter 2 of this volume, for details on how natural underground chambers were modified to result in this cave). Because the cave was regarded as the place *where* time began, the sight line from its mouth to the western horizon commemorated *when* time began. What a graphic embodiment of the "birth of the cosmos at Teotihuacan, the beginning of the present era" (to quote Millon 1992: 35).

Imagine, then, the formidable problem that confronted architects charged with the task of laying out their sacred city in accord with both the landscape and the skyscape. The Teotihuacan cosmovision undergirded in the urban arrangements of sky, of earth, of mountain, of cave, and of time formed the skeleton of a sacred canon that would reverberate throughout Mesoamerica for scores of generations to come.

Quadripartite spatial symbolism is one among several concepts in Mesoamerican cosmovision that I believe is traceable to Teotihuacan. The imitative axial alignments of cities all over the highlands to that of Teotihuacan (Aveni and Gibbs 1976), even the concept of positioning cities with respect to a mountain on the north (e.g., in Tenayuca and in Tenochtitlan), are difficult to deny. According to Sahagún, Quauhtepetl was the first place in the ritual of child sacrifice in the first month of the year, Atlcahualo. Here was an element of sacred geography that may have evolved into the north-equals-up, south-equals-down cosmic axis even as far away as Copán, but these are matters best left for discussion in the future.

In this chapter I will look at some specific space-time–related artifacts that reveal the details of this Teotihuacan classical canon, and I will use these artifacts to explore some possible ways Teotihuacan space-time elements were propagated through central Mexico all the way to the Petén.

THE SPACE-TIME PROPERTIES OF PECKED-CROSS PETROGLYPHS

Some years ago, we called attention to the widespread existence across Mesoamerica of a (usually) double-circular pattern centered on a pair of rectangular axes carved both on rock and in the floors of ceremonial buildings, mostly at Teotihuacan (Aveni, Hartung and Buckingham 1978). (For examples, see Figure 9.1 [a and b].) We have variously called these designs pecked crosses and pecked-cross circles. In later publications (e.g., Aveni and Hartung 1982, 1983, 1985, 1989a, 1989b) we updated discoveries of this petroglyphic symbol by a host of investigators. Meanwhile, Coggins (1980) suggested that this form of quadripartite symbol was part of an attempt by Early Classic Mexicans to introduce new concepts of the solar cycle to the central Petén region. She argues that prior to the intrusion, the Maya appeared to have isolated their esoteric, elite way of marking time by the Long Count from the empirical, less abstract, way of time reckoning via marking the position of the sun at the horizon. Thus, up until about 400 C.E., Maya astronomers were constructing specialized observatories, such as Group E structures (cf. Aveni and Hartung 1989) specifically for delineating the key positions of the sun. With the arrival of the foreigners, things changed; for example, as Coggins notes, carved stelae before the end of the fourth century celebrate dynastic events, while inscriptions emphasize the completion of pure time cycles. The establishment of katun-completion ceremonies in this area coincides with the demise of the practice of erecting the Group E observatories. Especially at Tikal, there is good evidence that twin-pyramid groups replaced Group E–type structures, at least as far as ritual function was concerned. Coggins believes the motive for this calendar reform was conditioned by the Mexicans' appreciation of a similarity between the structural principles of their 260-day calendar and the Maya katun round of thirteen 20-tun periods, a similarity that would have made it easier to propagate their own concepts of calendric ritual among their new subjects. In support of this idea, we find that the pecked circles tend to incorporate along their axes and quadrants numerical counts of nonastronomical origin, such as 20, 13, 9 and totals often approximating 260 as well as natural divisions of the solar year. For details, see Aveni (1989b).

Though we have continually refined our hypotheses concerning the meaning of the pecked crosses, we continue to argue that no single hypothesis fits all of the data and that at least three broad explanations are admissible: some of the petroglyphs could have been used to count time, some could have served as

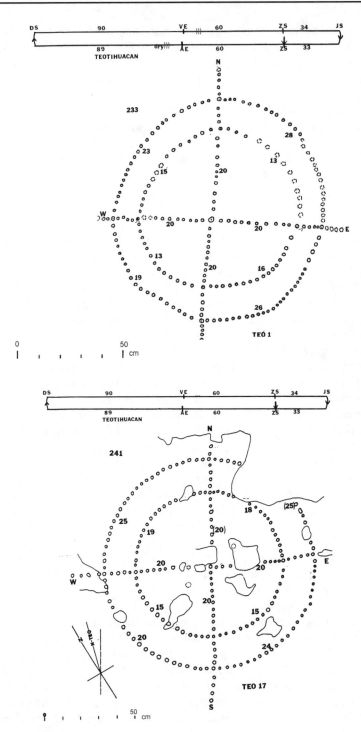

Fig. 9.1. a. TEO 1 petroglyph; b. TEO 17 petroglyph.

orientation devices, and some could have functioned as board games. Overlapping functions for a given design are not precluded, and I will not explore the last two hypotheses in this chapter.

PECKED CROSSES AT TEOTIHUACAN AND UAXACTÚN

The UAX 1 petroglyph from Uaxactún (Figure 9.2) was discovered and published (Smith 1950) long before the Teotihuacan mapping project reported its first two circles (Millon 1973). It bears such a striking resemblance in fine detail to the majority of the Teotihuacan pecked crosses that it would be worth quoting Smith's description in toto, which, though brief, is quite explicit:

> What has been called a calendrical circle was found on the Temple Court floor south of Construction A (figs. 8.15, a; 60,1). The design, made by small circular depressions in the floor, consist of two concentric circles divided into quadrants by two straight lines; it is very similar in outline to the wheel in the *Book of Chilam Balam of Kaua* (Bowditch 1910: fig. 64). The extremities of the straight lines point to the cardinal points. There is no consistency in the number of depressions or dots in each quadrant of the outer and inner circles, but the straight lines are arranged so that each has ten dots from the center to the inner circle, four dots from the inner circle to the outer, and four dots beyond the outer circle. Traces of two similar calendrical circles were found on the Temple Court floor south of Construction C. Although not exactly the same in size or in number of circular depressions in any quadrant as the one just described, each had two concentric circles divided into quadrants by two straight lines. In each case the lines were oriented and arranged in the same manner so that the depressions were divided into ten,

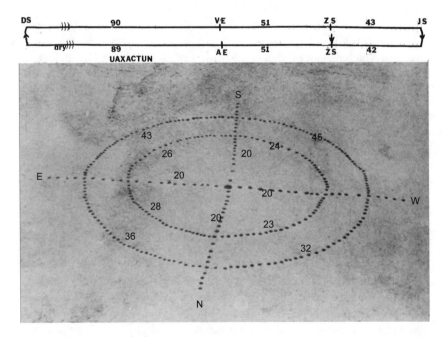

Fig. 9.2. UAX 1 petroglyph.

four, and four. There is no proof that the calendrical circles were made in Vault Ic,
but they could not have been made later than Ie, because If partially covers them.
(1950: 21–22)

Confinement of this design and its two (regrettably lost)[2] companions to the
early stages of the first vault phase, ca. 8.12.0.0.0 or 278 c.e. (Smith 1950: 86–87)
when the corbeled vault and Tzakol pottery are introduced, would place it early in
the construction of the building. The presence of Stela 26 (Long Count date 9.0.10.0.0)
in the layer atop the designs places a *termina post quem* date of 445 c.e. upon them.

Were the pecked crosses of Teotihuacan and Uaxactún used to keep time?
To explore this question we need to inquire how nature divides the year both in
the Central Mexican highlands and in the Petén. In Figure 9.3, I have charted out
the annual cycles and their breakdowns for both cities. Interestingly, at
Teotihuacan it is exactly 60 (or 3 x 20) days from the March equinox to the first
solar zenith passage, as well as from the second zenith passage to the September
equinox. But what is not so well known is that the east-west axial alignment of
Teotihuacan that is marked by a pair of pecked crosses (TEO 1 and 5) is such
that the Pyramid of the Sun faces the sunset 2 x 20 or 40 days after the vernal
equinox and 20 days before first zenith passage (the intervals are reversed when
the sun returns toward the south). Of all the manifold hypotheses that discuss the
orientation problem at Teotihuacan (see Millon 1992: 383–388; and Aveni 1980:
222–236 for a summary and assessment of them), this one is both the least discussed and, it seems to me, one of the most sensible and least contrived. There is
a rather extensive body of literature exploring the idea that 20-day solar periods
were figured into horizon observational astronomy across Mesoamerica (cf.
Aveni, Calnek, and Hartung 1988; Tichy 1976).

At Uaxactún, the interval between the equinox and the first solar passage
across the zenith is reduced to 51 days. Also the interval between solar zenith
passages, which includes the June solstice, which is 67 days at Teotihuacan, is
equal to 85 days at Uaxactún, i.e., the sun spends 298 days south of the zenith at
noon and 67 days north of it at Teotihuacan, while the year is similarly bifurcated into the intervals 280 and 85 days in the central Petén. This last number is
close to the universal quarter-year interval discussed above. Finally, intervals
between the dates when the sun passes the zenith can be divided into 33 + 34 =
67 days at Teotihuacan and 43 + 42 = 85 days at Uaxactún, assuming one had
wished to mark the solar stopping point between the two annual zenith passages.
All of these periods and subperiods would be the very numbers one might antici-
pate finding in artifacts hypothesized to have tallied observable solar time.

Figure 9.2 tabulates the count and arrangement of elements that make up
the UAX 1 petroglyph, which exhibits two unusual aspects. Note first the large
number of elements that make up the whole design, and second, the asymmetry
of their distribution, particularly on the outer circle: there are eighty-eight on the
northern (top) half as opposed to sixty-eight, or twenty less, on the southern half.
If we compare the observable solar year intervals indicated in Figure 9.3 with the
breakdown of elements on various parts of the design, we also discover that the
way the counts are grouped is quite supportive of the hypothesis that the
petroglyph functioned as a year calendar. First of all, the sum of the inner SE plus

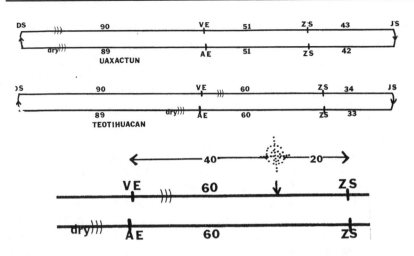

Fig. 9.3. Annual cycles at Teotihuacan and Uaxactún contrasted. The seasonal year cycle is segmented into intervals that separate solstices, equinoxes, and solar zenith passages. Also shown, in triple brackets, are the approximate wet/dry periods obtained from modern meteorological observations (World Weather Disc 1988). Note that in the Petén the dry period runs approximately from late fall to early spring while in highland Mexico it extends from just after the autumn to just after the spring equinox. [Inset: Alignment of east-west axis of Teotihuacan with sunset (arrow) divides the equinox-zenith sun period of 3 x 20 into 2 x 20 + 1 x 20 days.]

SW quadrants (26 + 24), as well as that of the inner NW plus NE quadrants (23 + 28), is close to the observed equinox-solar zenith interval in the Petén (51 days). Second, the sum of the SE plus SW outer quadrants (43 + 45) equals the observed interval between the autumn equinox and December solstice, as well as that between the December solstice and spring equinox (89–90 days). And finally, the intervals in the NW plus NE outer circle quadrants (32 + 36) add up to the interval between zenith passages, not at Uaxactún, but instead at *Teotihuacan* (60 days, cf. Figure 9.3).

If the point-by-point count on artifacts conceived as tally markers were used in practice to tabulate real solar time, that is, time as it is actually marked out by the course of the sun in the local environment, then one might expect to find slight asymmetries and inequalities due to modification by nonastronomical calendrical considerations.[3] At two locales as widely separated as Uaxactún and Teotihuacan, discernible differences in naturally-based calendars ought to be apparent, indeed to a degree even predictable.

ELEMENTS OF "TEOTIHUACAN STANDARD TIME"

PECKED CROSSES IN OTHER MEDIA

There are several potential resources in the written record for generating hypotheses about the flow of time in the Teotihuacan pecked crosses and its possible dissemination to other parts of Mesoamerica. The Maya calendar wheel in the *Book of Chilam Balam of Kaua* and the Mexican calendar in Durán (1971: plate 35) are both quadripartite calendar wheels, while those in *Codex Fejérváry-Mayer* (p. 1, Central Mexico) and *Codex Madrid* (pp. 75–76), (Maya) mark time on the periphery of a Maltese cross design. Elsewhere (Aveni 1980: 156–158, following Caso) I have described in detail how these devices actually might have worked. Here I shall elaborate only upon the one of them that is directly relevant to the present study.

The basic feature of the *Fejérváry* diagram is a floral symbol with two sets of four petals: a) a Maltese cross with large trapezoidal petals fitting a Cartesian frame, and b) a St. Andrew's cross consisting of four smaller rounded petals positioned at 45-degree angles between the petals of the Maltese cross. A square design forms the center of the pattern. The border of the entire design (Figure 9.4) is marked with circles whose count totals 260. The ritual count is divided into 20 named day cycles, counted in groups of 13 each. The first set of 13 commences with 1 Cipactli (alligator), which is located in the upper right-hand corner of the central quadrant. Moving counterclockwise, one proceeds to count 12 blue dots to the beginning of the next count of 13 which lands on 1 Ocelotl (jaguar). The third segment of the cycle passes across the top of the diagram ending on 1 Mazatl (deer) and one continues the pattern with Xochitl (flower), Acatl (reed), Miquiztli (death), Quiahuitl (rain), Malinalli (grass), Coatl (serpent), Tecpatl (flint knife), Ozomatli (monkey), Cuetzpallin (lizard), Ollin (movement), Itzcuintli (dog), Calli (house), Cozcacuauhtli (buzzard), Atl (water), Ehecatl (wind), Cuauhtli (eagle), and Tochtli (rabbit), finally returning to 1 Cipactli to close the ritual count. Graphically, the ritual cycle seems to enclose or enshrine all other matters, calendrical or otherwise, depicted within the count.

In addition to counting off the days of the 260-day calendar, we also can use the border of the design as a year-bearer calendar, that is, a system that names consecutive New Year's Days in the 365-day count. One begins at the top left with 1 Acatl, the name of the day for New Year's Day of that year and consequently the day that carries in or bears that year. Counting through the cycle of 20 day names eighteen times, with a remainder of 5 days, one arrives at the name of the day bearing the second year, Tecpatl. Likewise, New Year's Day of the third year is named Calli and that of the fourth year, Tochtli. The fifth year begins on the same day as the first, Acatl, thus closing the cycle (this is because $365 \times 4 = 1,460$ and 1,460 divided by 20 gives a remainder of zero). In the *Fejérváry-Mayer* cosmogram, one witnesses an attempt by cosmologists of ancient highland Mexico to unite various aspects of nature into a single cosmic framework. For each direction, we have a color, bird, plant, etc. pictured within and about the arms of the Maltese cross. Even parts of the body acquire a spatial cosmological interpretation, which, in a sense parallels Western classical systems of astrology.

What may one conclude about the shape and flow of time, the movement of events that transpire from this brief examination of this colorful geometrical drawing? Students of the calendar will note that the *Fejérváry-Mayer* diagram and its almost identical counterpart in the Maya *Codex Madrid* embody both the 260-day ritual count and the solar-based 365-day year. In each, time is counted

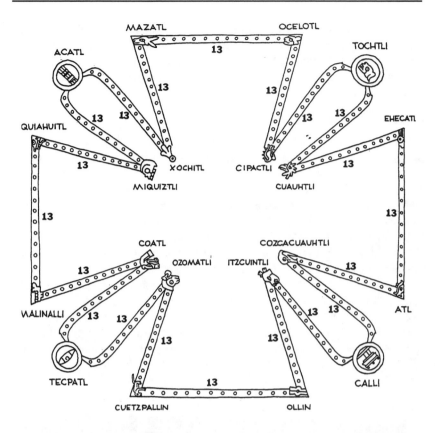

Fig. 9.4. *Codex Fejérváry-Mayer*, p. 1, showing the division of the calendar into 13 x 20 day units counted along the border.

in a counterclockwise course about the periphery of the diagram. The cosmogram unifies the two most important cycles of time by matching or fitting together the ritual and vague year cycles in a multivariate framework. Furthermore, it also offers a space-time unification (year bearers for directions, allocations of certain named days to zones along the horizon, even the counting of 260 days along the perimeter of the world). Indeed, the quadripartite "calendars" on page 1 of the *Codex Fejérváry-Mayer* is the symbol of completion par-excellence.

A much simpler-looking Maltese cross appears on page 34 of the *Codex Borbonicus* (Figure 9.5), where it adorns the top and side of a temple in which the New Fire ceremony is being celebrated. Four deities (?) with Maltese cross eyes bring bundles of sticks from the four directions to feed the New Fire that has been kindled in the center of the temple. Here the intent seems to be to implicate four directional aspects to the completion of the calendar round of fifty-two vague years that commensurate the 365- and 260-day periods. This function is consistent with the use of the symbol in the *Codex Fejérváry-Mayer* described above.

Such counting schemes seem extraordinarily simple when depicted on the symmetric, highly pictorial diagrams that appear in both the pre- and postcontact written record. It is when one moves to the somewhat more abstract medium of stone and stucco that we encounter seemingly inexplicable vagaries and variations in the makeup of the design.

OTHER FORMS OF THE MALTESE CROSS

Whenever an artifact dug out of the earth bears a resemblance *in detail* to a design or symbol in the Mesoamerican written record, common features, as well as differences, need to be pointed out. In a number of published works, we have suggested that TEO 2, a "petroglyph" pecked into the floor of Str–30E (N3W1), which lies on the west side of the Street of the Dead at Teotihuacan (Figure 9.6), distinctly resembles the famous cosmogram on page 1 of *Codex Fejérváry-Mayer*. Both forms consist of a Maltese cross with quadripartite and intercardinal elements. Let me first single out these two designs for detailed comparison before moving on to some of the other quadripartite petroglyphs I believe may have functioned as calendars. TEO 2 (See Aveni, Hartung, and Buckingham 1978 for details) is a triple cross centered on rectangular coordinate axes. We concluded that originally there had been 167 elements on the inner, 223 on the middle, and 260 on the outer cross patterns. With 142 points on the axes; this brings the total number of peck marks to 792. However, in the pattern on the outer rim and its

Fig. 9.5. New Fire Ceremony, *Codex Borbonicus*, p. 34.

numerical breakdowns we were able to discover some possible calendrical significance. The full count, like that on the *Féjerváry-Mayer* design, is 260, though the counting arrangement is different. The breakdown of the count on the petroglyph is: $1 + 18 + 1 + 13 + 1 + 13 + 1 + 18 + 1 + 18 \ldots = 260$, the "ones" falling at the vertices and on the axes, as labelled in Figure 9.6.[4] Some of these numbers resemble those indicated in the arrangement of the burials in the Temple of Quetzalcoatl reported by Cabrera, Sugiyama, and Cowgill (1991). A calendrical interval is implied in the axial count, which is $18 + 1 + 4 + 1 + 4 + 1 + 4 \ldots = 18 + 5 + 5 \ldots$; this effectively would enable an individual, starting at the center, to count 18 holes to get to the inner cross, 20 to get to the middle, and 25 to get to the outer.

Other curiosities in the TEO 2 petroglyph include the 4 (or 3 or 5) counts on the intercardinal axis between the middle and outer crosses. Points at the vertices of the inner cross also suggest a way to get to the middle cross, for example, by moving some sort of marker, thus further supporting the hypothesis that we are dealing at least in part with some sort of counting device. In sum, that the TEO 2 petroglyph specifically counts time is supported by the occurrence of 5s, 18s, 13s, 20s and 260s—all basic Mesoamerican calendrical numbers—and that the count of 260 goes around the periphery of the design.

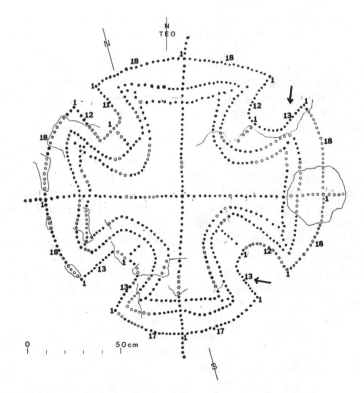

Fig. 9.6. TEO 2 petroglyph showing breakdown of count on the outer rim.

Since we initiated our study of pecked crosses in the early 1970s, we have noted that other such petroglyphs bear similarities to the Maltese cross design. The petroglyph excavated at the ruins of Río Grande, Tututepec, on the Oaxaca Coast (Zarate 1986: fig. 3) is one example. It is located on a flat rectangular field stone of dimensions 2.20 meters by 1.80 meters, and consists of an outer circular design, but the interior is unmistakably in the form of the Maltese cross. Intercardinals issue from the vertices of this inner design to the pecked circle. As we have not seen either the stone or the site, it is impossible to comment further except to say that the 10–1–4–1–4 pattern is clearly discernible along one of the axes in Zarate's photo. The site has been dated ceramically from 200–300 B.C.E. to 300–700 C.E.

The design ACA reported in our 1978 paper also resembles TEO 2. It is located at the edge of the village of Santa Cruz, Acalpixcan, 5 kilometers southeast of Xochimilco on the south shore of Lake Texcoco. Situated on a flat rock about 25 meters above the lake shore, it may have functioned in part as an alignment device. The contours on the eastern rim of the design bend and turn in much the same manner as we observe in TEO 2. In both cases, eighteen holes occur on the axis between the center and the first circle. Finally, more than one of the several pecked crosses recently excavated on the southeast side of the Pyramid of the Sun by Matos, and studied by Morante (1996), appear to resemble the Maltese cross design.

As stated above, the Maltese cross form is also found in the iconography adorning buildings at Tikal, where it appears above the Teotihuacan *tablero talud* on Str. 5D–43. Pasztory (1978: 110 and 141, note 6) likens 5D–43 to the radial design form prevalent in the Middle Classic and more readily detectable in the form of round buildings. She points out that the Maltese cross on the building resembles the Maya completion glyph and that such structures likely symbolized the completion of time cycles.

Figure 9.7 depicts forms of the design in the Teotihuacan motif index of Langley (1986). His trefoil classification (#214, Ref. 252, p. 295) appears on pottery as a horizontally bisected half Maltese cross (see also Thompson 1971: figs. 22–55, for Maya references to this common form as the sign for completion), an assignation not inconsistent with its connection to the New Fire ceremony. Langley states on page 295 that it occurs always in a floral context at Teotihuacan. His quatrefoil, #161 (all on figurines or vessels, Refs. 106, 687, but esp. 219) is identified as a "Teutonic Cross" (p. 317). This also can be seen in a photo by Sejourné (1959).

In this section I have called attention to the Maltese cross element, a particular form of quadripartite design, in petroglyphs, codices, and in the iconography of buildings. I also have stressed the similarity of structural detail between the design of the petroglyph TEO 2 and the cosmogram on page 1 of the *Codex Fejérváry-Mayer*. The likeness between cross petroglyphs and calendar wheels seems compelling, for TEO 2 and the *Fejérváry-Mayer* cosmogram are distinctly similar in detail, even down to the 260-day count along the outer perimeter. The completion of a round of time is the central theme that integrates these designs together.

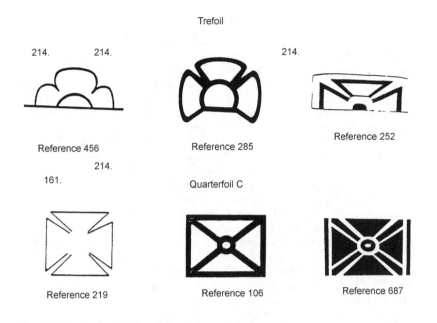

Trefoil

214.   214.   214.

Reference 456   Reference 285

Reference 252

214.
161.   Quarterfoil C

Reference 219   Reference 106   Reference 687

Fig. 9.7. Langley's (1986) trefoil and quatrefoil elements.

Summary

Does our failure to devise a fixed calendrical counting method common to all petroglyphs suggest that the petroglyphs could not have been so used? Imagine walking into a clock shop and confronting a wide variety of timepieces. Some have round faces with Roman numerals, others windows through which to view digital readouts. Even our calendars come in a variety of temporal formats. Most train the eye to move along from left to right, but others can be read in a downward direction and in some we flip the pages day by day. Likewise, it is not unreasonable to suppose that time would be counted in slightly different ways in temporal devices we find in the written documents. Given the flexibility and artistic license present in so much Mesoamerican iconography, there may well have been individual variations and flexibility on how to map the moving sun on a pecked circle.

Whether the inheritors of the Teotihuacan space-time canon expressed through the quadripartite completion symbol adopted ideas about such symbolism and cosmic models of space-time based upon it, or whether they only acquired a way to count the days; whether the diffusion of information was actively sought or forcibly intruded—none of these questions can be decided exclusively by the sort of research I have conducted on these artifacts. What does ring clear from the archaeological record is that the flow of information, as far as pecked crosses are concerned, was directed out of the Teotihuacan Valley—the place where time began.

NOTES

1. This idea of using one natural event (here the commencement of a star cycle) to reckon another (the start of the year of the seasons) is well known to students of world calendars. Basically one marks time with whatever signals nature conveniently offers. For example, one of the oddest of all cyclic pairings is that encountered in the calendar of the Trobriand Islanders of Southeast Asia. The primary event in the Trobriand calendar is the appearance of a worm! If ever there were a case of man adapting his own clock to one of nature's most reliable biological rhythms, the relationship between Trobriander and *palolo* worm is it. This worm, an inhabitant of Pacific coral reefs, executes a "circa-lunar" rhythm. Once a year for three or four nights, the posterior parts of the worm wriggle dramatically on the surface of the water and let loose their genital products. The spawning marine annelid is seen on the surface of the sea at the southern extremity of the island chain every year following the full moon that falls between October 15 and November 15 (our time). Trobrianders name this important month Milamala after the worm, and celebrate a great festival in its honor to inaugurate the planting season. (They also eat the worm roasted and prize it as a delicacy.) For a further discussion of such cyclic pairings, see Aveni (1989).

2. With Gordon Willey's kind assistance, a search of the Peabody Museum files for unpublished photographs of the missing UAX 2 and 3 petroglyphs was undertaken by me in the late '70s, though without success. Smith does tell us, however, that the $10-(1)-4-(1)-4 = 20$ count so common to the Teotihuacan petroglyphs also was present on the other two examples.

3. The modification of the length of our (originally) lunar months to 30, 31, 28, or 29-day lengths in the modern calendar is a good example.

4. Figure 9.6 shows the reconstructed count, which totals 247. However, if one were to modify partially destroyed segments to be in perfect accord with those that survive intact (the pair of 18s at the top or north side of the design and the pair of 13s at the east side (arrows) then the number 260 is reached.

REFERENCES

Aveni, Anthony F.
1980. *Skywatchers of Ancient Mexico*. Austin: University of Texas Press.
1989a. *Empires of Time*. New York: Basic Books.
1989b. "Pecked Cross Petroglyphs at Xihuingo." *Archaeoastronomy* (Supplement to the *Journal for the History of Astronomy*) 20, no. 14: S73-S115.
1993. *Ancient Astronomers*. Montreal and Washington, DC: St. Rémy Press and the Smithsonian Institution.

Aveni, Anthony F., Edward Calnek, and Horst Hartung
1988. "Myth, Environment and the Orientation of the Templo Mayor at Tenochtitlan." *American Antiquity* 53: 287–309.

Aveni, Anthony F., and Horst Hartung
1982. "New Observations of the Pecked Cross Petroglyph." *Lateinamerika Studien* (Munich) 10: 1025–1041.
1983. "Note on the Discovery of Two New Pecked Cross Petroglyphs." *Archeoastronomy Bulletin* 5, no. 3: 21–3.
1985. "Las cruces punteadas en Mesoamérica: Versíon actualizada." In *Cuadernos de Arquitectura Mesoamericana* 4: 3–13.
1989. "Uaxactun, Guatemala, Group E and Similar Assemblages: An Archaeoastronomical Reconsideration." In A. Aveni, ed., *World Archaeoastronomy* Cambridge: Cambridge University Press, pp. 441–460.

Aveni Anthony F., Horst Hartung, and Beth Buckingham
1978. "The Pecked Cross Symbol in Ancient Mesoamerica." *Science* 202: 267–279.

Aveni, Anthony F., and Sharon Gibbs
1976. "On the Orientation of Precolumbian Buildings in Central Mexico." *American Antiquity* 41: 510-517.

Baird, Ellen T.
1989. "Star Wars at Cacaxtla." In R. Diehl and J. Berlo, eds., *Mesoamerica After the Decline of Teotihuacan, A.D. 700–900.* Washington, DC: Dumbarton Oaks, pp. 105–122.

Berlo, Janet Catherine, ed.
1992. *Art, Ideology, and the City.* Washington, DC: Dumbarton Oaks.

Cabrera Castro, Rubén, Saburo Sugiyama, and George L. Cowgill
1991. "The Templo de Quetzalcoatl Project at Teotihuacan." *Ancient Mesoamerica* 2: 77–92.

Codex Borbonicus
1974. Bibliothèque de l'Assemblée Nationale, Paris (Y 120). Facsimile edition. Graz: ADV, Codices Selecti, vol. XLIV.

Codex Fejérváry-Mayer
1971. M 12014 City of Liverpool Museums. Facsimile edition. Codices Selecti, vol. XXVI. Graz: ADV.

Coggins, Clemency
1980. "The Shape of Time: Some Political Implications of a Four-Part Figure." *American Antiquity* 45: 727–739.

Diehl, Richard A., and Janet Catherine Berlo, eds.
1989. *Mesoamerica After the Decline of Teotihuacan: A.D. 700–900.* Washington, DC: Dumbarton Oaks.

Durán, Fray Diego
1971. *The Book of the Gods and Rites and the Ancient Calendar.* Translated and edited by F. Horcasitas and D. Heyden. Norman: University of Oklahoma Press.

Gamio, Manuel
1922. *La población del valle de Teotihuacan.* Vol. 1. Mexico: SEP, Dirección de Talleres Gráficos.

Langley, James C.
1986. *Symbolic Notation of Teotihuacan: Elements of Writing in a Mesoamerican Culture of the Classic Period.* Oxford: BAR International Series 313.

Linné, Sigvald
1934. *Archaeological Research at Teotihuacán, Mexico.* The Ethnological Museum of Sweden New Series Publication no. 1. Stockholm: Victor Pettersons Bokindustriaktiebolag.

Millon, René
1992. "Teotihuacan Studies: From 1950 to 1990 and Beyond." In J. C. Berlo, ed., *Art, Ideology and the City of Teotichuacan.* Washington, DC: Dumbarton Oaks.

Millon, René, ed.
1973. *Urbanization at Teotihuacan.* 2 vols. Austin: University of Texas Press.

Morante López , Rubén B.
1996. "Evidencias del conocimiento astronómico en Teotihuacan." Ph.D. diss. in Anthropology, Facultad de Filosofía y Letras, UNAM, Mexico, D.F.

Pasztory, Esther

1978. "Artistic Traditions of the Middle Classic Period." In E. Pasztory, ed., *Middle Classic Mesoamerica: AD 400–700*. New York: Columbia University Press, pp. 108–142.

Schele Linda, and David Friedel

1990. *A Forest of Kings: The Untold Story of the Ancient Maya*. New York: Morrow.

Sejourné, Laurette

1959. *Un palacio en la Ciudad de los Dioses, Teotihuacán*. Mexico: INAH.

Smith, A. Ledyard

1950. *Uaxactun Guatemala: Excavations of 1931–1937*. Washington, DC: Carnegie Institution Publication no. 588.

Thompson J. Eric S.

1971. *A Catalog of Maya Hieroglyphs*. Norman: University of Oklahoma Press.

Tichy, Franz

1976. *Orientación de las pirámides e iglesias en el altiplano mexicano*. Puebla, Mexico: Fundacíon Alemana para la Investigación Científica, Comunicaciones: Proyecto Puebla-Tlaxcala Suplemento no. 4.

Tobriner, Stephen

1972. "The Fertile Mountain: An Investigation of Cerro Gordo's Importance to the Town Plan and Icongraphy of Teotihuacan." In *Teotihuacán XI Mesa Redonda*. Mexico: SMA, pp. 103–115.

World Weather Disc

1988. Seattle: Worldwide Airfield Summaries.

Worthy, Morgan, and Roy S. Dickens Jr.

1983. "The Mesoamerican Pecked Cross as a Calendrical Device." *American Antiquity* 48: 573–576.

Zarate M., R.

1986. "Tres piedras labradas en la regíon oaxaqueña." *Cuadernos de Arquitectura Mesoamericana* 4, no. 7: 75–77.

10

▼

THE TURQUOISE HEARTH

FIRE, SELF SACRIFICE, AND THE CENTRAL MEXICAN CULT OF WAR

KARL TAUBE

In many respects, the great Classic-period city of Teotihuacan can be regarded as the canonical source of Postclassic Nahuatl culture. The civic and religious architecture of the Toltec and Aztec cultures share many traits with earlier Teotihuacan, including the use of balustrades and beam-and-mortar roofs, frequently ornamented with projecting *almena* sculptures. Such specific iconographic motifs as speech scrolls, Mexican year signs, and bivalve shells with coyote-like heads and limbs are well documented in both Teotihuacan and Aztec art.[1] In addition, some of the better-known Postclassic Central Mexican gods, including Tlaloc and Quetzalcoatl, can be readily traced to earlier Teotihuacan. Although many of these cited examples could be explained through shared ancestry, it is also clear that the Aztecs were not simply unconscious inheritors of previous traditions. Instead, they were very aware of Teotihuacan as a specific, ancient place exhibiting its own unique qualities and characteristics. Thus, along with contact-period Native accounts describing the ancient city, there are also archaistic Aztec evocations of Teotihuacan art and architecture (see Umberger 1987; Matos Moctezuma

This research greatly benefited from my interaction with the participants of the 1996 Moses Mesoamerican Archive conference at Princeton University, and I owe a special thanks to the coordinator of this event, Davíd Carrasco. I also wish to thank the following participants for their comments and suggestions both during and after the conference: Anthony F. Aveni, Elizabeth H. Boone, Davíd Carrasco, Alfredo López Austin, Leonardo López Luján, Saburo Sugiyama, and David Stuart. Carlos Trenary generously provided me with information regarding Mesoamerican meteor lore. In addition, Anthony Aveni, Frances Berdan, Stephen Houston, and John Pohl offered valuable comments regarding an earlier version of this manuscript.

and López Luján 1993). The Aztecs also traced many of the more essential traits of their solar war cult to ancient Teotihuacan (Taube 1992c). In this study, I discuss some of the more important themes shared between Teotihuacan and later Aztec warfare symbolism, including fire, self-sacrifice, and the metamorphosis and resurrection of the warrior soul.

Although this study focuses upon Central Mexican ideology and belief, a considerable amount of material will also derive from ancient Maya epigraphy and art, particularly of the Late Classic period. As general contemporaries of Teotihuacan, the Classic Maya were very much aware of the art and ideology of this great center. Even at the end of the Late Classic period, when Teotihuacan was no longer a major force in Mesoamerica, the Maya continued to celebrate Teotihuacan iconography and symbolism. In Classic Maya art, Teotihuacan imagery tends to appear not as piecemeal items in isolation, but rather within a complex of related motifs, such as Teotihuacan Tlalocs, Mexican year signs, chevrons, and many other elements. In Maya art, this foreign Mexican imagery commonly focuses on the symbolism of war. Possessing both a very naturalistic art style and the most developed writing system of ancient Mesoamerica, the Classic Maya have much to tell us of Teotihuacan. Thus objects occurring in the highly developed but rather opaque art of Teotihuacan stand out in striking clarity, and still poorly known entities are described glyphically in Mayan.

Along with presenting vivid insights into the iconography of Teotihuacan, Late Classic Maya art can also provide a crucial link to Late Postclassic Central Mexican symbolism and art. Take, for example, the Central Mexican *aztaxelli* headpiece of paired heron feathers, which serves as a important marker of Late Postclassic war-related deities, including Tezcatlipoca and Mixcoatl-Camaxtli (Figures 10.1 [a], 10.15 [b], and 10.28 [b]). In Late Classic Maya art, this same feather headpiece is worn in identical position on Aguateca Stela 2 and Dos Pilas Stela 16 (Figure 10.1 [b and c]). The protagonist upon these very similar monuments, Ruler 3 of Dos Pilas, is portrayed as a Teotihuacan warrior wielding a spearthrower, a weapon generally identified with foreign, Central Mexican warfare in the Maya area. Among the many readily identifiable Mexican elements appearing in his costume are his Tlaloc mask, Mexican year signs, and thick collar edged with bivalves. Although the *aztaxelli* headpiece is yet to be documented for Teotihuacan, its occurrence with Teotihuacan war imagery does imply a Central Mexican origin.

THE WAR SERPENT AND THE XIUHCOATL

Much of this study revolves around the Temple of Quetzalcoatl within the great Ciudadela compound at Teotihuacan. Excavations by Rubén Cabrera Castro, George Cowgill, and Saburo Sugiyama (Cabrera Castro et al. 1991; Sugiyama 1989a, 1989b, 1995) have revealed that probably over two hundred individuals were sacrificed for the dedication of this temple (ca. 200 C.E.). The majority were dressed with the costume and gear of Teotihuacan warriors, including back mirrors, obsidian-tipped darts, and, in many cases, thick shell collars adorned with imitation human maxillae. The presence of these many victims in militaristic costume suggests that the Temple of Quetzalcoatl was closely related to the office of war (Taube 1992c). But along with the sacrificed warriors, the remarkable sculptural façades on the temple sides also included a powerful emblem of war.

Two types of massive tenoned heads project from the sides of the Temple of Quetzalcoatl. Whereas one entity is clearly the Plumed Serpent, the other has a distinct muzzlelike snout with a slightly upturned nose and a set of large, closely spaced fangs, quite unlike the dentition of the Plumed Serpent (Figure 10.2 [a]). In addition, this second being is not covered with plumage but flat, angular plates, creating a scalelike surface. Both Sugiyama (1992, 1993, 1995) and I (Taube 1992c) note that this rather static-appearing head represents a headdress.[2] Similar examples occurring in Classic Maya art indicate that it is a zoomorphic war helmet composed of cut shell platelets (Figures 10.2 [e and f], 10.8 [a], and 10.9 [d and e]). Since the creature appearing on this headdress is deeply embedded in the context of Teotihuacan war iconography in Classic Maya art, I have termed it the War Serpent. Aside from the Temple of Quetzalcoatl, this entity occurs as a platelet

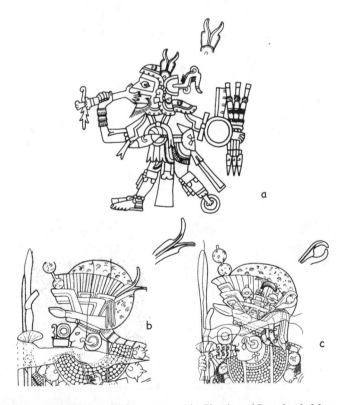

Fig. 10.1. The *aztaxelli* heron feather ornament in Classic and Postclassic Mesoamerican iconography; a. Tezcatlipoca as warrior with *aztaxelli* ornament, Late Postclassic Central Mexico, *Codex Fejérváry-Mayer*, p. 44; b. Ruler 3 of Dos Pilas with Teotihuacan-style war regalia and *aztaxelli* ornament, Aguateca Stela 2 (drawing courtesy of Ian Graham); c. Dos Pilas Ruler 3 with *aztaxelli* ornament (drawing courtesy of Ian Graham).

headdress in other contexts at Teotihuacan (Figure 10.2 [b and c]). It will be subsequently noted that the Teotihuacan examples commonly appear upon ceramic figurines portraying mortuary warrior bundles.

The War Serpent platelet headdress is but a more elaborate, zoomorphic form of the simple "pillbox" mosaic helmet of Classic Mesoamerica. Both the simple and War Serpent types appear on Piedras Negras Lintel 2, a panel portraying Maya elite in Teotihuacan-style military dress (see Schele and Miller 1986: plate 40). Citing archaeological examples of cut-shell platelets from Teotihuacan, Kaminaljuyú, and Tikal, Janet Berlo (1976: 36–37) first suggested that the Classic-

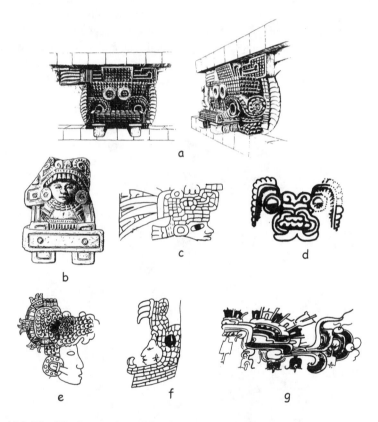

Fig. 10.2. The War Serpent in Teotihuacan and Classic Maya art; a. Two views of War Serpent from the Temple of Quetzalcoatl (from Caso and Bernal 1952: fig. 184); b. Teotihuacan bundle figure wearing War Serpent headdress (from Seler 1902–1923, V: 457); c. War Serpent platelet helmet, detail of painted wooden box in Teotihuacan style (after Berrin and Pasztory 1993: no. 55); d. Frontally facing War Serpent head, detail of Teotihuacan carved vase (after Seler 1902–1923, V: 516); e. Platelet War Serpent helmet—note feathered eye and burning torches on ears—Tikal Stela 31 (after Jones and Satterthwaite 1982: fig. 51); f. Ruler wearing platelet War Serpent helmet, detail of sherd from Nohmul, Belize (from Taube 1992c: fig. 6b); g. War Serpent trailing flames, detail of Late Classic Maya vase (from Taube 1992c: fig. 7c).

period platelet helmets were of shell mosaic. Berlo (58) also noted that Piedras Negras Burial 5 contained the remains of such a helmet, here in the form of 209 cut spondylous shell plaques (see Coe 1959: 59, figs. 53–54 and 64). In fact, examples of such headdresses have been excavated at a number of Maya sites, including Nebaj, Kaminaljuyú, and Copán (see Kidder, Jennings, and Shook 1946: figs. 22, 31, 161 [a,d], and 163 [d and e]; Smith and Kidder 1951: figs. 42, 69 [d]; Viel and Cheek 1983: fig. S–9e). The remains of a shell platelet helmet was found at Teotihuacan, apparently from the compound at Yayahuala (see Séjourné 1966: lám. 16).

The Teotihuacan platelet helmet illustrated by Laurette Séjourné (1966: lám. 16) is accompanied by a pair of cut-shell goggles, such as frequently appear in Teotihuacan art. These goggles are also on the brows of the War Serpent headdresses from the Temple of Quetzalcoatl (Figure 10.2 [a]). Moreover, the War Serpent often has goggled eyes in Teotihuacan art (Figures 10.2 [d], 10.18 [d–h], and 10.20 [a]). In both Teotihuacan and Classic Maya art, the goggles are commonly found with individuals wearing platelet helmets of both simple and zoomorphic

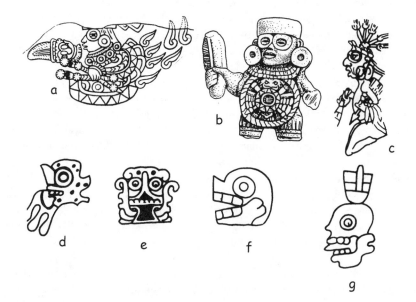

Fig. 10.3. Warrior goggles and skulls in Classic Mesoamerican art; a. Flaming warrior with goggles, Tepantitla (from Miller 1973: fig. 195); b. Warrior with goggles, spear-thrower, and shield over abdomen (after von Winning 1987, I: chap. 7, fig. 9b); c. Kneeling warrior with goggles, Pollinapan, Tuxtla region, Veracruz (after Valenzuela 1945: plate 2); d. Bleeding skull, detail of Teotihuacan vessel (after von Winning 1987: I: chap. 13, fig. 5b); e. Frontally facing skull, detail of Teotihuacan mural (after Miller 1973: fig. 47); f. Skull, detail of Teotihuacan vessel (after von Winning 1987, I: chap. 13, fig. 5a); g. Skull in glyphic compound, La Ventilla (after Cabrera Castro 1996: fig. 3).

forms (eg., Lintel 2, Temple 1, Tikal). At Teotihuacan, these goggles were an important component of military costume, and are often worn across the face of Teotihuacan and other Classic-period warriors (Figure 10.2 [a–c]). Of course, they are quite like the eyes of the Teotihuacan Tlaloc. It is noteworthy, however, that although fanged feline rain gods can be traced to the earlier Formative period, they lack goggle eyes (see Taube 1996). The goggle eyes of the Teotihuacan Tlaloc probably label him as a warrior or, to take it further, a god of war. Like the German term *blitzkrieg*, "lightning war," the thunderbolt was likened to a powerful weapon (see Paulinyi 1997). In a mural from the Tetitla compound, the lightning bolt of Tlaloc is rendered as an undulating *atlatl* dart (Miller 1973: figs. 248–249).

Aside from labeling warriors in Teotihuacan art, the white shell goggles probably had other, more esoteric meanings. When worn as facial armor, they would have presented a quite frightening and anonymous face, particularly when worn simultaneously by an onslaught of warriors. In addition, these goggles also resemble the eye orbits of skulls. At Teotihuacan, human skulls are often rendered with eye orbits as circular goggles (Figure 10.3 [d–g]). Along with serving as practical armor, the white shell goggles of Teotihuacan warriors probably presented an intimidating, other worldly appearance to opponents.

In Classic Maya art, the War Serpent commonly emanates smoke and fire, and appears rising out of a burning bowl on Yaxchilán Lintel 25. Similarly, the War Serpent also occurs with flame volutes at Teotihuacan (Figure 10.18 [g–h]). Both Caso and Bernal (1952: 113–114) and I (Taube 1992c) have suggested that the War Serpent from the Temple of Quetzalcoatl is an ancestral form of the Xiuhcoatl fire serpent of Postclassic Central Mexico. In the temple depictions, a long horizontal element lies atop of the War Serpent headdress (Figure 10.4 [a]). Whereas one end is curved, the other terminates in a featherlike tuft. As a headdress device, this horizontal element may well have had feathers. In Teotihuacan sculpture, however, flames have very similar undulating lines, and it is likely that this headdress element alludes to a burning. James Langley (1992: 272) notes that feathers can be used to designate flames in Teotihuacan art, a convention also known for later Aztec iconography (see Figure 10.14 [d]). One Teotihuacan mural portrays a very similar form, in this case fashioned of a fibrous plant material bent over on itself and bound in the middle (Figure 10.4 [b]). This object is quite like the green burning torches appearing in the murals from Tetitla, Teotihuacan (Figure 10.4 [c and d]).

Aside from Teotihuacan, similar torch bundles occur in Late Classic Maya art, frequently accompanied by Teotihuacan-derived iconography. Comparable objects appear on Copán Altar Q, a monument portraying the sixteen rulers of the Copán dynasty. Whereas the founder, K'inich Yax K'uk' Mo', wields a War Serpent shield and a burning dart, his successors hold probable torches, as if passing down the founding fire of the dynasty. A number of these torches have the same bent-over end appearing with Teotihuacan examples (Figure 10.4 [f]). In one Late Classic Maya vessel scene, a figure wields a burning torch above the head of the Teotihuacan Tlaloc (Figure 10.4 [g]). Along with the cited Copán and Teotihuacan examples, this torch appears to have a rounded, bent-over end. A still more complex fire bundle appears in a Late Classic Maya vessel scene portraying Teotihuacan motifs in the context of fire offerings (see Kerr 1990: 192). Whereas the center is of pliant plant material, it is surrounded by thicker and shorter elements, quite possibly paper or sticks of the fiercely burning, pitch-filled *ocote* wood (Figure 10.5 [e]).

One of the more common forms of the Teotihuacan torch bundle has the same type of knot appearing with the trapeze and ray motif, also known as the Mexican year sign (Figure 10.5 [a–d]). In Postclassic Mixtec writing, this device designates the year bearers, and by extension years, of the 365-day calendar.

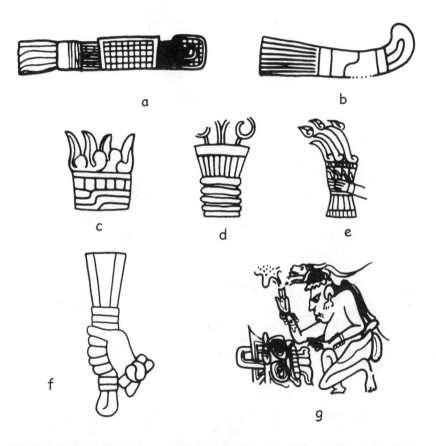

Fig. 10.4. Torches in Teotihuacan and Classic Maya art; a. Probable torch topping headdress of War Serpent helmet from Temple of Quetzalcoatl (after Caso and Bernal 1952: fig. 184); b. Probable torch of plant material, detail of Teotihuacan mural (after Miller 1973: fig. 367); c–d. Burning torches, detail of murals from Tetitla (after Miller 1973: figs. 296, 298); e. Burning torch (from Taube 1992b: fig. 10b); f. Probable torch, Copán Altar Q, Late Classic Maya (drawing by author); g. Figure holding burning torch, detail of Late Classic Maya codex-style vase (after Robicsek and Hales 1981: vessel 145).

Hasso von Winning (1977: 18) and James Langley (1992: 273) interpret the Teotihuacan sign as a tied bundle of firewood. However, the distal ends commonly flare outward, suggesting a more flexible plant substance (Figure 10.5 [a and d]). In one example, a line transcects the upper end of the bundle, creating smaller elements at the tips of the bound vertical material (Figure 10.5 [c]). This form is markedly similar to Late Classic Maya examples of Mexican year-sign bundles, which tend to be tipped with a series of small, ball-like elements (Figure

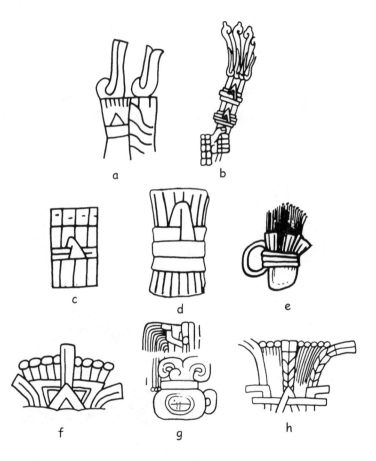

Fig. 10.5. Torches and vegetal bundles in Teotihuacan and Classic Maya art; a. Pair of burning torches, Teotihuacan (after Langley 1986: fig. 8a); b. Burning torch held by Teotihuacan goddess (after Berrin and Pasztory 1993: no. 4); c. Bundle with Mexican year-sign knot, Teotihuacan (after Langley 1986: 239); d. Bundle with Mexican year-sign knot, ceramic *adorno*, Teotihuacan (after Langley 1992: fig. 36); e. Probable profile representation of bundle with Mexican year-sign knot, detail of Late Classic Maya vase (after Kerr 1990: 192); f. Late Classic Maya Mexican year-sign bundle, Yaxchilán Lintel 17 (after Graham and von Euw 1977: 43); g. Mexican year-sign bundle in burning brazier, text from Temple 26, Copán (after drawing courtesy of David Stuart); h. Mexican year-sign bundle from lower stairway block, Copán Temple 26 (drawing by author).

10.5 [e–h]). The Maya torch bundles are clearly of pliant, flexible material. In one Copán text, the bundle drapes over a burning brazier, suggesting that it is as much a fire offering as a burning torch (Figure 10.5 [g]). It is quite likely that the aforementioned bundle in the Late Classic fire-offering scene is a rare view of the year-sign bundle in profile, with the prominent loop representing the central vertical element of the knot (Figure 10.5 [e]). At Yaxchilán, these Mexican year-sign bundles are commonly parts of headdresses worn in bloodletting and subsequent fire-offering scenes, often accompanied by representations of the War Serpent and the Teotihuacan Tlaloc (see the Yaxchilán Lintels 17, 24, and 25, and the "New

Fig. 10.6. The beaded vegetal bundle in Classic Maya and Aztec art; a. War Serpent surrounded by beaded vegetal sign, Kan crosses, and Teotihuacan Tlalocs, interior of Late Classic Maya bowl (after Hellmuth 1975: plate 51b); b. Detail of Teotihuacan Tlaloc with vegetal material and year-sign headdress; c. Profile of headdress with three jade disks and three Mexican year-sign bundles, Yaxchilán Lintel 17 (after Graham and von Euw 1977: 43); d. Headdress of Aztec Tlaloc impersonator with Mexican year sign, three *yauhtli* bundles, and three jade disks, detail from *Codex Borbonicus*, p. 30.

Stela" of Lady Evening Star). One Late Classic Petén-style bowl portrays the War Serpent surrounded by the beaded-plant motif, flames, Teotihuacan Tlalocs, and the Mexican year sign (Figure 10.6 [a]). The three rain gods on the bowl rim wear the Mexican year-sign bundle as their headdress, a convention known from other Classic Maya scenes (Figure 10.6 [b]).

The bundle of pliant material with beaded ends continues in Postclassic Central Mexican iconography, frequently with representations of the Xiuhcoatl fire serpent. At Early Postclassic Tula, an early form of the Xiuhcoatl—complete with a smoking mouth—appears on representations of back mirrors (Figure 10.10 [h]). The arched serpent bodies are of the same plant material tipped with balls. In Late Postclassic iconography, the beaded motif continues to tip the tails of the Xiuhcoatl, suggesting that this creature is virtually a personified bundle of this plant material (Figures 10.7 [a and c], 10.12 [h], and 10.13 [b–e]). The tail is bound by one or more broad knotted bands topped by the central pointed element of the Mexican year sign or, in a number of cases, the entire year sign (Figure 10.7 [a and c]). With the Mexican year-sign knot, they are essentially identical to Classic-period year-sign bundles (eg., Figure 10.7 [b]). In this regard, it should be noted that in Nahuatl, *xihuitl* has a range of meanings, including "year," as well as "herb," "comet (meteor)," and "turquoise."

The material composing the bundled year sign remains to be discussed. Aztec color representations portray the plant as green and tipped with yellow dots. Along with the cited Xiuhcoatl examples, this same yellow and green veg-etation appears as paper-wrapped bundles tied to the headdresses of the Tlaloc and Chicomecoatl impersonators in the famed *Codex Borbonicus* illustrations of Ochpaniztli. In the case of the Chicomecoatl maize goddess impersonators, the central headdress element is the bound Mexican year-sign bundle, quite like the previously cited Classic and Late Postclassic examples (Figure 10.7 [d]). Accord-ing to Seler (1902–1923, II: 722), the green and yellow plant motif on the Xiuhcoatl tail represents grass. However, explicit Aztec representations of grass (*zacatl*) are notably different, and tend to have large tufts resembling cattails (I: 194). Al-though it is possible that the material is of *malinalli* grass of the *Muhlenbergia* group, *malinalli* tends to be repesented with a bone jaw or skull and lanceolate-shaped flowers (see Peterson 1983).

In the Aztec *Codex Mendoza*, the green and yellow plant material appears as a tied bundle in the toponym for Yauhtepec, or "*yauhtli* mountain" (Figure 10.7 [e]). Although lacking the central point of the Mexican year sign, this paper-wrapped bundle is virtually identical to the green and yellow examples appearing on Xiuhcoatl tails (eg., Figure 10.13 [b and d]). A very similar wrapped plant bundle—complete with the capping yellow dots—appears in the *Codex Magliabechiano* as the name of Yauhtecatl, meaning "he from Yauhtepec." He evidently wears the same plant material both as a headband and a wreath around his neck, costume elements shared with most of the other pulque gods illustrated in the *Magliabechiano*.

The *yauhtli* plant is *Tagetes lucida*, a type of sweet-scented marigold (Sullivan 1997: 83, note 19). The yellow dots appearing on the *yauhtli* bundle refer to the small yellow flowers of this plant. Simeón (1988: 145–146) provides the following definition for *yauhtli*: "Planta que tiene el olor y el sabor de anís; se la echaba en el fuego en ves de incienso." According to Seler (1902–1923, I: 186, note 1) one meaning of the term *iauh* is "incense plant" (*Weihrauchkraut*). The use of *yauhtli* as incense immediately recalls the Copán scene of the vegetal year-sign bundle in

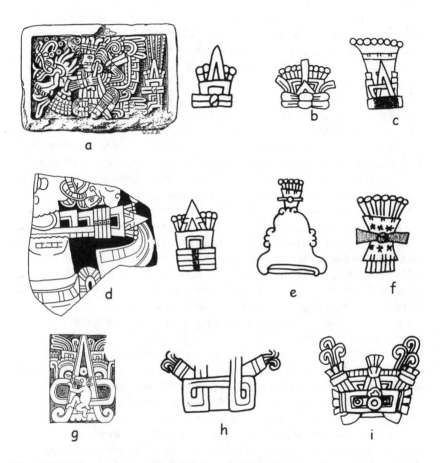

Fig. 10.7 Mexican year-sign and *yauhtli* elements in Mesoamerican iconography; a. Aztec relief depicting Xiuhcoatl with Mexican year sign and *yauhtli* tail (from Seler 1902–1923, II: 717); b. Mexican year-sign bundle, Yaxchilán Lintel 17 (see Figure 9.7[c]); c. Aztec Mexican year-sign *yauhtli* bundle, detail of headdress worn by Chicomecoatl impersonator, *Codex Borbonicus*, p. 30; d. Xiuhcoatl with *yauhtli* Mexican year-sign tail, detail of fragmentary Coyolxauhqui monument, Templo Mayor (from Taube 1993: 49); e. The toponym Yauhtepec, or "*yauhtli* mountain," *Codex Mendoza*, fol. 8r; f) Name glyph of pulque god Yauhtecatl, "he of Yauhtepec," *Codex Magliabechiano*, fol. 51r); g. Conflation of Mexican year sign and serpent face in sign for year 1 Rabbit (from Miller and Taube 1993: 113); h. Headdress with central Mexican year sign and two diagonal torches, detail from Early Classic Yehnal platform, Copán (drawing courtesy of Robert Sharer); i. Headdress with Mexican year sign and two diagonal torches, detail of ceramic censer from Xico, Valley of Mexico (after Berlo 1984: plate 45a).

a burning censer (Figure 10.5 [g]). Although it is widely known that Teotihuacan strongly influenced Classic Maya visual art, was sight the only sense involved? Certain exotic smells, such as from incense, can certainly provide powerful emotive responses in ritual, particularly when they are identified with distant, revered places. The use of incense from the Holy Land in Catholic ritual readily comes to mind.

Sahagún (1950–1982, book 11: 145–146) places *yauhtli* under the classification of "herb," or *xihuitl*, and notes that "with it there is incensing, there is washing." As a *xihuitl* plant used as an important form of incense, *yauhtli* is very well-suited for the Xiuhcoatl fire serpent. During the Xocotlhuetzi rites dedicated to the fire gods Xiuhtecuhtli and Xocotl, *yauhtli* was thrown into the face of the victims before they were hurled upon the sacrificial pyre (book 2: 17 and 115). The *yauhtli* headbands and wreaths found with the pulque gods, or *centzon totochtin* ("four hundred rabbits"), may also relate to warrior sacrifice. The *centzon totochtin* are probably but aspects of the *centzon huitznahua* ("four hundred southerners"), the four hundred half brothers of Huitzilopochtli defeated at Coatepec (see Taube 1993: 3). However, the *yauhtli* ornaments worn by the pulque gods could also refer to powers of fertility and abundance. Francisco Hernández (1959, I: 324) glosses *yauhtli* as "hierba de nubes." Bernard Ortiz de Montellano (1980 and 1990) notes that *yauhtli* incense was strongly identified with Tlaloc and other Aztec gods of water and fertility. The appearance of the green and yellow plant in the *Codex Borbonicus* scenes of Ochpaniztli is entirely appropriate for the agricultural role of *yauhtli* (Figures 10.6 [d], and 10.7 [c]). The Ochpaniztli festival concerns first harvest, and is filled with references to rain and maize. It will be recalled that in Late Classic Maya art, the Teotihuacan Tlaloc often wears a Mexican year-sign bundle as his headdress; in many instances, this bundle may be of *yauhtli* (Figure 10.6 [b]).

Although the link between the Aztec and Classic Maya headdresses may seem somewhat tenuous, there is a striking degree of correspondence. One of the headdresses rendered in profile on Yaxchilán Lintel 17 apparently has three *yauhtli* year-sign bundles framing three jade disks on a broad headband (Figure 10.6 [c]). The Tlaloc impersonator representing the world center on page 30 of the *Codex Borbonicus* wears a headdress of three green jade disks, three *yauhtli* bundles, and a Mexican year sign (Figure 10.6 [d]). The positioning of these Aztec *yauhtli* bundles—two flanking and one central crowning form—is essentially identical to the bundles appearing on the Yaxchilán headdress.

Some of the most ancient representations of the War Serpent, roughly contemporaneous with the examples from the Temple of Quetzalcoatl, appear as headdresses of Miccaotli-period Teotihuacan warrior figurines (Figure 10.20 [f]).[3] The schematic, frontally facing headdresses are notably similar to the aforementioned Mexican year sign, and also resemble personified forms of this device appearing in Late Postclassic Mixtec art (Figure 10.7 [g]). In the case of the Mixtec examples, the personified Mexican year sign is probably the Xiuhcoatl, which can have similar feather tufts on its shoulders (Taube 1992: 67, fig. 9 [d–e]). One of the early Teotihuacan figurines originally had a pair of diagonal elements on either side of the headdress (Figure 10.20 [f]). Although it is conceivable that these are feathers, they more likely represent torches, analogous to the examples appearing atop the War Serpents from the Temple of Quetzalcoatl. Teotihuacan-style censers from Xico, in the vicinity of Chalco, portray a Mexican year-sign headdress flanked by diagonal burning torches (Figure 10.7 [i]). At Copán, the same form of head-dress—complete with diagonal, burning torches and a central year sign—appears on a recently excavated stucco façade from the Early Classic Yehnal platform (Figure 10.7 [i]).

As the name implies, the faunal characteristics of the War Serpent are at least partly serpentine. At Teotihuacan and in the Maya region, it commonly has a long, bifurcated serpent tongue (Figures 10.2 [d], 10.9 [c], 10.11 [a and b], 10.18 [d–f, h], and 10.20 [b]). An Early Classic Teotihuacan-style vessel from Escuintla portrays a burning figure with a War Serpent headdress and a long serpent tail (see Hellmuth 1975: plate 20 [a–c]). In Late Classic Maya art, the serpent attributes are especially pronounced, with the creature often displaying a rattle-snake tail (Figures 10.8 [b] and 10.18 [b]). On Naranjo Stela 2, the Late Classic Maya king Smoking Squirrel appears in Teotihuacan war costume, with a War Serpent headdress and a smoking rattlesnake tail (for detail of headdress, see Figure 10.9 [f]). The Classic Maya term for this being is *waxaklahun u bah chan*, meaning "18 its image snake" (Figure 10.18 [a]) (Freidel, Schele, and Parker 1993: 308–310; for the *u bah* reading see Houston and Stuart 1997). Although the meaning of this curious term remains poorly known, the number 18 appears to have been closely identified with the War Serpent and the Temple of Quetzalcoatl. In their reconstructions of the front western façade of the Temple of Quetzalcoatl, both Marquina (1951: 85) and Sugiyama (1989a: fig. 2) place eighteen images of the War Serpent on either side of the stairway. In addition, eighteen is a significant and repetitive number for the group burials within the Temple of Quetzalcoatl. Each of the mass burials known as Graves 4, 190, and 204 contained eighteen individuals dressed in Teotihuacan-style military costume (Sugiyama 1995: 101, 108, 113). In addition, eighteen greenstone cones—otherwise unique in ancient Mesoamerica—were found grouped within the central multiple burial of the Temple of Quetzalcoatl (Berrin and Pasztory 1993: note 173).

Aside from its serpentine characteristics, the War Serpent also has a strongly feline component based on the jaguar. Along with the thick muzzle and large canines, the creature frequently displays jaguar ears (Figires 10.2 [c–e], 10.8 [a and c], 10.10 [a], 10.18 [f and h], and 10.20 [c]). An example from Monte Albán Stela 1 portrays a Teotihuacan warrior atop a War Serpent with a jaguar head, long serpent tongue, and a rattlesnake tail (Figure 10.8 [a]). An apparently burning serpent arches before the warrior bust. This representation is notably similar to a Late Classic Maya vessel scene, which represents a Teotihuacan-style warrior holding a curving War Serpent staff while riding atop a larger War Serpent with a burning rattlesnake tail (Figure 10.8 [b]). At Teotihuacan, the War Serpent is especially feline, and usually has clawed jaguar limbs (Figures 10.11 [a] and 10.18 [f and h]). Although the Maya version typically has a snake body, a monument in the Dallas Museum of Art portrays the War Serpent not only with a a feline ear, but an entire jaguar body, complete with spots and tail (Figure 10.10 [a]; for the entire figure, see Mayer 1989: plate 104).

In Teotihuacan-style iconography, butterflies are frequently portrayed with jaguar mouths (eg., Figure 10.8 [f]). Quite probably, this refers to the fierce, militaristic aspect of this being in Central Mexican thought, a topic subsequently to be discussed in detail. In this regard, it is noteworthy that along with displaying serpent and jaguar attributes, the War Serpent also has strong butterfly traits. Thus the thick snout frequently sports long tasseled elements closely resembling Teotihuacan representations of butterfly antennae (Figures 10.9 [a, c–e], and 10.11 [b]). At Teotihuacan, the War Serpent commonly has the feather-edged eye

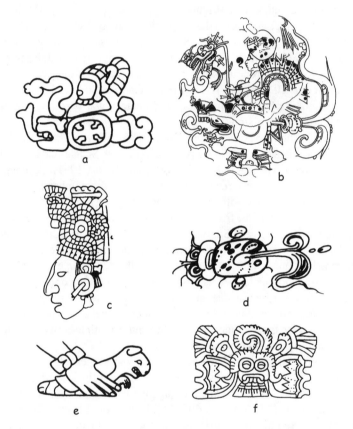

Fig. 10.8. Conflation of jaguar, serpent, and butterfly imagery in Classic Mesoamerican art; a. Bust of helmeted warrior atop War Serpent with jaguar head and rattlesnake tail, detail of Zapotec text from Stela 1, Monte Albán (after Marcus 1983: fig. 5.8); b. Warrior figure atop War Serpent with burning rattlesnake tail, interior of codex-style bowl, Late Classic Maya (after Robicsek and Hales 1981: vessel 107); c. Palenque ruler wearing War Serpent headdress with jaguar ears, detail of recently discovered monument (drawing after photograph by author); d. Probable cocoon with butterfly crenelations and jaguar pelt markings, detail of Late Classic Maya codex-style vase (after Kerr 1990: 218); e. Olmec portrayal of probable pupate form of butterfly with jaguarlike head, detail of carved jade pendant from Costa Rica (after Parsons 1993: fig. 19.1); f. Butterfly with goggled eyes and jaguar maw, detail of carved Teotihuacan vessel (from Taube 1992c: fig. 18a).

Fig. 10.9. Butterfly attributes of the War Serpent; a. War Serpent with antennae-like projections (from Taube 1992c: fig. 21b); b. Frontally facing butterfly with curving proboscis and antennae, detail of Aztec stone box (after Franco 1959: plate 7.2); c. Maya ruler wearing War Serpent headdress with projecting antennae, Piedras Negras Stela 7 (after Maler 1901: plate 16); d. War Serpent with projecting antennae, Lintel 2 of Temple 1, Tikal (detail of drawing courtesy of Linda Schele); e. Maya ruler wearing War Serpent with antennae-like tufts on snout, Stela 2, Naranjo (after Graham and von Euw 1975: 13); f. Butterfly with curving proboscis and crenelated edging (after Kerr 1992: 393); g. Itzpapalotl, the Obsidian Butterfly, with crenelated edging for butterfly wing, *Codex Vaticanus B*, p. 63; h. Butterfly with crenelated motif serving as wings, interior of Aztec plate (after Franco 1959: plate 17.1).

of butterflies, a convention shared with the War Serpent headdress from Tikal Stela 31, which also displays burning torches on its large jaguar ears (Figures 10.2 [b, d, and e], 10.10 [d and e], 10.11 [a], and 10.20 [a]). One Teotihuacan vessel portrays a creature with a War Serpent head and butterfly wings and tail (Figure 10.18 [g]). In Late Classic Maya art, the War Serpent usually has the crenelated edging also found with Maya representations of Teotihuacan-style butterflies (Figures 10.2 [g], 10.6 [a], 10.8 [b], 10.9 [d–f], and 10.10 [b]). The same edging is found with the War Serpent headdress from the Ixtapaluca Plaque of Late Classic Central Mexico (Figure 10.10 [f]). This butterfly crenelation continues in Late Postclassic Central Mexican iconography. On page 63 of the *Vaticanus B*, it constitutes the wings of Itzpapalotl, the

Obsidian Butterfly (Figure 10.9 [g]; see also Figure 10.30 [c]). A fragmentary
Aztec bowl contains another example of the butterfly wing crenelation (Figure
10.9 [h]). One Late Classic codex-style vessel portrays curious bundle-like elements with flames, and the butterfly crenelation (Figure 10.8 [d]). Also marked
with jaguar spots, these devices may well represent the cocoons of the jaguar
butterfly.

A frontally facing butterfly face—complete with antennae and a curving,
asymmetrical proboscis—appears on an Aztec-style stone box (Figure 10.9 [b]). In
his detailed study of Central Mexican butterfly iconography, José Luis Franco (1959:
22) noted that this image is strikingly similar to Teotihuacan artistic conventions. In

Fig. 10.10. The development of the Classic War Serpent into the Postclassic Xiuhcoatl; a.
Jaguar War Serpent with sharply upturned snout (after Mayer 1989: plate 104); b. War
Serpent with upturned snout (after Schele and Miller 1986: plate 5); c. War Serpent
profile, Xcalumkin Jamb 6 (after Graham and von Euw 1992: 168); d. War Serpent with
face halved, Tepantitla (from Miller 1973: fig. 193); e. War Serpent headdress with face
halved (after Séjourné 1966: fig. 81); f. Headdress of War Serpent with face halved, Itxapaluca
Plaque (from Taube 1992c: fig. 112c); g. Headdress of War Serpent with face halved, Stela
3, Xochicalco (from Sáenz 1961: plate 4); h. Early Postclassic Xiuhcoatl with upturned
snout, detail of portrayal of Toltec-style mirror, Tula (after Tozzer 1957: fig. 248); i.
Xiuhcoatl from turquoise rim of Toltec-style mirror, Chichén Itzá (from Taube 1992c: fig.
11e); j. Xiuhcoatl from mirror rim, Casas Grandes (after di Peso 1974, VII: fig. 656–657).

particular, it is very much like the Teotihuacan and Classic Maya War Serpent headdress (eg., Figure 10.9 [a and c]). Thus it has the antennae, fangs, upwardly turned snout, and the comma-shaped eyes of the War Serpent. Moreover, the cheeks of the Aztec being are segmented, quite like the platelet mosaic surface of the War Serpent helmet. But although the Late Postclassic Aztec butterfly image is very much like the Classic War Serpent, it differs in one significant detail: the face has a curving butterfly proboscis, a trait not found with the Classic War Serpent.

Although the War Serpent has strong butterfly attributes, it is actually a supernatural caterpillar. The larval butterfly before metamorphosis, the caterpillar is ideally suited to embody concepts of transformation and rebirth, a central theme of the Central Mexican cult of war. In Mesoamerica, worm or grublike creatures thematically overlap with snakes. For example, the *Florentine Codex* refers to the rather unpleasant parasitic worm known as *tzoncoatl*, or "anus snake" (Sahagún 1950–1982, book 11: 98). But along with their long, tubular bodies, caterpillars also possess legs, which are particularly developed in the frontal thoracic region, recalling the prominent forelimbs of many Teotihuacan War Serpents (Figures 10.11 [a and b] and 10.18 [f]). In ancient Mesoamerican art, caterpillars as well as butterflies can appear with feline characteristics. A Middle Formative Olmec jade pendant discovered at Talamanca de Tibas, Costa Rica, portrays a caterpillar in partial metamorphosis, as if freshly removed from its chrysalis or cocoon (Figure 10.8 [a]). Along with its pupate body, rudimentary wings, and clawed forelimbs, the creature has an eared, jaguarlike head. It will be subsequently noted that like the War Serpent, the Xiuhcoatl also represents a caterpillarlike being.

Scenes in Late Classic and Early Postclassic Mesoamerican art document the development of the War Serpent into the Late Postclassic Xiuhcoatl. In many Late Classic Maya depictions, the War Serpent already has the sharply backturned nose found with the Xiuhcoatl (Figure 10.10 [a–c]). Moreover, by splitting frontal images of the War Serpent in half, it is possible to create profiles of this being (Figure 10.10 [d–g]). Late Classic examples from Teotihuacan and other Central Mexican sites are very similar to the Xiuhcoatl appearing on Early Postclassic Toltec back mirrors. Fashioned in turquoise mosaic, or *xihuitl*, these Toltec examples are true early *xiuhcocoa*, or "turquoise serpents" (Figures 10.10 [h–j] and 10.27 [a]).

Aside from the Xiuhcoatl serpents on the rims of back mirrors, there are more elaborate, anthropomorphized examples in Early Postclassic Toltec art (Figure 10.11 [c–e]). As with the profile examples on back mirrors, these frontally facing figures appear to be rising up on forelimbs. In addition, the petaled eyes of some of these figures are entirely comparable to Classic War Serpents and the Xiuhcoatl appearing on Early Postclassic Toltec back mirrors (Figures 10.10 [d, i, j] and 10.11 [d]). Long ago, Herbert Spinden (1913: 221–222) compared a Chichén Itzá example to the Classic-period War Serpent, including the Ixtapaluca Plaque and depictions from Piedras Negras. Terming this entity the "jaguar serpent bird," Tozzer (1957: 123–124) noted its presence at Tula as well as Chichén Itzá, and the Classic-period examples previously noted by Spinden. However, Laurette Séjourné (1966: 103) further argued that the Early Postclassic examples from Tula and Chichén Itzá ultimately derived from Teotihuacan, where there are clear earlier forms of this

Fig. 10.11. The development of the Classic War Serpent into an Early Postclassic form of the Xiuhcoatl; a. War Serpent, detail of Teotihuacan vessel (from Séjourné 1956: fig. 33); b. War Serpent figure, detail of Xico censer (after Berlo 1984: plate 50); c. Crouching figure with goggles and butterfly nosepiece, Chichén Itzá (from Seler 1902–1923, V: 367); d. Figure with goggles and butterfly nosepiece, Tula (drawn after photograph by author); e. Figure with goggles and butterfly nosepiece, Chichén Itzá (after Tozzer 1959: fig. 317); f. Aztec butterfly flame with long, bifurcated tongue, compare with *Codex Borbonicus*, figs. 11c–e, p. 18.

being (Figure 10.11 [a]). An excellent example appears on an Early Classic Teotihuacan-style censer from Xico (Figure 10.11 [b]). Along with a jaguar maw and clawed forelimbs, the figure has a serpent tongue, prominent feathered butterfly eyes, and a pair of antennae-like tufts. Following Tozzer, Séjourné (1966) and Kubler (1972) considered this crouching being as part jaguar, snake, and bird. However, along with the Classic-period War Serpent, the Early Postclassic form also has strong butterfly attributes. In many instances, the Toltec period figures wear butterfly nosepieces, quite like examples known for Classic Teotihuacan. In addition, the bifurcated tongues are often extremely long, and closely resemble the long "tongues" found with Late Postclassic Central Mexican butterflies (Figures 10.11 [f], 10.29 [c, d, and g], and 10.30 [b]).

   In Mesoamerican art, the head of the "jaguar-serpent-bird" motif tends to occur as a headdress worn by anthropomorphic warrior figures. In this regard, butterfly attributes are entirely apt. According to Aztec belief, the souls of slain warriors were reborn as the *tonatiuh ilhuicac yauh*, supernatural butterflies and birds who accompany the rising diurnal sun to zenith (see Sahagún 1950–1982, book 3: 49; book 6: 162–163; and book 10: 192). Both Séjourné (1962: 141–146) and Kubler (1967: 9) suggested that at Classic Teotihuacan, butterflies also represented souls of the deceased. Berlo (1983) has made a compelling case that much of the Aztec warrior butterfly complex was indeed present at Teotihuacan, and notes the common presence of butterfly nosepieces, wings, antennae, proboscii, and other butterfly attributes with Teotihuacan warriors. It is noteworthy that along with the winged nosepieces, the Toltec-period figures wear goggles, despite the fact that such facial gear was no longer a part of Early Postclassic warrior costume. I suspect that the nosepieces and goggles label these Toltec-period figures as the souls of long dead warriors, those of ancient Teotihuacan.

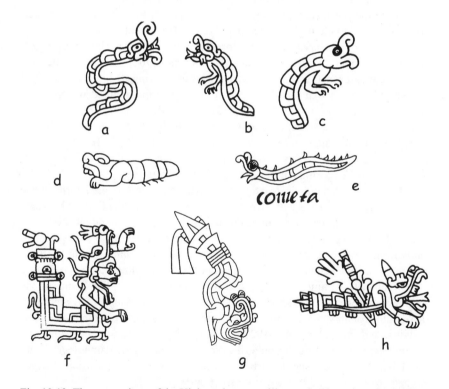

Fig. 10.12. The comparison of the Xiuhcoatl to caterpillars; a–b. Place signs for Ocuilan, *Codex Mendoza*, fols. 34r, 10v; c. Title of Aztec general, the *tocuiltecatl*, *Codex Mendoza*, fol. 65r; d. Probable caterpillar with prominent forelimbs and diminutive rear legs, *Codex Cospi*, p. 25; e. Illustration of *xihuitl* meteor as butterfly-headed caterpillar, *Codex Telleriano-Remensis*, fol. 39v; f. Burning Xiuhcoatl with forelimbs and segmented body, *Codex Borgia*, p. 44; g. Aztec diving Xiuhcoatl with forelimbs and segmented body (after Nicholson and Quiñones Keber 1983: note 8); h. Xiuhcoatl, or *yahui*, with forelimbs and diminutive rear legs, *Fons Mexicains 20*.

It has been noted that the War Serpent has butterfly attributes, and probably represents a caterpillarlike being. In the case of the Postclassic Xiuhcoatl, the caterpillar attributes are still more developed. During the Late Postclassic period, the fire serpent tends to have a strangely segmented body (Figures 10.7 [a and c], 10.12 [f–h], and 10.13 [a–f]). Among the toponyms in the Aztec *Codex Mendoza* is Ocuilan, *ocuila* signifying "caterpillar" or "worm" in Nahuatl. The place name is rendered as a caterpillar with a butterfly head, a bifurcated serpent tongue, fangs, and a segmented body that is virtually identical to that of the Xiuhcoatl. In the *Codex Mendoza*, the caterpillar is also represented in the title for one type of Aztec general, *tocuiltecatl* (Figure 10.12 [c]). Although this has been glossed as "Keeper of the Worm on Blade of Maize" (Berdan and Anawalt 1992, II: 200), the butterfly head denotes a caterpillar. Both this example and one of the Ocuilan signs have prominent forelimbs, a trait also appearing with a probable caterpillar in the *Codex Cospi* (Figure 10.12 [d]). In Late Postclassic Central Mexico, Xiuhcoatl serpents typically have only clawed forelimbs, with no rear legs (Figures 10.7 [a] and 10.12 [f and g]). As I have mentioned for the War Serpent, these forelimbs probably allude to the highly developed thoracic legs of caterpillars.

Aside from the larval body and forelimbs, the Late Postclassic Xiuhcoatl often displays overt butterfly attributes. As Séjourné (1962: 141, fig. 7) notes, the Aztec Xiuhcoatl can appear with crenelated butterfly wings (Figure 10.13 [d and e]). The *Codices Azoyu 1* and *2*—Guerrero manuscripts painted under strong Aztec influence—also portray Xiuhcoatl serpents with strong butterfly attributes. In this case, the fire serpents have segmented bodies and butterfly heads, although often with fangs and serpent tongues (Figure 10.13 [a–c]). The heads of the *Codex Azoyú 2* examples also have eye crests, recalling the crests of the War Serpent and Toltec period Xiuhcoatl (Figure 10.13 [b and c]).

Among the Postclassic Mixtec of Oaxaca, there is a related form of the Xiuhcoatl, here known as *yahui* (Smith 1973: 60–64). Like the Central Mexican Xiuhcoatl, this creature also tends to be red with a segmented, pupate body and sharply back-turned snout. Although *yahui* is suspiciously similar to the Nahuatl *yauhtli*, only rarely does the Mixtec creature have a *yauhtli* bundle tail (eg., Figure 10.12 [h]). Instead, it tends to be tipped with a burning flint blade (Figure 10.13 [f and g]). At times, the *yahui* can also appear with winglike flames on the shoulder, a convention also known for the Central Mexican Xiuhcoatl (Figure 10.7 [a]). Quite probably, these shoulder elements simultaneously refer to both butterfly wings and fire. Seler (1902–1923, IV: 713–714) noted that in Late Postclassic Central Mexican iconography, butterflies commonly designate flames (eg., Figure 10.11 [f]). In fact, the shoulder flames appearing on an aforementioned Aztec Xiuhcoatl are actually a stylized butterfly (Figure 10.7 [a]).

The Mixtec *Fons Mexicains 20* depicts a *yahui* Xiuhcoatl with small, rudimentary feet on its belly, recalling the feet of the *Codex Cospi* caterpillar and the grublike creature appearing on page 47 of the Mixtec *Codex Vindobonensis* (Figure 10.12 [h]). A Cholula polychrome vessel portrays a flying butterfly with the same feet found with the Mixtec *yahui*, and it appears that they represent the diminutive legs of caterpillars and related creatures (see Franco 1959: lám. XII: 1). In the early colonial *Codex Sánchez Solís*, the personal name of Lady 4 Wind is a smoking *yahui* with butterfly wings (Figure 10.13 [g]). The accompanying gloss, *ticuhua yahui*, signifies "butterfly *yahui*." On page 35 of the *Codex Nuttall*, a smoking butterfly *yahui* also serves as the personal name of Lady 9 Crocodile.

CATERPILLARS AND METEORS IN MESOAMERICA:

Aside from shared physical traits, caterpillars and the Xiuhcoatl may appear to have little in common. However, both were viewed as fiery, celestial beings in the form of meteors, that is, shooting stars. Mention has been made of the Mixtec *yahui* with its burning tail. According to Pohl (1994: 44), the *yahui* is a form of shooting star, and is considered by contemporary Mixtec as flying "luminescent balls." In one colonial Mixtec dictionary, *yahui nduvua* is glossed as *cometa* or "comet" (44). Similarly, there is the Xiuhcoatl, or "*xihuitl*-snake." Colonial Nahuatl sources commonly define *xihuitl* as *cometa*. However, in his detailed study of Mesoamerican comet and meteor lore, Ulrich Köhler (1989: 289) notes that in

Fig. 10.13. Xiuhcoatl serpents with butterfly traits; a) Xiuhcoatl with butterfly head, *Codex Azoyú 1*, fol. 26; b–c. Xiuhcoatl serpents with crested butterfly heads, *Codex Azoyú 2* (after Anawalt 1996: fig. 21); d. Aztec Xiuhcoatl with butterfly wing, *Codex Borbonicus*, p. 20; e. Xiuhcoatl with butterfly wing, *Codex Telleriano-Remensis*, fol. 24r; f. Mixed flying *yahui* with diminutive, flamelike wing, after *Codex Nuttall*, p. 69; g. Personal name of Lady 4 Wind Butterfly-Yahui, *Codex Sánchez Solís*, p. 22 (after Smith 1973: fig. 4c).

colonial and contemporary Spanish, *cometa* can refer to meteors as well as comets. In addition, among the contemporary Sierra Nahua of Veracruz, *xihuitl* is the specific term for meteors and meteorites (296). A detailed description of a *xihuitl* appears in an account of the terrible omens presaging the Spanish conquest:

> It became three parts and began from where the sun set and went toward where he arose. It went as if showering sparks, for a great distance it went extending; far out did its tail reach (Sahagún 1950–1982, book 8: 18).

As Köhler (1989: 295) notes, this account best corresponds to a meteor shower, not a comet.

Given the caterpillar body of the Xiuhcoatl, it is noteworthy that the Aztecs regarded shooting stars and meteorites as caterpillars. Köhler (1989: 295) cites a number of Aztec examples of meteoric caterpillars, including the belief that shooting stars cause caterpillar or grublike worms. The *Florentine Codex* mentions the *citlalocuilin* ("star worm/caterpillar"): "It is said that they are named 'star-arrow,' and what they are on is called 'shot by a star' (Sahagún 1950–1982, book XI.: 100). A more detailed account appears in another passage describing astronomical phenomena:

> It is said that the passing of a shooting star rose and fell neither without purpose nor in vain. It brought a worm [*ocuillo*] to something. And of [the animal] wounded by a shooting star, they said: "It hath been wounded by a shooting star; it hath received a worm (Sahagún 1950–1982, book VII: 13).

Köhler (1986: 295) also calls attention to the illustrations of a *xihuitl* meteor in the *Telleriano-Remensis* and cognate *Vaticanus A* codices (Figure 10.12 [e]). This segmented, snakelike being clearly has a butterfly head, thereby labeling it as a caterpillar.

Aside from the Aztec examples of meteoric caterpillars, Köhler notes that contemporary Sierra Nahuas of Los Reyes, Veracruz, believe that caterpillars appear where *xihuitl* meteorites fall:

> where a *xihuitl*, the term applied both for meteor and meteorite, arrives on the earth, black caterpillars will appear, which are about 3 cm long and are piled together into a heap the size of a hand. These caterpillars are called *citlalocuile*, "star-caterpillars," as well as *citlalcuitlatl*, "star shit," and the heap looks indeed like excrement (1989: 296).

Along with the instances cited by Köhler, there are many other examples of caterpillarlike meteoric beings in Mesoamerican lore. A common Nahuatl term for obsidian is *citlalcuitlatl*, or "star excrement" (Karttunen 1983: 35). In a dictionary of contemporary Nahuatl of the Sierra de Zacapoaxtla, Puebla, *sitalcuita* is glossed as "la suciedad de estrella, gusanos en la tierra" (Key and Ritchie de Key 1953: 203). This concept of *citlalcuitlatl* as meteoric, wormlike creatures of black obsidian is very similar to Köhler's Veracruz account of meteorites. Manuel Gamio (1922, I: 316) recorded the following belief from the community of Santiago, in the vicinity of Teotihuacan: "Dicen que en el lugar en donde calle un bólido (citlalcuítlatl o meztcuítlatl) se forma un gusano azul." This description of a blue meteorite "worm" recalls the turquoise Xiuhcoatl of Postclassic Central Mexico. Among the Otomí, meteorites, or "star excrement," cause flesh-penetrating worms, a concept virtually identical to the Aztec *citlalocuilin* (Galinier 1990: 527).

The belief in wormlike meteorites is also found in the Maya region. In Mopan Mayan, the term for a caterpillar tent ("pabellón de orugas") is *ta' xülab*, which can be glossed as "star excrement," a concept vitually identical to the cited Nahua and Otomí beliefs of metorites being wormlike excrement of the stars (Ulrich and Dixon de Ulrich 1976: 197). Among the the Tojolabal Maya of highland Chiapas there are the *sansewal*, little black worms created from meteorites. The following account describes the shooting star, or *sk'oy k'anal*, and the *sansewal:*

> Some say that this concerns metallic objects of stone like glass or mirrors that fall, during the night, from the sky as a light with a tail . . . Others say that they are the same as *sansewal*. They are little black worms that fall from the sky during the night (Lenkersdorf 1979: 325; author's translation).

Lenkersdorf provides the following entry for the *sansewal*:

> lightning, shooting star, light that appears at night in the mountains . . . They are stars that fall as shooting stars. They are little worms of fire that move and still are not like stone, but rather like little black serpents, like little worms. In the sky they shine like a lamp. Upon falling to earth they divide (1979: 312; author's translation).

As fiery, meteoric creatures having both serpent and wormlike attributes, the *sansewal* are strikingly similar to the Xiuhcoatl.

As the "meteor serpent," the Xiuhcoatl is a caterpillarlike embodiment of a shooting star. Among Tzeltalan-speaking peoples of highland Chiapas, a probable borrowed form of the Nahuatl term *xihuitl* designates caterpillars and grublike creatures. In contemporary Tzotzil, *xuvit* signifies "worm" or "maggot" (Hurley and Ruiz Sanchez 1986: 227; Laughlin 1975: 327). An early colonial Tzotzil dictionary of Zinacantan glosses *xuvit* as "caterpillar, maggot, or worm infesting meat, cheese, etc." (Laughlin 1988, I: 304). The 1571 Tzeltal dictionary of Domingo de Ara has the following entry for *xuuit*: "oruga, Gusano. Xuuitil" (Ruz 1986: 418). The last term, *xuuitil*, is extremely similar to the Nahuatl *xihuitl*. In the contemporary Nahuatl of Tetelcingo, Morelos, *xiuhocuilin* is a term for caterpillar (Brewer and Brewer 1971: 246).

According to the *Historia de los mexicanos por sus pinturas*, the fifth level of the sky was the realm of the fire serpents who emit "comets," in other words, meteors: "En el quinto había culebras de fuego, que hizo el dios de fuego, y de ellas salen los cometas y señales del cielo" (Garibay 1979: 69). The stars frequently appearing on the snout and body of the Xiuhcoatl fire serpent probably refer to these meteors and "signs of the sky" (Figures 10.12 [f and g], 10.13 [a, d, and e], 10.15 [d], and 10.17 [f–h]). In the *Vaticanus A*, this fifth level is rendered as a series of spherical stars with darts, representing an Aztec term for meteor, *citlalin tlamina*, or "star shoots dart" (Figure 10.16 [a and b]). The *Vaticanus A* glosses this region as Ilhuicatl Mamalhuazocan, or "Heaven of the Fire Drill" (Nicholson 1971: table 2). According to Alfredo López Austin (1988, I: 210), this fifth level is the lowest of the true heavens, where supernatural forces fall to earth, "the place where divine influences acquire their circling impulse in order to descend . . . The luminous heavenly bodies made their influence in the form of shooting arrows." The "shooting arrows" described by López Austin are fiery meteors—potent, highly charged manifestations of celestial power.

The concept of the fifth celestial level as the place of fire and fire drilling is not limited to the Aztecs. In an incantation concerning "traveler-siezure," the colonial Yucatec *Ritual of the Bacabs* describes the fifth level of the sky:

> He [traveler-seizure] comes from the fifth layer of the sky, the offspring of the *ko* in the Tzab (the "snake rattles constellation," the Pleiades) . . .
>   He would be the offspring of the fire-colored rainbow, the offspring of the fire there in the sky, the offspring of the fire there in the clouds, the force of the friction at the tip of the fire[-drill] (Roys 1965: 7).

The concept of the fifth celestial realm as the place of fire and fire-making may have also been present among the Classic Maya. One Classic Maya supernatural place known as Na Ho Chaan, or First Five Sky, is portrayed with long, twisted cords (see Freidel, Schele, and Parker 1993: fig. 2.31). Although these elements have been interpreted as umbilical cords or as the ropes used in birthing (Freidel, Schele, and Parker 1993: 99, 105; Miller 1982; Taube 1994a), there is another possibility. In Teotihuacan and later Aztec iconography, fire drills can be accompanied by a twisted rope, undoubtedly referring to the tightly twisted rope of the pump drill (Coggins 1987: 459; for examples, see von Winning 1979). It is likely that the twisted chords appearing with Na Ho Chaan also allude to the spinning force of the drill, fire making, and creation.

At Teotihuacan, the twisted-cord motif not only appears with depictions of flames, but also occurs on monumental stone braziers (Figure 10.14 [c]). In support of the fire drill identification, Heyden (1977: 215, fig. 9.17) cites Monument 46 from Castillo de Teayo, a stela carved in strong Aztec style.[4] The maize goddess appearing on this monument has a headdress with the twisted rope and the vertical bar of the drill stick (Figure 10.14 [d]). Heyden compares this headdress to the "new fire" reliefs from Teotihuacan (eg., Figure 10.14 [b]). She also notes that in the case of the Aztec headdress, the curving feathers flanking the rope and drill stick represent flames, a convention previously mentioned for Teotihuacan. In one Late Classic Maya fire-offering scene, the ruler wears a headdress with a prominent twisted cord emerging out of the *to* sign of beaded curls (Figure 10.14 [f]). As the fire drill rope, the twisted cord appears as the curious "cruller" of the Jaguar God of the Underworld, who has been recently identified as the Classic Maya god of fire (Stuart 1994) (Figure 10.14 [g]). David Stuart (personal communication, 1997) notes that as one of the Tikal Paddlers, the Jaguar God of the Underworld is a well-known denizen of Na Ho Chaan. In the *Codex Dresden*, the central fire of burning braziers and torches is rendered as tightly twisted cords, quite possibly alluding to the swirling, twisting nature of rising flames (Figure 10.14 [h]).[5]

Although twisted chords can refer to fire and fire making in both Central Mexican and Maya iconography, this does not necessarily contradict the overlapping meaning of umbilical chords and birth ropes. The making of fire is tantamount to creation and birth. Seler (1963, I: 76) notes that in the Aztec *Vaticanus A*, the primordial couple are portrayed as a pair of personified drill sticks. The friction and subsequent fire created by the vertical drill bit in the hole of the second stick mimics the act of copulation and conception. López Austin (1988: I: 209–210) suggests that the Aztec fifth level of heaven was the immediate source of the *tonalli*, or "soul," the place where it descends in meteoric fashion into the developing fetus on earth.[6]

At Early Postclassic Chichén Itzá, there are two large radial platforms displaying representations of both the aforementioned Xiuhcoatl warriors and flexible vegetal

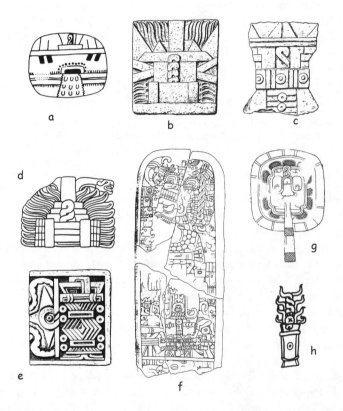

Fig. 10.14. The twisted-cord motif as a fire-making sign; a. Twisted cord with vertical drill stick, detail of Teotihuacan style, stucco painted vessel (after Hellmuth 1975: plate 43); b. Teotihuacan relief of twisted cord with flames (from Seler 1902–1923, V: 430); c. Relief on front of Teotihuacan stone censer (from Seler 1902–1923, V: 429); d. Twisted cord with serpents and feathers as flames, detail of Aztec-style sculpture from Castillo de Teayo (after Solís 1981: plate 47); e. Twisted cord with star, stick, and vegetal year bundle, Chichén Itzá (from Seler 1902–1923, V: 367); f. Late Classic Maya ruler performing fire offering—note twisted cord in headdress—Stela 13, Yaxha (drawing courtesy of Ian Graham); g. Shield representing the Jaguar God of the Underworld with twisted "cruller," detail of Naranjo Stela 21 (drawing courtesy of Ian Graham); h. Burning censer with flames as twisted cords, *Codex Dresden*, p. 28.

bundles with Mexican year signs (Figs. 10.11 [b] and 10.14 [e]).[7] At the side of each year-sign bundle, there is a vertical drill stick wrapped with twisted chord, here combined with a star sign (Figure 10.14 [e]). Although this star has commonly been interpreted as Venus, it may well refer to the starry, meteoric origin of new fire.

In ancient Central Mexican thought, fire drills and the making of new fire appear to have been closely linked to fiery meteors, that is, fire of celestial origin.[8] Thus the Classical Nahuatl term for fire making was *uetzi in tlequauhuitl*, "the fire drill falls." The same verb *uetzi* is also used to refer to the falling of a shooting star, as in the phrase *xihuitl uetzi* (Molina 1977: 159). The identification of fire drilling with meteors may well derive from the sparks that fly from the twirling fire drill, fleeting but potent sources of fire that resemble shooting stars. It will be recalled that in the aforementioned *Florentine Codex* description of a *xihuitl* meteor shower, it was compared to a shower of sparks, or *tlexuchtli pipixauhtiuh* in Nahuatl (Sahagún 1950–1982, book 8: 18).

In a discussion of Mixcoatl, the starry deity of slain warriors, Seler (1902–1923, IV: 72) noted that this being overlaps with the fire god, Xiuhtecuhtli:

> This divinity [Mixcoatl] is the representative of the eternally circling stars, of the firmament that turns around the pole, and for that reason also the god who has bored fire, the first creator of fire; he therefore coincides in some way with the fire god, the deity of the fire in the hearth who resides in the center of the world (translation in Seler 1990–96, V: 41).

It has been noted that *xihuitl* has a range of meanings in Classical Nahuatl, including, turquoise, meteor, year, and herb.[9] Although Xiuhtecuhtli is readily glossed as "turquoise lord," it probably had a related meaning of "meteor lord." In the *Primeros Memoriales*, the Xiuhcoatl meteor serpent is described as the *nahualli* co-essence of Xiuhtecuhtli (Sullivan 1997: 100). The precious blue nuggets of turquoise obtained from the distant American Southwest may have been considered as meteoric in origin, in other words, "sky stone."

Lined with a series of drilled holes, the horizontal, "female" portion of the fire drill strongly resembles worm-eaten wood (eg., Figure 10.15 [d]). In Classic Nahuatl, wood damaged by wood worms was referred to as *ocuilqualoc*, *ocuila* being the word for worm or caterpillar (Molina 1977: 76). In Mesoamerican thought, worms, grubs, and other caterpillarlike creatures are often credited with the power of drilling. In the *Leyenda de los soles* account of creation of people, Quetzalcoatl has his conch drilled by worms or caterpillars (*ocuilme*) (Bierhorst 1992: 145, see ms. p. 76, line 30, for Nahuatl). In Mayan languages, the words for drills and fire drilling are often the same as for larval wood worms. Thus in Yucatec, *hax* signifies both fire drilling and the holes made by wood worms (Barrera Vásquez 1980: 188). In the colonial Tzeltal Domingo de Ara dictionary, *ghoch* is glossed as "roer la madera los gusanos," and *ghochobte*, "ladrado," or "drill" (Ruz 1986: 292). Apparently the act of fire drilling was compared to the burrowing of worms, although in this case the worms are fiery, meteoric beings derived from stars.[10]

In many Late Postclassic Central Mexican representations of fire making, fire is drilled on the segmented, larval body of the Xiuhcoatl meteor serpent (Figure 10.15). In addition, a massive stone head of Xiuhcoatl found near the Templo

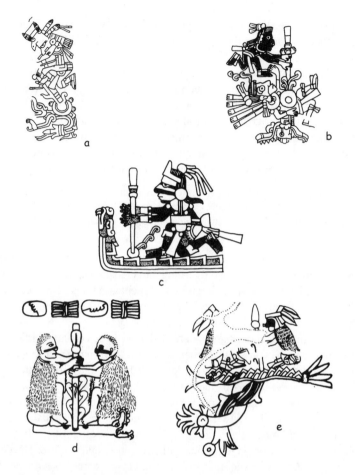

Fig. 10.15. The making of new fire atop the meteoric Xiuhcoatl fire serpent; a. Xiuhtecuhtli drilling fire on mirror atop back of Xiuhcoatl, *Codex Borgia*, p. 2; b. Figure drilling fire atop mirror with Xiuhcoatl below victim, *Codex Borgia*, p. 33; c. Xiuhtecuhti drilling fire on back of fire serpent, *Codex Laud*, p. 8; d. Chichimec drilling fire on Xiuhcoatl fire stick, *Mapa de Cuauhtinchan No. 2* (after Yoneda 1991: 127); e. Chichimec drilling fire on back of Xiuhcoatl, *Mapa de Cuauhtinchan No. 1* (after Yoneda 1991: 112).

Mayor bears the date 4 Acatl (Reed). Seler (1902–1923, II: 899) notes that 4 Reed was the most appropriate day for the drilling of new fire, and according to Chimalpahin, was the day on which new fire was drilled in the 1507 year of 2 Reed. At times, a pair of drill sticks appears on the head of the Xiuhcoatl (Figure 10.13 [e]). In highland Mexican New Fire scenes, a reed dart usually serves as the vertical drill, possibly referring to the concept of *citlalin tlamina*—fiery, meteoric darts shot by stars. Like the flaming dart wielded by K'inich Yax K'uk' Mo' on Copán Altar Q, the drill sticks were considered as weapons of war. Along with being compared to the fire drill, the Xiuhcoatl was also considered as a spear thrower. In one Aztec account, Huitzilopochtli creates war with his Xiuhcoatl and fire drill: "He cast at men the turquoise serpent, the fire drill—war" (Sahagún 1950–1982, book 1: 167).

The concept of shooting stars as the weapon of Huitzilopochtli is entirely consistent with Mesoamerican concepts of meteors, widely viewed as omnipotent weapons of supernatural beings. According to Seler (1902–1923, IV: 72–73), meteors were darts shot by the Central Mexican star god Mixcoatl. The contemporary Nahuas of Veracruz consider meteors as protective arrows of the stars (Sandstrom 1991: 248). For the Huichol of Nayarit, a pair of large stars in the northern and southern skies shoot meteors at venomous snakes:

> They [the pair of stars] are simply termed rulave, and are stars that sometimes fall down and get broken against rocks when trying to kill a serpent (Sp. *culebra*); in other words, meteors . . . these two stand immobile, guarding the world (Lumholtz 1900: 58).

Among the types of shooting stars known for the contemporary Otomí, there are the *piso*, which prevent stones from turning into jaguars (Galinier 1990: 526). The Huastec consider pieces of obsidian as the spent weapons of protective stars; "obsidian chips are also interpreted as pieces of stars left by red and blue flashes emitted by stars to punish brujos" (Alcorn 1984: 141).

In Mesoamerica, shooting stars are widely seen as celestial darts. Mention has been made of the Classical Nahuatl term *citlalin tlamina* and Aztec portrayals of meteoric darts shot from stars (Figure 10.16 [a and b]). In Mixtec codices, there are similar depictions of darts protruding from burning balls. This sign serves as the personal name of Lord 9 Flower, a brother of the famed Lord 8 Deer of Tilantongo (Figure 10.16 [c–f]). In view of the burning ball and dart, this individual could best be referred to as Lord 9 Flower Shooting Star.[11] In the Maya region, meteors are strongly identified with projectiles and warfare. Thus in colonial Yucatec, the term for shooting star or "cometa que corre," is *halal ek'*, meaning "arrow or dart star" (Barrera Vásquez 1980: 175). The colonial Tzotzil of Zinacantan referred to a meteor as *yolob vits*, or "mountain arrow" (Laughlin 1988, II: 423). The Quiché Maya term for shooting star is *ch'abi q'aq'*, meaning "flaming arrow" (Tedlock 1992: 28). In addition, Barbara Tedlock (1992) notes that one colonial Quiché term for meteor was *ch'olanic ch'umil*, or "star makes war." In this regard, David Stuart (personal communication, 1997) notes that two common Classic Maya logographs for war events, the "Earth Star" and "Shell Star" signs, may represent a meteor shower falling from a star (for examples of signs, see Lounsbury 1982: fig. 2). The parallel lines of dots falling from the stars are very similar to ancient Maya representations of sparks (Figure 10.4 [g]; see also, *Codex Madrid*, pp. 38b, 51a, 79b, 87b).

An emblem of celestial fire and warfare, the Xiuhcoatl often appears as an *atlatl*, a shooter of starry darts. The Xiuhcoatl commonly displays a series of stars on its snout, probably representing a shower of meteors (Figures 10.7 [a], 10.13 [a, d, and e], 10.15 [d], and 10.17 [f–h]). In the well-known *Codex Borbonicus* scene of Huitzilopochtli wielding his turquoise Xiuhcoatl *atlatl*, the weapon is ornamented with stars, surely referring to the meteoric darts shot by this bellicose god (Figure 10.17 [a]). The starry *xiuhcoatl* spear-thrower brandished by Huitzilopochtli and other gods in the *Borbonicus* explains the curious series of dots often appearing on the curving tips of Classic-period representations of spear-throwers in both Teotihuacan and Classic Maya art (Figure 10.17 [c–e]). As in the case of the *Borbonicus* examples, these dots probably depict stars, thereby portraying the weapons as shooters of meteoric darts.[12] The sharply turned snout of the Late Postclassic Xiuhcoatl may also refer to the spear-thrower. In the *Codex Borgia*, this curving, starry element can appear as a separate device affixed to the tip of the snout, and it is also possible to sever Aztec examples from

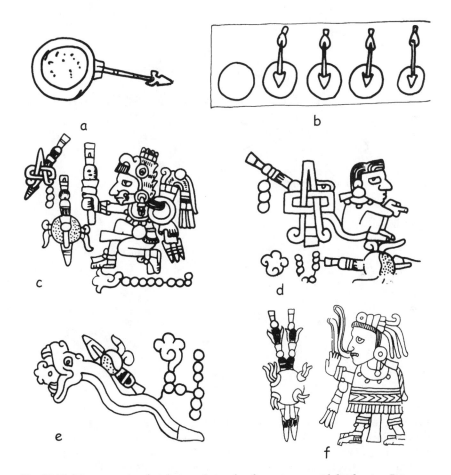

Fig. 10.16. Meteors as star-shot darts; a. Aztec sign for meteor, or *citlalin tlamina*, *Primeros Memoriales*, fol. 282r; b. Ilhuicatl Mamalhuazocan, the Aztec fifth level of heaven, as the place of shooting stars, *Codex Vaticanus A*, fol. 1v; c–d. Mixtec lord 9 Flower Shooting Star, *Codex Nuttall*, p. 26, *Codex Bodley*, p 7; e. Name of Lord 9 Flower Shooting Star with serpent, *Codex Bodley*, p. 12; f. Lord 9 Flower Shooting Star with personal name, *Codex Vindobonensis* obverse, p. 7.

the nose (Figure 10.17 [f–h]). This curving form closely resembles the bent tip of the spear-thrower, and with the circular stars, probably refers to the Xiuhcoatl as the shooter of starry darts.

The concept of meteors as star darts probably relates to the widespread Mesoamerican belief that dart points and other obsidian objects found in fields are the spent meteoric remains of star arrows. Mention has been made of the Huastec belief that obsidian chips derive from meteors. Bonnie Bade (personal communication, 1997) informs me that according to the Mixtec of San Miguel Cuevas, obsidian chips are stars that fall from the sky. The contemporary Quiché Maya also regard obsidian as meteoric in origin: "since it is believed that obsidian occurs wherever a meteor has landed, arrowheads, obsidian blades, and meteorites

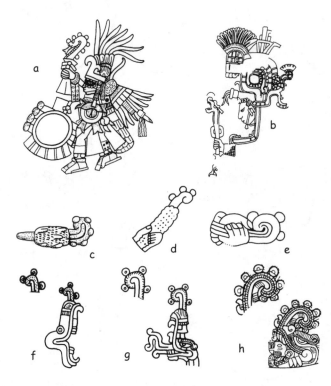

Fig. 10.17. Classic and Postclassic portrayals of starry spear-throwers and the Xiuhcoatl; a. Huitzilopochtli wielding Xiuhcoatl spear-thrower marked with stars, *Codex Borbonicus*, p. 34; b. Late Classic Maya ruler holding burning War Serpent *atlatl*, Bonampak Stela 1 (from Taube 1992c: fig. 6d); c. Spear-thrower ornamented with stars, Teotihuacan (after Séjourné 1959: fig. 135); d. Spear-thrower with stars, "ball-court marker" from Mundo Perdido, Tikal (after Freidel, Schele, and Parker 1993: fig. 7.9); e. Spear-thrower with stars, detail of text from Tikal Stela 31 (after Jones and Satterthwaite 1982: fig. 51a); f–g. Xiuhcoatl serpents with snout element resembling starry *atlatl*, *Codex Borgia*, pp. 46, 49; h. Aztec Xiuhcoatl with curving snout resembling starry *atlatl*, detail of Aztec Calendar Stone (see Figure 10.28).

are saved and placed together in the traditional household shrine known as the *meb'il*" (Tedlock 1992: 28). In a sixteenth-century Zinacanteco dictionary, *tzo k'anal* is glossed as *cometa*, which Laughlin (1988, I: 173) interprets as "meteor, meteorite." In Tzotzil, the same term also refers to obsidian. Laughlin provides the following entry for the contemporary Zinacanteco term for obsidian, *co k'anal*: "Obsidian is thought to have dropped by shooting stars as they fall and return to the sky" (1975: 93). Whereas *k'an* signifies "star," *co* is given the rather curious entry of "excrement, shit, guts/person, caterpillar" (93). Thus this Tzotzil phrase for obsidian may signify "caterpillar star excrement." This recalls the nearby Tojolabal concept of *sansewal* meteorites as black wormlike creatures that turn into glassy "mirror stone," quite possibly obsidian.[13]

The identification of meteors with obsidian may well derive from the use of this stone as projectile points. When found unhafted in fields, points and other obsidian fragments could have been readily regarded as the remains of celestial arrows or darts. However, is this an ancient concept or only a recent explanation by modern Mesoamerican peoples? Yet another meaning of obsidian, as excrement, indicates that it probably is also a pre-Hispanic as well as contemporary belief. Mention has been made of the Tzotzil term for meteorites and obsidian, *tzo k'anal*, "star excrement." Although this phrase is only glossed as *cometa* in the sixteenth-century Zinacanteco dictionary, other Mayan languages indicate that at the contact period, obsidian was referred to as excrement. Along with being the Yucatec term for feces, *ta* is also glossed as "lancet" in early colonial Yucatec dictionaries (Schele and Miller 1983: 10). Schele and Miller note therein that such lancets were surely of obsidian. More specifically, they were probably prismatic obsidian blades, such as are commonly found over much of ancient Mesoamerica. In Lacandón—a language very closely related to Yucatec—*tah* refers specifically to obsidian. In addition, David Stuart (personal communication, 1995) notes that one Late Classic Maya text from Copán refers phonetically refers to obsidian as *ta:h* (Figure 10.18 [a]).

In a great deal of the Mesoamerican meteor lore that has been cited, meteorites are regarded as star feces. Karttunen (1983: 35) notes that in some regions of Central Mexico, obsidian is referred to as "caca de estrella," essentially the Nahuatl term for obsidian and meteorite, *citlalcuitlatl*. On page 92 of the *Vaticanus B*, the fierce, celestial being known as Itzpapalotl, or Obsidian Butterfly, has a starry curl extruding from the tip of its abdomen (Figure 10.30 [a]). Clearly enough, this depicts *citlalcuitlatl* as the meteoric excrement of the Obsidian Butterfly. Carlos Trenary (1987–1988) notes that the concept of meteorites as star excrement is not limited to Mesoamerica, but occurs in many parts of the world. The contact period identification of obsidian with feces strongly suggests that in pre-Hispanic Mesoamerica, this stone was also regarded as meteoric excrement of the stars. The concept of obsidian as a meteor stone may have important implications for the symbolic role of obsidian in Teotihuacan warfare. Volleys of obsidian-tipped projectiles may well have been compared to meteor showers, a celestial "rain of darts."

Much of the present discussion has revolved around the Xiuhcoatl fire serpent as an embodiment of meteors and meteor showers. However, was the War

Serpent similarly regarded as a meteoric being in Classic Mesoamerica? The war-like, igneous, and caterpillar qualities of this creature are certainly consistent with Mesoamerican conceptions of shooting stars and meteorites. Like the Xiuhcoatl, the War Serpent can trail flames, often as a prominent burning tail, recalling the long tails of shooting stars (Figures 10.2 [g], 10.8 [b], and 10.17 [e]). The War Serpent also often seems to be in flight, and even can transport warriors on its back (Figure 10.8 [a and b]). Bonampak Stela 3 portrays the War Serpent as a

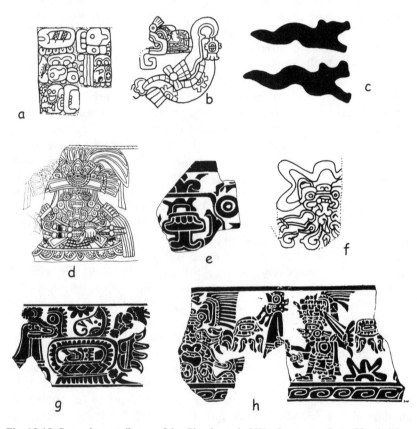

Fig. 10.18. Secondary attributes of the Classic-period War Serpent; a. Late Classic Maya text describing the obsidian and flint eyes of the War Serpent, detail of text from Copán Stela 11 (detail of drawing courtesy of Linda Schele); b. War Serpent with star markings and curving obsidian blade, Acanceh, Early Classic Maya (from Taube 1992c: fig. 8a); c. Probable War Serpents in form of obsidian eccentrics, from burials within the Temple of Quetzalcoatl, Teotihuacan (after Cabrera Castro, Sugiyama, and Cowgill 1991: fig. 10); d. War Serpent with curving obsidian blades at base and in headdress, Tepantitla (from Miller 1973: fig. 193); e. Teotihuacan vessel sherd of War Serpent with star on snout (from von Winning 1987, II: chap. 1, fig. 9q); f. Sherd of War Serpent with star and flames (after Seler 1902–1923, V: plate LXI); g. Star above butterfly with War Serpent head (from von Winning 1987, II: chap. 9, fig. 5); h. Teotihuacan vessel scene of War Serpent, stars, and flaming eyes (from von Winning 1987, I: chap. 13, fig. 5b).

spear-thrower, a trait also known for the Xiuhcoatl. Dressed in the guise of the War Serpent, Chaan Muan wields an *atlatl* in the form of a War Serpent with a burning tail (Figure 10.17 [b]). Andrea Stone (1989: 158) argues that the burning and sharply bent War Serpent staff appearing in another Late Classic Maya scene also represents a spear-thrower (Figure 10.8 [b]). Among the Classic Maya, the War Serpent was identified with obsidian. David Stuart (personal communication, 1995) notes that a portion of Copán Stela 11 can be read *ta:h uwu:t tok' uwu:t waxaklahun u bah chan*, meaning "obsidian is its eye, flint is its eye, the eighteen its image snake" (Figure 10.18 [a]). The Early Classic stucco façade at Acanceh, Yucatán, portrays a star-marked War Serpent coiled around a sickle-shaped weapon, a type of obsidian sacrificial knife known for Teotihuacan (see Berrin and Pasztory 1993: no. 168). The blade handle is bound with fibrous material, quite possibly a *yauhtli* bundle (Figure 10.18 [b]). One Late Classic carved column from the northern Maya lowlands portrays a ruler wielding the curving, sickle-like blade while dressed in War Serpent costume. As in the case of the Acanceh example, a stylized blood or heart element drips from the tip of the blade (see Mayer 1995: plate 83).

At Teotihuacan, the War Serpent is clearly identified with obsidian, warfare, fire, and stars. The two so-called Red Tlaloc War Serpents at Tepantitla are on beds of the aforementioned curving obsidian blades, with more of these knives in their headdresses (Figure 10.18 [d]). The upper portion of this mural portrays an *atlatl*-wielding warrior trailing flames from his body (Figure 10.3 [a]). With their upturned snouts and prominent ears, the small, eccentric obsidian serpents found in the Temple of Quetzalcoatl excavations are probable representations of the War Serpent, and recall the aforementioned meteoric *sansewal* serpent-worms of the Tojolabal Maya as well as the Nahuatl *citlalcuitlatl* obsidian worms (Figure 10.18 [c]). In addition, the War Serpent frequently appears with stars at Teotihuacan (Figure 10.18 [e–h]). One vessel scene portrays a burning shell platelet War Serpent with a warrior and stars (Figure 10.18 [h]). A fragmentary but still discernable star occurs immediately above the head of the War Serpent. It is possible that the flaming eyes hovering in the center of the scene represent meteors; in later Central Mexican iconography, stars are frequently depicted as eyes (for examples, see Figures 10.12 [f and g], 10.13 [a ,d, and e], 10.17 [f–h], and 10.30 [d and e]). Another Teotihuacan vessel portrays the War Serpent as the personification of a flaming star, quite probably a depiction of a fiery meteor (Figure 10.18 [f]). A fragmentary back mirror published by von Winning (1990: fig. 10) poytrays a frontally facing War Serpent surrounded by a ring of stars, possibly an early version of the Toltec style mirrors marked with the Xiuhcoatl meteor serpents.

SELF-SACRIFICE, FIRE, AND TRANSFORMATION

Among the more striking traits shared between the religious systems of Teotihuacan and the later Toltec and Aztec cultures is the conception of the warrior soul as a flaming butterfly. In Aztec belief, these are the *tonatiuh ilhuicac yauh*, who accompany the sun in its daily ascent into the sky. Both Séjourné (1962: 141–146) and Berlo (1982: 99; 1983) have noted that like the later Aztec, the inhabitants of Teotihuacan identified butterflies with both fire and warfare, and considered them the souls of dead warriors. It is especially intriguing that the Aztecs traced this concept to the ancient ruins of Teotihuacan. In the *Florentine Codex*, the resurrection of the soul as a butterfly is ascribed specifically to Teotihuacan:

> And so they named the place Teotihuacan, because it was the burial place of the rulers. For it was said: When we die, it is not true that we die, we are resurrected. . . . In this manner they spoke to the dead when one died; . . . "Awaken! It hath reddened; the dawn hath set in. Already singeth the flame-colored cock, the flame-colored swallow; already flieth the flame-colored butterfly (Sahagún 1950–1982, book 10: 192).

In this text, the rebirth of souls as fiery birds and butterflies is compared to the dawning of the sun. To the Aztecs, Teotihuacan was the place of the first dawning of this creation, the fiery birth of Nahui Ollin, the Fifth Sun.

In Teotihuacan, Toltec, and Aztec art, warriors are frequently represented as butterflies. Thus at Teotihuacan, warrior figures often wear butterfly headdresses and nosepieces in the form of stylized butterflies. One of the more common emblems of Toltec warriors was a large butterfly pectoral, apparently made of turquoise mosaic. For Aztec warriors, large butterfly images were often worn on the back as a form of insignia (see *Primeros Memoriales*, fol. 72r, 74r, 74v, 78v). The curious association of fierce warriors with butterflies may partly derive from the identification of these creatures with the diurnal sun, flowers, and fire.[14] However, the Aztecs also considered the natural event of a moth falling into a flame as a metaphor for self-sacrifice, an act of supreme courage.[15] The following is a Classical Nahuatl description of self-sacrifice recorded by Andrés de Olmos:

> As the butterfly becomes the flame, he lovingly metamorphoses into a rib cage, into a skull. Before the people, above the people, he awaits, publicly he whipped himself, he flogged himself. Then he falls inward there to suffer the stone repeatedly. Heedlessly as the moth he ascends, he falls inward (Maxwell and Hanson 1992: 178).

The concept of self-sacrifice epitomizes the code of the warrior, willing to offer his life for the common good.

The virtues of bravery and selflessness are powerfully expressed in the Aztec myth of the first dawning at Teotihuacan. It is not the rich and haughty Tecuciztecatl, but the humble and self-effacing Nanahuatzin who, like a moth, freely throws himself into the terrible flames to become the sun. According to the *Florentine Codex* and the *Leyenda de los soles*, the eagle and jaguar received their dark body markings from the same sacrificial pyre (Sahagún 1950–1982, book 7: 6; Bierhorst 1992: 148). The *Florentine Codex* mentions that these markings constituted signs of their personal valor and bravery at the sacrificial pyre. For the Aztecs, the eagle and jaguar were the military orders par excellence. The placement of these creatures at the birth of the sun indicates that to the Aztecs, much of their solar war cult originated in the sacrificial fire at Teotihuacan (Taube 1992c: 78).

The self-immolation of Nanahuatzin and Tecuciztecatl and their consequent rebirth relates to burial practices known for Teotihuacan and the later Aztecs. In the funerary rituals of Teotihuacan and the Aztecs, fire served as the transformative process for the metamorphosis and resurrection of the warrior soul. For the Aztecs, both slain warriors and kings were wrapped in bundles to be burned (see Durán 1994: 307, 385–386). An excellent representation of a burning funerary bundle appears in the *Codex Xolotl*, here illustrating the cremation of the Tepanec king Tezozomoc on the day Nahui Ollin (Figure 10.19 [a]). Although not a common Mixtec mortuary practice, bundle cremations also appear in the Mixtec codices (Figure 10.19 [b]). In Aztec funerary ceremonies for rulers as well as warriors lost in distant battles, images of mortuary bundles were also fashioned over a core of ocote (*ocotl*), the pitch-filled wood used for torches and for starting fires. Like the bundled dead, these ocote bundles were also burned (Durán 1994: 150–151, 284–285, 294). Aside from allowing the bundles to burn well, the ocote may have represented the fiery, potent nature of these beings. The *Codex Magliabechiano* portrays one of these ocote warrior bundle images, here arrayed in paper copies of the turquoise jewelry befitting great warriors and nobility (Figure 10.19 [c]). According to Durán (150, 294), both the images of Aztec rulers and slain warriors were placed in structures termed *tlacochcalli*, or "house of darts." The strikingly similar treatment of dead warriors and kings was undoubtedly a powerful and profound means of linking these two great offices of Aztec society. In death, kings were treated as valiant warriors, and slain warriors as great kings.

Among the more important annual Aztec rituals pertaining to the souls of warriors was Hueymiccailhuitl, or great feast of the dead, performed during the *vientena* of Xocotlhuetzi. Dedicated to the gods Xiuhtecuhtli and Xocotl as well as deceased adults, one of the major events of this *veintena* was the aforementioned casting of live captives into a large sacrificial hearth, immediately recalling the mythological episode at Teotihuacan (Sahagún 1950–1982, book II: 17–18, 111–117). Durán (1971: 205) notes that this sacrificial fire was called the "divine brazier," quite possibly the same "divine brazier" in which the bundled body of king Ahuiztotl was burned (see Durán 1994: 386). The Spanish description of a "divine brazier" also recalls the Nahuatl term for the mythic hearth at Teotihuacan, *teotexcalli*, or "divine oven" (Sahagún 1950–1982, book VII: 4).[16]

Aside from the fire offering of warriors to Xiuhtecuhtli, Xocotlhuetzi also concerned images of the deity Xocotl, also known as Otontecuhtli. This figure appeared as a warrior bundle adorned with paper butterflies, referring to the butterfly soul released during the burning of the bundle (Figure 10.19 [d and e]). Xocotlhuetzi signifies "the descent of Xocotl," and among the prominent rites during this *veintena* was the removal of the Xocotl warrior bundle image from atop a tall pole (Figure 10.19 [e]). Seler (1902–1923, IV: 68) describes the Xocotlhuetzi rites and the Xocotl pole:

> It was for the male deceased and for a god who was called Xocotl ("Younger Brother"?) or Otontecuhtli ("Prince of the Otomí"). Some have identified him with the god of fire, but he had white color and black design on his face and is further characterized by having two butterflies stuck in his hair; he is the picture of the dead warrior. His mummy bundle or his likeness in bird form was erected on high masts and torn down by the young. He came down, he came to earth, he came as fast as a meteor down to earth (translation in Seler 1990–1996, V: 41).

Both the Aztec *Codex Borbonicus* and the *Tonalamatl Aubin* portray the Xocotl pole for the *trecena* 1 Flint, dedicated to the sun god, Tonatiuh, and the god of death, Mictlantecuhtli. In view of the solar and death gods, it is appropriate that these scenes concern the fate of the warriors who died for the sun. Thus the upper right corner of page 10 of the *Borbonicus* scene portrays the warrior bundle so prominent in the Xocotlhuetzi rites. In addition, the base of the Xocotl pole is flanked with the turquoise jewelry worn by the warrior bundle effigies, including *xiuhuitzolli* crowns, *yacaxihuitl* nosepieces, and *xolocozcatl* pectoral.

Although Seler sees no direct relation of Xocotl to Xiuhtecuhtli, others consider him a fire god (eg., Galinier 1990: 244; Sullivan 1997: 98–99, note 29). His shared appearance in Xocotlhuetzi and his identification with fiery butterflies, and warrior bundles indicate a close relation to the fire god. Although of different color, the horizontal facial bands of Xocotl are strikingly similar to the facial marking of Xiuhtecuhtli. In addition, Xocotl commonly has a headdress containing a pair of sticks ornamented with paper butterflies (Figure 10.19 [e]; for other examples, see *Primeros Memoriales*, fol. 262r; *Codex Mendoza*, fol. 10v, for Xocotlan toponym). These sticks are probable variants of the pair of fire drill sticks commonly worn in the headdress of Xiuhtecuhtli. As the image of a warrior

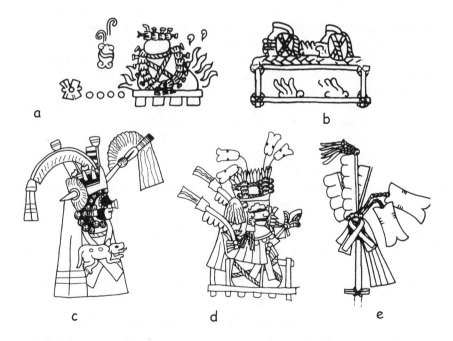

Fig. 10.19. Mortuary bundles and warrior effigy bundles in Late Postclassic Mesoamerica; a. The bundle cremation of Tezozomoc, *Codex Xolotl*, plate 8; b. Mixtec bundle cremation atop wooden frame, *Codex Bodley*, p. 29; c. Aztec warrior effigy bundle, *Codex Magliabechiano*, p. 60r; d. Bundle effigy of Xocotl, *Codex Telleriano-Remensis* fol. 2v; e. Bundle effigy atop Xocotlhuetzi pole, *Codex Borbonicus*, p. 28.

mortuary bundle, Xocotl is identified with the *xiuhuitzolli* crown and other turquoise ornaments appearing with warrior bundles and Xiuhtecuhtli. In fact, both the *xiuhuitzolli* crown and the *yacaxihuitl* nose ornament appear as the personal name of Motecuhzoma II, or Motecuhzoma Xocoyotzin, which Seler (1902–1923, II: 731–736) interpreted as the sign for the spirit of the warrior (Figure 10.28 [b]). Although the name Xocoyotzin appears to have little to do with Xiuhtecuhtli, it is entirely apt for Xocotl as a play on the term for "the younger" (*xocoyotzin*). In other words, the name glyph for Motecuhzoma II is that of Xocotl.

The meaning of the name *Xocotl* is poorly known. Although Seler tentatively suggested that it signified "younger brother," it also may be closely related to the term *ocotl*, that is, the pitch-filled wood used in firemaking. According to Galinier, Xocotl, or Otontecuhtli, was the god of ocote wood: "según la tradición prehispánica, Otontecuhtli tenía como doble a Ocotecuhtli, el Señor de Ocote" (1990: 244). In addtion, it will be recalled that the Aztec images of warrior bundles contained a core of ocote wood (e.g., Figure 10.19 [c]). It is possible that Xocotl represents a particular aspect of fire. To pursue the suggestion presented by Seler, Xocotl may represent meteoric fire, that is, the fire acquired from the starry souls of dead warriors.[17]

In the major accounts of Xocotlhuetzi, the Xocotl pole is well-integrated with the fire sacrifice of the captive warriors. It is entirely conceivable that the pole represents the "world tree" as the central world axis, the aforementioned *tlalxicco* of the fire god. However, the pole may also allude to a massive fire drill, with the Xocotl warrior image placed atop the vertical male stick.[18] During rites of fire making, the spinning vertical stick may have been compared to the world axis, the source of divine forces, here in the form of the engendering spark. It will be recalled that Seler (1902–1923, IV: 72) compared the turning of the stars around the central northern pole to the making of fire. In the *Florentine Codex*'s descriptions of the Xocotl pole, it is said to be festooned with heavy ropes, recalling the twisted cord of the pump drill and the Classic Maya place of Na Ho Chaan.[19] The descent (*uetzi*) of the Xocotl image was tantamount to the making or "descent" of fire, *uetzi in tlequauhuitl*. The victorious youth who obtained the Xocotl effigy was immediately escorted to the pyre where the captives had been sacrificed:

> he who had captured the *xocotl* . . . came down. When he had descended, when he had came down, thereupon the old men [fire priests] seized him; they took him up to the place of sacrifice. There they gave him gifts (Sahagún 1950–1982, book II: 116).

More than just a festival to honor desceased adults, Xocotlhuetzi is a complex and subtle body of symbolic imagery pertaining to fire, self-sacrifice, and the celestial souls of dead warriors.

Much of the essential symbolism pertaining to Xocotlhuetzi also appears with Aztec conceptions of the first dawning at Teotihuacan. Along with the sacrificial pyre, the prominent Xocotl warrior bundle also relates to the Aztec origin of the Fifth Sun. In the Aztec myth, the gods were sacrificed at the birth of the sun. According to the *Leyenda de los soles* (Bierhorst 1992: 149) and Mendieta (1980: 79), this occurred after the morning star, Tlahuizcalpantecuhtli, was shot by the solar darts of the newly born sun.[20] In the Mendieta account, the gods killed themselves in defeat after the slaying of their companion. From the mantles of these dead gods, the first god bundles were made by their worshippers:

> and these devotees and servants of these said gods wrapped these cloths around certain sticks, and made a notch or hole in the stick; they put as the heart some green stones and serpent and jaguar skin, and this bundle they called *tlaquimillolli* (Mendieta 1980: 80; author's translation).

Fashioned from the gods defeated at the first solar battle at Teotihuacan, these are the original warrior bundles. With their core of wood, they are quite like the Aztec effigy warrior bundles containing ocote in place of the body.

For Classic-period Teotihuacan, there is abundant evidence for warrior bundles, which constituted a major funerary cult at this site (see Headrick 1996). Although Paul Westheim (1965: 96–97) first suggested that the well-known stone masks of Teotihuacan may have been funerary, he did not interpret them as items worn on bundles destined for cremation. At Teotihuacan, the clearest representations of funerary bundles are represented in ceramic, not stone. By far the most commonly found depictions occur as two types of ceramic figurines. One form, often designated as a "half-conical figure," represents a seated individual with cloth covering the lower body, creating a conelike effect (Figures 10.20 [a and b] and 10.21 [c]). Séjourné (1966: 245) interpreted certain of the half-conical figurines as funerary bundles. However, according to Séjourné, these bundles were not burned, and thus are distinct from the aforementioned Aztec crematory bundles. Often wearing War Serpent headdresses, these figures typically appear as inert, lifeless objects. In one instance, the figure occurs as a static bundle carried by an anthropomorphic jaguar (Figure 10.20 [b]). The half-conical figures are probably related to a large, hollow ceramic sculpture discovered on the north side of the Ciudadela (Figure 10.20 [c]). Like the half-conical figures, it lacks limbs and has a broad, flaring base. Supplied with a detachable ceramic mask, this curious figure has been interpreted as a mortuary bundle (Múnera 1991; Berrin and Pasztory 1993, note 60; Headrick 1996). In style and proportion, the detachable mask is virtually identical to the stone examples, indicating that they were probably also bound to funerary bundles.

One of the examples cited by Séjourné is the second major type of funerary bundle figurine, often referred to as a "throne figure" (Figures 10.1 [b], 10.6 [f], and 10.20 [d–f]). This is essentially a more elaborate form of the half-conical figure, with the mortuary bundle placed on a wooden frame or scaffold. In the case of the early example illustrated by Séjourné, the platform appears to have a base of horizontal faggots of wood (Figure 10.20 [e]). Aside from Séjourné, Harold McBride (1969) and Annabeth Headrick (1996: 212) have interpreted throne figurines as representations of mortuary bundles. I suspect that the wooden platform found with these examples is for burning the bundle. Similar wooden platforms are found with burning mortuary bundles appearing in Late Postclassic scenes of cremations (Figure 10.19 [a and b]). In addition, one early Teotihuacan censer portrays an expanded version of the throne figure, with the censer bowl separating the conical figure from the platform (Figure 10.22 [a]).[21] When set afire, this censer would portray the mortuary bundle burning on the wooden scaffold.

At Teotihuacan, there is archaeological evidence for the burning of mortuary bundles (Séjourné 1959: 56; Serrano and Lagunas 1975; Serrano 1993; Sempowski and Spence 1994: 145–146). In this case, the cloth-wrapped bundle apparently was placed in a burning burial pit:

> Fire was used to burn certain materials at the bottom of the pit before proceeding with a burial, which may be noted by the presence of carbon fragments under the skeleton. It is also striking that mica sheets and slate disks decorated with red and ocher lines frequently accompany a body; in some cases, as at La Ventilla, true mica beds were found on which the burial was deposited (Serrano 1993: 112).[22]

Fig. 10.20. Teotihuacan representations of funerary bundles; a. Figurine of funerary bundle with War Serpent headdress and mirror pectoral (after Covarrubias 1966: fig. 54); b. Jaguar holding mortuary bundle with War Serpent headdress (after Séjourné 1959: fig. 84c); c. Ceramic funerary bundle figure with detachable mask (after Berrin and Pasztory 1993: no. 60); d. Early figurine of mortuary bundle upon probable wood platform (after Séjourné 1966: fig. 163); e. Early mortuary bundle figurine with schematic War Serpent headdress (from Taube 1992c: fig. 10d); f. Funerary bundle figurine with mirror pectoral (from Taube 1992a).

The slate disks are the remains of pyrite mosaic mirrors, such as are commonly found on the figurine mortuary bundles (Figure 10.20 [a and f]; see Taube 1992a).[23] One fragmentary Teotihuacan vessel portrays a probable masked mortuary bundle placed on flames (Figure 10.22 [c]). A curved, burning torch stands at one side of the masked bundle. This scene may well represent the burial practice of placing the bundled dead in a burning pit.

Mention has been made of the early censer with the mortuary bundle and wooden frame (Figure 10.22 [a]). This censer is probably a rare purcursor to the

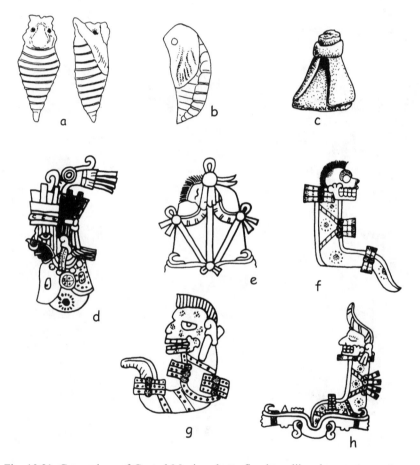

Fig. 10.21. Comparison of Central Mexican butterfly chrysalii and pupae to mortuary bundles; a. Chrysalis of *Protesilaus epidaus tepicus* (after Beutelspacher 1984: fig. 42); b. Pupa of *Baronia brevicornis* Salvin (after Beutelspacher 1984: fig. 35); c. Fragmentary Miccaotli-phase bundle figurine, Teotihuacan (after Séjourné 1966: fig. 162); d. Mortuary bundle of Mixcoatl with shoulder mantle, *Codex Vaticanus B*, p. 61; e. Funerary bundle with shoulder mantle, *Codex Fejérváry-Mayer*, p. 40; f–h. Mortuary bundles resembling pupae or wormlike beings, *Codex Fejérváry-Mayer*, p. 25, *Codex Vaticanus B*, p. 9, *Codex Laud*, p. 27.

well-known composite censers of Classic-period Teotihuacan. As in the case of the Miccaotli-period example, these later censers are also representations of the mortuary bundle, with the frequently masked figure on the conical lid representing the individual to be burned. An Early Classic example from the Escuintla area of Guatemala appears with not only the wood frame, but the mirror pectoral as well (Figure 10.22 [b]). With the mortuary figure as the lid, the Classic-period censers replicate the aforementioned practice of placing the mortuary bundle in the burning pit. Just as the interior of the funerary pit is set afire, the incense or other fire offering is lit within the censer basin. The mortuary bundle lid is then placed atop the burning offering, thereby copying the crematory burials. This would explain the abundance of butterfly imagery appearing on Teotihuacan-style censer lids. According to Berlo (1983), the elaborate censers of Teotihuacan and Escuintla concern a funerary cult centered on the butterfly soul of the dead warrior. These censers summoned the resurrected butterfly soul by reenacting the funerary rites of cremation. A number of examples from the Escuintla region portray the censer lid as the reborn butterfly (Figure 10.22 [d]). In this case, the large pyrite mirror pectoral seems to serve as both the body of the fiery butterfly and the burning hearth.

In a discussion of Teotihuacan composite censers, Berlo notes that butterflies are an ideal means of expressing rebirth and metamorphosis: "The butterfly is a natural choice for a transformational symbol. During its life, it changes from caterpillar to pupa wrapped in hard chrysalis, to butterfly: a process of birth, apparent death, and resurrection as a elegant airborn creature" (1982: 99). If this be the case, what are warrior bundles? They are the chrysalii or cocoons of warrior butterfly souls. Fire is the transformational means by which the moribund bundle metamorphosizes into the flaming butterfly spirit. With the burning of the enveloping shroud, the butterfly soul emerges as flame out of the funerary pyre. For Teotihuacan and Late Postclassic images of mortuary bundles, a cloth frequently covers the shoulder area of the bundle (Figures 10.20 [a–c, e] and 10.21 [c–e]). This corresponds to the wing region of the chrysalis, which resembles a shoulder mantle (Figure 10.21 [a and b]). Durán (1994: 294) mentions that the effigy funerary bundle of Axayacatl was capped with a small cape known as the *papalotilmantli*, or "butterfly mantle." Aside from the shoulder mantles appearing on many funerary bundles, there are also representations of strange, wormlike mortuary bundles, quite possibly referring to the pupate quality of the bundled corpse (Figure 10.21 [f–h]).

THE TURQUOISE ENCLOSURE

In Aztec accounts of the birth of the Fifth Sun, the Pyramids of the Sun and Moon are the places where Nanahuatzin and Tecuciztecatl did penance before their self-immolation. However, where was the place of the climactic, fiery sacrifice and rebirth? In one passage of the *Florentine Codex*, this sacrificial hearth is referred to as the *xiuhtetzaqualco*, or "turquoise enclosure" (Sahagún 1950–1982, book 1: 84). The same source describes this turquoise hearth as the pivotal *tlalxicco*, or "earth navel," the dwelling place of Xiuhtecuhtli-Huehueteotl (book 6: 88–89). The great Ciudadela constitutes the one major enclosure at Teotihuacan.

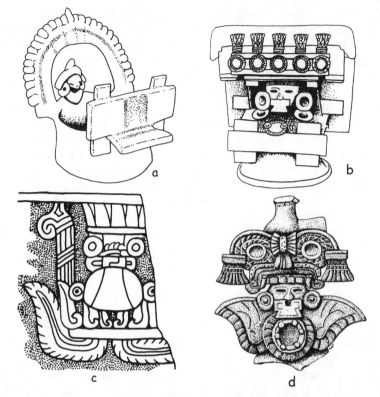

Fig. 10.22. Teotihuacan-style funerary bundles and censers; a. Early Teotihuacan censer with bundle figure and scaffold found with "throne" figurines, drawing by author from item on display in Museo Arqueológico de Teotihuacan; b. Escuintla-style censer lid in form of masked bundle with wooden frame—note mica mirror pectoral (after Berjonneau et al. 1985: plate 172); c. Mortuary bundle atop flames, detail of carved vessel on display in Museo Arqueológico de Teotihuacan; d. Escuintla-style censer lid portraying butterfly soul—note mirror serving as torso (from von Winning 1987, I: chap. 9, fig. 21a).

Cowgill suggests that the Ciudadela constitutes the cosmological center of the Teotihuacan world: "the Ciudadela was on the axis of the East and West Avenues and adjacent to the intersection of that axis with the Street of the Dead, and there is every reason to believe that this location signified not only the center of the four quarters of Teotihuacan, but the intersection of cosmic axes" (1983: 333).

Along with being the possible symbolic center of the Teotihuacan world, the Ciudadela also contains the Temple of Quetzalcoatl and its many sacrificed warriors. Elizabeth Boone (1996) notes that the early colonial map of San Francisco Mazapan contains an illustration of the Ciudadela and the Temple of Quetzalcoatl with an accompanying gloss in Nahuatl, which can be interpreted as "place of those who died in honor of the sun" (Figure 10.23 [a]). This term immediatly recalls the Aztec *tonatiuh ilhuicac yauh*, the deceased warriors who accompany the sun to zenith. According to Boone, this may allude to the ancient mass

sacrifice at the dedication of the Temple of Quetzalcoatl. However, it could simultaneously refer to the sacrificial place where the sun was born, that is, the turquoise hearth. In the early colonial illustration, a large sun hovers directly above
the Temple of Quetzalcoatl (Figure 10.23 [a and b]). As a sun above a pyramidal
mound, this is notably similar to a sign for Teotihuacan appearing in the *Codex
Xolotl* (Figure 10.23 [c]). Although the *Codex Xolotl* sign could be interpreted as
a representation of the Pyramid of the Sun, the major event at this site was not the
preparatory penance of Nanahuatzin, but his fiery resurrection as the sun.

Saburo Sugiyama (personal communication, 1996) notes that the largest
known workshop of the composite ceramic censers, containing some 20,000 fragments and complete examples, lies in the northwest portion of the Ciudadela (see
Berrin and Pasztory 1993: note 77). This censer workshop was clearly part of the
Ciudadela complex and its associated rituals. Not only did a stairway connect the
workshop to the Ciudadela, but portions of similar censers were found in the
residential areas behind the Temple of Quetzalcoatl. It would appear that the
censer cult of dead warriors was an important component of the symbolism and
rituals performed in the Ciudadela. Both the Teotihuacanos as well as later Aztecs
may have regarded the Ciudadela and the Temple of Quetzalcoatl as the place of
warriors who died for the sun.

Along with being an account of creation, the myth of the birth of the Fifth
Sun at Teotihuacan expresses some of the most essential aspects of the Aztec
solar war cult, including self-sacrifice, fire, butterflies, mortuary bundles, and
rebirth. In contrast to the Aztec origin myth of Huitzilopochtli, the Fifth Sun myth
is probably of considerable antiquity in Mesoamerica. I have suggested that a
probable Classic version of this myth appears on a Teotihuacan-style Escuintla
vessel (Figure 10.24 [a]) (Taube 1992c: 79). The center of the scene portrays a
rimmed burning hearth flanked above and below by two War Serpent faces. The
pair of gesticulating individuals on either side of the central fire may be early
versions of Nanahuatzin and Tecuciztecatl, the gods who became the sun and
moon.

A version of the Fifth Sun creation myth may also have been present at Late
Classic Xochicalco. Two of the three stelae from Structure A seem to constitute a
pair, and portray busts of individuals wearing War Serpent headdresses above
rectangular enclosures (Figure 10.24 [b and c]).[24] The two figures are topped by
large day names with broad fans of radiating feathers. In the case of Stela 3, the
date is 4 Motion, or in Nahuatl, Nahui Ollin, the name of the sun born at Teotihuacan.
In the first analysis of these stelae, excavator César Sáenz (1961: 58) interpreted
this date as an explicit reference to the Fifth Sun created at Teotihuacan. The
other monument, Stela 1, has the date 7 Reptile's Eye. Unfortunately, the meaning
of this date is poorly known, as the Reptile's Eye sign has yet to be correlated
with any of the known twenty day names of Late Postclassic Central Mexico.
Another, recently excavated Xochicalco monument may refer to the creation of
the moon. The sculpture portrays a lunar crescent with a complex hierogphyphic
sign (Figure 10.24 [d]). Along with containing a lifeless human head, the glyph is
topped with flames, both elements suggesting the fiery self-sacrifice at
Teotihuacan. The upwardly pointed feet at either side may refer to the ascent of

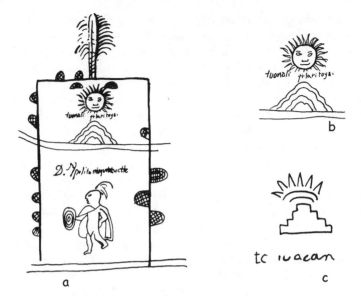

Fig. 10.23. Early colonial portrayals of Teotihuacan; a. Plan of Ciudadela and Temple of Quetzalcoatl, *Plano de San Francisco Mazapan* (after Gamio 1922, I: plate 148); b. Detail of Temple of Quetzalcoatl; c. Toponym for Teotihuacan, *Codex Xolotl*, plate 6.

the newly born moon. At the base of the sign are the remains of a coefficient, with only a portion of the bar for the number 5 surviving. The complex glyph may have contained the curl of the Reptile's Eye sign above the human head. However, a far clearer representation of the Reptile's Eye sign with a lunar crescent occurs on an Early Classic Escuintla vessel (Figure 10.24 [e]). The glyph and lunar crescent form the torso of a male with upraised arms, a probable rare representation of the moon god. Whereas Xochicalco Stela 3 represents the sun, Stela 1 probably depicts the moon.

Both the Stela 1 and 3 figures are atop rectangular enclosures marked with the Saint Andrew's cross, also known by the Mayanist term of "Kan cross" in Mesoamerican studies. During the Late Postclassic period, this element served as an Aztec sign for turquoise, recalling the description of the turquoise enclosure at Teotihuacan. For the Classic period, however, the Kan cross probably did not refer to turquoise, as this exotic stone was not common in Mesoamerica until the Postclassic period. Nonetheless, some of the other major meanings of this sign, including "fire" and "centrality," were already present in Classic Mesoamerica. A text from Tomb 5 at Huijazoo suggests that the Late Classic Zapotec regarded the Kan cross as a fire sign. In this text, the sign sprouts flames, much as if it were a burning hearth (Figure 10.25 [a]). The Classic-period Huehueteotl censer from Cerro de las Mesas, Veracruz, has a series of Kan crosses encircling the rim of the surmounting brazier, recalling the Aztec description of the fire god residing in center of the turquoise enclosure hearth, the *tlalxicco* earth navel (Figure 10.25 [b]).

Recent research indicates that the ancient Maya regarded the central axis mundi and surrounding world as a three-stone hearth placed on the carapace of a turtle (Freidel, Schele, and Parker 1993: 65–67, 80–82). In a number of instances, the center of the turtle shell is marked with the Kan cross (Figure 10.25 [c]). In Late Classic Maya scenes illustrating Teotihuacan iconography, the Kan cross often appears in contexts of fire and centrality. For the previously discussed Late Classic Maya scene of fire offering, a brazier and probable *yauhtli* bundle appear with an enclosure marked with Kan crosses (Figure 10.25 [d]). The *yauhtli* bundle Tlalocs appearing on the rim of the previously described Petén-style bowl are also accompanied by curving bands of Kan crosses and vegetal material, effectively making an enclosure around the central, burning War Serpent (Figure 10.6 [a]). Marked with Kan crosses, the rectangular elements at the base of Xochicalco

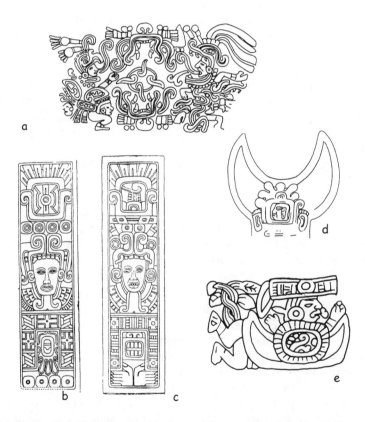

Fig. 10.24. Possible Classic-period versions of the creation of the sun and moon at Teotihuacan; a. Escuintla-style vessel illustrating pair of individuals flanking hearth with War Serpents (from Taube 1992c: fig. 21b); b–c. Stelae 3 and 1, Xochicalco (from Sáenz 1961: plates 4 and 2); d. Lunar sign with glyph of lifeless head and flames, Xochicalco (after de la Fuente et al. 1995: illus. 22); e. Figure with lunar crescent and Reptile's Eye sign, detail of Esquintla-style vessel (after Berrin and Pasztory 1993: no. 178).

Stelae 1 and 3 probably refer to an early form of the turquoise enclosure, a place identified with fire and centrality.

The *Codex Nuttall* of the Late Postclassic Mixtec contains a probable representation of the creation of the sun and moon at Teotihuacan. This scene is squarely embedded in the early mythological and legendary portion of the codex, and precedes an account of the deity 9 Wind, the Mixtec version of Ehecatl-Quetzalcoatl. However, it should be noted that the mythological scene on page 17 of the *Codex Nuttall* is *not* the native Mixtec account of solar creation, but rather, represents an intentional borrowing of Central Mexican mythology. John Pohl (1994: 103–106) notes that the principal protagonist of the *Codex Nuttall*, Lord 8 Deer, consciously identified himself with Central Mexican Chichimec individuals, rites, and iconography. The left half of page 17 of the *Nuttall* and the neighboring right portion of page 18 represent a series of Mixtec gods convening at a great burning pyre. A pair of individuals seated atop mountains flank the sides of the pyre (Figure 10.26 [a]). Whereas one of the figures is named 4 Motion, the other has the name 7 Reed. Clearly enough, 4 Motion is identical to Nahui Ollin, the name of the sun born at Teotihuacan. In the Central Mexican *Historia de los reyes de Culhuacan*, 7 Reed is the name of the moon (Caso 1959: 91). The scene on page 17 of the *Codex Nuttall* probably represents the Central Mexican sun and moon gods engaged in penance on their two mountains, the Pyramids of the Sun and Moon.[25] At the base of the pyre there is the Mixtec sign for town surmounted by a U-shaped enclosure marked with two merlons on either side. This enclosure is painted the color of turquoise, probably referring to the *xiuhtetzaqualco* containing the sacrificial pyre.

The mythological scene on *Nuttall* pages 17 and 18 apparently represents the assembling of the gods at the creation of the sun and moon at Teotihuacan. In the immediately following scene on page 18, there is the first appearance of the sun in the manuscript. Hovering in the sky with an aged creator couple, it is explicitly marked with the Motion or Ollin sign, despite the fact that the Mixtec sun god was named 1 Death, not 4 Motion. On page 21 of the *Nuttall*, there is a clear contrast between a sun marked with the Motion sign and another with the day name Death, that is, the Mixtec sun.[26] The sun first appearing on page 18 is an explicit reference to Nahui Ollin, the sun born at Teotihuacan.

Another probable reference to the birth of the Fifth Sun at Teotihuacan appears on page 46 of the *Codex Borgia*. This complex scene is dominated by an enclosure formed of four burning Xiuhcoatl serpents surrounding a central turquoise hearth (Figure 10.26 [b]). Combined, the serpents and central hearth represent the turquoise enclosure. In the center of the hearth, there is a vessel containing a figure with upraised arms. An aspect of Quetzalcoatl, this character appears no less than six times on page 46 of the *Borgia*. Both Seler (1963, I: 149) and I (Taube 1992b) have interpreted this scene as a version of the self-immolation of Nanahuatzin and the creation of the sun. However, page 46 of the *Borgia* has also been viewed as a depiction of the New Fire rites, such as were performed every fifty-two years by the Aztecs (Anders, Jansen, and Reyes García 1993: 241). Indeed, page 46 contains an explicit representation of fire drilling upon the abdomen of Xiuhtecuhtli. The use of Xiuhtecuhtli probably relates to the Aztec practice of drilling the new fire on the chest of a captive warrior whose name contained the term *xihuitl* (Sahagún 1950–1982, book 7: 31).

The two cited interpretations of page 46 of the *Codex Borgia* are by no means contradictory; the New Fire rites reenacted the birth of the sun at Teotihuacan. The body of the captive warrior was entirely consumed in the flames of the new fire, the same fate as Nanahuatzin and Tecuciztecatl (see Sahagún 1950–1982, book 7: 26). During the nocturnal New Fire ceremonies, a series of deity impersonators assembled at the place of fire making, recalling the convening of the gods in darkness at Teotihuacan (27). In the New Fire scene on page 34 of *Codex Borbonicus*, the series of god impersonators file toward the new fire

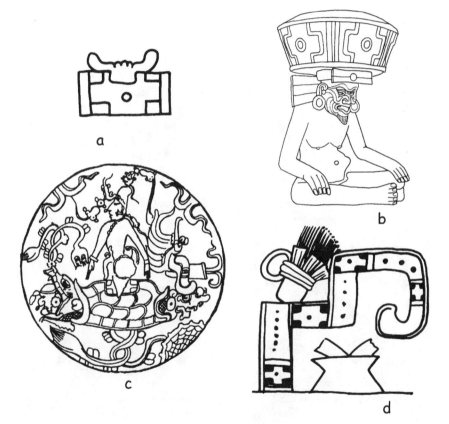

Fig. 10.25. The Kan cross as a Classic-period sign for fire and centrality; a. Kan cross with flames, detail of text from Tomb 5, Huijazoo (after Miller 1995: plate 35); b. Huehueteotl censer with Kan crosses on rim, Cerro de las Mesas (from Taube 1992b: fig. 66c); c. Maya maize god rising out of Kan cross in center of turtle carapace, interior of Late Classic bowl (from Freidel, Schele, and Parker 1993: fig. 6:20b); d. Censer and probable *yauhtli* bundle with enclosure marked with Kan crosses, detail of Late Classic Maya vase (after Kerr 1990: 192).

burning in the Tlillancalco, the house of darkness. This procession of god impersonators is notably similar to the assembly of gods in the aforementioned scene
on pages 17 and 18 of the *Nuttall*. Four individuals holding bundles of firewood
stand within the house of darkness (Figure 10.26 [c]). According to Seler (1902–
1923, II: 763), these figures are dressed as the warrior spirits who accompany the
sun, the *tonatiuh iluicac yauh*. In support, Seler notes that the *xiuhuitzolli*
crown, *xolocozcatl* pendant, and paper costume is notably similar to the warrior
bundle effigy appearing in the *Codex Magliabechiano* (Figure 10.19 [c]). It will
be recalled that such bundle effigies contained a core of ocote, and were probable
embodiments of Xocotl, a god of deceased warriors and the making of new fire.The
central, burning hearth is painted turquoise blue, once again alluding to the turquoise enclosure (Figure 10.26 [c]).

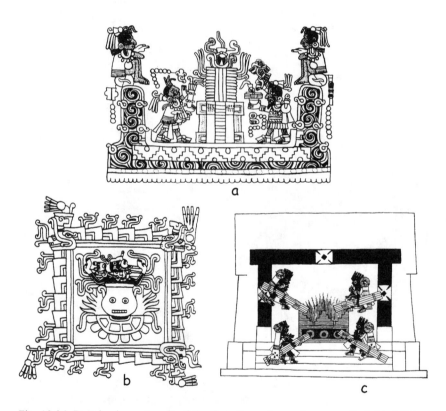

Fig. 10.26. Postclassic portrayals of the fiery turquoise enclosure; a. Probable Mixtec
portrayal of the Teotihuacan solar creation myth, with central hearth atop U-shaped
turquoise enclosure, *Codex Nuttall*, p. 17 (from Anders, Jansen, and Reyes García 1993);
b. Figure in hearth as turquoise-rimmed mirror surrounded by four Xiuhcoatl serpents,
Codex Borgia, p. 46 (from Taube 199c: fig. 22b); c. Turquoise hearth of Aztec New Fire
rites, *Codex Borbonicus* p. 34 (from Seler 1902–1923, II: 762).

BURNING HEARTHS AND SOLAR MIRRORS

The burning turquoise hearth appearing on page 46 of the *Codex Borgia* represents a particular form of artifact, a turquoise-rimmed back mirror (Taube 1983: 123; 1992a: 186). The spoked and petalled rim of the turquoise hearth and the four encircling Xiuhcoatl fire serpents are diagnostic of Early Postclassic Toltec-style back mirrors (Figure 10.27 [a and b]). The central pyrite mosaic mirror corresponds to the sacrifical pyre. An Early Postclassic bas-relief from Tula portrays a petalled back mirror flanked by flames, much as if it were a burning hearth (Figure 10.27 [b]). It is noteworthy that the four burning Xiuhcoatl serpents on *Borgia* page 46 have the directional colors of blue, yellow, white, and red, thereby marking the central hearth as the *tlalxicco* world axis. By extension, the four Xiuhcoatl serpents occuring on the rim of Toltec-style back mirrors probably also define the central pyrite mirror as the world center.

A relatively common sculptural theme in Late Classic Mesoamerica is a standing figure with a War Serpent headdress and a circular mirror over the lower abdomen (Figure 10.27 [c]; for other examples, see Taube 1992c: fig. 9.20). These mirrors not only mark the the navel of the standing figure, but probably also allude to the *tlalxicco* world navel as a hearth (Taube 1992c: 81). At Teotihuacan, a number of the large, hollow ceramic "host figures" contain figurines in the region of the navel (for examples of host figures, see Berrin and Pasztory 1993: 210–215). Two of these smaller, interior figurines have the corroded remains of miniature pyrite mirrors in the center of their bodies, a reference to the *tlalxicco* hearth as a pyrite mirror (Figure 10.27 [d and e]). For one of these figures, the pyrite mirror forms the abdomen of an anthropomorphic butterfly. This figure is very much like the aforementioned Escuintla censer lids portraying warrior butterfly souls (Figure 10.22 [d]). In both instances, the mirror represents both the burning hearth and the body of the rising, reborn butterfly.

Coggins (1987: 465) suggests that new fire was drilled on mirrors, and cites the archaeological presence of burned mirrors at Chichén Itzá. In scenes of fire drilling, the fire drill is often upon a circular mirror placed atop the Xiuhcoatl (Figure 10.15 [a–c]). One Aztec sculpture portrays a coiled Xiuhcoatl with burning mirrors on its body, which Hermann Beyer (1965: fig. 208) identified as a *tezcacoatl* (mirror snake) form of the Xiuhcoatl (for mirror detail, see Taube 1992a: fig. 14b). It will be recalled that in the Tojalabal description of shooting stars, meteorites were compared to both glass and mirrors. Along with obsidian, iron pyrite may have been considered as a meteoritic stone in ancient Mesoamerica. Today, iron pyrite nodules are among the most common type of "pseudo-meteorites," that is, objects mistaken for the remains of shooting stars (Brown 1973: 177). In addition, as an iron ore, pyrite produces strong sparks when struck with stone, which was undoubtedly a common process in the initial stages of lithic reduction for the preparation of iron pyrite mirrors.

Although Toltec-style turquoise mirrors do allude to starry, meteoric fire, this is but the generative spark for the great solar pyre. The principal meaning of such mirrors is the hearth and birthplace of the sun, and by extension, the burning sun itself. The Toltec-style back mirrors with four encircling Xiuhcoatl were extremely widespread in Mesoamerica, and are well-documented at Chichén Itzá, Tula, and even distant Casas Grandes in northern Chihuahua, near the border of the American Southwest (see Figures 10.10 [h–j] and 10.27 [a and b]).

Some of the symbolism of the Toltec-style turquoise mirrors apparently continues in contemporary Navajo creation mythology of the American Southwest. According to Navajo belief, the sun was created by fire drilled upon a turquoise disk: "[T]he First Pair made the sun of a large turquoise disk surrounded by red rain, lightning, and various kinds of snakes. It was heated by Black God's fire drill" (Reichard 1963: 17). Surrounded by serpents, this turquoise sun disk is notably like the Toltec mirror with its Xiuhcoatl rim.[27] Born of fire and comet, Black God is the shambling old god of fire, who hurls his fire drill as a powerful weapon (Reichard 1963: 196, 399–403). Black God is also a starry being, and is marked with

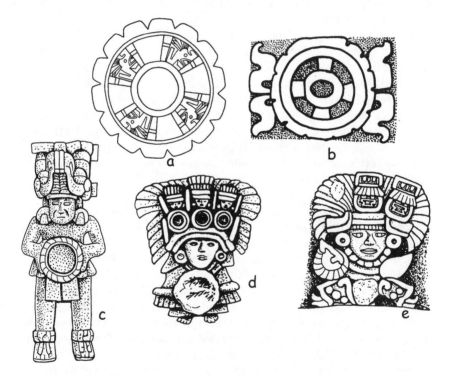

Fig. 10.27. Mirrors, fire, and centrality in Central Mexico; a. Schematic drawing of Toltec-style turquoise mirror with four Xiuhcoatl serpents on rim (from Taube 1992a: fig. 19d); b. Burning Toltec-style mirror, Tula (after de la Fuente, Trejo, and Solana 1988: no. 144); c. Standing figure with War Serpent headdress and mirror on abdomen, Late Classic Puebla (from Taube 1992c: fig. 20c); d. Figure holding corroded miniature pyrite mirror on abdomen as *tlalxicco* (detail after Séjourné 1966: fig. 193); e. Butterfly figure from interior of host figure sculpture with miniature pyrite mirror as abdomen (from Taube 1992: fig. 23b).

the Pleiades on his body (402; see also Haile 1947: 2).[28] According to Haile (5), certain Navajo use the appearance of the Pleiades to plan the fall or winter Mountainway ceremonial, which features the drilling of fire and a fire dance atop a mountain. The identification of the Pleiades with fire drilling recalls both the colonial Yucatec account of the fifth level of heaven and the Aztec new fire rites of the 52-year cycle, timed according to the zenith passage of the Pleiades in mid-November (Sahagún 1950–1982, book 4: 143; Broda 1982: 134). Among the Hopi of Walpi, Arizona, close neighbors of the Navajo, new fire is drilled in mid-November during the initiation rites of Wuwuchim (Fewkes 1900 and 1922; Parsons 1936: 964–965).[29] For the Wuwuchim rites recorded by Alexander Stephen in 1891, the Pleiades had a major role. From November 12 to 14, the Pleiades and Orion were carefully watched, particularly the zenith position of the Pleiades near midnight (Parsons 1936: 969, 973, 977).

THE AZTEC CALENDAR STONE

Aside from contemporary Navajo lore, the concept of solar turquoise disks is well-documented among the Aztecs. For example, there is the Aztec phrase *xiuhchimaltonatimomanaquiuh*. The *Florentine Codex* paraphrases this as follows: "The *xiuh*-means blue; *chimal*-means shield, that is round, *tonati*-means the sun; *momanaquiuh* means it will come to emerge" (Sahagún 1950–1982, book 1: 81–82). Thus this phrase describes the dawn rising of the blue turquoise solar disk. The great Aztec Calendar Stone constitutes an especially massive turquoise sun disk (Figure 10.28). Noting the series of turquoise signs encircling the edge of the central sun, Herbert Spinden (cited in Saville 1922: 75) interpreted the Calendar Stone as a solar disk fashioned of turquoise mosaic (Figure 10.28 [b]). However, in view of the pair of Xiuhcoatl serpents circling the edge of the disk, the Calendar Stone can be more closely related to the Toltec-style mirror with its turquoise Xiuhcoatl rim. With this comparison, the central Nahui Ollin sign would correspond to the pyrite mirror face (Taube 1983: 125).

The Xiuhcoatl serpents of the Toltec-style mirrors and the Calendar Stone are the fiery, meteoric beings that lit the original solar pyre. Durán describes the dedicatory rites of an important solar monument on the day preceding Nahui Ollin:

> [T]he priests took from the shrine of Huitzilopochtli a serpent made from paper coiled around a pole, all made of [red arara] feathers . . . A priest carried the snake, twisted around a pole. He then set it on fire and walked around the stone, incensing it with the smoke. While it was burning, he climbed to the top of the monument and threw the still smoldering serpent upon all the blood that bathed the stone. At this moment a great paper mantle was brought and was cast upon the stone. It burned together with the serpent until there was nothing left of it and the blood was consumed or had dried (1994: 190–191).

Heyden (1977: 191, note 4) notes that this serpent is the same type of feathered Xiuhcoatl torch used in the rites of Panquetzalli, where the burning Xiuhcoatl descends from the temple of Huitzilopochtli. In the dedication of this sun stone, the Xiuhcoatl was used to light a solar fire atop the blood of captive warriors, a vivid reenactment of the original sacrificial pyre at Teotihuacan.

Aside from the ceremony performed for the sun stone of Motecuhzoma I, Durán also describes the dedication of a solar monument commissioned by the following ruler, Axayacatl:

> [B]efore the sacrifice [of 700 warriors] a fire priest came out of the temple carrying a great incense burner in the form of a serpent, which they called *xiuhcoatl*, "fire serpent," and which was already lit. The fire priest walked around the stone four times, so that the smoke from the incense bathed it, and finally he placed this upon the Stone, where it finished burning (1994: 190–191).

For both the Motecuhzoma I and Axayacatl stones, the solar images were lit by burning Xiuhcoatl serpents, thereby endowing them with heat and life. It is also noteworthy that the Xiuhcoatl serpents are carried entirely around the sculptures, recalling the Xiuhcoatl encircling the rims of Toltec-style mirrors and the Aztec Calendar Stone. Of course, the act of lighting these solar images replicated the fiery birth of the sun at Teotihuacan.

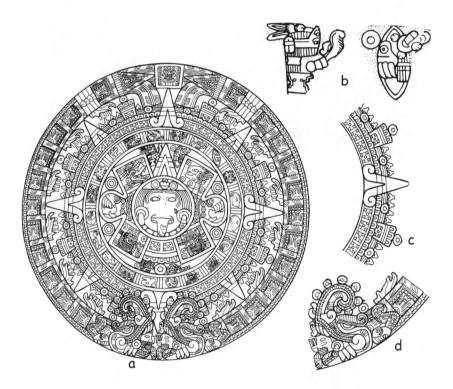

Fig. 10.28. The Aztec Calendar Stone and the birth of the sun at Teotihuacan; a. Aztec Calendar Stone with Nahui Ollin in center (drawing courtesy of Emily Umberger); b. Glyphs at upper portion of Nahui Ollin sign, signs for Xocotl and the *trecena* 1 Flint; c. Detail of turquoise ring enclosing Nahui Ollin sign; d. Detail of Xiuhcoatl with fiery butterflies on segmented body and winglike flame on shoulder.

Along with representing the descending Xiuhcoatl serpents that lit the original solar pyre, the Calendar Stone also depicts the mythic emergence of the new
sun at Teotihuacan. More than simply a solar sign, the date of Nahui Ollin en-
circled by the turquoise ring alludes to Teotihuacan and the turquoise enclosure.
It will be recalled that this enclosure refers to the pivotal hearth of Xiuhtecuhtli,
who resides in the *tlalxicco* earth navel. Seler (1902–1923, II: 799) suggested that
the four flanges of the central Nahui Ollin refer to the four cardinal directions as
well as previous creations, a concept also noted by subsequent authors (e.g.,
Beyer 1965: 188–200; Sáenz 1961: 58). As Sáenz (1961) notes, these four directions
mark the Ollin sign as the world center. In addition, the ring of twenty day names
encircling the Nahui Ollin probably also mark centrality (Figure 10.28 [a]). Since
each of the twenty day names designates a particular direction, this series defines
the Ollin sign as the central place surrounded by the four directions. However, the
Calendar Stone is not simply a depiction of the earth navel. Durán (1994: 191)
notes that the aforementioned sun stone of Motecuhzoma I represented the sun
at high noon. As a burning hearth lying in the center place of the earth, the
tlalxicco mirror is reflected into the center of the sky as the sun at zenith. In other
words, the Calendar Stone not only represents the fiery birth of the sun god, but
also the sun at full glory, in the center of the turquoise blue diurnal sky.

Mention has been made of the flying warrior souls who accompany the
rising sun to zenith, which appears to have been the special paradisical realm of
the butterfly and bird warrior spirits. According to the *Florentine Codex*, after
passing the sun to the western female *mociuaquetzque* warriors at zenith, the
male spirit warriors dispersed to enjoy the nectar of celestial flowers:

> [The male warrior spirits] rose up; they came ascending to meet the noonday sun
> there . . . There these eagle-ocelot warriors, those who had died in war, delivered
> the sun into the hands of the women. And then [the warriors] scattered out
> everywhere, sipping, sucking the different flowers (Sahagún 1950–1982, book 6:
> 163).

The burning of funerary bundles at Teotihuacan and with the later Aztecs concerns the concept of the metamorphosed butterfly accompanying the reborn sun
at dawn. Aztec funerary practices reveal the close link between deceased warriors, kings, and the sun. According to Durán (1994: 386), the cremated remains of
Ahuizotl's funerary bundle was buried next to a solar stone. In another passage,
Durán mentions that the burned remains of the bundle effigies in commemoration
of three slain brothers of Motecuhzoma II were also buried near the Calendar
Stone: "The ashes were gathered and buried in the Altar of the Eagles (as they
called it), next to the Sun Stone" (428). It is probably no coincidence that in the
Codex Xolotl, the funerary bundle of Tezozomoc is burned on the day 4 Ollin, the
name of the sun created at Teotihuacan (Figure 10.4 [g]).

The Calendar Stone displays several hieroglyphic signs alluding to the mythic
birth of the sun at Teotihuacan and the soul of the dead warrior. At the uppermost
portion of the disk—between the *yauhtli*-marked tails of the descending
xiuhcocoa—there is the date 13 Acatl within a square enclosure, designating the
Aztec year 13 Reed (Figure 10.28 [a]). As Seler (1902–1923, IV: 63–64) notes, 13
Reed is the specific year in which the sun was created at Teotihuacan. Two other

glyphs appear below, at the upper portion of the Ollin sign (Figure 10.28 [b]). One sign is the Xocotl glyph of Motecuhzoma II, complete with the *xiuhuitzolli* crown, *yacaxihuitl* nosepiece, as well as the *aztexelli* feather ornament of warriors. The accompanying glyph is the date 1 Flint, the *trecena* devoted to the sun and death gods and the soul of the dead warrior. In fact, Seler (1902–1923, II: 800) interpreted the Xocotl sign as a reference to the dead warriors who accompany the sun. In view of the accompanying date of 1 Flint, it is likely that the Xocotl glyph is a reference to the slain warriors who accompany the sun.

Rather than being a static depiction of the sun, the Calendar Stone is a dynamic portrayal of transformation and resurrection. The encircling, larval Xiuhcoatl serpents sprouting winglike flames on their shoulder and backs, possibly alluding to the spark that grows and matures into fluttering butterfly flames, which also appear in each segment of the Xiuhcoatl bodies (Figure 10.28 [a and e]).

Fig. 10.29. The Ollin sign and butterflies; a. Four-flanged Ollin sign from center of Calendar Stone (detail of drawing courtesy of Emily Umberger); b. Date 1 Ollin, *Primeros Memoriales,* fol. 302v; c. Aztec ceramic butterfly stamp (after Franco 1959: plate 15.5); d. Aztec butterfly, *Codex Magliabechiano*, p. 8v; e. Butterfly rising out of petalled mirror, Teotihuacan (after Langley 1992: fig. 25); f) Butterfly emerging out of solar sign, personal name of Mixtec Lady 3 Jaguar, *Codex Bodley*, p. 16; h. Flaming butterfly rising out of burning vessel, *Codex Borgia*, p. 66.

However, the central Nahui Ollin sign presents the most striking reference to metamorphosis and rebirth (Figure 10.29 [a]). With its four-flanged form, the Ollin sign is strikingly similar to Aztec representations of butterflies, a comparison that has been already made by Beutelspacher (1984: 16). The Ollin sign appearing in the *Primeros Memoriales* is virtually identical to an Aztec butterfly seal, save that the latter is supplied with antennae and an eye (Figure 10.29 [b and c]). According to Durán (1971: 187), the Ollin sign represents a butterfly. The Calendar Stone represents the newborn sun rising as a fiery butterfly out of the burning hearth. A related image occurs at Teotihuacan, where a butterfly with star markings rises out of a circular, petal-rimmed mirror (Figure 10.29 [e]). In Late Postclassic Central Mexican iconography, flames may be represented as a butterfly rising out of a burning hearth (Figure 10.29 [g]). One Mixtec noblewoman, Lady 3 Jaguar, has the personal name Butterfly Sun Jewel (Caso 1979, II: 320). In the *Codex Bodley*, this personal name is rendered as a butterfly rising out of solar disk, essentially the central theme of the Aztec Calendar Stone (Figure 10.29 [f]).

Aside from the Calendar Stone, there were surely other Aztec representations of butterflies rising out of solar disks. Durán mentions a complex depiction of the sun within the warrior House of the Eagles:

> [A]bove an altar there hung on the wall a painting done with brush on cloth: the image of the sun: This figure was in the form of a butterfly with wings and around it a golden circle emitting radiant beams and glowing lines (1971: 188).

The House of the Eagles was dedicated to the Eagle and Jaguar Warriors. It was their sacred charge to support and maintain the movement of the sun, a path that truly began at the blazing sacrificial hearth of Teotihuacan.

Conclusions

To the Aztecs, Teotihuacan was not only the place where time began, but was also the origin of a basic creed—the active role of the warrior, and by extension society, in the support of the sun. Certain aspects of the Aztec solar war cult were inherited from the earlier Classic-period traditions of Teotihuacan. Much of this continuity revolves around the symbolism of fire, including the hearth and centrality, the burning of warrior bundles, and the concept of the warrior soul as a fiery butterfly. However, other elements of the Aztec solar war cult were probably later Postclassic innovations, such as the Eagle and Jaguar military orders, which have no clear, immediate predecessors at Teotihuacan. In addition, although the Aztec regarded the Pyramids of the Sun and Moon as the places where Nanahuatzin and Tecuciztecatl performed their penance, it is by no means certain whether these structures were identified with the sun and moon during Classic-period Teotihuacan. However, the map of San Francisco Mazapan suggests that the Aztecs did regard the Ciudadela as a place of solar sacrifice, a theme consistent with the mass burials within the Temple of Quetzalcoatl and the mass production of composite censers. Both the mass graves and the censers may well relate to a Classic form of the Aztec *tonatiuh ilhuicac yauh*, the warrior souls who follow the sun. It is probable that the Ciudadela is the turquoise enclosure of Aztec myth, as well as the *tlalxicco* center of the Teotihuacan world.

The War Serpent helmets upon the sides of the Temple of Quetzalcoatl refer to both fire and warfare, and demonstrate the pivotal role of these two themes in Teotihuacan worldview. Both the War Serpent and its Postclassic descendant, the Xiuhcoatl, portray supernatural caterpillars, the pupate butterfly before metamorphosis. Although the Teotihuacan and Classic Maya forms of the War Serpent are clearly the same essential being, there are subtle differences. Whereas the Classic Maya creature is strongly serpentine, the Teotihuacan War Serpent tends to display jaguar attributes with greater frequency, including prominent ears and clawed forelimbs. Nonetheless, the illustrated example from Xico and the "Red Tlalocs" from Tepantitla reveal that the Central Mexican form is by no means an ordinary jaguar, but displays the petalled eyes of butterflies (Figures 10.10 [d], 10.11 [b], and 10.18 [d]). Along with physical characteristics, such as the upwardly turned nose, the War Serpent and Xiuhcoatl also share secondary attributes, much of this related to fire and warfare. Thus there are vegetal, Mexican year-sign bundles, probable depictions of bound *yauhtli* incense. In addition, both the War Serpent and the Xiuhcoatl were identified with shooting stars, widely regarded as flaming darts of celestial fire. However, the Xiuhcoatl and the earlier War Serpent differ in one major sense. Whereas the Xiuhcoatl was closely identified with turquoise, this stone was notably rare in Classic Mesoamerica. Instead, obsidian appears to have been the stone of the War Serpent. Nonetheless, it is likely that both obsidian and turquoise were closely identified with shooting stars and meteorites.

It has been noted that in Mesoamerica, meteorites are widely considered as caterpillars or grublike beings, sources of celestial fire, and presumably the sparks created in ritual fire making. However, aside from the work of Trenary (1987–1988) and Köhler (1989), there has surprisingly little interest in the symbolism of shooting stars and meteorites in ancient or contemporary Mesoamerica. Instead, Venus has dominated studies of Mesoamerican starlore, including the importance of Venus in warfare. Indeed, Venus is the "great star" of ancient Mesoamerica, but clearly there are other equally impressive celestial phenomena. As burning celestial darts, shooting stars are excellent symbols for omnipotent, divine weaponry and warfare. Moreover, meteors and meteor showers are frequently dazzling and even frightening events. The following is an eyewitness account by Professor Thomson who witnessed the Leonid meteor shower on November 12, 1833, in Nashville, Tennessee:

> [I]t was the most sublime and brilliant sight that I have ever witnessed. The largest of the falling bodies appeared about the size of Jupiter or Venus when brightest. The sky presented the appearance of a shower of stars and omens of dreadful events (cited in Brown 1973: 205).

As annual events, the seasonal appearance of the Leonids, Perseids, and other meteor showers may have been closely watched by ancient Mesoamerican peoples.[30]

In ancient Mesoamerica, two star groups appear to have been closely identified with meteors and fire making: the Pleiades and the belt of Orion. Mention has been made of the Pleiades with relation to the Yucatec Maya fifth level of heaven and the use of these stars to time the drilling of new fire in ancient Central Mexico and the contemporary American Southwest. Along with representing blazing meteors, the Xiuhcoatl was probably also related to the Pleiades. Each of the descending Xiuhcoatl on the Aztec Calendar Stone have seven stars on their snouts, the conventional number of stars counted for the Pleiades. Located close to the Pleiades, there is the sword and belt of Orion, which Coe (1975: 25–26) has persuasively identified as the Aztec *mamalhuaztli* ("fire drill") constellation. It will be recalled that during the Hopi Wuwichim new fire rites at Walpi, both the Pleiades and Orion are closely observed.

Aside from Orion and the Pleiades, shooting stars and meteorites are also closely related to another celestial phenomenon, lightning. Decorated with turquoise mosaic and seven pyrite disks, an undulating flint thunderbolt from the Aztec Templo Mayor appears to be a conflation of lightning and meteor symbolism (see Weigand 1977: 27). The celestial fire of lightning surely overlaps with the fire symbolism of meteors. For the Lacandon Maya, shooting stars are the castaway cigars of the Chacs, the gods of rain and lightning (Thompson 1970: 113). According to Tozzer (1907: 157), the Yucatec Maya regard meteorites (*chink'aak'*, or "hanging fire") as the points of arrows shot by the Chacs. Among the Tojolabal, *sansewal* refers to lightning (*relampago*) as well as fiery meteorites. In eighteenth-century Europe, meteorite falls were generally dismissed as "thunderstones," that is, stones created by lightning striking the earth (Burke 1986: 14). The close relation of meteors to lightning partly derives from the thunderous effect of blazing meteoric fireballs, or bolides, when they enter the atmosphere.[31] At times, such entries can create a deafening series of explosive sounds.

> If a bolide breaks into smaller fragments . . . each component may set off its own set of cannonades and detonations so that the observers on the ground are treated to an impressive and sometimes frightening tattoo of noises. Such sounds can often be heard more than a hundred kilometers distance from the final impact point (Brown 1973: 163).

Along with lightning, the Tlaloc war complex of Classic Mesoamerica may have also encompassed the symbolism of shooting stars and meteorites.

It has been noted that in Late Postclassic Central Mexican thought, the souls of slain warriors were identified both with butterflies and the night stars. The two soul forms, butterflies and stars, are not necessarily contradictory, as the stars represent the nocturnal form of the butterfly souls. Seler (1902–1923, IV: 722–723) notes that butterflies can be represented with starry eyeballs (eg., Figure 10.29 [d]):

> This eye was introduced because the butterfly pictures were fire butterflies, symbols of the flame and the spirits of the dead, and these, dwelling in the sky, were considered as stars (translation in Seler 1990–1996, V: 316).

In Late Postclassic iconography, stars are frequently depicted with wings, conflations of the butterfly and star aspects of the warrior soul (Figure 10.30 [c–e, g]). Aztec forms of these butterfly stars are frequently supplied with stone blades, and thereby refer to the fierce star goddess Itzpapalotl, the obsidian butterfly (Figure 10.30 [e and g]) (Seler 1902–1923, IV: 723–724). Among the back emblems donned by Aztec warriors was that of Itzpapalotl, which displays the pair of sticks and paper butterflies found with Xocotl, the god of slain warriors (Figure 10.30 [b]). Itzpapalotl is also closely identified with Mixcoatl and the Centzon Mimixcoa, the warrior spirit stars, as well as the women warrior souls of the west (Seler 1902–23, IV: 76–80; 1963, I: 137–42). A warlike, starry being of slain warriors, the Obsidian Butterfly is centered in the symbolism of shooting stars and meteorites.

In Late Postclassic art, the butterfly stars are frequently accompanied by stars hanging on long stalks (Figure 10.30 [d and e]). Seler (1902–1923, IV: 23) suggests that these curious elements represent "falling stars," in other words,

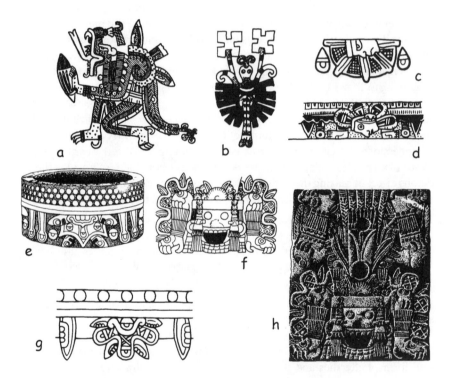

Fig. 10.30. Warrior butterflies, stars, and the goddess Itzpapalotl, Obsidian Butterfly; a. Itzpapalotl excreting a starry stream, or *citlalcuitlatl, Codex Vaticanus B*, p. 92 (from Seler 1902–23, IV: 721); b. Aztec Itzpapalotl warrior standard, *Primeros Memoriales,* fol. 78v; c. Butterfly warrior soul as night star, detail of Mixtec carved bone, Tomb 7, Oaxaca (after Caso 1969: fig. 193); d. Starry butterfly warrior soul flanked by shooting stars, detail of Mitla mural (after Seler 1902–1923, IV: 318); e. Schematic Itzpapalotl star flanked by pairs of shooting stars, Aztec carved stone vessel (after Seler 1902–1923, IV: 318); f. Detail of Aztec sculpture of diving Itzpapalotl with obsidian blades on cross-hatched wings (after Seler 1963, I: fig. 365); g. Schematic Itzpapalotl star sign flanked by obsidian blades, detail of side of Aztec Calendar Stone (after Beyer 1965: fig. 240); h. Aztec sculpture of diving Itzpapalotl with obsidian blades on cross-hatched wings (from Seler 1963, I: fig. 365).

meteors. His intepretation is surely correct, as falling rain is similarly depicted in Aztec art (Figure 10.30 [e]). In many Aztec portrayals, stone blades appear instead of the falling stars, the same blades that are found on the wings of Itzpapalotl and the butterfly stars (Figure 10.30 [e, g–h]).[32] On the starry side of the Aztec Calendar Stone, these blades alternate with the Itzpapolotl star, which also emanates knives (Figure 10.30 [g]). The markings on these blades are indentical to those found on the diving Itzpapalotl diving figure (Figure 10.30 [h]). This particular blade serves as an Aztec sign for obsidian, and appears for the place names Çtzihuinquilocan and Itzucan in the Aztec *Codex Mendoza* (fol. 30r, 42r). Like the pendant stars, the celestial blades refer to meteors, or *citlalcuitlatl*, recalling the *Vaticanus B* scene of Itzpapalotl defecating a stream of starry excrement (Figure 10.30 [a]). However, Itzpapalotl is also related to the spark-producing flint as well as obsidian. According to the *Leyenda de los soles*, the fiery warrior spirits, the *xiuhteteuctin*, burned Itzpapalotl, and from her remains obtained a white flint blade for the star god, Mixcoatl (Bierhorst 1992: 152). In a version reported by Mendieta (1980: 77), the flint blade was hurled to earth by Citlalicue, the star-skirted Milky Way.[33]

Much of the warfare imagery discussed in this chapter concerns rebirth and fire as a transformative agent. The fiery resurrection of the sun at Teotihuacan is replicated in the burning of warrior bundles, which transform the dead into flying butterfly spirits of the sun. The butterfly is a perfect metaphor for this process of transformation and metamorphosis, with the warrior bundle symbolized by the dormant chrysalis or cocoon. Two Aztec rites, Xocotlhuetzi and the New Fire ceremony, evoked the mythic birth of the sun at Teotihuacan through the fire sacrifice of warriors. The Calendar Stone also portrays the birth of the sun, with the sun rising as a butterfly out of the burning, turquoise hearth. At Teotihuacan and among the later Aztecs, there was an intentional blurring of the living and dead warrior. Mention has been made of the skull-like shell goggles donned by Teotihuacan warriors. The Central Mexican warrior bundles or their effigies of ceramic or cloth, wood and paper, were probably considered as semi-animate beings to be conjured and supplicated though fire offerings. This negation of the violence and finality of death surely contributed to the ethos of the courageous warrior. Self-sacrifice on the field of battle simply began a metamorphosis, as sure and effortless as a caterpillar transforming into a butterfly.

NOTES

1. For Aztec examples of legged mollusks, see the *Florentine Codex*, book 11, folio 64.

2. Although both Sugiyama and I identify the Temple of Quetzalcoatl form as a headdress, our interpretations differ considerably. Sugiyama (1989b, 1992) initially viewed it a representation of the Feathered Serpent, essentially an inanimate form of the plumed serpent heads projecting from the temple façade. However, in a co-authored paper with Alfredo López Austin and Leonardo López Luján and subsequent studies, Sugiyama considers the headdress to represent a caiman, or Cipactli. According to this interpretation, the headdress refers to the first day of the twenty day names and the beginning of the calendar (López Austin, López Luján, and Sugiyama 1991; Sugiyama 1993: 116). However, Cipactli has yet to be identified as a day name at Teotihuacan. In fact, the only explicit representations of caimans at Teotihuacan appear in the Mythological Animals

Mural, and these examples appear to have little in common with the Temple of Quetzalcoatl headdress (see de la Fuente 1995: lám 5).

3. A form of the War Serpent may have been present in Formative Mesoamerican art. One possible image appears on a vessel attributed to Tlapacoya, a Central Mexican site well known for its Olmec-style Formative vessels. Like the War Serpent, the frontally facing image has a large muzzle, fangs, and featherlike edging (see Gay 1972: fig. 33). Unfortunately, since the entire vessel is not illustrated, it is difficult to date the image reliably.

Possible Late Preclassic examples of War Serpent headdresses can be found on early, hollow, Remojadas-style figures from Veracruz (see Taube 1988: plate V–13).

4. Heyden (1977: fig. 18) illustrates another Aztec Chicomecoatl maize goddess displaying a drill stick and twisted ropes in the center of the headdress. It is noteworthy that this headdress is clearly a version of that worn by the Chicomecoatl impersonator appearing in the aforementioned *Borbonicus* scene, that is, the headdress with the central *yauhtli* bundle bound with the Mexican year sign (Figure 10.6 [d]).

5. In the northern Maya lowlands, War Serpents can appear as long, twisted ropes (such as in Itzimte Stelae 1 and 7; for unprovenanced examples, see Mayer 1995: plate 83). In the case of Itzimte Stela 1, the smoking serpent ropes appear on a ruler wearing a Tlaloc mask.

6. For the Tzutuhil Maya of Guatemala, there is the term *q'aaq'al*, derived from the word for fire, *q'aaq'*. The *q'aaq'al* refers to a shooting star, which is regarded as a sign for the soul of an infant or child (Mendoza and Mendoza 1996: 332).

7. Whereas one of the radial platforms is oriented to the principal north side of the Castillo, the other occurs at the east side of the Temple of the High Priest's Grave, which in many respects constitutes an early form of the larger Castillo. The imagery of this recently excavated structure is almost identical to the platform north of the Castillo, and also has crouching anthropomorphic Xiuhcoatl figures along with the Mexican year-sign bundle and the starry rope and drill stick. Coggins (1987) and I (Taube 1994b) argue that structures with radial stairways are widely identified with fire making in the Maya area. Both of these radial platforms may well have been loci for creating new fire at Chichén Itzá.

A similar pattern also occurs in the Mundo Perdido of Classic-period Tikal. At the base of another large radial pyramid, 5C–54, there is a radial, *talud-tablero* platform. Along with the two cited examples from Chichén Itzá, this platform is marked with stars and in addition, the shell goggles of Teotihuacan warriors.

8. Among contemporary Nahuas of northern Veracruz, fire is believed to have originated in the sky (Sandstrom 1991: 249).

9. Karttunen (1983: 324) notes that in Nahuatl, the terms for "turquoise" and "comet" are slightly different. For comet (i.e., meteor), *xihuitl* has a long vowel *i*. However, in view of the identification of the Xiuhcoatl with meteors, it appears that the two terms were in fact closely related.

10. Whereas the Nahautl term *tlemoyotl* is a term for "spark," with *tletl* meaning "fire," *moyon* signifies the swarming of ants, worms, and other similar creatures (Karttunen 1983: 154 and 308).

11. I am indebted to Monica Bellas Jensen for pointing out the example from the *Codex Vindobonenis* (Figure 10.15 [f]).

12. Saville (1925: plates 9 and 10) illustrates two Late Postclassic wooden spearthrowers marked with a series of stars on their shafts, probably designating them as star shooters.

13. In appearance, intact prismatic obsidian blades do resemble black worms or caterpillars.

14. Hill (1992: 131–132) notes the widespread identification of flowers with flames in Uto-Aztecan languages, including Nahuatl, Yaqui, and the O'odham of the American Southwest.

15. In Classical Nahuatl, there is the phrase *tlepapalochiua*, meaning "to be placed in a flame like a butterfly," a metaphor for being put in danger (Siméon 1988: 704).

16. Durán (1994: 205) mentions that the god impersonators to be sacrificed during Xocotlhuetzi were lined in a row next to the great hearth. Similarly, the *Florentine Codex* describes the gods standing in two lines at the sides of the sacrificial hearth at Teotihuacan (Sahagún 1950–1982, book 7: 5).

17. Whereas in Jacaltec Mayan, the word for ocote is *tah*, the term for meteorite is *tahwi* (Ramírez Pérez, Montejo, and Hurtado 1996: 248). In Mayan languages, the words for ocote and obsidian are often very similar if not identical (see Schele and Miller 1983: tables 1 and 2). It will be recalled that obsidian chips are often considered as meteorites, or "star excrement," among Mesoamerican peoples. One Kekchi Mayan dictionary defines *cha* as "splinter of glass for bloodletting," *chaj* as "ocote," and *chahim* as "star." In addition, *chajal* is glossed as "certain caterpillar (*gusano*) of a butterfly (Sedat 1955: 60–61)."

18. Aside from the Xocotl beam, the pole of the well-known *volador* dance is very much like a massive pump drill. In this case, the twisted ropes wrapped around the pole cause the descending dancers to spin, quite like the spinning motion of the drill. The *volador* dancers are frequently portrayed as bird-men, and in a number of sources the image topping the Xocotl pole is also described as a bird. Both the Xocotl image and the avian *voladores* dancers may refer to the souls of warriors, which are referred to as birds as well as butterflies. Galinier (1990: 396) notes that the contemporary Otomí consider the *volador* pole as a symbolic world axis, the "ladder of heaven." Among the Otomí, the fiery hearth also serves as the center of the world (145).

19. During a fire ceremony performed by the contemporary Otomí of San Pedro Tlachichilco, a pine tree covered with twisted wool threads is erected next to the central hearth. Armed with miniature bows, a group of boys known as "Apaches" shoot down *ídolos* tied to the multicolored cords (Galinier 1990: 242). Although making no mention of the twisted cords nor the warrior youths taking down the deity images, Galinier (1990: 244) compares this tree to the Xocotlhuetzi pole.

20. The Mendieta account refers to the morning star simply as Citli, or "star."

21. Marked with clay pellets, the curving element arching over the top of the Teotihuacan censer is notably similar to examples occurring on roughly contemporaneous Protoclassic censers from Colima (see Kubler 1986: 328–329). However, in this case the pellet-marked arch is typically a bicephalic serpent from which other serpents descend. This arch probably represents the sky as a bicephalic feathered serpent, with the falling snakes probably alluding to lightning, meteors, or perhaps both. An Early Classic censer lid from Tetitla, Teotihuacan, portrays another curving arch marked with feather edging (see Berlo 1984: plate 26). In this case the arch is marked with a series of eyes, a common means of representing stars in ancient Mesoamerica.

22. The Classical Nahuatl term for mica is *metzcuitlatl*, meaning "excrement of the moon" (Sahagún 1950–1982, book 11: 235). In the aformentioned quote by Gamio, this same term is used to refer to meteorites in the region of Teotihuacan. During Classic-period Teotihuacan, mica was frequently used to represent the shining face of miniature mirrors (e.g., Figure 10.22 [b]).

23. It appears that for Late Postclassic mortuary bundles, the golden pyrite mirror was replaced with a gold disk. The mortuary god bundles appearing on *Vaticanus B* pages 60 to 62 all wear gold disk pectorals (Figure 10.21 [d]). For the Tarascans of Michoacán, a circular gold shield was worn behind the bundle of the deceased Cazonci ruler (Craine and Riendorp 1970: 47)

24. Also placed in the Structure A stelae cache were objects in pure Teotihuacan style, including three stone statuettes, a fragmentary stone mask, and most striking of all, a stone Huehueteotl censer (see Sáenz 1961: figs. 8, 10, and 12). This collection of objects probably

constituted an intentional allusion to the great center, Teotihuacan, a theme apparently also expressed by the three stelae.

25. However, John Pohl (personal communication 1997) notes that scenes in the *Codex Nuttall* are tied to specific features in the local landscape of the Mixteca. Although it is quite possible that the Teotihuacan solar creation myth may have been used to describe a particular local place, the town of two hills and the turquoise enclosure are yet to be documented for Oaxaca.

26. This contrast between the 4 Motion and 1 Death suns could have temporal significance in the *Codex Nuttall*. Here the sun of 4 Motion may have been used to designate the ancient "sun" or time of Classic-period Teotihuacan, whereas 1 Death may have represented the current sun of the Postclassic Mixtec.

27. During the Navajo Mountainway rites, there is the manipulation of solar images fashioned from circular, store-bought glass mirrors (Haile 1946: 35–37; Wyman 1975: 27).

28. According to Berard Haile (1947: 2), the Pleiades appear on the left temple of Black God, who is the deity of gleaming starlight as well as fire.

29. During the 1891 Wuwuchim rites, the vigil of November 13 was particularly dramatic in that only the Agave and Horn Societies who previously drilled the new fire were allowed out:

> When the Pleiades come over head, the marching ceases, at least so I understand. No women look out, no one stirs abroad save the Agaves and the Horns...
>
> As the night grew later the pace waxed swifter until, as the Pleiades reached their zenith, both Horns and Agaves were encircling Walpi at a furious run, and this they maintained until the Pleiades and Orion were in the place they occupied when the Singers and Wü'wüchîmtü finished their songs on the previous nights at the [kiva] hatch, or about 12:30 (Parsons 1936: 977).

The frenetic circling of Walpi recalls the act of fire making, the spinning of the fire drill.

30. Although an annual event, the Leonid meteor showers vary in intensity, with especially strong displays averaging every 33.25 years (Burke 1986: 84–85). According to elderly Otomí informants, particularly impressive meteor showers, or "lluvia de estrellas" occur every thirty years, a fairly close approximation of the Leonid cycle (Galinier 1990: 527).

31. A recent newspaper article entitled "Flashing Meteor Sparks Panic in West Texas," describes a bolide witnessed on October 9, 1997: "A meteor flashing across the sky yesterday sent a ripple of fear through West Texas, where alarmed residents flooded police lines with reports of an explosion, a shuddering boom, and a burst of smoke" (*San Francisco Chronicle*, October 10, 1997, page A3).

The Niels Boehr Institute of Copenhagen subsequently described a major meteoric fall two months later on December 9, 1997, in southern Greenland: "The flashes observed in conjunction with the meteorite were so bright as to turn night into daylight at a distance of 60 miles, and can be compared to the light of a nuclear explosion in the atmosphere" (*New York Times*, December 19, 1997, page A11).

32. Although the place of Itzpapalotl, Tamoanchan, is typically represented as a severed tree, it appears as a furry caterpillar on page 63 of the *Vaticanus B*.

33. It has been suggested that the eccentric serpents at Teotihuacan may represent meteoritic beings. Similarly, it is possible that Classic Maya obsidian and flint eccentrics may have also related to meteor symbolism. Among the more common forms of flint and obsidian eccentrics at Piedras Negras are oblong, serrated forms that closely resemble multilegged caterpillars (see Coe 1959: figs. 4e, 5j, 9j, 10k and u, 12a–c, 16f, 17i, 21s and u, 24h, t, and u, 25a and p, 29a and n, 30b, 31u–w, and 32a–c). In addition, Charles Bouscaren (personal communication, 1997) notes that one elaborate Late

Classic serpentine eccentric may be a multilegged caterpillar, complete with projecting antennae (see Schele and Miller 1986: plate 114).

REFERENCES

Alcorn, Janice
1984. *Huastec Mayan Ethnobotany*. Austin: University of Texas Press.

Anawalt, Patricia Rieff
1996. "Aztec Knotted and Netted Capes: Colonial Interpretations vs. Indigenous Primary Data." *Ancient Mesoamerica* 7, no. 2: 187–206.

Anders, Ferdinand, Maarten Jansen, and Luis Reyes García
1993. *Los templos del cielo y de la oscuridad, oráculos y liturgia: Libro explicativo del llamado Códice Borgia*. Madrid/Graz/Mexico: SEQC/ADV/FCE.

Barrera Vásquez, ed.
1980. *Diccionario Maya Cordemex*. Mérida, Mexico: Ediciones Cordemex.

Berdan, Francis F., and Patricia Rieff Anawalt, eds.
1992. *The Codex Mendoza*. 4 vols. Berkeley: University of California Press.

Berlo, Janet C.
1976. "The Teotihuacan Trapeze and Ray Sign: A Study of the Diffusion of Symbols." M.F.A. thesis, Department of the History of Art, Yale University, New Haven, CT.
1982. "Artistic Specialization at Teotihuacan: The Ceramic Incense Burner." In A. Cordy-Collins, ed., *Pre-Columbian Art History: Selected Readings*. Palo Alto, CA: Peek Publications, pp. 83–100.
1983. "The Warrior and the Butterfly: Central Mexican Ideologies of Sacred Warfare and Teotihuacan Iconography." In J. C. Berlo, ed., *Text and Image in Pre-Columbian Art*: *Essays on the Interrelationship of the Visual and Verbal Arts*. Oxford: BAR International Series 180, pp. 79–117.
1984. *Teotihuacan Art Abroad: A Study of Metropolitan Style and Provincial Transformation in Incensario Workshops*. 2 vols. Oxford: BAR International Series 199.

Berjonneau, Gerald, Emile Deletaille, and Jean-Louis Sonnery
1985. *Rediscovered Masterpieces: Mexico-Guatemala-Honduras*. Boulogne: Editions Arts.

Bernal, Ignacio
1969. *100 Great Masterpieces of the Mexican National Museum of Anthropology*. New York: Harry N. Abrams.

Berrin, Kathleen, and Esther Pasztory
1993. *Teotihuacan: Art from the City of the Gods*. London and New York: Thames and Hudson.

Beutelspacher Baigts, Carlos Rommel
1984. *Mariposas de México*. Mexico: La Prensa Médica Mexicana.

Beyer, Hermann
1965. "El llamado 'calendario Azteca': Descripción e interpretación del cuauhxicalli de la 'Casa de las Águilas.' " *El México Antiguo* 10: 134–256.

Bierhorst, John
1992. *History and Mythology of the Aztecs: The Codex Chimalpopoca*. Tuscon: University of Arizona Press.

Boone, Elizabeth H.
1996. "Venerable Place of Beginnings: The Aztec Understanding of Teotihuacan." Paper presented at "The Classic Heritage: From Teotihuacan to the Templo Mayor"

Conference, October 17, Moses Mesoamerican Archive and Research Project, Princeton University.

Brewer, Forrest, and Jean W. Brewer
1971. *Vocabulario de Tetelcingo, Morelos*. Mexico: Summer Institute of Linguistics.

Broda, Johanna
1982. "La fiesta azteca del fuego nuevo y el culto de la pléyades." In F. Tichy, ed., *Space and Time in the Cosmovision of Mesoamerica*. Munich: Wilhelm Fenk, pp. 129–158.

Brown, Peter Lancaster
1973. *Comets, Meteorites, and Men*. New York: Tamplinger Publishing Company.

Burke, John G.
1986. *Cosmic Debris: Meteorites in History*. Berkeley: University of California Press.

Cabrera Castro, Rubén
1996. "Caracteres glíficos Teotihuacanos en un piso de La Ventilla." In B. de la Fuente, ed., *La pintura mural prehispánica en México, Teotihuacán I*. Mexico: UNAM, vol. 2, pp. 401–427.

Cabrera Castro, Rubén, Saburo Sugiyama, and George Cowgill
1991. "The Templo de Quetzalcoatl Project at Teotihuacan." *Ancient Mesoamerica* 2: 77–92.

Caso, Alfonso
1949. "Una urna con el dios mariposa." *El México Antiguo* 7: 78–95.
1959. "Nombres calendáricos de los dioses." *El México Antiguo* 9: 77–99.
1969. *El tesoro de Monte Albán*. Mexico: INAH, Memorias, 3.
1979. *Reyes y reinos de la Mixteca*. 2 vols. Mexico: FCE.

Caso, Alfonso, and Ignacio Bernal
1952. Urnas de Oaxaca. Mexico: INAH, Memorias, 2.

Coe, Michael D.
1975. "Native Astronomy in Mesoamerica." In A. F. Aveni, ed., *Archaeoastronomy in Pre-Columbian America*. Austin: University of Texas Press, pp. 3–31.

Coe, William R.
1959. *Piedras Negras Archaeology: Artifacts, Caches, and Burials*. Philadelphia: The University of Pennsylvania.

Coggins, Clemency Chase
1975. "Painting and Drawing Styles at Tikal: An Historical and Iconographic Reconstruction." Ph.D. dissertation, Harvard University, Cambrisge, MA. Ann Arbor, MI: University Microfilms.
1987. "New Fire at Chichen Itza." In *Memorias del Primer Coloquio Internacional de Mayistas*. Mexico: UNAM, pp. 427–484.

Covarrubias, Miguel
1966. *Indian Art of Mexico and Central America*. New York: Alfred A. Knopf.

Cowgill, George L.
1983. "Rulership and the Ciudadela: Political Inferences from Teotihuacan Architecture." In R. M. Leventhal and A. L. Kolata, eds., *Civilization in the Americas: Essays in Honor of Gordon R. Willey*. Cambridge, MA: Peabody Museum of Archaeology and Ethnology, Harvard University, pp. 313–343.

Craine, Eugene R., and Reginald C. Reindorp
1970. *The Chronicles of Michoacán*. Norman: University of Oklahoma Press.

de la Fuente, Beatriz
1995. "Zona 4: Animales mitológicos." In B. de la Fuente, ed., *La pintura mural prehispánica en México, Teotihuacán* 1. Mexico: UNAM, vol. 1, pp. 92–101.

de la Fuente, Beatriz, Silvia Trejo, and Nelly Gutierrez Solana
1988. *Escultura en piedra de Tula.* Mexico: UNAM.

de la Fuente, Beatriz, Silvia Garza Tarazona, Norberto González Crespo, Arnold Lebeuf, Miguel León Portilla, and Javier Wimer
1995. *La Acrópolis de Xochicalco.* Mexico: Instituto de Cultura de Morelos.

Di Peso, Charles C.
1974. "Medio Period Copper Artifacts." In Charles C. Di Peso, John B. Rinaldo, and Gloria J. Fenner. *Casas Grandes: A Fallen Trading Center of the Gran Chichimeca.* Dragoon, AZ: Amerind Foundation, vol. 7, pp. 500–532.

Durán, Diego
1971. *Book of the Gods and Rites and the Ancient Calendar.* Norman: University of Oklahoma Press.
1994. *The History of the Indies of New Spain.* Norman: University of Oklahoma Press.

Fewkes, J. Walter
1900. "The New-Fire Ceremony at Walpi." *American Anthropologist,* n.s., 2: 80–138.
1922. "Fire Worship of the Hopi Indians." In *Smithsonian Report, 1920.* Washington, DC: Smithsonian Institution, pp. 589–610.

Franco, José Luis
1959. "Representaciones de la mariposa en Mesoamérica." *El México Antiguo* 9: 195–244.

Freidel, David, Linda Schele, and Joy Parker
1993. *Maya Cosmos: Three Thousand Years on the Shaman's Path.* New York: William Morrow and Co.

Galinier, Jacques
1990. *La mitad del mundo: Cuerpo y cosmos en los rituales otomies.* Mexico: UNAM.

Gamio, Manuel
1922. *La población del Valle de Teotihuacan.* Mexico: Secretaría de Agricultura y Fomento.

Garibay, Ángel María
1979. *Teogonía e historia de los mexicanos: Tres opúsculos del siglo XVI.* Mexico: Editorial Porrúa.

Gay, Carlo T. E.
1972. *Chalcacingo.* Portland, OR: International Scholarly Book Services.

Graham, Ian
1967. *Archaeological Explorations in El Peten, Guatemala.* New Orleans, LA: Tulane University, Middle American Research Institute Publication 33.

Graham, Ian, and Eric von Euw
1975. *Naranjo.* Corpus of Maya Hieroglyphic Inscriptions 2, no.1. Cambridge, MA: Peabody Museum of Archaeology and Ethnology, Harvard University.
1977. *Yaxchilan.* Corpus of Maya Hieroglyphic Inscriptions 3, no. 1. Cambridge, MA: Peabody Museum of Archaeology and Ethnology, Harvard University.
1992. *Uxmal, Xcalumkin.* Corpus of Maya Hieroglyphic Inscriptions 4, no. 3. Cambridge, MA: Peabody Museum of Archaeology and Ethnology, Harvard University.

Haile, Berard
1946. *The Navajo Fire Dance.* Saint Michaels, AZ: Saint Michaels Press.

1947. *Starlore Among the Navajo*. Santa Fe, NM: Museum of Navajo Ceremonial Art.

Headrick, Annabeth
1996. "The Teotihuacan Trinity: UnMASKing the Political Structure." Ph.D. dissertation, Department of Art History, University of Texas at Austin.

Hellmuth, Nicholas M.
1975. *The Escuintla Hoards: Teotihuacan Art in Guatemala*. Guatemala: Foundation for Latin American Research Progress Report 1, no.2.

Hernández, Franciso
1959. *Historia natural de la Nueva España*. 2 vols. Mexico: Editorial Pedro Robledo.

Heyden, Doris
1977. "The Year Sign in Ancient Mexico: A Hypothesis as to Its Origin and Meaning." In A. Cordy-Collins and J. Stern, eds., *Pre-Columbian Art History: Selected Readings*. Palo Alto, CA: Peek Publications, pp. 213–237.

Hill, Jane H.
1992. "The Flower World of Old Uto-Aztecan." *Journal of Anthropological Research* 48: 117–144.

Houston, Stephen, and David Stuart
1997. "The Ancient Maya Self: Personhood and Portraiture in the Classic Period." Unpublished ms. in possession of author.

Hurley, Alfa, and Agustín Ruíz Sánchez
1986. *Diccionario Tzotzil de San Andrés con variaciones dialectales*. Mexico: Instituto Lingüístico de Verano.

Jones, Christopher, and Linton Satterthwaite
1982 *The Monuments and Inscriptions of Tikal: The Carved Monuments*. Philadelphia: University of Pennsylvania, University Museum Monograph 44.

Karttunen, Frances
1983. *An Analytical Dictionary of Nahuatl*. Austin: University of Texas Press.

Kerr, Justin
1990. *The Maya Vase Book: A Corpus of Rollout Photographs of Maya Vases 2*. New York: Kerr Associates.
1992. *The Maya Vase Book: A Corpus of Rollout Photographs of Maya Vases 3*. New York: Kerr Associates.

Key, Harold, and Mary Ritchie de Key
1953. *Vocabulario de la Sierra de Zacapoaxtla, Puebla*. Mexico: Summer Institute of Linguistics.

Kidder, Alfred V., Jesse D. Jennings, and Edwin M. Shook
1946. *Excavations at Kaminaljuyu, Guatemala*. Washington, DC: Carnegie Institution Publication no. 561.

Köhler, Ulrich
1989. "Comets and Falling Stars in the Perceptions of Mesoamerican Indians." In A. F. Aveni, ed., *World Archaeoastronomy*. Cambridge: Cambridge University Press, pp. 289–299.

Kubler, George
1967. *The Iconography of the Art of Teotihuacan*. Studies in Pre-Columbian Art and Archaeology 4. Washington DC: Dumbarton Oaks.
1972. "Jaguars in the Valley of Mexico." In E. P. Benson, ed., *The Cult of the Feline*. Washington, DC: Dumbarton Oaks, pp. 19–44.

Kubler, George, ed.
1986. *Pre-Columbian Art of Mexico and Central America*. New Haven, CT: Yale University Art Gallery.

Langley, James
1986. *Symbolic Notation of Teotihuacan*. Oxford: BAR International Series 313.
1992. "Teotihuacan Sign Clusters: Emblem or Articulation?" In J. C. Berlo, ed., *Art, Ideology, and the City of Teotihuacan*. Washington, DC: Dumbarton Oaks, pp. 247–80

Laughlin, Robert M.
1975. *The Great Tzotzil Dictionary of San Lorenzo Zinacantán*. Washington, DC: Smithsonian Institution Press.
1988. *The Great Tzotzil Dictionary of Santo Domingo Zinacantán*. Contributions to Anthropology 31. Washington, DC: Smithsonian Institution.

Lenkersdorf, Carlos
1979. *Diccionario Tojolabal-Español*. 2 vols. Mexico: Editorial Nuestro Tiempo.

López Austin, Alfredo
1988. *The Human Body and Ideology: Concepts of the Ancient Nahuas*. 2 vols. Salt Lake City: University of Utah Press.

López Austin, Alfredo, Leonardo López Luján, and Saburo Sugiyama
1991. "The Temple of Quetzalcoatl at Teotihuacan: Its Possible Ideological Significance." *Ancient Mesoamerica* 2, no. 1: 93-105.

Lounsbury, Floyd
1982. "Astronomical Knowledge and Its Uses at Bonampak." In A. Aveni, ed., *Archaeoastronomy in the New World*. Cambridge: Cambridge University Press, pp. 143–186.

Lumholtz, Carl
1900. *Symbolism of the Huichol Indians*. Memoirs of the American Museum of Natural History 1. New York.

Maler, Teobert
1901. *Researches in the Central Portion of the Usumatsintla Valley*. Memoirs of the Peabody Museum of American Archaeology and Ethnology, Harvard University, vol. 2, no. 1. Cambridge, MA

Marcus, Joyce
1983. "Stone Monuments and Murals of Monte Albán IIIa." In K. V. Flannery and Joyce Marcus, eds., *The Cloud People: Divergent Evolution of the Zapotec and Mixtec Civilizations*. New York: Academic Press, pp. 137–143.

Marquina, Ignacio
1951. *Arquitectura prehispánica*. Mexico: INAH, Memorias, 1.

Mathews, Peter
1980. "Notes on the Dynastic Sequence of Bonampak, Part 1." In M. G. Robertson, ed., *Third Palenque Round Table, 1978*, part 2. Austin: University of Texas Press, pp. 60–73.

Matos Moctezuma, Eduardo, and Leonardo López Luján
1993. "Teotihuacan and Its Mexica Legacy." In K. Berrin and E. Pasztory, eds., *Teotihuacan: Art from the City of the Gods*. New York: Thames and Hudson, pp. 156–165.

Maxwell, Judith M., and Craig A. Hanson
1992. *Of the Manners of Speaking That the Old Ones Had: The Metaphors of Andrés de Olmos in the TULAL Manuscript 'Arte para Aprender la Lengua Mexicana' 1547*. Salt Lake City: University of Utah Press.

Mayer, Karl Herbert
1989. *Maya Monuments: Sculptures of Unknown Provenance, Supplement 2*. Berlin: Verlag von Flemming.
1995. *Maya Monuments: Sculptures of Unknown Provenance, Supplement 4*. Graz: Academic Publishers.

McBride, Harlold W.
1969. "Teotihuacan Style Pottery and Figurines from Colima." *Katunob* 7, no. 3: 86–91.

Mendieta, Geronimo de
1980. *Historia eclesiastica indiana*. Mexico: Editorial Porrúa.

Mendoza, Francisco Pérez, and Miguel Hernández Mendoza
1996. *Diccionario Tz'utujil*. Antigua: Proyecto Lingüístico Francisco Marroquín.

Miller, Arthur G.
1973. *The Mural Painting of Teotihuacan*. Washington, DC: Dumbarton Oaks.
1982. *On the Edge of the Sea: Mural Painting at Tancah-Tulum, Quintana Roo, Mexico*. Washington, DC: Dumbarton Oaks.

Molina, Alonso de
1977. *Vocabulario en lengua Castellana y Mexicana y Mexicana Castellana*. 2nd ed. Mexico: Editorial Porrúa.

Múnera, Carlos
1991. "Una representación de bulto mortuorio." In R. Cabrera C., I. Rodríguez G., and N. Morelos G., eds., *Teotihuacán 1980–1982: Nuevas interpretaciones*. Mexico: INAH, pp. 335–341.

Nicholson, Henry B.
1971. "Religion in Pre-Hispanic Central Mexico." In R. A. Wauchope, gen. ed.; G. Ekholm and I. Bernal, vol. eds., *Handbook of Middle American Indians*. Vol. 10, Part 1: *Archaeology of Northern Mesoamerica*. Austin: University of Texas Press, pp. 395–446.

Nicholson, Henry B., and Eloise Quiñones Keber
1983. *Art of Ancient Mexico: Treasures of Tenochtitlan*. Washington, DC: National Gallery of Art.

Nicholson, Henry B., and Rainer Berger
1968. *Two Aztec Wood Idols: Iconographic and Chronologic Analysis*. Studies in Pre-Columbian Art and Archaeology 5. Washington, DC: Dumbarton Oaks.

Ortiz de Montellano, Bernardo
1980. "Las hierbas de Tlaloc." *Estudios de Cultura Náhuatl* 14: 287–314.
1990. *Aztec Medicine, Health, and Nutrition*. New Brunswick, NJ: Rutgers University Press.

Parsons, Elsie Clews, ed.
1936. *Hopi Journal of Alexander M. Stephen*. New York: Columbia University Press.

Parsons, Lee A.
1993. "The Izapa Style and the Tibas Jade." In F. W. Lange, ed., *Pre-Columbian Jade: New Geological and Cultural Interpretations*. Salt Lake City: University of Utah Press, pp. 251–259.

Paulinyi, Paul
1997. "El rayo del dios de la lluvia: Imágenes de serpientes ígneas en el arte teotihuacano." *Mexicon* 19, no. 2: 27–33.

Peterson, Jeanette Favrot
1983. "Sacrificial Earth: The Iconography and Function of Malinalli Grass in Aztec Culture." In J. F. Peterson, ed., *Flora and Fauna in Pre-Columbian Cultures:*

Iconography and Function. Oxford: BAR International Series 171, pp. 113–148.

Pohl, John
1994. *The Politics of Symbolism in the Mixtec Codices.* Nashville, TN: Vanderbilt University Publications in Anthropology 46.

Ramírez Pérez, José, Andrés Montejo, and Baltazar Díaz Hurtado
1996. *Diccionario del idioma Jakalteko.* Antigua: Proyecto Lingüístico Francisco Marroquín.

Reichard, Gladys A.
1963. *Navajo Indian Religion: A Study of Symbolism.* 2nd ed. New York: Bollingen Foundation.

Robicsek, Francis, and Donald M. Hales
1981. *The Maya Book of the Dead: The Ceramic Codex.* Charlottesville: University of Virginia Art Museum.

Roys, Ralph
1965. *Ritual of the Bacabs.* Norman: University of Oklahoma Press.

Ruz, Mario Humberto, ed.
1986. *Vocabulario de lengua Tzeltal según el orden de Copanabastla.* Mexico: UNAM.

Sáenz, César A.
1961. "Tres estelas de Xochicalco." *Revista Mexicana de Estudios Antropológicos* 17: 39–65.

Sahagún, Fray Bernardino
1950–1982. *Florentine Codex: General History of the Things of New Spain.* Translated by A. J. O. Anderson and C. E. Dibble. Santa Fe, NM: The School of American Research/ University of Utah.

Sandstrom, Alan R.
1991. *Corn Is Our Blood: Culture and Ethnic Identity in a Contemporary Aztec Village.* Norman: University of Oklahoma Press.

Saville, Marshall H.
1922. *Turquoise Mosaic Art in Ancient Mexico.* Contributions of the Museum of the American Indian 6. New York: The Heye Foundation.
1925. *The Wood-Carver's Art in Ancient Mexico.* Contributions of the Museum of the American Indian 9. New York: The Heye Foundation.

Schele, Linda, and Jeffrey H. Miller
1983. *The Mirror, the Rabbit, and the Bundle: "Accession" Expressions from the Classic Maya Inscriptions.* Studies in Pre-Columbian Art and Archaeology 25. Washington, DC: Dumbarton Oaks.

Schele, Linda, and Mary Ellen Miller
1986. *The Blood of Kings: Dynasty and Ritual in Maya Art.* Fort Worth, TX: The Kimbell Art Museum.

Sedat, Guillermo
1955. *Nuevo diccionario de las lenguas K'ekchi' y Española.* Guatemala: Chamelco.

Séjourné, Laurette
1959. *Un palacio en la Ciudad de los Dioses: Exploraciones en 1955–1958.* Mexico: INAH.
1962. "Interpretación de un jeroglífico teotihuacano." *Cuadernos Americanos* 124: 137–158.
1964. "La simbólica del fuego." *Cuadernos Americanos* 135: 149–178.
1966. *El lenguaje de las formas en Teotihuacán.* Mexico: INAH.

Seler, Eduard E.
1902–1923. *Gesammelte Abhandlungen zur Amerikanischen Sprach-und Alterthumskunde.* 5 vols. Berlin: Ascher und Co.
1963. *Comentarios al Códice Borgia.* 3 vols. Trans. M. Fenk. Mexico: FCE.
1990–1996. *Collected Works in Mesoamerican Linguistics and Archaeology.* F. E. Comparato, gen. ed. Culver City, CA: Labyrinthos.

Sempowski, Martha L., and Michael W. Spence
1994. *Mortuary Practices and Skeletal Remains at Teotihuacan.* Salt Lake City: University of Utah Press.

Serrano, Carlos
1993. "Funerary Practices and Human Sacrifice in Teotihuacan Burials." In K. Berrin and E. Pasztory, eds., *Teotihuacan: Art from the City of the Gods.* London and New York: Thames and Hudson, pp. 109–115.

Serrano, Carlos, and Zaíd Lagunas
1975. "Sistema de enterramiento y notas sobre el material osteológico de La Ventilla, Teotihuacán, Mexico." *Anales del INAH,* época 7a, 4: 105–44.

Siméon, Rémi
1988. *Diccionario de la lengua Náhuatl o Mexicana.* Mexico: Siglo Veintiuno Editores.

Smith, A. Ledyard, and Alfred Kidder
1951. *Excavations at Nebaj, Guatemala.* Washington, DC: Carnegie Institution Publication no. 594.

Smith, Mary Elizabeth
1973. "The Relationship Between Mixtec Manuscript Painting and the Mixtec Language: A Study of Some Personal Names in Codices Muro and Sánchez Solís." In E. P. Benson, ed., *Mesoamerican Writing Systems.* Washington, DC: Dumbarton Oaks, pp. 47–98.

Solís, Felipe
1981. *Escultura del Castillo de Teayo, Veracruz, Mexico.* Mexico: UNAM.

Spinden, Herbert J.
1913. *A Study of Maya Art, Its Subject Matter and Historical Development.* Memoirs of the Peabody Museum of American Archaeology and Ethnology, Harvard University, vol. 4. Cambridge, MA.

Stone, Andrea
1989. "Disconnection, Foreign Insignia, and Political Expansion: The Warrior Stelae of Piedras Negras." In R. A. Diehl and J. C. Berlo, eds., *Mesoamerica After the Decline of Teotihuacan, A.D. 700–900.* Washington, DC: Dumbarton Oaks, pp. 153–172.

Stuart, David
1994. " 'The Fire Enters His House': Architecture and Ritual in Classic Maya Texts." In S. D. Houston, ed., *Function and Meaning in Classic Maya Architecture.* Washington, DC: Dumbarton Oaks, in press.

Sugiyama, Saburo
1989a."Burials Dedicated to the Old Temple of Quetzalcoatl at Teotihuacan, Mexico." *American Antiquity* 54, no.1: 85–106.
1989b. "Iconographic Interpretation of the Temple of Quetzalcoatl at Teotihuacan." *Mexicon* 9, no. 4: 68–74.
1992. "Rulership, Warfare, and Human Sacrifice at the Ciudadela: An Iconographic Study of Feathered Serpent Representations." In J. C. Berlo, ed., *Art, Ideology, and the City of Teotihuacan.* Washington, DC: Dumbarton Oaks, pp. 205–230.

1993. "Wordview Materialized in Teotihuacán, Mexico." *Latin American Antiquity* 4, no.3: 103–129.

1995. "Mass Human Sacrifice and Symbolism of the Feathered Serpent Pyramid in Teotihuacan, Mexico." Ph.D. dissertation, Anthropology Dept., Arizona State University, Tempe.

Sullivan, Thelma
1997. *Primeros Memoriales*. Norman: University of Oklahoma Press.

Taube, Karl
1983. "The Teotihuacan Spider Woman." *Journal of Latin American Lore* 9, no. 2: 107-189.
1988. *The Albers Collection of Pre-Columbian Art*. New York: Hudson Hills Press.
1992a. "The Iconography of Mirrors at Teotihuacan." In J. C. Berlo, ed., *Art, Ideology, and the City of Teotihuacan*. Washington, DC: Dumbarton Oaks, pp. 169–204.
1992b. *The Major Gods of Ancient Yucatan*. Studies in Pre-Columbian Art and Archaeology 32. Washington, DC: Dumbarton Oaks.
1992c. "The Temple of Quetzalcoatl and the Cult of Sacred Warfare at Teotihuacan." *Res: Anthropology and Aesthetics* 21: 53–87.
1993. *Aztec and Maya Myths*. London: British Museum Press.
1994a. "The Birth Vase: Natal Imagery in Ancient Maya Myth and Ritual." In Justin Kerr, *The Maya Vase Book 4*. New York: Kerr Associates, pp. 652–685.
1994b. "The Jade Hearth: Centrality, Rulership and the Classic Maya Temple." In S. Houston, ed., *Function and Meaning in Classic Maya Architecture*. Washington, DC: Dumbarton Oaks.
1996. "The Rainmakers: The Olmec and Their Contribution to Mesoamerican Belief and Ritual." In J. Guthrie, ed., *The Olmec World: Ritual and Rulership*. Princeton: The Art Museum, Princeton University, pp. 83-103.

Tedlock, Barbara
1992. "The Road of Light: Theory and Practice of Mayan Skywatching." In A. Aveni, ed., *The Sky in Mayan Literature*. New York: Oxford University Press, pp. 18–42.

Thompson, J. Eric S.
1970. *Maya History and Religion*. Norman: University of Oklahoma Press.

Tozzer, Alfred M.
1907. *A Comparative Study of the Mayas and the Lacandones*. New York: Archaeological Institute of America.
1941. *Landa's Relación de las Cosas de Yucatán*. Papers of the Peabody Museum of American Archaeology and Ethnology, Harvard University, vol. 18. Cambridge, MA.
1957. *Chichen Itza and Its Cenote of Sacrifice: A Comparative Study of Contemporaneous Maya and Toltec*. Memoirs of the Peabody Museum of American Archaeology and Ethnology, Harvard University, vols. 11–12. Cambridge, MA.

Trenary, Carlos
1987–1988. "Universal Meteor Metaphors and their Occurrence in Mesoamerican Astronomy." *Archaeoastronomy* 10: 99–116.

Ulrich, E. Matthew, and Rosemary Dixon de Ulrich
1976. *Diccionario Maya Mopán/Español, Español/Maya Mopán*. Guatemala: Instituto Lingüístico de Verano.

Umberger, Emily
1987. "Antiques, Revivals, and References to the Past in Aztec Art." *Res: Anthropology and Aesthetics* 13: 62–105.

Valenzuela, Juan
1945. "La segunda temporada de exploraciones en la región de las Tuxtlas, estado de Veracruz." *Anales del INAH* 1: 81–105.

Viel, René, and Charles D. Cheek
1983. "Sepulturas." In *Introducción a la arqueología de Copán, Honduras 1*. Tegucigalpa: Instituto Hondureño de Antropología e Historia, pp. 551–628.

von Winning, Hasso
1977."The Old Fire God and His Symbolism at Teotihuacan." *Indiana* 4: 7–61.
1979. "The 'Binding of the Years' and the 'New Fire' at Teotihuacan." *Indiana* 5: 15-32.
1987. *La iconografía de Teotihuacán: Los dioses y los signos*. 2 vols. Mexico: UNAM.
1990. "Altmexikanische Pyritspiegel mit reliefierter Rüchseite." In B. Illius and M. Laubscher, eds., *Circumpacifica: Festschrift für Thomas S. Barthel*. Frankfurt am Main: Peter Lang, pp. 189–215.

Westheim, Paul
1965. *The Art of Ancient Mexico*. Garden City, NJ: Doubleday and Co.

Weigand, Phil C.
1997. "La turquesa." *Arqueología Mexicana* 5, no. 27: 26–33.

Wyman, Leland C.
1975. *The Mountainway of the Navajo*. Tuscon: University of Arizona Press.

Yoneda, Keiko
1981. *Los Mapas de Cuauhtinchan y la historia cartográfica prehispánica*. Mexico: FCE.

▼

11

Tollan Cholollan and the Legacy of Legitimacy During the Classic-Postclassic Transition

Geoffrey G. McCafferty

Recent cultural-historical syntheses of the Mexican central plateau have represented Cholula, the *other* great urban center of the Classic period, in one of two ways. In some studies, Cholula has been considered as a secondary center within the larger Teotihuacan empire, sometimes even as a sister city (e.g., Adams 1991; Weaver 1993). In such a scenario, Cholula is perceived as a faint carbon copy of Teotihuacan, with little to offer in comparison to its grander sibling. Alternatively, Cholula has been recognized as a separate polity (Miller 1996; Millon 1988), but with a material culture considered to be an "impoverished" imitation of Teotihuacan (Dumond and Müller 1972:1209). In this scenario, too, it is unnecessary to look further because Teotihuacan is bigger, better, and far more accessible. To a considerable extent, the same analogy applies to the Postclassic period as well, and thus Cholula has tended to reside in the shadows of Teotihuacan, Tula, and Tenochtitlan.

Research contribution to these interpretations was supported by a Mellon Foundation Post-Doctoral Fellowship at Brown University, and by Brown University Undergraduate Research and Teaching Assistantship (UTRA) grants. The original research reported was directed by Arqlgo. Sergio Suárez Cruz of the Puebla Regional Center of Mexico's National Institute of Anthropology and History. The ideas expressed have resulted in part from numerous discussions of Cholula's complex history, especially with Rex Koontz and members of the University of Texas Maya Meetings discussion group on Epiclassic interactions. Thanks also to Davíd Carrasco, Mickey Lind, and H. B. Nicholson for their long-standing interests in Cholula. An oral presentation on this topic at the 1998 Texas Meetings was dedicated to Linda Schele, who has encouraged me to bring Cholula out from the shadows. Special thanks go to Sharisse McCafferty for illustrations, serenity, and patience.

My objective is not necessarily to bring Cholula into the spotlight, but to at least bring it out from the shadows. Specifically, I will consider Cholula in relation to Teotihuacan during the Classic period, examining dynamic strategies through which Cholulteca art and architecture communicated cultural affiliation and difference with its neighbor in the Basin of Mexico. Furthermore, I will outline Cholula's historical trajectory into the Postclassic to argue that whereas the Mexica looked to a mythical Tollan for legitimation, perhaps in partial reference to Teotihuacan, Tollan Cholollan provided the cultural continuity to transform the Classic into the Postclassic. Finally, I will consider the roots of Cholula's cultural longevity that allowed it to survive the "collapse" of other centers, to propose an alternative model that combines religion and trade in a unique blend that materialized as the Mixteca-Puebla stylistic tradition and was linked inextricably to the cult of Quetzalcoatl (Ringle, Gallereta Negrón, and Bey 1998; see also López Austin and López Luján, chapter 1 of this volume; and Nicholson, chapter 4 of this volume).

CHOLULA AS AXIS MUNDI

Cholula is located in the Puebla/Tlaxcala Valley, east of the Basin of Mexico and on the outskirts of the sprawling modern city of Puebla (Figure 11.1). It is situated on the floor of a broad and exceedingly fertile plain, noted by colonial chroniclers as among the most productive agricultural regions in New Spain (Bonfil Batalla 1973; Rojas 1927). In pre-Hispanic times, the well-watered area even included a marshy lake to the northeast of the city that probably attracted migratory waterfowl and may have permitted *chinampa* agriculture (Messmacher 1967; Mountjoy and Peterson 1973). Cholula sits atop an excellent clay source, from which ceramics were produced well into the twentieth century (Bonfil Batalla 1973). Brick making remains an economically important (though archaeologically destructive) industry. Finally, Cholula is positioned on crossroads linking the Basin of Mexico, the Gulf Coast, the Tehuacan Valley, and the Mixteca Baja, and as a consequence the city developed into an important mercantile center (Durán 1971: 138–139, 278; Pineda 1970).[1]

These resources, however, fail to explain why Cholula arose as an important religious center, the site of the Great Pyramid, or Tlachihualtepetl ("man-made mountain"), the largest and oldest continuously used shrine of the pre-Columbian world (Figure 11.2) (Marquina 1970; McCafferty 1996a and n.d.). When the Great Pyramid was begun in the Terminal Formative period, its nascent ceremonial complex was probably no different from dozens of comparable small centers throughout the Puebla/Tlaxcala region (García Cook 1981). But something happened, such that Cholula flourished while other centers within the eight-hundred-square-kilometer area that became the Cholula kingdom were abandoned (Lind 1995).

Two "cosmo-magical" principles, to borrow a term from Paul Wheatley (1971), provide clues as to why Cholula became such an important center. First, the Great Pyramid was built over a natural spring, a cosmic opening into the underworld (cf. Heyden 1981). Waters from the spring still flow out to the east of the pyramid, and a small chapel on the side of the mound covers a deep well that allows modern worshipers to sample the sacred waters. Pre-Hispanic access to the underworld may have been available via tunnels into the pyramid, mentioned in Sahagún's (1950–1982, Introductory Volume: 48) account of the pyramid long before archaeologists began their own tunneling (Marquina 1970: 33). A chamber deep in the heart of the pyramid may have been used for ritual communion with the supernatural (Eduardo Merlo, personal communication; McCafferty 1996a: 5), and remains of a possible "tunnel" with pre-Columbian architectural features is exposed on the northeast side of the pyramid.

The second clue involves the orientation of the Great Pyramid itself. The pyramid is aligned at 24°–26° north of west (Marquina 1970; Tichy 1981: 223), facing the setting sun at the summer solstice. At that time of year, the sun sets behind the twin volcanoes Popocatépetl and Iztaccíhuatl, which therefore block out the fading sun's rays and focus the dying light on the Great Pyramid on the longest day of the solar year. A temple atop that pyramid would be the last point illuminated in the valley, and would be visible from throughout the region.

Interestingly, when Fray Diego Durán wrote about the Great Pyramid in the mid-1500s it was in a chapter on mountain worship (1971: 259). Petitioners as-

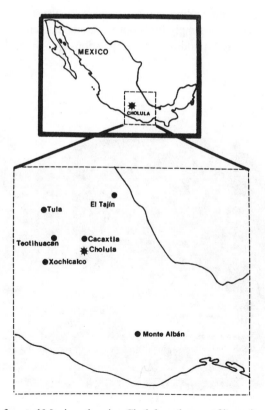

Fig. 11.1. Map of central Mexico, showing Cholula and some of its major eontemporaries during the Classic-Postclassic transition.

cended the pyramid to pray to the Lord of Created Things, that is, the solar deity Tonacatecuhtli. The Great Pyramid is identified in several colonial manuscripts as 7 Flower (Simons 1968: 65–66, lám. 4; *Historia tolteca-chichimeca* 1976: 9v–10r, 14r), the calendrical name for the Mixtec solar deity that parallels Tonacatecuhtli (Furst 1978:164). It is therefore likely that at least during the Postclassic period the pyramid was associated with the primordial sun, though the orientation of the pyramid suggests that this meaning may have considerable time depth.

By building an earthen pyramid, a "man-made mountain," over a spring, the ancient Cholultecas physically created an *altepetl*, or "water-mountain," the fundamental concept of the central Mexican polity (Lockhart 1992; also Matos Moctezuma, chapter 6 of this volume). By constructing a mountain over a spring, the Cholultecas also created Coatepetl, a "serpent hill" like a cosmic elevator shaft linking the underworld with the heavens (Gillespie 1989: 87). As David Carrasco (1992: 135) has described it: "The [Great P]yramid was believed to be the opening to celestial forces as well as the covering over the primordial waters of the underworld." Finally, the Great Pyramid became Sustenance Mountain, a source of fertility and abundance that during the Classic period may have been associated with the Teotihuacan Great Goddess (Berlo 1993; Manzanilla, chapter 2 of this volume).

It is unclear what sociopolitical processes went into the emergence of Cholula as a religious center—we simply have not yet conducted enough problem-oriented research focused on addressing the question. One thing that is obvious,

Fig. 11.2. The Great Pyramid of Cholula, from the west, showing Stages 3 A, B, and C as well as the Church of the Virgen de los Remedios on top of the pyramid.

however, is that Cholula was built around a fundamental principle that was in some ways similar to, but in others different from (and perhaps even intentionally contrasted with) Teotihuacan. The Great Pyramid, the urban grid of Cholula, and even field boundaries throughout the Cholula kingdom are oriented at 24°–26° north-of-west (Marquina 1970; Tichy 1981: 223), and are therefore clearly differentiated from the orientation of Teotihuacan and its hinterland. This was undoubtedly an important factor in the construction of the symbolic landscape relating to state-level ideology, though the specific meanings of the material discourse remain to be explicated.

THE GREAT PYRAMID OF CHOLULA

The Great Pyramid, *Tlachihualtepetl*, is the best-known monument from Cholula. In a recent reinterpretation of its construction history, I argue that the Great Pyramid was built in four major stages, plus at least nine partial modifications (Figure 11.3) (McCafferty 1996a). The ceremonial precinct was built up over a 1,700-year period between approximately 500 B.C.E. and 1200 C.E., though it must be emphasized that the Cholula chronology remains problematic (McCafferty 1996b). Since the pyramid continued as an important shrine during the Late Postclassic period, and later became a major pilgrimage site dedicated to the Virgen de los Remedios (Olivera 1970), the Great Pyramid continues as an axis mundi after at least 2,500 years.

Throughout this long history, however, meanings accrued and became transformed as the Great Pyramid evolved as a dynamic symbolic landscape (McCafferty n.d.). Just as the grid orientation may have expressed a discourse of difference relative to Teotihuacan, architectural and decorative elements of the pyramid sometimes shared Teotihuacan canons, but sometimes they were quite distinct. Following Debra Nagao (1989), the "public proclamations" of Cholula monumental architecture were an ongoing dialogue about affiliation and discord.

Stage 1 of the Great Pyramid, for example, featured Teotihuacan-style *taludtablero* architecture with *tablero* murals of a skeletal head, depicted frontally, with a larval body stretched to the side (Marquina 1970: 39, lám. 1) (Figure 11.4). This may represent cyclical death and rebirth through metaphoric reference to a butterfly's life-cycle (Berlo 1983). The configuration of a frontal head and profile body, however, also recalls the *tablero* of the Pyramid of the Feathered Serpent at Teotihuacan. Through architecture and monumental art, the builders of this initial stage of the pyramid may have claimed political/ideological affiliation with Teotihuacan.

The second stage of the Great Pyramid is like no other in Mesoamerica (Margain 1971: 69). It measured 180 meters on a side, rising in nine levels to 35 meters in height, where an upper platform measured 90 meters square (Marquina 1970: 39). What is unique about this structure is that each side is made up entirely of steps, so that access to the top would have been possible from any direction. There was a prominent raised stairway of fifty-two steps on the north side of the pyramid. The use of such cosmologically significant numbers as architectural units implies yet another level of meaning for this incarnation of the Great Pyramid. Yet, while the calendrical principles expressed may have some relationship to

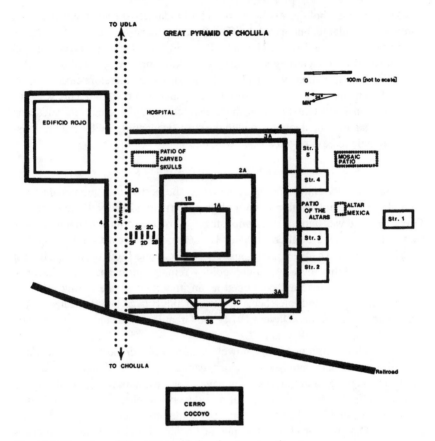

Fig. 11.3. Plan view of Great Pyramid showing construction stages.

the Pyramid of the Feathered Serpent at Teotihuacan (López Austin, López Luján, and Sugiyama 1991; also see Sugiyama, chapter 3 of this volume, and Taube, chapter 10 of this volume), the architectural medium of that message was distinct. Affiliation with Teotihuacan may have been symbolically rejected as Cholulteca architects chose to ignore the *talud-tablero* style that had become iconic of the Teotihuacan canon to experiment with alternative forms, including the four-sided pyramid that was later prominent at Maya sites such as Chichén Itzá. In fact, a late modification (Stage 2G) features a painted *tablero* of black rectangles outlined in white, resembling the Temple of the Niches at El Tajín (Marquina 1970: 40–41), suggesting that during this period cultural affiliations may have already been oriented toward the Gulf Coast.

Stage 3A of the Great Pyramid expanded to 350 meters on a side, and reached a height of about 65 meters (Marquina 1970: 41). Note that this is over twice the volume of Teotihuacan's Pyramid of the Sun. Architectual façades again used a Teotihuacan-style *talud/tablero* form. The chronology of this construction phase is problematic, however, though it has been been assumed that the presence of the *talud-tablero* architecture indicates contemporaneity with Teotihuacan. But if Stage 2G is related to a Tajínoid Gulf Coast influence (as is the Edificio Rojo, discussed below), then, based on new dates from El Tajín (Brueggemann and Ortega Guevara 1989), Teotihuacan may have been declining if not already abandoned at the time that Stage 3A was built. Though far from conclusive, it may be that the architects of Stage 3A were attempting a symbolic "proclamation" of Cholula's role as legitimate heir to Teotihuacan's cosmic centrality.

Besides the Great Pyramid, several other Classic-period pyramids still exist throughout Cholula, rising like islands in a sea of urban development. Cerro Cocoyo (now known as Acozoc) lies due west of the Great Pyramid, across a wide clearing that was most likely the central plaza of the Classic ceremonial center. To the southwest is a tall adobe nucleus—all that remains of another pyramid whose façades have been stripped away, presumably to make adobe bricks. Northeast of the Great Pyramid is the Edificio Rojo, a large pyramid platform with a well-preserved staircase and stucco façade bearing stylistic similarities to El Tajín (Rex

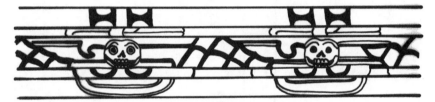

Fig. 11.4. "Chapulin" mural from Stage 1B of Great Pyramid.

Koontz, personal communication). It is well-preserved because the structure was engulfed by the Epiclassic expansion of the "man-made mountain." Across town, about 2 kilometers west of the Great Pyramid, is the Cerrito de Guadalupe, whose base is also made of a nucleus of adobe brick, indicating that this may be yet another unexplored pyramid. Cortés (1986: 75) noted over 430 temples in Cholula at the time of the Conquest, and many of these may have originally been Classic-period structures. Yet while there is considerable evidence for monumental construction, the settlement size for Classic-period Cholula was only about 4 square kilometers, with an estimated population of perhaps 20–25,000 (McCafferty 1996b: 304).

Aside from architectural comparisons, evidence to evaluate interaction between Cholula and Teotihuacan during the Classic period has been scant. Both Eduardo Noguera (1954) and Florencia Müller (1970, 1978), in their respective volumes on Cholula ceramics, noted similarities in pottery and figurine styles between the two areas. Noguera pointed to greater similarities in the Early Classic, noting that the Cholultecas may have been ethnically related to the people of Teotihuacan, but he suggested that there was greater divergence between the two cultures later in the sequence (Noguera 1954: 188).

The R–106 Classic Household

In 1993, rescue excavation R–106 by Arqlgo. Sergio Suárez C. of the INAH Centro Regional de Puebla encountered a Classic-period house, dubbed the "Transito" site, within the urban zone of Cholula (McCafferty and Suárez C. 1994). Four radiocarbon samples date the occupation to the Late Classic, between 400 and 650 c.e. (McCafferty 1996b). Architectural features and material culture from the Transito site now provide an unprecedented opportunity to compare Cholula domestic practices with those of Teotihuacan.

The house was small, with only two rooms separated by a well-formed doorway (Figure 11.5). Intrusive middens and other postdepositional disturbances (and a lack of time) hindered further delimitation of the structure, but exterior walls were identified on the west and east sides, while exterior features were located to the south. The house floors were made of a thick stucco; the low remains of adobe walls also had remnants of plaster. Outside the structure wall on the west was a high density of obsidian production debris, probably refuse from a workshop (Edelstein 1995). Because the floor was less than 50 centimeters beneath the ground surface, plow disturbance had thoroughly mixed artifacts above the floor,

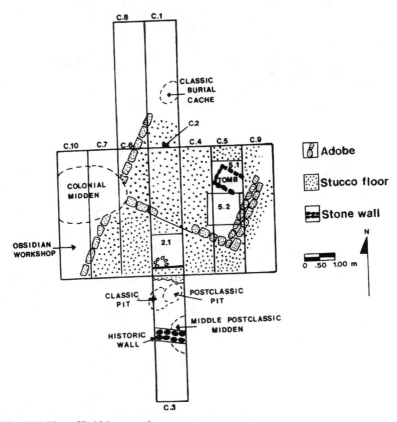

Fig. 11.5. Plan of R-106 excavation.

to the extent that there were even plow scars in the plaster surface. In order to obtain a more representative sample of artifacts with which to date the structure, a series of 1 meter by 1 meter units were excavated through the floor in areas where the unbroken floor surface indicated the potential for sealed deposits.

By chance, the first test pit encountered an area where several earlier stucco floors had been removed in antiquity in order to excavate down to a burial chamber. This crypt's walls were lined with stone on three sides, while on the unlined west end it extended slightly under the exterior structure wall. Fragmentary skeletal remains of two secondary burials were found on the earthen floor of the tomb, while the excavated context of superimposed floors and sequential tomb entry suggested that the interments may have been from different generations of the same lineage (McCafferty and Suárez 1994). Six Tepontla Burnished Gray Brown vessels were found in a niche hollowed out beneath the structure wall. Other items included two greenstone beads, an obsidian projectile point, a bone spindle whorl, and several figurines. Most of these items, however, were located in the fill above the burials so it is unclear if all were, in fact, offerings. The material remains from the tomb, tomb fill, and from the other pits beneath the house floor included unmixed artifacts from the Classic period. Ceramic types included a monochrome serving ware (Tepontla Burnished Gray Brown), an orangish utilitarian ware (Acozoc Tan Orange), and Teotihuacan Thin Orange, including several variations that may be local imitations (McCafferty 1996b: 307). Strong similarities exist between these types and Classic Teotihuacan ceramics in vessel form and surface treatment. Teotihuacan Thin Orange comprised about 8 percent of all rim sherds found beneath the house floor. Figurines were also stylistically similar to Teotihuacan, especially for the Tlamimilolpa and Xolalpan phases (Charles Kolb, personal communication).

Obsidian from beneath the floor and from the workshop debris was nearly all green (Edelstein 1995), and therefore was obtained from the Cerro de las Navajas source near Pachuca, Hidalgo. Notably, obsidian waste flakes represented all phases of the reduction sequence, including flakes with external matrix indicative of the initial phase of the core preparation process. This suggests that Cholula may have had direct access to Pachuca sources that bypassed the suggested Teotihuacan "monopoly" (Santley 1983).

Extrapolating from the R–106 evidence suggests that Cholula and Teotihuacan may have shared certain fundamental elements of domestic culture, including pottery styles and certain foodways, obsidian resource procurement areas and redistribution networks, and household ritual as indicated by the figurines (cf. Brumfiel 1996). This suggests that the two populations were culturally similar and may have shared ethnic origins.

Yet other factors present important differences. Several components of Teotihuacan material culture are absent at R–106 (and are very rare at Cholula in general), such as *candeleros* and other censer types representative of Teotihuacan's state religion (Berlo 1982). The Transito site structure walls were aligned at 24° north of west, conforming to the grid orientation of Cholula but in contrast to Teotihuacan. The building was probably a single-family dwelling, based on its simple, two-room floor plan, in further contrast to the multifamily apartment compounds common to Teotihuacan. The mortuary practice of secondary burials in a prepared, stone-lined tomb is unknown from Teotihuacan (Serrano S. 1993; but see García Cook, Arias M.G., and Abascal M. 1976 for a comparable stone-lined crypt from Tlaxcala). Single-family houses with well-built tombs such as that found at R–106 imply a very different conception of the individual and lineage than that of Teotihuacan (cf. Cowgill 1993). These data suggest that despite fundamental cultural similarities an ideology of distinction may have existed between Cholula and Teotihuacan during the Late Classic period whereby political and state-level religious differences were projected, perhaps to mask deeper cultural patterns.

Classic-Postclassic Continuity at Cholula

Throughout the central plateau, the end of the Classic period represents a time of dramatic change, including the abandonment of ceremonial centers associated with the "old" regime. So although Teotihuacan remained the principal population center of the Epiclassic Basin of Mexico, the ceremonial structures along the Avenue of the Dead were desecrated and destroyed (Millon 1988). Traditional interpretations of Cholula's ceremonial center have followed this model, too, with explanations of volcanic eruption, flooding, and general social upheaval all used to account for a hypothetical abandonment of the Great Pyramid and perhaps even the city itself (Dumond and Müller 1972; García Cook 1981; García Cook and Merino C. 1990; Mountjoy 1987; Müller 1978; Suárez C. and Martínez A. 1993; but see Sanders 1989).

I disagree, and instead argue for a model of cultural continuity as originally proposed by Noguera (1954) and Marquina (1951), based on their initial research results. Under this interpretation, Cholula continued as an important ceremonial center throughout the Classic to Postclassic transition, albeit with substantial change in material culture, probably as the result of changing ethnic composition and religious orientation.

During the Epiclassic, major additions were made to the exterior of Stage 3 of the Great Pyramid on at least the south and west sides, particularly at the Patio of the Altars (McCafferty 1996a). The patio was built up in a sequence of six construction stages bounded by long platforms, the earliest of which were attached to the Teotihuacan-style *talud/tablero* of Stage 3A. The platform façades retain a similar style of greca-decorated taluds throughout the construction sequence (Acosta 1970a). It was on an early phase of the Patio of the Altars that the famous Bebedores mural was painted, depicting 50 meters of drunken revelry (Marquina 1971; Müller 1972).

The "Altar Mexica"[2] is located about 3 meters beneath the surface of the final phase of the Patio of the Altars (Figure 11.6). It contained skeletal remains of several ceremonially interred individuals (López A., Lagunas R., and Serrano S. 1976), with Cocoyotla Black-on-Natural ceramics that clearly indicate that the altar dates to the Epiclassic period (McCafferty 1996b). This "late" pottery should not be considered an anomaly, since similar ceramics were encountered as an offering beneath Altar 2 of the Patio of the Altars (Acosta 1970b), and at Edificio 1 south of the Patio (Matos and López V. 1967). In fact, a stratigraphic profile indicates that virtually all of the deposition in this area was post-Classic (Müller 1970: 132, fig. 22). So although lacking absolute dates for support, or even many primary depositional contexts for independent confirmation, I contend that much of the southern ceremonial precinct was built following the end of the Classic period.

Decoration at the Patio of the Altars is in an eclectic style that combines traits from the Gulf Coast, Mixteca Alta, and even the Maya region (McCafferty n.d.). Carved stone stela/altar groups feature volute borders around blank central panels in a style strongly reminiscent of El Tajín (Acosta 1970c). Murals with polychrome diagonal bands, and architectural *taludes* of continuous grecas are both typical architectural elements in Mixtec painted manuscripts (McCafferty 1994). An extensive "mat" motif on the *tablero* of Pyramid Stage 3B may also relate to Mixtec iconography, but the most vivid archaeological parallels come from Maya sites such as Copán and Chichén Itzá (Fash 1991: 130–134). Another mat motif from Cholula was depicted as a polychrome mural at the Patio of the Altars (Marquina 1970: lám. 3). A final mural of note was a polychrome feathered serpent (Acosta 1970d).

Fig. 11.6. "Altar Mexica."

Stylistic information from the ceremonial precinct proclaims a dynamic program of affiliation. Upon a Teotihuacan-style *talud-tablero* architectural background (Stage 3A), diverse styles were overlain in a palimpset of multi-ethnic internationalism.

THE OLMECA-XICALLANCA AT CHOLULA

The presence of possible Gulf Coast and Maya influences at Cholula during the Epiclassic period is notable because it corresponds with ethnohistorical accounts of the arrival and settlement at the city by members of the Olmeca-Xicallanca ethnic group, with probable ties to the southern Gulf Coast. According to Ixtlilxochitl (1975–1977, I: 530–531), Cholula was inhabited by "giants," or *quinametinime*, when the Olmeca-Xicallanca arrived and defeated them. The "giants" are generally interpreted as the ancestral Teotihuacanos (Davies 1977: 46). The Olmeca-Xicallanca then built the Great Pyramid (or at least the final stages of it) with the help of their lord Quetzalcoatl, and resided in Cholula until the destruction of the Third Age of the World by wind.

Clearly this legend is steeped in myth, but there may be important kernals of historical fact wrapped in fancy. Feathered-serpent imagery at the Patio of the Altars, for example, is the first known appearance of Quetzalcoatl iconography at the Great Pyramid,[3] though it later became prominent on polychrome pottery of the Postclassic period. The arrival of Quetzalcoatl's cult at Cholula and its coincidence with the final building phases of the Great Pyramid suggest that changes in the material culture relate to ethnic change associated with the arrival of the Olmeca-Xicallanca.

Gulf Coast and Maya stylistic elements at the ceremonial center may also indicate cultural importations. The vivid murals at the nearby site of Cacaxtla support a theme of ethnic conflict involving individuals displaying Maya physical and iconographic traits (McCafferty and McCafferty 1994; McVicker 1985; Quirarte 1983), and the site was identified as a stronghold of the Olmeca-Xicallanca in colonial accounts (Abascal et al. 1976; Muñoz Camargo 1948). At Cholula, an elaborate burial from a platform on the south side of the Great Pyramid contained an adult male with distinctively Maya-style tabular oblique cranial deformation and teeth inlaid with greenstone and pyrite that Sergio Suárez C. (1985; McCafferty 1992a) interprets as a Maya merchant/priest. Additionally, early polychrome pottery from Cholula features close similarities to ceramics from Isla de Sacrificios, Veracruz (McCafferty 1996b).

All of this evidence suggests intriguing possibilities as to cultural changes that may have taken place in Cholula following the end of the Classic period. Extracting history from myth is a delicate balancing act, and the legendary Olmeca-Xicallanca are a particularly ephemeral group to identify (Chadwick 1966; Davies 1977; Jiménez Moreno 1942; Olivera and Reyes 1969). The name suggests an origin in the southern Gulf Coast, around the port-of-trade known as Xicalango, located near the mouth of the Coatzalcoalcos River. Thus they may have been related to the Chontal and/or Putún Maya, and were associated with long-distance coastal traders (Webb 1973). I suggest that the Olmeca-Xicallanca were the culture brokers who transformed Classic canons into the international style of the Postclassic, and Cholula was the crucible in which the metamorphosis transpired.

THE PATIO OF THE CARVED SKULLS

The *Historia tolteca-chichimeca* (1976) depicts the arrival of Nahua Tolteca-Chichimeca in Cholula in the Early Postclassic period, ca. 1200 C.E. The Tolteca-Chichimeca encountered the Olmeca-Xicallanca at Tollan Cholollan Tlachihualtepetl, "the Great City of Cholula and the Man-Made Mountain." In a scene depicting the Great Pyramid (*Historia tolteca-chichimeca* 1976: fol. 7v) (Figure 11.7), the two lords of the Tolteca-Chichimeca meet one of the two high-

priests of the Olmeca-Xicallanca, the Aquiach Amapane, at his palace on a platform of the Great Pyramid. Based on the orientation of the spring flowing from
beneath the pyramid, it can be inferred that the palace is on the northeast corner
of the mound (McCafferty 1996a).

Eduardo Noguera (1937) excavated a palace on the northeast corner of the
Great Pyramid in the 1930s, and among other things he discovered the Altar of the
Carved Skulls, a miniature pyramid altar that is nearly identical to the Altar Mexica
from the south side of the Great Pyramid. The Altar of the Carved Skulls contained the skeletal remains of two adults, a male and a female, with exotic grave
goods including Cocoyotla Black-on-Natural vessels similar to those from the
Altar Mexica to further support their contemporaneity. The altar was located in a
courtyard, with staircases to raised platforms on at least two sides (Figure 11.8).
Interestingly, while the courtyard was oriented at 24° north of west, consistent
with the Cholula ceremonial zone, the Altar itself was oriented at 16°, more typical
of Teotihuacan's and Tula's alignment.

In 1994, Sergio Suárez C. directed small-scale excavations at the patio surrounding the Altar of the Carved Skulls during consolidation of the platform
(McCafferty 1996b: 310–312; McCafferty and Suárez C. 1995). Six stages of construction were identified, including an earlier altar that was partially demolished
when the later patio was built. The patio seems to have been just one phase of a

Fig. 11.7. Great Pyramid Tlachihualtepetl, showing location of the palace of Aquiach
Amapane (*Historia tolteca-chichimeca* 1976: folio 7v).

long sequence of palace construction on the platform, where both earlier and later structures are identifiable from exposed floor surfaces. This sequence suggests continuous occupation of a prominent and undoubtedly prestigious location on the side of the Great Pyramid, but also a succession of change. Judging from the occupants of the Altar of the Carved Skulls, the altars may have been ancestral shrines for lineage founders. If so, then the partial demolition of Altar 2 when the courtyard was remodelled could indicate a dynastic change. Because the "new" altar was then built to a distinctive orientation, it may again suggest claims on the Teotihuacan legacy.

The material evidence from the Patio of the Carved Skulls excavation reveals a surprising combination of Classic and Postclassic elements. The two most important serving wares present are Tepontla Burnished Gray Brown, the major type found in Classic contexts such as the Transito site, and Cocoyotla Black-on-Natural, the bichrome sometimes referred to as Aztec I Black-on-Orange. Also

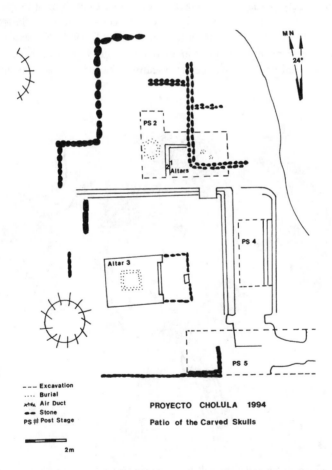

Fig. 11.8. Plan of Patio of the Carved Skulls excavation.

present were flat-bottomed bowls with stamp-impressed designs (*fondos sellados*), that also continue into the Early Postclassic period. The predominant utilitarian ware was the Classic period Acozoc Tan Orange, but significant amounts of Postclassic Momoxpan Orange and San Andrés Red were also present. The co-occurence of Classic and Early Postclassic diagnostics associated with all six of the construction stages argues for a gradual transition between Classic and Postclassic populations, and not a dramatic cultural break caused by site abandonment.

Other aspects of the material culture provide additional information on the cultural processes of the transition. Import pottery, though rare in the small samples recovered, indicated that contact with the Gulf Coast may have been more significant than with the Basin of Mexico—only a single sherd of Mazapan Red-on-Buff was recovered. Figurines are flattened and mold-made, and generally represent females. One fragment of a figurine headdress features a floral band in a pattern very similar to the figurines discovered at Xochitecatl near Cacaxtla (Serra Puche 1996; Spranz 1982). Green obsidian is almost absent from the Patio of the Carved Skulls (Edelstein 1995), in marked contrast to the pattern at the Transito site, and the predominant gray and black obsidians probably come from sources in the Orizaba area between Puebla and the Gulf Coast.

Archaeological evidence from the Patio of the Carved Skulls supports a reorientation of foreign interaction toward the Gulf Coast, even as symbolic statements via architectural orientation proclaimed affiliation with Teotihuacan. This pattern parallels the "public proclamations" of the architectural program of Stage 2 of the Great Pyramid, with stylistic elements associated with the Gulf Coast and only later, in Stage 3A, a return to Teotihuacan-style *talud-tablero* façades. It also suggests a gradual integration of new elements with the established canons of the Classic period. It must be pointed out, however, that this was a very small-scale investigation, and these interpretations will remain tentative until additional research can take place.[4]

Origins of the Mixteca-Puebla Tradition at Cholula

Noguera (1954: 219–224) noted that polychrome pottery was fairly common on the surface of the Great Pyramid, but was absent from its interior. Only a single sherd of Cholula polychrome was found at the Patio of the Carved Skulls, but it was prominent in other parts of the northeast platform. The origin of the polychrome ceramic tradition has been a source of confusion in cultural-historical reconstructions of Postclassic Cholula (McCafferty 1994; Nicholson 1982; Nicholson and Quiñones Keber 1994; Smith and Heath-Smith 1980). Noguera (1954) distinguished three Postclassic phases based on distinct polychrome assemblages. Müller (1978) viewed all polychromes as occurring in the Late Postclassic Cholulteca III phase, beginning in 1325 C.E. As a result, contexts with polychrome were dated as *late*, and thus few Early Postclassic assemblages were recognized, leading to the conclusion that Cholula was depopulated until the Late Postclassic (Dumond and Müller 1972; Müller 1978).

Several recent studies have challenged Müller's sequence for the origins of Cholula polychrome. Primary depositional contexts from the Universidad de las

Américas identified assemblages with very different concentrations of polychrome types, suggesting that they did not all occur at the same time (Barrientos 1980; Lind 1994; McCafferty 1992b; Mountjoy and Peterson 1973). Suárez C. (1994) excavated a well with polychrome and Black-on-Natural pottery dating to 900–1000 C.E., based on two radiocarbon dates. Based on a seriation of domestic contexts from the UA–1 site, the Postclassic can now be divided into five phases, each with a distinctive ceramic complex (McCafferty 1992b, 1994, 1996b).

As a result of this research, we can now suggest that polychrome pottery was being produced at least by 900 C.E. (and therefore the Patio of the Carved Skulls predates this development). These early polychromes correspond to an incipient form of what would become the Mixteca-Puebla stylistic tradition (Figure 11.9). Based on the cultural mix in Cholula at this time, it can be inferred that the Mixteca-Puebla style was a product of the combination of Gulf Coast and Oaxacan elements with canons from Classic Cholula. The Mixteca-Puebla tradition became the "international" style of the Postclassic (Robertson 1970), the iconographic vocabulary of elite communication and religious representation (Nicholson 1960 and 1982; Nicholson and Quiñones Keber 1994).

LATE POSTCLASSIC CHOLULA

With the arrival of the Tolteca-Chichimeca groups ca. 1200 C.E., the Great Pyramid of Cholula lost its primacy as the focus of Cholula's religious administration. A new ceremonial center was built in what is now the plaza of San Pedro Cholula, with the major pyramid dedicated to Quetzalcoatl (*Historia tolteca-chichimeca* 1976; Marquina 1970; Rojas 1927). The Great Pyramid retained some importance, as mentioned above in relation to mountain worship, and also as a shrine to a rain deity, Chiconauquiahuitl (9 Rain) (Rojas 1927).

There is some evidence that the abandonment of the Great Pyramid was not a peaceful transition. The sculptures of the final phase of the Patio of the Altars were thrown down, shattered, and then scattered (Acosta 1970b). An Early Postclassic house at UA–1 was burned, and over 100 projectile points were discovered in the small area excavated (McCafferty 1992b), suggesting possible warfare. No finished façade has ever been found for the final stage of the Great Pyramid, suggesting that it was either never completed, or else it may have been stripped off for later construction purposes (McCafferty 1996a). If the stripping

Phase	Dates	Complex
Late Cholollan	1400–1520 C.E.	UA-79 Feature 10
Early Cholollan	1200–1400 C.E.	UA-70 midden
Late Tlachihualtepetl	1050–1200 C.E.	UA-1 Structure 1
Middle Tlachihualtepetl	900–1050 C.E.	San Pedro well
Early Tlachihualtepetl	700–900 C.E.	Patio of Carved Skulls

Table 11.1. Postclassic Chronology and Ceramic Complexes.

Fig. 11.9. Early Postclassic polychrome with portrait of figure in feathered headdress (Ocotlan Red Rim subtype Cristina Matte, UA–1 #10927).

of a captive was an act of humiliation and a pan-Mesoamerican indication of defeat (McCafferty and McCafferty 1994), could the stripping of a pyramid be evidence that it too was in disgrace? Leonardo López Luján (1998) notes that the pyramid of Tlatelolco was kept in a state of filth and disuse after its city's defeat by the Tenochca; perhaps a similar concept was at work at the Great Pyramid. Following the indigenous description of a pyramid as a *cue* (Diáz del Castillo 1963: 19), derived from *cueitl* ("skirt"), perhaps removing the dressed-stone façade was the metaphoric equivalent of "undressing" the pyramid.

Late Postclassic Cholula was the center for the cult of Quetzalcoatl, and ethnohistoric accounts provide abundant evidence for its religious significance (Durán 1971; Rojas 1927; Sahagún 1950–1982, book 1; Torquemada 1975–1983; see also Nicholson, chaper 4 of this volume). Bernal Diáz de Castillo (1963: 202) noted that the Pyramid of Quetzalcoatl was taller than the Templo Mayor of Tenochtitlan. Nobles from throughout central Mexico came to Cholula for political legitimation (Rojas 1927), while the Tenochca lords went to great lengths to smuggle nobles from Cholula into their own coronation ceremonies (Durán 1994). Peregrinations to the Temple of Quetzalcoatl were so extensive that Spanish chroniclers described Cholula as the Rome or Mecca of New Spain (Rojas 1927; Sahagún 1950–1982, Introductory Volume). In the 1581 *Descripción de Cholula*, Gabriel de Rojas (1927) commented that many of the houses in the city were empty, reserved for the periodic visits of foreign nobles during religious festivals. As a center of priestly knowledge, Cholula probably housed an extensive library of genealogical codices as well as religious texts such as the *Codex Borgia* (Nicholson 1966).

Ethnohistorical accounts also describe the administrative organization of the pre-Hispanic city (Rojas 1927; summarized in Carrasco 1971; Lind 1990). Dual high priests, the Aquiach and the Tlalchiach, administered the the religious affairs of the state, especially those associated with the temple of Quetzalcoatl. Civic matters were controlled by a council of elders, probably lineage heads representing different *calpultin* (lineage-based neighborhoods). Additional political organizations probably also existed, resulting in factional competition. Díaz del Castillo captured a hint of this complexity when he wrote that, following the Cholula massacre at the hand of Cortés and his followers, "certain *Caciques* and *papas* of Cholula [came forth] who belonged to other districts and claimed to have taken no part in the plot—for it is a large city and they were a separate party or faction" (1963: 200). It is very possible that these other factions were descendants of the Olmeca-Xicallanca, living in what is now San Andrés Cholula (Olivera and Reyes 1969).

In addition to the religious importance of Cholula, it was also a major commercial center. *Pochteca* merchants affiliated with the cult of Quetzalcoatl-Yacatecuhtli traveled throughout Mesoamerica acquiring precious objects to exchange in the Cholula marketplace (Durán 1971; Pineda 1970), and in the process they distributed objects of the Mixteca-Puebla style. Bernardino de Sahagún (1950–1982, book 9) recorded detailed information on the organization of the *pochteca* from a perspective of Aztec state-control, but the organization of merchants at Cholula seems to have been more open to individual initiative. Long-distance entrepeneurs journeyed for years at a time to acquire wealth that they then used to finance religious ceremonies dedicated to Quetzalcoatl.

Postclassic Cholula was organized around dual principles of religion and trade. Although it did take part in the "flowery wars" in opposition to the Triple Alliance (Durán 1994), militarism never seems to have been an important facet of its political strategy. Instead, Cholula maintained prestige based on its religious preeminence relating to Quetzalcoatl, its international economy funded by the *pochteca* using Mixteca-Puebla iconography as currency, and its historical legacy dating back to the age of the giants.

<h2 style="text-align:center">CONCLUSION</h2>

The model of Postclassic Cholula and its political economy is quite different from that of other pre-Columbian states. Cholula was organized around a religious administration of the Temple of Quetzalcoatl, closely linked to long-distance trade. It seems to have developed a unique strategy for establishing a far-flung empire based around religion, using the material media of ceramics, textiles, featherwork, and metalwork, all symbolically charged with Mixteca-Puebla iconography for use in elite communication.

In this respect, Cholula may have been distinct from the better-known political models of the Aztec or Maya. Militarism was never an important theme in the iconography of Cholula. In fact, a better comparison might be Polanyi's model of a port-of-trade (Berdan 1978; Chapman 1957), a neutral territory on the fringe of more "powerful" states where merchants from even warring kingdoms could interact in safety. The merchants, however, were protected under the evangelical umbrella of the cult of Quetzalcoatl, and their stock in trade, exotic objects crafted in the Mixteca-Puebla style, served to spread that cult as they created a prestige economy of elite goods, what Mary Helms (1995) calls the "kingly ideal." An ethnographic analogue to this process may be found in Islamic Africa, where the Hausa created a commercial "diaspora" that included religious icons along with other items (Curtin 1984).

This model may have deep historical roots, dating back into the Classic period, but it crystallized in the Epiclassic. With the arrival of the Olmeca-Xicallanca, Cholula became the highland hub of an international trading empire, probably connected with the other great port-of-trade described in colonial sources, Xicalango. Through the combination of trade and religion, Cholula was able to not only survive the sociopolitical upheavals of the Classic-period collapse, but, through dynamic transformation, reinvent itself as a new entity based on cultural diversity, supernatural authority, and international trade.

How does this model relate to the Teotihuacan canon of statecraft? Archaeological evidence from Teotihuacan clearly indicates that it was created around cosmological principles, establishing itself in the Early Classic period as an axis mundi revolving around the Pyramids of the Sun and the Moon. Far-flung pockets of Teotihuacan-style iconography indicate that the ideas, if not the actual Teotihuacanos, were internationally recognized sources of legitimacy (Fash and Fash, chapter 14 of this volume), while distribution of Teotihuacan-controlled consumer goods such as green obsidian and Thin Orange pottery suggests a commercial network that may have been comparable to the Postclassic *pochteca*. In sum, Teotihuacan seems to have relied on religion and trade as the machinery of empire. Cholula may therefore provide a model, with ethnohistoric detail, for understanding the inner workings of Classic Teotihuacan.

The end of Teotihuacan as a ceremonial center is dramatically documented by the burning and destruction along the Avenue of the Dead (Millon 1988), ushering in what has been called the "Classic collapse." In contrast to previous models that suggested that Cholula itself was similarly diminished (e.g., Dumond and Müller 1972; Mountjoy 1987), recent evidence indicates that the Cholula ceremonial precinct flourished during the Epiclassic period, with new construction at the Great Pyramid and the Patio of the Altars. Furthermore, in contrast to the architectural elements that marked an ideology of distinction from Teotihuacan in the Classic period, the rulers of Cholula overtly emphasized Teotihuacan forms in the Epiclassic as a symbolic proclamation that Cholula had inherited the symbolic authority of its neighbor. Cholula emerged from the Classic period as the primary religious center of central Mexico, the Rome of Anahuac. Through mythic memory of the *quinametinime*, Cholultecas reinforced their historical legacy while asserting dominance over the "giants." Nobility from throughout Mesoamerica sought legitimation from Cholula, either by actually visiting the shrine of Quetzalcoatl on pilgrimage to make offerings and thereby receive recognition of their authority, or symbolically by consuming and displaying objects using the Mixteca-Puebla iconographic vocabulary.

The cultural longevity of Cholula was not based on static norms, however. At least by the Postclassic period, it was a multicultural society that celebrated its international atmosphere. Tollan Chololian Tlachihualtepetl was a dynamic city that based its legacy on historical roots from the Classic period, but affirmed its legitimacy through cosmological principles manifested in the Great Pyramid and embodied in Quetzalcoatl. As such, Cholula offers important insights into the possible structure of earlier empires, such as Teotihuacan.

NOTES

1. As Davíd Carrasco points out, "crossroads" can signify more than simply an intersection of exchange networks, but also include the cultural interactions that occur at a market center. Thus Cholula would have been a hub of diversity where innovative cultural combinations would have developed.

2. The so-called Altar Mexica contained Cocoyotla Black-on-Natural vessels that were identified as similar to Aztec I Black-on-Orange ceramics, and thus the feature acquired the "Mexica" misnomer, even though it dates to approximately five hundred years before the Late Postclassic Aztec culture.

3. Iconography relating to Ehecatl-Quetzalcoatl also appears at this time on stamp-impressed grater bowls (McCafferty, Spencer, and Suárez Cruz 1998).

4. Additional investigations at the Patio of the Carved Skulls and associated areas of the platform were planned for 1999. These excavations will concentrate on exploring the transition between the Epiclassic and Early Postclassic, particularly through the development of Mixteca-Puebla–style polychrome pottery.

REFERENCES

Abascal, Rafael, Patricio Davila, Peter J. Schmidt, and Diana de Davila
1976. "La arqueologia de sur-oeste de Tlaxcala, primera parte." In *Communicaciones, Proyecto Puebla/Tlaxcala, Supplemento 2*. Puebla, Mexico: Fundación Alemana para la Investigación Científica.

Acosta, Jorge R.
1970a. "Sección 3." In I. Marquina, ed., *Proyecto Cholula*. Mexico: INAH, Serie Investigaciones 19, pp. 47–56.
1970b. "El Altar 2." In I. Marquina, ed., *Proyecto Cholula*. Mexico: INAH, Serie Investigaciones 19, pp. 103–110.
1970c. "El Altar 1." In I. Marquina, ed., *Proyecto Cholula*. Mexico: INAH, Serie Investigaciones 19, pp. 93–102.
1970d. "Patio Sureste." In I. Marquina, ed., *Proyecto Cholula*. Mexico: INAH, Serie Investigaciones 19, pp. 57–66.

Adams, Richard E. W.
1991. *Prehistoric Mesoamerica*. Norman: University of Oklahoma Press.

Barrientos, Catalina
1980. "Análisis de la cerámica del elemento 10 de UA–79." Unpublished tesis de licenciatura, Department of Anthropology, Universidad de las Américas, Cholula, Puebla, Mexico.

Berdan, Frances F.
1978. "Ports of Trade in Mesoamerica: A Reappraisal." In D. L. Browman, ed., *Cultural Continuity in Mesoamerica*. The Hague: Mouton, pp. 179-198.

Berlo, Janet Catherine
1983. "The Warrior and the Butterfly: Central Mexican Ideologies of Sacred Warfare and

Teotihuacan Iconography." In J. C. Berlo, ed., *Text and Image in Pre-Columbian Art*. Oxford: BAR International Series 180, pp. 79–118.

1993. "Icons and Ideologies at Teotihuacan: The Great Goddess Reconsidered." In J. C. Berlo, ed., *Art, Ideology, and the City of Teotihuacan*. Washington, DC: Dumbarton Oaks, pp. 129–168.

Bonfil Batalla, Guillermo
1973. *Cholula: La ciudad sagrada en la era industrial*. Mexico: UNAM-IIH.

Brueggeman, Juergen, and René Ortega Guevara
1989. "El Proyecto Tajín." *Arqueología* 5: 153–174.

Brumfiel, Elizabeth M.
1996. "Figurines and the Aztec State: Testing the Effectiveness of Ideological Domination." In R. P. Wright, ed., *Gender and Archaeology*. Philadelphia: University of Pennsylvania Press, pp. 143–166.

Carrasco, Davíd
1992. *Quetzalcoatl and the Irony of Empire: Myths and Prophecies of the Aztec Tradition*. 2nd editon. Chicago: University of Chicago Press.

Carrasco, Pedro
1971. "Los barrios antiguos de Cholula." *Estudios y documentos de la región de Puebla-Tlaxcala*. Puebla, Mexico: Instituto Poblano de Antropología e Historia, vol. III, pp. 9–87.

Chadwick, Robert E. L.
1966. "The 'Olmeca-Xicallanca' of Teotihuacan: A Preliminary Study." *Notas Meso-americanas* 7–8: 1–24.

Chapman, Anne C.
1957. "Port of Trade Enclaves in Aztec and Maya Civilizations." In K. Polanyi, C. Arensberg, and H. W. Pearson, eds., *Trade and Market in the Early Empires*. New York: The Free Press, pp. 114–153.

Cortés, Hernán
1986. *Letters from Mexico*. Translated and edited by A. Pagden. New Haven, CT: Yale University Press. Originally written in 1520–1526.

Cowgill, George
1993. "Distinguished Lecture in Archaeology: Beyond Criticizing New Archaeology." *American Anthropologist* 95: 551–573.

Curtin, Phillip D.
1984. *Cross-Cultural Trade in World Prehistory*. Cambridge: Cambridge University Press.

Davies, Nigel
1977. *The Toltecs, Until the Fall of Tula*. Norman: University of Oklahoma Press.

Diáz del Castillo, Bernal
1963. *The Conquest of New Spain*. Translated by J. M. Cohen. Harmondsworth, UK: Penguin Books. Originally written in 1580.

Dumond, Don, and Florencia Müller
1972. "Classic to Post-Classic in Highland Central Mexico." *Science* 175: 1208–1215.

Durán, Diego
1971. *The Book of the Gods and Rites and the Ancient Calendar*. Translated by F. Horcasitas and D. Heyden. Norman: University of Oklahoma Press. Originally written in 1576–1579.

1994. *The History of the Indies of New Spain*. Translated, annotated, and with introduction by D. Heyden. Norman: University of Oklahoma Press.

Edelstein, Ruth
1995. "Obsidian Exploitation and Political Economic Dynamics on the Classic Period Through Colonial Era Central Plateau: An Analysis of a Lithic Collection from Cholula, Puebla, Mexico." Unpublished master's thesis, Department of Anthropology, McMaster University, Hamilton, Ontario, Canada.

Fash, William L.
1991. *Scribes, Warriors, and Kings: The City of Copán and the Ancient Maya*. New York: Thames and Hudson.

Furst, Jill Leslie
1978. *Codex Vindobonensis Mexicanus I: A Commentary*. Albany: SUNY, Institute for Mesoamerican Studies, Publication 4.

García Cook, Angel
1981. "The Historical Importance of Tlaxcala in the Cultural Development of the Central Highlands." In V. R. Bricker and J. A. Sabloff, eds., *Handbook of Middle American Indians, Supplement 1: Archaeology*. Austin: University of Texas Press, pp. 244–276.

García Cook, Angel, Martha Arias M. G., and Rafael Abascal M.
1976. "Una tumba de la fase Tenanyecac en Tlaxcala, México." In *Comunicaciones, Proyecto Puebla-Tlaxcala, Suplemento III*. Puebla, Mexico: Fundación Alemana para la Investigación Científica.

García Cook, Angel, and Beatriz Leonor Merino Carrión
1990. "El 'Epiclásico' en la región poblano-tlaxcalteca." In F. Sodi Miranda, ed., *Mesoamerica y norte de México: Siglo IX–XII*. Mexico: Museo Nacional de Antropología, INAH, pp. 257–280.

Gillespie, Susan D.
1989. *The Aztec Kings: The Construction of Rulership in Mexica History*. Tucson: University of Arizona Press.

Helms, Mary
1995. *Craft and the Kingly Ideal: Art, Trade, and Power*. Austin: University of Texas Press.

Heyden, Doris
1981. "Caves, Gods, and Myths: World-View and Planning in Teotihuacan." In E. P. Benson, ed., *Mesoamerican Sites and World Views*. Washington, DC: Dumbarton Oaks, pp. 1–40.

Historia tolteca-chichimeca
1976. Edited and translated by P. Kirchhoff, L. Odena G., and L. Reyes G. Mexico: INAH. Originally written between 1547–1560.

Ixtlilxóchitl, Fernando de Alva
1975–1977. *Obras historicas*. 2 vols. Edited and with an introduction by E. O'Gorman. Mexico: INAM-IIH. Originally written in 1625.

Jiménez Moreno, Wigberto
1942. "El enigma de los olmecas." *Cuadernos Americanos* 1, no. 5: 113–145.

Lind, Michael
1990. "The Great City Square: Government in Ancient Cholula." Paper presented at the Mesoamerican Network Meeting, Riverside, CA.

1994. "Cholula and Mixteca Polychromes: Two Mixteca-Puebla Regional Sub-Styles." In H. B. Nicholson and E. Quiñones Keber, eds., *Mixteca-Puebla: Discoveries and Research in Mesoamerican Art and Archaeology*. Culver City, CA: Labyrinthos Press, pp. 79–100.

1995. "The Obverse of the Codex of Cholula: Defining the Settlement System in the Kingdom of Cholula." Paper presented at the 60th Annual Meeting of the Society for American Archaeology, Minneapolis, MN.

Lockhart, James
1992. *The Nahuas After the Conquest: A Social and Cultural History of the Indians of Central Mexico, Sixteenth Through Eighteenth Centuries*. Stanford, CA: Stanford University Press.

López Alonso, Sergio, Zaid Lagunas Rodríguez, and Carlos Serrano Sánchez
1976. *Enterramientos humanos de la Zona Arqueológica de Cholula, Puebla*. Mexico: INAH/SEP, Colección Científica 44.

López Austin, Alfredo, Leonardo López Luján, and Saburo Sugiyama
1991. "The Temple of Quetzalcoatl at Teotihuacan: Its Possible Ideological Significance." *Ancient Mesoamerica* 2, no. 1: 93–106.

López Luján, Leonardo
1998. "Recreating the Cosmos: Seventeen Aztec Dedication Caches." In S. Mock, ed., *The Sowing and the Dawning: Termination, Dedication, and Transformation in the Archaeological and Ethnographic Record of Mesoamerica*. Albuquerque: University of New Mexico Press, pp. 176-187.

Margain, Carlos R.
1971. "Pre-Columbian Architecture of Central Mexico. In R. A. Wauchope, gen. ed.; G. F. Ekholm and I. Bernal, vol. eds., *Handbook of Middle American Indians*, Volume 10, Part I: *Archaeology of Northern Mesoamerica*. Austin: University of Texas Press, pp. 45–91.

Marquina, Ignacio
1951. *Arquitectura prehispánica*. Mexico: INAH/SEP, Memorias, 1.
1970. "Pirámide de Cholula." In I. Marquina, ed., *Proyecto, Cholula*. Mexico: INAH, Serie Investigaciones 19, pp. 31–46.
1971. "La pintura en Cholula." *Artes de Mexico*, no. 140.

Matos Moctezuma, Eduardo, and Pablo López V.
1967. "El Edificio No. 1 de Cholula." In M. Messmacher, ed., *Cholula, Reporte Preliminar*. Mexico: Editorial Nueva Antropología, pp. 39–43.

McCafferty, Geoffrey G.
1992a. "Book review of *Un entierro del clásico superior en Cholula, Puebla*, by Sergio Suárez C., and *Últimos descubrimientos de entierros postclásicos en Cholula, Puebla*, by Sergio Suárez C." *American Antiquity* 57, no. 2: 378–379.
1992b. "The Material Culture of Postclassic Cholula, Mexico: Contextual Analysis of the UA–1 Domestic Compounds." Unpublished Ph.D. dissertation, Department of Anthropology, State University of New York at Binghamton.
1994. "The Mixteca-Puebla Stylistic Tradition at Early Postclassic Cholula. In H. B. Nicholson and E. Quiñones Keber, eds. *Mixteca-Puebla: Discoveries and Research in Mesoamerican Art and Archaeology*. Culver City, CA: Labyrinthos Press, pp. 53–78.
1996a. "Reinterpreting the Great Pyramid of Cholula, Mexico." *Ancient Mesoamerica* 7, no. 1: 1–17.
1996b. "The Ceramics and Chronology of Cholula, Mexico." *Ancient Mesoamerica* 7, no. 2: 299–323.

n.d. "Mountain of Heaven, Mountain of Earth: The Great Pyramid of Cholula as Sacred Landscape." In R. Koontz, K. Reese-Taylor, and A. Headrick, eds., *Landscape and Power in Ancient Mesoamerica*. Boulder, CO: Westview Press, in press.

McCafferty, Geoffrey G., Jane Spencer, and Sergio Suárez Cruz
1998. "Stamp-Bottom Bowls and the Origins of the Mixteca-Puebla Stylistic Tradition at Epiclassic Cholula, Puebla, Mexico." Paper presented at the 63rd Annual Meeting of the Society for American Archaeology, Seattle, WA.

McCafferty, Geoffrey G., and Sergio Suárez Cruz
1994. "Cholula and Teotihuacan in the Early Classic Period: Recent Investigations at the Transito Site (R106)." Paper presented at the 59th Annual Meeting of the Society for American Archaeology, Anaheim, CA.
1995. The Classic/Postclassic Transition at Cholula: Recent Investigations at the Great Pyramid." Paper presented at the 60th Annual Meeting of the Society for American Archaeology, Minneapolis, MN.

McCafferty, Sharisse D., and Geoffrey G. McCafferty
1994. "The Conquered Women of Cacaxtla: Gender Identity or Gender Ideology?" *Ancient Mesoamerica* 5, no. 2: 159–172.

McVicker, Donald
1985. "The 'Mayanized' Mexicans." *American Antiquity* 50, no. 1: 82–101.

Messmacher, Miguel
1967. "Los patrones de asentamiento y la arquitectura en Cholula." In M. Messmacher, ed., *Cholula, Reporte Preliminar*. Mexico: Editorial Nueva Antropología, pp. 6–17.

Miller, Mary Ellen
1996. *The Art of Mesoamerica*. 2nd ed. New York: Thames and Hudson.

Millon, René
1988. "The Last Years of Teotihuacan Dominance." In N. Yoffee and G. L. Cowgill, eds., *The Collapse of Ancient States and Civilizations*. Tucson: University of Arizona Press, pp. 102–164.

Mountjoy, Joseph
1987. "The Collapse of the Classic at Cholula as Seen from Cerro Zapotecas." *Notas Mesoamericanas* 10: 119–151.

Mountjoy, Joseph, and David A. Peterson
1973. *Man and Land in Prehispanic Cholula*. Nashville, TN: Vanderbilt University Publications in Anthropology no. 4.

Müller, Florencia
1970. "La cerámica de Cholula." In I. Marquina, ed., *Proyecto Cholula*. Mexico: INAH, Serie Investigaciones 19, pp.129–142.
1972. "Estudio iconográfico del Mural de los Bebedores, Cholula, Puebla." In J. Litvak King and N. Castillo Tejero, eds., *Religión en Mesoámerica*. Mexico: SMA, pp. 141–146.
1978. *La alfarería de Cholula*. Mexico: INAH, Serie Arqueología.

Muñoz Camargo, Diego
1948. *Historia de Tlaxcala*. Mexico: Ateneo Nacional de Ciencias y Artes de México.

Nagao, Debra
1989. "Public Proclamation in the Art of Cacaxtla and Xochicalco." In R. A. Diehl and J. C. Berlo, eds., *Mesoamerica After the Decline of Teotihuacan, A.D. 700–900*. Washington, DC: Dumbarton Oaks, pp. 83–104.

Nicholson, H. B.
1960. "The Mixteca-Puebla Concept in Mesoamerican Archaeology: A Re-Examination."
In A. F. C. Wallace, ed., *Men and Cultures: Selected Papers from the Fifth International
Congress of Anthropological and Ethnological Sciences, Philadelphia, September 1–9,
1956*. Philadelphia: University of Pennsylvania Press, pp. 612–617.
1966. "The Problem of the Provenience of the Members of the 'Codex Borgia Group': A
Summary." In A. Pompa y Pompa, ed., *Summa antropológica en homenaje a Roberto
J. Weitlaner*. Mexico: INAH, pp. 145–158.
1982. "The Mixteca-Puebla Concept Re-Visited." In E. H. Boone, ed., *The Art and Iconography of Late Post-Classic Central Mexico*. Washington, DC: Dumbarton Oaks,
pp. 227–254.

Nicholson, H. B., and Eloise Quiñones Keber
1994. "Introduction." In H. B. Nicholson and E. Quiñones Keber, eds., *Mixteca-Puebla:
Discoveries and Research in Mesoamerican Art and Archaeology*. Culver City, CA:
Labyrinthos Press, pp. vii–xv.

Noguera, Eduardo
1937. *El altar de los cráneos esculpidos de Cholula*. Mexico: Talleres Gráficos de la
Nación.
1954. *La cerámica arqueológica de Cholula*. Mexico: Editorial Guaranía.

Olivera de V., Mercedes
1970. "La importancia religiosa de Cholula." In I. Marquina, ed., *Proyecto Cholula*. Mexico:
INAH, Serie Investigaciones 19, pp. 211–242.

Olivera de V., Mercedes, and Cayetano Reyes
1969. "Los choloques y los cholultecas: Apuntes sobre las relaciones étnicas en Cholula
hasta el siglo XVI." *Anales del INAH* (época 7a) 1: 247–274.

Pineda, Juan de
1970. "Carta al rey sobre la ciudad de Cholula en 1593" (edited by Pedro Carrasco).
Tlalocan 6: 176–192.

Quirarte, Jacinto
1983. "Outside Influence at Cacaxtla." In A. G. Miller, ed., *Highland-Lowland Interaction
in Mesoamerica: Interdisciplinary Approaches*. Washington, DC: Dumbarton Oaks,
pp. 201–221.

Ringle, William M., Tomás Gallareta Negrón, and George J. Bey III
1998. "The Return of Quetzalcoatl: Evidence for the Spread of a World Religion During
the Epiclassic Period." *Ancient Mesoamerica* 9: 183–232.

Robertson, Donald
1970. "The Tulum Murals: The International Style of the Late Postclassic." In *Verhandlungen
des XXXVIII Internationalen Amerikanistenkongresses. Stuttgart-München, 12. bis 18.
August 1968*. Munich: Kommissionsverlag K. Renner, vol. II, pp. 77–88.

Rojas, Gabriel de
1927. "Descripción de Cholula." *Revista Mexicana de Estudios Históricos* 1, no. 6: 158–
170. Originally written in 1581.

Sahagún, Fray Bernadino de
1950–1982. *Florentine Codex: General History of the Things of New Spain*. 13 vols.
Edited and translated by A. J. O. Anderson and C. E. Dibble. Santa Fe, NM: The
School of American Research/University of Utah. Originally written between 1547–
1585.

Sanders, William T.
1989. "The Epiclassic as a Stage in Mesoamerican Prehistory: An Evaluation. In Richard A. Diehl and Janet Catherine Berlo, eds., *Mesoamerica After the Decline of Teotihuacan, A.D. 700–900*. Washington, DC: Dumbarton Oaks, pp. 211–218.

Santley, Robert
1983. "Obsidian Trade and Teotihuacan Influence in Mesoamerica. In A. G. Miller, ed., *Highland-Lowland Interaction in Mesoamerica: Interdisciplinary Approaches*. Washington, DC: Dumbarton Oaks, pp. 69–124.

Serra Puche, Mari Carmen
1996. "Feminine Places." Paper presented at the "Re-Discovering Gender in the Americas" Conference, Dumbarton Oaks, Washington, DC.

Serrano S., Carlos
1993. "Funerary Practices and Human Sacrifice in Teotihuacan Burials." In K. Berrin and E. Pasztory, eds., *Teotihuacan: Art from the City of the Gods*. New York: Thames and Hudson, pp. 108–115.

Simons, Bente Bittman
1968. *Los Mapas de Cuauhtinchan y la Historia tolteca-chichimeca*. Mexico: INAH, Serie Investigaciones 15.

Smith, Michael E., and Cynthia M. Heath-Smith
1980. "Waves of Influence in Postclassic Mesoamerica? A Critique of the Mixteca-Puebla Concept." *Anthropology* 4, no. 2: 15–50.

Spranz, Bodo
1982. "Archaeology and the Art of Mexican Picture Writing." In E. H. Boone, ed., *The Art and Iconography of Late Post-Classic Central Mexico*. Washington, DC: Dumbarton Oaks, pp. 159–174.

Suárez Cruz, Sergio
1985. *Un entierro del clásico superior en Cholula, Puebla*. Mexico: INAH Centro Regional de Puebla, Cuaderno de Trabajo 6.
1994. "Polícroma laca de Cholula." In H. B. Nicholson and E. Quiñones Keber, eds., *Mixteca-Puebla: Discoveries and Research in Mesoamerican Art and Archaeology*. Culver City, CA: Labyrinthos Press, pp. 45-51.

Suárez C., Sergio, and Silvia Martínez A.
1993. *Monografía de Cholula, Puebla*. Puebla, Mexico: H. Ayuntamiento Municipal Constitucional de San Pedro Cholula.

Tichy, Franz
1981. "Order and Relationship of Space and Time in Mesoamerica: Myth or Reality?" In E. P. Benson, ed., *Mesoamerican Sites and World-Views*. Washington, DC: Dumbarton Oaks, pp. 217–245.

Torquemada, Fray Juan de
1975–1983. *Monarquía indiana*. 7 vols. Edited by M. León-Portilla. Mexico: UNAM-IIH. Originally written in 1615.

Weaver, Muriel Porter
1993. *The Aztecs, Maya, and Their Predecessors: Archaeology of Mesoamerica*. 3rd edition. San Diego, CA: Academic Press.

Webb, Malcom C.
1973. "The Peten Maya Decline Viewed in the Perspective of State Formation." In T. P. Culbert, ed., *The Classic Maya Collapse*. Albuquerque, NM: The School of

American Research, pp. 367–404.

Wheatley, Paul
1971. *The Pivot of the Four Quarters: A Preliminary Enquiry into the Origins and Character of the Ancient Chinese City*. Chicago: Aldine.

PART FOUR

▼

CLASSIC TEOTIHUACAN
IN THE CONTEXT OF
MESOAMERICAN SCHOLARSHIP AND
INTELLECTUAL HISTORY

12

▼

VENERABLE PLACE OF BEGINNINGS

THE AZTEC UNDERSTANDING OF TEOTIHUACAN

ELIZABETH HILL BOONE

Teotihuacan, the city named by the Aztecs "the home of the gods," seeped early into the human imagination as an old, great, and sacred place. After the decline of the culture that created it and gave it life, Teotihuacan remained a vast, visible ruin, well-known to those peoples who came later. Unlike some other cities reduced to ruins, it was never "lost" or completely abandoned, which means that it was never "rediscovered," either by Mesoamericans or by explorers from Europe. It was reimagined, however, especially by the Aztecs. Teotihuacan's original people, long dead, were unknown to the Aztecs, just as they are still unknown to us. We hypothesize their social structure, we speculate about their political system, and we argue about what language they spoke, but we lack definitive answers. We are like the Aztecs in this respect, for we walk and explore the ruins, we excavate ceramic vessels and sculptures, and we try to conjure up the people who made them. We create stories of the Teotihuacan past.

The Aztecs told stories about Teotihuacan. They imagined the great ruined city in their own distinctive way, and they drew it materially and metaphorically into the heart of their ritual precinct in Tenochtitlan. It is their view of Teotihuacan that has shaped the way we see the city and its people.

In this essay, I share with you my understanding of the Aztec image of Teotihuacan, that venerable place of beginnings. A survey of the existing pictorial codices and the alphabetic chronicles yields only small and scattered pieces of what the Aztecs must have said about the city and how they pictured it, but it is enough to give us an idea of the larger view. The codices and chronicles also tell us something about the Acolhua city-state that came to occupy Teotihuacan in the Late Postclassic. Finally, we can assess the physical presence of Teotihuacan in the Aztec capital, manifest in buildings and artifacts uncovered at the Templo

371

Mayor. These lines of evidence can help us understand just how important Teotihuacan was to the Mexica Aztecs.

BIRTHPLACE OF THE FIFTH SUN

It begins with the beginning. For it was at Teotihuacan, according to Bernardino de Sahagún's noble informants and the author of the *Leyenda de los soles*, that the Fifth Sun was created. The author of the *Leyenda de los soles*, who was reading from a pictorial codex, tells us:

> The name of this sun is Naui Ollin (4 Movement). It is ours, it belongs to us who live today. This is its image, that which is here, because the Sun fell in the fire in the divine hearth [*teotexcalli*] of Teotihuacan (*Codex Chimalpoca* 1975: 121).

Sahagún mentions the creation of the sun at Teotihuacan in two passages: briefly at the beginning of this third book, "The Origin of the Gods," and later in Book 7 when he discusses the sun and the moon. Book 3 begins:

> How the gods had their beginning . . . cannot be known. This is plain: that there in Teotihuacan, they say, is the place; the time was when there still was darkness. There all the gods assembled and consulted among themselves who would bear upon his back the burden of rule, who would be the sun. . . . But when the sun came to appear, then all [the gods] died there. Through them the sun was made to revive. None remained who did not die. . . . And thus the ancient ones thought it (1959–1972, book 3: 1).

In Book 7 (4–8, 42–58), Sahagún gives a fuller version:

> It is told that when yet [all] was in darkness, when yet no sun had shone and no dawn had broken—it is said—the gods gathered themselves together and took counsel among themselves there at Teotihuacan. They spoke; they said among themselves: "Come hither, O gods! Who will carry the burden? Who will take it upon himself to be the sun, to bring the dawn?" (4).

The well-known story relates how two gods volunteered to be the sun and the moon: the fine and rich Tecuciztecatl and the poor, pustule-covered one, Nanauatzin. They did penance for four days. Sahagún says that "for these two, for each one singly, a hill was made. There they remained, performing penance for four nights. They are now called pyramids—the pyramid of the sun and the pyramid of the moon" (4–5). After the four days of penance, it was time for one to jump into the great fire that burned in the hearth that was called *teotexcalli* ("divine hearth"). Four times Tecuciztecatl tried and failed. Then Nanauatzin, in a single great leap, threw himself into the fire, where "his body crackled and sizzled" (6). Then Tecuciztecatl himself jumped in. There followed the eagle and the jaguar, who emerged respectively scorched and sooted. Nanahuatzin rose to become the sun, and Tecuciztecatl later became the moon. Because the sun stalled motionless in the heavens, all the gods who had gathered there then gave their own lives to revive the sun and set it in motion (7–8).

We are being told several things here by Father Sahagún. The first is that Teotihuacan is the place where the fifth and present age was begun, where the Fifth Sun was created by the sacrifice of the gods, initially the two (Nanauatzin and Tecuciztecatl) and then all the others. It was the place where the sun and moon were born as celestial bodies, and the place where the assembled gods died. It was also the place where the eagle and the jaguar (the future Aztec warriors) first risked their lives for the sake of the sun. There at Teotihuacan was also the divine hearth, the metaphoric center of the divine household.

The two great pyramids at Teotihuacan are named for us: *ytzacual tonatiuh* ("tower or hill of the sun") and *ytzacual metztli* ("tower or hill of the moon") (book 7: 45, 47). It has been imagined, although no sixteenth-century source indicates this, that the gods were thought to have gathered around the rim of the Ciudadela (perhaps on the fifteen shrines there) to watch the great fire burning in the divine hearth in its center.

Other documentary sources also name the great pyramids at Teotihuacan. The map of San Francisco Mazapan (Figure 12.1) is one of three related maps that record the sixteenth-century ownership of farmland in what had formerly been the main precinct of the ancient city.[1] Oriented with east at the top, the map shows the layout of the Classic-period ceremonial center as it was known in 1560 (Arreola 1922). Sixteenth-century roads and buildings are pictured and are named with Nahuatl glosses, as are the indigenous owners of the fields. In the lower left corner, the Pyramid of the Moon is shown as a five-stepped pyramid with a circular moon painted just above its summit. A Nahuatl gloss identifies it as *meztli ytzacual*; other glosses note that there are many caves in the immediate area (555). As George Kubler (1980: 48) observes, these caves approximate the location of the Quetzalpapalotl Palace with its underground structures. The Avenue of the Dead parallels the lower edge of the map, extending from the Moon complex past the Pyramid of the Sun and on past the Ciudadela to the right; a Nahuatl gloss labels it *micca otlica* (Road of the Dead). The Pyramid of the Sun is represented as a four- or five-stepped pyramid oriented "upside down" (with its base toward the top and its summit toward the avenue) just east of the avenue near the centerfold of the map; vegetation grows from its ruined mass. As the largest mound on the map, there can be no mistaking its identity, although the gloss next to it refers not to the pyramid but to the boundary of sixteenth-century fields.

The right side of the map is dominated by the large rectangle of the Ciudadela, the edges of the compound flanked by small mounds. In the middle of the Ciudadela, above the standing image of the then-current landowner, a smaller pyramid rises just where the Temple of the Feathered Serpent now stands. A European-style sun disk, complete with rays and frontal face, is painted just above it;[2] the adjacent Nahuatl gloss reads *tonali itlaltiloyan*, which José Arreola (1922: 555) translated as "place of burials in honor of the sun." Here, Rubén Cabrera Castro, Saburo Sugiyama, George Cowgill, and their teams found the spectacular mass graves of sacrificial victims, numbering some two hundred so far.[3] This gloss strongly suggests that the Aztecs knew about these or other similar graves. The Aztecs may even have thought them to be the graves of those ancient gods who died in honor of the sun at the beginning of the Fifth Age.

This map of the tiny indigenous community of San Francisco Mazapan, a barrio of San Juan Teotihuacan, still preserves in 1560 the sacred geography of the place where the Fifth Sun was born. The ancient mounds underlie and shape the agricultural plots that were later planted around and over them. The inhabitants of the area have retained memory of the Pyramids of the Sun and Moon and the Avenue of the Dead, even after the disruption of the Spanish Conquest; they seem aware, too, of the human sacrifices once offered and buried in the Ciudadela.

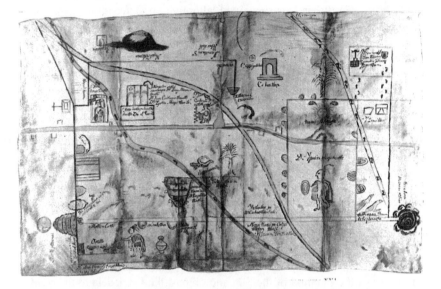

Fig. 12.1. Mazapan Map of Teotihuacan (after Arreola 1922: 555).

WHERE GOVERNMENT WAS CREATED AND FROM WHERE THE PEOPLE DISPERSED

Teotihuacan makes a second appearance in an entirely different Aztec legend, a legend that also speaks of the early period when the Aztecs were still wandering Chichimecs. Sahagún, in Book 10 (1959–1982: 189–197), tells of the origin of the Mexica:[4]

> In the distant past, which no one can still reckon, which no one can still remember, those who came here to disperse [their descendants]—the grandfathers, the grandmothers, those called the ones who arrived [first], the ones who came [first], those who came sweeping the way, those who came with hair bound, those who came to rule in this land (190).

The legends tells how the people arrived in boats on the northern Gulf Coast; then, led by their priests and wise men (*tlamatinime*), they arrived at Tamoanchan, where they tarried. Soon thereafter, the wise men and priests left and abandoned the people at Tamoanchan; they took away the painted books and left the people without guides for living. Those who remained behind had to re-create the sacred books all over again and had to record time anew. It was about this time, also, that the people learned how to ferment maguey juice and make the divine pulque.

Eventually the people left Tamoanchan. As Sahagún records: "And they departed from there, from Tamoanchan. Offerings were made at a place named Teotihuacan. And there all the people raised pyramids for the sun and the moon; then they made many small pyramids where offerings were made. And there leaders were elected, wherefore it is called Teotihuacan" (1959–1982, book 10: 191). Sahagún's Spanish text adds: "And in this town they elected those that ruled over others, and because of this they called it *teutioacã*, that is to say *vey tioacã*: place where lords were made" (191). Sahagún's Nahuatl text continues:

> And when the rulers died, they buried them there. Then they built a pyramid over them. The pyramids now stand like small mountains, though made by hand. There is a hollow where they removed the stone to build the pyramids. And they built the pyramids of the sun and the moon very large, just like mountains. It is unbelievable when it is said they are made by hands, but giants still lived there then. Also it is very apparent from the artificial mountains at Cholollan; they are of sand, of adobe. It is apparent they are only constructed, only made. And so they named it Teotihuacan, because it was the burial place of the rulers (191–192).

Summarizing the arrival, stay, and departure of these pre-Aztec people, Sahagún records that:

> Then they set themselves in motion; all moved—the boys, the old men, the young women, the old women. They went very slowly, very deliberately; they went to settle together there at Teotihuacan. There law was established, there rulers were installed. The wise men, the sorcerers, the *nononotzaleque* were installed as rulers. The leading men were installed. Then they departed; they moved very slowly. Their leaders accompanied them; they went leading each [group. The members] of each group understood their own language. Each had its leader, its ruler. To them went speaking the one they worshipped. And the Tolteca [were] the ones who took the very lead (book 10: 194).

From Teotihuacan, the people eventually dispersed. They diverged according to whether they were Tolteca, Otomí, Mexica, Chichimeca, Michoaque, Tepaneca, Acolhuaque, Chalca, Huejotzinca, or Tlaxcalteca, each group going separately from Teotihuacan toward their eventual homeland (195).

What does this tale reveal to us about the Aztec view of Teotihuacan? It is clear the Aztecs knew that the pyramids were not natural geological features but had been constructed. Sahagún's noble informants address the astonishing size of the pyramids, and the nearly inconceivable amount of labor that was involved in their building, by invoking the presence of giants, implying that these giants built the pyramids.[5] Sahagún's sources also recognize an equivalency between the structures at Teotihuacan and Cholula; they see these places as like kinds.

More than this, however, the story gives us two new and important insights into the Aztec understanding of Teotihuacan. It shows us, first, that the Aztecs considered Teotihuacan to be an ancient place where the Aztec system of government was constituted. There at Teotihuacan the *tlatoque*, the hereditary rulers, were elected or made, seemingly for the first time. The clear implication is that before this moment, the people were led by *tlamatinime* (wise men), sorcerers, and priests in an unofficial capacity, but that now the position of *tlatoani* was codified and the people came to be led by *tlatoque*. At Teotihuacan, too, Sahagún notes that "law was established," meaning that the Aztec legal system was drawn up. Moreover, the people went to Teotihuacan as a single group; once there they divided themselves into different groups, each having its language, its hereditary ruler, and its patron deity. Thus, at Teotihuacan the people established the governmental system and form of rule that was to characterize the Aztec political system below the level of empire: people organized in *altepetl* ruled by *tlatoque* and governed under a civil legal system. They came as generic Chichimecs and left as Mexica, Acolhua, Chalca, etc.

The second important point the story makes is that Teotihuacan was a jumping-off point, a point of departure, for many of the peoples who inhabited Central Mexico in the Late Postclassic. The people came to Teotihuacan from the mythical Tamoanchan as a single group, but there they divided, and from there they dispersed in many directions, the Tolteca leading the way. Sahagún tells how the Otomí left for the forest (where they have since lived) and the different people went off across the plains and deserts (1959–1982, book 10: 195). Thus, Teotihuacan is a point of origin and departure for the peoples of Central Mexico; it is the place from which they dispersed. In this particular account, Teotihuacan supplants Chicomoztoc as the place of emergence and dispersal, for Sahagún notes that the peoples went to Chicomoztoc, dwelled there a long time and made offerings there, but did not actually emerge from Chicomoztoc. As he says: "all the people glorify themselves; they say that they were created at Chicomoztoc, that from Chicomoztoc they came forth. But there was no emerging from Chicomoztoc; [it was] merely that offerings were made at Chicomoztoc when they lived in the desert. And thereupon there was departing" (195–196).[6] Thus, Sahagún characterizes Teotihuacan as being like Chicomoztoc, Tollan, and Cholula, all ancestral places from which the Nahuas and others came.

TEOTIHUACAN OF THE TOLTECS

This equivalency of Teotihuacan, Chicomoztoc, Tollan, and Cholula brings to mind an old debate, argued spiritedly over fifty years ago and decided in the negative: To what extent can Teotihuacan be considered Tollan? Prior to 1941, most Mesoamericanists identified the Tollan of the Nahuatl legends with Teotihuacan. This was prior to significant excavations at Tula and before Wigberto Jiménez Moreno (1941) successfully argued that the Tollan of Ce Acatl Topiltzin Quetzalcoatl existed geographically as Tula, Hidalgo. Now most Mesoamericanists identify Tula, Hidalgo, as the Tollan of the Toltecs. I do not intend here to try to refute Jiménez Moreno's argument and to replace Tula with Teotihuacan. Instead, I feel it is time to expand our imagining of the word "Tollan," to recognize it as a concept and a metaphor rather than a single specific location, and to understand that the place existed in multiples. There is evidence that Teotihuacan was itself called Tollan, and there is evidence that the Aztecs did consider it an ancient Toltec city, perhaps the greatest of all the Toltec cities.

Fernando de Alva Ixtlilxochitl, that son of the Texcocan royal house, whose ancestors had ruled the Aztec *altepetl* of Teotihuacan, mentions the old city as a major Toltec polity. He tells us that, in ancient times, when the Toltec ruler Topiltzin was forced to flee Tula, he traveled and passed through a number of towns, among them Teotihuacan (Alva Ixtlilxochitl 1985, 1: 281). Alva Ixtlilxochitl (283) also mentions Teotihuacan as one of the dozen Toltec market cities, cities in which the largest periodic markets were held; Tula, Tulantzinco, and Cholula were some of the others. When he describes how one of the Acolhua founders explored the Valley of Mexico, he says that the founder passed by Teotihuacan, calling it "a very large city of the Toltecs" (294). In speaking of the many towns and cities the Toltecs built, Alva Ixtlilxochitl also says:

> Among the most notable was Teotihuacan, city and place of the god. This city was grander and more powerful than Tula, for being the sanctuary of the Toltecs. It had enormously grand, and very tall temples, and the most impressive buildings in the world [*los más terribles en el mundo*], which even today can be appreciated in their ruined state, and other great curiosities (272).

Then the chronicler proceeds to speak of other Toltec cities, cities like Tuluca, Cuauhnahuac, and Cholula. It is clear that Teotihuacan counted for the Aztecs as one of the major Toltec cities.

But was it Tollan in the Aztec mind? Yes, I would say it definitely was *a* Tollan, one of several. The evidence is pictorial.[7] On page 2 of the *Mapa Quinatzin* (Figure 12.2), which pictures the Texcocan palace and explains the structure of governance, the Texcocan ruler Nezahualcoyotl sits facing his son Nezahualpilli

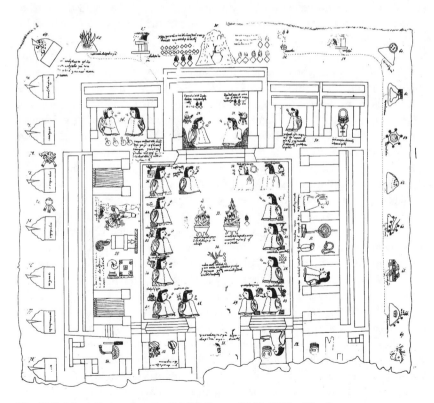

Fig. 12.2. *Mapa Quinatzin*, page 2 (after the ca. 1849–1851 edition).

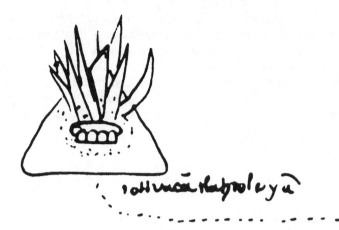

Fig. 12.3. Detail of the place sign for Teotihuacan in the *Mapa Quinatzin*, p. 2.

in the central, uppermost building. Below them, within the atrium of the rectangular palace, sit the fourteen *tlatoque* who are their vassals. Around the outside edge of the palace, as a frame, are place glyphs of the lands and *altepetl* of the realm, oriented with their bases toward the palace. On the left side of the top row, Teotihuacan and Otumba are pictured side by side; both were judicial seats of the Acolhua domain and are glossed as such. The place glyph of Teotihuacan is closest to the upper left corner (Figure 12.3). It is pictured as a hill marked with reeds or rushes (*tollin*) and a tooth or *tlantli* sign. Glyphically, it reads *tollan*. The accompanying Nahuatl gloss says *teotihuacn tlahtoyan*, "Teotihuacan tribunal" (Offner 1983: 61). The artist of the *Mapa Quinatzin* clearly recognized Teotihuacan as Tollan.

Tollan to the Aztecs was more than the home of the Toltec ruler Topiltzin Quetzalcoatl in Tula, Hidalgo. Tollan was a place of fertility and abundance, a place of origin, and a place where many people lived—a metropolis. Doris Heyden (1983: 94–97) has pointed out that Tollan, which means "Among the reeds, rushes, or cattails," symbolized an earthly paradise, where water and land meet, where edible animals and plants are abundant. This abundance encouraged many people to settle in places of reeds, and Tollan came to mean a metropolis. As Heyden (1983: 94) notes, Ángel María Garibay K. (1969, 4: 360) defined Tollan as the "toponomy of a great city, city in general."

Cholula was known as Tollan, its name often given as Tollan Chollolan. One sees this pictorially in the *Historia tolteca-chichimeca* (Figure 12.4), where Cholula's place sign features cattail reeds growing from swirling waters. The map of the *Relación geográfica* of Cholula also pictures it as a place of reeds and swirling waters (Figure 12.5);[8] the accompanying alphabetic text says that "Tullam ... means congregation of many officials; this is what the Indians of ancient times and scholars say, although others say that *tullam* signifies a multitude of people, similar to masses of *tule* which are rushes" (Heyden 1983: 97). The *Relación* also states that Cholula was where rulers came for investiture, where they had their nose, ears, or lower lip pierced to hold the jeweled insignia of rulership (Smith 1973: 72; Heyden 1983: 97).

In Aztec times, the Mixtecs considered Mexico-Tenochtitlan to be a Tollan. Mary Elizabeth Smith (1973: 72) has noted that the Mixtec name for Mexico-Tenochtitlan is *ñuu co' yo* (Town of Marsh Grass) and has shown that "in the sixteenth-century *Codex Sierra*, the place sign for Mexico City is a frieze with cattails."[9] The *Codex Sierra* lists a series of payments made by the city of Santa Catarina Texupan in the Mixteca Alta in the years 1550 to 1564. It refers pictorially to Mexico City seven times, picturing it each time as a place of reeds. In Figure 12.6, for example, the town paid twenty pesos to Francisco Sánchez, Regidor, who traveled to Mexico City with officials from the nearby town of Acalán in order that these towns would not be merged; the process also required a written letter (*Codex Sierra* 1982: 37).

Fig. 12.4. Place sign for Cholula in the *Historia tolteca-chichimeca* 1976: p. 29, fol. 16v

Fig. 12.5. Place sign for Cholula from the map of the *Relación geográfica de Cholula*. Courtesy of the Benson Latin American Collection, University of Texas at Austin (JGI xxiv-1).

As Bente Bittmann Simons (1967–1968: 295) points out, the cities of Teotihuacan, Cholula, Tula, and Tenochtitlan all carried the appellative "Tollan." The name implied a large and diversely populated city, a metropolis, and, because of the Toltec connections, the name meant a place of great agricultural and intellectual achievement. In the pictorial and alphabetic records that tell of the pre-Aztec peoples, Tollan is also a place of origin, like Chicomoztoc, from which people came. Corroborating evidence even comes from the relatively distant Maya world. David Stuart (chapter 15 of this volume) suggests that the Maya had a similar conceptualization of Tollan as a greatly esteemed ancestral place. He also argues that a place of reeds pictured in some Classic-period Maya texts refers to Teotihuacan as a Maya version of Tollan.

These data show how natural it would be for the Aztecs to think of Teotihuacan as a Tollan. It was the place where the Fifth Sun, the present age, was born. It was a place where the people prospered, where the Aztec system of governance was established, were laws were laid down. Teotihuacan, Cholula, and Tula were also places from which the wandering peoples dispersed; they were places of origin, ancestral homelands.

I am clearly not alone in thinking that we should reconsider reserving the Tollan concept only for Tula, Hidalgo. Davíd Carrasco (1982: 109, 126) has proposed that Teotihuacan was the first Tollan, because it was "the first great place in central

Fig. 12.6. Tenochtitlan as a place of reeds in the *Codex Sierra* 1933: p. 22.

Mexico where a fully integrated, harmonious, rich, and well-fed society operated under the authority of supernatural forces and cosmo-magical formulas." He argues that the abundance and order of Teotihuacan "gave birth to the concept of Tollan, a capital city which organized the world into an effective space." Carrasco (126–147) sees Xochicalco, Cholula, and Chichén Itzá as subsequent Tollans. Dana Leibsohn (1993: 96), arguing from the evidence in *Historia tolteca-chichimeca*, sees Cholula bound with Tollan as "places of extraordinary affluence and legendary holiness . . . [that] fuse in the utopian model from which they both derive." Jerome Offner (1983: 307–308, note 10) also sees Teotihuacan as the first Tollan, of which he says the other, Postclassic Tollans were pale imitators. Nigel Davies (1977: 24–70), Doris Heyden (1983: 94–97), and Emily Umberger (1987a: 69–70) have spoken of many Tollans, including one identified as Teotihuacan. And Susan Gillespie (1989: 203–207) questions whether the so-called Toltec diaspora out of Central Mexico into the Yucatán really came from Tula. With increasing evidence from the Classic-period Maya inscriptions that the Maya looked to distant Teotihuacan as a place of origins, it is clearly time to reassess the relation between the Toltecs, Tollan, and Teotihuacan.

OTHER IDENTITIES

The *Mapa Quinatzin* (Figures 12.2 and 12.3) represents Teotihuacan as the place "Among the Cattail Reeds," but this was not Teotihuacan's only toponym. The Aztecs also pictured it glyphically as two pyramids and as the sun disk. In Alonso de Santa Cruz's map of Mexico City and its environs of 1550 (Figure 12.7), a pair of three-stepped pyramids stands for Teotihuacan; the site is correctly located on the map in the northeastern part of the valley, near a significant water source and on the road to Otumba.

A pair of pyramids (with four stages each) also identifies Teotihuacan on map 1 of the *Codex Xolotl* (Figure 12.8), where the pyramids are accompanied by a cave. Doris Heyden (1975: 141) has suggested that this cave is probably the one beneath the Pyramid of the Sun, which was discovered in 1971, but it may also refer simply to the many caves in the precinct, which were known in the sixteenth century. Heyden (140) also suggests that the face that is part of the cave symbol may refer to or represent the oracle said to be at Teotihuacan (see discussion below). What is striking about this representation of Teotihuacan is that it is not portrayed here as a ruined Toltec city. Fernando de Alva Ixtlilxochitl (1985, 1: 294), who used the *Codex Xolotl* in writing his alphabetic history, explained that Nopaltzin "passed through Teotihuacan, the very large city that belonged to the Toltecs." But there is no Toltec glyph here. Other ruined Toltec cities—Tula in the

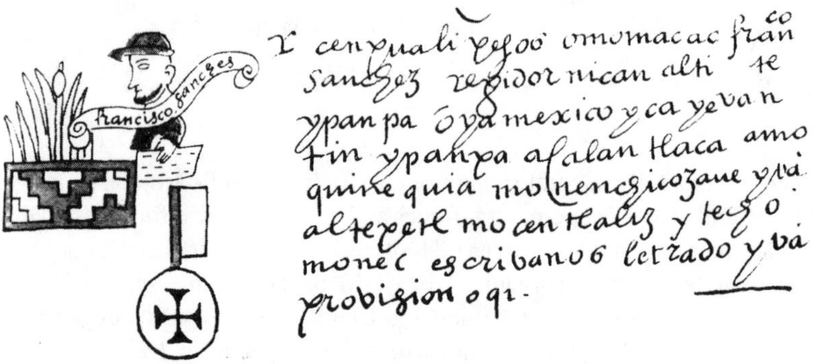

Fig. 12.7. Place sign of Teotihuacan from the Santa Cruz Map of 1550 (Alonso de Santa Cruz 1974[?]).

west, Cahuac in the northeast (Figure 12.9), and a site near Tepetlaoztoc—are identified by a cluster of features that includes at least one stepped pyramid, a scattering of broken rocks to represent the site's decayed state, and a stand of curved grass to indicate weeds at the site. These Toltec places are also identified by the glyph for the Tolteca: a clump of green rushes, with a human chin below. The *Xolotl* artist pictures Teotihuacan neither as ruined nor as Toltec. Why? I suspect this is because Teotihuacan functions in the *Codex Xolotl* story as an active polity instead of a deserted Toltec site.

Elsewhere in the *Codex Xolotl* Teotihuacan figures as an *altepetl* of the Acolhua realm. Although its ancient ceremonial core may have decayed, Teotihuacan was not completely abandoned and empty in Aztec times, but became a thriving city active in Acolhua affairs. It is pictured thusly on map 3 in the *Codex Xolotl* (Figure 12.10), where the two pyramids compose the place sign for the site, and its ruler is pictured above. Elsewhere, on map 6 (Figure 12.11), Teotihuacan is identified by a single pyramid, presumably the Pyramid of the Sun, from which the sun can be seen rising;[10] the site is glossed "Teotiuacan." On two other *Xolotl* maps (5 and 8) Teotihuacan's place sign is simply the face of the sun (Figure 12.12), the sun Europeanized as a frontal face with curved rays radiating out from the disk. Clearly this sun disk refers to the largest pyramid of the site and to the birth of the sun there at the beginning of the era. The Aztecs thus consistently thought of Teotihuacan, and represented it glyphically, as the city of the enormous human-made pyramids and the place where the sun was born; it was the old city where it all began.

Aztec Teotihuacan

Despite the Aztec characterization of Teotihuacan as an esteemed ancient place, there was a significant Aztec presence in the city in the Late Postclassic. In the last two centuries before the Spanish invasion, Teotihuacan was an independent *altepetl*, one of the cities of the Acolhua sphere that provided goods and services to the Texcocan royal palace for half the year (Offner 1983: 39, 61). The *Codex Xolotl* includes Teotihuacan first as a Chichimec polity and then as a

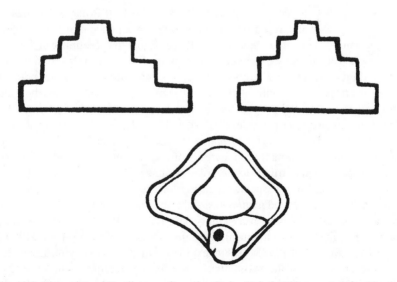

Fig. 12.8. Place sign of Teotihuacan from the *Codex Xolotl* 1980: map 1 (after Heyden 1975: fig. 10).

Fig. 12.9 Place sign of the ruined Toltec city of Cahuac, *Codex Xolotl* 1980: map 1. Drawing by Lori Boornazian Diel.

member of the Acolhua domain (Dibble 1980: 78, 85, 99–100). In map 3, Teotihuacan joins Tepetlaoztoc and Tepeapulco as polities still independent of Xolotl's control; the animal skins of its ruler (Figure 12.10) signal that Teotihuacan, like the others, was still culturally Chichimec. By the time of Teotihuacan's appearance on map 6 (Figure 12.11), the polity had been brought into the Acolhua political sphere and its populace civilized, for Teotihuacan's ruler Acolhua wears the white cotton *tilmatl* of settled people. Teotihuacan here is presented as joining other *altepetl* in recognizing the new rule of Ixtlilxochitl (Dibble 1980: 83–87). Teotihuacan is not mentioned in the *Codex Mendoza* or other Mexica tribute lists probably because it was never formally conquered by the Mexica emperors and did not pay a significant amount of tribute to the Triple Alliance. The *Relación geográfica* of Teotihuacan records pre-Hispanic tribute to Moctezuma as "some coarse maguey-fiber cloaks, that are called *ichtilmates*, and some loads of maguey spines, which are called *metzontli*" given every eighty days (Acuña 1986: 235). Teotihuacan was (and remains) a center for maguey-farming (Evans 1988: 9, 45, 47–48, 1990).

Alva Ixtlilxochitl (1985, II: 89) explains that Nezahualcoyotl designated Teotihuacan as one of the two judicial seats for the Acolhua realm outside of Texcoco proper. The Texcocan lord named Otumba (the old Otomí capital) as the place where the commoners went to have their legal appeals heard, and he chose

Teotihuacan as the tribunal where the lords and nobles would go for their legal affairs (Offner 1983: 60–61, 65, 67). The *Relación geográfica* of Teotihuacan records a number of the laws in effect there (Nuttall 1926: 72–73; Acuña 1986: 236–237).[11] One can imagine how lords and nobles must have flocked to Aztec Teotihuacan, restoring it, in some small way, to the intellectual capital it was during the Classic period. Diego Durán (1994: 330) records that when the Texcocan lord Nezahualpilli

Fig. 12.10. Place sign of Teotihuacan, with its ruler, *Codex Xolotl*, map 3. Drawing by Lori Boornazian Diel.

Fig. 12.11. Place sign of Teotihuacan, with its ruler, *Codex Xolotl*, map 6. Drawing by Lori Boornazian Diel.

came to Mexico-Tenochtitlan to observe the dedication of the Templo Mayor in 1487, the lord of Teotihuacan was one of those who accompanied him.[12] Then when the Texcocan realm was divided between three competing heirs during the reign of Moctezuma Xocoyotzin, Ixtlilxochitl chose Teotihuacan and Otumba as his capitals (Alva Ixtlilxochitl 1985, I: 484; Offner 1983: 240). The *Relación* describes the Aztec inhabitants of Teotihuacan as "a polished people of good understanding," in sharp contrast to the duller people of the other towns in the neighborhood (Acuña 1986: 233). Because it had been an autonomous *altepetl*,

Fig. 12.12. Place sign of Teotihuacan, with its ruler, *Codex Xolotl*, map 8. Drawing by Lori Boornazian Diel.

Teotihuacan had *cabecera* ('head") status in sixteenth-century New Spain (Acuña 1986: 233).

The *Relación geográfica* additionally tells of a great oracle there (Acuña 1986: 234), another reason for lords and commoners both to flock to the city. The accompanying map (Figure 12.13) shows the Classic precinct of Teotihuacan just outside what must have been the Aztec city and then the Spanish town. The precinct features the two largest pyramids in their respective locations, flanked along the Avenue of the Dead by other smaller structures. The Spanish gloss places the Oracle of Moctezuma here in the Classic-period ritual precinct. The mountain, Cerro Gordo, to which the avenue is oriented, is shown; it is labeled Tenan (Our Mother), because as the *Relación* says, "it has given birth to many other mountains" (Nuttall 1926: 76; Acuña 1986: 233).

By this time, Aztec gods had replaced their Classic-period and Toltec predecessors. The *Relación* describes a colossal stone cult image at the summit of the largest pyramid; it faced west and was named Tonacatecuhtli. A smaller platform in front of the pyramid bore the stone image of Mictlantecuhtli, who faced east. On top of the Moon Pyramid stood a monumental image of the Moon God; there were six other "brethren of the Moon" in a large temple nearby. To these moon deities, the *Relación* says, the priests of Moctezuma, and the lord of Mexico himself, came to offer sacrifices every twenty days (Nuttall 1926: 68; Acuña 1986: 235–236).[13] The Moon Pyramid complex might then have been the very site of the famous oracle.

AZTEC UNDERSTANDING

This is what we know about the Aztec understanding of Teotihuacan from the ethnohistorical sources, from pictures and words of the Aztecs. The sources show us how the Aztecs venerated Teotihuacan as the place where the Fifth Sun was created, where the gods first sacrificed themselves, and where the future warriors first showed their valor by risking their lives for the sun. They knew the ancient Teotihuacan to be the place where government as they knew it was established, where rulers were installed for the first time, where the first laws were made, and where the Chichimecs divided themselves and distinguished themselves as Acolhua, Mexica, Chalca, etc. It was a place where rulers were buried. It was a great Toltec city, one of the mythical Tollans. The modern, Aztec city reflected some of these meanings, for it was a judicial seat for Acolhua lords, and it was home to a powerful oracle.

But the Aztecs did more than just talk about ancient Teotihuacan. They metaphorically brought it to the heart of their empire by incorporating Teotihuacan features and elements into the program of the Templo Mayor. They had surely

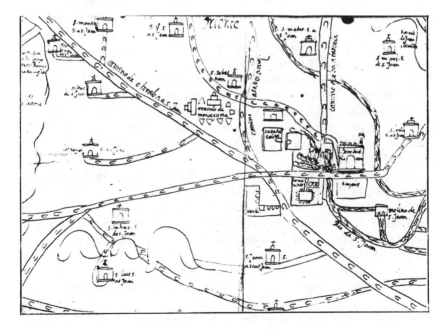

Fig. 12.13. Detail of the map accompanying the *Relación geográfica de San Juan Teotihuacan*, 1580, showing the plan of the ancient ceremonial precinct (after Gamio 1922: lám. 140).

made excavations at the ancient site, for they understood its Classic architecture, mural paintings, and sculpture. Antique Teotihuacan objects as well as new forms fashioned by the Aztecs in the earlier Teotihuacan style became part of the ritual precinct and of other sacred locations in Tenochtitlan.

The Aztecs copied Teotihuacan sculptures and embraced them as their own. A prime example is the Xiuhtecuhtli scepter found north of Shrine C in 1981 during the recent Templo Mayor excavations (Matos 1988: 99–101; López Austin 1987: 255. As Alfredo López Austin (1987), Emily Umberger (1987a: 88–89), and others have pointed out, this seated, bent-over figure is an Aztec translation of Teotihuacan's old fire god braziers. Umberger (85–90) has additionally identified several other Aztec sculptures, including two partially skeletal figures, as archaizing references to Teotihuacan prototypes.

Aztec builders also imitated Teotihuacan temples. Two of the most dramatic examples are found on either side of the twin temples to Huitzilopochtli and Tlaloc. There, Aztec architects re-created two Teotihuacan-style temples, now called the Red Temple and Shrine C. These temples replicate in a simplified manner and on a smaller scale the layout, form, *talud-tablero* wall treatment, sculptural embellishments, and painted wall decorations of Teotihuacan's religious architecture. In at least two other locations around the ritual precinct, they built other pseudo-Teotihuacan temples.[14]

Within the pyramid body of the Templo Mayor, the Aztecs carefully placed Teotihuacan objects among the offerings. These prized objects were antiques that had been excavated from the ancient city, or else they were modern copies, some carved or rendered so perfectly in the ancient style that they are indistinguishable from their prototypes. Three exquisitely carved Teotihuacan masks have come from the pyramid of the Templo Mayor. One was excavated by Leopoldo Batres in 1900; its near twin and a third mask in a different Teotihuacan style were found by Eduardo Matos Moctezuma's team between 1978 and 1992. Stone figurines have come from both excavations, as have Teotihuacan-style ceramics.[15] Matos and Leonardo López Lújan (1993: 162) report that forty-one Teotihuacan and twenty-three Teotihuacanoid-style pieces were uncovered in the latter excavations. Teotihuacan clearly was an important component of the Templo Mayor offerings.

By placing Teotihuacan objects and Teotihuacan copies and references in the Templo Mayor, the Aztecs brought the beginning to the present and thereby made it their own. They built the foundation for their stone and mortar edifice on elements of the Teotihuacan past, just as they built their political and social system on those ancient social foundations established at Teotihuacan. By flanking the Templo Mayor with two Teotihuacan-style buildings, they framed their own religious performances with the imagined memory of those ancient rituals at Teotihuacan. By bringing the "place where the Fifth Sun was created" to the Templo Mayor, the Aztecs metaphorically took ownership of this Sun, for whose continuance their sacrifices and offerings were responsible.

I end this essay with a single serpentine figurine (Figure 12.14), which sums up several of these points. The figurine, now housed in the Museum für Völkerkunde in Hamburg, has been studied by Emily Umberger (1987a: 84–85), whose interpretation I follow here. It is a Teotihuacan figurine of unknown provenience that either was found or was preserved by an Aztec citizen, who then carved two dates on the antique figure's chest (Figure 12.15). The dates are 13 Reed on the right, and 1 Flint on the left, the flint knife embellished with flowing blood.[16] As Umberger (1987b: 437) points out, we can identify the year 13 Reed as the year of the sun's birth at Teotihuacan; it appears thusly on the so-called Calendar Stone. One Flint is the year of Huitzilopochtli's birth; it is also the year when the Aztecs initiated great undertakings: it was the year the Mexica left Aztlan; the year their first monarch, Acamapichtli, took office; and the year Itzcoatl was inaugurated, the year they defeated the Tepanecs to initiate the Triple Alliance empire. One Flint was, thus, for the Aztecs the year of beginnings. As Umberger argues, "When inscribed together with the date of the sun's birth, it probably signifies the birth of the 'Mexica sun' in a political sense, and the ascendance of the Mexica as the people of the sun" (1987a: 84). The conjunction

Fig. 12.14. Teotihuacan greenstone figurine with the dates 1 Flint and 13 Reed carved on the chest. Museum für Völkerkunde, Hamburg.

of these two dates draws together Aztec beginnings with the beginning of the Fifth Age. Further, it equates Huitzilopochtli with the Fifth Sun born at Teotihuacan and thereby reinforces the ideology of Huitzilopochtli as the sun. Metaphorically and on many levels, it says to us that the Aztec world began when the Fifth Sun began, there with the dawning at Teotihuacan.

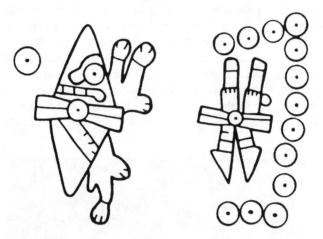

Fig. 12.15. Detail of the carved dates 1 Flint and 13 Reed (after drawing by Umberger 1987a: fig. 23).

Notes

1. The map is published without provenience by Arreola (1922: plate opposite 552), who describes it as being painted "on the back of an old piece of parchment" and notes that it was copied from a lost original (553). Glass (1975: no. 314) gives the map's location as "Pueblo," presumably meaning that the document is still in San Juan Teotihuacan; Kubler (1980: 43) says its location is unknown. The other maps are the Ayer Map of Teotihuacan in the Newberry Library (Glass 1975: no. 312) and the Saville Map of Teotihuacan in the American Museum of Natural History (Glass 1975: no. 313). Kubler (1980) analyzes the three maps, following Arreola's translation of the Nahuatl glosses on the Mazapan map. Glass (1975: no. 314) and Kubler both assign the Mazapan map to the nineteenth century, but Kubler (1980: 44) judges it to be the closest to the lost original because it contains the most written and pictorial information. The 1560 date on the Mazapan map is understood to be the date of the original.

2. The Saville Map likewise pictures the face of the sun above this pyramid (see Glass 1975: fig. 58).

3. See, for example, Sugiyama (1989); Cabrera Castro, Sugiyama, and Cowgill (1991).

4. See also the translation by López Austin (1985).

5. This remark about giants living in an earlier age reminds us that a race of giants were said to have occupied the earth during the First Sun or cosmic age. The *Leyenda de los soles* and the *Historia de los mexicanos por sus pinturas* date this first age as enduring from 2,028 to 1,352 years before the Fifth and present Sun was set into motion at Teotihuacan; see Nicholson (1971: 398–399). The bones of large Pleistocene fauna, such as mammoths and mastodons, have been found near Teotihuacan and at other sites in the Valley of

Mexico, and it may be that the Aztecs thought these were the bones of the ancient giants. See Aveleyra and Maldonado-Koerdell (1953).

6. The *Codex Mexicanus* (1952: 22–23) and the *Codex Azcatitlan* (1994: 8) also show the Aztecs arriving at and departing from Chicomoztoc, although the *Mexicanus* assigns a tribe to each of the seven caves, which suggests that they emerged from these caves.

7. Jerome Offner (1983: 61) pointed this out.

8. For Cholula as a Tollan, see Bittmann Simons (1968: 295), Kubler (1968), Smith (1973: 70), and Leibsohn (1993: 95–98).

9. See *Codex Sierra* (1982: 22, 33, 34, 38, 41, 47, 59).

10. George Kubler (1980: 45), who pointed out the identity of the Teotihuacan place signs in the *Codex Xolotl*, suggested that this sun indicated the summer solstice, to which he mistakenly thought the site was oriented. Aveni (1988: 459) has argued instead that Teotihuacan's alignment marks the setting point of the Pleiades; see also Aveni (chapter 9 of this volume).

11. This list from Teotihuacan and the manuscript "Estas son los leyes" are two of our principal sources for understanding Aztec legalism; see Offner (1983: 65–69).

12. Dyckerhoff and Prem (1990: 51) pointed this out when they noted that Teotihuacan was one of the toponyms that could take *hue* ("old, great") as a prefix; here Durán calls it Ueitihuacan.

13. I should state here that I doubt that Moctezuma, *huey tlatoani* of Mexico-Tenochtitlan, came every twenty days to Teotihuacan; no other source says that he did, and I imagine the author of the *Relación* to be embellishing here out of civic pride. As important as the site was, it would have been too long a journey to make on foot and in canoe with any frequency. My guess is that special feasts were held every twenty days; these would have been the eighteen monthly feasts, and perhaps Moctezuma journeyed out there once or twice.

14. See Matos (1964), Gussinyer (1970, 1972), Boone (1985: 179; 1987: 52–53, 56), Heyden (1987: 125), Umberger (1987a: 86–88), Matos and López Luján 1993: 159–161).

15. See Batres (1902: 17, 19, 24), Umberger (1987a: 67), Berrin and Pasztory (1993: note 185), Matos and López Luján (1993: fig. 1).

16. Umberger (1987a: 85) identified the fingers emanating from the flint knife as speech scrolls, but I think they are more clearly blood or another liquid. Although neither date has a framing cartouche to signal definitively that it is a year date rather than a day date, the context strongly suggests these are year dates.

References

Acuña, Rene, ed.
1986. *Relaciones geográficas del siglo XVI*. Vol. 7: *México, tomo segundo*. Mexico: UNAM.

Alva Ixtlilxochitl, Fernando de
1985. *Obras históricas*. 2 vols. Edited by E. O'Gorman. Mexico: UNAM.

Arreola, José María
1922. "Códices y documentos en mexicano." In M. Gamio, ed., *La población del Valle de Teotihuacan*. Mexico: SEP, tomo 1, vol. 2, pp. 549–594.

Aveleyra Arroya de Anda, Luis, and Manuel Maldonado-Koerdell
1953. "The Association of Artifacts with Mammoth in the Valley of Mexico." *American Antiquity* 18: 332–340.

Aveni, Anthony
1988. "The Thom Paradigm in the Americas: The Case of the Cross-Circle Designs." In C. Ruggles, ed., *Records in Stone*. Cambridge: Cambridge University Press, pp. 442–472.

Batres, Leopoldo
1902. *Archaeological Expolrations in Escalerillas Street, City of Mexico, by Leopoldo Batres, General Inspector of Archaeological Monuments, Year 1900.* Mexico: J. Aguilar Vera and Co.

Berrin, Kathleen, and Esther Pasztory, eds.
1993. *Teotihuacan: Art from the City of the Gods.* New York: Thames and Hudson, and the Fine Arts Museums of San Francisco.

Bittmann Simons, Bente
1967–1968. "The Codex of Cholula: A Preliminary Study." *Tlalocan* 5: 267–339.

Boone, Elizabeth H.
1985. "The Color of Mesoamerican Architecture and Sculpture." In E. H. Boone, ed., *Painted Architecture and Polychrome Monumental Sculpture in Mesoamerica.* Washington, DC: Dumbarton Oaks, pp. 173–186.
1987. "Templo Mayor Reseach, 1521–1978." In E. H. Boone, ed., *The Aztec Templo Mayor.* Washington, DC: Dumbarton Oaks, pp. 5–69.

Cabrera Castro, Rubén, Saburo Sugiyama, and George Cowgill
1991. "The Templo de Quetzalcoatl Project at Teotihuacan: A Preliminary Report." *Ancient Mesoamerica* 2: 77–92.

Carrasco, Davíd
1982. *Quetzalcoatl and the Irony of Empire: Myths and Prophecies in the Aztec Tradition.* Chicago: University of Chicago Press. 2nd ed. published 1992.

Codex Azcatitlan
1994. Facsimile with commentary by R. H. Barlow, edited by M. Graulich. 2 vols. Paris: Bibliothèque Nationale de France.

Codex Chimalpopoca
1975. *Códice Chimalpopoca: Anales de Cuauhtitlán y Leyenda de los soles.* Translated and edited by P. F. Velázquez. Mexico: UNAM-IIH.

Codex Mendoza
1992. Edited by F. F. Berdan and P. R. Anawalt. 4 vols. Berkeley: University of California Press.

Codex Mexicanus
1952. *Codex Mexicanus Nos. 23–24 de la Bibliothèque Nationale de Paris.* Edited by Ernest Mengin. *Journal de la Société des Américanistes,* n.s., 41: 387–498, with the facsimile published as a supplement.

Codex Sierra
1933. *Códice Sierra: Traducción al español de su texto náhuatl y explicación de sus pinturas jeroglíficas por el doctor Nicolás León.* Mexico: Museo Nacional de Arqueología, Historia y Etnografía.

Codex Xolotl
1980. *Códice Xolotl.* 2 vols. Edited by C. E. Dibble. Mexico: UNAM-IIH.

Davies, Nigel
1977. *Until the Fall of Tula.* Norman: University of Oklahoma Press.
1984. "The Aztec Concept of History: Teotihuacan and Tula." In Jacqueline de Durand-Forest, ed. *The Native Sources and the History of the Valley of Mexico.* Oxford: BAR International Series 204, pp. 207–214.

Dibble, Charles E., ed.
1980. *Códice Xolotl.* 2 vols. Mexico: UNAM-IIH.

Durán, Diego
1994. *The History of the Indies of New Spain*. Translated and edited by D. Heyden. Norman: University of Oklahoma Press.

Dyckerhoff, Ursula, and Hanns J. Prem
1990. *Toponyme und Ethnonyme im Klassischen Aztekischen*. Acta Mesoamericana 4. Berlin: Verlag von Flemming.

Evans, Susan Toby
1988. "Cihuatecpan: The Village in its Ecological and Historical Context." In S. T. Evans, ed., *Excavations at Cihuatecpan: An Aztec Village in the Teotihuacan Valley*, Nashville, TN: Vanderbilt University Publications in Anthropology 36, pp. 1–49.
1990. "The Productivity of Maguey Terrace Agriculture in Central Mexico During the Aztec Period." *Latin American Antiquity* 1: 117–132.

Gamio, Manuel, ed.
1922. *La población del Valle de Teotihuacan*. Tomo 1, Vol. 2: *Tercer parte, La éopca colonial*. Mexico: SEP.

Garibay K., Ángel María, ed.
1969. *Historia general de las cosas de Nueva España*, by Bernardino de Sahagún. 4 vols. Mexico: Editorial Porrúa.

Gillespie, Susan D.
1989. *The Aztec Kings: The Construction of Rulership in Mexica History*. Tucson: University of Arizona Press.

Glass, John B.
1975. "A Census of Native Middle American Pictorial Manuscripts." In R. A. Wauchope, gen. ed.; H. F. Cline, vol. ed., *Handbook of Middle American Indians*, Vol. 14: *Guide to Ethnohistorical Sources, Part 3*. Austin: University of Texas Press, pp. 81–252.

Gussinyer, Jordi
1970. "Un adoratorio azteca decorado con pinturas." *Boletín del INAH* 40: 30–35.
1972. "Rescate de un adoratorio azteca en México, D.F." *Boletín del INAH*, segunda época, 2: 21–30.

Heyden, Doris
1975. "An Interpretation of the Cave Underneath the Pyramid of the Sun in Teotihuacan, Mexico." *American Antiquity* 40: 131–147.
1983. "Reeds and Rushes: From Survival to Sovereigns." In J. F. Peterson, eds., *Flora and Fauna Imagery in Precolumbian Cultures: Iconography and Function. Proceedings of the 44th International Congress of Americanists, Manchester, 1982*. London: BAR International Series 171, pp. 93–148.
1987. "Symbolism of Ceramics from the Templo Mayor." In E. H. Boone, ed., *The Aztec Templo Mayor*. Washington, DC: Dumbarton Oaks, pp. 109–130.

Historia tolteca-chichimeca
1976. Edited by P. Kirchhoff, L. Odena Güemes, and L. Reyes García. Mexico: INAH.

Jiménez Moreno, Wigberto
1941. "Tula y los Toltecas según las fuentes históricas." *Revista Mexicana de Estudios Antropológicos* 5: 79–83.

Kubler, George
1968. "The Colonial Plan of Cholula." In *Actas y memorias: XXXVII Congreso Internacional de Americanistas, Mar de la Plata, Argentina, 1966*. Buenos Aires: Buenos Aires Library, vol. 1, pp. 209–223.

1980. "The Mazapan Maps of Teotihuacan in 1560." In G. Kutscher, A. Mönnich, and W. Zeller, eds., *Gedenkschrift Walter Lehmann*. 3 vols. Berlin: Gebr. Mann/Ibero-Amerikanisches Institut, vol. 2, pp. 43–55.

Leibsohn, Dana
1993. "The Historia Tolteca-Chichimeca: Recollecting Identity in a Nahua Manuscript." Ph.D. dissertation, University of California at Los Angeles.

López Austin, Alfredo
1985. "El texto sahaguntino sobre los mexicas." *Anales de Antropología* 22: 287–335.
1987. "The Masked God of Fire." In E. H. Boone, ed., *The Aztec Templo Mayor*. Washington, DC: Dumbarton Oaks, pp. 257–291.

Mapa Quinatzin
c. 1849–1851. *Mappe Quinatzin. Cour Chichimèque & Histoire de Tezcuco, pl. 2*. Edited by J. M. A. Aubin. Paris: Lith. de Jules Desportes.

Matos Moctezuma, Eduardo
1964. "El adoratorio decorado de las Calles de Argentina." *Anales del INAH* 17: 127–138.
1988. *The Great Temple of the Aztecs: Treasures of Tenochtitlan*. New York: Thames and Hudson.

Matos Moctezuma, Eduardo, and Leonardo López Luján
1993. "Teotihuacan and Its Mexica Legacy." In K. Berrin and E. Pasztory, eds., *Teotihuacan: Art from the City of the Gods*. New York: Thames and Hudson/The Fine Arts Museums of San Francisco, pp. 156–165.

Nicholson, H. B.
1971. "Religion in Pre-Hispanic Central Mexico." In R. A. Wauchope, gen. ed.; G. Ekholm and I. Bernal, vol. eds., *Handbook of Middle American Indians*, Vol. 11, Part 2: *Archaeology of Northern Mesoamerica*. Austin: University of Texas Press, pp. 395–446.

Nuttall, Zelia, ed. and trans.
1926. *Official Reports on the Towns of Tequizistlan, Tepechpan, Acolman, and San Juan Teotihuacan Sent by Francisco de Castañeda to His Magesty, Philip II, and the Council of the Indies, in 1580*. Papers of the Peabody Museum of American Archaeology and Ethnology, Harvard University, vol. 11, no. 2. Cambrige, MA.

Offner, Jerome A.
1983. *Law and Politics in Aztec Texcoco*. Cambridge: Cambridge University Press.

Sahagún, Fray Bernardino de
1959–1982. *Florentine Codex: General History of the Things of New Spain*. 12 books and Introduction. Translated and edited by C. E. Dibble and A. J. O. Anderson. Santa Fe, NM: The School of American Research/University of Utah.

Santa Cruz, Alonso de
[1974?] *The Alonso de Santa Cruz Map of Mexico City and Environs Dating from 1550*. Edited by A. B. Elsasser. Berkeley: Lowie [now Phoebe Appleton Hearst] Museum of Anthroplogy, University of California.

Smith, Mary Elizabeth
1973. *Picture Writing from Ancient Southern Mexico: Mixtec Place Signs and Maps*. Norman: University of Oklahoma Press.

Sugiyama, Saburo
1989. "Burials Dedicated to the Old Temple of Quetzalcoatl at Teotihuacan." *American Antiquity* 54: 85–106.

Umberger, Emily

1987a. "Antiques, Revivals, and References to the Past in Aztec Art." *Res: Anthropology and Aesthetics* 13: 62–105.

1987b. "Events Commemorated on Date Plaques at the Templo Mayor: Further Thoughts on the Solar Metaphor." In E. H. Boone, ed., *The Aztec Templo Mayor*. Washington, DC: Dumbarton Oaks, pp. 411–449.

13

▼

CALENDRICS AND RITUAL LANDSCAPE AT TEOTIHUACAN

THEMES OF CONTINUITY IN MESOAMERICAN "COSMOVISION"

JOHANNA BRODA

In this study I explore, from an anthropological and archaeoastronomical per-spective, aspects of calendrics and ritual landscape at Teotihuacan dealing with the basic orientation and grid plan of Teotihuacan, i.e., the alignment group of 15° 30' (15.5°) and the fixed calendrical cycle of 260 days implied in this alignment. This fixed 260-day cycle is not to be confused with the rotating sacred almanac of 260 days (*tonalpohualli, tzolkin*) that was permutated in ever-revolving cycles with the vague year to form the fifty-two-year Calendar Round.

I first became interested in this problem years ago when studying the calendrical, ethnohistorical, and ethnographic characteristics of the Feast of the Holy Cross (May 3) in present-day Mexico (Broda 1983). At the Second Oxford Conference that Anthony F. Aveni organized in Mérida in 1986 (Aveni ed. 1989), I presented a paper on this highly syncretistic Indian feast proposing that it was one of the most significant dates of the Mesoamerican agricultural calendar and that this structural characteristic still conveys a particular importance to this contemporaneous Indian feast at the present day (Broda 1986). When analyzing more deeply the implications of this date, and its corresponding alignment of 15° 30' (correlated with the dates of April 30, August 13, October 30, and February 12),[1] I came across the problem of the Teotihuacan orientation that belongs to this alignment. I was not able to elucidate this issue at the time. Since then, I have continued to investigate the issue in archaeoastronomical, archaeological, and modern ethnographic data (Broda 1993, 1995, n.d.).

If now I am taking up again this complex matter, great advances have been made over the past years not only in the ongoing archaeological studies on Teotihuacan, but also in archaeoastronomical research in the central highlands. Several important new field investigations have been carried out that permit us to discuss the issue today with much more evidence than was available ten years ago.

CALENDRICS AND ARCHAEOASTRONOMY

Studies on the Mesoamerican calendar system, whose origins are documented archaeologically for the first millenium B.C.E., have registered considerable advances over the past two decades due to the new interdisciplinary field of archaeoastronomy. To the analysis of calendrical inscriptions on stelae and of written texts, archaeoastronomy has added a new dimension consisting in the systematic investigation of the orientation principle in Mesoamerican architecture and in the planning of towns and ceremonial centers. Time and space were coordinated in the landscape by means of the orientation of buildings and settlements. The most important dates of the annual course of the sun were tracked on the local horizon by means of a horizon reference system. These orientations constitute a calendrical principle different from the one represented on stelae and in codices. The "script" used was, in this case, architecture itself and its coordination with the natural environment. A system of codes was created within the living landscape. Isolated buildings, architectural assemblages, and settlement patterns show particular alignments; in some cases, these alignments were coordinated with specific points of the landscape: with mountains or other natural elements like springs and caves, as well as with artificial markers in the form of petreglyphs, reliefs, or buildings constructed deliberately in these places. These points on the horizon or the orientation of temples to the rising or setting phenomena of the sun and certain stars were also coordinated with cult practice. The same might be said for the rites and observations carried out in subterranean chambers—artificial caves in the womb of the earth. The elaborate cult activities were kept in tune with agricultural cycles due to the fact that the basic structure of the festival calendar was the solar year and ritual functioned to regulate and control social and economic life.

COSMOVISION AND RITUAL LANDSCAPE

Alignment studies of Mesoamerican temples and ceremonial centers that apply the general methodology of archaeoastronomy to archaeological evidence, provide a rich field for the research of pre-Hispanic cosmovision. It is a different way of investigating that cosmovision in the material remains of archaeology, not only through texts or iconography, and it complements the important findings of the latter studies.

Yet, it is necessary to point out that after more than two decades of the constitution of the new field of archaeoastronomy, we see more clearly now that it is not possible to study only alignments and that they were not a profane expression of astronomical observation. They were immersed in the cultural context, and for the ancient Mesoamericans precise observation of nature was inextricably tied to ritual and magic (Broda 1993; Aveni ed. 1989).

In this perspective, the study of "ritual or ceremonial landscapes" is of great interest. This concept was introduced by Davíd Carrasco (1982, 1991) as an agenda for several previous Mesoamerican Archive meetings, and has proved to be a useful tool for research. It refers to the culturally transformed natural land-scape in which there existed sanctuaries and local shrines where certain rites were performed that were meaningful in terms of cosmovision and of indig-enous observation of nature (cf. Broda 1991a, 1991b, 1993, 1996a). I prefer this term to the one of "sacred geography," which in a way implies that cosmological concepts by themselves created the cultural landscape and not the rites performed there; these rituals established a link to society and state organization.

By "cosmovision" we understand the structured view in which ancient Mesoamericans combined into a coherent whole the notions about the natural environment in which they lived, and about the cosmos in which they situated themselves (Broda 1991a: 462). The archaeoastronomical approach and method-ology, combined with calendrical studies and the anthropological perspective, permit us to study the ways in which cosmological concepts were transformed into material forms, implying at the same time that there existed social and political institutions and agents that were capable of putting these religious concepts into practice.

Monumental architecture such as that which existed at Teotihuacan had an eminently ideological function. It was designed to "impress" people, to transmit a message of grandiosity to spectators, and in this way this "cosmic ideology" also expressed the exercise of power of the Teotihuacan rulers—whether it was the collective rulership of priests or any other form of state government. In this sense, ritual landscape reproduced not only the concepts of cosmovision, about man's place in nature and the cosmos, but was also closely tied to state ideology that imbued the physical landscape with political and religious significance.

Ritual was the means by which society took possession of the symbolic landscape. Ritual established the link between the abstract concepts of cosmovision and the human actors. It was the concrete process by which myth was transformed into social reality. Although we know very little about the ac-tual rites that were performed in the ceremonial precinct of Teotihuacan, it is necessary to imagine the imposing temples peopled by lavishly dressed per-formers who used colorful insignia and offerings to carry out the ceremonies that gave life and meaning to the architecture and duly impressed the congre-gated people who were thereby confirmed in their role as subjects.

These ancient cults of fertility and the earth were, since the Preclassic pe-riod, violent rituals that included human sacrifice and blood offerings; during Teotihuacan times, apparently, this cult reached a climax based on the sacrifice of war captives, military expansion, and power exercised within the hierarchical order of its own society.

TOPOGRAPHY AND SACRED GEOGRAPHY: CAVES, MOUNTAINS, AND WATER

Stephen Tobriner proposed in 1972 that Cerro Gordo, the big mountain to the north of Teotihuacan and its main water supply, may have determined the orientation of the Street of the Dead. The latter actually points two degrees to the west of the summit (Aveni 1980: 234; Tobriner 1972). The Pyramid of the Sun, as seen from the south end of the city, seems to imitate the silhouette of Cerro Gordo, which according to the sixteenth-century *Relaciones geográficas* was called Tenan ("mother of people" in Nahuatl) (Acuña ed. 1986, 2: 233), a highly significant name applied in later times to mother and earth goddesses, some of them mountains, in the sixteenth-century Aztec Basin of Mexico (Broda 1991b).

In 1970 the cave underneath the Pyramid of the Sun was discovered—although it seems probable that it might have been known before to local people, as were some subterranean shafts inside the construction of the Pyramid of the Moon (Manzanilla 1996). The latter are being explored only recently in an ongoing excavation by Rubén Cabrera and Saburo Sugiyama, and the cave underneath the Pyramid of the Sun was described by Doris Heyden (1975) in a now-classic article that brilliantly combines the analysis of archaeological data with the interpretation of the cosmological and ritual significance of this cave (see also Heyden 1981; Taube 1986). The study of caves and geological formations underneath the northern part of Teotihuacan was taken up in the past years by Linda Manzanilla directing an interdisciplinary study group that detected that the geological formation of tunnel-shaped volcanic caves was not only used for extracting building materials for the huge building program of the city, but that these artificially enlarged caves also had great cosmological significance.[2]

Manzanilla (1996) has shown how the geological particularities of lava formations in the Teotihuacan Valley provided the material basis for the construction of monumental buildings, and how economic and environmental factors blended with sacred geography in which great cosmological importance was attributed to caves as the entrances to the underworld.

René Millon (1992), in his recent comprehensive review article on Teotihuacan studies, also stresses the paramount importance of the cave underneath the Pyramid of the Sun. The cave shows architectural alterations all along its extension, as well as numerous remains of offerings that involved fire, water, fish, and shell, as well as miniature ceramic dishes (385–387). Millon points out that "the cave . . . was modified . . . in various ways by the Teotihuacanos in the Tzacualli phase and earlier to produce a passageway much more sinuous and serpentine that the natural cave. The cave must have been centrally important in Teotihuacan religion because its entrance determined the locus and center line of the Sun Pyramid. Every aspect of the modified cave manifests ritual"(387, fig. 10).

The cosmological importance of the water cult also existed at Teotihuacan. The course of the Río San Juan, Teotihuacan's main water supply, was artificially modified. Sugiyama (1993: 110) points out that this modification consisted of creating a channel more than 2,500 meters long and 15.40 meters wide, which ran north-south and east-west in accordance with the layout of the central part of the city. The Río San Lorenzo apparently was also deviated according to this general plan. The Cuidadela seems to have been the focus of such an artificially irrigated scheme, with a large well at its center (Sugiyama 1993: 111, 112; Rodríguez G. 1982: 56, 67–68). Within this perspective, the recent excavation by Eduardo Matos (see chapter 6 of this volume) of the platform around the Sun Pyramid, and his proposition that a broad canal might have surrounded the latter is highly intriguing, and might have been an additional aspect of the complementarity of the cult of the sun, the earth (the underworld) and water at Teotihuacan.

These elements of cosmovision and ritual landscape connect Teotihuacan with previous cultures as well as with later traditions of Postclassic societies in Central Mexico (Broda 1987; Knab 1991; Aramoni 1990). In the Postclassic, the cult of caves and mountains is widely documented in the central highlands (Broda 1991a). According to Fray Bernardino de Sahagún (1956, 3: 344–345), mountains were conceived as hollow vessels filled with water, and caves were the entrances to this subterranean realm filled with water. The Aztecs believed that there existed a subterranean connection with the sea. The latter was for them the embodiment of absolute fertility; they called it *huey atl* ("the great water") or *teoatl* ("divine water"). They also claimed that the Templo Mayor of Tenochtitlan was founded upon two rocks with two sacred caves that contained four sacred qualities of waters. These concepts were fundamental for the great cosmic and political paradigm of the Templo Mayor (Broda 1987). The sea at Teotihuacan— whose symbols are omnipresent on its beautiful murals—also seems to have embodied absolute fertility, and in this sense there appears to have existed a great continuity from Teotihuacan to Tenochtitlan.

On the other hand, this tradition goes back to the Preclassic, the most important example in the central highlands comes from the Olmec site of Chalcatzingo, with its magnificent relief carvings on the cliffs of its sacred mountain towering over the site. The most famous of these relief carvings portrays a dignitary or priest sitting inside a cave surrounded by the symbols of clouds and raindrops (Angulo 1987). The Olmec site of Chalcatzingo (900–600 B.C.E.) also had a later Teotihuacan occupation, as well as a Postclassic Tlalhuica one (Grove ed. 1987), a fact which shows that the sanctuary at the foot of the magic mountain continued to be used throughout almost two millenia.[3]

Another important site in Morelos is Xochicalco. It dates from the Epiclassic, the time after Teotihuacan's decline. The Central Acropolis of Xochicalco was a mountain with several caves that were artificially enlarged to create a system of galleries inside the mountain. Just as in Teotihuacan, the origin of these caves is partly due to the purpose of extracting stone as building materials for the site, but on the other hand at least two of these (artificial) caves also had eminently ritual and calendrical functions. These are the famous "astronomical" caves of Xochicalco that were transformed into observatories by building vertical tubes into their ceiling; only one of them has been preserved (cf. Morante 1993, 1995).

ORIENTATIONS AND GRID PLAN OF TEOTIHUACAN

Teotihuacan was constructed according to a rectangular plan that defies local topography. As Anthony F. Aveni noted in his *Skywatchers of Ancient Mexico*,

> the course of the Río San Juan and its tributaries was modified to fit the plan. . .
> The grid orientation must have been of extreme importance because the Teotihuacan
> architects retained it with great precision even in the hillside barrios on the outskirts of the ceremonial center . . . Indeed, the overall appearance of the city
> suggests that its designers left little to chance (1980: 222–223).

As the Teotihuacan Mapping Project directed by René Millon (1973) has shown, the streets of the ancient holy city align in two sets of directions: a north-south orientation 15° 28' east of north, which is also the orientation of Teotihuacan's main axis, the Street of the Dead, and an east-west orientation of 16° 30' south of east, which, however, was not so prominent.[4] As Aveni points out (see Figure 13.1), "We look southward along the north-south axis from the top of the Pyramid of the Moon at the northern end of the ruins. The archaeological evidence suggests that the deviation of 1° from a perfect right angle between the two is probably not accidental. Many building complexes and residential compounds within the city follow the first orientation while others obey the second" (1980: 223).

A number of explanations have been proposed for this deviation from the cardinal points.[5] Some of them are complementary; some are, in fact, contradictory. It would lead too far to review all of them in detail.

For the argument of the present study, I am assuming, as Aveni has pointed out, that the difference observable at Teotihuacan between the north-south orientation of 15° 28' and the E-W orientation of 16° 30', was *not* accidental. In this study we are mainly concerned with investigating the alignment of the Street of the Dead, as the main north-south axis of the city. In fact, the latter is exactly perpendicular to the east-west axis of the Pyramid of the Sun.

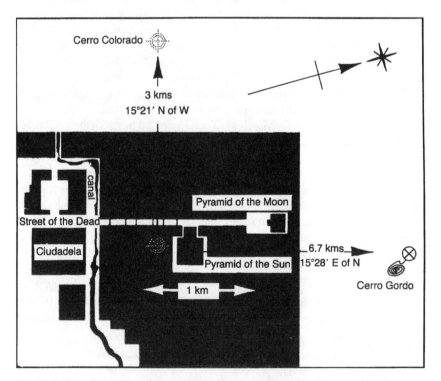

Fig. 13.1. Plan of Teotihuacan showing the position of its principal structures and pecked-circles TEO1 and TEO2. Their alignment is perpendicular to the Street of the Dead and coincides with the axis of the Sun Pyramid. Another cross petroglyph coinciding with this alignment was situated on Cerro Gordo. (Plan according to Aveni 1980: 223; diagram by P.Dunham.)

According to René Millon (1992: 386–387), the cave underneath the Pyramid of the Sun, with its entrance in line with the axis of the monumental pyramid, was responsable for the orientation of Sun Pyramid as well as the Street of the Dead. Rubén Morante (1996a: 92), in his recent detailed study of alignments and astronomy at Teotihuacan, also proposes that the fundamental structure that accounts for the orientation of Teotihuacan was the Pyramid of the Sun. Chronologically, it was also one of the first constructions, and certainly the most monumental one, of the ceremonial precinct.

From the entrance to the sacred cave a sight line to the western horizon bears the exact azimuth of 285° 30'. This sight line runs parallel to the one marked by two conspicuous pecked circles: TEO1 incised on the floor of a structure near the Sun Pyramid, and TEO5 at a distance of 3 kilometers engraved on the boulders of Cerro Colorado on the western horizon. On this sight line it was possible (within one degree of difference) to observe the heliacal setting of the constellation of the Pleiades at the beginning of April (14° 40' north of west) around 150 C.E. when the major construction period of Teotihuacan was initiated (Tzacualli 1–150 C.E.) (Aveni 1980: 225–226) (Figure 13.1).

On the other hand, as Aveni has pointed out, the heliacal rising of the Pleiades occurred exactly on the date of the first local zenith passage of the sun (May 18), after forty days of invisibility. The observation of this coincidence seems to have motivated the constructors of the city to attribute a particular importance to this constellation. (Aveni 1980: 109–117, table 9, 223–226, 233; Aveni 1993: 117; Dow 1967).

We know that the Pleiades played an important role in Mesoamerican cosmology and astronomy. Jorge Angulo (1991) suggested that they were represented on the floor of Pórtico no. 24 at Tetitla, Teotihuacan. The cult of the Pleiades is well documented from Postclassic times. For the Aztecs at Tenochtitlan the midnight meridian passage of the constellation marked the time when their major calendrical cycle of fifty-two years was completed and the celebration of the New Fire Ceremony initiated a new calendar round. This event during fall coincided with the antizenith position of the sun, being exactly six months apart from the solar zenith passage at the latitude of Tenochtitlan (as well as of Teotihuacan) (Broda 1982b).

Due to precession, the Pleiades rise every seventy years one day earlier (Aveni, personal communication). Therefore, the rising and setting phenomena do not keep in tune with the solar cycle over a long period of time. The heliacal rising and setting of the Pleiades ocurred at Teotihuacan approximately twenty days earlier than at Aztec Tenochtitlan; today the difference is approximately twenty-nine days, as compared to the year 100 C.E. (Broda 1982b: 143, note 22, table 2; Aveni 1980: 110).

During Aztec times, around 1500 C.E. the heliacal setting of the Pleiades ocurred in the last days of April. As I have argued (1982b), for the Aztecs the disappearance of the Pleiades announced the zenith of the sun (May 17) as well as the coming of the rains. This event was further associated all over Mesoamerica to Venus as Evening Star, and to fertility and the rains (cf. Šprajc 1996a, 1996b).

David Drucker (1977), while collaborating in the Teotihuacan Mapping Project, established that observers at the cave entrance at the foot of the Sun Pyramid could see the sun set on the western horizon on April 29 and August 12 (April 30 and August 13 (?) [J.B.]). The interval between these dates was 105 and 260 days, respectively. Drucker also pointed out that these dates fell fifty-two days before and after summer solstice, and that the 260-day and 105-day intervals were significant as basic divisions of the vague year of 365 days.[6]

Another hypothesis with regards to the orientation of the Street of the Dead was proposed by the geographer Vincent Malmström (1978, 1981, 1992) (see below). Malmström enhanced the fact that the date corresponding to the (perpendicular of the) alignment of the Street of the Dead (285.5°) was August 13, and that this day coincided with the legendary date that the Classic Mayas established for the beginning of their present era—"the day that 'time' began," according to the Maya Long Count. Thus, Malmström hypothesized that by adopting this date the Teotihuacanos commemorated the beginning of the present era according to the Classic Maya calendar.

Millon considers that the conjunction of these factors is convincing: "In my view no single observation or calculation is sufficient to make the case. But the combination of these observations and calculations when related to the cave *is* persuasive" (1992: 388, note 58). According to Millon,

> the sightline from the cave entrance to the hills on the western horizon (15° 30' north of west) commemorated and celebrated [thereby]: the beginning of the present era, the birth of the cosmos, the day that time began; the zenith passage . . . in part of the Maya area; and, by extension, . . . the 260-day sacred almanac, and the 52-year calendar round (388).

Millon stresses, however, that "what transformed these early observations from the esoteric and parochial to wider significance" was the huge program of public work, of monumental buildings and a great avenue that was undertaken during the first century C.E. This was achieved "to commemorate permanently the city's unique cosmological significance" (388), thus converting Teotihuacan into a paradigm to be imitated by contemporary and later cultures.

THE LATITUDE OF 15° N AND THE CALENDAR OF 260 DAYS

The 15.5° orientation is neither a solstitial nor an equinoctial alignment, marked by the sun's extremes on the horizon, nor by the east-west line; it is instead a calendrical alignment that only corresponds to significant solar dates at the latitude of 15° N. Only there it is linked to the zenith passages of the sun (Figure 13.2).

At the latitude of 15°, the sun passes the zenith on April 30 and August 13, thus delimiting two fixed periods of 105/260 days within the annual cycle. At this latitude, two major archaeological sites are situated: Preclassic Izapa and the great Classic center of Copán (latitude 14° 52'). Several authors have proposed that the calendar of 260 days, as a solar count, originated at this latitude.[7] Malmström (1973, 1978, 1981, 1989, 1992) has insistently put forward the hypothesis that the 260-day ritual calendar was invented at Izapa as early as the fourteenth century B.C.E.

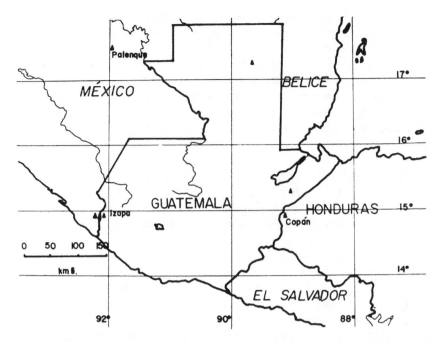

Fig. 13.2. Latitude of 15°N. Archaeological sites of Izapa, Chiapas, and Copán, Honduras.

(1978: 108), while it was further developed centuries later at the great Classic center of calendrical learning at Copán.

Malmström proposed that the 260-day count was diffused to virtually all parts of Mesoamerica where traces of the 15° alignment (285°) are found (1981: 251, table 22.1). However, the concrete arqueological proofs for this diffusion have not been adduced so far. Malmström (1991) dedicates special interest to Edzná, a large urban site in Yucatán whose construction was initiated as early as 150 B.C.E. He proposed that its major structure, "5 Pisos" with an alignment of 285° 30', was one of the earliest and most important Mesoamerican calendrical structures. The particular interest of Edzná lies in the fact that it is located in southwestern Yucatán, practically on the same latitude as Teotihuacan!

Malmström hypothesizes that the August 13 (sunset) date initiated the 260-days yearly count and that it was the most important calendrical date of the year.[8] The Classic Maya designated it as 4 Ahau 8 Cumku, the mythical beginning of time and the zero date of their Long Count. It corresponds to August 13, 3114 B.C.E. according to the Goodman-Martínez-Thompson correlation of the Maya and Christian calendars.

In the case of Teotihuacan, Malström stresses that the orientation of the Street of the Dead also corresponded to the date of August 13. According to this author, the Teotihuacanos adopted the Maya calendar, making it the foundation of the design of their city in spite of the fact that there, as well as in most other places to which the 260-day calendar was diffused, the orientation of 15° 30' did not correspond anymore to the period between the local zenith passages. He suggests that this orientation was "a learned pattern of behavior which diffused along with the ritual almanac itself" (1981: 258).

In the context of recently increasing evidence for closer contacts between the Maya area and the central highlands than were known before, Malmström's hypotheses acquire new interest. Yet, his argument is not sufficiently documented by archaeological data. As long as there can not be adduced more substantial historical and archaeological evidence, the coincidences of calendrical properties may only be noted as such, and must not be taken as an explanation nor a proof.

The "origin" of the calendar of 260 days remains so far a mystery. Izapa, although it is a very important Preclassic site and has extremely interesting iconographic data on cosmology (cf. Coggins 1982; Florescano 1995), has been too little explored archaeologically and therefore its ancestral role to Maya culture remains uncertain.

From the Classic period onwards, however, increasing evidence has accumulated on contacts between the Maya and Central Mexico. At the Epiclassic sites of Xochicalco and Cacaxtla certain Maya traits are present, but have not been explained sufficiently so far. With respect to Teotihuacan, the relations rather worked the other way around, however. After about 350 c.e. (Tlamimilolpa period), Teotihuacan culural elements were conspicuous in many sites throughout Mesoamerica, particularly in the Maya lowlands. Teotihuacan influence on the Maya has been noted in political terms, as reflected in the iconography at such important sites as Tikal (Coggins 1975; Pasztory 1988) and Copán (see William and Barbara Fash, chapter 14 of this volume). Drucker (n.d.b) interpreted the pecked crosses found at Seibal and Uaxactún as an indication of Teotihuacan's influence on the Maya, particularly at Tikal, and also argues that Teotihuacan contacts can be detected in the eighth-century inscriptions of Copán. This evidence argues, according to Drucker, for the importation of Teotihuacan solar models into the Maya region. Of particular interest are the new data on historical relations between Teotihuacan and Copán, although so far they are not of a calendrical nature (see chapter 14 of this volume).

At Copán there exists evidence for an ancient grid plan. As Aveni has pointed out, "a 7 km long base-line between Stela 12 on the east side of the Copán Valley and Stela 10 on the west is directed 9° 00' north of west. It passes over the archaeological site at the extreme south end of the West Court where the buildings are oriented in approximately the same direction. The implied association between building orientations and a long-distance base-line parallels the case at Teotihuacan" (1980: 240). As viewed from Stela 12, the sun sets over Stela 10 on April 12 and September 1.

As Merrill (1945) was the first to notice, sunsets along the Stela 12–10 base line occurred approximately midway in time between the equinoxes and Copán solar zenith passages. The April event occurred twenty-one days after vernal equinox and nineteen days before zenith passage, while the September event took place nineteen days after the second zenith passage and twenty-one days before autumnal equinox (Aveni 1980: 242–243). The base line thus established a sequence of two twenty-day periods between the equinoxes and the zenith passages, respectively. It indirectly emphasized the two dates of the zenith passages at Copán, i.e., April 30 and August 13. It is also noteworthy that these dates coincide with calendrical periods still important in the Aztec calendar correlation given by Sahagún (1950-1982; 1956): If the year began on February 12 (Gregorian date), the fourth month IV Huey tozoztli started on April 13 and the eleventh month XI Ochpaniztli on August 31 (cf. Broda 1983: 149, table 2; Tichy 1991). During Huey tozoztli the Aztecs celebrated their sowing festival, dedicated to the maize goddess Chicomecoatl, a ritual date that is still important in many Indian communities of modern Mexico, Guatemala, and Honduras (Broda n.d.).

In the area around Copán, Honduras, where the Chortí—a particularly conservative Maya group—live, the syncretistic Catholic feasts associated to these dates are still of extraordinary importance. Between April 25 (San Marcos) and May 3 (Feast of the Holy Cross), the Chortí continue to celebrate their ancestral ceremonies in petition for rain (Wisdom 1940).

In a suggestive article entitled "The Planet Venus and Temple 22 at Copan," Closs, Aveni, and Crowley (1984) pointed out that "because of its preservation of pre-European forms, the Chortí celebration is the best model we have for the ancient ceremonies dedicated to the coming of the rains. In fact, these ceremonies may derive from the ancient rituals performed in Copán at the time Temple 22 was in use" (234). Temple 22 was particularly related to Venus, maize, and the Sky Monster and/or Feathered Serpent.

As far as cosmological symbolism and calendrics are concerned, it therefore seems an urgent task to initiate a systematic comparison between Copán and Teotihuacan. Another facet of these fascinating issues might be the possible association, at both sites, of the Feathered Serpent and Venus to the calendrical matters (and dates) discussed in this chapter.

Rich ethnographic evidence on the Chortí of the area around Copán was provided by Rafael Girard (1962)[9] who reported a fixed agricultural cycle of 260 days beginning on February 8 with the preparation of the fields and ending on October 25 with harvest. He described at great length the ceremonies performed throughout the year, and interpreted their cosmological associations. He also referred to the link between the petition for rain (from April 25 to May 3), the solar zenith passage, the observation of Venus, and the disappearance of the Pleiades—a symbolic cluster that I have studied in the Aztec case (Broda 1982b) and that might be interesting to compare with Teotihuacan.

In his extensive work on calendrical matters, Franz Tichy (1981: 237; 1991: 122–131) explored the astonishing symmetry of the calendar reported by Girard, starting after the *nemontemi* on February 12; a 260-day cycle that is dependant upon five astronomically significant dates. These dates are: vernal equinox, first zenith passage (April 30), summer solstice, second zenith passage (August 13), and autumnal equinox.

This calendar is characterized at the latitude of 15°N by regular internal divisions of time of 36, 40, and 52 days. Tichy pointed out that between the 260-day fixed cycle of Copán and the central highlands there existed an astonishing symmetry involving the same intervals as among the Chortí; however, in Central Mexico the order is reversed, consisting of 52, 40, and 36 days.

Tichy's work (cf. 1991) explores many strands of the possible associations between architectural alignments, significant sequences of azimuths, and periods of time. On this basis, he hypothesized that a series of "orientation calendars" existed in Mesoamerica. He has insisted since 1976 on the importance of the zenith observation, and on the existence of a possibly fixed *tonalpohualli* closely tied to solar observation and to the agricultural cycle that, however, was adapted to local conditions depending on the geographic latitude.[10] This work should be taken into account for future studies.

THE FIXED CYCLE OF 260 DAYS AND THE ALIGNMENT GROUP OF 15° TO 16°

However, much more can be said with respect to the interesting alignment group of 15°–16° (15.5°), and it constitutes the central issue of this chapter. I have discussed this alignment in previous work, putting forward a series of calendrical hypotheses (Broda 1993). One of these propositions was that in Mesoamerican cosmovision the greatest importance was attributed to the dates themselves, i.e., the precise days of the solar cycle (*xiuhpohualli*). These dates, in turn, were fixed by alignments in the horizon reference system. However, the alignments corresponding to these dates vary slightly according to the horizon elevation and other local environmental factors.[11] Therefore, I suggest that the calendrical dates were more meaningful than the alignments themselves (1993: 260).

With respect to Teotihuacan, I assume, as noted above, that the orientation of 15.5° (Street of the Dead, Pyramid of the Sun) reflects most closely the purpose of the builders of Teotihuacan. I propose, therefore, that the alignment of 17° (16°–18°), to which belonged the east-west axis of the city, as well as the Ciudadela, falls already outside the range of this purposeful orientation, i.e., it might have had a different meaning. Since during this time of the year (approximately at the middle between the solstices and the equinoxes), the daily movement of the sun is relatively fast, the difference of one or two degrees is significant.

The orientation of the Street of the Dead being north-south, the relevant azimuth of this alignment is, in fact, the perpendicular to it; the latter coincides, as we have seen, with the east-west axis of the Pyramid of the Sun. This east-west orientation corresponds to the four azimuths of the annual cycle of 74° 30', 105° 30', 254° 30', and 285° 30'. Two of these azimuths correspond to *sunrise* and two to *sunset*. The azimuth of 105° 30' corresponds to sunrise on February 12 and October 30; and the azimuth of 74° 30' to sunrise on April 30 and August 13; while the azimuth of 285° 30' applies to sunset on April 30 and August 13, and the azimuth of 254° 30' to sunset on October 30 and February 12 (Figure 13.3, Table 13.1).

In terms of calendrical studies there is a common agreement that the calendar system consisting of the combination of the two cycles of 365 and 260 days was one of the main cultural traits shared by all Mesoamerican cultures and that it is first documented in full use around 600 B.C.E. at Monte Albán (Broda 1996b). On the other hand, this calendar system is abundantly recorded in Aztec historical sources for the fifteenth and sixteenth century. For the preceding two millennia that it was in use, it is documented in the archaeological and iconographic evi-

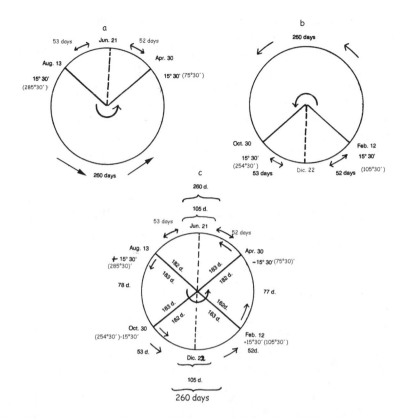

Fig. 13.3. Subdivisions of the year of 365 days into 260 + 52 + 53 days (dates February 12–April 30–August 13–October 30), from Broda 1993.

dence. Here, archaeoastronomical alignment studies of individual structures and building assemblages have added important new evidence for the application of calendrical knowledge in the generation of sacred architecture.

The Teotihuacan alignment is frequently present at contemporary sites that were influenced by Teotihuacan, some of them as far away as Uaxactún in the Petén, or Alta Vista at the Tropic of Cancer (Aveni and Gibbs 1976; Aveni 1980: app. A). It also occurs at Epiclassic Xochicalco and Teotenango (Tichy 1991: 99), at Postclassic sites like Tula, Tenayuca, and Tepoztlan (Aveni 1980: 237, app. A; Ponce de León 1983), as well as at the Aztec sanctuary of Malinalco (Galindo 1990; Broda 1977). However, if we separate the 15°–16° orientation from the azimuth of 16°–18°, the number of sites will be reduced. I am proposing to take into account the horizon elevation in each case and to calculate the exact date to which the orientation corresponded. The relevant dates, as we have argued, are February 12, April 30, August 13, and October 30.

The central hypothesis presented here is that these four dates corresponded to four extremely important feasts of the annual agricultural cycle, which also had important socioeconomic as well as cosmological connotations. To develop this hypothesis, I have drawn upon data from the last Aztec period from which there exists abundant ritual evidence.

The importance of the four dates in the pre-Hispanic calendar was as follows:[12]

1. February 12 was the initial day of the Aztec calendar, according to our best historical source, Fray Bernardino de Sahagún (1956, 2: 274).
2. April 30 corresponded to the Aztec sowing festival, the initiation of their cycle of maize cultivation, as well as to the coming of the rains, an extremely important symbolism for the agricultural peoples of Mesoamerica. Ceremonies for the petition of rain and crop fertility were carried out at

Dates April 30–August 13–October 30–February 12
Subdivisions of the year in 260, 105, 77/78, and 182/183 days

AZ 15°30'   **Dates April 30–August 13–October 30–February 12**
A, B:

	August 13	
	April 29	
	260 days	

	August 13	October 30
	October 29	February 11
	78 days	105 days (52+53)

	February 12	
	October 29	
	260 days	

	February 12	April 30
	April 29	August 12
	77 days	105 days (52 + 53)

C:

	April 30	February 12
	October 29	August 12
	183 days	182 days
	[(52 + 53) + 78]	

	October 30	August 13
	April 29	February 11
	182 days	183 days
	[(52 + 53) + 77]	

1 year: $183 + 182 = 365$ days $182 + 183 = 365$ days

Table 13.1. The orientation group of 15° 30'. (Dates of April 30–August 13–October 30–February 12.) (Subdivisions of the year into 260, 105, 77/78, and 182/183 days.)

the shrines on mountaintops as I have analyzed elsewhere at great length (Broda 1971, 1983, 1991a, 1991b, 1996a, 1996b).

3. August 13, on the other hand, happens to have been the initial day of the Maya Long Count, as was pointed out by Malmström (1978, 1981, 1989); and finally,

4. October 30 marked the end of the agricultural cycle and the beginning of harvest in Aztec ritual (Broda 1983, 1993).

On the basis of this evidence, I have concluded in my earlier studies that these four dates were extremely important in terms of the internal structure of the Mesoamerican solar calendar as well as in ritual terms. They divided the year into four symmetrical parts (into fixed subdivisions of $260 + 105$ $(52 + 53) = 365$ days), a circumstance that was significant in Aztec times. However, the calendrical pattern seems to go back to the Preclassic as I have suggested previously (1993; see below) and seems to have been particularly relevant at Teotihuacan, as is argued in the present chapter.

Another astonishing circumstance about these four dates consists in the fact that their importance for the internal structure of the annual calendrical cycle, in a way, can still be perceived in the agricultural festival calendar of traditional Indian communities of Mexico and Guatemala. These Catholic feasts introduced by the Spaniards after the Conquest, and which became particularly conspicuous in syncretistic terms, are: 1) La Virgen de la Candelaria on February 2;[13] 2) the Feast of the Holy Cross on May 3 (its rites often start on April 25, the Day of San Marcos); 3) the "Asunción de la Virgen" on August 15, a very important Catholic Feast; and 4) October 30 (or rather November 1 and 2), the Catholic All Saints' Day and the Day of the Dead, another sequence of outstanding syncretistic feasts in modern Mexico (Broda 1995, n.d.).

These feasts constitute the basic framework for the celebration of agricultural rites in traditional Indian communities, complex ceremonies that naturally show a great variation in their specific details; however, it is a variation within the basic symbolism of these agrarian rites that preserve many elements of pre-Hispanic cosmovision. These ceremonies are dedicated to maize, rains, and mountains, and are closely related to concepts of still-existing ritual landscapes. I have been studying this subject since 1980, and have collected a rich corpus of ethnographic evidence since then; however, it would lead too far to go into more detail here (cf. Broda 1983, 1987, 1991a, 1993, 1995, n.d.). Yet, for the formulation of my calendrical hypothesis with respect to the importance of these four dates in pre-Hispanic cosmovision, this ethnographic strand of investigation has been fundamental.

But let us return to the archaeological evidence. At the other extreme of Mesoamerican history, I have hypothesized (1993) that at the important Preclassic site of Cuicuilco—the first monumental ceremonial center in the Basin of Mexico and direct antecedent of Teotihuacan—there existed a remarkable horizon calendar. From its monumental round pyramid, the big volcanoes Popocatépetl and Iztaccíhuatl, as well as several other conspicuous mountains of the eastern horizon, functioned as natural markers indicating the time of the solstices (winter solstice at the northern slope of Popocatépetl), the equinoxes (or rather, mid-year days at Mt. Papayo), as well as the dates of February 12, April 30, August 13, and October 30 on the horizon line of Iztaccíhuatl and Mt. Tlaloc (Figure 13.4).

The horizon calendar of Cuicuilco provided the possibility of fixing a 260-day cycle between February 12 and October 30 on the southern end of the broad profile of Iztaccíhuatl, and the symmetrical dates of April 30/August 13 on Mt. Tlaloc, respectively. Thus, from the monumental round pyramid of Cuicuilco, it was possible to track a 260-day calendar on the local horizon, delimited by the dates investigated in this chapter, and which, in this case, seems to go back to Preclassic origins (Broda 1993: 275–285).

The remarkable natural properties of the eastern horizon as contemplated from Cuicuilco induce us to think that the site was consciously selected for the purpose of these observations, which stood at the origin of calendrical practice and the construction of the Mesoamerican calendrical and geometrical system during the first millenium B.C.E. The great volcanoes were used, in this case, as natural markers on the horizon. Cuicuilco is not just any archaeological site, but is considered to have been the first truly monumental pyramid and proto-urban settlement of the Valley of Mexico that preceded Teotihuacan.

In this context, a hypothesis put forward by Munro S. Edmonson (1988) in his comprehensive, however speculative, study on the evolution of Mesoamerican calendrical systems, is of special interest. Edmonson proposes that it is at Cuicuilco that we find the first evidence of the existence of the Calendar Round (composed of the 365-day year and the cycle of 260 days), which he postulates to have originated in the eighth century B.C.E. (initial date: June 22, summer solstice, 739 B.C.E.) and to have been ancestral to all later variants of this calendar (17, 20, 113–117).[14]

This hypothesis is intriguing; however, it needs to be substantiated by further archaeological evidence. Yet we might mention in this context that in 1996, the Instituto Nacional de Antropología e Historia (INAH) initiated new excavations at the pyramid of Cuicuilco that was covered by lava from the eruption of the volcano Xitle more than two thousand years ago. These excavations, conducted by Mario Pérez Campa, have uncovered from the lava flow an enormous stone stela with strange incisions (circles, etc.) that, according to Mora, might be calendrical inscriptions ancestral in time (Pérez Campa 1998). This more than 4-

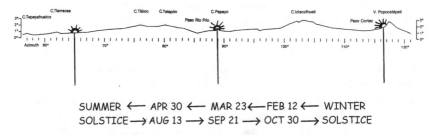

Fig. 13.4. Cuicuilco: Eastern horizon (Broda 1993, horizon profile courtesy of Franz Tichy).

meter-high stone column seems to belong to the earliest occupation of Cuicuilco some three thousand years ago. It has an inclination of 6° 30' that apparently is intentional; due to this inclination the sun illuminates the stela totally during May, on its movement towards the north and again during August, on its way back to the south (Pérez Campa 1997: 60). If these observations by archaeologist Pérez Campa can be substantiated by further evidence in the future, this may indicate that the stela permitted to register the dates of April 30 and August 13 and thus, the calendrical cycles 105/260 days reviewed in this chapter.

Hypothesizing that Cuicuilco was an important center of calendrical learning during late Preclassic times, its direct influence on Teotihuacan may have been decisive. It is generally assumed that after Cuicuilco was destroyed by the eruptions of Xitle, its population migrated to the Valley of Teotihuacan where it contributed to the rise of that metropolis.

Another amazing peculiarity about Cuicuilco refers to the fact that almost two millennia later in the complex history of the cultural landscape of the basin, the Aztecs still attributed a particular importance to this geographical spot. They built a sanctuary at nearby Zacatepetl where they worshipped the ancient mother- and earth-goddess, as well as Mixcoatl, their Chichimec ancestral deity related to Venus. This temple permitted the Aztecs to make exactly the same horizon observations as from the Preclassic pyramid of Cuicuilco. This sanctuary was called Ixillan Tonan, "there at the navel of our mother." It reminds us of the name of Cerro Gordo at Teotihuacan, which was Tenan, "the mother of people." Next to Zacatepetl there exist other archaeological remains at a place called Tenantongo. Nearby San Ángel was called Tenanitla in the sixteenth century (Broda 1991a: 106–107). All these places apparently were related to the worship of the ancient mother and earth goddess.

Another Aztec site dedicated to the cult of the earth- and mother-goddess was Malinalco, situated to the south of the Valley of Mexico (cf. Broda 1977, 1996a). At this important rock sanctuary, the horizon observation of a fixed cycle of 260 days is documented as well. There, the axis of one of the main chambers (Temple IV), hewn from the "life rock" of the mountain, points with an alignment of 105° 09' to a vertical cliff of the nearby eastern horizon where the sun rises on February 12, and again 260 days later on October 29/October 30.[15] This event was documented by Jesús Galindo (1990) in an excellent archaeoastronomical study. The fact that February 12 was the first day of the Aztec year, and that the sun returned to this horizon marker exactly 260 days later, surely was not a mere coincidence. The important Aztec sanctuary of Malinalco clearly documents a deliberate integration of the temple architecture into the mountainous landscape based on horizon observations. The most significant calendrical period that was tracked on the horizon was the fixed period of 260 days between February 12 and October 29.

In his recent book of synthesis on Mesoamerican archaeoastronomy, Galindo (1994) also insists on the calendrical importance of the division of the year into the fixed cycles of 260/105 days, based on the four above-mentioned dates, and reviews a number of archaeological sites where these alignments can be observed.

New Evidence from Teotihuacan

But let us return to Teotihuacan and interpret in the light of the above-mentioned archaeoastronomical studies the new evidence from the site. The comparative material presented serves to better evaluate the importance of the recent findings.[16]

SUBTERRANEAN ASTRONOMICAL OBSERVATORIES

One of the most important pieces of new evidence from Teotihuacan refers to the three caves that were recently discovered and excavated (cf. Rubén Cabrera Castro, chapter 7 in this volume). They are not only interesting in terms of the cave-cult, but above all because they were subterranean observatories. These caves doubtlessly had an astronomical function. Thus, the cosmological concept of the cave as the womb of the earth and the entrance to the underworld was combined at Teotihuacan with astronomical observation and calendrical practice.[17] Probably, they were crucial for the development of calendrics at Teotihuacan, a subject on which there had existed so little evidence so far. From the point of view of the present study, the particular interest of these observatories is that they seem to have been designed particularly to mark the periods of time we are concerned with in this study, i.e., the fixed cycles of 105/260 days running from April 30 to August 13 and from August 13 to April 29.

The first detailed archaeoastronomical study of these observatories was undertaken by Rubén Morante López in recent years, first at Xochicalco[18] and then at Teotihuacan.[19] According to the detailed field observations carried out by Morante at Xochicalco (1993),[20] its astronomical tube was oriented with great precision to observe the two zenith passages of the sun, as well as the period of 105 days between April 30 and August 12 when the rays of the sun enter directly into the cave; while during the remaining 260 days of the year the beam of sunlight cannot be seen from the subterranean ritual chamber.

The observatory of Xochicalco is the most sophisticated construction that is known so far. At the Epiclassic site of Xochicalco, it was probably copied from the earlier and less elaborate subterranean chambers of Teotihuacan (Morante 1995, n.d.a). At Teotihuacan, these astronomical caves have only recently been excavated.

During the Proyecto Arqueológico Teotihuacan 1980–1982, directed by Rubén Cabrera, Cave 1 was discovered some 270 meters to the southeast of the Pyramid of the Sun. It was excavated and studied by Enrique Soruco Sáenz (1985, 1991). During the Proyecto Especial Teotihuacan 1993–1994, directed by Eduardo Matos Moctezuma, two new caves were registered very close to Cave 1. They were explored by Natalia Moragas and studied in archaeoastronomical terms by Rubén Morante (1996a, n.d.a), as noted above. These caves were artificially excavated from the volcanic rock during the Early Tlamimilolpa phase (around 200 C.E.); apparently they were abandoned in the next phase (Xolalpan, around 450 C.E.) (Morante n.d.a). Caves 1 and 2 both contain a rudimentary clay altar with an erect stone slab or stela (without inscription). Cave 1, according to Soruco (1985, 1991), permitted the making of calendrical observations of the year of 365 days, the zenith passages, the solstices and equinoxes, as well as the dates of February 9 and November 1. Note that the latter dates are very close to October 30 and February 12. Morante (1996a: 171, 181; n.d.a) additionally observed in 1994–1995 that the first rays of the sun enter Cave 1 by April 29/30 illuminating the edge of the rudimentary stela found in situ. He points out that this date is highly significant at Teotihuacan as well as at Xochicalco: at both places it corresponds to the first day that sunlight enters the observatory.

Morante (1996a: 181–182), comparing the results on his studies of the subterranean observatories of Xochicalco, Teotihuacan, and Monte Albán (where there exists another artificial tube), reaches the conclusion that in all three cases, these observatories, based on the principle of the camara oscura,[21] permit the observation of the period between the end of April and the middle of August, i.e., from April 29 to August 13. The observatories also served to register the zenith passages of the sun, which, however, varied locally according to latitude. The observatories of Teotihuacan, Xochicalco, and Monte Albán marked regular periods of days grouped around the solstices. These periods were 52/53 days at Teotihuacan and Xochicalco, and 65 days at Monte Albán, respectively. This indicates, according to Morante, the use of the *tonalpohualli* as the basic counting device in these subterranean chambers (182).

Morante points out that a clear evolution of these observational instruments can be perceived. "Starting with the caves of Teotihuacan, the constructions become more sophisticated. The tallest chimney is that from Xochicalco, which also has the most complex constructive system"(182). It is also the latest in time. The three observatories offer the possibility of detecting the tropical year (of 365.2422 days) by means of the variations in the projection of light produced on the ground of the observatories in the four-year annual cycle (182). Starting from April 30, the sun enters the subterranean chamber of Xochicalco for 105 days, while for the remaining 260 days the visibility of the direct rays of the sun is obstructed. In leap years, the chimney allowed the observation of intervals of 261/105 days, a fact that may have made it possible to correct the calendar, at least theoretically.[22]

For reasons of space, it is not possible to reproduce here in more detail the steps of the observations undertaken by Morante in Caves 1 and 2 of Teotihuacan, which should be consulted directly in his detailed work (1996a: 165–194). According to this author, Cave 2, besides other dates, also marked the periods of 105 days from April 30 to August 12, and 260 days from August 13 to April 29, on the altar with the stela found in situ inside the cave; other periods of time that are indicated inside are 52/53 days, around the summer solstice, and periods of 20 days around February 12 and October 30, respectively (180; n.d.a); all of these periods have calendrical significance, as pointed out already. These dates, as we have seen, corresponded to the 15.5° alignment of the sacred city. Thus, the important evidence from the astronomical caves corroborates the calendrical significance and intentional design of this alignment.

SOLAR OBSERVATIONS AT THE PYRAMID OF THE SUN: WINTER SOLSTICE AND FEBRUARY 12

*A Solstitial Alignment.*The Pyramid of the Sun has two extraordinary solar orientations. The fact that the pyramid as well as the sacred city in general possess a solstitial alignment to Mexico's highest mountain, Pico de Orizaba, was noted before by Malmström (1978) on the basis of map analysis; it was recently confirmed by Morante's observations in the field (1996a: 57–60) (Figure 13.5).

The winter-solstice sunrise over Pico de Orizaba is, however, not directly visible from the Sun Pyramid; the nearby range of the hills of Apan hide it from sight. An intermediate point of observation on these hills is required; it was localized by Morante (59, 86, fig. 3.3) at Cerro Ocotalito. However, so far, no archaeological site is reported from there.

Morante describes a peculiar experience during his fieldwork when he observed, on a cold winter sunrise of December 22, a sun pillar at the summit of the pyramid exactly in the direction of Pico de Orizaba (1996a: 57–60). This sun pillar—a triangular visual phenomenon produced by crystals of ice (on the Pico de Orizaba) acting as a kind of mirror that causes the reflection of light—may have on occasions conjured the luminous image of that preeminent volcano, and surely would have been interpreted by the priests of Teotihuacan as a great hierophany.

February 12 and the Beginning of the Year. As we have seen, the sun sets perpendicular to the alignment of the Street of the Dead on April 30 and August 13, while it rises to the east on February 12 and October 30. In fact, as several authors have pointed out (Aveni 1980; Millon 1992; Galindo 1994) and Rubén Morante (1996a) has studied recently in great detail, the Pyramid of the Sun has exactly this orientation; it certainly was of fundamental importance. As crucial as its western sight line, mentioned above, should have been the view toward sunrise. In fact, several codices—the *Mapa Quinatzin*, and the map included in the *Relación geográfica de Mazapan* (1580)—give as the symbol for Teotihuacan the sun rising behind its main pyramid (see Elizabeth Boone, chapter 12 in this volume). However, it has to be noted that the point on the horizon where the sun,

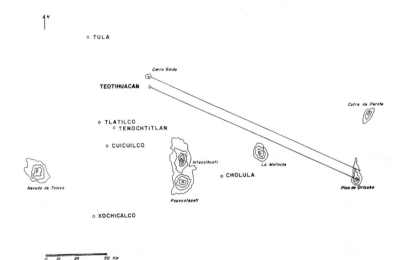

Fig. 13.5. Winter solstice alignment from the Valley of Teotihuacan toward Pico de Orizaba, Mexico's highest peak (according to Morante 1996: fig. 2.1).

rises on February 12—a hill called Mesas Quebradas according to Morante (1996a: 86, fig. 3.3)—is not a conspicuous peak on the horizon.

February 12, which is another one of the four dates corresponding to the alignment of 15.5°, was an extremely important date in the sixteenth-century Aztec calendar. According to interesting information given by Fray Bernardino de Sahagún (1956, 2: 274), it was the initial day of the *xiuhpohualli*, the year of 365 days. Franz Tichy (1980, 1981, 1991), in his research on pre-Hispanic calendrical matters in relation to cultural geography, alignment studies, and archaeoastronomy, also reached the conclusion that in structural terms, February 12 was the initial day of the solar year count. Thus, Tichy's reconstruction of the Aztec calendar coincides with Sahagún's correlation, although it was obtained in an entirely different way.

February 12 was the first day of the Aztec month of Atlcahualo, when the Aztecs offered child sacrifices at the mountaintops in petition for rain (Broda 1971, 1991b, 1993). Thus, Atlcahualo was an important month within the annual ritual cycle of the cult of maize, rain, and mountains. Child sacrifices were the most ancient human sacrifices in Mesoamerica; at Teotihuacan they were reported by Leopoldo Batres (1906: 40) from the corners of the terraces of the Sun Pyramid. Among the Aztecs, infant sacrifices were particularly related to nobles and kings. The next important feast with child sacrifices was Huey tozoztli, when the king opened the agricultural cycle, i.e., the sowing season. This Aztec sowing festival fell on April 30—another one of the four dates correlated with 15.5°—and it was celebrated by the kings of the Triple Alliance at the summit of Mt. Tlaloc where there existed a sanctuary, the remains of which are still visible today. Child sacrifices were thus related to royal and dynastic beginnings, a fact that enhanced the importance of the months of Atlcahualo and Huey tozoztli.

Linda Manzanilla (1996), in a fascinating study on the concept of the underworld at Teotihuacan, reproduces the following ethnographic information obtained in 1989 from the inhabitants of the vicinity of the archaeological site. Various old-aged informants mentioned the myth that "in ancient times, during February, one could see a man proceed from the inside of the Sun Pyramid carrying maize, amaranth, beans, and squash in his arms. Many [informants] added that, underneath the structure, there existed *chinampa*-type irrigated fields where these food products were harvested" (42).

This information coincides with the image that the inside of mountains was fertile land with an abundance of water, greenness, food plants, and other riches—known to the Aztecs as Tlalocan, the paradise of the rain god Tlaloc—which is represented on the famous Tepantitla murals of Teotihuacan. Viewed from this perspective, the famous murals might actually represent the Teotihuacano's visualization of the subterranean space underneath the Pyramid of the Sun. This image was recurrent in pre-Hispanic cosmovision throughout the centuries, and is still one of the most frequent concepts shared by traditional peasants of the central highlands (Broda 1991a; Robles 1995, n.d.). What is really striking in this case is that this image is still connected today at the modern village of San Juan Teotihuacan with the month of February.

The Temple of Quetzalcoatl as a Calendrical Marker?: February 12 Sunrise. Another interesting hypothesis proposed by Morante in his voluminous work on Teotihuacan (1996a: 209–228), concerns the possible use of the Temple of Quetzalcoatl and the Ciudadela as another set of calendrical markers. It might not have been the only function of that great complex of buildings, maybe not even the principal one. Although Morante took into account the data of the recent excavations of the Teotihuacan Project conducted by Rubén Cabrera, his rather complex reconstruction of the original height and dimensions of the Temple of Quetzalcoatl still remains hypothetical and needs to be taken with certain caution, last but not least because of the spectacular implications it contains.

Based on his field observations in the period between 1993 and 1995, Morante proposes that the Temple of Quetzalcoatl and the Ciudadela may have functioned as a huge astronomical marker, as he argues at great length in his aforementioned study (1996a:195–228). Like Sugiyama (1993) he reaches the conclusion that numerology implying the principal calendrical periods was involved in the building of the Temple of Quetzalcoatl. In the course of his argument, he hypothesizes that, as observed from Structure 1 C across the huge plaza of the Ciudadela, the sun would have risen on February 12/13 right at the (hypothetically reconstructed) summit of the Pyramid of Quetzalcoatl (Morante 1996a: 215–217).

Morante (217) further suggests the possibility that from the different buildings of the Great Plaza of the Cuidadela, the Teotihuacanos might have observed the five *nemontemi* anteceding February 12, with the Ciudadela and the Temple of Quetzalcoatl serving as a huge calendrical structure in which the latter temple provided an artificial horizon that permitted making day-to-day observations of the sun's movement during this crucial time of the year.

The proposition with respect to the day-to-day observation of the *nemontemi* seems rather speculative; however, it does not stand out alone, as Morante's field observations at several other important sites show. At the Aztec site of Mt. Tlaloc at an altitude of 4,120 meters,[23] he observed the same situation when the sun moves horizontally from one day to the other along the broad summit of La Malinche, which as viewed from Mt. Tlaloc is seen in line with the Pico de Orizaba, thus announcing the *nemontemi* and the beginning of the indigenous year on February 12 (Morante n.d.b). In another interesting article on Mt. Tlaloc, Iwaniszewski (1994) also proposes that the same days were observed. On the other hand, Morante also traced the same days on the eastern horizon of Xochicalco, when the sun passes over the summit of nearby Cerro Jumil, as seen from the Temple of the Feathered Serpent, in what seems to have been an artificially worked horizon line (Morante 1993). Yet another observation of this kind could be made from the important Postclassic site of Tenayuca in the Basin of Mexico; as seen from there, the sun passes over Mt. Tlaloc on February 12 and October 30, an observation that has been recorded by Ponce de León (1983) and Morante (n.d.b).[24] Šprajc (n.d.) also refers to the same circumstances in an interesting recent paper on the calendrical properties of the pyramid of Tenayuca. It is noteworthy that the magnificent temples of Quetzalcoatl at Teotihuacan and Xochicalco, as well as the Postclassic pyramid of Tenayuca, all three bear as their principal decoration serpent motifs (Morante 1996a: 217).

With respect to the Ciudadela, Drucker (1974, as cited by Sugiyama 1993: 114) analyzed "architectural references for the possible calendric implications of the layout of the Ciudadela. He proposed that the 15 temple pyramids atop the four platforms served for calendric counts of the *tonalpohualli* and the Venus cycle." Sugiyama points out that although Drucker's proposition about the Ciudadela remains hypothetical, some results of his own measurement-unit study tend to support Drucker's basic idea that the "builders of the Ciudadela purposefully encoded calendric numbers in the location and the sizes of buildings" (Sugiyama 1993: 114).[25]

Alfredo López Austin, Leonardo López Luján, and Saburo Sugiyama (1991), interpreting the Temple of Quetzalcoatl, have also proposed that this pyramid was related to calendrics; they suggest that it was primarily dedicated to the myth of the origin of time. These authors, particularly Sugiyama (1993), have stressed the numerological properties with calendric implications of the Pyramid of Quetzalcoatl: the main numbers employed are 13, 18, 20, 52, and 260. They all point to symbolic associations with the calendar of 260 days. Sugiyama has further suggested that there existed a TEO measurement unit of 83 meters that implied the use of 260 and multiples of 260 as units that were basic in the proportions of the buildings erected during the grand construction program of the site.

Pecked Circles in the Ritual Landscape. This leads us to consider a final point in this chapter: the relation that might have existed between the design of the city and the symbolism of the pecked circles.

Another important feature of the ritual landscape created at Teotihuacan were the so-called pecked circles—peculiar petroglyphs in the shape of circles with pecked dots delineating the circles and their axes. Numerous pecked circles were discovered at Teotihuacan and its surroundings, in the Basin of Mexico and adjacent valleys, as well as in distant places such as Alta Vista on the Tropic of Cancer to the north (Aveni, Hartung, and Kelley 1982) or at Uaxactún in the Petén to the south (Aveni 1980: 277; ed. 1989). It is generally assumed that they were created by the Teotihuacan state and denote its cultural influence over these faraway regions at the limits of the sphere of influence (Aveni 1980: 237; chapter 9 of this volume).

Pecked circles at Teotihuacan are situated within the urban settlement, in the ceremonial precinct, as well as on the hills and mountains surrounding the Valley of Teotihuacan. It was suggested that they might have to do with the urban planning of the site (Millon 1973); however, their nature seems to be rather numerological and calendric, maybe partly astronomical. At Teotihuacan, they were used so often and are of such different shapes, that so far it has not been possible to find a unified explanation for their design and purpose (Aveni 1988). Recently, Morante has suggested that they were used as counting devices (1997).

It is not possible in this study to discuss the varied aspects of pecked circles, nor to describe the recent discovery to the south of the Sun Pyramid of eighteen pecked circles and twenty-eight other designs engraved into the broad stucco platform (cf. Morante 1996a: 134–164; 1997). I will only mention a calendrical aspect of these designs that is relevant for the present discussion.

The pecked circles have been studied by numerous investigators.[26] Among them, Aveni[27] has undertaken the most comprehensive research on them over the past two decades, and any future study has to depart from this work. Recently, Morante (1996a: 137–145) includes new evidence on the pecked circles; he registers forty-six of them only at Teotihuacan as well as twenty-eight other engraved designs (146–149). Several authors have noted before that cycles of 260 dots seem to have been particularly relevant in some, although not all, pecked crosses. David Drucker was perhaps the first to have insisted on this circumstance, when TEO1 and TEO2 were discovered within the Teotihuacan Mapping Project. Drucker (n.d.b) explored pecked circles TEO1, 2, 3, and 5 assuming that they were in some general way connected to the solar calendar, the seasonal round of planting and harvesting, and perhaps even involved the 260/105-day division of the year.[28]

Stanislaw Iwaniszewski (1991), on the other hand, observed that TEO1 and TEO2, on the stuccoed floors of buildings in the vicinity of the Pyramid of the Sun, pointed to interesting azimuths on their east-west axis. TEO1, according to measurements taken by this author, points to the four annual dates of February 5, April 29, August 13, and November 11 (azimuths 285° 02' and 107° 52', respectively). However, he admits that due to the deterioration of the petroglyphs, errors of $\pm 2°$, i.e., of approximately ± 6 days, are possible (279, 280, gráfica 4) (Figure 13.6).

TEO2, which consists of three concentric Maltese crosses, actually is the most elegant one of these designs (Iwaniszewski 1991: 283, gráfica 5) (Figure 13.7). Its east-west axis points again to the four annual dates of February 13, April 28, August 14, and October 30 (admitting the same possibility of error as in the case of TEO1), denoting intervals of days of $(74 + 108 + 77 =) 260$ and 106 days, respectively (282).

Taking into account the possibility of a correction of $\pm 2°$ (± 6 days) mentioned by Iwaniszewski, I propose that the intended dates of TEO1 and TEO2 might rather have been February 12, April 30, August 13, and October 30 and the azimuth of $\pm 15.5°$.[29] In case this interpretation is correct, these two conspicuous pecked circles might actually reveal a close link to the fixed cycle of 260 days and the basic Teotihuacan alignment referred to in this chapter.

Aveni published in 1978 a survey of the pecked circles known at that time. There he indicates, among other data, the averaged orientation of the axes relative to astronomical north (Aveni, Hartung, and Buckingham 1978: table 1, 269–271). In his later publications, he does not repeat these data. For TEO1 and TEO2, he registers the average azimuth of 17° 50' and 16° 11', respectively. He further lists six pecked circles at Teotihuacan (TEO 3, 4, 9, 10, and 12) with azimuths between 15° and 17°; two in the surroundings (TEP3, TEX) with an azimuth of 14°; as well as three pecked crosses at Uaxactún (UAX1, 2, 3) with the azimuth of 17° 30'.[30] The above-mentioned circles are classified, as far as their general description, as belonging to the TEO1 class of pecked circles. Aveni, Hartung, and Buckingham observe that "the axes of the cross pattern of TEO1 appear to be aligned closely with the Teotihuacan grid which is oriented about 15.5° east of north" (1978: 271). The line connecting TEO1 to TEO5 is oriented almost exactly perpendicular to the Street of the Dead, thus defining the east-west axis. According to Aveni, the Category 1 symbols (TEO 1, 2, 3, 4, 9, 10, 12, 20) all seem to be oriented within the grid plan of the city. TEO1 had long ago been implicated in such a scheme (Dow 1967). However, Aveni comments: "But what of the large number of designs in the buildings on the western side of the Street

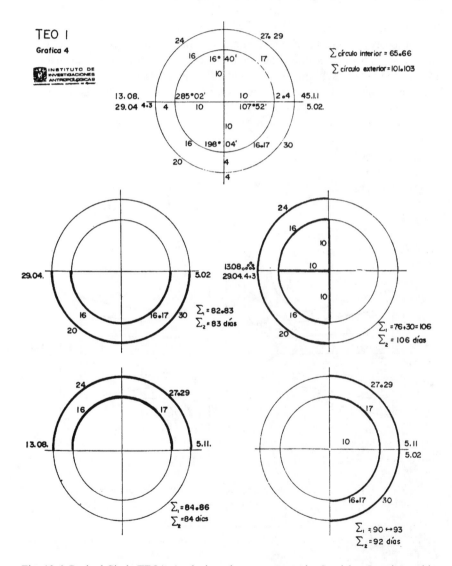

Fig. 13.6. Pecked Circle TEO1: Analysis and measurements by Stanislaw Iwaniszewski 1991: 47.

opposite TEO1? We would hypothesize an eastward alignment or orientation by prolonging the 15.5°(south of east) cardinally deviated axis to the horizon and then searching that vicinity for a matching petroglyph, similar to TEO5 on the western horizon. But this is work for the future"(Aveni 1988: 465).

I do not pretend to have found a unified solution to the intricate problem of the pecked-cross symbol; however, the examples cited show that at least some of them were related to the issues discussed in this chapter. It is further evidence, besides the other examples analyzed, for the links that existed between calendrical counts, the fixed cycle of 260 days, and the basic Teotihuacan alignment.

Conclusions

The new evidence points to a paramount interest of ancient Teotihuacanos in creating a planned artificial human order as an imposition upon the chaos of the natural elements. In this sense, the words of Paul Kirchhoff, which I rescued years ago from his so far unpublished notebooks, seem prophetic. According to this eminent scholar,

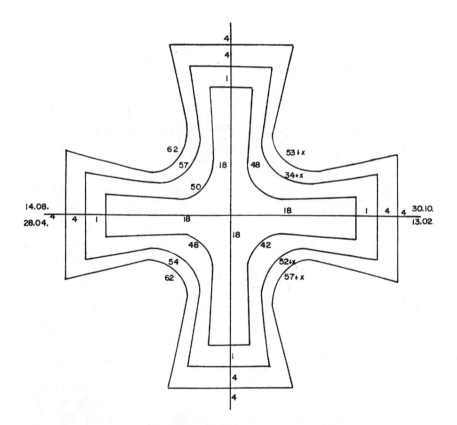

Fig. 13.7. Pecked Cross TEO2: Analysis and measurements by Stanislaw Iwaniszewski 1991: 47.

Ancient Mexico is a world of order, in which everything and everybody has his proper place. Thus, ancient Mexico could not have existed without an enormous mass of people that work according to what they are told to do. Man has formed for himself a very orderly image of the world. It is a world in which man has formed a unity in everything. Everything has its perfect place, there is a formula for everything; it is also a world that terrifies us because of its universality.

Religion is conceived as a unity with the universe, a fact that gives great security to man. Everything has a visible structure, everything has a center. One world is destroyed and another world surges to the surface; everything is predestined. All things have their place because thus it has been prophesized. Architecture and calendrics are structuring principles: the calendar is a two fold structuring principle, with time and with space. These cultures do not know chaos.

One discovers things that seem disorderly according to our judgment, but afterwards one discovers a much more fantastic order, e.g. that there exist a multiplicity of parallel calendars. The orderly structure can be seen in everything (Kirchhoff, n.d., author's translation).

These comments by Paul Kirchhoff seem pertinent as concluding remarks. Calendrical and archaeoastronomical studies situate Teotihuacan within the context of other Mesoamerican cultures. Teotihuacan participated in this cultural tradition. Although we still count on too little calendrical and textual evidence from Teotihuacan, and it is of a different kind than in the Maya area, nevertheless recent ongoing research has established that there existed many common elements that Teotihuacan shared with the rest of Mesoamerica, also in terms of the calendrical tradition that combined the 365-day annual cycle with the 260-day ritual almanac.

Within the general perspective of this study, calendrics offer a particularly rich field of research. In the past years, increasing evidence has accumulated that permits us to get a glimpse of how calendric and solar observations might have operated and how the calendar was developed that formed one of the main cultural achievements of the peoples of Mesoamerica.

In this study we have put forward a hypothesis to explain the basic orientation of Teotihuacan in terms of calendrical observation, citing the new archaeoastronomical evidence from Teotihuacan, and adducing abundant comparative data in order to substantiate the argument. I have *not* proposed that this is the explanation for the origin of the *tonalpohualli*, the sacred almanac that rotated in relation to the solar year. Instead, we have dealt here with the fixed observational periods of 260/105 days delimited by the dates of February 12, April 30, August 13, and October 30. This fixed cycle of 260 days corresponded to the basic orientation scheme of the great city, and created a fourfold structure that divided time and space and was related to four highly significant cosmological as well as agricultural dates. It was significant, maybe since the Preclassic, and existed at Teotihuacan as well as at the Aztec capital of Tenochtitlan.

This internal structuring was so important in economic as well as cosmological terms that it seems to have been repeated in endless cases in the orientation of Mesoamerican sites after Teotihuacan. Probably, this orientation at later sites commemorated the cosmological scheme of the great Classic city of Teotihuacan; it might even have commemorated the mythical foundation of the present era as conceived by the Classic Maya; but it also had important agricultural and seasonal implications that linked these dates to economic and social life, thus regenerating continuously through ritual its actuality and practical significance.

In this sense calendrics at Teotihuacan were also intimately linked to geography, climate, and agricultural cycles and to a cosmovision in which the deities of sustenance, water, earth, caves, mountains, fire, lightning, and thunderstorms were crucial agents of the universe. Sacred geography was an important creation of these early states, by which cosmological concepts were projected into nature, and the state agencies and priesthoods transformed the natural environment according to the ideological canons of their cosmovision. Volcanic caves underneath the surface of the Valley of Mexico were important places of rituals directed to conjure fertility and water by means of magic by analogy, depositing marine and other water elements in these caves. Calendric rituals were imbued by these ancient symbols and kept alive a tradition that the Teotihuacanos inherited from earlier cultures; greatly elaborating upon it, they created new traditions that survived the collapse of their metropolis and were handed down to Postclassic cultures.

However, I do not mean to imply that there only existed continuities from the Classic to the Postclassic. History as a social process deals with continuities implicit in the permanence of cultural traditions within one area, as well as discontinuities and particular local developments. Obviously, continuities as well as changes and innovations occurred within the one great cultural tradition that was ancient Mesoamerica.

NOTES

1. All dates given in this study are Gregorian dates, including the ones referring to historical (archaeological) periods before the Gregorian Calendar Reform (1582). Ten days have been added to correct the corresponding Julian dates.

2. Manzanilla 1996 and chapter 2 in this volume; Manzanilla, Barba, Chávez, Arzate, and Flores 1989; Barba 1995.

3. Today, the inhabitants of the nearby village of Chalcatzingo continue to consider the mountain a sacred place and perform rites of petition for rain, ascending its summit during the Feast of the Holy Cross on May 3.

4. Millon 1973; Aveni 1980; Wallrath and Rangel 1991.

5. Dow 1967; Millon 1973, 1992; Drucker 1977, n.d.a, b, c; Aveni 1980; Aveni and Hartung 1991; Chiuh and Morrrison 1980; Malmström 1978, 1981, 1992; Tichy 1982, 1991; Iwaniszewski 1991; Morante 1996a.

6. David Drucker (1977), as quoted in Millon (1992: 387), has made some very interesting contributions to orientation studies of Teotihuacan, as well as to the study of pecked crosses that were discovered by the Teotihuacan Mapping Project (Drucker 1974, 1977, n.d.b, c). Unfortunately, several of these papers were never published. Another provocative theory proposed by Drucker (n.d.a) refers to the assumption of a continuity in the calendrical count between Teotihuacan and Tenochtitlan, an argument that I find rather convincing. The more detailed analysis of his rather complicated papers, which are not easily accessible, is beyond the scope of this chapter. I especially want to thank Darcie Flanagan, who kindly made some of these unpublished manuscripts available to me.

7. Nuttall 1928; Apenes 1936; Larsen 1936; Merill 1945.

8. In this case he refers to the *tzolkin* or rotating cycle that was combined with the solar year count.

9. Since this author was not a professional anthropologist and his writings contain digressions on Maya history that are mere speculation, his work has not been taken into account in the academic discussion. Nevertheless, his ethnographic data are very interesting, although they need to be taken with due caution.

10. Tichy (1982; 1991: 95–99) has also explored the orientation of Teotihuacan, emphazising the azimuth of 17° rather than 15.5°. He insists on the internal symmetry that this azimuth produces in terms of dividing the annual cycle into regular angular units. In this chapter it is argued, however, that such a conspicuous symmetry applied rather to the azimuth of 15.5° and its corresponding dates; the latter vary slightly from those corresponding to the alignment of 17°. However, there exist a number of coincidences with Tichy's analysis. I want to acknowledge the fruitful and stimulating exchange of ideas that I have maintained with Franz Tichy over the years. I also want to thank him for his comments on the present chapter.

11. Due to these circumstances, one must always allow for a slight margin in azimuths and their corresponding local dates. See, for example, the explanation about the equinoxes by Aveni (Aveni, Calnek, and Hartung 1988: 290); the discussion in Aveni 1980, ch. III, appendices B, D, and E; or the comments on the measurement of the horizon of Malinalco by Galindo (1990: S25–S32, notes 1 and 2).

12. All dates have been converted into Gregorian dates, see note 1.

13. This is the only feast that corresponds to the original Julian date given by Sahagún for the beginning of the year (1956, 2: 274). While Sahagún's data were collected before the Gregorian Calendar Reform in 1582, ten days were added after the reform. Therefore, in Gregorian dates the indigenous year beginning fell on February 12, as is generally assumed in this chapter. However, the important Christian feast is, in this case February 2, not February 12.

14. This early evidence is an earspool from Cuicuilco (Site Museum at Cuicuilco) with the (Olmec) calendar date "2 Lord," which Edmonson correlates with the date 679 B.C.E. According to the same author, this finding "indicates the presence among the Olmecs, probably dating to the seventh century B.C.E., of a fully developed calendar round that is obviously cognate with and almost certainly ancestral to all the other calendars [known from Mesoamerica]." Edmonson further puts forward the hypothesis that at Cuicuilco the true solar year was already calculated with 365.2462 days, which was later corrected to 365.2422 days (the same as the Gregorian year) in 433 B.C.E. (1988: 113–117).

15. Galindo 1990; Romero Quiroz 1987; Aveni 1980: 313; Broda 1977.

16. For the following evidence on Teotihuacan, I am relying on the work of Rubén Morante (see notes 18 and 19), particularly on some of the conclusions of his extremely valuable field observations that form part of his yet unpublished Ph.D. dissertation. However, the argument and conclusions of this chapter are entirely my own responsibility.

17. An intriguing proof for this association of concepts constitutes the ladder of human femurs that according to Morante (1996b) provided the access, or rather the descent into Cave 1. Morante reconstructed this ladder of femurs and proved experimentally its feasibility.

18. This research was carried out between 1987 and 1992 and presented as a M.A. thesis, under my direction, at the Escuela Nacional de Antropología (Morante 1993). See also Morante (1990, 1995).

19. The first detailed study of astronomy at Teotihuacan was carried out by Rubén Morante and presented as a Ph.D. dissertation, under my direction, at UNAM (Morante 1996a). This work is based on his archaeoastronomical field observations

and measurements undertaken between 1993 and 1996. It is impossible to refer to all the wealth of data that Morante in this intereresting thesis presents here; I will only mention those results that are particularly important from the point of view of the argument of this chapter.

20. Earlier studies of this observatory were undertaken by Tichy (1978, 1980), Aveni and Hartung (1981), and Broda (1982a).

21. That the observatory of Xochicalco was based on the principle of the camara oscura was first pointed out by Franz Tichy (1978, 1980).

22. Tichy (1978, 1980) was the first to have proposed out the possibility of correcting the calendar by means of these observations.

23. This site is situated on the eastern mountain range of the Basin of Mexico and dated back to earlier Toltec and possibly Teotihuacan times (Broda 1971, 1991a, 1991b; Iwaniszewski 1986b, 1994; Morante n.d.b).

24. This alignment is really the continuation of the Pico de Orizaba–Mt. Tlaloc alignment, a circumstance that needs to be explored further.

25. Drucker's study on the Ciudadela (1974) should be systematically compared with the recent calendrical hypothesis proposed by Morante (1996a) on the basis of his field observations and reconstruction of the original height of the Temple of Quetzalcoatl.

26. Aveni 1980, 1988, 1989, and chapter 9 in this volume; Aveni and Hartung 1982, 1991; Aveni, Hartung, and Buckingham 1978; Aveni, Hartung, and Kelley 1982; Drucker 1977, n.d.b, c; Wallrath and Rangel 1991; Tichy 1991; Iwaniszewski 1991, 1993; Galindo 1994; Morante 1996a, n.d.c; among other authors.

27. See note 26.

28. TEO2 was considered by Drucker (n.d.c) to have been a true calendrical calculating device on which he bases some of his provocative theories on calendrical continuities between Teotihuacan and Tenochtitlan.

29. Beyond the general concepts implicated in these four dates, one should perhaps not look for too much precision in these designs.

30. With respect to these pecked circles, Aveni observed: "Perhaps . . . these could have been intended to indicate the sanctity of the TEO grid alignment; e.g., UAX 1, 2, and 3 line up in the direction of the Teotihuacan grid, though they are located hundreds of km from Teotihuacan" (1988: 465).

References

Acuña, René, ed.
1986. *Relaciones geográficas del siglo XVI: México*. Vol. 2. Mexico: UNAM-IIA.

Angulo Villaseñor, Jorge
1987. "Los relieves del grupo 'IA' en la montaña sagrada de Chalcatzingo." In B. Dahlgren, C. Navarrete, L. Ochoa, M. C. Serra Puche, Y. Sugiura, eds., *Homenaje a Román Piña Chan*. Mexico: UNAM-IIA, pp. 191–228.
1991. "Identificación de una constelación en la pintura teotihuacana." In J. Broda, S. Iwaniszewski, and L. Maupomé, eds., *Arqueoastronomía y etnoastronomía en Mesoamérica*. Mexico: UNAM-IIH, pp. 309–328.

Apenes, Ole
1936. "Possible Derivation of the 260-Day Period of the Maya Calendar." *Ethnos* 1, no. 1: 5–8.

Aramoni, María Elena
1990. *Talokan tata, talokan nana: Nuestras raíces*. Mexico: CNCA/Dirección General de Publicaciones.

Aveni, Anthony F.
1980. *Skywatchers of Ancient Mexico*. Austin: University of Texas Press.
1988. "The Thom Paradigm in the Americas: The Case of the Cross-Circle Designs." In C. Ruggles, ed., *Records in Stone*. Cambridge: University of Cambridge Press, pp. 442–472.
1989. "Pecked Cross Petroglyphs at Xihuingo." *Archaeoastronomy* (Supplement to the *Journal for the History of Astronomy*) 20, no. 14: S73-S115.
1993. *Ancient Astronomies: Exploring the Ancient World*. Montreal/Washington, DC: St. Rémy Press/Smithsonian Institution.

Aveni, Anthony F., ed.
1988. *New Directions in American Archaeoastronomy*. Oxford: BAR International Series 454.
1989. *World Archaeoastronomy*. Cambridge: Cambridge University Press.

Aveni, Anthony F., Edward Calnek, and Horst Hartung
1988. "Myth, Environment, and the Orientation of the Templo Mayor of Tenochtitlan." *American Antiquity* 53, no. 2: 287–309.

Aveni, Anthony F., and Sharon L. Gibbs
1976. "On the Orientation of Pre-Columbian Buildings in Central Mexico." *American Antiquity* 41, no. 4: 510–517.

Aveni, Anthony F., and Horst Hartung
1981. "The Observation of the Sun at the Time of Passage Through the Zenith in Mesoamerica." *Archaeoastronomy* 3: 51–70.
1982. "New Observations of the Pecked Cross Petroglyph." In F. Tichy, ed., *Space and Time in the Cosmovision of Mesoamerica*. Lateinamerika-Studien 10. Munich: Wilhelm Fink-Verlag, pp. 25–41.
1991. "Observaciones sobre el planeamiento de Teotihuacan: El llamado trazo cuadricular y las orientaciones a los puntos cardinales." *Cuadernos de Arquitectura Mesoamericana* 13: 23–36.

Aveni, Anthony F., Horst Hartung, and Beth Buckingham
1978. "The Pecked Cross Symbol in Ancient Mesoamerica." *Science* 202: 267–279.

Aveni, Anthony F., Horst Hartung, and J. Charles Kelley
1982. "Alta Vista (Chalchihuites), Astronomical Implications of a Mesoamerican Ceremonial Outpost at the Tropic of Cancer." *American Antiquity* 47, no. 2: 316–335.

Barba Pingarrón, Luis A.
1995. "El impacto humano en la paleogegrafía de Teotihuacan." Ph.D. thesis in Anthropology, Facultad de Filsofía y Letras, UNAM, Mexico, D.F.

Batres, Leopoldo
1906. *Teotihuacan*. Mexico: Fidencio -S. Soria.

Berlo, Janet Catherine, ed.
1992. *Art, Ideology, and the City of Teotihuacan*. Washington, DC: Dumbarton Oaks.

Broda, Johanna
1971. "Las fiestas aztecas de los dioses de la lluvia." *Revista Española de Antropología Americana* 6: 245–327.
1977. "Malinalco: Santuario solar y calendárico de los aztecas." Unpublished manuscript.
1982a. "Astronomy,Cosmovision and Ideology in Prehispanic Mesoamerica." In A. F. Aveni and G. Urton, eds., *Ethnoastronomy and Archaeoastronomy in the American Tropics*. New York: Annals of the New York Academy of Sciences 385, pp. 81–110.
1982b. "La fiesta azteca del Fuego Nuevo y el culto de las Pleyades." In F. Tichy, ed.,

Space and Time in the Cosmovision of Mesoamerica. Lateinamerika-Studien 10. Munich: Wilhelm Fink Verlag, pp. 129–158.

1983. "Ciclos agrícolas en el culto: Un problema de la correlación del calendario mexica." In A. F.Aveni and G. Brotherston, eds., *Calendars in Mesoamerica and Peru: Native American Computations of Time*. Oxford: BAR International Series 174, pp. 145–165.

1986. "Significant Dates of the Mesoamerican Agricultural Calendar and Archaeoastronomy." Paper read at the 2nd Oxford International Conference on Archaeoastronomy, Mérida, January 1986 (Abstract in Aveni, ed. 1989: 494).

1987. "Templo Mayor as Ritual Space." In Johanna Broda, Davíd Carrasco, and Eduardo Matos. *The Great Temple of Tenochtitlan: Center and Periphery in the Aztec World*. Berkeley: University of California Press.

1991a. "Cosmovisión y observación de la naturaleza: El ejemplo del culto de los cerros." In J. Broda, S. Iwaniszewski, and L. Maupomé, eds., *Arqueoastronomía y etnoastronomía en Mesoamérica*. Mexico: UNAM-IIH, pp. 461–500.

1991b. "The Sacred Landscape of Aztec Calendar Festivals: Myth, Nature and Society." In D. Carrasco, ed., *To Change Place: Aztec Ceremonial Landscapes*. Niwot: University Press of Colorado, pp. 74–120.

1993. "Astronomical Knowledge, Calendrics, and Sacred Geography in Ancient Mesoamerica." In C. Ruggles and N. Saunders, eds., *Astronomies and Cultures* Niwot: University Press of Colorado, pp. 253–295.

1995. "La historia y la etnografía," In *Reflexiones sobre el oficio del historiador*. Mexico: UNAM-IIH, pp. 11–36.

1996a. "Paisajes rituales del Altiplano central." In *Arqueología Mexicana* 4, no. 20: 40–49.

1996b. "Calendarios, cosmovisión y observación de la naturaleza." In S. Lombardo and E. Nalda, eds., *Temas mesoamericanos*. Mexico: INAH, pp. 427–470.

n.d. "La etnografía de la Fiesta de la Santa Cruz: Una perspectiva histórica." In J. Broda and F. Báez-Jorge, eds., *Cosmovisión, ritual e identidad de los pueblos indígenas de México*. Mexico: FCE, in preparation.

Broda, Johanna, and Félix Báez-Jorge, eds.
n.d. *Cosmovisión, ritual e identidad de los pueblos indígenas de México*. Mexico: FCE, in preparation.

Carrasco, Davíd
1982. *Quetzalcoatl and the Irony of Empire*. Chicago: University of Chicago Press.

Carrasco, Davíd, ed.
1991. *To Change Place: Aztec Ceremonial Landscapes*. Niwot: University of Colorado Press.

Chiu, Bella C., and Philip Morrison
1980. "Astronomical Origin of the Offset Street Grid at Teotihuacan." *Archaeoastronomy* (Supplement to the *Journal for the History of Astronomy*) 11, no. 2: S55-S64.

Closs, Michael P., Anthony F. Aveni, and Bruce Crowley
1984. "The Planet Venus and Temple 22 at Copán." In A. Mönnich, B. Riese, G. Vollmer, and W. Zeller, eds., *Gedenkschrift Gerdt Kutscher*. 2 vols. Berlin: Gebr. Mann/Ibero-Amerikanisches Institut, vol. 1, pp. 221–247.

Coggins, Clemency C.
1975. "Painting and Drawing Styles at Tikal: An Historical and Iconographical Reconstruction." Ph.D. dissertation, Harvard University, Cambridge, MA. Ann Arbor, MI: University Microfilms, no. 76–3783.

1982. "The Zenith, the Mountain, the Center, and the Sea." In Anthony F. Aveni and Gary Urton, eds., *Ethnoastronomy and Archaeoastronomy in the American Tropics*. Annals of the New York Academy of Sciences 385. New York: The Academy, pp. 111–124.

Dow, James W.

1967. "Astronomical Orientations at Teotihuacan, A Case Study in Astroarchaeology." *American Antiquity* 32, no. 3: 326–334.

Drucker, David R.

1974. "Renovating a Reconstruction: The Ciudadela at Teotihuacan, Mexico: Construction Sequence, Layout, and Possible Uses of the Structure." Ph.D. dissertation, University of Rochester, Rochester, N.Y. Ann Arbor, MI: University Microfilms.

1977. "A Solar Orientation Framework for Teotihuacan." In *Los procesos de cambio en Mesoamérica y áreas circumvecinas. XV Mesa Redonda, Sociedad Mexicana de Antropología y Universidad de Guanajuato, julio 31 al 6 de agosto 1977, Guanajuato.* Mexico: SMA, vol. 2, pp. 277–284.

n.d.a. "The Founding of Mexico Tenochtitlan and the Dedication of its Main Temple." Unpublished manuscript, written 1986.

n.d.b. "The Teotihuacan Pecked Crosses: Models and Meanings." Unpublished manuscript, written 1986.

n.d.c. "Dating a Teotihuacan Pecked Cross: Teo2." Unpublished manuscript.

Edmonson, Munro S.

1988. *The Book of the Year: Middle American Calendrical Systems.* Salt Lake City: University of Utah Press.

Florescano, Enrique

1995. *El mito de Quetzalcóatl.* Mexico: FCE.

Galindo Trejo, Jesús

1990. "Solar Observations in Ancient Mexico: Malinalco." *Archaeoastronomy* (Supplement of the *Journal for the History of Astronomy*), no. 15: S17-S36.

1994. *Arqueoastronomía en la América antigua.* Madrid: Consejo Nacional de Ciencia y Tecnología/Editorial Equipo Sirius.

Girard, Rafael

1962. *Los mayas eternos.* Mexico: Libro Mex.

Grove, David, ed.

1987. *Ancient Chalcatzingo.* Austin: University of Texas Press.

Heyden, Doris

1975. "An Interpretation of the Cave Underneath the Pyramid of the Sun in Teotihuacan, Mexico." *American Antiquity* 40: 131–147.

1981. "Caves, Gods, and Myths: World Views and Planning in Teotihuacan." In E. P. Benson, *Mesoamerican Sites and World Views.* Washington, DC: Dumbarton Oaks, pp. 1–39.

Iwaniszewski, Stanislaw

1986a. "De Nahualac al Cerro Ehécatl: Una tradición prehispánica más en Petlacala." In *Arqueología y etnohistoria del Estado de Guerrero.* Mexico: INAH/Gobierno del Estado de Guerrero, pp. 497–518.

1986b. "La arqueología de alta montaña en México y su estado actual." *Estudios de Cultura Náhuatl* 18: 249–273.

1991. "La arqueología y la astronomía en Teotihuacan." In J. Broda, S. Iwaniszewski, and L. Maupomé, eds., *Arqueoastronomía y etnoastronomía en Mesoamérica.* Mexico: UNAM-IIH, pp. 269–290.

1993. "Mesoamerican Cross-Circle Designs Revisited." In C. Ruggles, ed., *Archaeoastronomy in the 1990s.* Loughborough, UK: Group D Publications Ltd., pp. 288–297.

1994. "Archaeology and Archaeoastronomy of Mount Tlaloc, Mexico: A Reconsideration." *Latin American Antiquity* 5, no. 2: 158–176.

Kirchhoff, Paul

n.d. "Algunas notas sobre organización social y política." Unpublished ms., Papeles inéditos de Paul Kirchhoff, Biblioteca del Museo Regional de Antropología e Historia, Puebla, Mexico.

Knab, Tim J.

1991. "Geografía del inframundo." *Estudios de Cultura Náhuatl* 21: 31–57.

Larsen, Helga

1936. "The 260-Day Period as Related to the Agricultural Life of the Ancient Indians." *Ethnos* 1: 9–12.

López Austin, Alfredo, Leonardo López Luján, and Saburo Sugiyama

1991. "The Temple of Quetzalcoatl at Teotihuacan: Its Possible Ideological Significance." *Ancient Mesoamerica* 2: 93–105.

Malmström, Vincent H.

1973. "Origin of the Mesoamerican 260-Day Calendar." *Science* 181: 759–760.

1978. "A Reconstruction of the Chronology of Mesoamerican Calendrical Systems." *Journal for the History of Astronomy* 9: 105–116.

1981. "Architecture, Astronomy, and Calendrics in Precolumbian Mesoamerica." In R. A. Williamson, *Archaeoastronomy in the Americas.* Los Altos, CA: Ballena Press, pp. 249–261.

1989. "The Spatial Dimension in Preliterate Time Reckoning." *Geographical Review* 79, no. 4: 422–434.

1991. "Edzna: Earliest Astronomical Center of the Maya." In J. Broda, S. Iwaniszewski, and L. Maupomé, eds., *Arqueoastronomía y etnoastronomía en Mesoamérica.* Mexico: UNAM-IIH, pp. 37–47.

1992. "Geographical Diffusion and Calendrics in Pre-Columbian Mesoamerica." *Geographical Review* 82, no. 2: 113–127.

Manzanilla, Linda

1996. "El concepto de inframundo en Teotihuacan." *Cuicuilco* (Mexico: ENAH), nueva época, no. 6: 29–50.

Manzanilla, Linda, Luis Barba, Rogelio Chávez, J. Arzate, and L. Flores

1989. "El inframundo de Teotihuacan. Geofísica y arqueología." *Ciencia y desarrollo* 15, no. 85: 21–35.

Merrill, Robert H.

1945. "Maya Sun Calendar Dictum Disproved." *American Antiquity* 10, no. 3: 307–311.

Millon, René

1973. *Urbanization at Teotihuacan, Mexico.* Vol. 1, part 1: *The Teotihuacan Map.* Austin: University of Texas Press.

1992. "Teotihuacan Studies: From 1950 to 1990 and Beyond." In J. C. Berlo, ed., *Art, Ideology, and the City of Teotihuacan.* Washington, DC: Dumbarton Oaks, pp. 339–419.

Morante López, Rubén B.

1990. "En Xochicalco, el Popocatépetl marca el tiempo." *México Desconocido* 13, no. 164 (October): 28–32.

1993. "Evidencias del conocimiento astronómico en Xochicalco, Morelos." M.A. thesis, División de Estudios de Posgrado, ENAH, Mexico.

1995. "Los observatorios subterráneos." *La Palabra y el Hombre* 94: 35–71.

1996a. "Evidencias del conocimiento astronómico en Teotihuacan." Ph.D. dissertation in Anthropology, Facultad de Filosofía y Letras, UNAM, Mexico.

1996b. "El descenso al inframundo en Teotihuacan." *Estudios de Cultura Náhuatl* 26: 99–115.

1997. "El abaco teotihuacano." *Estudios de Cultura Náhuatl* 27: 419–433.

n.d.a "Subterranean Observatories in Teotihuacan, Mexico." Paper presented at 4th Oxford International Conference on Archaeoastronomy, Santa Fe, New Mexico, August 1996.

n.d.b. "Monte Tlaloc: La montaña sagrada de los chichimecas." In Johanna Broda, ed., *Paisajes labrados en la roca: Ritualidad indígena en los paisajes prehispánicos de Mesoamérica y los Andes*. Mexico: UNAM-IIH, in preparation.

Nuttall, Zelia

1928. *La observación del paso del sol por el zenit por los antiguos habitantes de la América tropical*. Mexico: Talleres Gráficos de la Nación.

Pasztory, Esther

1988. "The Aztec Tlaloc: God of Antiquity." In K. J. Josserand and K. Dakin, eds., *Smoke and Mist: Mesoamerican Studies in Memory of Thelma D. Sullivan*. Oxford: BAR International Series 402, pp. 289–327.

Pérez Campa, Mario

1997. "Descubren una gran estela ligada al culto agrícola en Cuicuilco, de 3 000 años de antiguidad" (interviewed by Francisco Ortiz Pardo). *Proceso* (Mexico), no. 1072 (May 18): 60.

1998. "La estela de Cuicuilco." *Antropología Mexicana* 5, no. 30 (March–April): 37.

Ponce de León, Arturo

1983. "Fechamiento arqueoastronómico en el altiplano de México." In A. F. Aveni and G. Brotherston, eds., *Calendars in Mesoamerica and Peru: Native Computations of Time*. Oxford: BAR International Series 174, pp. 73–99.

1991. "Propiedades geométrico-astronómicas en la arquitectura prehispánica." In J. Broda, S. Iwaniszewski, and L. Maupomé, eds., *Arqueoastronomía y etnoastronomia en Mesoamérica*. Mexico: UNAM-IIH, pp. 413–446.

Robles García, Alejandro

1995. "Geografía cultural del Suroeste de la Cuenca de Mexico: Estudios históricos sobre el Pedregal, Ajusco y M. Contreras." M.A. thesis, División de Estudios de Posgrado, ENAH, Mexico, D.F.

n.d. "Paisajes de lava y cosmovisión indígena: Estudios históricos y etnográficos sobre el paisaje cultural del Altiplano Central." Ph.D. dissertation, División de Estudios de Posgrado, ENAH, Mexico, D.F., in preparation.

Rodríguez García, Ignacio.

1982. "Frente 2." In R. Cabrera C., I. Rodríguez G., and N. Morelos G., eds., *Memoria del Proyecto Arqueológico Teotihuacán 80–82*. Mexico: INAH, pp 49–54.

Romero Quiroz, Javier

1987. *Solsticio de invierno en Malinalco*. Toluca: Universidad Autónoma del Estado de México.

Sahagún, Fray Bernardino de

1950–1982. *Florentine Codex: General History of the Things of New Spain*. 13 parts. Ed. and trans. A. J. O. Anderson and C. E. Dibble. Santa Fe, NM: The School of American Research/University of Utah.

1956. *Historia general de las cosas de Nueva España*. 4 vols. Ed. Ángel María Garibay. Mexico: Editorial Porrúa.

Soruco Sáenz, Enrique
1985. "Una cueva ceremonial en Teotihuacán." B.A. thesis, ENAH, Mexico, D.F.
1991. "Una cueva ceremonial en Teotihuacán y sus implicaciones astronómicas religiosas."
    In J. Broda, S. Iwaniszewski, and L. Maupomé, eds., *Arqueoastronomía y
    etnoastronomía en Mesoamérica*. Mexico: UNAM-IIH, pp. 291–296.

Šprajc, Ivan
1996a. *Venus, lluvia y maíz: Simbolismo y astronomía en la cosmovsión mesoamericana.*
    Mexico: INAH, Colección Científica.
1996b   . *La estrella de Quetzalcoatl: El planeta Venus en Mesoamérica.* Mexico: Editorial
    Diana.
n.d. "Calendario observacional de Tenayuca, Mexico." Unpublished manuscript.

Sugiyama, Saburo
1993. "Worldview Materialized in Teotihuacan, Mexico." *Latin American Antiquity* 4, no.
    2: 103–129.

Taube, Karl
1986. "The Teotihuacan Cave of Origin." *Res: Anthropology and Aesthetics* 12: 51–82.

Tichy, Franz
1978. "El calendario solar como principio de organización del espacio para poblaciones y
    lugares sagrados." In *Comunicaciones Proyecto Puebla-Tlaxcala* no. 15. Puebla, Mexico:
    Fundación Alemana para la Investigación Científica, pp. 153–163.
1980. "Der Festkalender Sahagun's. Ein echter Sonnenkalender?" In H.-A. Steger and J.
    Schneider, eds., *Wirtschaft und gesellschaftliches Bewusstsein in Mexiko seit der
    Kolonialzeit*. Lateinamerika-Studien 6. Munich: Wilhelm Fink Verlag, pp. 115–137.
1981. "Order and Relationship of Space and Time in Mesoamerica: Myth or Reality." In
    E. P. Benson, ed., *Mesoamerican Sites and World-Views*. Washington, DC: Dumbarton
    Oaks, pp. 217–245.
1982. "The Axial Direction of Mesoamerican Ceremonial Centers on 17° North of West
    and their Associations to Calendar and Cosmovision." In F. Tichy, ed., *Space and Time
    in the Cosmovision of Mesoamerica*. Lateinamerika-Studien 10. Munich: Wilhelm Fink
    Verlag, pp. 63–84.
1991. *Die geordnete Welt indianischer Völker: Ein Beispiel von Raumordnung und
    Zeitordnung im Vorkolumbischen Mexiko*. Wiesbaden: Franz Steiner-Verlag.

Tobriner, Stephen
1972. "The Fertile Mountain: An Investigation of Cerro Gordo's Importance to the Town
    Plan and Iconography of Teotihuacan." In *Teotihuacán: XI Mesa Redonda*. Mexico:
    SMA, pp. 103–116.

Wallrath, Matthew, and Alfonso Rangel Ruíz
1991. "Xihuingo (Tepeapulco): Un centro de observación astronómica." In J. Broda, S.
    Iwaniszewski, and L. Maupomé, eds., *Arqueoastronomía y etnoastronomía en
    Mesoamérica*. Mexico: UNAM-IIH, pp. 413–446.

Wisdom, Charles
1940. *The Chorti Indians of Guatemala*. Chicago: University of Chicago Press.

▼

14

TEOTIHUACAN AND THE MAYA

A CLASSIC HERITAGE

WILLIAM L. FASH AND BARBARA W. FASH

The Isthmus of Tehuantepec served as the bridge between the ancient cultures of central and northern Mexico in the west, and their Maya and Central American counterparts to the east. Curiously, this geographic feature has too often served as a great divide in studies of ancient Mesoamerica, with some scholars insisting on the uniqueness of the Maya and their independent development of the hallmarks of civilization. Indeed, some Mayanists have been known to take a rather privileged view of the accomplishments of the culture they study, placing them on a pedestal as the culmination of civilized life in ancient Mexico and Central America. One of the most enduring legacies of that tendency is the chronological periods under which Mesoamerican scholars have labored for the past half century, some with more trepidation than others.

The term "Classic," of course, derives from scholars' admiration of Maya culture during the period of time when they inscribed stone monuments with dates in the so-called Long Count system of linear time-reckoning. This was originally thought to have spanned the years from 300 to 900 C.E., and the Long Count was—incorrectly, it turns out—believed to have been the exclusive invention of the

---

We would like to thank David Grove for instilling in us a deep curiosity about highland-lowland exchanges in Mesoamerica and portraits of foreign dignitaries, during our work at Chalcatzingo, Morelos, Mexico. We would also like to thank Davíd Carrasco for the opportunity to engage in such a lively and important dialogue with him and his colleagues on the Moses Mesoamerican Archive project at this enlightening conference. Finally, we would like to thank Davíd, and Joyce Marcus, for constructive criticisms of the first draft of this chapter, and numerous colleagues and students over the years with whom we have fruitfully discussed the nature of Teotihuacan-Maya interactions.

ancient Maya. Based on the abundance of dateable inscriptions, monumental architecture, and their distinctive, elaborate art style, the "Classic Maya" civilization was considered the height of cultural achievement in ancient Mesoamerica. All cultures before that time were considered "Pre-Classic," having failed to achieve those cultural heights, and the later cultures were considered "Post-Classic," decadent descendants of the wise astronomer-priests who had labored in their jungle temples for the most distinguished epoch of aboriginal New World history. We now know that the Long Count was not invented by the lowland Maya, and that it goes back to the first century C.E. if not earlier in the lowlands of Veracruz and adjacent parts of upland Chiapas, its creators in effect spanning the Isthmus of Tehuantepec. We also appreciate that the greatest city of the Classic period was Teotihuacan, constructed before the onset of Initial Series monument dedications in the Maya lowlands. Yet the Maya texts continue to color our considerations of the Classic legacy by the very names that we employ to discuss all of the cultures that were earlier, contemporaneous, or later than the Lowland Maya people who took the older and broader Mesoamerican inscribed stela and altar tradition to its greatest extreme.

It is abundantly clear that sustained and complex interactions between contemporaneous, often competing cultures in the highlands and lowlands were an integral part of the story of the rise and fall of civilizations in this part of the world. This has been documented from the time of the first highland and lowland kingdoms in the Preclassic (Flannery 1968; Flannery and Marcus 1994; Hirth 1984; Sharer and Grove 1989), through the Classic and Postclassic periods (Kidder, Jennings, and Shook 1946; Miller 1983). Indeed, such interaction—and rivalry— can even be seen in the demise of the (highland) Triple Alliance, when Malintzin and Aguilar (of the lowlands) were critical forces in the success of Cortés and his Tlaxcalan allies. Initially, the highlands seem to have the leading role in such interactions. During the Early Formative period, the Basin of Mexico, adjacent sectors of Morelos and Puebla, and the Valley of Oaxaca have the earliest evidence for public architecture, complex iconography in ceramics and other media, and evidence for long-distance exchange of specialized craft goods. In the final century of the second millennium B.C.E. up through the first half of the Middle Formative period, the lowland Olmec sites of Veracruz and Tabasco boasted the most labor-intensive public monuments and elite goods, but were simply one focus of an exchange system that included complex societies in virtually all regions of Mesoamerica (Sharer and Grove 1989). With the rise of Teotihuacan the highlands resumed and thereafter retained the pre-eminent position in Mesoamerican affairs. It was during the Classic period that Teotihuacan reified the legacy that most people equate with Mesoamerican civilization.

The timing of and roles played by the great metropolis of Teotihuacan in the origins, development, and decline of Classic Maya civilization has been a controversial topic in Mesoamerican studies for decades. The discovery of Early Classic (Tzakol 3) ceramics with Teotihuacan stylistic elements and forms in the early Carnegie Institution investigations at Uaxactún (Smith 1955) was highlighted when A.V. Kidder, Jesse Jennings, and Edwin Shook (1946) encountered spectacular graves stocked with Teotihuacan ceramics, slate-backed iron-ore mirrors, and other artifacts, placed in buildings of pure Teotihuacan-style at the highland Maya site of Kaminaljuyú. Kidder concluded that Kaminaljuyú became a Teotihuacan outpost after it was overtaken by warrior-merchants from the great city. The theoretical implications of this and broader economic models later pursued by Sanders and Price (1968) were that Teotihuacan played a primary role in the creation of Mesoamerican civilization; the Maya were relegated to secondary state status. Kaminaljuyú and Teotihuacan were considered to have played pivotal roles in the political history of what was thought to be the largest Classic Maya city, Tikal, by Clemency Coggins (1975; 1976; 1979), whose mentor Tatiana Proskouriakoff had early on signalled the importance of "the arrival of strangers" in the Petén, in her broader study of Maya history, finally published in 1993.

Not surprisingly, many Maya scholars reacted strongly against these initial interpretations of a direct role for Teotihuacanos in the political and economic fortunes of the Classic Maya. Several researchers pursued alternative explanations for the presence of Teotihuacan architectural forms (Kubler 1973; Laporte and Fialko 1995), ceramics and other artifacts (Demarest and Foias 1993), portraiture elements and conventions (Schele 1986; Schele and Freidel 1990; Stone 1989), and religious concepts (Schele and Freidel 1990) in the eastern third of Mesoamerica. Many scholars believed that the Maya simply borrowed some useful Teotihuacan ideas and technology and re-cast them in their own way, all the while remaining completely independent of any hegemonic intentions, bellicose incursions, or long-distance diplomatic initiatives from the great capital of Central Mexico, a point of view that David Stuart (chapter 15 of this volume) refers to as the "Internalist" perspective.

These two positions present useful points of departure for more detailed and inclusive interpretations of the legacy of Teotihuacan for Classic Maya civilization. Here we will consider some of the more provocative and useful aspects of the two perspectives in our own interpretations of the kinds and degrees of interaction that may have taken place between these two great and long-lived cultural traditions within the larger culture area of Mesoamerica. New data from Copán and other sites support the conclusion that the symbolism used by Maya kings of the Classic and Postclassic periods can be tied to larger Mesoamerican patterns, specifically to the desire to affirm their own ties to a powerful "Tollan" and its legacy as an urban center (Carrasco 1982; Stone 1989). The constellation of archaeological data strongly suggests the arrival of powerful Teotihuacanos at the sites of Tikal, Copán, and Kaminaljuyú within a period of fifty to seventy-five years during the Early Classic period. We believe that the historical records, pictorial depictions, and oral histories that surrounded these "arrivals" became grist for the mill of Late Classic Maya kings who sought to legitimize themselves as ruling lines did throughout Mesoamerica: by claiming descent from the Master Craftsmen—and warriors—of Tollan. In the case of Copán, they went even further, using a variety of media to emphasize their pedigree and to elevate their city to the exalted status of a new Tollan.

INITIAL VIEWS OF TEOTIHUACAN-MAYA INTERACTION

It came as a revelation to all Mesoamericanists when Kidder, Jennings, and Shook (1946) discovered compelling evidence for the presence of Teotihuacanos at the highland Maya site of Kaminaljuyú. Although Herbert Joseph Spinden (1933) had already adduced evidence for important shared material culture traditions throughout Mesoamerica in the Preclassic with what he called the "Q-complex," and the work at Uaxactún had likewise signalled important contacts during the Early Classic (Smith 1955), this was the first clear indication that the Classic Maya had direct interactions with their distant contemporaries in Teotihuacan. It also helped to solidify the chronological placement of the Teotihuacan ceramic sequence with respect to that of the Maya, which had been tied to the Long Count at Uaxactún, and to the Christian calendar by means of the Goodman-Martínez-Thompson correlation. As noted, the public buildings and tomb goods of Esperanza phase Kaminaljuyú were so strikingly similar to the architecture and artifacts of Teotihuacan that Kidder, Jennings, and Shook concluded that a cadre of warrior merchants from Teotihuacan had conquered Kaminaljuyú, and set up a public center whose buildings and burial goods mirrored those of their homeland.

Subsequently, the same argument was made but on a broader scale, derived from theoretical expectations rather than solely because of the archaeological finds at Kaminaljuyú. William Sanders and Barbara Price (1968) posited that the development of hydraulic agriculture caused early civilization to emergence first in the Basin of Mexico, specifically in the Teotihuacan Valley. In their view, Classic Maya civilization was a secondary development, derivative from the more urbanized, hydraulically-based state of Teotihuacan. Sanders later undertook a large-scale project in the Valley of Guatemala to prove his point, as well as to look at the broader sweep of cultural evolution in that region. Sanders (1978) used ethnohistoric materials from the Aztec to refine his models of the nature of interaction between Kaminaljuyú and Teotihuacan, positing that itinerant warrior-merchants from Teotihuacan (akin in status and function to the *pochteca* of the later Culhua-Mexica) established themselves in Kaminaljuyú in the fifth century C.E. In his view, they married women from a local elite lineage, and constructed public buildings that mimicked the form and underlying world view of Teotihuacan. Their descendants gradually became assimilated into the local aristocracy and adopted their material culture traditions, with progressively less evidence of Teotihuacan buildings, goods, and ideology with the passing of time.

The Kaminaljuyú case alerted Maya archaeologists and art historians to the possibility that further evidence for Teotihuacan contacts could be found in new investigations and already excavated material. William Coe (1972) reported on a vast array of evidence for "cultural contact between the Lowland Maya and Teotihuacan" at Tikal, in the form of inscribed stone monuments, architecture, imported obsidian and ceramics, and an incised vessel from Problematic Deposit 50 that showed a delegation of Teotihuacanos travelling from their homeland to a site with Maya-style architecture, where they are received by Maya noblemen. Joseph Ball (1974) reported on a ceramic cache from Becán that contained a Teotihuacan figurine inside a cylindrical slab-footed tripod vase, which he tied to a time of political trouble and invasion at the site. David Pendergast (1971) found a cache of green obsidian figurines at the site of Altun Ha so similar to those uncovered at Teotihuacan as to be virtually identical. He wondered how the entire assemblage could have been transferred, intact, from Teotihuacan, and placed in a single, deliberate offering there. Nicholas Hellmuth (1972) noted a Teotihuacan-style portrait on a stone monument from the Petén site of Yaxhá, and Teotihuacan decorative elements on Stela 6 from Copán (Hellmuth 1976) (Figure 14.1). Hellmuth (1978) and Janet Berlo (1989) subsequently demonstrated that the Escuintla region of highland Guatemala was closely tied to Teotihuacan, as evidenced by the sophistication and abundance of the Teotihuacan-style "theater censers" that were found there.

The first scholar to propose detailed interpretations of the role of historically named individuals in the relationships between Teotihuacan, Kaminaljuyú, and Tikal was Clemency Coggins (1975, 1976, 1979, 1983). Coggins suggested that the Tikal ruler Curl Snout hailed from Kaminaljuyú, and that his son and successor Stormy Sky immortalized that connection in his public monuments. In particular,

Fig. 14.1. Stela 6, Copán (drawing by B. Fash).

the figures on the two narrower sides of Tikal Stela 31 were seen as evidence for the presence of Teotihuacanos at Tikal, people who oversaw the transfer of power from the local lowland dynasty to one deriving from Kaminaljuyú and ultimately answering to Teotihuacan. She also suggested that the Maya imported a new form of calendar reckoning from Teotihuacan to the Maya lowlands to correspond with this political change (Coggins 1979, 1983).

Richard E. W. Adams (1986) pursued Coggins's suggestions and insights, after he found a set of royal tombs at the secondary center of Río Azul, Guatemala. Based on the presence of cylindrical slab-footed tripod vessels in the lateral tombs, Adams concluded that he had found the individuals portrayed on the sides of Tikal Stela 31. This provided evidence, he believed, of Teotihuacan's direct involvement in the fortunes of both Tikal and Río Azul. Unlike the case at Kaminaljuyú, there were fewer tomb vessels at Río Azul that were identical in decorative technique to vessels from Teotihuacan. Also lacking was architectural evidence that would indicate the presence of Teotihuacanos, or any glyphic references in the tombs or their furniture to the personal names cited on Stela 31.

Regarding the effect that the demise of Teotihuacan had upon the Classic Maya, Gordon Willey (1974) offered a thoughtful re-consideration of the "hiatus" phenomenon. Willey suggested that the famed decline in stela and altar dedication from 9.5.0.0.0 to 9.8.0.0.0 (534–593 C.E.) that affected Tikal and its immediate neighbors in the central core of the Maya lowlands was in essence a "rehearsal for the collapse." In Willey's view, the withdrawal of Teotihuacan influence and trade connections (due to its own declining fortunes and impending political collapse) caused Tikal and its allies many hardships. The disruptions occurring at this time presaged those that would bring the great dynasties to their knees at the end of the Classic period, when some scholars posited that disruption of trade routes by peoples to the west played a crucial role in the demise of the Classic Maya order (Adams 1973). Recently, Arlen and Diane Chase have proposed that the hiatus of Tikal and its neighbors was caused by the defeat of Tikal by Caracol in a war that took place in 562 C.E. (Chase and Chase 1987). The ongoing discussion regarding the date of the collapse of Teotihuacan, with archaeomagnetic dates indicating that it may have occurred as early as 550–600 C.E. (Wolfman 1990), may indicate that Willey's suggestion has more to recommend it than had recently been thought.

THE ELITE EMULATION HYPOTHESIS

The notion that Teotihuacan played a decisive or hegemonic role in the evolution of Classic Maya civilization was greeted by most Mayanists with skepticism bordering on exasperation. When their esteemed cultural tradition was branded a "secondary" development, many Mayanists reacted defensively. This response had a historic precedent, since the first such skirmish occurred when Mathew Stirling, Miguel Covarrubias, and Alfonso Caso had the audacity to suggest that the Olmec cultural tradition actually preceded the Classic Maya. J. Eric Thompson, considered the dean of Maya scholars for the middle decades of the twentieth century, reacted with a scorching essay, excoriating anyone who would consider the Maya to not have been the first civilization of Mesoamerica.

With the help of radiocarbon dating and a set of early Long Count monuments in Veracruz, Chiapas, and the Pacific slopes of Guatemala, Stirling, Covarrubias, and Caso were proven to be absolutely right about the primacy of Olmec civilization. Likewise, the chronometric dating of the origins of Teotihuacan was equally decisive in demonstrating that its meteoric rise occurred before the development of the Classic period Maya kingdoms.

However, archaeologists soon found a Preclassic city that rescued Maya civilization from the onus of being post-Teotihuacan, and in that sense "secondary." Discovered by Ian Graham in 1963, the site of El Mirador was demonstrated by Raymond Matheny (1980) and Arthur Demarest and William Fowler (1984) to have had its greatest florescence during the Late Preclassic period, several centuries prior to the explosive growth of Teotihuacan in the first century C.E. Subsequent research by Richard Hansen (1991) has revealed monumental architecture at the site of Nakbé, located near El Mirador, dating back to the Middle Preclassic period, ca. 500 B.C.E. (Hansen 1991). These developments indicate that the lowland Maya were in effect catching up with their predecessors and contemporaries in the Gulf Coast region, and the great highland kingdom of Monte Albán in the Valley of Oaxaca, during the Middle and Late Formative periods. This effectively demolished the idea that the lowland Maya evolved large, complex societies in response to the rise of the pristine state in Teotihuacan.

In keeping with this cultural crusade, the once uncontested position that warrior-merchants from Teotihuacan established an "outpost" or "colony" at Kaminaljuyú was brought into question by archaeologists and art historians alike. George Kubler (1973) discounted the thesis that architectural style could be considered a badge of ethnicity, or that the examples of *talud-tablero* architecture at Kaminaljuyú were so similar that the site could be considered a "colony" of the central Mexican metropolis. Subsequently, Arthur Demarest and Antonia Foias (1993) were able to show that very few pots found in the Maya region actually came from Teotihuacan, based on neutron activation analysis of ceramics from the Kaminaljuyú tombs and other Maya sites. Instead, the evidence suggests the majority of the Teotihuacan-style tomb vessels were made in the Maya area, imitating forms and in some cases surface decoration techniques from Central Mexico. Furthermore, Demarest and Foias noted that the actual form of the tomb chambers in Kaminaljuyú followed local canons, not Teotihuacan traditions. They concluded there was no direct evidence for populations of Teotihuacanos in the Maya area, nor for a controlling interest by them in any Classic Maya kingdom. They used these findings to call into question the validity of the concept of "horizon styles" for Mesoamerica, and suggested that the Maya were simply engaging in the tradition of elite emulation first posited by Flannery (1968). (It should be noted that the results of the long-term Valley of Oaxaca Human Ecology Project have resulted in a different view of the nature of interaction between that region and the lowlands of Veracruz and Tabasco than the initial model that Flannery proposed [Marcus 1989; Flannery and Marcus 1994, chapter 20].)

Following this tack, in keeping with what Stuart (chapter 15 of this volume) calls the "Internalist" school, some Mayanists have recently sought to discount the idea that Teotihuacan had ever had a direct role, let alone a controlling interest, in any lowland Maya polity. Linda Schele (1986) proposed that the Maya rulers displayed Teotihuacan imagery in their regalia to suit their own cult of "Venus-Tlaloc warfare," which she believed to be rooted in Classic Maya divination and Venus cycles. Following Mathews (1985), Schele and David Freidel (1990) concluded that the text of Uaxactún Stela 5 recorded the "conquest" of Uaxactún by a lord from Tikal by the name of Smoking Frog. They extended the interpretation based upon their reading of that monument, and the contents of one of the large tombs of Uaxactún, to posit that a new form of "unlimited war" derived from Teotihuacan martial tactics was ushered into the lowland Maya political arena with this event. David Stuart's new reading of the purported "conquest" statement as a simple declaration of the "arrival" of Smoking Frog suggests the need to reconsider the scenario proposed by Schele and Freidel for Uaxactún and Tikal (see chapter 15 of this volume, and below).

The hypothesis of elite emulation of a foreign power has also been proffered by Juan Pedro Laporte and Vilma Fialko (1995) to account for some *talud-tablero* buildings and a ball court marker in Classic Teotihuacan style in the "Lost World" compound at Tikal. They date these buildings to about a century earlier than the reigns of the rulers known as Curl Snout and Stormy Sky. One structure consisted of a small platform used to display a vertical stone marker identical in form to the so-called ball court marker or "composite stela" found at La Ventilla in Teotihuacan. Although they also found numerous vessels comparable to those of contemporary Teotihuacan, Laporte and Fialko remain convinced that the burial patterns in the Lost World compound are firmly grounded in lowland Maya tradition. They interpret the *talud-tablero* architecture, vertical ball court marker (with a Maya hieroglyphic inscription), and pottery as other examples of the Maya selectively imitating symbolism and acquiring elite goods that enhanced their local status. All of this, it bears repeating, occurred in the century prior to the purported "arrival" of Smoking Frog.

The meaning behind the use of Teotihuacan symbolism by the Classic Maya dynasties has been insightfully addressed by Andrea Stone (1989), in a seminal article on the use of "outsider" symbolism by the southern Maya lowland kings to symbolize their "disconnectedness" from the commoners. Stone elucidates the powerful meaning of Classic Maya claims to ties with the "Toltec" of their day from Teotihuacan by recalling the well-documented boasts by the Postclassic and early Colonial period Maya (from both the highlands and lowlands) of their descent from the Toltecs. She sees the great florescence of Teotihuacan imagery on lowland Maya stone monuments of the Late Classic period—even after the decline and fall of the Mexican city—as evidence for reverence of that great Classic period center by the Maya rulers. The majority of this imagery is found in warrior costumes associated with militaristic forays by ambitious rulers (Stone 1989; Pasztory 1997). In Stone's model, the Classic Maya were not merely emulating the Teotihuacanos—as posited by the tandems of Demarest and Foias, Schele and Freidel, and Laporte and Fialko—but rather they were claiming the Teotihuacan heritage as their own.

Stone's reading of the Late Classic Maya monuments is certainly in keeping with the broader pattern noted by Davíd Carrasco (1982, chapter 3), wherein

Mesoamerican peoples display the forces that legitimate them in their costuming and on their skins. In this way, they tried to absorb the power of their gods and symbols, as well as—in the case at hand—publicly exhibit their foreign affiliations. Carrasco revived scholars' interest in the many Tollans, the greatest being Tollan Teotihuacan, which established the archetype of the Mesoamerican urban, civilized center referred to as a "place of the reeds" (Carrasco 1982). By claiming dynastic ties to the ancestral Tollan, the Classic Maya (and their Postclassic successors; see Stone 1989) were pursuing the same strategy of legitimization subsequently pursued by the ambitious Mexica. Those upstart Chichimecs could only command attention and respect in the Valley of Mexico once they had secured a claim to Toltec ancestry, in their case through marriage with a Culhua princess. Ever thereafter, they proudly called themselves the Culhua Mexica.

Nonetheless, it is somewhat risky to explain this Late Classic enthusiasm for Central Mexican based solely on evidence from stone monuments commissioned by rulers. A broader look at other kinds of archaeological evidence from the Early Classic period in the Maya lowlands, including imported artifacts, burial practices, architectural styles, and even local settlement patterns, serves to reveal a factual basis for the Late Classic boasts of Teotihuacan heritage in the early histories of those kingdoms.

ARCHAEOLOGICAL EVIDENCE FOR EARLY CLASSIC TIES BETWEEN TEOTIHUACAN AND THE MAYA CENTERS OF TIKAL, COPÁN, AND KAMINALJUYÚ

Our own formal involvement with these issues began when we undertook the Hieroglyphic Stairway Project in Copán, in January of 1986 (Fash 1988). This multidisciplinary program for research and conservation of the longest extant hieroglyphic inscription of the aboriginal Americas included plans to test the veracity of the official history inscribed on the stairway, late in the city's history. This was to be achieved by tunnelling into the underlying pyramid and bringing to light the evidence provided by its ancestral buildings, texts, and offerings (Fash et al. 1992). This project received strong support from numerous quarters, and was expanded into the much larger and more complex Copán Acropolis Archaeological Project (1988–1995), or PAAC in Spanish, under the direction of the senior author. The PAAC employed the conservation and excavation methods developed on the Stairway project to other parts of the Main Acropolis of Copán that were at risk either because of natural causes (the river cut of the Acropolis) or lack of conservation measures by earlier investigators. These methods included the recovery, documentation, and re-fitting of the thousands of fragments of tenoned mosaic façade sculpture fragments that adorned the Late Classic Acropolis structures, a surprising number of which included Teotihuacan imagery (Fash 1992; Fash and Fash 1996). The PAAC also undertook extensive tunnelling to document the construction history of the entire artificial mass exposed in the river cut as a pre-requisite for its complete consolidation. This coincidentally enabled us to assess the historical record inscribed in the Late Classic texts and pictorial imagery through discovery and documentation of Early Classic architectural monuments and texts (Fash and Sharer 1991). As a result, the Main Acropolis at Copán is now one of the best understood of its kind in the Maya area, and remarkable progress has been achieved in the evaluation of the historical inscriptions based on the physical, archaeological remains of the rulers and monuments of record. One of the most illuminating aspects of the archaeological materials that we have documented is the evidence for strong ties with Teotihuacan.

The archaeological remains customarily cited as evidence for Teotihuacan connections with sites outside the Basin of Mexico are the presence of public architecture with *talud-tablero* façades, Pachuca green obsidian, Thin Orange ceramics, slate-backed pyrite mirrors, and cylindrical slab-footed tripod vessels, especially those with Teotihuacan-style incised designs and painted stucco surfaces. At Tikal, Copán, and Kaminaljuyú, the public architecture in Teotihuacan *talud-tablero* style is restricted to the Early Classic period, which is when the vast majority of the other artifact types that suggest connections are also found. The presently available evidence indicates that this complex of trade items and architectural styles appears first at Tikal at the beginning of the Early Classic period in the Lost World complex. It then shows up in the Copán Valley, finding its greatest expression and concentration in the area where the dynastic founder sets up his royal compound ca. 426 C.E. Shortly thereafter, it makes a dramatic appearance at Kaminaljuyú ca. 450 C.E.

The bulk of the Teotihuacan merchandise found in Copán arrived very early, coinciding with the reign of the founder of the Classic period Copán dynasty, K'inich Yax K'uk' Mo' ("Sun-Faced Blue-Green Quetzal Macaw"), and that of his son and successor, Ruler 2. In Copán, the Teotihuacan-style tripod vessels, Thin Orange ceramics, and slate-backed pyrite mirrors are found in association with elite burials of the Early Classic period, almost exclusively in the dynastic center. Green obsidian has been found in Early Classic contexts with the earliest public architecture of the Acropolis area, and in other Early Classic settlements in the valley. Thereafter it virtually disappears in the archaeological record until a much later appearance in a Postclassic settlement found to the southwest of the (by then abandoned) dynastic center. As in the case at Kaminaljuyú, the majority of the cylindrical slab-footed tripod vessels were probably manufactured by local artisans imitating Teotihuacan styles, however the Thin Orange bowls, Pachuca obsidian, and slate-backed mirrors were clearly imported.

The building that served as the axis mundi for the early Copán Acropolis at the time of these Teotihuacan imports has been given the field name "Hunal" by our co-workers on the Copán Acropolis Archaeological Project (Sharer 1996). This first public building was to serve as the pivot for all the subsequent versions of the Copán Acropolis, which expanded both vertically and horizontally from that nucleus. This building—the very core of the Copán kingdom—was constructed with a *talud-tablero* façade, and adorned with a superstructure that bore painted murals in the Teotihuacan style (Sharer 1997; G. Stuart 1997). Robert Sharer (1996, 1997) has made what we believe to be a very persuasive case that he has located the tomb of the founder of the dynasty memorialized on Copán's Altar Q, inside of this building at the heart of the Main Acropolis. Although the tomb itself is a Classic Maya vaulted chamber, the structure it was intruded into is clearly Teotihuacan-inspired. Sharer notes that it adheres more closely to the

Teotihuacan proportions of the *talud-tablero* than any other structure outside of the great city (Sharer 1997).

Shortly after the construction of Hunal, a ball court was built some 100 meters to the north, which exhibited four supernatural birds modelled in stucco on its exterior façades (Fash and Fash 1996). Each bird displays a Feathered Serpent head in its genital area that bear a remarkable similarity to those on the Temple of the Feathered Serpent at Teotihuacan (Figure 14.2). Adjacent to this earliest ball court was a stucco-embellished masonry structure that we have given the field name "Motmot." A cylindrical stone-lined grave (Burial XXXVII-8; Figure 14.3) very similar in size and form to those that characterize Teotihuacan burials (Manzanilla 1993; Serrano Sánchez 1993) was unearthed five meters in front of the Motmot structure, on its central axis. The hieroglyphic text on the floor marker used to ultimately seal this grave, and to dedicate the Motmot structure (cited as the "four sky" building, in keeping with the four sky bands modelled in stucco on its substructure façades), also refers to "four macaws," a probable allusion to the great birds with Feathered Serpent attributes adorning the adjacent ball court.

It is likely that the Teotihuacan-style cylindrical grave beneath this historic marker was originally built in association with the Motmot structure's predecessor, discovered inside of the latter's substructure and known as "Yax." After the initial construction of the burial chamber, the seated body of a young adult female was carefully placed on a reed mat on its floor. Some time later (possibly seven years later, to judge from dates on the marker text), the cist was re-entered, many of the upper body bones were displaced and burned, new offerings were placed with the deceased, the roof capstones were replaced, and a deer was burned atop the capstones as a final offering. The total offering complex was sealed off with the immense limestone floor marker, integrally set into the stucco plaza floor shared by Motmot and Ballcourt I. The probable association of the original construction of the cylindrical grave with Yax structure is important, because the fill of Yax was shown to have the greatest proportion of Central Mexican Pachuca green obsidian to other obsidian of any site or context outside of the Basin of Mexico (Aoyama 1996). It is also significant that the famous incised ceramic vessel from Tikal which shows a journey by Teotihuacan dignitaries from a site in their own homeland (with Teotihuacan-style architecture) to a Maya site (complete with resident Maya dignitaries and architecture) comes from Problematic Deposit 50, found inside of a pit which was extraordinarily similar in size, cylindrical shape, and content (including burned human bone) to the cylindrical grave in Copán and the dozens of documented examples at Teotihuacan.

Further critical evidence for early Teotihuacan links at Copán is the warrior burial (referred to as the "Tlaloc Warrior") placed axially in front of the building (field name "Margarita") that succeeded the central Acropolis structure of Hunal, dedicated by the second ruler. This adult male was laid to rest with dozens of projectile points in his grave, and shell (Storm God, or Tlaloc) goggles still in place on the forehead of the skull (G. Stuart 1997). A burial placed due east of the earliest ball court (Burial V-6; Cheek and Viel 1983) likewise had such shell goggles, as well as Thin Orange ceramics, a slate-backed pyrite mirror, and

Fig. 14.2. a. Stucco bird from Copán, Ballcourt I: feathered serpent head highlighted (drawing by B. Fash); b. Feathered serpent façade sculpture from Teotihuacan, Temple of the Feathered Serpent.

the remnants of a shell platelet headdress, in a square stone cist with wooden roof identical to those of Esperanza phase Kaminaljuyú.

The shell platelet headdress represents another important artifact complex evincing ties to Teotihuacan in the Early Classic elite tombs of Copán. Stone (1989) discusses the mosaic helmet headdresses made of spondylus shell platelets that are found in elite burials in sites in the Maya lowlands as part of the

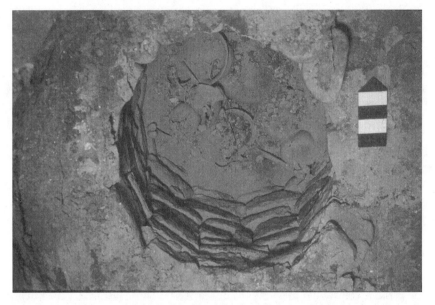

Fig. 14.3. Teotihuacan-style cylindrical burial, west of Motmot Structure.

Teotihuacan military costume seen at Piedras Negras and other sites. Karl Taube (personal communications) believes that these headdresses depict the Teotihuacan "War Serpent" deity (Taube 1992), and believes that such a shell platelet headdress was laid to rest with the occupant of the Early Classic "sub-Jaguar" tomb recently discovered by Loa Traxler (1997; see also G. Stuart 1997). The example from Burial V-6, placed in a Kaminaljuyú-style tomb just east of the first ball court, is yet another. The presence of this quintessential Teotihuacan symbol in the headgear of prominent Maya kings and nobles during the Early and Late Classic periods would appear to support Stone's interpretations of the imagery. The new excavations at the Copán Acropolis indicate that costume elements, architecture, and elite goods connected with Teotihuacan begin as early as 426 C.E., and continued until the end of the eighth century of the current era. This allows us to update her initial assessment that the earliest and longest lived appearance of Teotihuacan imagery at a Late Classic Maya site was at Piedras Negras, ca. 620–735 C.E. (Stone 1986: 164). It also poses the question, will the Early Classic tombs of Piedras Negras yield the same kind of archaeological and textual evidence for ties with Teotihuacan as has been found at Copán, Tikal, and Kaminaljuyú?

Regarding Tikal, David Stuart (chapter 15 of this volume) has made some provocative new decipherments on the claims by its Early Classic kings to Teotihuacan heritage. Stuart contends that the actor known as "Smoking Frog" or Siyah K'ak', "arrived" at (rather than having conquered) Uaxactún, after having already "arrived" at El Perú, a site located to the west of Uaxactún. Referred to as a "Lord of the West," he apparently made his entry to the Classic Maya kingdoms from the west, and worked his way east through the Maya lowlands. The texts inform us that the very day he made his appearance, the reigning king of Tikal known as Jaguar Paw, dies ("enters the water"). As Davíd Carrasco pointed out to us (personal communication, 1997), "arrivals" are often noted in Central Mexican historical texts. Even the arrival of Cortés was hailed in the codices prepared immediately after the conquest. These citations are all part of the important practice that José Piedra (1989) refers to as "the game of critical arrival." Further, Stuart suggests that after the death of Jaguar Paw, Smoking Frog may have served as a regent for the young Tikal ruler Curl Snout (Nun Yax Ayin). The inscriptions indicate that Curl Snout was the son of a man named "Atlatl Cauac," whom Stuart (chapter 15 of this volume) suggests may have been the paramount ruler of Teotihuacan itself. Certainly, Curl Snout's Teotihuacan-style portraits on Tikal Stelae 4 and 31 make perfect sense in that context.

If Stuart's readings are correct, these developments provide a very striking scenario for the takeover of Tikal by agents (or principals) of the great highland city. A century or so of intense interaction, marked by the construction and rebuilding of a number of large buildings in *talud-tablero* style in the Lost World compound, the carving and display of a "ball court marker" in La Ventilla style, and the importation of numerous craft goods from Teotihuacan, was followed by the grand entrance of a major "Lord of the West." Subsequently a young man named Curl-Nose, possibly the son of a Teotihuacan ruler named "Atlatl-Cauac," is seated on the throne of Tikal, and portrayed on Stela 4 (and somewhat later, on Stela 31) as a Teotihuacano. One begins to wonder how much military intelligence had been gathered by Teotihuacan merchants and emissaries in their visits to the great Maya metropolis, before it was decided that the time was ripe for action.

The latest and most easterly mention (if not actual sighting) of the enigmatic figure known to us as Smoking Frog is in Copán, where his name shows up on an Early Classic step dated to 439 C.E. (Sharer1996; D. Stuart 1997 and chapter 15 of this volume; G. Stuart 1997). There his name is associated with that of K'inich Yax K'uk' Mo', the first ruler of the Copán dynasty. Among the titles listed for the legendary Copán founder by his successors was that of "Lord of the West," just like Smoking Frog. Significantly, the "arrival" of K'inich Yax K'uk' Mo'in Copán is cited as a pivotal event on Altar Q, the king's list dedicated to the memory of the founder and named in his honor by the sixteenth and final ruler of the city (Stuart 1992). The abundance of Teotihuacan imagery on the portraits and architecture associated with the Copán lord K'inich Yax K'uk' Mo,' and his title as another "Lord of the West," show that both he and his successors were intent on affirming his pedigree and affiliations with the great Central Mexican metropolis. The abundance of artifactual evidence, foreign burial practices, and

Teotihuacan warrior accoutrements indicate that those affiliations were not a fiction of later vainglorious rulers.

Looking to broader patterns, one should note that the use of the title Lord of the West is similar to the Terminal Classic references to the "Mexican" mercenaries of the Cocom, the Ah Canul. They are identified simultaneously as "Maya men" and as people of West Zuyuá 1957: 107; Roys 1962: 36; Thompson 1970; Stone 1989: 167). It would seem then that the importance of association with Zuyuanism (see López Austin and López Luján, chapter 1 of this volume) among Maya rulers of the Terminal Classic stretches back to the Early Classic period in Copán and Tikal.

These threads of narrative and symbolism cannot be considered definitive proof of Teotihuacan ancestry for these important occupants of Maya thrones, in and of themselves. We must look to the archaeological record for confirmation of such claims (Marcus 1992), especially the strontium and DNA analyses of the human skeletal remains. No doubt further insights will be gained in the ongoing analysis of the grave of K'inich Yax K'uk' Mo' of Copán, the founder who is associated with Teotihuacan imagery by the later kings of that city. The two unique burial chambers at Copán with structural features that suggest the presence of actual residents from Kaminaljuyú (Burial V-6) and Teotihuacan (Burial XXXVII-8; Figure 14.3) are also noteworthy. The preponderance of green obsidian artifacts in the fill of the building associated with Burial XXXVII-8, and the cylindrical form of the grave placed on its central axis, constitute further direct archaeological evidence—independent of the historical record and pictorial imagery—for a direct connection between Teotihuacan and Copán, at the time of the latter's "founding."

It is important to note that green obsidian is also found in very high proportions at the Copán Valley hilltop site of Cerro de las Mesas, located two kilometers northwest of the Acropolis. The associated ceramics suggest that this occurrence may slightly pre-date the green obsidian found in association with Yax Structure, suggesting that this is the first site in the Copán region to make a connection with Teotihuacan merchants. Its defensible position is mirrored by three other hilltop sites in the Copán region that also have Early Classic ceramics pre-dating the founding of the Acropolis by K'inich Yax K'uk' Mo'. The first of these is the settlement located on the alluvial spur where the modern town of Copán Ruinas stands, long known to have Early Classic inscriptions (Morley 1920), including a reference to a ruler who apparently pre-dates K'inich Yax K'uk' Mo's dynasty (Stuart 1992). Another early hilltop settlement sits atop Cerro Chino, which is located intermediate between the Acropolis and Cerro de las Mesas. Yet another is the more distant and impressive hilltop site of Los Achiotes, under investigation by Marcello Andrea Canuto. This hilltop settlement pattern is in striking contrast to Late Classic practice, when the vast majority of the settlements were on or very near the alluvial bottomlands. In fact, none of the last three hilltop sites mentioned have Late Classic occupations of any magnitude, meaning the apparent need for such defensible localities in settlement planning had diminished.

These early defensible hilltop settlements imply an unsettled political landscape when K'inich Yax K'uk' Mo' set up his fiefdom, vital information not

available to us through the window of official history carved in stone. The settlement pattern data, ceramics, and green obsidian lead us to speculate that a faction
with ties to Teotihuacan established itself on the fortress-like hill of Cerro de las
Mesas, and unified the diverse competing noble lines, moreover establishing a
royal center in a thoroughly indefensible place, in the center of the Copán Valley
bottomlands. David Webster's (1977) hypothesis that warfare was critical in the
formation of Maya kingdoms would seem to have much in its favor in the case of
the Classic period Copán dynasty. What better way to resolve an internal conflict
than to place themselves in the hands of a veteran warrior-merchant, who validated his right to rule by his mercantile and militaristic connections with the
mighty Teotihuacan? The skeletal evidence that the man in the Hunal tomb had a
parry fracture on his right forearm is interpreted by Jane Buikstra (personal communications, 1997) as evidence for a battle wound. As Sharer (1997) notes, it is
also illuminating when we discuss archaeological confirmation of the pictorial
record, since K'inich Yax K'uk' Mo' is portrayed with a small rectangular shield

Fig. 14.4. Altar Q detail of K'inich Yax K'uk' Mo' showing shell goggle around eye,
feathered cape, and *cipactli* shield.

on his right arm on the front of Altar Q (Figure 14.4). Finally, it is significant that the strontium analysis of the bones of this individual indicate that he was, in fact, not a native of the Copán Valley (Sharer et al. 1998), adding important evidence in favor of his having been a "Lord of the West."

Although we cannot demonstrate that K'inich Yax K'uk' Mo' "took over" Copán by force, we believe that Sharer has made a strong case that he did set up his own palace compound, with his own public buildings, at some distance from the previous dynastic center. His use of Teotihuacan architecture, burial patterns, warrior accoutrements, green obsidian, Thin Orange pottery, and other Teotihuacan-style ceramics, indicate that whatever his origins may have been, he sought to create a "Tollan" at the eastern frontier of the Maya world that in some small way represented a microcosm of Teotihuacan. These archaeological data and conclusions find an interesting glyphic corroboration in the form of the *pu* (bullrush, or reed) sign infixed into the Copán emblem glyph as early as the reign of the fourth ruler (see Stuart, chapter 15 of this volume). Terminal Classic groups in Yucatán that claimed descent from the west or "Place of Zuyuá," maintained a mixture of names, some Maya, others Mexican in origin. Perhaps the two identities were often paired, to situate the ruling line in both realms. At the site of Piedras Negras, the ruler's accession stelae are void of Teotihuacan motifs, while the protagonists on the warrior stelae are laden with Teotihuacan accoutrements (Stone 1989).

It is intriguing and perhaps significant that there are no contemporary portraits of K'inich Yax K'uk' Mo' that have survived. (We should leave open the possibility that he also left buildings and perhaps other monuments in the area beneath the enormous construction mass of Structure 11, whose only tunnel excavation yielded a step inscribed by the seventh ruler claiming that this was the locus of the "lineage house of Yax K'uk' Mo'" [David Stuart, personal communication, 1987].) To be sure, his son and successor, and several much later rulers, do portray him and cite his exploits quite often. Why did the so-called "founder" not commission any portraits of himself? One possible explanation was offered to us by Karl Taube (personal communication, 1997): because that would not have adhered to the tradition of Teotihuacan, where, as we all know and lament, ruler portraits in stone are nonexistent, or at best extraordinarily rare. The "cult of personality" that so obsessed the Maya rulers in their stone monuments never took hold in Classic period Central Mexico. This same "faceless, nameless" tradition of Teotihuacan was followed by the Toltec of Tula, Hidalgo, where ruler portraits in stone also shine by their absence. Among the Mexica, as well, rulers were deemed less worthy of the sculptor's and muralist's art than the gods and the days who bore their destinies. Thus, we should not be surprised that Teotihuacanos were loathe to have their likeness carved in stone in the Maya world; the very idea went against the grain.

Later rulers portrayed K'inich Yax K'uk' Mo' with Storm God goggles over his eyes on a number of monuments: on Altar Q (Figure 14.4); on his portrait in the niche of the superstructure of Temple 16 by Ruler 16 (Fash 1992); on the ceramic figure from Tomb XXXVII-4 beneath the Hieroglyphic Stairway by Ruler 13 (Fash et al. 1992) (Figure 14.5), and; in Sharer's estimation, on the Teotihuacan-style polychrome pot from the Margarita Structure, by Ruler 2 or an immediate successor (Sharer 1996, 1997; G. Stuart 1997). Why, then, was he portrayed without them on the Motmot floor marker (Fash and Fash 1996: figure 2), dedicated by his son and successor so soon after his death? As B. Fash (1997) has suggested, perhaps it had to do with changing political currents of the time. After all, he was only in power for about a decade, according to both the texts and the archaeology of the Acropolis. His son and successor garnered enough support to continue the political consolidation of his realm, to judge from his frenetic building campaign and the fact that his father's royal compound would ever thereafter be the Main Acropolis of Copán. Robert Sharer and his colleagues (Sharer et al. 1998) believe that the aged woman laid to rest in the Margarita tomb, directly above that of Hunal, was the wife of the Copán founder, and the mother of Ruler 2. The strontium analysis of the Margarita tomb occupant indicates that this woman was from the Copán Valley, thus supporting Sharer's earlier interpretation that Yax K'uk' Mo' married a noblewoman from Copán (Sharer 1997). Their son apparently felt the need was stronger, or the potential payoff was greater, to build up his center in regal Maya fashion, rather than imperial Teotihuacan style. This pattern is also very much in keeping with what was to occur later at Kaminaljuyú, where the purported "takeover" was followed by intense displays of Teotihuacan architecture, symbolism, and craft goods, followed by their assimilation into the local elite "mainstream" in subsequent generations (Sanders 1978).

Kaminaljuyú's alleged "takeover" apparently occurred shortly after the arrival of K'inich Yax K'uk' Mo' in Copán. According to Sanders (1978), and Cheek (1977), the Teotihuacan contingent began its occupation and massive constructions of Teotihuacan-style buildings at Kaminaljuyú around 450 C.E. The two major temple-pyramids were re-built periodically, corresponding to the interment of important dignitaries at the foot of each of them, several times over the next fifty years. Thereafter the architecture reverts to local styles, and the importation of craft goods from Teotihuacan and even the production of local imitations of Teotihuacan ceramic styles and decorative techniques declines rapidly as the Teotihuacanos are assimilated into the local traditions and social context. Thus, present evidence indicates that for the three Early Classic Maya kingdoms for which there are clear indications of what archaeologists refer to as "site unit intrusions," the "intruders" used symbols and texts to claim direct affiliations with Teotihuacan. The evidence from strontium (Copán), texts (Tikal), and ethnohistoric analogy (Kaminaljuyú) has been used to affirm that these important historical individuals married women from the local aristocracy, and were eventually incorporated into the local royal bloodlines in ways familiar to royal houses the world over. There is no evidence—at present—to sustain the view that these historic individuals established long-lived "outposts" of a Teotihuacan "empire," sending tribute on an annual basis to the highland metropolis in contractual arrangements like those of the later Triple Alliance. However, we should note that any evidence for such arrangements would more likely to surface at Teotihuacan, than in the Maya area.

Fig. 14.5. Ceramic censer effigy lids; offerings outside of Burial XXXVII-4; a. Interpreted as image of K'inich Yax K'uk' Mo', founder of the Copán dynasty; b. Ruler in warrior costume with year signs in headdress (also holds a lancet, not pictured).

LATE CLASSIC COPÁN AS A TOLLAN

The many ways in which the Late Classic rulers of Copán capitalized on their connection with Teotihuacan in the official records on their public monuments (B. Fash 1992, 1997; W. Fash 1997; Stuart 1997 and chapter 15 of this volume) again recall the Aztec example of constant reminders of their Toltec heritage. Classic Maya rulers seem determined to prove that they were of Highland Mexican pedigree, by having themselves portrayed with goggles over the eyes, rectangular shields on one forearm and *atlatl* in the other hand, shell platelet "War Serpent" headdresses, and Mexican year signs and garters. Those monuments stand as testimony to the importance that Teotihuacan held in the minds of the Maya, both as a sacred urban center and as home to powerful military orders and strategies. To judge from their obsessive use of Teotihuacan military symbolism, the martial aspects seem to have been the most compelling and useful to the Maya during the Late Classic period, in all likelihood due to their concerns with maintaining authority in an increasingly bellicose political landscape.

In Late Classic Copán, there are numerous representations of Teotihuacan imagery in architectural sculpture in the dynastic center or "Principal Group." Only recently, however, have we come to realize that this imagery was also embellished on Late Classic vaulted masonry palaces and temples built in outlier communities. Until extensive excavations are carried out at the outlier sites, we can only speculate as to the nature of any interaction between their occupants and the people of highland Mexico. However we can pose a provocative question: to what degree was "Tollanization" (Carrasco 1982) at work in the Copán kingdom in the eighth century C.E.?

Intensive research in the retrieval, cataloguing, analysis, and re-fitting of thousands of fragments of tenoned stone mosaic façade sculptures from the Copán Acropolis has revealed that four major monumental buildings in the dynastic center of Copán displayed numerous motifs in their sculpture programs attributed to Central Mexico, and Teotihuacan in particular (Fash 1992): Structures 10L-16, -21, -21A, and -26 (Figures 14.6–14.9). Three other dynastic buildings in the royal residential area on the south flank of the Acropolis, Structures 10L-29, -33, and -41, reveal similar iconography. Additionally, Stela 6, located one-half kilometer west of the dynastic center and carved late in the reign of the 12th ruler ("Smoke Imix-God K"), has been identified as having a Teotihuacano costume (Figure 14.1). And as previously mentioned, the founder, K'inich Yax K'uk' Mo', is shown wearing goggle eye pieces and carrying a shield ornamented with a Teotihuacan War Serpent sign on his portrait on Altar Q (Figure 14.4). Beginning with the twelfth ruler on Stela 6 and working up through the reign of the sixteenth ruler who erected Structure 16, Structure 21A, and Altar Q, we note an increase in the amount and scale of this symbolism at Copán rather than a decline. This is in contradistinction to what was actually happening at the site of Teotihuacan, which had certainly fallen into decline by that point (Cowgill 1997).

Fig. 14.6. Outset stairway panel displaying skull rack surrounding a Tlaloc image, Copán, Structure 16; reconstruction by B. Fash and K. Taube.

The same pattern is seen at many other lowland Maya sites in the eighth and ninth centuries C.E. (Stone 1989; Schele and Freidel 1990; Pasztory 1997).

This pattern compels us to examine how ideology and art forms were shared across such great distances in earlier times, when Teotihuacan was in full flower. The Temple of the Feathered Serpent in Teotihuacan (built around 200 C.E.) and the cult of Quetzalcoatl (Nicholson 1957; Carrasco 1982) seems to have been vividly remembered by the sculptor who fashioned the earliest known stucco bird on Ballcourt I at Copán, dated to ca. 450 C.E. (Figure 14.2). One can easily note the similarity in the heads of the feathered serpents and the head emerging from the groin area of the Copán ball court bird (Fash and Fash 1996). H. B. Nicholson (1971) remarks on the sudden appearance of the Temple of the Feathered Serpent and its decorative frieze as an unprecedented "tour de force." Pasztory questions whether the stucco masks in the Maya area inspired the stone sculpture façade of the Temple of the Feathered Serpent (1997), however, it is intriguing to flip the question and ask whether the later shift to mosaic stone sculpture from plaster

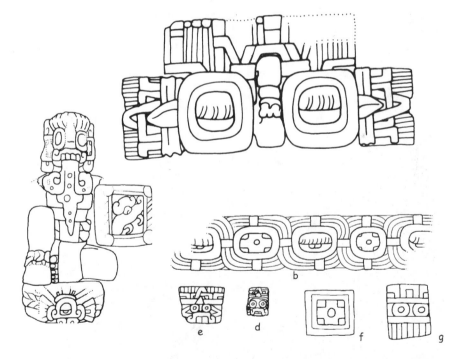

Fig. 14.7. Teotihuacan imagery from Temple 16; a. Goggle-eyed owl with tufted year signs (owl identification via personal communication with K. Taube); b. Interlocking eye and Kan cross; c. Tlaloc warrior and *cipactli* shield; d. Interior temple Tlaloc; e. Exterior façade Tlaloc with tufted year sign; f. Kan cross; g. Shell goggle shield.

antecedents at Copán was inspired by Teotihuacan. Once the Temple of the Feathered Serpent was buried, the later, Xolalpan mosaic sculptures that adorned temples from the West Plaza Complex, Street of the Dead Complex, and the Palace of Quetzalpapalotl could have served as templates for Late Classic Maya mosaic sculpture. In this regard, it is equally plausible that an Early Classic Copanec could have travelled to Teotihuacan on a pilgrimage and brought the Teotihuacan traditions back home, as that a Central Mexican merchant or emissary brought this specialized knowledge with him to Copán.

Even without the kinds of compelling evidence that have recently surfaced in the Copán Acropolis Archaeological Project investigations, the Classic Maya familiarity with Teotihuacan has long suggested interaction at the highest level (Pasztory 1997). Why did Maya rulers want to foster this connection and in what way did it help them to enhance their authority? Following Carrasco's (1982) reconstruction, if Teotihuacan was a pilgrimage place, a trade center, and also a place of craft production and "higher learning," then conceivably cities from all over Mesoamerica sent their people there to worship and to be trained in the

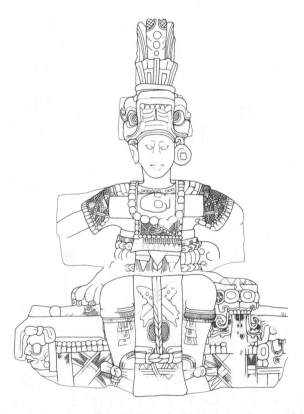

Fig. 14.8. Second seated figure from the Hieroglyphic Stairway, Structure 26, Copán. The warrior costume is of a Central Mexican style, showing a Tlaloc head, leg garters, and year signs.

esoteric arts, military tactics, and/or craft production. Once training was complete, they returned to their respective homelands as knowledgeable and possibly militarily proficient people. From there they could selectively impart this knowledge to their own people. This higher level of training seems to have been available only to the elite, but the commoners were either accepting of its superiority
or in awe of it.

The ancient Copanecs promoted their connections with Teotihuacan from
the founding of the Yax K'uk' Mo' dynasty until its demise. The evidence for
direct trade in the form of diverse Teotihuacan commodities is clear, as is the
presence of Teotihuacan-style architecture, burial practices, and warrior accoutrements. We suggest that in their case, the connections involved more than simply
an attempt at emulation, and propaganda for the legitimization of the ruling family.
The Altar Q text statement that the founder "arrived" from the west, suggests to
some that K'inich Yax K'uk' Mo' himself may have been from Teotihuacan. This is
reinforced by the likelihood that the burial inside the early-fifth-century Acropolis
building Hunal, with its *talud-tablero* sub-structure and Teotihuacan-style murals,

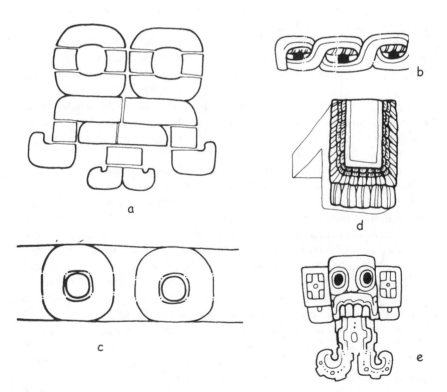

Fig. 14.9. a. Structure 21A Tlaloc mosaic; hypothetical reconstruction; b. Structure 21,
interlocking eye motif; c. Structure 26, *chalchihuites*; d. Structure 26, rectangular shields;
e. Structure 21, Tlaloc skull mosaic, hypothetical reconstruction.

is that of the founder. We do not yet have sufficient evidence to resolve whether K'inich Yax K'uk' Mo' was born and raised in Teotihuacan, or if instead he was one of many elites who "passed through" the great Tollan to be "enriched socially and culturally," thus preparing him for acceptance as a "civilized leader" (Carrasco 1982: 105). It is more than mildly suggestive, however, that the man in the Hunal tomb was not born and raised in Copán.

When, centuries later, the great Tollan Teotihuacan collapsed, the royal houses at sites such as Copán felt compelled to uphold their power and authority by reinforcing what their ties with the sacred city had been. Stone (1989) sees the great florescence of Teotihuacan imagery on lowland Maya stone monuments of the Late Classic period—even after the decline and fall of the Mexican city—as evidence for reverence of the great Classic period center of the arts and sciences by the Maya rulers. With the central locus of Teotihuacan in ruins, power shifted to the formerly subsidiary cities that revered the Teotihuacan ideology and respected its military regime, and may have had ancient blood ties to that capital. "Long after the society of Teotihuacan collapsed its iconography, institutions, symbols, and prestige as the center of the world continued to reverberate as the living substance of later cites" (Carrasco 1982: 118). Subsidiary cities had to proclaim ever more emphatically, that they were still invested with the power from the first Tollan (Carrasco 1982).

In fact, in Copán, the evidence indicates that in the late eighth century C.E., several prominent outlying settlements suddenly erected structures with Central Mexican iconography. This is predominant at the sites of Río Amarillo (located 20 km. east of the dynastic center), Rastrojón (2 kilometers east of the center), and Ostumán (3 kilometers west of the center). In those increasingly turbulent times, it seems the rulers felt empowered to be the new bestowers of the Tollan symbolism (if not the knowledge and training) to enhance the status of supportive lineage groups (Fash 1988; 1991).

This explosion of Teotihuacan imagery both in the dynastic center and the palatial compounds of supporting nobles made the Copán Principal Group and its outlying settlements a sort of microcosm of the earlier center of Teotihuacan as a "Place of the Reeds," extending out to the far reaches of the Copán kingdom as Teotihuacan once reached out to all of Mesoamerica. It is possible that many of the other lowland Maya kingdoms were vying "to fill the vacuum of power" (Stone 1989), using the same perquisite of calling themselves a "Tollan." Dennis Tedlock (1989) suggests that for the sixteenth-century Quiché, Copán was the eastern "Tollan" of the four Tollans mentioned in the *Popol vuh*, a place of great power where rulers went on pilgrimages to obtain the insignia of office. If he is correct then Copán succeeded, even after the demise of the ruling dynasty, in securing its legacy as a Tollan, a Place of the Reeds, a "Place of Origins" (Heyden 1975), or "Emergence" (Taube 1986). Could this be the motive behind the claim to authority by Ruler 15 ("Smoke Shell") in the temple inscription above the Hieroglyphic Stairway (Figure 14.10), with its use of glyphs imbedded with Teotihuacan symbols and characters (see Stuart, chapter 15 of this volume), as well as his abundant use of Central Mexican imagery on the stairs, balustrades, and temple façades (Figures 14.8 and 14.9)?

The Classic Heritage

But what of Teotihuacan's interest in the Maya? Why do we not see the first great "Place of the Reeds" reciprocating the Maya's reverence, and proclaiming its ties to the vibrant lowland kingdoms to the east? One possible explanation is that it would have gone against Mesoamerican principles of hierarchy for them to do so. It is exceedingly unlikely that the older city-states of the Valley of Mexico would have cited Mexico-Tenochtitlan, prior to the meteoric ascendance of that community following their defeat of the Tepanecs in the early fifteenth century. Likewise, Joyce Marcus (1976) long ago demonstrated that the largest Maya cities (e.g., Tikal, Calakmul, Copán, Palenque, etc.) only very rarely cited the smaller sites that were under their sway. Protocol required the smaller sites to be quite forthcoming about mentioning the larger ones, in an ascending ladder of citation. It does not bring prestige to oneself to mention lesser sites, unless their conquest was highly profitable or the stuff of legend.

Another, more compelling reason why Teotihuacan does not play up whatever "Maya connections" it had, is rooted not in cultural ecology or religious ideology, but simple logistics. Given the vast distance between the Teotihuacan Valley and the Maya lowlands, it seems doubtful that Teotihuacan could have controlled the affairs and economies of any major Maya kingdom for very long. The sophisticated administrative strategies of the later Mexica and Inka were still centuries away, and present evidence does indeed seem to support Demarest and Foias's conclusion that vast armies of Teotihuacanos were never stationed in the Maya lowlands. What we are left with is a history in which (at least three) prominent cities in the Maya lowlands were taken over by charismatic figures with strong ties to Teotihuacan, who married into the local Maya aristocracy, and within a few generations' time were completely absorbed into their local political contexts.

Thus, it seems, we were asking the wrong question. Instead of expecting to see the Maya painted on the murals or portrayed in Teotihuacan stone sculptures, we should instead look for their presence on the ground—in the streets and barrios of the great city. It is not unreasonable to hold out the hope that a purely Maya version of something like the Oaxaca barrio, or the Merchants' barrio (with ties to Veracruz and the western edges of the Maya world), may yet be discovered there. The fact that people from Oaxaca and Veracruz were represented in the metropolis certainly increases the likelihood that immigrants from other areas of Mesoamerica also migrated there, and stayed for extended periods of time.

Given that the strongest ties with Tikal, Copán, and Kaminaljuyú seem to have flourished in the first half of the Early Classic period, perhaps our hypothetical Maya barrio did not survive as late as the latter well-known examples, and thus is not as easily recognized by surface survey. If a Maya barrio one day surfaces in excavations, we may then obtain a glimpse of what material goods and/or services the Maya contributed to Teotihuacan, and which regions of the Maya world were represented there. In the meantime, the idea that the "Teotihuacan sky" was shaped by celestial phenomena visible only in the Maya world (Aveni, chapter 9 of this volume), alerts us to the kinds of ideological contributions that the rich Maya tradition could have bestowed upon the Teotihuacan intelligentsia.

Certainly, the record of the Quiché kings "obtaining the tools of kingship" from the Tollans of the four directions that is recorded in the *Popol vuh* makes it clear that royal visits to large, ancient cities to obtain the accoutrements of office were part of Maya rituals of accession. Teotihuacan was clearly the most powerful Tollan of the Classic period, and others would certainly have emulated its example and drawn from its rich traditions. Thus, even if K'inich Yax K'uk' Mo' was not himself from Teotihuacan, we can be confident that he had been there, and became knowledgeable in their ways.

His successors and numerous other Late Classic Maya proudly proclaimed their ties to the great city and civilization of central Mexico on numerous portraits of themselves, carved in stone and locked in time for all eternity. Clearly, the power of Teotihuacan to fire the imagination and strike fear in the heart of one's enemies was widespread. From interpreting both the imagery and the archaeological record, it is clear that the legacy was indeed one of finely made luxury goods, esoteric knowledge, military might, architectural, calendric and cosmological sophistication, in sum, all that one would expect of a city of master craftsmen, and a timeless cultural tradition. The objects found in royal tombs in the Classic Maya world provide solid evidence of the Maya's appreciation of Teotihuacan goods, and their desire to emulate them in their own workshops. The caches of Pachuca obsidian also signal a perceived need to offer, and to use, the clear green glass of Central Mexico. The prominent use of *talud-tablero* architecture demonstrates the quest to create spaces that evoked the great Tollan of the west, and the memory of the Lords of the West who had visited or even joined them.

Yet the legacy of this first great Tollan, it is clear, was not confined to its art, architecture, artifacts, or cosmology. The imagery on the Maya monuments indicates that warfare was an integral part of the collective perception, and later remembrances, of Teotihuacan. This legacy was the one most frequently commemorated at subsequent Tollans, such as Tula, Hidalgo, and later cities claiming Toltec heritage, including Mexico-Tenochtitlan. Like all civilizations, Classic Mesoamerica struggled with war even as it tried to define a cosmic peace. Zuyuanism may not have had its start at Teotihuacan, but certainly the lore of that city played a defining role in its codification and spread. The "language of Zuyuá" helped to reify that tradition, and was used by Postclassic Maya peoples of Yucatán to judge those worthy to rule (Roys 1967). We are left wondering if the magnificent paired scripts of the Temple of the Hieroglyphic Stairway (Figure 14.10) might represent Maya, and Zuyuá. We are hopeful that future research will profit from visualizing the Isthmus of Tehuantepec as a bridge rather than a barrier in assessments of the Classic Mesoamerican legacy.

REFERENCES

Adams, Richard E. W.

1973. "Maya Collapse: Transformation and Termination in the Ceramic Sequence at Altar de Sacrificios." In T. P. Culbert, ed., *The Classic Maya Collapse*. Albuquerque: University of New Mexico Press, pp. 133–163.

1986. "Rio Azul: Lost City of the Maya." *National Geographic* 169, no. 4 (April): 420–465.

Aoyama, Kazuo
1996. "Exchange, Craft Specialization, and Ancient Maya State Formation: A Study of Chipped Stone Artifacts from the Southeast Maya Lowlands (Copán Valley, La Entrada, Honduras)." Ph.D. diss., Anthropology Dept., University of Pittsburgh, Pittsburgh, PA.

Ball, Joseph
1974. "A Teotihuacan-Style Cache in the Maya Lowlands." *American Antiquity* 27, no. 1: 2–9.

Barrera Vásquez, Alfredo
1957. *Códice de Calkiní.* Campeche: Biblioteca Campechana 4.

Berlo, Janet
1989. "Art Historical Approaches to the Study of Teotihuacan-Related Ceramics from Escuintla, Guatemala." In F. J. Bové and L. Heller, eds., *New Frontiers in the Archaeology of the Pacific Coast of Southern Mesoamerica.* Anthropological Research Papers, 39. Tempe: Arizona State University, pp. 147–162.

Carrasco, Davíd
1982. *Quetzalcoatl and the Irony of Empire: Myths and Prophecy in the Aztec Tradition.* Chicago: University of Chicago Press.

Chase, Arlen F., and Diane Z. Chase
1987. *Investigations at the Classic Maya City of Caracol, Belize: 1986–1987.* San Francisco: Pre-Columbian Art Research Institute Monograph 3.

Cheek, Charles D.
1977. "Teotihuacan Influence at Kaminaljuyú." In W. T. Sanders and J. W. Michels, eds., *Teotihuacan and Kaminaljuyú: A Study in Prehistoric Culture Contact.* University Park: Pennsylvania State University Press, pp. 441–453.

Cheek, Charles D., and Rene Viel
1983. "Sepulturas." In C. F. Baudez, ed., *Introducción a la arqueología de Copán, Honduras.* Tegucigalpa: Secretaría del Estado en el Despacho de Cultura y Turismo, vol. 1, pp. 551–609.

Coe, William R.
1972. "Cultural Contact Between the Lowland Maya and Teotihuacan as Seen from Tikal, Petén, Guatemala." In *XI Mesa Redonda.* Mexico: SMA, vol. 2, pp. 257–271.

Coggins, Clemency
1975. "Painting and Drawing Styles at Tikal: An Historical and Iconographic Reconstruction." Ph.D. diss., Harvard University, Cambridge, MA.
1976. "Teotihuacan at Tikal in the Early Classic Period." In *Actes du XLIIe Congrès International des Américanistes: Paris, 2–9 septembre 1976.* Paris: Société des Américanistes, vol. 8, pp. 251–269.
1979. "A New Order and the Role of the Calendar: Some Characteristics of the Middle Classic Period at Tikal." In N. Hammond and G. Willey, eds., *Maya Archaeology and Ethnohistory.* Austin: University of Texas Press, pp. 38–50.
1983. "An Instrument of Expansion: Monte Alban, Teotihuacan, and Tikal." In A. G. Miller, ed., *Highland-Lowland Interaction in Mesoamerica: Interdisciplinary Approaches.* Washington, DC: Dumbarton Oaks, pp. 49–68.

Cowgill, George
1997. "Teotihuacan's Internal Politics and External Relations." Paper presented at the "A

Tale of Two Cities: Copán and Teotihuacan" Conference, Peabody Museum, Harvard University, Cambridge, MA.

Demarest, Arthur, and Antonia Foias
1993. "Mesoamerican Horizons and the Cultural Transformations of Maya Civilization." In D. S. Rice, ed., *Latin American Horizons*. Washington, DC: Dumbarton Oaks, pp. 147–191.

Demarest, Arthur, and William Fowler, eds.
1984. "Proyecto El Mirador de la Harvard University, 1982–1983." *Mesoamerica* 5, no. 7: 1–160.

Fash, Barbara
1992. "Late Classic Architectural Sculpture Themes at Copán." *Ancient Mesoamerica* 3: 89–102.
1997. "Teotihuacan Symbolism in the Classic Period Art of Copán." Paper presented at the "A Tale of Two Cities: Copán and Teotihuacan" Conference, Peabody Museum, Harvard University, Cambridge, MA.

Fash, William
1988. "A New Look at Maya Statecraft from Copán, Honduras." *Antiquity* 62: 157–169.
1991. *Scribes, Warriors, and Kings: The City of Copán and the Ancient Maya*. London: Thames and Hudson.
1997. "Official Histories and Archaeological Evidence in the Evaluation of the Copán-Teotihuacan Relationship." Paper presented at the "A Tale of Two Cities: Copán and Teotihuacan" Conference, Peabody Museum, Harvard University, Cambridge, MA.

Fash, William L., and Barbara W. Fash
1996. "Building a World View: Visual Communication in Classic Maya Architecture." *Res: Anthropology and Aesthetics* 29/30: 127–147.

Fash, William L., and Robert J. Sharer
1991. "Sociopolitical Developments and Methodological Issues at Copán, Honduras: A Conjunctive Perspective." *Latin American Antiquity* 2: 166–187.

Fash, William L., Richard V. Williamson, C. Rudy Larios Villalta, and Joel Palka
1992. "The Hieroglyphic Stairway and its Ancestors: Investigations of Copán Structure 10L-26." *Ancient Mesoamerica* 2: 105–115.

Flannery, Kent
1968. "The Olmec and the Valley of Oaxaca: A Model for Inter-regional Interaction in Formative Times." In E. Benson, ed., *Dumbarton Oaks Conference on the Olmec*. Washington, DC: Dumbarton Oaks, pp. 79–110.

Flannery, Kent, and Joyce Marcus
1994. *Ceramics from the Valley of Oaxaca*. Ann Arbor: University of Michigan, Museum of Anthropology, Memoir 27.

Hansen, Richard
1991. "On the Road to Nakbe." *Natural History* (May): 9–14.

Hellmuth, Nicholas
1972. "Excavations Begin at a Maya Site in Guatemala." *American Antiquity* 25: 148–149.
1976. "Evidence of Teotihuacan Contact in the Maya Lowlands: A Study in Iconography." M.A. thesis, Yale University, New Haven, CT.
1978. "Teotihuacan Art in the Escuintla, Guatema Region." In E. Pasztory, ed., *Middle Classic Mesoamerica, A.D. 400–700*. New York: Columbia University Press, pp. 71–85.

Heyden, Doris
1975. "An Interpretation of the Cave Underneath the Pyramid of the Sun in Teotihuacan, Mexico." *American Antiquity* 40, no. 2: 131–147.

Hirth, Kenneth G., ed.
1984. *Trade and Exchange in Early Mesoamerica*. Albuquerque: University of New Mexico Press.

Kidder, Alfred V., Jesse Jennings, and Edwin Shook
1946. *Excavations at Kaminaljuyu, Guatemala*. Washington, DC: Carnegie Institution Publication no. 501.

Kubler, George
1973. "Iconographic Aspects of Architectural Profiles at Teotihuacan and in Mesoamerica." In *The Iconography of Middle American Sculpture*. New York: Metropolitan Museum of Art, pp. 24–39.

Laporte, Juan Pedro, and Vilma Fialko
1995. "Un Reencuentro con Mundo Perdido, Guatemala." *Ancient Mesoamerica* 4: 44–94.

Manzanilla, Linda
1993. "Daily Life in the Teotihuacan Apartment Compounds." In K. Berrin and E. Pasztory, eds., *Teotihuacan, Art from the City of the Gods*. San Francisco: The Fine Arts Museums of San Francisco, pp. 90–99.

Marcus, Joyce
1976. *Emblem and State in the Classic Maya Lowlands*. Washington, DC: Dumbarton Oaks.
1992. *Mesoamerican Writing Systems: History, Myth, and Propaganda in Four Ancient Civilizations*. Princeton, NJ: Princeton University Press.
1989. "Zapotec Chiefdoms and the Nature of Formative Religions." In R. J. Sharer and D. C. Grove, eds., *Regional Perspectives on the Olmec*. Cambridge: Cambridge University Press, pp.148–197.

Matheny, Raymond
1980. *El Mirador, Peten, Guatemala, and Interim Report*. Papers of the New World Archaeological Foundation no. 45. Provo, UT.

Mathews, Peter
1985. "Maya Early Classic Monuments and Inscriptions." In G. R. Willey and P. Mathews, eds., *A Consideration of the Early Classic Period in the Maya Lowlands*. Albany: Institute for Mesoamerican Studies, SUNY.

Miller, Arthur G., ed.
1983. *Highland-Lowland Interaction in Mesoamerica: Interdisciplinary Approaches*. Washington, DC: Dumbarton Oaks.

Morley, Sylvanus G.
1920. *The Inscriptions at Copán*. Washington, DC: Carnegie Institution Publication no. 219.

Nicholson, H. B.
1957. "Topiltzin Quetzalcoatl of Tollan: A Problem in Mesoamerican History." Ph.D. diss., Anthropology Dept., Harvard University, Cambridge, MA.
1971. "Major Sculpture in Pre-Hispanic Central America." In R. A. Wauchope, gen. ed.; G. Ekholm and I. Bernal, vol. eds., *Handbook of Middle American Indians*, Vol. 10, Part 1: *Archaeology of Northern Mesoamerica*. Austin: University of Texas Press, pp. 92–134.

Pasztory, Esther
1997. *Teotihuacan: An Experiment in Living*. Norman: University of Oklahoma Press.

Pendergast, David
1971. "Evidence of Early Teotihuacan-Lowland Maya Contact at Altun Ha." *American Antiquity* 36, no. 4: 455–460.

Piedra, José
1989. "The Game of Critical Arrival." *Diacritics* 19: 34–61.

Proskouriakoff, Tatiana
1993. *Maya History*. Ed. R. A. Joyce. Austin: University of Texas Press.

Roys, Ralph L.
1963. "Literary Sources for the History of Mayapan." In H. E. D. Pollock, R. L. Roys, T. Proskouriakoff, and A. L. Smith. *Mayapan, Yucatan, Mexico*. Washington, DC: Carnegie Institution Publication no. 619, pp. 25–86.
1967. *The Book of Chilam Balam of Chumayel*. Norman: University of Oklahoma Press.

Sanders, William T.
1978. "Ethnographic Analogy and the Teotihuacan Horizon Style." In E. Pasztory, ed., *Middle Classic Mesoamerica, A.D. 400–700*. New York: Columbia University Press, pp. 35–44.

Sanders, William T., and Barbara Price
1968. *Mesoamerica: The Evolution of a Civilization*. New York: Random House.

Schele, Linda
1986. "The Tlaloc Heresy." Paper presented at the Blood of Kings Conference, the Kimball Art Museum, Fort Worth, TX.

Schele, Linda, and David Freidel
1990. *A Forest of Kings: The Untold Story of the Ancient Maya*. New York: William Morrow.

Serrano Sánchez, Carlos
1993. "Funerary Practices and Human Sacrifice in Teotihuacan Burials." In K. Berrin and E. Pasztory, eds., *Teotihuacan, Art from the City of the Gods*. San Francisco: The Fine Arts Museums of San Francisco, pp. 108–115.

Sharer, Robert
1996. "Patterns of Architectural Growth in the Early Classic Copán Acropolis." Paper presented at the 61st Annual Meeting of the Society for American Archaeology, New Orleans, LA.
1997. "K'inich Yax K'uk' Mo' and the Genesis of the Copán Acropolis." Paper presented at the "A Tale of Two Cities: Copán and Teotihuacan" Conference, Peabody Museum, Harvard University, Cambridge, MA.

Sharer, Robert, and David C. Grove, eds.
1989. *Regional Perspectives on the Olmec*. Cambridge: Cambridge University Press.

Sharer, Robert, David W. Sedat, Loa P. Traxler, Christine W. Carrelli, Ellen E. Bell, and Fernando López
1998. "Informe de la Temporada de 1998, Programa de Investigación de la Acrópolis Temprana." Report submitted to the Instituto Hondureño de Antropología e Historia, Tegucigalpa, Honduras.

Smith, Robert E.
1955. *Ceramic Sequence at Uaxactun, Guatemala*. 2 vols. New Orleans, LA: Tulane

University, Middle American Research Institute Publication 20.

Spinden, Herbert Joseph
1933. "Origin of Civilizations in Central America and Mexico." In D. Jenness, ed., *The American Aborigines, Their Origin and Antiquities*. Toronto: University of Toronto Press, pp. 217–246.

Stone, Andrea
1989. "Disconnection, Foreign Insignia, and Political Expansion: Teotihuacan and the Warrior Stelae of Piedras Negras." In R. Diehl and J. C. Berlo, ed., *Mesoamerica After the Decline of Teotihuacan, A.D. 700–900*. Washington, DC: Dumbarton Oaks, pp. 153–172.

Stuart, David
1992. "Hieroglyphs and Archaeology at Copán." *Ancient Mesoamerica* 3: 164–189.
1997. "Smoking Frog, K'inich Yax K'uk' Mo', and the Epigraphic Evidence for Ties Between Teotihuacan and the Classic Maya." Paper presented at the "A Tale of Two Cities: Copán and Teotihuacan" Conference, Peabody Museum, Harvard University, Cambridge, MA.

Stuart, George E.
1997. "Royal Crypts of Copán." *National Geographic* 192, no. 6 (December): 68–93.

Taube, Karl
1986. "The Teotihuacan Cave of Origin: The Iconography and Architecture of Emergence Mythology in Mesoamerica and the American Southwest." *Res: Anthropology and Aesthetics* 12: 51–82.
1992. "Temple of Quetzalcoatl and the Cult of Sacred War at Teotihuacan." *Res: Anthropology and Aesthetics* 21: 53–87.

Tedlock, Dennis
1989. *Writing and Reflection Among the Maya*. College Park: University of Maryland, Department of Spanish and Portuguese, 1992 Lecture Series Working Papers no. 4.

Thompson, J. Eric S.
1970. *Maya History and Religion*. Norman: University of Oklahoma Press.

Traxler, Loa
1997. "Connections Buried Beneath the Dancing Jaguars at Copán, Honduras." Paper presented at the "A Tale of Two Cities: Copán and Teotihuacan" Conference, Peabody Museum, Harvard University, Cambridge, MA.

Webster, David
1977. "Warfare and the Evolution of Maya Civilization." In R. E. W. Adams, ed., *The Origins of Maya Civilization*. Albuquerque: University of New Mexico Press, pp. 335–372.

Willey, Gordon R.
1974. "The Classic Maya Hiatus: A Rehearsal for the Collapse?" In N. Hammond, ed., *Mesoamerican Archaeology: New Approaches*. Austin: University of Texas Press, pp. 417–444.

Wolfman, Daniel
1990. "Mesoamerican Chronology and Archaeomagnetic Dating, A.D. 1–1200." In J. L. Eighmy and R. S. Sternberg, eds., *Archaeomagnetic Dating*. Tucson: University of Arizona Press, pp. 261–308.

15

▼

"THE ARRIVAL OF STRANGERS"

TEOTIHUACAN AND TOLLAN IN CLASSIC MAYA HISTORY

DAVID STUART

This chapter revisits a much-debated topic in Mesoamerican archaeology—the nature and scope of the political interaction between the highlands of Central Mexico and the Maya lowlands during the Classic period (ca. 250–850 C.E.). Beginning in the middle years of the twentieth century, scholars of Mesoamerican culture have pondered the archaeological evidence of intensive contact between these two regions, most clearly suggested by the presence of Teotihuacan ceramic styles and figural imagery at several Maya sites in the central Petén region of present-day Guatemala. The existence of some sort of close interaction is not questioned. Yet for some years now Mesoamericanists have offered very different explanations for this culture contact.

In general, the scholarship has polarized around two different propositions. The first posits an overt and disruptive Teotihuacan presence in the Maya lowlands in the late fourth century C.E., associated with military incursions if not political domination (Coggins 1975, 1979a, 1983; Proskouriakoff 1993). The second and more recently developed viewpoint suggests that Teotihuacan styles and material remains in the Maya area might better be seen as a local appropriation of prestigious or legitimating symbolism and its associated militaristic ideology. This has been advanced in varied ways by several scholars working in the Maya area (Berlo 1983; Schele 1986; Stone 1989; Schele and Freidel 1990; Demarest and Foias 1993). In this latter view, the evidence of Teotihuacan influence in the Maya area says very little about what actual power relations might have existed between the Mexican highlands and the Maya lowlands. Such characterizations of the two main schools of thought are simply drawn, to be sure, but I believe accurate in their essentials.[1]

Different assessments of Teotihuacan-Maya contact have proved difficult to resolve, due in part no doubt to the pitfalls of deriving specific cultural-historical interpretations from the sometimes ambiguous archaeological and stylistic evidence at hand. To complicate matters even more, the political and economic ties that existed between Teotihuacan and Maya polities, however we characterize them, presumably changed over the centuries as fortunes and societies on both ends shifted in their own localized way. At least on the basis of Postclassic patterns and lowland Classic Maya geo-political history, we know that Mesoamerican political interactions, alliances, and hierarchies could shift and realign themselves with surprising speed, sometimes within the course of a generation or two. Rather than insist on a dichotomous either-or model, it is possible that both the "externalist" and "internalist" models outlined above have merit and explanatory power when applied at different times in Classic history.

Where, then, does this leave our debate? In my view, traditional lines of archaeological evidence are limited in their capacity to provide an explanatory context for the sort of intensive culture contact so evident at Tikal and Copán. Advancing the discussion and debate requires a more detailed historical context that can only be provided from an analysis of the preserved hieroglyphic texts at Tikal, Copán, and other Maya centers. The potential importance of the hieroglyphic texts is clear, but it is surprising how seldom they have been used to clarify the history underlying Teotihuacan-Maya interactions. With the exception of Proskouriakoff (1993), most epigraphic work on central Petén history has assumed a more "internalist" perspective, often ignoring the Teotihuacan issue altogether (e.g., Mathews 1985). I offer a very different perspective in this essay, arguing that hieroglyphic texts at Tikal, Copán, and other Maya sites offer insights into Maya perceptions of a dynamic and often changing relationship with central Mexico. As we shall see, such sources strongly support a more "externalist" view that Teotihuacan played a very direct and even disruptive role in the political history of Maya kingdoms.

In addition to the historical details surrounding this highland-lowland encounter, Classic Maya inscriptions and iconography allow us to perceive how the Maya consciousness of Teotihuacan changed and developed over the course of four centuries, melding the formidable power and memory of that foreign city with their own political symbolism and ideology. It is therefore in the latter part of the Classic period, after the collapse of Teotihuacan, that the less direct "internalist" model comes into play. I will argue that Maya rulers kept open a claim to this earlier history, evoking Teotihuacan as both a place and an idea of political origin. This discussion will be based in large part on my earlier decipherment (Stuart 1994, 1996) of the Classic Maya name for Teotihuacan, "Place of Cattails" (equivalent to the Nahuatl name "Tollan"), and the implications that this has presented for Mesoamerican studies. Through the perspective of Classic Maya documents, I will confirm and elaborate on the antiquity of what might be called the "Tollan paradigm" of Mesoamerican political power and self-representation. Although this concept would later pervade Mesoamerica through many so-called Tollans (Carrasco 1982), I will suggest that Teotihuacan was the archetype, having played a direct and active role in founding political orders within the Maya area.

PART I: TEOTIHUACAN IN PETÉN HISTORY

A Teotihuacan presence in the Maya lowlands was evident from an early date, when archaeology in the region was just coming of age. The excavations at Uaxactún, Guatemala, conducted by the Carnegie Institution of Washington between 1926 and 1931, produced a wealth of information and an intellectual legacy that continues to be felt, perhaps most strongly through its establishment of a base-line ceramic chronology (Smith 1955). The Early Classic of Uaxactún was defined by Smith through the "Tzakol sphere," where certain trends in form and typology continue from the Late Preclassic but differ with the appearance of polychrome decoration and, during the Tzakol 3 phase in particular, a distinctive subcomplex of forms with clear Teotihuacan affiliations. Elite wares such as cylinder vessels with apron lids and slab-footed tripods were hallmarks of Central Mexican influence at Uaxactún. Some years later, excavations at Kaminaljuyú, in the distant Guatemalan highlands, revealed a ceramic assemblage with more pronounced Teotihuacan styles and decorative motifs, associated with the so-called Esperanza phase (Kidder, Jennings, and Shook 1946). *Talud-tablero* architectural platforms and a wide array of artifact remains indicated a strong

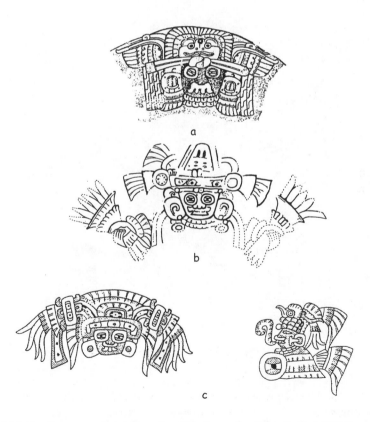

Fig. 15.1. Teotihuacan-style paintings from Tikal ceramics (from Culbert 1993b).

and very intimate connection between Kaminaljuyú and Teotihuacan during the Early Classic, the nature of which continued to be discussed and debated for many years (Sanders and Michels 1977).

Extensive excavations in the North Acropolis at Tikal between 1956 and 1970 further revealed a tremendous wealth of archaeological evidence of Teotihuacan contact in the central Petén, a pattern that has continued to be borne out by more recent excavations in other areas of the site during the 1980s (LaPorte and Fialko 1990). Highland ceramic forms and decorative modes similar to those encountered at Kaminaljuyú helped to define the Manik Complex at Tikal, which is generally affiliated with Tzakol phases of Uaxactún (Culbert 1993b; Coggins 1975). In the North Acropolis, several elite tombs contained varieties of Teotihuacan-style vessels, some locally manufactured and others probably imports. The painted decoration on numerous vessels combine Maya and highland elements, while several are largely indistinguishable from the Teotihuacan tradition (Figure 15.1).

Fig. 15.2. The figures from Stela 31 of Tikal. The ruler Siyah Chan K'awil is in the center, flanked by images of a "Teotihuacan" personage. The text captions name both as portraits of Nun Yax Ayin, father of the Tikal king. Drawing by W. R. Coe.

Fig. 15.3. Tikal Stela 32. Drawing by W. R. Coe (from Jones and Sattterthwaite 1982: fig.55a).

Most striking of all, perhaps, was the discovery of sculpted monuments bearing portraits of "Mexican" individuals, such as the well-preserved Stela 31 with its image of a warrior in Teotihuacan dress grasping a rectangular shield and an *atlatl* ("spear-thrower") (Figure 15.2). Stela 32, also found in the North Acropolis, shows a highland warrior wearing a so-called tassel headdress and is in even a more direct Teotihuacan style (Figure 15.3). Taken together with an assortment of other material evidence, it was clear by the mid–1960s that Teotihuacan played a very important and highly visible role in Early Classic Tikal's political and ceremonial life.[2]

Coggins's study of painting styles and ceramics at Tikal integrated numerous aspects of this evidence. She combined the archaeological data with the known historical rulers of the dynasty, working with the consultation of Tatiana Proskouriakoff (Coggins 1975: 140; Proskouriakoff 1993). Since then, work on the early facet of the Tikal dynasty has been expanded and refined by a number of scholars, among Schele (1976), Jones and Satterthwaite (1982), Mathews (1985), Fahsen (1987), Schele and Freidel (1990), Culbert (1993a), and Valdés, Fahsen, and Cosme (1997). Generally these all agree on the essential details of the ruler sequence and their associated dates. One significant development of late has been the decipherment of the specific name glyphs of Tikal kings. Previously, these figures have had only nicknames, such as "Stormy Sky," "Curl Nose," and so forth, but in the discussions below I prefer to employ their Maya names as I have deciphered them. These readings will be noted in the course of discussions below.

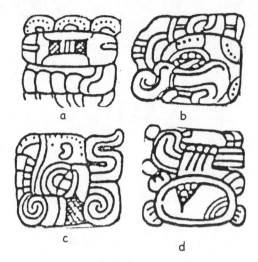

Fig. 15.4. Four prominent name glyphs in Early Classic Tikal history: a. Chak Tok 'Ich'ak; b. Nun Yax Ayin; c. Siyah K'ak'; d. "Spear-Thrower Owl" (variant). All are taken from the text of Stela 31.

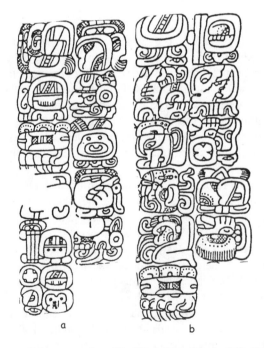

Fig. 15.5. Two sequential passages from Tikal Stela 31: a. Blocks C12–C17, recording the Period Ending 8.17.0.0.0 in connection with Chak Tok Ich'ak; b. Blocks C19–C24, recording the "11 Eb" date and an event involving Siyah K'ak' over one year later.

Proskouriakoff's 1993 treatment of early Tikal history remains one of the most compelling, despite being originally conceived nearly thirty years ago. In that work, she notes that the early Tikal king Great Paw (or Jaguar Paw, as he is called in more current literature) was among the earliest documented rulers of the Early Classic (Figure 15.4 [a]), and associates him with the Long Count date 8.14.0.0.0 (317 C.E.) as recorded on the back of Stela 31, the single most important text for studying early Tikal history.[3] I differ from her assessment, however, in suggesting that Jaguar Paw actually reigned somewhat later. On Stela 31 and possibly Stela 39, this ruler seems to be linked with the *k'atun* ending 8.17.0.0.0 (376 C.E.) (Figure 15.5 [a]). It is on this calendar station that he "fastens the stone," or performs the period-ending ritual (Stuart 1996). His accession date is unknown, but may be recorded on the early stela from the nearby secondary site of El Temblor, located to the east of Tikal.[4]

The next date recorded on Stela 31 (Figure 15.5 [b]) is written simply as "11 Eb," equivalent to 8.17.1.4.12 11 Eb 15 Mac, or January 16, 378 C.E. (a distance number in the text establishes its Long Count placement). This date is one of the most significant—and debated—in early Maya history, for reasons that will soon become clear. Less than a year later a new king assumes power, named Nun Yax Ayin (customarily known by the nicknames "Curl Nose" or "Curl Snout") (Figure

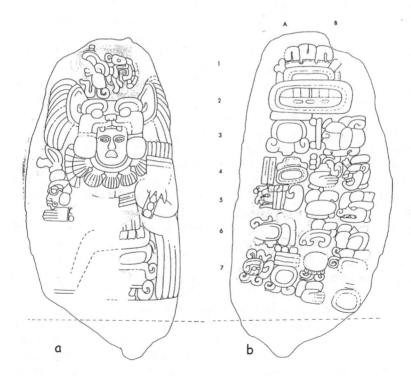

a					b

Fig. 15.6. Tikal Stela 4, front and back. Drawings by W. R. Coe (from Jones and Satterthaite 1982: fig. 5).

15.4 [b]). He is the individual most likely interred within Burial 10 in the North Acropolis, accompanied as we have seen by large numbers of Teotihuacan-style ceramics and artifacts (Coggins 1975). The archaeological record exemplified by this and other rich burials of about the same period suggested to Proskouriakoff and Coggins that such Mexican traits occurred around the time of Nun Yax Ayin's ascendancy to the throne.[5]

In support of this association, the diminutive Teotihuacan "warrior" shown twice on the sides of Stela 31 is named in the accompanying captions as Nun Yax Ayin himself. Stela 4 bears another portrait of him, again in Teotihuacan costume, and commemorates the *k'atun* ending 8.18.0.0.0 (396 C.E.) (Figure 15.6). On the basis of such strong archaeological and visual evidence, Nun Yax Ayin has been called a foreign king, or at least "one who consorted closely with highland people" (Proskouriakoff 1993: 11). That much seems clear, but the circumstances surrounding his sudden appearance at Tikal have heretofore been cloudy at best. A better understanding of just what happened requires a revisit to the 11 Eb event that occurred a year before his accession, commemorated in several inscriptions at Tikal and Uaxactún.

THE 11 EB EPISODE: A REEXAMINATION

In her important overview of Maya history, Proskouriakoff (1993) devoted one chapter to what she called "the arrival of strangers" in the Maya lowlands in the late fourth century C.E. The "strangers" were from the highlands and included the Tikal ruler Nun Yax Ayin (Proskouriakoff's "Curl Snout"), displayed in his three known portraits as having strong affinities to Teotihuacan. As Proskouriakoff noted, other names seemed to be recorded in the inscriptions of this time as well, and it is their respective roles in this history that are very illuminating.

Proskouriakoff recognized that the 11 Eb date falling shortly before the accession of Nun Yax Ayin was a pivotal event of some sort. It was recorded on Stela 31 of Tikal as well as on Stelae 5 and 22 of Uaxactún (one of the few historical dates repeated at different sites) (Figures 15.7 and 15.8). Subsequent to her death in 1984, a fourth reference to the 11 Eb date (as it will henceforth be referred to) came to light on the so-called Marcador stone from Tikal (Figure 15.9), bringing the total number of records to four. Its appearance on Uaxactún Stela 5 in particular caught Proskouriakoff's attention, for it was the one inscribed date on a sculpture depicting a striding warrior in Teotihuacan dress, holding an *atlatl*. There is no evidence that this is Nun Yax Ayin of Tikal; in fact the accompanying glyphs suggest it is someone else entirely. Yet it was immediately apparent to her that a foreigner with Central Mexican associations appeared in direct association with the 11 Eb date. No such association could be found before this date and within the reign of Jaguar Paw, suggesting to Proskouriakoff that this prominently commemorated day was somehow connected with the arrival of foreigners into the central Petén, perhaps specifically at Uaxactún. It must be stressed, however, that Proskouriakoff made no claims to read the inscriptions found with records of the 11 Eb date, leaving the matter somewhat open to question. She nonetheless summarized the importance of the date in this way:

Many questions remain unresolved in regard to this crucial incident of Maya history. Who were these strangers who appeared at this time in the Petén, bringing with them weapons originating in the Mexican highlands? How long had they been in the country, and from what direction did they come? Were any other Maya sites involved in the conflict that appears to have been instigated by Uaxactún? What really happened on this day to perpetuate it in the memory of the Uaxactún rulers? We are not yet equipped to answer such questions, for the undeciphered inscriptions give us only the barest of hints that something momentous was happening at this time, which can only be clarified by efforts of future archaeologists and epigraphers" (Proskouriakoff 1993: 8–9).

According to Tikal's Stela 31, Nun Yax Ayin was the son of an individual whose name glyph is written with two signs, one a hand grasping an *atlatl*, the other a *cauac* element with "tufts" at its four corners (Figure 15.10). "Atlatl Cauac" or "Spear-Thrower Owl" will be a focus of discussion later in this essay, but for now we can remark on the fact that he was *not* the king who preceded Nun Yax Ayin, whom we know to have been Jaguar Paw. Clearly we are faced with an unusual break in the customary father-to-son pattern succession to office. The

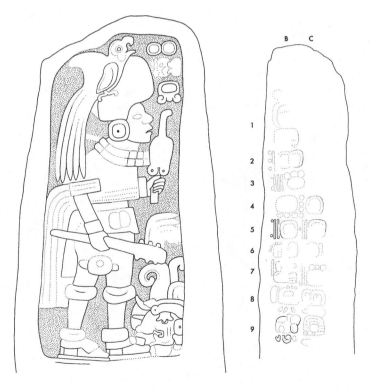

Fig. 15.7. Uaxactún Stela 5, front and side. The texts records the 11 Eb date and its associated event. Drawings by I. Graham (from Graham 1986: 143,145).

Fig. 15.8. Uaxactún Stela 22, side, recording the 11 Eb date and event. Drawing by I. Graham (from Graham 1986: 191).

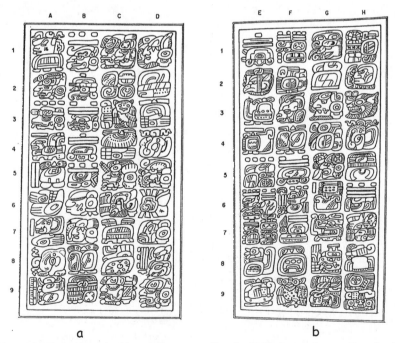

Fig. 15.9. Tikal "Marcador" inscriptions, recording the 11 Eb date and event. Drawing by P. Morales.

Fig. 15.10. Parentage statements from Tikal Stela 31, naming "Spear-Thrower Owl" as the father of Nun Yax Ayin: a. Blocks N2–N3; b. Blocks I3–J3 and K4–L4. Drawings by the author.

11 Eb event, with all of its indirect connections to Teotihuacan influence, stands directly at the time of this disruption, within a year before the accession of the "foreign king."

The four extant records of the 11 Eb episode at Uaxactún and Tikal are all very different in presentation, and thus present a number of difficulties to epigraphers. While they purport to record events occurring on the same day, they are not glyph-for-glyph restatements of the same information. The variation evident in these four records is potentially illuminating, since each text might contribute different pieces to the overall historical puzzle. One "constant" in

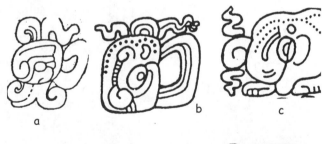

Fig. 15.11. Name variants of Siyah K'ak'; a. Tikal Stela 4, A7; b and c. Tikal "Marcador," D4 and H4; d. Tikal Stela 31, C22, D22 (with *Kalomte'* title).

these passages is the personal name of yet another figure called Smoke Frog or Smoking Frog in the recent literature, and who was first discussed in detail by Mathews (1985). In my view, his name glyph (Figure 15.11) is most likely to be read Siyah K'ak', or "Fire is Born," and as protagonist of the 11 Eb event in all four inscriptions, it stands to reason that he is a pivotal figure in understanding the nature of Maya-Teotihuacan relations in the late fourth century.[6]

After Proskouriakoff's perceptive first steps, the first concerted attempt to grapple with the difficult 11 Eb passages was by Mathews (1985), soon followed by Schele and Freidel (1990). Mathews saw two significant aspects of these records. First, the mutual appearance of the date at Uaxactún and Tikal suggested to him that it recorded a major interactive event between these sites. Second, with Stela 5 at Uaxactún apparently depicting a warrior, Mathews posited

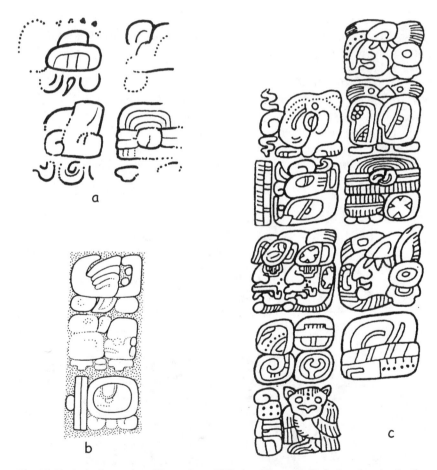

a

b

c

Fig. 15.12. Arrival records at Uaxactún and Tikal: a. Uaxactún Stela 5, redrawing by the author of side text, blocks B8–C9; b. Uaxactún Stela 22, B9–B11; and c. Tikal "Marcador" inscription, B8–C3.

that a war between the two centers was the event associated with the 11 Eb date. Noting the presence of the Tikal emblem with Siyah K'ak's name glyph on this same monument (see Figure 15.12 [a]), he suggested that Tikal was the more dominant site of the two. Mathews's work brought Schele and Freidel (1990) to the conclusion that Tikal's proposed war against Uaxactún was one of outright conquest, thus establishing Tikal as the center of political power in the central lowlands. In their reconstruction of events, Siyah K'ak' (Smoking Frog) was seen as a Tikal warrior who conquered and ruled over Uaxactún. These theories suggested by Mathews, Schele, and Freidel proposed that Tikal and Uaxactún were exclusive players in the localized historical scene. They therefore represent the "internalist" reaction of Mayanist scholarship in the mid–1980s to perceived overstatements of Teotihuacan's more direct and active role in the Maya area. Indeed, Mathews's 1985 work makes virtually no mention of Teotihuacan or "foreigners" in Tikal's history.

It is vital to note, however, that in reviewing the readable glyphs associated with 11 Eb and Siyah K'ak', I have concluded that the posited Tikal-Uaxactún war never actually happened, at least in connection with the date in question. The four relevant texts at Tikal and Uaxactún contain no known "war" glyph, several of which are found in later Maya inscriptions. Moreover, there is no firm evidence that Siyah K'ak' was from Tikal; his name glyph on Uaxactún Stela 5 is followed by the Tikal emblem sign, but without any accompanying title such as *ahaw*. It could well have a different role in that inscription, even specifying the location of the event itself. I raised similar doubts in an earlier treatment (Stuart 1995), confining my remarks to stating that the relevant inscriptions remained too opaque to allow any sort of firm alternative interpretation of the evidence. Now, however, more of the glyphs can be read, producing interesting historical results.

On Stelae 5 and 22 at Uaxactún, the event glyphs found with the 11 Eb date are clearly *hul-iy*, or "he, she, it arrived" (Figure 15.12 [a and b]). On Stela 5 this is more difficult to see due to the eroded state of the inscription, yet I believe the *hu*, *li*, and *ya* signs used to spell *hul-iy* are readily discernible. As confirmation of this, we find in the far better preserved text of Stela 22 that the verb is spelled *hul-li-ya*, an alternative form with the addition of the "hand-and-moon" *hul* sign in place of the syllabic spelling. Interestingly, Stela 22 is a much later monument dating to 495 C.E., and commemorates the earlier 11 Eb event in 378 as something of great historical importance.

The glyph for "to arrive" was brilliantly deciphered by Barbara Macleod (1990) in contexts where it is used to record moon ages within a twenty-nine or thirty-day lunar month. The moon age is expressed as a certain number of days since the moon "arrived," and the glyph on these Uaxactún inscriptions is precisely the same. Furthermore, Macleod also noticed that "arrive" verbs are used in connection with foreign women who marry into distant polities. The most famous example is the Lady of Dos Pilas who is said to have "arrived" at Naranjo in 682 C.E. Her arrival at Naranjo had a profound effect on the political fortunes of the local kingdom, apparently being the initial step in Naranjo's resurrection as an independent polity, years after its defeat at the hands of Caracol (see Schele and

Freidel 1990). Importantly, other similar "arrival" events documented in the royal histories revolve around the appearance of "outsiders" who bring with them significant political change.

Tikal's records of the 11 Eb "arrival" are more difficult to read than those at Uaxactún. As noted, it appears on the unusual Marcador stone excavated at Group 6C-XVI in Tikal (Fialko 1987) (Figures 15.9 and 15.12 [c]). This perfectly preserved monument bears two inscribed panels of Maya glyphs, yet in form it is little different from so-called ball-court markers at Teotihuacan. Iconographic decorations on the stone are also highland in origin. Significantly, the opening Long Count date in the inscription (A1-A5) is our familiar "arrival" date, 8.17.1.4.12 11 Eb 15 Mac, with Siyah K'ak' clearly named as the protagonist (A8-A9). It is difficult to find the glyph for "arrive." In the position where we would expect the "arrive" verb (B7) we instead find a head glyph that could conceivably be a variant form (suggested, perhaps, by a *hu*-sign prefixed to the face), though there is no firm confirmation of this. Regardless, the association of Siyah K'ak' and the 11 Eb date with a Teotihuacan monument is highly suggestive.

Of all the records of this pivotal event, that on Tikal Stela 31 is the most important and informative (Figure 15.5 [b]). The 11 Eb date is clearly written after the record of the 8.17.0.0.0 *k'atun* ending overseen by Jaguar Paw. The verb is not *hul*, but rather a complicated phrase introduced by the statement *tsuts-uy*, "it ended." This is followed by an unknown place glyph and two enigmatic glyphs that include, at least once, the sign *ok*, "foot, leg." In many Mayan languages, *ok* serves as a verb root for "walk" or "journey" (ex. Yucatec *ok-il*). Although no "arrive" statement is made explicit here, it is worth noting that the same sequence of glyphs appears in a completely different text on Lintel 3 of Temple IV at Tikal (D6-D7) where it is grouped with the statement "he arrived" (E1); clearly the statements must be at least thematically related. The protagonist on Stela 31 is Siyah K'ak', named in the next glyph and accompanied by a the title Och-K'in K'awil, or "West K'awil." A second sentence then follows, naming Jaguar Paw as its subject. The verb before his name is *och-ha'*, "enter the water," known from other contexts to be associated with death.[7] The inscription seems to be saying that on the very day Siyah K'ak' arrived, the king of Tikal died. It would be hard not to view Jaguar Paw's death as the result an episode of aggression, and a signal of great political change.

This detailed examination of a few inscriptions at Tikal and Uaxactún reveals that Proskouriakoff was, in typical fashion, very close to the truth when she posited that the 11 Eb date recorded the "arrival" of outsiders into the central Petén. Remarkably, she had no knowledge of the phonetic reading of the *hul* ("arrive") glyph identified by MacLeod, and made her supposition based on circumstantial but strong evidence. There seems every reason to believe, therefore, that the inscriptions make direct reference to the appearance of Teotihuacanos in the central Petén.

WHO WAS SIYAH K'AK'?

Judging by the importance accorded to the event by the scribes of Tikal and Uaxactún, the arrival of Siyah K'ak' on January 16, 378 C.E., was highly significant.

But the texts say almost nothing about the circumstances surrounding it. The only indication of the event's character is provided by Stela 31's mention of Jaguar Paw's death on the very same day (Figure 15.5 [b]). As aforementioned, I would interpret this as fairly clear evidence that the arrival was more than a simple visitation by outsiders. It may well have been accompanied by violence and the execution of the reigning Tikal lord, but it should be cautioned that the language of these texts is seldom so explicit.

Siyah K'ak' is named in other inscriptions at Tikal, including Stela 4 (See Schele and Freidel 1990: 153–155) (Figure 15.6 above). This stone bears the accession date of Nun Yax Ayin (379 C.E.), who is named as the protagonist of the monument and presumably the figure portrayed on the front. Following the record of the ruler's accession, we find the glyph *y-ahaw*, "the lord of," and then the name of Siyah K'ak'. The relationship expressed between the two names is highly significant, for we know of similar "lord of" statements from more easily understood periods of Maya history. First identified by Houston and Mathews (1985), the "lord of" glyph apparently expresses a hierarchical relationship of some sort between two rulers, where the second-named person (Siyah K'ak' in this case) is in some way superior to the first (Nun Yax Ayin). The same relationship would later exist between Ruler 1 of Dos Pilas and the overlord of Calakmul. Houston (1993: 139) notes that such statements constitute the best Maya evidence of "panregional organization," where high kings could reign under the patronage of others. We are forced to conclude from Stela 4 that Siyah K'ak' in some way dominated or sponsored Nun Yax Ayin at the time of the latter accession. Interestingly, the same relationship seems to be implied by the portion of Stela 31's text, which records Nun Yax Ayin's inauguration. The statement there is accompanied by the sentence (in blocks F13, E14) *u-chab-hi Siyah K'ak'*, or "Siyah K'ak' oversees it." When such language is used in other inscriptions, the implication is that one ruler "installs" another into office.[8]

It is likely that Siyah K'ak''s name also appears on a stela from the small site of Bejucal, located some 20 kilometers northwest of Tikal. The date on this monument is 8.17.17.0.0 11 Ahau 3 Tzec, corresponding to 393 C.E., and the remaining inscription records the stela's dedication by a local lord possibly named Yune' Balam, (literally, "Jaguar's Tail"). Although a bit eroded, a specified time interval of at least twelve years reckons back to an earlier date, possibly this ruler's accession to office (no accession glyph is legible, but such a structure is typical of texts of the period). Here Yune' Balam is called the "lord of" someone whose name glyph is partially effaced, but which includes the K'ak' sign and the title Kalomte'. Both are suggestive clues, since the important Kalomte' title is found with Siyah K'ak''s name on Tikal Stelae 4, 31, as well as on the Marcador. It is reasonable to suppose that this designates Siyah K'ak' as Yune' Balam's sponsor, like his contemporary Nun Yax Ayin at Tikal.

Moving further afield from Tikal, we find another reference to Siyah K'ak' on the inscription of Stela 15 from El Perú, a site located some 75 kilometers west of Tikal (Figure 15.13). This mention of Siyah K'ak' is in some ways the most fascinating of all, for it is found with the date 8.17.1.4.4 3 Kan 7 Mac, or January 8, 378 C.E., only eight days before his recorded "arrival" in the Tikal and Uaxactún texts. The El Perú inscription is missing several important fragments, including one that may state just what took place on this day. But later in the inscription, in what may be a back reference to the same date, there are remains of a verb that could be read as "arrive." If so, it suggests that Siyah K'ak' passed through El Perú on his way to the Tikal and Uaxactún area, moving from west to east. The length of his stay at El Perú is unknown, but could have been no more than a few days, of course. Stela 13 was erected nearly forty years later by a local El Perú ruler named K'inich Balam ("Great-Sun Jaguar") on 8.19.0.0.0.

Fig. 15.13. A passage from a stela at El Perú, Guatemala. Drawing by I. Graham.

The western origin of Siyah K'ak' seems to be indicated by the common usage of the "west" glyph (*ochk'in*) with his name, as found on Stela 31 at Tikal and Stela 22 of Uaxactún. Directional titles are common for Maya rulers, with east, west, and south glyphs sometimes encountered in combination with honorifics such as Kalomte'. I therefore hesitate to assign much conclusive significance to Siyah K'ak's "west" title, but taken together with his apparent movement across the central lowlands from El Perú towards Tikal and Uaxactún, it seems reasonable to suggest that it relates to the starting point of his journey. In discussions below, we shall discuss more examples of the very same "west" title in connection with other highland-related names at both Tikal and Copán.

On the face of the present evidence, I think that there is no choice but to conclude that Siyah K'ak' is a foreigner, and that he may well be instigator of the Teotihuacan presence in the region of Tikal. If allowed to speculate, I would go so far as to view him as leader of a military force that overthrew Tikal's dynasty in 378, killing its ruler Jaguar Paw and installing a new ruler, Nun Yax Ayin, in his place. It is perhaps significant that no monuments predating the arrival event were kept for veneration in Tikal's plazas as far as is known; the earliest remaining stela is Nun Yax Ayin's own accession monument, Stela 4. We shall never know the specific circumstances, but we can now be fairly certain that Siyah K'ak' was a significant vehicle by which considerable political and cultural changes occurred in the central Petén.[9]

"Spear-Thrower Owl": A Teotihuacan Ruler?

We have seen that another mysterious participant in early Tikal history was "Spear-Thrower Owl," who in other sources has been dubbed "Atlatl Shield" or "Atlatl Cauac."[10] To reiterate, on Stela 31 Spear-Thrower Owl is named as the father of the newly installed Tikal ruler Nun Yax Ayin (Figure 15.10), and is thus

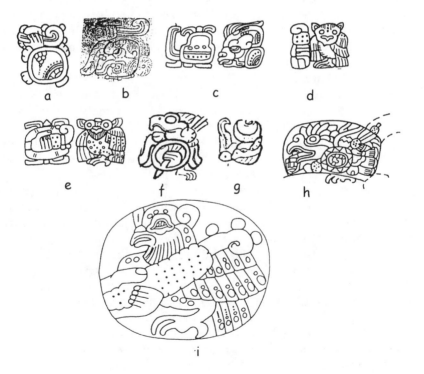

Fig. 15.14. Variants of the name "Spear-Thrower Owl" from Maya texts: a. Tikal Stela 31; b. Unprovenienced vessel K; c, d, and e. Tikal "Marcador" inscription; f. unprovenienced jade ear-spool; g. Tikal MT 32; h. Tikal Stela 31, in headdress held by ruler; i. In central medallion of Tikal "Marcador."

the grandfather of the later ruler Siyah Chan K'awil. Significantly, there is no evidence that Spear-Thrower Owl was ever crowned as ruler of Tikal. He therefore stands out as something of a disruptive element in the expected sequence of dynastic succession, as noted earlier.

Again, the foreign associations with this personage are very suggestive, as Proskouriakoff originally recognized (1993: 11; see also Jones 1991: 112). The components of his name glyph are a case in point (Figure 15.14). The spear-thrower or *atlatl* is a distinctively highland weapon, and the owl is strongly associated with militaristic themes in Teotihuacan iconography. Indeed, it is tempting to link the two components of the name to a frequent icon in Teotihuacan imagery known as the *lechuza y armas*, to be discussed momentarily (von Winning 1987; Berrin 1988). Some variants of the Spear-Thrower Owl name on the Marcador of Tikal and on a looted ear-spool are very similar to this Teotihuacan motif (Figure 15.14). The visual and historical link of this name to highland Mexico is inescapable, and I think generally agreed upon.[11]

In proposing that the Spear-Thrower Owl glyph at Tikal serves as a personal name, I go against previous interpretations by Proskouriakoff (1993) and Schele and Freidel (1990), who all viewed it as a general label or title, shared by more than one person. Proskouriakoff saw it as a glyph "designating the foreigners" (1993: 11). Schele and Freidel (1990: 156–157, 449–450) agreed with a Teotihuacan connection for the Spear-Thrower Owl glyph, and linked it to the larger highland-derived Tlaloc-Venus iconographic complex revolving around themes of conquest warfare and sacrifice. In their interpretation, this "*atlatl* shield" functioned as a war title of highland origin, and could be assumed by any one of several individuals in this period of Tikal history. They further suggested that this glyph appeared in conjunction with a new type of conquest warfare introduced from the highlands and employed by Tikal against neighboring Uaxactún in 378, the day of our 11 Eb "arrival" event. Later Grube and Schele (1994) posited a phonetic reading of the owl sign as *kuy*, "owl, omen," and reiterated the role of the Spear-Thrower Owl glyph as a war title.

Several key points cast doubt on the function of the Spear-Thrower Owl glyph as a title or general label, and suggest instead that it was the personal name of a politically important individual. On Stela 31 of Tikal, the Spear-Thrower Owl glyph (its "Atlatl Cauac" variant) occupies the position where Nun Yax Ayin's father must be named (Figure 15.10). Elsewhere on Stela 31, Spear-Thrower Owl bears the now-familiar title Kalomte', found with personal names throughout the entire body of Maya inscriptions. Moreover, Stela 31 mentions near the end of its text a death event (*och bih*), followed by the Spear-Thrower Owl glyph (Figure 15.15). Only a true personal name could serve in such a context. What is more, on the front of Stela 31 the Tikal ruler Siyah Chan K'awil holds aloft a headdress adorned with a Spear-Thrower Owl "medallion" at its top (Figure 15.16 [a]). The glyph is shown within a cartouche that is part of a maize-plant motif. In Early Classic Maya portraiture, such maize plants in the headdress contain personal names, precisely as shown in the Stela 31 example (Figure 15.16 [b]). Here the headdress is labeled with the name of its intended wearer, Spear-Thrower Owl, revealing that, contrary to other interpretations

Fig. 15.15. Passage from Tikal Stela 31, recording the death (*och-bih*, "road-entering") of "Spear-Thrower Owl."

(Schele and Freidel 1990: 156), it is about to be worn by Siyah Chan K'awil. Just why Spear-Thrower Owl's headdress is shown with no sign of the Spear-Thrower Owl himself is something of a mystery; as with Siyah K'ak', no known portraits of him exist.

Spear-Thrower Owl is associated with only a few events in Tikal's historical records. We first encounter him on the Marcador of Tikal, where he is named three times. According to the text, Spear-Thrower Owl sees or in some way sanctions the arrival of Siyah K'ak' in 378 c.e.[12] This might be construed as evidence that Spear-Thrower Owl was at Tikal or Uaxactún at the time of the arrival, but this is not necessarily the case. Parallel examples in other inscriptions describe the same sort of action (*y-ita-hi*), and convey the notion that the subject in some way "looks on" the principal event, either figuratively or literally. Although he is somehow involved in the arrival episode, the first date associated with him actually falls a few years earlier and also is recorded on the Marcador (Figure 15.17). This is 8.16.17.9.0 11 Ahau 3 Uayeb (374 c.e.), which is clearly given as an accession date. Spear-Thrower Owl is therefore seated in office as ruler, but where? To reiterate, Jaguar Paw was almost certainly ruler at Tikal at this time, leading up to the arrival of Siyah K'ak'. In fact, Spear-Thrower Owl lives on for a considerable amount of time. He is named in association with the dedication of the Marcador monument at Tikal on 8.18.17.14.9, a date within the reign of his son at Tikal, Nun Yax Ayin. Finally, his death is recorded on Stela 31 as occurring on 9.0.3.9.18., well into the reign of his grandson, Siyah Chan K'awil (Stormy Sky). In sum, Spear-Thrower Owl, father of a Tikal ruler, was himself a king, and reigned *somewhere* for over six decades (374–439 c.e.).

Although difficult to prove, one very real possibility to consider is that Spear-Thrower Owl was ruler of Teotihuacan. Unlike the other characters in our plot such as Siyah K'ak' and Nun Yax Ayin, Spear-Thrower Owl's name, however it may eventually be read, is probably not Mayan. Visually, at least, it evokes a "foreignness" unlike any other personal name in Maya history, and is likely a variation on the common Teotihuacan emblematic device known as the *lechuza y armas* (Figure 15.18). But most suggestive of all is the established fact that Spear-Thrower Owl is father to Nun Yax Ayin, the one king at Tikal who is singled out for his highland style of costume. Is it far-fetched to believe that the father of Nun Yax Ayin, the one supposed "foreigner," was himself of the highlands? I think not.

a

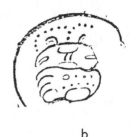

b

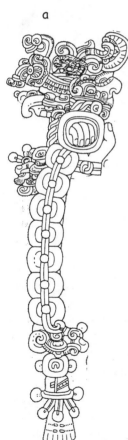

Fig. 15.16. Royal names in headdresses: a. Tikal Stela 31, front; b. On unprovenienced ceramic cache vessel from Tikal area (from Berjonneau, Deletaille, and Sonnery 1985: fig. 354).

Fig. 15.17. Passage from the Tikal "Marcador" inscription, recording inauguration of "Spear-Thrower Owl" as a ruler.

Considering that Spear-Thrower Owl was a high ruler, the idea of his being a Teotihuacan king has a certain appeal.

As noted, the *lechuza y armas* symbol so common in Teotihuacan iconography is clearly related to the Spear-Thrower Owl name. It appears both on ceramic vessels and as circular medallions worn on the collars of warrior figurines (Figure 15.18). Von Winning (1987, 1: 90) cites these as evidence for it being a heraldic symbol of some sort, or else the designation of a militaristic order within Teotihuacan, comparable to the Jaguar or Eagle Knights of the Mexica Aztec. On the basis of the controlled Tikal evidence, I suggest instead that the distinctive *lechuza y armas* emblem may be a personal name glyph even in Teotihuacan, serving to label the figures with which they are found. If Spear-Thrower Owl was a Teotihuacan ruler, the presence of his "name tag" would allow us to identify such figures as portraits of the warrior-king.[13] On one cylindrical tripod illustrated by von Winning, the *lechuza y armas* motif is shown as the body or person of a helmeted warrior (Figure 15.18 [b]), suggesting strongly that his identity is somehow conveyed by the icon. If these and other examples in Teotihuacan art are indeed personal name glyphs, as the Maya evidence would strongly suggest, our view of writing and its uses at Teotihuacan would change dramatically, as would our notion of the "impersonality" of political rule at that site. Other names might conceivably exist, now recognized solely as categories of repeating "motifs." But speculations are best left for another time.

Returning to our Maya evidence at Tikal, the image on Stela 31, with its depiction of Siyah Chan K'awil lifting up the headdress of Spear-Thrower Owl, might now be interpreted as a scene of headdress presentation not unlike others encountered in Maya art. As Khris Villela notes (personal communication, 1998), Maya accession rites that involve the presentation of headbands and headdresses by allied lords are similar to Sahagún's accounts of accession rites among the Mexica Aztec, where rulers of outlying provinces were active participants in the crowning ceremony. Although I speculate, Siyah Chan K'awil may hold Spear-Thrower Owl's headdress aloft as a sign of his political alliance, or perhaps sub-servience, to the foreign ruler.

A common title of Spear-Thrower Owl is Kalomte', also used by Siyah K'ak' on occasion. In later Maya history, this title conveys a supreme status within a political hierarchy. It is the office for high kings of Late Classic Tikal and possibly Calakmul, and Simon Martin has suggested that it serves to mark

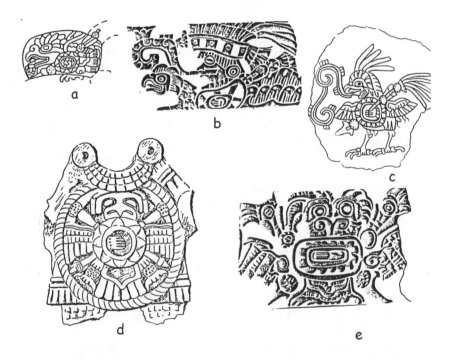

Fig. 15.18. Teotihuacan *lechuza y armas* emblems: A ruler's name?: a. Tikal, Stela 31 headdress; b through e. From various Teotihuacan sources (from von Winning 1987).

overlords or "emperors" of conquered territories (personal communication, 1995). Lacking a decipherment of the term *kalomte'*, it is difficult to be precise about the literal meaning of the glyph, yet the pattern of its use is clear enough in the later sources. It would suggest that both Spear-Thrower Owl and Siyah K'ak' both held considerable political power, perhaps involving the control of distant locales. This interpretation is in keeping with my proposal that Spear-Thrower Owl is the name of the Teotihuacan ruler. Siyah K'ak', in turn, having arrived at Tikal, may have been the local representative of Mexican control in the central Petén, a role that would agree with his being named as an overlord in historical texts in the central Petén region, such as at Bejucal.

Spear-Thrower Owl's birth date is not known. A few years after his accession to office in 374 C.E., the closely affiliated character Siyah K'ak' arrives at Tikal and assumes a powerful role there, possibly as some sort of regional political leader (Kalomte'). Siyah K'ak', as we have seen, had an important "overseeing" role in the inauguration of Spear-Thrower Owl's son at Tikal. Now, if we are to believe that Spear-Thrower Owl acceded to his throne in 374 and died in 439 (sixty-five years later), then logic would dictate that the son, Nun Yax Ayin, must have been very young at the time of his own inauguration at Tikal in 379.[14] There is support for this from both written and artistic evidence. On the right side of Stela 31, the caption accompanying Nun Yax Ayin's portrait states that he was a " '*k'atun*' lord," or that he was less than twenty years old as depicted. Significant, I think, is the diminutive size of this portrait relative to that of Siyah Chan K'awil, the later ruler (Figure 15.2). Comparable arrangements of figural portraits on Tikal stelae show that adult body size is both naturalistic and consistent. Stela 40, for example, is startlingly similar to Stela 31 in its design and execution, and was arguably carved by the same hand (Valdés, Fahsen, and Cosme 1997). The parents of the ruler, shown also on the sides, are full-sized. Not so on Stela 31, where the diminutive Nun Yax Ayin looks as though he may indeed be a "child warrior," depicted as he looked at the time of his own inauguration.[15] Siyah K'ak's own role as an "overseer" of the Nun Yax Ayin's accession and ruler over local satellite centers suggests that Siyah K'ak' served as a sort of regent for the child-king from Teotihuacan. Spear-Thrower Owl may have sent his son to rule once Siyah K'ak' laid the groundwork at Tikal and consolidated much of the power within his own hands.

The history I have discussed up to this point is certainly a detailed one, combining both firm facts and speculative assertions. In order to clarify my overall interpretation and present the more solidly grounded facts as I understand them, a few points of summary are here offered, with events arranged in chronological order (specific sources are given in italics):

In 374 C.E., an individual named Spear-Thrower Owl assumes the throne, though the location is unspecified (*Tikal Marcador*).

Another figure named Siyah K'ak' arrives at Tikal and/or Uaxactún on January 14, 378 C.E., apparently with the direct or indirect sanction of Spear-Thrower Owl (*Tikal Marcador, Stela 31; Uaxactún Stelae 5, 22*).

On the very same day of the "arrival," the Tikal ruler Jaguar Paw dies, or "enters water" (*Tikal Stela 31*).

Siyah K'ak's arrival is from the west, having days earlier arrived (?) at El Perú (*El Perú Stela 15*). This may relate to the common use of the "west" glyph in his glyphic name phrase.

Within a year after Siyah K'ak's arrival, Nun Yax Ayin ("Curl Nose") assumes the rulership of Tikal, introducing overt Teotihuacan imagery into the monumental art (*Tikal Stelae 4, 31*). His father is Spear-Thrower Owl, and not the previous Tikal king Jaguar Paw (*Stela 31, side texts*).

Nun Yax Ayin may have been a boy at the time of his inauguration (*Stela 31*). Siyah K'ak' in some way oversees his inauguration (*Stela 31*), and may have also been dominant over the local ruler of Bejucal, a small site on Tikal's periphery (*Bejucal Stela 1*).

Spear-Thrower Owl has very strong Teotihuacan associations, and his name is depicted as a so-called heraldic emblem in much Teotihuacan iconogra-

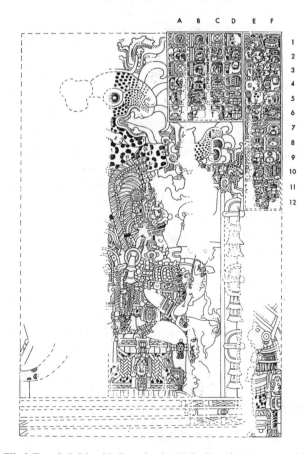

Fig. 15.19. Tikal, Temple I, Lintel 3. Drawing by W. R. Coe (from Jones and Satterthwaite 1982: fig. 70).

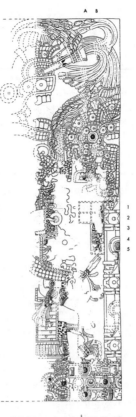

Fig. 15.20. Tikal, Temple I, Lintel 2. Drawing by W. R. Coe (from Jones and Satterthwaite 1982: fig. 69).

phy. Evidence suggests that he was perhaps ruler of that site. He dies in 439 C.E. (*Tikal Stela 31*), during the reign at Tikal of his grandson, Siyah Chan K'awil (Stormy Sky).

I posit this sketch of history with some hesitation, since it would be impossible in this essay to discuss all of the relevant details of the Early Classic Tikal inscriptions; this will be done in another study now under preparation.

That said, much of what is presented here stands in contrast to previous studies of Tikal's history. Most important perhaps is the revision of the nature of the 11 Eb event as "arrival," much as Proskouriakoff originally reasoned. If this is true, it is difficult to reconcile with the supposed Tikal-Uaxactún war posited by Mathews (1985) and Schele and Freidel (1990). Rather, I view this as the single most important political or military episode of early Classic Maya history, when Teotihuacan established itself as a dominant force in the politics and elite culture of the central Petén. There is now ample evidence, I believe, to support the interpretation that the arrival was a highly disruptive occasion, if not a violent one. The direct instrument of this change was Siyah K'ak', who seems to have wielded considerable influence and power at Tikal and Uaxactún in the years subsequent to his arrival. His placement at Tikal allowed for the installation of Nun Yax Ayin, the son of the possible Teotihuacan ruler Spear-Thrower Owl. This new dynasty of Tikal, as far as we know, continues unbroken for many years, through the reigns of Siyah Chan K'awil and Kan Boar, after which we come to the opaque history surrounding the so-called hiatus and the Early-to-Late Classic transition.

Later still, in the midst of the Tikal's Late Classic rivalry against Calakmul and its allies, the early history rooted in Teotihuacan would continue to be recalled and commemorated. Ruler C, first identified by Jones (1977), was named Nun Yax Ayin, in remembrance of the intrusive king of centuries past. Most interesting also are the surviving wooden door lintels of Temple 1, dedicated by the king Hasaw Chan K'awil (Ruler A). Lintel 3 records the thirteen *k'atun* anniversary (in 695 C.E.) of Spear-Thrower Owl's death (Figure 15.19), stating that on this day Hasaw Chan K'awil "conjured the Holy One." The adjacent door lintel of this temple, Lintel 2 (Figure 15.20), depicts a seated Teotihuacan warrior above a toponymic register of cacti and cattails (Taube 1992; Stuart 1994). Given the anniversary celebrated in the temple, it is tempting to see this as a portrait of Spear-Thrower Owl himself, but this again is conjecture.

PART II: TEOTIHUACAN IN COPÁN HISTORY

Whereas Tikal and Uaxactún were the first Classic Maya sites to receive much attention on the question of Teotihuacan influence, Copán, on the southeast frontier of the Maya area, has recently emerged as an additional vantage point for studying Teotihuacan associations (Fash and Fash, chapter 14 of this volume). As with Tikal, Copán is a well-excavated site with extensive ceramic, artifactual, iconographic, and architectural allusions to Central Mexico. This begins in the Early Classic period, as recently revealed by excavations of the Early Copán Acropolis Project under the general direction of Robert Sharer of the University of Pennsylvania. Late Classic references to central Mexico are almost as numerous, though of a very different character. The dynastic history of Copán is now well understood (W. Fash 1991; Stuart 1992), providing much of the context we need to understand the nature of these foreign references. As we shall see, Copán exhibits both important similarities and differences with the situation as described in the central lowlands.

The pivotal figure of Copán's history was K'inich Yax K'uk' Mo' ("Great Sun Green Quetzal-Macaw"), an Early Classic ruler who is represented by later kings as the first in the dynastic sequence. A few tantalizing references exist here and there to "pre-dynastic" names in Copán's history, but these are far too fragmentary to be of much use (Stuart 1992). They do suggest that K'inich Yax K'uk' Mo' was not the first ruler of the place we know of as Copán, but he was apparently considered the "founder" of the institution of Copán kingship as defined throughout the Late Classic. He is consistently mentioned in the later texts as a divine ancestor, evoked as a source of political power up to the reign of the sixteenth and very last known king, Yax Pasah (Stuart 1992; Schele 1992).

K'inich Yax K'uk' Mo's portraits, while rare, often depict him in Central

Mexican costume (Coggins 1988; Schele 1992; Stuart 1994; Fash and Fash, chapter 13 of this volume). Altar Q has one of the most explicit of these images (See Fash and Fash, this volume: fig. 14.4), showing him with goggles and a square shield bearing the War Serpent. No other king's portrait has such features, which can be traced to a number of other retrospective images associated with Structure 10L–16 and possibly 26. A ceramic effigy burner used and ritually destroyed during the dedication of the tomb of Ruler 12, discovered within Structure 10L–26, also has his goggled portrait; eleven other effigy censers also show similar portraits, but none with the goggles we associate with the founder. The costume itself led Coggins (1988) to surmise that he was indeed an outsider, originating either from Kaminaljuyú, Tikal, or Teotihuacan.

In a startling parallel to early Petén history, the text on Copán's Altar Q mentions the "arrival" of K'inich Yax K'uk' Mo' in 426 C.E., specifically 8.19.10.11.0 8 Ahau 18 Yaxk'in (Figure 15.21 [a]). Actually this is the second of two closely placed dates on the altar, the other falling three days before on 8.19.10.10.17 5 Caban 15 Yaxk'in.[16] On this earlier day, K'uk' Mo' Ahaw ("Quetzal Macaw Lord") is said to have "taken the K'awil"—a phrase used else-

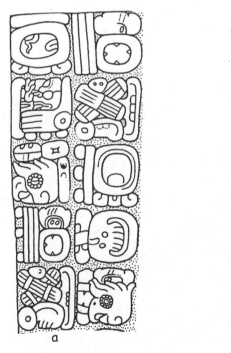

Fig. 15.21. Copán and Quiriguá records of K'inich Yax K'uk' Mo's "arrival": a. Copán, Altar Q (drawing by the author); b. Quiriguá, Zoomorph P. (drawing by N. Grube).

where for accession to office. (I assume that K'uk' Mo' Ahaw is an alternative name for K'inich Yax K'uk' Mo', perhaps used before his becoming a ruler.) Both events are said to have taken place in a certain building or structure labeled by a distinctive crossed-bundles element (Figure 15.22), of which more will be said below. Purely on the basis of the textual material, the implication is that K'inich

a   b

Fig. 15.22. A house name (?) with Teotihuacan associations: a. Copán, Altar Q; b. Tikal, Stela 31.

Yax K'uk Mo' was somehow an outsider. In light of the similar conclusions drawn from the iconographic evidence already described, there seems every reason to believe that he was not native to the local political scene, at least as the Late Classic Copanecs describe him.

These same two dates in 426 C.E. are mentioned on Zoomorph P at Quiriguá, but with a different twist (Figure 15.21 [b and c]). There, we read that on 5 Caban 15 Yaxk'in "he came" to the same "crossed-bundles building" mentioned on Altar Q (I use this name as a convenient term of reference only; it is an undeciphered glyph). Three days later on 8 Ahau 18 Yaxk'in, a local Quiriguá ruler dedicated a stone monument, an act that was overseen and sanctioned by K'inich Yax K'uk' Mo', who is called a "Lord of Copán." One wonders if we are reading of a journey here, not unlike Siyah K'ak's eastward trek through the Petén many years before. K'inich Yax K'uk' Mo' "came" to Quiriguá on September 5 of 426, then three days later "came" to Copán. Such a scenario is tempting but may be difficult to support, since the place name associated with both arrivals specifies a building, not a community.

The "crossed-bundles building" was a place of major importance for K'inich Yax K'uk' Mo' and itself carries strong Teotihuacan associations. In working with this glyph a number of years ago, Schele and I noted its almost constant appearance with K'inich Yax K'uk' Mo's name in the Copán texts, and called it the "founder's glyph" (see Schele 1992), though this is a bit misleading. Later kings also make use of the glyph with their names, stating that they are the "*n*th of the house" after K'inich Yax K'uk' Mo', the number specifying their place in the dynastic sequence. In one text, K'inich Yax K'uk' Mo' is named as "lord" of this house, presumably because he was the first to be associated with it. One of the enigmatic aspects of the glyph, however, is that it is found in the inscriptions of a great many sites, including Copán, Quiriguá, Tikal, Machaquila, and Yaxchilán. It is clear that the glyph is a proper name for a building of some sort, since its last element is always-*nah*, or "structure," found with architectural names throughout the Maya inscriptions (Stuart and Houston 1994: fig. 104). The other elements of the glyph, including the crossed-torch bundles element and *te'*, give the proper name.[17] But what building or buildings does it name? Altar Q's inscription prominently features the glyph, and its placement before the stairway of Structure 10L–16 suggests that it might refer to this structure. This would be a fitting association, given that Structure 10L–16 and its antecedents were temples associated with the veneration of K'inich Yax K'uk' Mo' (see Fash and Fash, chapter 14 of this volume). If true, then the glyph might be the name for an important type of ancestral shrine found at many sites.

The Teotihuacan connections of this building name are fairly consistent even outside of its intimate link to K'inich Yax K'uk' Mo' at Copán. At Río Amarillo, an important satellite of Copán during Late Classic times, Structure 5 was decorated with large stone mosaic panels of this very same glyph, along with *wits* "mountain" masks and Tlaloc heads (William Saturno, personal communication, 1997). Its placement on the exterior walls of the building emphasize its true use as a building name, and the association with Tlalocs repeats similar connections found at Copán with Structures 10L–16 and 10L–33 (Schele 1992). Mexican "year signs" also appear in association with it in Copán's architecture. At distant Yaxchilán, Lintel 25 names the same house as the location of Itsamnah Balam I's (Shield Jaguar I) accession and its associated "conjuring" ceremony. The Teotihuacan War Serpent is the dominant image in the accompanying ritual scene. Furthermore, at Tikal, the "crossed-bundles building" is named on MT 35 as the place where the "foreign" ruler Nun Yax Ayin does something a number of months before his accession to office. I would suggest that this association with Teotihuacan symbolism is an important clue to the overarching significance of the building name, which appears to be central to many rituals involving rulership and political foundation.[18]

K'inich Yax K'uk' Mo' often carries the title Ochk'in Kalomte' ("West Kalomte' ") identical to the honorifics we have seen associated with Siyah K'ak' and Spear-Thrower Owl at Tikal (Figure 15.23). These prominent figures are all "outsiders" who would seem to have western or highland origins, and I believe the pattern can not be coincidental. Significantly, one other name that is a West Kalomte' is not a historical person at all, but rather a god or supernatural known as the War Serpent. A version of this character appears on the square shield held by K'inich Yax K'uk Mo' on the side of Altar Q, and is seen on Yaxchilán, Lintel 25, mentioned briefly above. The War Serpent is indeed prominent in Teotihuacan-related art and inscriptions throughout the Maya area. Karl Taube (chapter 10 of this volume) has written extensively on the War Serpent, and makes a compelling case that it is a direct iconographic allusion to Teotihuacan, or more precisely to a cult of sacred warfare associated with that metropolis in the Early Classic period. The War Serpent appears in a variety of artistic contexts, but is perhaps most common in Maya sources as the helmet or headdress of warriors. He is distinguished usually by a shell platelet "skin," a curved brow-ridge, and a prominent row of front teeth. He may in fact combine serpent and coyote characteristics, although Taube has suggested serpent and jaguar associations in his analyses. His hieroglyphic name in Maya was recognized some years ago in independent work by the author and by Schele (cited in Schele and Freidel 1990), among others. It appears in several inscriptions, but two noteworthy cases are found on the Marcador of Tikal and Stela 6 of Copán—two monuments with strong Teotihuacan associations.[19] The name is Waxaklahun U-bah Chan, or "Eighteen Are the Snake's Heads." While certainly obscure to us in meaning, it is intriguing to consider the possibility that this relates in some way to the eighteen heads of the very same War Serpent on the terraces of the Temple of Quetzalcoatl at Teotihuacan.

Fig. 15.23. The name of K'inich Yax K'uk' Mo' with the title "west Kalomte'," Copán, Hieroglyphic Stairway. Drawing after B. Fash.

K'inich Yax K'uk' Mo' remains an enigmatic character for us, viewing him as we do through the distant and removed lens of later Copán art and inscriptions. This stands in contrast to the situation at Tikal, where the history and characters I sketched were for the most part contemporary with the sources. Little can be said of his personal or political history, except that the Period Ending 9.0.0.0.0 8 Ahau 13 Ceh features heavily in later references to him (on Stela 63, among a few other texts). On this date, the beginning of the current *bak'tun* was a cosmic founding or renewal event, and its association of the "founder" K'inich Yax K'uk' Mo' seems more than coincidental. The end result produces for us, perhaps as it did for the later Classic Maya, a vaguely defined, almost "primordial" persona. When coupled with his non-Maya "otherness," K'inich Yax K'uk' Mo' becomes a symbolic figure that fuses temporal, geographical, and ethnic distance, when at the same time he stands as the focal point for the entire dynastic history of the polity. Paradoxically, he seems a culture-hero of another culture.

THE TEMPLE OF THE HIEROGLYPHIC STAIRWAY

By now it should be clear that Copán makes frequent use of Teotihuacan-derived iconographic motifs on its Late Classic architectural façades. Several buildings carry such symbolism, among them Structures 10L–16, 21, 26, and 29 (B. Fash 1992), and present variations on a single complex of repeating motifs and icons, including Tlaloc masks, isolated goggles, highland-costumed warriors, coiled ropes, and Kan crosses, among other symbols. Structure 10L–16 already has been mentioned as a centrally placed ritual structure evoking the memory of the dynastic founder, but Structure 10L–26 is equally imposing a structure, famous for its ornate Hieroglyphic Stairway. Its general design is different from that of Structure 10L–16, but it clearly served as a shrine devoted to an evocation of the historical past (Stuart 1994; W. Fash et al. 1992).

Fig. 15.24. Restored left section of the Temple Inscription from Copán. Drawing by the author.

The stairway inscription is the longest known from the Maya area and presents a detailed account of the dynastic history of Copán, including mentions of K'inich Yax K'uk' Mo.' It was originally built by Ruler 13 of Copán and conceived as a funerary monument for the twelfth ruler. Ruler 15 later expanded on his predecessors structure, rebuilding portions of the steps and the temple above (Stuart 1994). Unfortunately little was preserved of the upper temple when first investigated by Maudslay in the nineteenth century, and the only clear vestiges of its existence were a very large assortment of sculptured stone from its outer façade (B. Fash 1992: fig. 16) and interior walls. Whereas the exterior of the temple displayed explicit Teotihuacan iconography, the interior decoration incorporated the same visual sensibility and symbolic vocabulary into a highly ornate full-figure hieroglyphic inscription (Figure 15.24). Called simply the "Temple Inscription," this text constitutes one of the finest examples of Maya scribal art, and is perhaps one of the most intriguing Maya inscriptions ever discovered. Its significance lies not so much in its content, but in the way Teotihuacan-derived symbols were uniquely manipulated to form a type of "writing" not seen anywhere else in the Mesoamerica.

Portions of the Temple Inscription were taken to the Peabody Museum at Harvard shortly after Structure 10L–26 was first excavated, with numerous other blocks left at Copán. Still others were identified during surface excavations on Structure 10L–26 in 1987. The numerous fragments of the inscription remained unarticulated until 1992, when Barbara Fash and I made a renewed effort to reconstruct the text as much as possible, using those pieces still at Copán and photographs of the blocks stored at the Peabody Museum. Work continued intermittently until 1996, when the inscribed wall was rearticulated and placed within the Museo de Escultura Maya at Copán.[20] The wall originally stood at the back of the inner temple and held a wide, shallow niche. The glyphs run down the sides and across the top of this niche, which originally may have held a painted or sculpted image of some sort.

Nearly all the glyphs of the Temple Inscription are full-figure, making their decipherment difficult. What is more, many of the glyphs are in a highly unusual style exhibiting a blend of Teotihuacan and Maya forms. Some of the signs are completely unrecognizable as "proper" Maya glyphs, containing Teotihuacan-style elements and figures, and are unique in the corpus of Maya inscriptions. Other glyphs are conventional and legible as Maya. While unusual, the inscriptions visual style does conform to the visual program of the temple's outer iconography, which was very heavily decorated with Tlaloc masks, goggles, and seated Teotihuacan-style warriors. Many of these same elements appear in the full-figure glyphs, giving them a very strange appearance indeed.

In the course of drawing the individual fragments, it soon became apparent that the Teotihuacan-style glyphs and the more conventional Maya glyphs were equal in number and were placed in alternating columns. What is more, these columns are read individually, not in the conventional double-column format of most Maya texts. The resulting format presents two separate but parallel texts that are visually interwoven, one "Teotihuacan" and one Maya. Most surprising of all, further close inspection shows that the two inscriptions are presented as individual pairs of blocks, giving a single text written in two very different-looking scripts.

An examination of the horizontal portion of the inscription (Figure 15.24) demonstrates this highly unusual format. Column pE of the horizontal band shows two "Teotihuacan" glyphs, the first composed of the number 18 and a small Tlaloc figure, the second a hybrid Tlaloc and God K (K'awil) figure. The column immediately to the right, pF, displays two standard Maya glyphs: a full-figure number 18 and, below, a "jog" gopher (ba) and God K. From the Maya signs it is abundantly clear that this is the name of Waxaklahun Ubah K'awil (18-[u]ba-K'awil). Jumping ahead to column pI, we find a frontal-view Tlaloc with a numerical coefficient of 2 above a second glyph representing a seated figure with a staff and a coefficient of 11. The column to the right, pJ, displays the Maya head variant of 2 above a *k'atun* glyph, and below, a clearly recognizable full-figure version of "11 tuns." I would posit, then, that the frontal-view Tlaloc functions as an equivalent in some manner to the *k'atun* (7,200-day) period, and that the seated figure with the staff serves as a *tun* equivalent. In column pK, the combination of 8 and a goggled-eyed figure in a cartouche is placed next to "8 Ahau" in pL, and similarly in pM, an 8 attached to an incomplete zoomorphic creature appears next to "8 Zotz." When combined, these calendrical glyphs give the date 9.16.5.0.0 8 Ahau 8 Zotz, the dedication date of the temple and also of Stela M, placed at the foot of the Hieroglyphic Stairway.

The pattern holds remarkably well for many of the glyphs, yet for other juxtaposed pairs the equivalencies are not so evident. In column pG, for example, two Teotihuacan-style glyphs seem to have no clear relationship to the name of Ruler 14 that appears to their side in column pH. Despite some ambiguous pairings, however, there can be little doubt that the Temple Inscription is made of two roughly parallel texts, one in a "Teotihuacan" script, apparently to be read first, and a "translation," if you will, in standard Maya. Because of its clear affinities to Maya conventions, one might consider the Teotihuacan glyphs as an elaborate "type-face" or "font" that was deemed visually and thematically appropriate to the temple and its Teotihuacan flavor. As mentioned, this inscription is unique in its visual presentation and structure, and stands as one of the most fascinating Maya texts in existence. Much work remains to be done on the full implications of this exciting inscription.

An important aspect of the Temple Inscription is its obvious dichotomous structure, wherein the Teotihuacan and Maya glyphs are viewed as completely separate, with their own repertoire of signs and aesthetic qualities. There is an almost alien sense to these glyphs that was acknowledged by the ancient scribe who composed it, and appreciated by the audience that read it (or tried to!). This tends to confirm that the Teotihuacan style was considered distinct in some manner from that of the ordinary Maya canon. Like K'inich Yax K'uk' Mo', the temple evokes the idea of ethnic otherness, of another place.

The interpretation of this temple as an ancestral dynastic shrine seems inescapable, given the textual record of the stairway leading up to it. The inscription recounts the events in the lives of all of the known Copán kings, beginning with K'inich Yax K'uk' Mo'. Significantly, the earliest dates and historical events of the stairway inscription were inscribed on the upper steps, where the text began. As Houston has argued, the architectural settings of hieroglyphic stairways take advantage of this temporal aspect, taking the reader back in time as he or she nears the temple above. The ascent of the pyramid constitutes a sort of "time travel," with the summit being an origin point. In the case of Structure 10L-26, an ascent to the summit would involve not only a journey to a previous era, but to a place cloaked in the imagery of highland Mexico. In the case of the histories of Copán and Tikal, the past was a foreign country.

MAYA IMAGES OF POLITICAL FOUNDATION AND PRIMORDIAL HISTORY

Much of this Copán evidence agrees with Stone's (1989) powerful interpretations of Late Classic warrior stelae from Piedras Negras, where Teotihuacan-like symbolism and dress are a constant theme. She suggests that such symbolism was seen by the Classic Maya as decidedly foreign, consciously appropriated within certain artistic contexts to emphasize their own ranked "disconnection" from society at large. The two parallel inscriptions from the temple of Structure 10L-26, however difficult they may be to read and interpret, perhaps best illustrate this inherent "otherness" of Teotihuacan symbolism in the Maya world, but I would argue that there is a strong temporal dimension to such evocations as well. By the Late Classic, Teotihuacan was no longer the dominant force it once was in Mesoamerica, or at least in the Maya area, and may even have "collapsed" at or before the time the Copán buildings were constructed. The evocation of Teotihuacan by a Maya artist or ruler therefore cannot help but call to mind the historical past and Teotihuacan's place in it.

Such nuanced symbolism is suggested further, I believe, by the drastic differences we find between references to Teotihuacan in Maya art and writing from Early Classic and Late Classic times. Tikal's direct use of Teotihuacan icons and imagery in the Early Classic certainly reveals its close (I argue) political association with the highlands, but it is important here to emphasize that this is a contemporary association. Teotihuacan costumes and religious iconography are often indistinguishable from the imagery produced at Teotihuacan itself. The Late Classic Maya uses of Teotihuacan symbols become progressively more distant from their Central Mexican origins. Elements such as the "year sign" device and visages of Tlaloc are more hybrid in form, making use of very Maya aesthetic conventions, as the architectural decorations at Copán demonstrate. As the interactions between the central highlands and the Maya area changed throughout the Classic period, becoming less intimate and direct, the manner in which Maya artisans and rulers represented Central Mexican visual forms changed as well, becoming more infused local Maya conventions, while at the same time emphasizing notions of distance and disconnection.

Maya images of historical events and people from the distant past lend weight to this interpretation, for they regularly use Teotihuacan-derived symbolism to lend them what might be called an "aged look." Panel 2 from Piedras Negras is one example (Figure 15.25). Its scene depicts several warriors all dressed in a Teotihuacan mode, as shown by the trapeze-and-ray helmet devices, square shields, and a standing goggled figure. The inscription of this panel records the

Long Count date in the year 658 C.E. and an anniversary ceremony that year celebrated by Ruler 2 of Piedras Negras. The text next goes on to recall the same ceremony involving an Early Classic ruler in 510 C.E. There is no way to be sure which date goes with the scene depicted, but it is significant that the many named figures on the scene, including several individuals from Yaxchilán and Bonampak as well as a "young lord" from Piedras Negras, are nowhere recorded in other Late Classic inscriptions. I believe that the scene probably depicts the earlier of the two featured ceremonies—a "historical" scene in the distant past.

Fig. 15.25. Piedras Negras Panel 2. Drawing by the author.

Another Piedras Negras monument, Stela 40, bears a highly unusual scene of a scattering ruler above what appears to be a large ancestral "bust" figure inside an open tomb (Figure 15.26). "Earth" markings on the ground where the ruler kneels indicates that the lower image is in some subterranean structure or crypt. In any event, the ancestral image wears a mosaic Teotihuacan War Serpent head-dress (Stone 1989). I would not claim that this marks the figure as being from Teotihuacan, but would think that at the very least it shows the entombed figure to be one of the past, in contrast to the living king who is shown above. Similarly, a recently excavated panel from Palenque dates to the Late Classic, probably to the reign of Kan Balam II in the late seventh or early eight century C.E., yet bears a date falling on 490 C.E., firmly in the Early Classic. It is difficult to determine what happened on this day, but it may have been the historical foundation of what we today call Palenque, whose ancient name was Lakamha' (Stuart and Houston 1994). According to the inscription, the scene is of the Early Classic ruler Akul Anab, who wears a War Serpent headdress and other Teotihuacan imagery in his costume.

Finally, returning to Copán, the Fashes (chapter 14 of this volume) point out something altogether striking about how the image of K'inich Yax K'uk' Mo' changed in Copán art. We have seen that he is overtly connected with Mexican imagery in the Late Classic art, as Coggins (1988) has pointed out. However, the

more recent discovery of an Early Classic disc altar beneath the Hieroglyphic
Stairway—the so called Motmot marker—shows us the most contemporary portrait of this founder king. It was presumably created by the second ruler, K'inich
Yax K'uk' Mo's son, who is shown on the right-hand side, facing his father.
There is nothing in the founder's portrait to suggest any connection at all to
Teotihuacan or a foreign association. Based on the quantity of Teotihuacan-
derived artifacts found in the excavations of the early acropolis, I feel Copán's
historical connections with the highlands were real but somehow "played down"
in the contemporary portraits of K'inich Yax K'uk' Mo'. By the Late Classic,
centuries later, the founder is consistently shown in a Teotihuacan mode, com-
municating a definite ethnic otherness for the founder. However, the contrast
with the Early Classic portrait suggests also that his Mexican dress and style
may be used to evoke the related notion of the primordial past, the time of "foundation."

Fig. 15.26. Piedras Negras Stela 40. Photograph courtesy of the University Museum,
University of Pennsylvania.

These examples suggest that Maya representations of the past may have consciously tapped into an archaistic Teotihuacan "look." Yet not all instances of Teotihuacan-style costumery in the later Maya art are so explicitly connected to early historical events. The elaborate butterfly-jaguar warrior costumes of Dos Pilas Stela 2 and Yaxchilán Lintel 25 are worn by contemporary rulers who stand above captives, yet it is possible that these too allude to the past in some way as conscious historical "reenactments" of a time when the warrior culture of high-land Mexico was a more visible force in the Maya area. The reasons militaristic images are so central to the hybrid Teotihuacan-Maya style are complex and beyond the scope of this study (Stone 1989), yet I believe that their significance at Copán and many other sites is sometimes secondary to the greater archaistic effect of lending age and remoteness to portraits and architecture. Significantly, Copán's texts all but ignore military themes and subjects, making the militaristic imagery of Temples 26 and 16 all the more unusual and remote. It was probably quite intentional there as a means of expressing the temporal distance of the founding father and his possible non-Maya ethnicity.

PLACE OF CATTAILS: THE MAYA NAME FOR TEOTIHUACAN

Thus far we have examined the different characterizations of Teotihuacan as found in two important Maya cities. Both present in their official histories and political art a strong connection to the Mexican highlands that is rooted in specific historical events concerning the establishment of new political orders.

In her perceptive study of Teotihuacan imagery in the Piedras Negras monuments, Stone (1989) makes an important point that the "disconnection" evident in their use of non-Maya symbolism is strikingly similar to a pattern widely seen in Postclassic Mesoamerican sources, where "foreigners" are repeatedly mentioned as major players in politics and in mythologies of origin. Among the Postclassic Maya, we need look no further than the powerful Itzá, who are identified as arriving in Yucatán from the land of Zuyuá, located to the west. Even the mere claim to a foreign affiliation was important for elites who wished to identify themselves as something apart from society at large. As Stone notes, "Claims for foreign affiliation were a favored form of propping up elite hierarchies in Yucatan from at least the Terminal Classic" (1989: 167). She posits that the Late Classic stelae at Piedras Negras do much the same thing, infusing a "Mexican-ness" into the Maya representations of political and military authority. Stone is convincing in showing the time-depth of these ideas, and sees them as being based on "ideological manipulation rather than historical events." As the above discussions make clear, I agree with her important observations, but would differ in assessing the origins of such powerful symbolism. For the Classic Maya, I would argue that claims of foreign descent *were* based on historical realities of the late fourth and early fifth centuries, when intrusions and arrivals from the highlands occurred with some frequency.

The cultural intersections presented in the Classic texts and iconography therefore reflect some important themes that would repeat themselves in Mesoamerican mythic histories. An origin from some removed locale, a journey with stops along the way, the arrival at the new settlement where order is established and the world renewed—all these elements can be found to some degree or another in a number of historical chronicles from the Postclassic era. I suggest that the inklings of history that we read of at Tikal and Copán represent precursors of this paradigm, but would insist again on its basis in certain historical realities, particularly as seen in the central Petén histories.

In the Postclassic and colonial histories throughout Mesoamerica, an elemental concept that exerts a powerful historical and cultural presence was Tollan or Tula, the "Place of Cattails." It represented a place of origin and foundation for a great many political powers, ranging from the Mexica Aztec imperial dynasty to the comparatively diminutive kingdom of the Cakchiquel Maya. It is cited throughout Yucatán and Oaxaca, as well, as a paradigmatic place of beginnings for political, social, and cultural institutions. The people of Tollan, the Toltec, represented for the Mexica Aztec all that was cultured and civilized, a model to be emulated by all rulers and elites. The subject of Tollan and its historical and mythic dimensions have been explored elsewhere many times (e.g., Carrasco 1982), and it is generally considered to be a Postclassic phenomenon in Mesoamerica. The identity of the historical Tollan has been debated for decades, but the general consensus now holds that the present-day archaeological site of Tula, Hidalgo, is likely to be "the" Tollan. In fact, the written sources speak of many Tollans, suggesting that the name might best be considered an alternative term for "city" (Carrasco 1982).

Surprisingly, perhaps, Classic Maya sources present important evidence concerning the original identity of the Place of Cattails. Several iconographic scenes from the Maya region use the Maya "cattail, reed" sign as a toponym, in each case in direct association with Teotihuacan-derived symbolism.

Lintel 2 of Temple I at Tikal (Figure 15.20) was earlier mentioned as a possible portrait of Spear-Thrower Owl, who I conjecture to have been a Teotihuacan ruler. Aside from this particular speculation, Taube (1992) pointed out the toponymic band at the base of the scene displays images of plants native to the central highlands. These he identifies as the barrel cactus and grass (Figure 15.27 [a]). The scene on the lintel is dominated by the Teotihuacan War Serpent, who stands behind and above a seated ruler with the accouterments of a highland warrior. According to Taube, the intent is to show the Maya ruler, literally or figuratively, as in the arid highlands where such plants are native. I wholeheartedly agree with Taube's interpretation, but there is one slight modification to offer. The plant motif he identifies as grass is more precisely a representation of a cattail or reed. The Maya form of this sign is common in both iconography and hieroglyphic writing (Figure 15.27 [b]) is visually related to the Aztec day-sign "Reed." As a Maya hieroglyph it functions as the syllable *pu* (Stuart 1987). In several Mayan languages, *pu* or *puh* means "reed, cattail," or "bulrush."

This Maya cattail glyph, abstracted in some cases to an unnaturalistic design, occurs in close association with other examples of Teotihuacan-style iconography. On the stucco façade of Acanceh, Yucatán, this sign alternates with highly unusual representations of animals outfitted in Teotihuacan-like costume and associated symbols (Figure 15.28). The cattail glyphs here may have a locational function, much as Taube suggested on the Tikal lintel. In a similar way, large stacked cattail signs decorate the background of another Maya sculpture from the Palenque region (Figure 15.29). The fragmentary tablet depicts seated figures who flank a standing individual in the center. The objects held in the hands of the two kneeling men are bowls containing large Teotihuacan Tlaloc heads. The standing figure, though incomplete, is dressed in Teotihuacan-style costume replete with War Serpent sandals.

Finally, I point out the presence of the cattail glyph as part of the name phrases of two prominent historical figures mentioned in this paper. At Copán, the name K'inich Yax K'uk' Mo' is accompanied by a Copán emblem glyph, standard in all respects save for the inclusion of the *pu* sign along with the ever-present bat

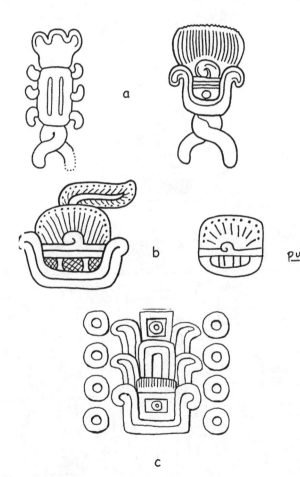

Fig. 15.27. "Reed" glyphs: a. A barrel cactus and a reed, from the toponymic register of Tikal, Temple I, Lintel 2; b. Reed glyph from stucco frieze at Acanceh, Yucatán, compared with *pu* hieroglyph; c. Mexica day sign Acatl.

head (Figure 15.30 [a]). This may have a purely phonetic role in the spelling of the Copán polity name, but it is possible that it labels the dynastic founder as of the "cattail place." Similarly, we find the *pu* sign in a title of Nun Yax Ayin of Tikal, on the side of Stela 31 (Figure 15.30 [b]). The same ambiguity exists as to the function of the sign, for it may be present to represent solely the sound *pu* in combination with other signs.

Taken together, the evidence shows that the cattail glyph is noticeably placed in scenes evoking Teotihuacan styles and associations. Arguably, it specifies the location of such scenes as occurring in the Place of the Cattails, or Tollan. It follows that Copán and other Maya sites of the Classic period presented their stories of ancestral origin and political foundation in much the same way as later Maya groups in Yucatán and Guatemala, who in the ethnohistoric sources make reference to Central Mexico and Tula as places where elite authority was derived. The well-known legends and representations of Tollan as a place of origin have up to now been associated with Postclassic sources almost exclusively, but I

Fig. 15.28. Portion of the stucco frieze from Acanceh, Yucatán (from Seler 1902–23: plate 11).

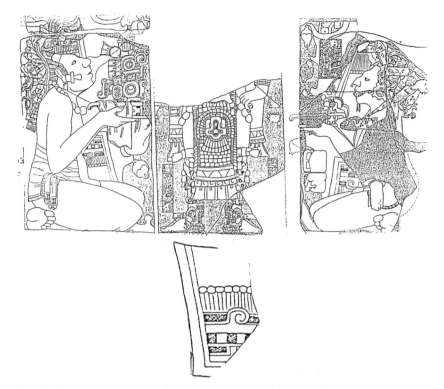

Fig. 15.29. The "Jonuta Panel" from Palenque, with detail of "reed" design.

Fig. 15.30. "Reed" glyphs in with the names of K'inich Yax K'uk' Mo' of Copán and Nun Yax Ayin of Tikal: a. Copán, Stela 11, drawing by B. Fash; b. Tikal, Stela 31, drawing by W. R. Coe.

would like to entertain the likelihood that such ideas and conceptualizations have considerable more time-depth in the Maya area and probably other areas of Mesoamerica. Many "Tulas" are known from later Mesoamerica, but my own Maya perspective leads me to agree that Teotihuacan was held as the first ideal city, the primordial Tollan.

CONCLUSIONS

The notion that that Classic Maya political centers such as Copán and Tikal claimed a certain "Toltec" heritage based on historical events challenges a number of strongly held assumptions about Maya culture history. We can no longer be satisfied with simply viewing the Maya use of Teotihuacan symbolism as the appropriation of foreign visual forms that communicate aspects of elite ideology and militarism. These ideas are true enough, but I sense much more lies behind the artistic and archaeological evidence of this interaction. Here I have used written sources from the Classic period to suggest that the Teotihuacan presence in the Maya lowlands was intense and sometimes disruptive during the Early Classic period, with profound political changes at Tikal. My interpretations are based on relatively recent decipherments, but agree with the overall picture presented earlier by Proskouriakoff (1993) and Coggins (1979a). If Teotihuacan was in some manner politically dominant in this region during the Early Classic, as I believe it was, Maya kings would nonetheless continue to refer to the great highland center for centuries to come in their own political and ritual texts, even long after Teotihuacan declined. It became an idealized concept more than anything else, a place from which people and forces came to leave their mark on the Maya world. It represented a paradigm through which Maya rulers could define themselves and their historical pedigree. From a wider Mesoamerican perspective, such a pattern strikes a familiar cord, and in its structure much of what I have presented reflects long-established understandings of indigenous history and its conceptualization. What is novel, I hope, is the demonstration that the Classic Maya were participants in this long-lived paradigm of historicism, where highlands and lowlands participated in ancient patterns of contact and movement, and of mutual influence and awareness. Late Classic Maya dynasties and the elite communities that surrounded them defined themselves at least in part through the remembrance of the old and distant "Place of Cattails," what the later Nahua would know as Tollan-Teotihuacan.

NOTES

1. These varied interpretations of the lowland Maya evidence strikingly recall a similar debate that followed the excavations of Mounds A and B at Kaminaljuyú (Kidder, Jennings, and Shook 1946), where evidence of Mexican contact during the Esperanza phase was strong and seemingly pervasive. Kidder et al. suggested a military conquest of Kaminaljuyú by Teotihuacan warrior-merchants, whereas Borhegyi (1956) later emphasized the absorption of a Teotihuacan "cosmopolitan" fashion by local elites. Borhegyi (1965) would later reject this alternative in favor of the conquest scenario. Economic dimensions of the relationship between highland Guatemala and Teotihuacan were emphasized by Sanders and Price (1968), and subsequent work at Kaminaljuyu advanced such theories in more detail (Sanders and Michels 1977).

2. Even with the excavations of numerous other central Petén sites, the concentration at Tikal of Teotihuacan styles remains striking and simply unparalleled. In their studies of Altar de Sacrificios and Seibal, for example, Adams (1971) and Sabloff (1975) noted relatively little evidence of Teotihuacan-associated ceramics during the Early Classic. Rather, such material seems spatially grouped around the central and northern Petén region, including sites such as Tikal, Uaxactún, as well as Río Azul. Lincoln (1985) offers a reassessment of Early Classic ceramic chronology, suggesting that the Tzakol 3 phase of the central Petén was perhaps a localized "elite/ceremonial subcomplex" that overlapped significantly with both Tzakol 1 and 2. This chronological revision remains to be confirmed, but it is safe to say that the northern Petén, and Tikal and Uaxactún in particular, constituted the lowland focus of this highland contact. It was not very widespread.

3. As noted, the names "Great Paw" or "Jaguar Paw" are only convenient labels and do not purport to be true translations of the original Mayan name. It is difficult to say what the original name might have been, but three elements are consistent: *chak*, *to* or *tok* (?), and the "paw" element. The paw can be replaced by a head variant showing a skull, with the jaguar paw protruding as its nose. In other contexts, the simple paw can have the value *ich'ak*, or "claw," but the odd head variant here may indicate something different. If I were to offer a tentative hieroglyphic transcription of the name, it would be Chak-Tok-Ich'Ak. This may be a member of a distinctive class of personal names where colors such as *chak* ("red") pair with *tok* ("cloud?") and a variable final sign. Due to the ambiguities, however, I prefer for the time being to retain the nickname "Jaguar Paw."

4. The El Temblor stela was recorded some years ago by Ian Graham, and photographs and drawings are now on file in the archive of the Corpus of Maya Hieroglyphic Inscriptions Program at the Peabody Museum. The monument was damaged by looters and is incomplete, but bears parts of an inscription on its two narrow sides. One side gives a Long Count date that is difficult to reconstruct with much assurance, followed by a verb for "accession." On the other side, records of other events include the accession of Jaguar Paw of Tikal, but unfortunately again the date is too damaged to read. Whatever the date, it would have to fall some time before the Period Ending 8.17.0.0.0. recorded on Tikal Stela 31.

5. The more recent excavations at the Mundo Perdido area of Tikal suggest a Teotihuacan influence in Manik-phase ceramics before this date in the late fourth century (LaPorte and Fialko 1990). This does not run counter to Proskouriakoff's suppostion that the 11 Eb date was important to this phenomenon, however, for the greatest concentration of such highland material still appears at around this time, tied into dynastic history through the North Acropolis excavations (Coggins 1975). I should caution, also, that the internal seriation of Tzakol-Manik ceramics may eventually be reworked, as Lincoln (1985) has called into question the exclusivity of its subphases. The dating revisions of Teotihuacan influence as proposed at the Mundo Perdido seem to rely on the original seriations, and should be evaluated anew once the chronology is more refined.

6. In its simplest form, his name glyph contains two signs, the "birth frog" and "fire." Their order varies, but more complex examples of the name reveal the actual reading. On Stela 4 at Tikal, the birth frog is expanded into a full birth glyph, *SIH-ya-ha*, showing the spelling of the verbal suffix -*ah* after the root *sih*, "be born." Other names at Tikal are known to use this verb, such as Siyah Chan K'awil, where the verb endings can drop off on accasion. Given these parallels, I opt to read the name in full as Siyah K'ak', or "Fire Is Born."

7. The death associations for the *och-ha'* or "enters water" glyph derive from the significance of the underworld as a watery place of death and resurrection (e.g,. Schele and Miller 1986: 267; Hellmuth 1987). Significantly, this glyph is the one event written in the short text painted on the wall of a tomb at Río Azul, Guatemala, apparently referring to the demise of the tomb's occupant.

8. Stela 18 of Tikal also names Siyah K'ak', but the inscription is almost completely gone. The date is 8.18.0.0.0 (396 C.E.), when Nun Yax Ayin was ruler. The text closes in much the same way as Stela 4, stating that the king is "the lord of" Siyah K'ak'.

9. Mention should be made of another probable reference to Siyah K'ak' in a much later Tikal text (MT34) inscribed on a Late Classic bone "hairpin" excavated in Burial 116, illustrated by Jones (1987: fig.6). This was one of a set of six such needles, all bearing short statements with dates, names, and events revolving around this early period of Tikal's history. Nun Yax Ayin is named on one (MT35) as is perhaps also Spear-Thrower Owl (MT32). The date associated with Siyah K'ak' on MT34 is probably 8.17.0.15.7 9 Manik 10 Xul, or 145 days before his arrival as recorded at Tikal and Uaxactún. If so, this would be the earliest known event to be associated with him. The event is unclear, but I wonder in speculation if it may refer to his "departure" toward the Petén. I will discuss these interesting texts at length in another study.

10. I can not offer a literal translation of the name, but prefer to use the label "Spear-Thrower Owl" used by Schele and Freidel (1990), at least for the time being. The other nicknames cited here are less accurate descriptions of the name glyph, since "shield" and "cauac" are both problematic identifications. Mathews (cited in Schele and Freidel 1990: 450) has proposed that the "cauac" element is phonetic *ku* used to spell the documented word for owl, variously *ku*, *kuh*, or *kuy*. Grube and Schele greatly expand on Mathews's reading. In the case of this Tikal name, however, I hesitate to accept the *ku* reading, since the form of the "cauac" sign is so different from other *ku* syllables. Rather, I think this sign after the spear-thrower element remains to be deciphered, although it is clearly in free substitution for the owl, as Schele originally demonstrated.

11. Very recently Justin Kerr kindly shared with me his photographs of an Early Classic Tzakol 3 lidded tripod bearing an important reference to Spear-Thrower Owl (Kerr no. 7528). There the name is written with the standard spear-thrower and the head variant of "cauac," similar in some ways to the head used in the name on the Tikal Marcador stone, and thus strengthening the identification of that name as equivalent. Simon Martin noted the same connection when studying the vessel (Martin, personal communication 1997).

12. This interpretation of the Marcador passage, while tentative, is based upon the verb *yi-ta-(hi)* that precedes the name of Spear-Thrower Owl, after the record of the arrival. I once considered that this served as a relationship expression for "sibling," but this now seems unlikely. Despite the revision, the older reading has gained a strong foothold in the literature, and was even used to posit specific kin relations between some of these actors in Tikal history (Schele and Freidel 1990). There is no doubt in my view, however, that it is a verb with no "sibling" connection whatsoever. This verb is found in many inscriptions where it gives the sense that the subject is witnessing or overseeing the action stated previously. It is just possible that the root of the verb is *ita* < *il-ta*, "look at" (cf. colonial Tzotzil, *it-o*, "look here!"). This reading will be explored further in a paper now under preparation.

13. Stela 32 of Tikal (Figure 15.3) shows the small but recognizable remains of a crested owl on the chest of the warrior, precisely where the *lechuza y armas* medallions are found on the ceramic figurines illustrated. Virginia Fields (cited in Schele and Freidel 1990: 449–450) has linked this to the Spear-Thrower Owl glyph, leading me to suggest, albeit tentatively, that this likewise is a portrait of Nun Yax Ayin's father.

14. A fact pointed out to me by Bridget Hodder Stuart.

15. Lest this sound too far-fetched, I would point out that a similar "disjunction" of figural time frames is found on the panels of the Cross Group at Palenque. There each panel shows two facing views of the ruler Kan Balam II. One portrait is of him on the day of his accession, the other smaller one as a six-year-old child. Again, the scale of the figures is highly naturalistic, as I suggest might be the case on Stela 31.

16. The similarity of this Calendar Round date to 5 Caban 10 Yaxk'in, the accession date of Nun Yax Ayin of Tikal, is interesting but likely coincidental.

17. The building name is probably found in Early Classic inscriptions at Tikal, Tres Islas, and Río Azul as *wi-te-nah*. The equivalence is based on the common Teotihuacan associations of both glyphs, the apparent fact that they are building names, and that *wi-* occurs with the crossed-bundles version on Lintel 25 of Yaxchilán. Interestingly, in a possible parallel to its Copán occurrence with K'inich Yax K'uk' Mo', the *wi-te-nah* house name appears on Stela 31 of Tikal in connection with the inauguration statement of Yax Nun Ayin.

18. The sign representing the crossed torch bundles is not yet deciphered in my view, but may point to the structure serving as a place of ritual fire and burning. Such an interpretation needs to be considered further, but it is in agreement with the fire-related themes Taube suggests for Structure 10L–16 at Copán (personal communication, 1996) and in Taube's chapter in the present volume.

19. The War Serpent is also named twice on the set of bones from Tikal Burial 116, which appear to relate episodes of Early Classic Tikal history around the time of the "arrival event" (see note 8).

20. Karl Taube and Barbara Fash were important contributors to the reconstruction work in 1996. I would like to thank James Fitzsimmons of Harvard University and Jennifer Smit of the University of Michigan for their help in the recording and photography of the assembled text.

REFERENCES

Adams, Richard E. W.
1971. *The Ceramics of Altar de Sacrificios*. Papers of the Peabody Museum of Archaeology and Ethnology, Harvard University, vol. 63, no. 1. Cambridge, MA.

Berlo, Janet
1983. *Teotihuacan Art Abroad: A Study of Metropolitan Style and Provincial Transformation in Incensario Workshops*. Oxford: BAR International Series 199.

Berrin, Kathleen, ed.
1988. *Feathered Serpents and Flowering Trees: Reconstructing the Murals of Teotihuacan*. San Francisco: The Fine Arts Museums of San Francisco.

Borhegyi, Stephan F. de
1956. "The Developoment of Folk and Complex Cultures in the Southern Maya Area." *American Antiquity* 21, no. 4:343–356.
1965. "Archaeological Synthesis of the Guatemalan Highlands." In R. A. Wauchope, gen. ed.; G. Willey, vol. ed., *Handbook of Middle American Indians*. Vol. 2, Part 1: *The Archaeology of Southern Mesoamerica*. Austin: University of Texas Press, pp. 3–58.

Borjenneau, Gerald, Emile Deletaille, and Jean-Loius Sonnery
1985. *Rediscovered Masterpieces of Mesoamerica: Mexico-Guatemala-Honduras*. Boulogne: Editions Arts.

Carrasco, Davíd
1982. *Quetzalcoatl and the Irony of Empire: Myths and Prophesies in the Aztec Tradition*. Chicago: University of Chicago Press.

Coggins, Clemency C.
1975. "Painting and Drawing Styles at Tikal: An Historical and Iconographic Reconstruction." Ph.D. dissertation, Department of Fine Arts, Harvard University, Cambridge, MA.

1979a. "A New Order and the Role of the Calendar: Some Characteristics of the Middle Classic Period at Tikal." In N. Hammond and G. R. Willey, eds., *Maya Archaeology and Ethnohistory*. Austin: University of Texas Press, pp. 38–50.

1979b. "Teotihuacan and Tikal in the Early Classic Period." In *Actes du XLIIe Congrès International des Américanistes, Congrès du Centenaire, Paris, 2-9 septembre 1976*. Paris: Société des Américanistes, vol. 8, pp. 251–269.

1983. "An Instrument of Expansion: Monte Alban, Teotihuacan, and Tikal." In A. Miller, ed., *Highland-Lowland Interaction in Mesoamerica: Interdisciplinary Approaches*. Washington, DC: Dumbarton Oaks, pp. 49–68.

1988. "On the Historical Significance of Decorated Ceramics at Copan and Quirgua and Related Maya Sites." In E. H. Boone and G. R. Willey, eds., *The Southeast Classic Maya Zone*. Washington, DC: Dumbarton Oaks, pp. 95–124.

Culbert, T. Patrick
1993a. "Polities in the Northeast Peten, Guatemala." In T. P. Culbert, ed., *Classic Maya Political History: Hieroglyphic and Archaeological Evidence*. Cambridge: Cambridge University Press, pp. 128–146.

1993b. *The Ceramics of Tikal: Vessels from the Burials, Caches, and Problematical Deposits*. Tikal Report no. 25, Part A. Philadelphia: The University Museum, University of Pennsylvania.

Demarest, Arthur A., and Antonia E. Foias
1993. "Mesoamerican Horizons and the Cultural Transformations of Maya Civilization." In D. S. Rice, ed., *Latin American Horizons*. Washington, DC: Dumbarton Oaks, pp. 147–192.

Fahsen, Federico
1987. "Los personajes de Tikal en el Clásico Temprano: La evidencia epigráfica." In *Primer Simposio Mundial sobre Epigrafía Maya, agosto 19–21, 1986*. Guatemala: Asociación Tikal, pp. 47–60.

Fash, Barbara W.
1992. "Late Classic Architectural Sculpture Themes at Copán." *Ancient Mesoamerica* 3, no. 1: 89–104.

Fash, William L.
1991. *Scribes, Warriors, and Kings: The City of Copán and the Ancient Maya*. London and New York: Thames and Hudson.

Fash, William L., Richard V. Williamson, Carlos Rudy Larios, and Joel Palka
1992. "The Hieroglyphic Stairway and Its Ancestors: Investigations of Copán Structure 10L–26." *Ancient Mesoamerica* 3, no. 1: 105–116.

Fialko C., Vilma
1987. "El marcador de juego de pelota de Tikal: Nuevas referencias epigráficas para el Clásico Temprano." In *Primer Simposio Mundial sobre Epigrafía Maya, agosto 19–21, 1986*. Guatemala: Asociación Tikal, pp. 61–80.

Graham, Ian
1986. *Corpus of Maya Hieroglyphic Inscriptions*. Volume 5, part 3: *Uaxactún*. Cambridge, MA: Peabody Museum of Archaeology and Ethnology, Harvard University.

Grube, Nikolai, and Linda Schele
1994. "Kuy, the Owl of Omen and War." *Mexicon* 16, no. 1: 10–17.

Hellmuth, Nicholas M.
1987. *Surface of the Underwaterworld: Iconography of the Gods of Early Classic Maya*

Art in Peten, Guatemala. 2 vols. Culver City, CA: Foundation for Latin American Anthropological Research.

Houston, Stephen D.
1993. *Hieroglyphs and History at Dos Pilas: Dynastic Politics of the Classic Maya*. Austin: University of Texas Press.

Houston, Stephen D., and Peter Mathews
1985. *The Dynastic Sequence of Dos Pilas, Guatemala*. San Francisco: Pre-Columbian Art Research Center, Monograph 1.

Jones, Christopher
1977. "Inauguration Dates of Three Late Classic Rulers of Tikal, Guatemala." *American Antiquity* 42, no.1: 28-60.
1987. "The Life and Times of Ah Cacau, Ruler of Tikal." In *Primer Simposio Mundial sobre Epigrafía Maya, agosto 19–21, 1986*. Guatemala: Asociación Tikal, pp. 107-120.
1991. "Cycles of Growth at Tikal." In T. P. Culbert, ed., *Classic Maya Political History: Hieroglyphic and Archaeological Evidence*. Cambridge: Cambridge University Press, pp. 102–127.
1992. "The Life and Times of Ah Cacau, Ruler of Tikal." In *Primer Simposio Mundial sobre Epigrafía Maya, agosto 19–21, 1986*. Guatemala: Asociación Tikal, pp. 107–120.

Jones, Christopher, and Linton Satterthwaite
1982. *The Monuments and Inscriptions of Tikal: The Carved Monuments*. Tikal Report no. 33, Part A. Philadelphia: University Museum, University of Pennsylvania.

Kidder, Alfred V., Jesse D. Jennings, and Edwin M. Shook
1946. *Excavations at Kaminaljuyu, Guatemala*. Washington, DC: Carnegie Institution Publication no. 561.

Laporte, Juan Pedro, and Vilma Fialko
1990. "New Perspectives on Old Problems: Dynastic References for the Early Classic at Tikal." In F. S. Clancy and P. D. Harrison, eds., *Vision and Revision in Maya Studies*. Albuquerque: University of New Mexico Press, pp. 33–66.

Laporte, Juan Pedro, and Lilian Vega de Zea
1987. "Aspectos dinásticos para el Clásico Temprano de Mundo Perdido, Tikal." In *Primer Simposio Mundial sobre Epigrafía Maya, agosto 19–21, 1986*. Guatemala: Asociación Tikal, pp. 127–140.

Lincoln, Charles E.
1985. "Ceramics and Ceramic Chronology." In G. R. Willey and P. Mathews, eds., *A Consideration of the Early Classic Period in the Maya Lowlands*. Albany: SUNY, Institute of Mesoamerican Studies Publication 10, pp. 55–54.

Mathews, Peter
1985. "Maya Early Classic Monuments and Inscriptions." In G. R. Willey and P. Mathews, eds., *A Consideration of the Early Classic Period in the Maya Lowlands*. Albany: SUNY, Institute of Mesoamerican Studies Publication 10, pp. 5–54.

Proskouriakoff, Tatiana
1993. *Maya History*. Austin: University of Texas Press.

Sabloff, Jeremy A.
1975. "Ceramics." In *Excavations at Seibal, Department of Peten, Guatemala*. Memoirs of the Peabody Musuem of Archaeology and Ethnology, Harvard University, vol. 13, no. 2. Cambridge, MA.

Sanders, William T., and Joseph W. Michels, eds.
1977. *Teotihuacan and Kaminaljuyu: A Study in Prehistoric Culture Contact*. University
Park: Pennsylvania State University Press.

Sanders, William T., and Barbara Price
1968. *Mesoamerica: The Evolution of a Civilization*. New York: Random House.

Schele, Linda
1976. "Tikal: A Summary of the Early Classic Texts Resulting from Consultation of Linda
Schele, Peter Mathews, Dicey Taylor, and Floyd Lounsbury." Unpublished paper.
1984. "Human Sacrifice Among the Classic Maya." In E. H. Boone, ed., *Ritual Human
Sacrifice in Mesoamerica*. Washington, DC: Dumbarton Oaks, pp. 7–48.
1986. "The Tlaloc Complex in the Classic Period: War and the Interaction Between the
Lowland Maya and Teotihuacan." Paper presented at the Blood of Kings Symposium,
The Kimball Art Museum, Fort Worth.
1992. "The Founders of Lineages at Copán and Other Maya Sites." *Ancient Mesoamerica*
3, no. 1: 135–144.

Schele, Linda, and David Friedel
1990. *A Forest of Kings: The Untold Story of the Ancient Maya*. New York: William
Morrow.

Schele, Linda, and Mary Ellen Miller
1986. *The Blood of Kings: Dynasty and Ritual in Maya Art*. Fort Worth: The Kimbell Art
Museum.

Seler, Eduard
1902–1923. "Die Stuckfassade von Acanceh in Yucatan." In E. Seler, *Gesammelte
Abhandlungen zur amerikanischen sprach- und Alterthumskunde*. Berlin: Ascher/
Behrend, vol. 5, pp. 389-404.

Smith, Robert E.
1955. *Ceramic Sequence at Uaxactun, Guatemala*. 2 vols. New Orleans: Tulane University, Middle American Research Institute Publication 20.

Stone, Andrea
1989. "Disconnection, Foreign Insignia, and Political Expansion: Teotihuacan and the Warrior
Stelae of Piedras Negras." In R. A. Diehl and J. C. Berlo, eds., *Mesoamerican After the
Decline of Teotihuacan, A.D. 700–900*. Washington, DC: Dumbarton Oaks, pp. 153–172.

Stuart, David
1992. "Hieroglyphs and Archaeology at Copán." *Ancient Mesoamerica* 3, no. 1: 169–184.
1993. "Historical Inscriptions and the Maya Collapse." In Jeremy Sabloff and John S.
Henderson, eds., *Lowland Maya Civilization in the Eighth Century A.D.* Washington,
DC: Dumbarton Oaks, pp. 321–354.
1994. "The Texts of Temple 26: The Presentation of History at a Classic Maya Dynastic
Shrine." Paper prepared for the SAR Advanced Seminar "Copán: The Rise and Fall of
a Classic Maya Kingdom," The School of American Research, Santa Fe, NM.
1995. "A Study of Maya Inscriptions." Ph.D. dissertation, Department of Anthropology,
Vanderbilt University, Nashville, TN. Ann Arbor, MI: University Microfilms International.
1996. "Kings of Stone: A Consideration of Stelae in Maya Ritual and Representation."
Res: Anthropology and Aesthetics 29/30: 149–171.

Stuart, David, and Stephen Houston
1994. *Classic Maya Place Names*. Studies in Pre-Columbian Art and Archaeology, no. 34.
Washington, DC: Dumbarton Oaks.

Taube, Karl A.
1992. "The Temple of Quetzalcoatl and the Cult of Sacred War at Teotihuacan." *Res: Anthropology and Aesthetics* 21: 53–87.

Valdés, Juan Antonio, Federico Fahsen, and Gaspar Antonio Cosme
1997. *Estela 40 de Tikal: Hallazgo y lectura.* Guatemala: Instituto de Antropología e Historia de Guatemala.

von Winning, Hasso
1987. *La iconografía de Teotihuacán: Los dioses y los signos.* 2 vols. Mexico: UNAM.

▼

16

PARALLEL CONSUMPTIVE COSMOLOGIES

PHILIP P. ARNOLD

While flipping through the TV channels recently I happened upon a show on the Arts and Entertainment (A&E) network dedicated to Teotihuacan. It was part of the *Ancient Mysteries* series hosted by Leonard Nimoy (who earned his fame playing Spock in the popular television series *Star Trek* in the 1960s). *Ancient Mysteries* travels the globe in order to discover and reveal the most bizarre features of our ancient human past for the entertainment of the viewing public. During the Teotihuacan episode we were treated to flashy camera work that featured stunning time-lapse photography of the Pyramids of the Sun and Moon moving quickly through the course of a day and night, misty camera effects of what seemed like ancient young Mexican men moving with determined faces through the silent urban center to reenact a heart sacrifice, and Nimoy's deep-throated narration punctuated by the appearance of scholarly experts to lend his interpretations an air of credibility.[1] All these efforts were skillfully orchestrated to capitalize on Teotihuacan's mystery.

Nimoy's interpretation consistently focused on a crass "blood and guts" sensationalistic presentation of Mesoamerican culture. This approach heightened the mysteriousness, or total "Otherness," of Teotihuacan, thus making its presence on TV more titillating for the audience. In recent years these docudramas have effectively rendered remote cultures into consumables. Through the camera, viewers could see what Nimoy referred to as a Teotihuacano obsession with creating an "utopian paradise." In *Ancient Mysteries'* interpretation, Teotihuacan is mysteriously and magically re-created by an incongruity between a Mesoamerican celebration of violence and an obsessive preoccupation with utopia. As a consequence, the meaning of Teotihuacan is simultaneously "opaque" in its otherness while being "transparently" dramatized on TV for all to see.

It may seem odd to start a serious examination of Teotihuacan with a discussion of Nimoy on television but, as I will argue, there are some serious issues involving the relationship of human consumption and interpretation that are revealed most powerfully in a popular context. Finding what was wrong with *Ancient Mysteries'* interpretations of Teotihuacan would be like shooting fish in a barrel, yet its presence in my living room was a reality that constituted an expression of a consumptive cosmology distinct from, yet in intimate contact with, a Mesoamerican consumptive cosmos.

I.

Teotihuacan is indeed remote from our world. At best, its language, ethnic make-up, and religious worldview (to name just a few) are the subjects of well-informed guesses. In recent years, anthropologists and others have wondered whether it is possible to know another culture at all, let alone one at such a temporal and cultural distance as Teotihuacan.

Whatever Teotihuacan was for its residents, however, it was almost certainly not a utopia (i.e., "no place"). Everything about the site seems to reveal a locative emphasis.[2] Johanna Broda's work (chapter 12 in this volume) painstakingly moves us through a living landscape at Teotihuacan in which the contours of earthly forms were conjoined with the sky into architecture and rituals. Their calendar was not an abstract succession of endless chronological moments (as it would be for a utopian viewpoint), but based on observation of celestial bodies in relationship to the landscape.[3] Likewise Doris Heyden has emphasized how material features of the site, in particular cave symbolism and the underworld, served as a religious organizing principle for Teotihuacan.[4] A locative meaning for Teotihuacan reveals the earth to be its primary feature of religious life. These initial considerations of Teotihuacan adhere closely to Charles Long's definition of religion as orientation "in the ultimate sense, that is, how one comes to terms with the ultimate significance of one's place in the world."[5]

Work at Teotihuacan over the last fifteen years or so has revealed a much greater understanding of its cosmological significance. Most striking is the eating symbolism associated with caves, sacrificed warriors, and urban calendrics. Understandings of the *cipactli* have been enlarged by recent excavations and interpretations. The *cipactli* seems to form the locus for a variety of associations with other beings that include Tlaloc, Chalchiuhtlicue, the *tlaloque*, and Tlaltecuhtli, to name a few. The *cipactli* also forms a Mesoamerican "genus" that includes subterranean toads, alligators, crocodiles, snakes, and sawfish. Symbolically, the *cipactli* is connected with shells, greenstone, rain, water, earth, and the underworld. Broda's work has systematically articulated the connections between the Tlaloc cult and material life to present a coherent Mesoamerican cosmovision.[6] My own work has focused on Aztec ritual cosmology as an "eating landscape."[7] More recently, Davíd Carrasco has explored the mythic and iconographic dimensions of what he calls "Cosmic Jaws."[8]

Holding together the *cipactli* genus of animals (toad, crocodile, alligator, and sawfish) is the mouth with exaggerated upper teeth. These animals are also associated with water. In the excavations at the Temple of Quetzalcoatl by Cabrera,

Sugiyama, and Cowgill were found around two hundred sacrificed warriors numerically distributed in a pattern reminiscent of a calendrical order.[9] Many of these warriors had shell collars with pendants fashioned to imitate human jaws made of shell teeth set in stucco. A few of the burials had real jaws. Other objects included greenstone beads, ear-spools, nose pendants, figurines, conical objects, obsidian blades, figurines, shells, and remains of wood and textiles.[10]

There is a pronounced symmetry between warrior sacrifice and shell jaws. The emphasis was placed on the upper jaw, or maxilla, and was connected with the voracious mouths of the iconography of the temple. That they are made of shell is also suggestive of a connection between fertility and warfare. Perhaps this is also indicated by the east-west axis of the burials. Doris Heyden's important article on the cave underneath the Pyramid of the Sun contains in it a number of examples that depict caves as open mouths with teeth.[11] The fact that these warriors were buried, or entombed in the earth, may also symbolize fertility. Could these sacrificial burials indicate an extension of cave symbolism and eating cosmology? Can we more fully integrate what we term "military" and "ecological" features of Mesoamerican life? Are Teotihuacan warriors understood as the human extensions of the voracious jaws of an eating cosmos? Or is their life and death struggle seen as a feeding activity for the earth?

Cabrera, Sugiyama, and Cowgill make some tentative comparative steps toward Shang Chinese archaeology, in which similar sacrificial finds have been found.[12] While cross-cultural work of this sort is an encouraging prospect, it seems that Mesoamerica may be in a better position to inform the work of archaeologists working in China than the reverse. The depth and duration of the sacrificial cult throughout Mesoamerica could have an even more profound impact than it currently does on cultural studies all over the world. There is, however, a more significant comparative work to be done. Following J. Z. Smith, historians of religion must be "rigourously self-conscious" regarding our own interpretive frameworks, which implies that cross-cultural work begins by determining the distance between ancient Mesoamerica and ourselves.[13]

The *cipactli* also had direct associations with time. According to Alfredo López Austin, Leonardo López Luján, and Saburo Sugiyama, the Temple of Quetzalcoatl is a monument to time.[14] The *cipactli* was the first cosmogonic force of creation and, in combination with the symbolism of Quetzalcoatl, represented the divine-temporal-destiny-force that was borne by the deity and by human beings. Forces that animate life carry with them a "temporal burden" that was articulated in ritual celebrations which surrounded the Mesoamerican calendar systems. Quetzalcoatl was depicted with a *cipactli* headdress, which at once symbolized the authority of Teotihuacan and its burden (or responsibility) of a mythic cosmogony, and was encoded in stone on the Temple of Quetzalcoatl.

Sugiyama has extended this temporal building plan into the urban design of Teotihuacan.[15] Combining the unit of 83 centimeters with other numbers of astronomical significance (52 [x 10], 73, 260, 584, and 819), the urban planners of Teotihuacan created a city of time. Like the yard of ancient Europe, 83 centimeters was a bodily measurement from heart to fingers, or from shoulder-blade to fingers. Moreover, the north-south axis of the city was symbolically conceived of as traversing upper- and underworlds. Time was materially articulated and located in the ceremonial space of Teotihuacan.

One is prompted to ask, what kind of time does Teotihuacan exhibit? Time was surely not the abstract chronological succession of moments from one to the next that seems to dominate our modern notions, but was instead an *embodied* time located in a particular physical place. Likewise, the Nahuatl term for time, *cahu(i)-tl*, was used also in terms that describe space. Molina, for example, translates the "space of time" as *cahuitl* and the "space of place" as *tlacauhtli, cauhtica*, and *tlacauilli*.[16] Anthony Aveni has also continually emphasized the locative character of Mesoamerican calendrical systems throughout his work. Time reckoning was an orientational activity with reference to material features of the landscape.[17] Units of time were not abstractions but fixed to the movement of beings, in the form of stars and planets. Mesoamerican time materially oriented human beings with reference to the seasons, rain, drought, migration of animals, and assorted other phenomena.

But Sugiyama's suggestion of a bodily unit of measure in this ceremonial space brings other located temporal structures to mind. There are other locations for time that more directly adhere to the human body. Music, rhythm, and dance are also temporal units. Unlike the nearly mute condition of the site today, Teotihuacan 1,500 years ago was a vital place full of rich sights, smells, and sounds. Ritual performances, sacrifices, etc. all have a bodily-temporal dimension. They meaningfully articulate a living connection with the world. Could the city itself, as a monument to time, be seen as a coherent bodily structure enlivened by the ceremonial activity of its inhabitants? As humans were embodied, could the earth or the city have also been understood as a coherent bodily structure?

II.

There is no question about the prestige of Teotihuacan in the Mesoamerican world. It has been called the "Rome of Anahuac." For this volume, Davíd Carrasco has ask us to consider it as a canon of Mesoamerica. Certainly its architectural forms are seen in numerous sites, testifying to its enormous influence in urban centers throughout the pre-Columbian world.

H. B. Nicholson's work on Quetzalcoatl, over a forty-year period, documents the dynamism and richness of one type of canon that emerged from Teotihuacan.[18] Indeed, the persistence of Tollan as the paradigmatic city seems to have originated with the Classic legacy. This presents a promising methodology for examining the intersite heritage in order to help formulate how religious understandings were merged with each other and transformed in their movement through the archaeological record. For example Geoffrey McCafferty's contribution to this volume reintroduces us to the dynamics between the neglected, yet vitally important, site of Cholula and Teotihuacan. Heyden's and Sugiyama's contributions here likewise draw on a variety of orientations and iconographic representations that persist through Mesoamerica.

But what sort of canon is a city? It is more than a book, or series of sacred texts, from which the category of "canon" emerged. Teotihuacan was a "locative canon," or an image of the cosmos articulated in stone and image. It therefore stands in contrast to the more familiar written canon, or "utopian" canon, which, as the Bible and other sacred books did, allowed for colonial and modern people to disengage from their homes and occupy other places. Teotihuacan was a canon in which various revelations of the sacred, whatever they were, were an ongoing possibility—a place where revelation was not finished in the world. Indeed its locative status relied on the possibility of new orientations to new manifestations of the sacred.

There is a marked distinction between book cultures (i.e., including those of us who aspire to write) and locative ones, which revolve around the proper place in which to situate the hierophany—or the manifestation of the sacred. In the first case, the sacred is at once located in books and, following Mircea Eliade, in human beings through history.[19] The meaning of places, or material life in general, is relegated to a profane or "fallen" status. Teotihuacan's legacy stands in marked contrast to this modern view of religion. It was an articulation of a place at the center of the cosmos that organized, or founded, the rest of material existence.

A debate between those who see an ancient earth-based cult and those who see a warrior cult has emerged in our discussions of Teotihuacan. My intention here is to draw these insights together in an abbreviated fashion by conceiving of Teotihuacan, as well as much of Mesoamerica in general, as a consumptive cosmos. Implied in both its fertility and warrior cosmological expressions was that the continuance of human life, indeed all material existence, was predicated on killing. As with Mauss's understanding of the "gift," the logic of sacrifice, which finds its most virulent expressesions with the Aztecs, can be seen as fiercely dedicated to a reciprocity of living beings.[20] Indeed, most religions have had to deal with the fact that eating requires that something be killed. In Mesoamerica this ironic feature of human life took on a unique character.

Karl Taube's work in this volume, for example, highlights the violence inherently involved in consuming a living landscape. Tlaloc appeared in the Maya context as a voraciously consumptive figure of war who was seemingly removed from his agricultural origins. Yet, following some of the recent archaeological excavations, it seems likely that Teotihuacanos may have conceived of warfare as also a consumptive activity and therefore in a dynamic relationship with earthly fertility.

Not only are these interpretive positions important for our growing understanding of Teotihuacan but, perhaps more significantly, for an ability to push our understandings of things such as religion, land, time, warfare, cities, and consumption. Our current interpretive vantage point is decidedly not that of Mesoamericans and, most likely, shares with Nimoy's in being more a projection of a culture of "consumerism" (i.e., a more fully abstract and dislocated ideology of consumption) than an understanding generated from inside of the Mesoamerican world. Indeed, the hermeneutical conundrum with which we are necessarily involved is helpful insofar as we are able to adjudicate the *distance* between our cultural constitution and theirs—inevitably our categories can not be theirs, our material world can not be theirs—and in that distance we can challenge our own cultural presuppositions.

The key anthropological insight in a hermeneutical interplay between our modern existences and the Teotihuacanos' is that we are capable of knowing them only in so far as our cultural constitution will allow. We may see something in that distant world that offers insights into our current cultural challenges. When we are trying, with all diligence, to understand the meaning of Teotihuacan for the Teotihuacanos, we are simultaneously asking ourselves what the world means—we are subjecting their perceived meanings to our own cultural grids.

As Charles Long has pointed out, another culture's *first creation*, that mode of being in the world that is internal to their cohesion and identity, is unavailable to an outsider. Whether they existed in a remote corner of the world—at some other time and place—or whether they are sitting beside us, another culture's first creation is not available. Ironically, throughout the history of anthropology and the history of religions, however, another's first creation is the object of our efforts. For some this is a depressing and possibly debilitating realization. For Long, however, outsiders are involved in another level of cultural identity that, at times, is even more important. As interpreters, we are involved in the others *second creation*—or how the "other" is signified.[21] In the present context, we are intimately involved with the ongoing creation of Teotihuacan and its inhabitants. Ultimately, one's own cultural identity is risked in the interplay of intimate levels of being *with* the other. There is, then, a level of commitment to Teotihuacan in their signified, second-creation status. The meaning of that place is bound up with our own orientation too—"the ultimate significance of one's place in the world."

The *Ancient Mysteries*' depiction of Teotihuacan as attempting to create a utopian paradise (yet failing), ends up sounding like an apologia for the modern fulfillment of our own utopian dream. It characterizes the Mesoamericans as failed moderns whose wrong turn was in ritually enacting the violence of reproduction. Put more economically, from the vantage point of consumerism (i.e., Nimoy, his audience, and modern culture), Teotihuacan couldn't realize its utopian dream because of its understanding of their occupying a living consumptive cosmos. We have parallel consumptive cosmologies that directly challenge the presuppositions of each other's existence. This interpretive dynamic is lost, however, when we assume to peer, unhindered, into the cultural existence of another. Without accounting for the distance between our own cultural constitution and Teotihuacan's, we have relinquished an opportunity to challenge our catagorical structuring of reality.

I have chosen to highlight the interplay of consumptive cosmologies because, from a U.S. consumer's perspective, this is what most urgently pressures and challenges my assumed cultural understandings. Taking seriously the consumptive cosmology of Mesoamerica reinserts the proper place of religion into the material world. Rather than religion as defined by a series of beliefs, or even institutions, it is primarily a means of adjudicating the human place in time, eating, fertility, warfare, etc.—or the "materiality" of religion and human life. In addition, there are some serious questions concerning the viability of a modern consumerist worldview that may help explain a fervent interest in "archaic" societies. Serious consideration of Teotihuacan should push us to different, and perhaps more viable, considerations of the meaning of the world. Thus the "ancient mysteries" of Mesoamerica can offer us the possibility of a locative, consumptive cosmos that, with special care and attention to interpretive strategies, could also be a feature of our modern cultural landscape.

NOTES

1. As it happens, one of our own conference members was a scholarly "talking head" for the program. It is not my intention to accuse anyone of "stooping" to television for popular consumption. Indeed, an intelligent analysis of difficult data should be available to the public. I am interested in simply calling attention to the consumptive worldview that surrounds our contemporary interpretive activities.

2. The useful categorical distinction between "utopian" and "locative" originates with Jonathan Z. Smith's work. See his *Map Is Not Territory: Studies in the History of Religions* (Leiden: E.J. Brill, 1978), and *Imaging Religion: From Babylon to Jonestown*, in Chicago Studies in the History of Judaism, Jacob Neusner, ed. (Chicago: University of Chicago Press, 1982). For an analysis of this distinction with a different emphasis, see my "Paper Ties to Land: Indigenous and Colonial Material Orientations to the Valley of Mexico," *History of Religions* 35 (August 1995) no. 1: 27–60.

3. See Anthony F. Aveni, chapter 9 in this volume, and his "The Pecked Cross Symbol in Ancient Mesoamerica," *Science* 202 (1978): 267–279, co-authored with Horst Hartung and B. Buckingham.

4. See her contribution to this volume as well as her "An Interpretation of the Cave Underneath the Pyramid of the Sun in Teotihuacan, Mexico," *American Antiquity* 40, no. 2 (1975): 131–147.

5. Charles H. Long, *Significations: Signs, Symbols, and Images in the Interpretation of Religion* (Philadelphia: Fortress Press, 1986), p. 7.

6. Johanna Broda, "Astronomy, Cosmovisión, and Ideology in Pre-Hispanic Mesoamerica," in *Ethnoastronomy and Archaeoastronomy in the American Tropics*, edited by Anthony F. Aveni and Gary Urton (New York: Annals of the New York Academy of Sciences 385, 1982), pp. 81–110; and Broda, "The Sacred Landscapes of Aztec Calendar Festivals: Myth, Nature, and Society," in *Aztec Ceremonial Landscapes: To Change Place*, edited by Davíd Carrasco (Niwot: University Press of Colorado, 1999), pp. 74–120.

7. Philip P. Arnold, *Eating Landscape: The Aztec and European Occupation of Tlalocan* (Niwot: University Press of Colorado, 1999); and "Eating Landscape: Human Sacrifice and Sustenance in Aztec Mexico," in *To Change Place: Aztec Ceremonial Landscapes,* edited by Davíd Carrasco (Niwot: University Press of Colorado, 1991), pp. 219–232.

8. Davíd Carrasco, "Cosmic Jaws: We Eat the Gods and the Gods Eat Us," *Journal of the American Academy of Religion* LXIII, no. 3 (Fall 1995): 429–463.

9. Rubén Cabrera Castro, Saburo Sugiyama, and George Cowgill, "The Templo de Quetzalcoatl Project at Teotihuacan: A Preliminary Report," *Ancient Mesoamerica* 2 (1991): 77–92.

10. These investigators hypothesize that the interior burial chambers may have contained the remains of a person or persons of high status, while military retainers were placed in burials around the periphery and facing outward as if to guard the interior contents of the temple.

11. Note 4 above; also see Linda Manzanilla's contribution to this volume for a thorough analysis of cave symbolism at Teotihuacan.

12. Castro, Sugiyama, and Cowgill 1991, note 9 above.

13. As Jonathan Z. Smith has said, "The student of religion, and most particularly the historian of religion, must be relentlessly self-conscious. Indeed, this self-consciousness

constitutes his primary expertise, his foremost object of study." (*Imagining Religion* [note 2 above], p. xi).

14. Alfredo López Austin, Leonardo López Luján, and Saburo Sugiyama, "The Temple of Quetzalcoatl at Teotihuacan, Its Possible Ideological Significance," *Ancient Mesoamerica* 2 (1991): 93–105.

15. Saburo Sugiyama, "Worldview Materialized in Teotihuacan, Mexico," *Latin American Antiquity* 4, no. 2 (1993): 103–129.

16. Fray Alonso de Molina, *Vocabulario en lengua castellana y mexicana y mexicana y castellana* (Mexico City: Editorial Porrúa, 1977), pp. 58v and 59r.

17. For example, see Anthony F. Aveni, *Sky Watchers of Ancient Mexico* (Austin: University of Texas Press, 1980); "The Role of Astronomical Orientation in the Delineation of World View: A Center and Periphery Model," in *Imagination of Matter: Religion and Ecology in Mesoamerican Tradition*, edited by Davíd Carrasco (Oxford: BAR International Series no. 515, 1989), pp. 85–102; and "Mapping the Ritual Landscape: Debt Payment to Tlaloc During the Month of Atlcahualo," in *To Change Place: Aztec Ceremonial Landscapes*, edited by Davíd Carrasco (Niwot: University Press of Colorado, 1991), pp. 58–73.

18. See his "Topiltzin Quetzalcoatl of Tollan: A Problem in Mesoamerican Ethnohistory," Ph.D. dissertation, Harvard University, 1957, and his contribution to this volume.

19. Davíd Carrasco, *Quetzalcoatl and the Irony of Empire: Myths and Prophecies in the Aztec Tradition* (Chicago: University of Chicago Press, 1982).

20. Mircea Eliade, *The Myth of the Eternal Return, or, Cosmos and History*, translated by Willard R. Trask (Princeton, NJ: Princeton University Press, 1954).

21. Marcel Mauss, *The Gift: Forms and Functions of Exchange in Archaic Societies*, translated by Ian Cunnison (New York: W. W. Norton & Co., 1967).

22. See his "The Oppressive Elements in Religion and the Religions of the Oppressed," in *Significations* (note 5 above), pp. 158–172.

EDITORS AND CONTRIBUTORS

Davíd Carrasco is Director of the Moses Mesoamerican Archive and Professor of History of Religions at Princeton University. His previous works include *Daily Life of the Aztecs: People of the Sun and Earth* (with Scott Sessions); *Moctezuma's Mexico: Visions of the Aztec World* (with Eduardo Matos Moctezuma); *To Change Place: Aztec Ceremonial Landscapes, Religions of Mesoamerica: Cosmovision and Ceremonial Centers*; and *Quetzalcoatl and the Irony of Empire: Myths and Prophecies in Aztec Tradition*. He is currently chief editor of the *Oxford Encyclopedia of Mesoamerican Cultures*, a multivolume reference work to be published in the year 2000.

Lindsay Jones is an associate professor in the Division of Comparative Studies in the Humanities at Ohio State University. A historian of religions concerned both with the specifics of Mesoamerica and with the broader issues in the cross-cultural study of religion, particularly matters of sacred space and architecture, Jones is the author of *Twin City Tales: A Hermeneutical Reassessment of Tula and Chichén Itzá* and the forthcoming *The Hermeneutics of Sacred Architecture: Experience, Interpretation, Comparison*.

Scott Sessions is a research associate at Amherst College working on the African-American Religion Documentary History Project and a doctoral candidate in the Department of Religion at Princeton University. He has worked for many years as a researcher and administrative assistant for the Moses Mesoamerican Archive and is development editor of the *Oxford Encyclopedia of Mesoamerican Cultures*.

Philip P. Arnold, Assistant Professor of American Religions at Syracuse University, earned his Ph.D. in the History of Religions from the University of Chicago in 1992. His research interests are on the implications for religion that emerge from the contact between indigenous and colonial/modern peoples in the New World. Focusing his work on the religious meanings of land in the Aztec, Lakota, and Haudenosaunee (Iroquois) traditions, he is author of *Eating Landscape: The Aztec and European Occupation of Tlalocan*.

Anthony F. Aveni is Russel B. Colgate Professor of Astronomy and Anthropology at Colgate University and the author of numerous articles and several books on Mesoamerica that focus especially on cosmology, astronomy, and timekeeping, among them, *Skywatchers of Ancient Mexico* and *Stairways to the Stars: Skywatching in Three Great Ancient Cutures*. He is also the author of *Behind the Crystal Ball: Magic, Science, and the Occult from Antiquity Through the New Age* and *Empires of Time: Calendars, Clocks, and Cultures*. In 1982 he was named National Professor of the Year by the Council for the Advancement and Support of Education, Washington, D.C.

Elizabeth Hill Boone is Martha and Donald Robertson Chair in Latin American Art at Tulane University. Her publications include *The Codex Magliabechiano*;

Incarnations of the Aztec Supernatural; *The Aztec World*; *Writing Without Words: Alternative Literacies in Mesoamerica and the Andes* (with Walter Mignolo); and a forthcoming book on Mexican pictorial histories.

Johanna Broda is an anthropologist and ethnohistorian with the Instituto de Investigaciones Históricas at the Universidad Nacional Autónoma de México. Her numerous publications on Mesoamerican society and culture include *Continuidad y cambio en la sociedad indígena de México después de la conquista*; *The Great Temple of Tenochtitlan: Center and Periphery in the Aztec World* (with Davíd Carrasco and Eduardo Matos Moctezuma); *Economía política e ideología en el México prehispánico* (with Pedro Carrasco); and *Graniceros: Cosmovisión y meteorología indígenas de Mesoamérica* (with Beatriz Albores).

Rubén Cabrera Castro is an archaeologist with the Instituto Nacional de Antropología e Historia and curator of the Teotihuacan Archaeological Zone, where he has worked for nearly twenty years. He has directed the Teotihuacan (1980–1982), La Ventilla (1992–1994), Ateteco (1998—), and Pyramid of the Moon (1998—) Projects and codirected the Temple of Quetzalcoatl Project (1988–1989). He is the author of several articles appearing in various edited volumes, exhibition catalogs, and journals, and coauthor of *El proyecto Templo de Quetzalcoatl* (with Oralia Cabrera).

Doris Heyden is an art historian and historian of religion at the Etnología y Antropología Social facility of the Instituto Nacional de Antropología e Historia in San Ángel, Mexico City. Her numerous publications include *The Eagle, the Cactus, the Rock: The Roots of México-Tenochtitlan's Foundation Myth and Symbol*; *Pre-Columbian Architecture of Mesoamerica* (with Paul Gendrop); and richly annotated translations of Diego Durán's *History of the Indians of New Spain* and *Book of the Gods and Rites and The Ancient Calendar* (with Fernando Horcasitas).

Barbara W. Fash is a research associate at the Peabody Museum of Archaeology and Ethnology at Harvard University and Director of the Hieroglyphic Stairway Project at Copán, Honduras. Specializing in Mesoamerican art and archaeology and museum studies, she conceived, designed, and installed the exhibits in the Copán Sculpture Museum, which opened in 1996. Her detailed illustrations of the site's major monuments have appeared in numerous publications and she has co-written articles appearing in *Natural History*, *Res: Anthropology and Aesthetics*, *Ancient Mesoamerica*, and the *Journal of Field Archaeology*.

William L. Fash is Charles P. Bowditch Professor of Mexican and Central American Archaeology in the Department of Anthropology at Harvard University. He is also Director of the Copán Mosaics Project and the Copán Acropolis Archaeological Project, and the author of *Scribes, Warriors, and Kings: The City of Copán and the Ancient Maya* and *The Archaeological Map of the Copán Valley*.

Alfredo López Austin is Professor of Mesoamerican History at the Instituto de Investigaciones Antropológicas of the Universidad Nacional Autónoma de

México. His numerous publications include *Tamoanchan and Tlalocan, Places of Mist*; *The Myths of the Opossum*; *The Rabbit on the Face of the Moon*; *The Human Body and Ideology: Concepts of the Ancient Nahuas*; *Hombre-dios*; and *El pasado indígena* (with Leonardo López Luján).

Leonardo López Luján is an archaeologist and professor working at the Templo Mayor Museum. Among his numerous publications on Mesoamerican religions and politics are *The Offerings of the Templo Mayor of Tenochtitlan*; *Xochicalco y Tula* (with Robert Cobean and Alba Guadalupe Mastache); *El pasado indígena* (with Alfredo López Austin); and *Historia antigua de México* (with Linda Manzanilla).

Linda Manzanilla, Director of the Instituto de Investigaciones Antropológicas of the Universidad Nacional Autónoma de México, specializes in the archaeology of the world's earliest urban sites. Among her recent publications are *Emergence and Change in Early Urban Societies* and *Anatomía de un conjunto residencial teotihuacano en Oztoyahualco*.

Eduardo Matos Moctezuma is Director of the Templo Mayor Museum and the Proyecto de Arqueología Urbana in Mexico City. His numerous publications include *Teotihuacan: The City of Gods*; *Life and Death at the Templo Mayor*; *Treasures of the Great Temple*; *The Aztecs*; and *Moctezuma's Mexico: Visions of the Aztec World* (with Davíd Carrasco).

Geoffrey G. McCafferty has conducted archaeological investigations at Cholula since 1980, and is currently planning additional fieldwork there on the "Classic heritage" problem. He is Assistant Professor of Archaeology at the University of Calgary, Alberta, Canada, and holds a Ph.D. in anthropology from SUNY Binghamton.

Hector Neff is Senior Research Scientist at the Missouri University Research Reactor Center, University of Missouri, Columbia. He holds a Ph.D. in anthropology from the University of California, Santa Barbara. His research interests include Mesoamerican archaeology and chemistry-based archaeological provenance determination.

H. B. Nicholson is Professor of Anthropology, Emeritus, University of California, Los Angeles, whose numerous publications include *Mixteca-Puebla: Discoveries and Research in Mesoamerican Art and Archaeology* (with Eloise Quiñones Keber) and *The Work of Bernardino de Sahagún: Pioneer Ethnographer of Sixteenth-Century Aztec Mexico* (with J. Jorge Klor de Alva and Eloise Quiñones Keber). He has also played instrumental roles in such major publishing projects as the *Handbook of Middle American Indians*, the *Collected Works in Mesoamerican Linguistics and Archaeology of Eduard Seler*, and the forthcoming *Oxford Encyclopedia of Mesoamerican Cultures*.

David Stuart is a lecturer in the Department of Anthropology and the Peabody Museum of Archaeology and Ethnology at Harvard University. Specializing in symbolic archaeology, historical linguistics, and ancient writing systems, he has written several essays and journal articles and is co-author (with Stephen Houston) of *Classic Maya Place Names*.

Saburo Sugiyama is an archaeologist and associate professor at Aichi Prefectural University, Nagakute, Japan, who has worked in the Teotihuacan Archaeological Zone for several years. He received his Ph.D. in anthropology from Arizona State University and has written and co-written articles in journals such as *Latin American Antiquity* and *Ancient Mesoamerica*.

Karl A. Taube, Professor of Anthopology at the University of California at Riverside, specializes in the iconographic and writing systems of ancient Mesoamerica. Among his publications are *The Major Gods of Ancient Yucatan*; *Aztec and Maya Myths*; and *The Gods and Symbols of Ancient Mexico and the Maya* (with Mary Ellen Miller).

INDEX

▼

Page numbers in italics refer to illustrations.